DAVID O. MCKAY LIBRARY

P9-CJE-679

THE NEW ENGLAND SOUL

MAR 5 2002

PROPERT
DAVID O. McKAY LIBRARY
BYU-IDAHO
REXBURG ID 83460-0405

WITHDRAWN

JUN 17 2024

DAVID O. McKAY LIBRARY
BYU-IDAHO

JUN 17 2024

THE
NEW ENGLAND
SOUL

Preaching and Religious Culture in Colonial New England

HARRY S. STOUT

OXFORD UNIVERSITY PRESS
New York   Oxford

Oxford University Press

Oxford   New York   Toronto
Delhi   Bombay   Calcutta   Madras   Karachi
Petaling Jaya   Singapore   Hong Kong   Tokyo
Nairobi   Dar es Salaam   Cape Town
Melbourne   Auckland

and associated companies in
Berlin   Ibadan

Copyright © 1986 by Oxford University Press, Inc.

First published in 1986 by Oxford University Press, Inc.,
200 Madison Avenue, New York, New York 10016

First issued as an Oxford University Press paperback, 1988

Oxford is a registered trademark of Oxford University Press

All rights reserved. No part of this publication may be reproduced,
stored in a retrieval system, or transmitted, in any form or by any means,
electronic, mechanical, photocopying, recording, or otherwise,
without the prior permission of Oxford University Press, Inc.

Library of Congress Cataloging-in-Publication Data
Stout, Harry S.
The New England soul.
Bibliography: p.   Includes index.
1. Preaching—New England—History.
2. New England—Religious life and customs. I. Title.
BV 4208.U6S75   1986   251'.00974   85-29853
ISBN 0-19-503958-0
ISBN 0-19-505645-0 (PBK.)

2   4   6   8   10   9   7   5   3   1

Printed in the United States of America

For
Richard W. Gray, D.D.
1911–1979
and
Susan J. Stout

Acknowledgments

In the years that I have been engaged in writing this book I have accumulated many intellectual debts that I happily acknowledge. I began my graduate work on Puritanism at Princeton Theological Seminary where I benefitted from the encouragement and counsel of Edward Dowey and the late Lefferts A. Loetscher. At Kent State University where I completed graduate study, my teachers William H. Kenney III, Lawrence S. Kaplan, Henry Leonard, and Jerome Friedman gave unstintingly of their time and attention amid tumultuous circumstances. To Robert P. Swierenga, who first took me under his wing as a troubled college sophomore and continued to nurture me throughout my graduate studies, I owe my career as a historian. Through this book I hope to express something of my regard for him and my indebtedness to his inspiration and scholarship.

Like most historians today, I have benefitted from a variety of institutions that support modern scholarship. A Research Fellowship from the National Endowment for the Humanities in 1976–77 enabled me to begin the long process of visiting sermon archives. The following year I received an Andrew Mellon Fellowship from the University of Pennsylvania where I benefitted from the time and opportunity to share my ideas with a stimulating group of early Americanists. A visiting appointment at Calvin College in 1981 supplied a congenial environment in which I could test some early chapters on my former undergraduate teachers. Throughout my research and writing, the history department and Research Foundation at the University of Connecticut did everything possible to encourage me: they unhesitatingly paid for microfilms and photocopy, furnished travel awards, and provided me with reduced teaching loads that made writing possible.

Throughout my periods of travel I found research libraries unfailingly helpful and good natured, despite my blanket request "to see all your colonial sermon manuscripts." I am particularly indebted to the curators and staffs of the following institutions for short-term fellowships that allowed extended access to their superb collections: the American Antiquarian Society, in particular John B. Hench; the Huntington Library, in particular Martin L. Ridge; and the Newberry Library, in particular Richard Jensen. I have also benefitted from the courtesy and cooperative spirit of other archivists and libraries including the Historical Society of Pennsylvania, Philadelphia; the Congregational Library, Boston; The Essex Institute Historical Collections, Salem, Massachusetts; the Connecticut Historical Society, Hartford; the Connecticut State Library, Hartford; the New London Historical Society; the Mansfield Historical Society; and, last but not least, the Beinecke Library at Yale University. For their photocopy and microfilm services, I am grateful to the Massachusetts Historical Society, Boston; the New York Historical Society; and the Concord (Massachusetts) Free Library.

To friends and colleagues I owe more than I can say for their encouragement and criticism. At an early age in my thinking I benefitted greatly from the suggestions of Philip J. Greven and William G. McLoughlin. Drafts of the chapters have been read and criticized by Sacvan Bercovitch, T. H. Breen, David D. Hall, Karen O. Kupperman, and Mark A. Noll. Richard D. Brown, George M. Marsden, and R. Kent Newmyer gave new meaning to the terms friendship and collegiality by reading an excessively long preliminary draft of the book in its entirety. Whatever errors remain, however, are my responsibility.

As the book moved from pencil draft to final form, another group of friends and assistants provided long hours of labor on the manuscript. A mere listing of my graduate assistants hardly does justice to the contributions they made in copyediting and reference checking. They are: Louise Chipley, Rebecca Guild, Patti Bacon, Li Yan, and, especially, James F. Cooper. A special thanks goes to Deborah H. DeFord, my word processor, who expertly prepared the manuscript and compiled the index. Throughout she demonstrated an interest beyond the call of duty, besides a rare wisdom and patience. Cynthia A. Read at Oxford University Press applied her considerable talents to preparing the work for publication; the final product is much the better for her attention.

On more occasions than I could possibly enumerate I have been sustained and inspired by my parents H. Stober Stout and Norma W. Stout. Despite frequent evidence to the contrary, they never stopped believing the ancient promise that if you bring up a child in the way he should go, when he is old he will not depart from it. My children, Deborah and James, have reached the ages where they know how much this book has meant to me and have encouraged me throughout despite the assurance there will be "no big royalties."

Of all my acknowledgments, two stand out and are named in the dedication. From Richard W. Gray, pastor throughout my youth and again in the twilight of his powerful ministry, I received a gift of prophetic preaching whose impression is stamped on every page of this book.

My greatest debt is reserved for my wife Susan who alone has been with me at each stage along the way. Her support, encouragement, and companionship have been the rudder of my life in ways that only she can know.

April 1986 H. S. S.
Storrs, Connecticut

Contents

V MEMORY, 1764–1776

ABBREVIATIONS

AAS	American Antiquarian Society, Worcester, Massachusetts
BL	Beinecke Rare Book and Manuscript Library, Yale University, New Haven, Connecticut
CHS	Connecticut Historical Society, Hartford, Connecticut
CL	Congregational Library, Boston, Massachusetts
CSL	Connecticut State Library, Hartford, Connecticut
EI	Essex Institute Historical Collections, Salem, Massachusetts
HC	Harvard College, Cambridge, Massachusetts
HL	Huntington Library and Art Gallery, San Marino, California
HSP	Historical Society of Pennsylvania, Philadelphia, Pennsylvania
MHS	Massachusetts Historical Society, Boston, Massachusetts
NL	Newberry Library, Chicago, Illinois
NYHS	New York Historical Society, New York, New York
YC	Yale College, New Haven, Connecticut

NOTE

In quotations from original sources, contractions have been extended and the use of u and v, i and j has been standardized. I have not included an ellipsis for matter omitted from the end of a quotation unless it distorted the writer's meaning. Because of the serendipity of sermon notes, some punctuation has been silently added to ensure intelligibility, and periods have been substituted for colons and terminal dashes. Bible quotations are taken from the Authorized (King James) Version.

THE NEW ENGLAND SOUL

Introduction

A major theme in recent social scientific literature is the role that communications media and the "information revolution" play in shaping and delimiting our cultural horizons.[1] As never before we realize that societies, like individuals, act within a limited range of choices that depends upon the amount and types of information they receive. This study explores a seventeenth- and eighteenth-century medium of communications—the New England sermon—whose topical range and social influence were so powerful in shaping cultural values, meanings, and a sense of corporate purpose that even television pales in comparison.

Unlike modern mass media, the sermon stood alone in local New England contexts as the only regular (at least weekly) medium of public communication. As a channel of information, it combined religious, educational, and journalistic functions, and supplied all the key terms necessary to understand existence in this world and the next. As the only event in public assembly that regularly brought the entire community together, it also represented the central ritual of social order and control. Seldom, if ever before, did so many people hear the same message of purpose and direction over so long a period of time as did the New England "Puritans."[2]

The seventeenth-century founders of New England set out to create a unique and self-perpetuating "people of the Word," and by extending the sermon to all significant facets of life—social and political, as well as religious—they achieved exactly that. Throughout the colonial era the regular "planting" of churches in most towns kept pace with the growth of population so that by the time of the Revolution there were 720 Congregational churches in New England. In like manner the number of college-educated, ordained ministers grew with the population, resulting in a constant ratio of preachers to general population that was among the lowest—if not the lowest—in the Protestant world.[3] Twice on Sunday and often once during the week, every minister in New England delivered sermons lasting between one and two hours in length. Collectively over the entire span of the colonial period, sermons totaled over five million separate messages in a society whose population never exceeded one-

3

half million and whose principal city never grew beyond seventeen thousand. The average weekly churchgoer in New England (and there were far more churchgoers than church members) listened to something like seven thousand sermons in a lifetime, totaling somewhere around fifteen thousand hours of concentrated listening.[4] These striking statistics become even more significant when it is recalled that until the last decade of the colonial era there were at the local level few, if any, competing public speakers offering alternative messages. For all intents and purposes, the sermon was the only regular voice of authority.

Despite the impressive volume of Puritan studies in the past fifty years, there has been no overall synthesis of preaching and religious culture that spans the colonial era. Studies based on the sermons are segmented and limited by time, event, or category. Some studies trace the evolution of the sermon over several "generations"; others isolate key "events" like the Half-way Covenant, the Glorious Revolution, the Great Awakening, or the Revolution; and still others examine discrete types or categories of sermons such as fast and thanksgiving sermons, election day sermons, funeral and execution sermons, and ordination sermons. Only when all these periods and perspectives are brought together will it be possible to appreciate the changes, continuities, and variations within this most powerful and durable of New England institutions.

In addition to the limitations of segmentation, one other shortcoming in existing sermon studies is so pervasive as to require more extended comment. Underlying almost every study of colonial preaching is the assumption that printed sermons are the best comprehensive index to "what was said and done publicly." This assumption goes back to Perry Miller who in his magisterial reconstruction of Puritan ideas and values relied almost exclusively on printed sermons to convey the changes and nuances of the "New England mind."[5] Since that time scholars have questioned his interpretations but followed his method, preferring centrally located and microfilmed printed sermons to the chaotic and far more extensive body of manuscript sermons preserved in historical societies across the nation. Only from the vantage point of unpublished sermons, however, can the full range of colonial preaching be understood.

Published sermons present limitations because they are not necessarily representative of regular preaching, nor can we be certain they are the best index to what the clergy offered the public on a weekly basis. The vast majority of published sermons (at least after the first generation) originated as "occasional" or weekday sermons, which were expanded after delivery for publication. As such they provide an inexact and even misleading guide to what was being said publicly in most churches on most Sundays. By the Revolutionary era, 85 percent of printed sermons were of the occasional variety (especially fast and election sermons). In the real world of colonial public assembly, such sermons often occurred only six or seven times a year in the life of any particular church—a figure representing less than 10 percent of the total sermons preached.[6] Unpublished regular sermons were more "public" communications than their printed counterparts. Not everyone in New England *read* sermons, certainly not routinely, but nearly everyone *heard* them, week in, week out. The most accurate guide we therefore have to what people actually heard are the handwritten sermon notes that ministers carried with them into the pulpit.[7]

Rather than limit my analysis of preaching to one period within New England's colonial past or to a single type of sermon, I have sought to examine the sermons in all their variety and to present an overview of the sermon as an institution shaping and directing New England culture for a century and a half. While I cannot pretend to have examined all the printed and unprinted sermons surviving from the colonial era, I have spent nine years reading all types of sermons, over two thousand of them, and I believe they represent a comprehensive index to what was being said and done publicly in colonial New England.

To organize the mass of sermonic literature into a workable chronological sequence, I have divided the colonial clergy into five cohorts or "generations." The term generation is a shorthand device to distinguish groups of ministers according to their date of graduation from college—the meaning colonial ministers themselves attached to the term. My own dating conforms closely to theirs (see table).[8]

Colonial New England Ministry by Generation

First generation	Trained in England, ca. 1600–1640
Second generation	Trained at Harvard College, 1642–1675
Third generation	Trained at Harvard College, 1676–1709
Fourth generation	Trained at Harvard and Yale colleges, 1710–1744
Fifth generation	Trained at Harvard, Yale, and Princeton colleges, 1745–1776

After studying all types of sermons across five generations of preaching and exploring the overall system of belief they contain, I arrived at an organizing principle that reflects the five parts of classical rhetoric as taught in the manuals of Cicero and Quintillian.[9] In those texts, the first part was called "Invention" (*inventio*), referring to the process by which the speaker "discovered" the subject matter and rhetorical strategies of the oration. With subject matter firmly in mind, the speaker proceeded to the second stage of speech preparation, "Arrangement" (*dispositio*), or "the distribution of arguments in proper order." Having settled on the subject matter and arranged it in proper order, the orator turned to "Style" (*elocutio*), or "the fitting of the proper language to the invented matter." All of these operations preceded the study of "Delivery" (*pronuntiatio*), or "the control of voice and body in a manner suitable to the dignity of the subject matter and the style." Finally, since speakers initially spoke without notes, they had to practice "Memory" (*memoria*), or "the firm mental grasp of [subject] matter and words."[10]

In employing the terminology of classical rhetoric to organize my book, I do not mean to imply a rhetorical determinism. These are simply labels that happen to describe, as briefly and clearly as any, what I take to be the distinctive rhetorical qualities of each generation. The founders invented a meaning for New England and the children maintained and built upon it. Third-generation ministers, living in a tolerant, "anglicized" age, promulgated the same doctrines as their predecessors but adorned them with a "polite" style that registered the influence of English manners and the "New Learning." Fourth-generation ministers, spanning the years of religious "awakening" and war with France, learned anew the importance of delivery both in theory and fact. Finally, fifth-generation ministers, living through Independence, built their case for resistance and revolution on the memory of the founders and New England's inherited covenant mission. Each generation had its distinct challenges and emphases, but in their collective careers we observe a continuity and unity like that of an unfolding oration.

The continuity in sermon substance was the most surprising finding to emerge from my research. If there was a "decline" and resultant "secularization" of Puritanism, it was not evident in the regular life of the churches. The majority of inhabitants continued to go to church, and their ministers persisted in the subject matter of their sermons. No shift from piety to moralism was evident. Indeed, it appears that models of secularization stem from historians' failure to appreciate the functional distinctions made by colonial ministers (and their congregations) between regular sabbath preaching and occasional weekday sermons. Beginning with the founders, each generation of New England ministers invented and institutionalized a growing range of occasional sermons that allowed for pulpit commentary on social and political themes without corrupting the enduring concern of regular preaching, which was the salvation of the soul. The message and meaning of occasional sermons could and did change over time as New England's social and political circumstances changed, but regular preaching—the preaching colonists heard most of the time—remained consistently otherworldly. By conflating the themes of regular and occasional preaching, and by emphasizing printed occasional sermons to the virtual exclusion of regular sermon notes, historians have extracted a pattern of meaning that distorts the larger spiritual context in which political ideas were expressed and given meaning.

The implications of enduring spirituality in the pulpit and pew are especially important for understanding the "meaning of America" as it unfolded in the Revolutionary era. By 1776, Congregational ministers in New England were delivering over two thousand discourses a week and publishing them at an unprecedented rate that outnumbered secular pamphlets (from all the colonies) by a ratio of more than four to one.[11] Unlike most pamphlets, which were composed in private for a limited, informed audience of the educated elite, printed sermons originated in speech and more accurately express Revolutionary sentiments as they were heard by the main body of New England patriots. The more one reads these sermons the more one finds unsatisfactory the suggestion that ideas of secular "republicanism," "civil millennialism," or class-conscious "popular ideology" were the primary ideological triggers of radical resistance and violence in the Revolution.[12] Such temporal concerns may have motivated other colonists, and they certainly engaged "Americans" after 1776, but they were not the ideological core around which the Revolution in New England revolved. In Revolutionary New England, ministers continued to monopolize public communications, and the terms they most often employed to justify resistance and to instill hope emanated from the Scriptures and from New England's enduring identity as an embattled people of the Word who were commissioned to uphold a sacred and exclusive covenant between themselves and God. The idea of a national covenant supplied the "liberties" New Englanders would die protecting, as well as the "conditions" that promised deliverance and victory over all enemies. It also provided the innermost impulsion toward radical thought and violent resistance to British "tyranny" in New England.

Covenant theology as it evolved over five generations of New World preaching comprised a view of history and corporate identity that could best be labeled "providential." In this view God entered into covenants with nations, as well as with individuals, and promised that he would uphold them by his providential might if they would acknowledge no other sovereign and observe the terms of obedience contained in his Word. Covenanted peoples like those of ancient Israel and New England were the hub around which sacred (i.e., real) history revolved. Such peoples might be ignored or reviled by the world and figure insignificantly in the great empires of profane history, but viewed through the sacred lens of providential history they were seen as God's special instruments entrusted with the task of preparing the way for messianic deliverance. As Israel witnessed to God's active involvement with nations in ancient times and brought forth the Christ, so New England's experience confirmed God's continuing involvement with nations that would persist until Christ's return to earth, when history itself would cease and be swallowed up in eternity. Within this historical covenant perspective, resistance to England was only secondarily about constitutional rights and political liberties. Ultimately, resistance became necessary the minute England declared the colonies' duty of "unlimited submission" in "all cases whatsoever" and, in so doing, set itself alongside God's Word as a competing sovereign. Such demands were "tyrannical" and left New Englanders no choice but to resist unto death or forfeit their identity as a covenant people. As explained from the pulpit, New Englanders' revolution was first and foremost a battle to preserve their historic identity and unique messianic destiny.

To the extent that providential history contained a blueprint for the future as well as a record of the past it can be labeled "millennial." But in recent literature on colonial New England preaching, this term has been abused through overemphasis. Throughout the colonial period, ministers rarely preached specifically on millennial prophecies pointing to the end of time, and when they did it was generally in the most undogmatic and speculative of terms. For the most part, they did not base their preaching on the assumption that history would stop tomorrow, and in this respect they differed radically from popular millennarian movements in Europe and post-Revolutionary America whose plans of action were governed exclusively by apocalyptic considerations. The past was the tried-and-true key invariably invoked by ministers to interpret the present. Initially this past was largely limited to Israel's experience as recounted in the Old Testament which, New England colonists believed, was a "type" or model for their own experience as God's "New Israel." Within one generation, New England's own record of providential threatenings and deliverances was engrafted onto Israel's, with the same revelatory significance. When apocalyptic sentiments did appear in colonial preaching—usually in moments of grave danger (war) or ecstatic joy (revival)—they served as speculative additions to the bedrock of history.

Once we recognize and acknowledge the enduring hold of concepts like the covenant, *Sola Scriptura* (Scripture alone), and providential mission on pulpit discourse and the public imagination, it is easier to understand the ease with which most New Englanders accepted the Revolution and its republican principles. In the course of 150 years virtually all of the inherited Old World assumptions governing social order and authority were challenged and overturned. Gradually but irresistibly, institutions established on the basis of aristocratic privilege were transformed into engines of democratization. In the churches this transformation was shown most dramatically in the mid-eighteenth-century revivals inaugurated by Jonathan Edwards and George Whitefield; in politics it appeared in popular assemblies and "mob" revolts beginning with the "Glorious Revolution" of 1689 and continuing through the American Revolution. Yet as remarkable and far-reaching as these changes were, they did not result in the widespread violence or civil war characteristic of most "modern" revolutions. Instead, New Englanders experienced radical changes in social and political organization secure in the conviction that, at base, the essential underpinnings of their society remained unchanged. They believed that in 1776 they were the same people of the Word that they had been in 1630, and their revolution was less a rejection than a fulfillment of the founders' dream of creating a holy nation subject in every regard to the claims of God's Word.

That New England audiences were able to preserve the myth that they were a special people and maintain a continuity with their past was attributable largely to the exegetical inventiveness of their ministers. Scriptural texts were always the last word in New England culture, but ministers exercised the freedom to turn at different times to different portions of the Bible for typological identification and direction. Instead of giving up their sacred legacy and identification with ancient Israel when "outward" circumstances changed, as in the Half-way Covenant or the Glorious Revolution, ministers shifted their textual reference points to other portions of Israel's history better suited to their current situation. During the early years of New England's "theocracy" and rule by "visible saints," for example, ministers had turned for support and precedent to times in Israel's past when God intervened directly on behalf of his chosen people and spoke to them directly through his prophets. Later, with the revocation of Massachusetts's charter and New England's integration into Britain's royal network, their typological identification shifted to "Israel's constitution" during the Davidic monarchy. Finally, with Independence, attention moved once more to the "Jewish Republic" that had existed before the Jewish people demanded that God give them a king like the other nations. By the Revolutionary era, the lesson audiences were taught to learn from Israel's variegated political experience was that as long as God's Word continued to be proclaimed faithfully in local churches it did not really matter what form of government or social organization prevailed. Neither theocracies, constitutional monarchies, nor democratic republics could guarantee the continuation of God's national covenant with a peculiar people. All of these forms had notable successes and equally notable failures; each could succeed only to the extent that the people were virtuous and continued to trust in God.

Before entering the world of the New England sermon, a caveat is in order. Outside of New England the sermons treated here cannot be viewed as representative of religious rhetoric in the New World, though they do encompass some widespread beliefs. New Englanders perceived themselves as the predestined founders of the American Republic and the custodians of its providential mission, but that fiction cannot be maintained in fact. The recent surge of scholarship on the Middle Colonies and Chesapeake confirms how atypical and nonrepresentative New England was in certain key social, cultural, economic, political, and demographic respects. Other speakers and audiences in other colonies could and did take entirely different meanings from their New World.

Such a caveat is apt to annoy nonscholarly readers who seek only a deeper understanding of the role that religious rhetoric and institutions played in shaping the meaning of America. But, like the fine points of Puritan theology, such qualifications are necessary lest we fall into the trap of reading America as New England writ large. Even in 1776, the new nation was simply too big, its citizens too varied, and its traditions too diverse to support so simple a reduction. At the same time, however, it would be a mistake to understate the importance of New England's religious culture to the evolving American Republic and, more particularly, the influence of Puritan rhetoric on the American identity. In light of the continued impact of New England on nineteenth-century American culture, the implications to be drawn from this study are obviously more than *merely* regional.[13] New England's peculiar identity, conceived by the Puritan founders, nurtured by their lineal and intellectual descendants in the eighteenth century and cast in literary form by their Yankee stepchildren, helped sustain a national dream of messianic destiny and national election that apparently has yet to run its course. Other colonists had similar dreams to be sure, but no other colonies fused them so persistently and thoroughly to events and institutions as did the New England Puritans. Only in New England did the sermon enjoy such a powerful role in directing thought. And so, the reader can see in colonial New England a model—as clear as any that exists in American history—of the way in which religion came to permeate a national identity at its deepest cultural and intellectual levels.

PART I

INVENTION, 1620–1665

[1]

The Institutional Setting of the Sermon

The mission and meaning of New England were established from the outset of colonization when Governor John Winthrop informed the first settlers of Massachusetts Bay that they had taken out a divine "Commission" to make their New World society a godly "Citty vpon a hill" that would be a beacon for lost humanity.[1] For that city to grow and enjoy God's covenant protections, God's Word would have to be preeminent. This meant, in turn, that the sermon would have to hold uncontested sway over the hearts and minds of its listeners. In establishing such a place for the sermon Winthrop and his fellow founders faced two major challenges. First they had to protect the sermon from encroaching institutions or grasping individuals, whether they be among the laity, the magistracy, or the ministry. And second, they had to invent avenues of expression whereby the sermon could speak to all areas of life—social, political, and economic—without corrupting its primary religious function of saving souls for eternity. As we shall see in this chapter, both of these challenges were resolved in the first decades of settlement. The institutional problem of fixing the sermon at the center of public assembly and social order was solved in the creation of the "Congregational Way," with its peculiar balance of powers between church and state, and between clergy and laity. The rhetorical problem of expanding the sermon's purview to include all aspects of public life was solved through the medium of weekday or "occasional" sermons. By organizing New England towns around autonomous local churches, and by authorizing ministers—and only ministers—to speak on all occasions of public note, the founders established patterns of community that would ensure the sermon's place at the center of New England society, and with it, New England's identity as a unique "people of the Word."

PURITY, POWER, LIBERTY:
AN EXPERIMENT IN FUSION

The meetinghouse stood at the center of the New England town, its only public building and the most significant mark the community would

13

make on its landscape. No sooner were towns incorporated than committees were formed to survey the land and engage a builder to proceed with the task of erecting a "place of assembly" on elevated ground at a point as nearly equidistant from the surrounding homes as possible. In all, New England towns would erect over 220 such structures in the seventeenth century and another 2,000 in the eighteenth.[2] Symbolically they proclaimed to all that religion was the chief business of the community and the highest priority of its people.

The first meetinghouses were singularly inelegant. Even when allowances are made for the primitive circumstances of early settlement and the lack of finished materials, the modern viewer is struck by the builders' complete disregard for beauty and adornment. Little more than a cabin of rough-hewn logs enclosed by crude palisades, the meetinghouse could be distinguished from private houses only by virtue of its location at the village center. The cold, dark interior contained only planked pews horizontally positioned before a pulpit or "desk" fastened to the north wall. Architecturally and aesthetically, the meetinghouse was nothing more than the "Lord's Barn."

The Puritans' rejection of decorated architecture, like their rejection of ornament in speech, bespoke their broader rejection of English culture that earned for them the sobriquet "nonconformists."[3] But if we see in their speech and architecture only the negation of what the Puritans opposed, we may miss the positive thrust of their message and the source of their appeal. Puritan speech and architecture reflected an alternative cultural and theological system whose expressed goal was the creation of a Bible commonwealth governed in all regards by the precepts of Holy Writ. The austere construction of the meetinghouse conveyed the Puritans' determination to recapture the simplicity and purity of the "primitive" New Testament church, uncorrupted by the intervening centuries of "humane" inventions, "arbitrary" authorities, and "superstitious" customs. The meetinghouse's position at the center of the community also signified submission to God's power, the power that came to a people who subordinated all human authorities and institutions to the infallible rule of *Sola Scriptura*. The supernatural power represented by the meetinghouse was deliberately veiled to the external eye and became manifest only in those moments when, in a room filled to capacity, the community assembled to worship God and hear him speak through his Word. In those moments the meetinghouse ceased to be merely a building and became a church where God made his power and presence felt among the assembled. The buildings meant nothing because the church—the gathered body of believers—meant everything.

The twin motifs of purity and power informed the essence of preaching on church organization, and social teaching for one and one-half centuries of New England's colonial experience. Neither of these themes was unknown in Europe but no single church embodied both. Some churches like the "Separate" or "Brownist" churches understood the scriptural truth that for churches to be pure they must be "gathered" out from the world and established on the basis of voluntary commitments and the "covenant of grace." But these churches separated so entirely from the world that they were in no position to influence its operations; they were so heavenly minded, Puritans argued, that they were no earthly good. Other churches like the Anglican and the Presbyterian understood the church's obligation to the nation and its duty to preserve social order according to the God-ordained distinctions between superior and inferior, but they failed to keep their churches pure according to the covenant teachings of Scripture. They relied on human traditions and hierachies that retained many of the "papist" heresies condemned by the Reformers. New England's "Congregational" founders dedicated themselves to the mission of fusing what had been hopelessly fragmented in England and, in so doing, pointed the way to a national renewal and divine favor.[4]

For the experiment in fusion to work, the founders required the precondition of "liberty," or the freedom to start from scratch in constructing a model society. In fact, liberty constituted a third organizing theme of Puritan culture. As power and purity defined the axis of Puritan culture, so liberty bespoke the open space those ideals needed to take root and grow. In England, the opposition of Charles I and Archbishop Laud made it clear that national reform and renewal would have to originate outside of England, in a place where there were no entrenched interests or institutions at odds with the ideal of *Sola Scriptura*. New England, the founders hoped, would be such a place of liberty—not the liberty of unrestrained freedom, but "gospel liberty" harnessed to the duties and dictates of God's Word as understood by the congregations and their ministers. From the start of New World settlement, "liberty" was a sacred term to the Puritans, but it was always used in an instrumental rather than an ultimate sense; it meant the necessary precondition for establishing a pure and powerful holy commonwealth. Purity, power, and liberty constituted a sacred trinity of thought and action; each depended on the other for balance and meaning.

THE SUFFICIENCY OF INDEPENDENT CHURCHES

New England's mission began with the church. The cathedrals in Europe were beautiful to the eye and mighty in splendor but stood in the shadows of more powerful institutions housed in palaces, courthouses, and countinghouses. And, like the buildings in which they worshiped, many members of the Church of England existed in the shadows of ignorance and superstition. In New England, the church would be central. The eyes of the faithful would be opened fully to the truths of God's Word; and with light would come power, and through that power the entire society would be transformed into a people with the soul of a church.

The Puritan founders devoted so much of their creative energies to the church because the entire New World experiment hung on its design. As

they fashioned axioms and rules to uphold pure churches, they were
defining the social assumptions and the division of power that would
undergird every other institution. As Boston's "teacher" and most famous
minister John Cotton explained in a letter to Lord Say and Sele in 1636,
"Noe man fashioneth his house to his hangings, but his hangings to his
house. It is better that the commonwealth be fashioned to the setting forth
of Gods house, which is his church: than to accommodate the church
frame to the civill state." In his classic sermon to the departing Winthrop
fleet, *God's Promise to His Plantation*, Cotton had warned that God's
promises of blessing and peace to a professing people hinged on a due
regard for the "ordinances" of worship, including biblical preaching, discipline, and the sacraments: "As soon as God's Ordinances cease, your
Security ceaseth likewise; but if God plant his Ordinances among you,
fear not, he will maintain them."[5] If the proper rules governing the organization and running of the church were not set from the start, then other
institutions would fail or be corrupted, and the divine commission would
lapse as it had in the Old World.

The immediate requirement before everyone's eyes was that the
churches be pure according to the pattern of the New Testament apostolic
church. In determining how that purity could be institutionalized, the
founders unavoidably confronted the corollary question of power. If
God's Word was sovereign, what did this mean for human authority both
in the church and outside? Sovereignty, by its nature, was unitary and
indivisible. If God's Word was sovereign then *all* human powers and
authorities would have to be limited. Accordingly, Cotton declared that
"all power that is on earth be limited, Church-power or other." This was
partly a deduction from the logic of sovereignty and partly an observation
drawn from sinful human nature. If allowed equality with God, man
would seize "what ever power he hath received. . . . If he have liberty, he
will think why may he not use it."[6] The only solution to the problem of
"tyranny" was a scheme of church government and social order whereby
power would be distributed throughout the body of believers in such a
way that no single individual or group of individuals could seize control
and exert a God-like authority over the rest. All individuals and institutions would be subordinate to the dictates and determinations of God's
sovereign will as revealed in Scripture.

Most immediately, the limitation of human authority meant that
churches must be independent of state control. In England, God's authority in the church was compromised by the crown's claim to absolute control over the church both in the appointment of officers and the determination of correct doctrine. This claim was, in Governor Winthrop's
word, "arbitrary." "God onely hathe this prerogative," he went on,
"whose Sovereintye is absolute, and whose will is a perfecte Rule and
Reason it selfe; so as for men to usurpe such Authority, is tiranye, and
impietye."[7] In New England the churches would be "independent." As

formally codified in *The Cambridge Platform* of 1649, this meant that civil magistrates ordinarily were forbidden to "meddle" in the selection and appointment of church officers, in the administration of church discipline, or in the determination of correct doctrine. Nor could the state "compell" church membership or regulate the preaching of the Word and administration of the sacraments.[8] These crucial functions were left to the churches alone.

If the state did not control and govern the church, who did? One possibility, long the rule in Europe, was to lodge administrative control in the hands of a national board of bishops (the episcopacy) or presbyters (the presbytery). But this too posed the threat of a tyranny of the few over the faithful—which the Puritans knew from painful experience. Studying the origins of the New Testament church, the founders concluded that the church was nothing more (or less) than a local assembly (*ecclesia*) of God's people gathered out of the synagogues and pagan temples to hear the gospel proclaimed in their midst. Any ruling authority outside of the individual congregation was by definition not a part of the church and hence in competition with it. For God's Word to function freely, and for each member to feel an integral part of the church's operations, each congregation must be self-sufficient, containing within itself all the offices and powers necessary for self-regulation. New England's official apologist, John Cotton, termed this form of church government "Congregational," meaning that all authority would be located within particular congregations.[9]

The problem still remained of how local churches could be established and, once established, how order and discipline could be preserved from within. The answer to the question of establishment was found in the Puritan concept of covenant. From the start of their movement in England, Puritans had used covenant theology to interpret Scripture and to explain the terms by which God saved sinners (the covenant of grace) and called individual nations to be his own people (the federal covenant).[10] In New England the founders would apply that same concept to the establishment of local churches. In a sermon delivered to the church at Salem in June 1636, Cotton defended the principle of church covenanting with a text from Jeremiah 50:5 ("Come, and let us cleave unto the Lord in a perpetual and everlasting covenant which shall never be forgotten"). He concluded:

> That which doth make a people a joined people with God, that doth [also] make a church. [and] what is that? The covenant of grace doth make a people, a joined people with God, and therefore a Church of God. And therefore you shall find that when the Lord establishes Israel for a Church unto himself, He maketh this covenant; not only that in Mount Horeb, but He doth make another covenant with them in the plains of Moab, Deut. 29. 10, 17. And so by this means they come to be established to be a church unto the living God.[11]

Churches were nothing more than local covenants whereby people voluntarily "joined" themselves to one another and God in a visible assembly; there was no need for some higher agency or authority beyond local church officers. The mere fact that people came together to worship God made them a church of God. As John Winthrop explained, all "true churches" were founded on an "implicate covenant" between the local assembly, their officers, and God. The problem was that many churches, including the Church of England, failed to recognize the covenant explicitly and were compromised by other sources of power lying outside the local covenanted body. They did not see that what made their church a church was their commitment to one another and to God, not presbyters' or bishops' ordination.[12]

In Puritan terminology, believers in all times and ages constituted the "matter" of a church, and the local covenant was the "form" by which one subgroup of this universal church officially stood before God as a corporate entity and publicly vowed to be a "particular" church. These covenants were always written by the individual congregation, though in practice they all sounded similar. The prototype for all church covenants in New England was that of the Salem church founded in 1629 on the eve of the Great Migration. After months of mutual study and examination, the members came together and agreed to the simple proposition that "we Covenant with the Lord and one with an other; and doe bynd our selves in the presence of God, to walke together in all his waies, according as he is pleased to reveale himself unto us in his Blessed word of truth."[13] This brief sentence describes all the attributes of a true church—a group of believers committing themselves to one another and to God, and standing in absolute submission to the "Blessed word of truth" contained in the Scriptures. The freedom to make simple pledges like this would bring to New England the greatest folk migration in the history of the New World.

To ensure pure church members, congregations founded after Salem built into their period of mutual examination and confession the requirement that prospective members submit a "relation" or "testimony" of saving grace.[14] Since the church covenant was nothing more than a corporate extension of each member's personal covenant of grace, it followed that membership must be limited to true believers or "visible saints." Church membership in New England was not an automatic privilege but a sacred commitment limited to "such, as have not only attained the knowledge of the principles of Religion, and are free from gros[s] and open scandals, but also do together with the profession of their faith and Repentance, walk in blameles[s] obedience to the Word." While recognizing that some "hypocrites inwardly" might escape detection and situate themselves within the body of believers, the churches restricted membership to achieve purity; it was an attempt to make the local "visible church" correspond as closely as possible to the "invisible" or universal church whose "matter" was known only to God. In theory—and generally in practice—prospective members were given the benefit of "charitable discretion," and few were turned away.[15] But the requirement signified the founders' intention to create discriminating churches of committed members who, by virtue of their purity, would elicit God's special "interest" and favor.

Once formed into autonomous local churches, congregations still faced the problem of maintaining internal order and discipline and ensuring that God's Word would be faithfully and powerfully proclaimed. A church gathered in submission to God's Word meant little if there was no living voice to explain and apply that Word. While the assembled "brethren" constituted the "essence and being" of a church and reserved for themselves the "priviledge" of consent in all matters touching upon their assembly, they could not be a complete organism until they ordained ruling officers. These officers included a pastor "to exhort," a teacher "to attend to doctrine," and ruling elders "to joyn with the *Pastor* and *Teacher* in those acts of *spiritual Rule* which are distinct from the ministry of the word and Sacraments." To free the ministers and elders for preaching and spiritual oversight, the office of deacon was also included to manage the physical operations of the church and care for the poor and widows. The selection of rulers was left solely to the consent of the brethren, but once ordained, congregations were expected to "becom[e] subject, *and* most willingly submit to their ministry in the Lord, whom they have so chosen."[16] Covenanting with their ministers and elders, congregations promised to sacrifice their own will and obey the teachings of their spiritual superiors as long as these were compatible with Scripture.

The ministers enjoyed awesome powers in New England society; they alone could speak for God in public assemblies of the entire congregation. Their sermons were the only voice of authority that congregations were pledged to obey unconditionally. Yet, because sermons had to be based on *Sola Scriptura*, even the ministers' authority was limited. Their authority was by virtue of their specialized knowledge of the Scriptures and their ordination, not through any special perfections or infallible inspiration. The printed Bible was the bridge linking ministers to congregations, and all who internalized its vocabulary, rhythms, and doctrines could participate in a common community of discourse.[17] In cases where ministers abused that text or lived in a scandalous manner unbecoming their high office, congregations could dismiss them. Congregational vows of submission were not vows of apathy but of constant supervision and vigilance. Congregations were obliged not only to obey the voice of the sermon but also to read their Bibles and make sure their ministers held true to biblical doctrines. Though no friend to "democracy," John Cotton upheld the congregation's responsibility to monitor the minister and limit the range of his authority:

It is therefore fit for every man to be studious of the bounds which the Lord hath set. And for the People, in whom fundamentally all power lyes, to give as much power as God in his word gives to men. And it is meet that Magistrates in the Commonwealth, and so Officers in Churches should desire to know the utmost bounds of their own power, and it is safe for both. All intrenchment upon the bounds which God hath not given, they are not enlargements, but burdens and snares.[18]

THE "CONGREGATIONAL WAY" OF CHURCH ORDER

When word of the "Congregational Way" reached England many nonconformists initially sympathetic to the Great Migration, which they had hoped would provide a model to emulate at home, began to question whether their New World brethren had become too infected with the separatist teachings of the "New Plymouth men" in neighboring Plymouth colony.[19] The New England system of autonomous church government and discrimination in the admission of church members, in their opinion, conceded too much to purity at the expense of comprehensive social order and national uniformity. In England, where large portions of the population were illiterate (hence incapable of regulating themselves according to *Sola Scriptura*), and where there was a broad spectrum of dissenting ideas in opposition to *any* established church, the New England Way would be inevitably separatist and anarchic; isolated churches would spring into being with no national center or established uniformity. Furthermore, the critics pointed out, while Puritans claimed Scripture as their sole authority, there was no explicit precedent for local covenanting in the New Testament. How then could New England ministers and magistrates claim their way was nonseparatist, let alone scriptural? Or, by implication, how could they expect England to follow their example?

In response to English criticisms as well as dissenting voices in their own midst, the leading founders insisted that New England must be judged by the shape of its entire society, not simply by its churches. As important as the churches were, they were only one part of the total social experiment. Any final evaluation of their way must take into account the configuration of the whole "nation" or society. And here the coercive and establishmentarian aspects of the New England Way became readily, even painfully, apparent.

Much as the founders insisted upon Congregational independency, they never meant by that term an absolute separation of church and state in which government was unconcerned with the religious life of its people. On the contrary, government existed primarily for religious reasons and represented, in effect, the coercive arm of the churches. The state could not compel church membership or determine doctrinal orthodoxy. It was, however, responsible for preserving uniformity of worship as determined by the churches generally and for punishing such "outward" transgressions of God's law as "Idolatry, Blasphemy, Heresy, venting corrupt and pernicious opinions . . . open contempt of the word preached, prophanation of the Lords day, [or] disturbing the peaceable administration and exercise of the worship and holy things of God."[20] These sins against the "first table" of the Law were not simply moral or religious offenses but civil offenses as codified in the Massachusetts *Body of Liberties* (1641) and Connecticut's *Fundamental Laws* (1636).[21] Offenders were prosecuted in civil court and punished by fine, imprisonment, banishment, or (in theory at least) death. The state also had the positive responsibility to promote actively the proclamation of God's Word by compelling church attendance and by providing support for the ministry and meetinghouses. In the Puritan state, religious freedom would be tolerated no further than the boundaries of "gospel order" determined by the Congregational churches. Those who were not prepared to accept those boundaries were at liberty to live elsewhere.

The Puritans' suppression of heterodoxy was in keeping with their instrumental sense of liberty as the freedom to establish and maintain a Bible commonwealth. The state existed to wield power in the interests of gospel purity, and that meant prosecution of religious offenses as well as civil. In his famous quarrel with the Massachusetts Bay ministers, Roger Williams protested that "if thou huntest any for cause of *conscience*, how canst thou say thou followest the *Lambe* of *God* who so abhorr'd that practice?" John Cotton replied that the individual conscience was at liberty only insofar as it was "rightly informed." Any further concession to liberty would be licentious. If an enemy of the New England Way should "*persist* in the Errour of his way, and be therefore punished; He is not *persecuted* for Cause of *Conscience*, but for sinning *against* his Owne *Conscience*."[22] In New England, where all institutions were purified according to biblical precept and ordered by visible saints, there was no inherent contradiction between civic loyalty and godly sanctification. Thus, when a person knowingly transgressed the law of the land or blasphemed its public institutions, that person sinned against his or her conscience, and it would be a perversion of charity *not* to punish him or her. "Such things as a man may tolerate when he cannot remove them, he cannot tolerate without sin when he may remove them."[23] If Christ did not prosecute evil, it was because his church did not have the power to prosecute in the times of the Roman Empire. In New England, the churches had such a power through the agency of the state, and it would be sinful not to use it for the suppression of evil.

Governor Winthrop and his assistants expanded the franchise in 1631 to include all male church members, and in 1632 provided that all civil officers would be elected by the freemen.[24] Once called to office, a ruler's only responsibility was to the Word of God, not to the people who called him to office. The provision for popular election, Thomas Shepard insisted, was not an admission of popular sovereignty but a measure designed to facilitate the "gover[nment] of the Lord over a people." Because of sin, individuals were inclined to "look unto present profit" and personal "ambition"—qualities that were sure to undermine a public spirit of corporate unity. Shepard likened the power of self-interest to a

"raging Sea which would overwhelm all if they have not bankes." Laws
and magistrates existed to contain that sea and confine the people within
the safe banks of God's "strict government," even at the cost of popular
"impatience."[25] In this "theocracy," or rule of God's Word, rulers could
and did enact unpopular legislation in accordance with scriptural precept,
and it was the responsibility of the people to honor these laws whether
they liked them or not.

The selection of provincial officers by popular election and codification
of biblically inspired laws were only part of Puritan government. To be
consistent with the decentralized Congregational ideals of mutual covenanting and local autonomy, most day-to-day governing powers were
delegated to individual towns.[26] Once established, each New England
town, like the church it encompassed, was a self-sufficient entity that governed and regulated itself in all regards. The responsibilities of internal
regulation and self-defense were entrusted to the town, which by covenant and mutual consent appointed leaders and enforced laws consistent
with God's Word. The town meeting, consisting of all landowners,
appointed "selectmen" from among the "better sort" to run affairs
throughout the year but reserved the right to approve all legislation at its
quarterly or semiannual meetings.[27] Only in cases of irreconcilable division did the provincial government intervene to render a judgment. In
matters of local defense the same assumptions prevailed. All males
between the ages of fifteen and fifty-five were formed into local "trained-
bands" in which they retained the covenant privilege of electing their
captain and officers, subject to confirmation by the General Court.[28] In the
militia, as in the churches and governments, the goals of voluntary obedience and covenant commitment determined the form authority would
assume.

The series of covenants that joined church, town, and commonwealth
into one great chain of order also included the household—parents, children, and servants.[29] Although the smallest of New England institutions,
the family was, next to the church, the most important. Those who arrived
in New England unattached to families were required to attach themselves to a household and submit to the discipline of the husband and
wife. Ministers routinely referred to the family as a "little church" or a
"little commonwealth," by which they meant a microcosm of the covenantal relationships governing church and state.[30] Within the Puritan
household the father assumed the role of the minister in leading family
devotions and organizing discussions around the weekly sermon. Husband and wife together modeled the magisterial function in running the
household and eliciting the unquestioning obedience of its members. In
this way children would be prepared to assume larger covenant obligations in adulthood and instinctively defer to their superiors in church and
state.[31]

It is clear that the New England Way did not seek purity at the expense
of power and uniformity so much as it redistributed power among many
hands in local contexts. The English critics were correct in believing that

such a way could never work in England, but they failed to see how well suited it was to the open spaces of the New World. By locating power in the particular towns and defining institutions in terms of local covenants and mutual commitments, the dangers of mobility and atomism—the chief threats to stability in the New World—were minimized. This was particularly true in the case of the local church. In England, church members belonged to a national parish system and so were free to move at will from one local branch of the national church to another without losing membership status or privilege. As Governor Winthrop explained, "If a man enters no covenant, then is he not tyed to one Churche more then to another, and then may he departe without leave or offense."[32] The genius of the Congregational Way lay in the local covenant, which ensured local commitment. As churches came into being only by means of a local covenant, so individual members could be released from their sacred oath only with the concurrence of the local body. In practice such a release or "dismission" was granted only in relatively rare circumstances. Persons leaving without the consent of the body sacrificed not only church membership but also property title, which was contingent on local residence. Through measures like these, which combined economic and spiritual restraints, New England towns achieved extraordinarily high levels of persistence and social cohesion. Townspeople endured disagreements and bickerings to be sure, but compared to other seventeenth-century societies the New England Way was remarkable for its record of internal peace, order, and uniformity.[33]

THE SERMON AND SOCIAL ORDER

New England's unique social structure of interlocking institutions governed by a single nucleus of covenanted saints gave congregations the coercive powers necessary to impose their brand of piety on society, and it also endowed the sermon with unprecedented range and influence. Although spoken exclusively by the ordained ministers, the sermon's source was not ministerial wisdom but Scripture, and its powers were the common possession of ministers, magistrates, and congregations. Besides dominating Sunday worship services, sermons were delivered at every significant event in the life of communities. In the Old World, social habits and institutions were legitimized by a broad range of authorities and rituals, such as royal processions, coronations, and martial parades. In New England there would be no competing voices or rituals, and the sermon would become as important for social meaning as for spiritual enlightenment. It not only interpreted God's plan of redemption and told the people how they must live as a church but also defined and legitimated the meaning of their lives as citizen and magistrate, superior and inferior, soldier, parent, child, and laborer. Sermons were authority incarnate.

The responsibility to provide social direction placed added demands on the sermon, but the structure of Puritan society rendered this job easier than it would have been in the Old World. In England, where many laws and customs had evolved through "tradition" rather than express biblical warrant, ministers could not preach the duty of unlimited submission to authority without compromising the doctrine of *Sola Scriptura*. Sometimes civil disobedience and nonconformity were necessary to honor the higher morality of God's Word. But in New England, all laws and customs proceeded from biblical texts, and all social arrangements were founded on voluntary covenant. Ministers did not have to make distinctions between submission to the civil order and submission to the Word of God. There was, in their view, no conflict between Christ and the culture they had created. Thus in guiding their listeners to the way of sanctification and the "covenant of thanksgiving," ministers needed only to urge them to follow the Way set forth by civil and ecclesiastical "fathers." Civil obedience and corporate loyalty could not earn salvation but could be taken as a positive "sign" of election. Conversely, a willful rebellion against the social order was indicative of an endangered soul.

With the sermon's provenance expanded to include social and cultural functions previously reserved for other dignitaries and institutions, the ministers encountered far more opportunities to preach. They discovered that these social occasions required a rhetoric and mode of persuasion different from the evangelical message they had concentrated on in England. Their central theme had always been what God had done for humanity on the cross and in the lives of his elect. Their emotional levers were God's unconditional love and mercy to an undeserving, sin-sick people. As social and cultural custodians, however, their primary focus shifted from God's mercy to man's responsibility to honor the conditional terms of God's national covenant. Here the emotional levers were fear and the possibility of divine desertion. Unlike personal salvation, which was granted not earned, national covenants required good works on the part of the citizens.

The tension between these two opposite emphases had been reconciled theoretically in England, but practical implementation was another story.[34] Puritan faith was a minority religion, so there was no danger of confusing or conflating the logic of the unconditionality of God's decrees in matters of personal salvation with the logic of man's conditional obedience in matters of national covenant keeping. The Puritans, quite simply, were not responsible for shaping or upholding a national policy. In the New World environment, however, three thousand miles away from English rule and institutions, the balance in preaching shifted to include frequent proclamations on social order, conditional obedience, and corporate mission. Inevitably, this raised anew the problem of purity versus power.

The latent tensions between the sermon as a proclamation of God's free grace and the sermon as an instrument of social direction became dramatically manifest in 1636 when the recently arrived prophetess Anne Hutchinson publicly accused the New England ministers (save her teacher John Cotton and brother-in-law John Wheelwright) of preaching a "covenant of works."[35] Hutchinson had come to spiritual maturity under Cotton's Old World preaching, which was rigorously evangelical and unequivocal in its insistence that there is "no condition [of obedience] before Faith . . . whereby a man can close with Jesus Christ"; she therefore viewed the new emphasis on civil loyalty and public obedience only as a corruption of the gospel.[36] Such obedience, she argued was no "evidence" of justification and, worse yet, could actually lead unwitting listeners down the soul-destroying path of works righteousness. Assurance of salvation lay solely in the internal testimony of the Holy Spirit; any other ground, including outward conformity to the New England Way, was as apt to be a sign of hypocrisy as true "effectual calling."

According to the laws of New England, Hutchinson's public accusations constituted a civil offense and in 1637 she was tried for heresy. The first charge against her was that she made her private reservations grounds for a public attack on the ministry. Though a "private person" was permitted and even required to question the minister "for information" and clarification, it had to be done quietly and without public "reproach." If everyone was allowed equal opportunity for public oratory, gospel order would disintegrate into a Babel of competing voices all claiming to speak in the name and place of God. In Hutchinson's case this breach of the rules of public speech was widened still further by the fact that she was a woman speaking out of her "place."[37] But even worse than the social consequences of her speech were the possible spiritual repercussions. Her words threatened to undermine all faith in the New England Way, which depended on a bridge of trust and mutual commitment linking minister, congregation, and Word into one united organism. Without that trust, social and spiritual order would collapse; there were no other external institutions to rely upon.

Early in her trial it became apparent that Hutchinson's defense and public support depended in no small measure on the tacit support of John Cotton. Congregations wanted to trust their ministers as much as the ministers wanted that trust, and the people would support Hutchinson as long as their beloved teacher spoke on her behalf. Like Hutchinson, Cotton did not at first appreciate or understand the added social demands placed on the sermon in the New World. Before proceeding in earnest against Hutchinson, the ministers first met in a synod with Cotton to explain and justify their novel creation. After protracted debate Cotton was led to see how obedience to New England's biblically deduced institutions constituted a form of "sanctification" and that so long as such obedience was not made the "ground" of justification in place of Christ's free sacrifice "the Soule may gather Knowledge of his estate, from such Evidences of Sanctification."[38] Armed with this concession from Cotton, the magistrates proceeded against Hutchinson as a united front. Having lost Cotton's support, Hutchinson invoked instead the "immediate revelation" of the Holy Spirit. Such a claim to personal revelation supplanted the principle of *Sola Scriptura* that both ministers and congregations were pledged to uphold and resulted in her conviction and sentence of banishment. In a parallel church trial Hutchinson's congregation followed the lead of the ministers and, excepting her children, voted unanimously for her excommunication. The "Antinomian controversy" thus ended as abruptly as it began, and the "Antinomian party" disintegrated.

Interestingly, the fact that Anne Hutchinson's story lived on in New England history into the eighteenth century is attributable mainly to the ministers.[39] Hutchinson never became a popular martyr or folk hero, but she did live on in elite memories. Her accusations had touched fears the ministers themselves were feeling. Hutchinson was not the only one concerned about confusing grace and works. The new social responsibilities of the sermon had multiplied so quickly and were so pressing that ministers themselves wondered if they had moved too close to preaching works righteousness. Hutchinson forced them to confront that question head-on and legitimate their social preaching. Her accusations lingered in their memories and furnished material for self-justifying sermons over the next decade and beyond. Their middle way was precarious, and the smallest slip to either side would plunge them either into an abyss of power without purity or (as Anne Hutchinson or Roger Williams would have preferred) of purity without power.

Reacting to the prodding of Anne Hutchinson, New England's ministers entered an intensive period of institutional self-examination that would continue throughout the colonial era. They needed to know that the Way they proclaimed was pleasing to God and not a perversion of his Word. In a series of sermons delivered shortly after the Antinomian controversy, Concord's Peter Bulkeley rehearsed again the careful distinctions between federal covenants and the covenant of grace. Bulkeley was moderator of the Cambridge Synod of 1637 that persuaded Cotton to oppose Anne Hutchinson. In *The Gospel-Covenant* he carried the same arguments to his congregation. With painstaking care, he demonstrated that the separate and contradictory logics of the two covenants were appropriate in their proper spheres and that neither could stand without the other. Without coercive powers, pure institutions were impotent, whereas powerful institutions without converted leaders and sanctified governing principles became the rivals of God, not his servants. Only by preserving both logics could New England become the model society that Winthrop had envisioned aboard the *Arabella*. In terms similar to Winthrop's, Bulkeley urged his congregation to remember that

the Lord looks for more from thee, then from other people; more zeale for God, more love to his truth, more justice, and equity in thy wayes; thou shouldst be a special people, an onely people, none like thee in all the earth. Oh be so, in loving the Gospel and the Ministers of it. . . . Take heed lest for neglect of either, God remove thy Candlesticke out of the midst of thee; lest being now *as a Citie upon an hill*, which many seek unto, thou be left like a *Beacon upon the top of a mountaine*, desolate and forsaken.[40]

THE OCCASIONAL SERMON AND SOCIAL PREACHING

In distinguishing the separate but overlapping covenants of grace and national peoplehood, context meant everything. As social guardians, ministers could preach a message of civic obedience and works righteousness as long as they made it plain that their message concerned corporate and temporal blessings, not eternal salvation. As gospel heralds, they had to remind their hearers that good works were no more than a form of "thankfulness" that came *after* God's gift of grace and did nothing to earn salvation. These distinctions were clear enough in theory but left a pressing rhetorical problem. Both personal and corporate covenants were proclaimed through the same medium—the sermon. Both were rooted in scriptural texts, both employed the common term "covenant." How were audiences to know which logic was being employed in any particular sermon? To avoid dangerous confusions and endless qualifications, the founders had to find a rhetorical signal or clue to let listeners know what type of sermon and what type of covenant logic they could expect to hear from the pulpit. That signal would come to be the "occasional" or weekday sermon.

Occasional sermons were not unknown in England, but the founders invested them with a new legal status and scope. From the first days of New World settlement, fast days were observed and weekday sermons invoked to secure God's corporate blessings on dangerous ocean crossings, church foundings, and civic order. On Sundays, ministers would be gospel heralds proclaiming the way of personal salvation through faith in Christ; and on weekdays—as the occasion required—they would become social guardians telling the nation who they were and what they must do to retain God's special covenant interest. Through this simple but comprehensive rhetorical division of labor based on the day of the week, the sermon could retain both its purity and power in guiding the spiritual and civic lives of its listeners. By carefully separating the themes of personal salvation and corporate conditions, and by limiting explicit corporate commentary to weekdays, the people would not become confused or misled, and God's Word would be brought to bear on all aspects of life.

Since all society fell under the mastery of God's Word, it was necessary that there be provision for formal presentation of that Word at every significant event in the life of the community. More than any other custom or institution, the occasional sermon symbolized New England's claim to peculiar peoplehood and proclaimed that in all events bearing on public life, God's Word would be preeminent.

Of all the occasions New Englanders observed for purposes of weekday sermon attendance, the most versatile and numerous were the fast days. In England, the Puritans observed fasts as an alternative to Anglican holy days, but their observances enjoyed neither the force of law nor the participation of the whole nation. In New England, the fast day was a public event called by civil or ministerial authority and imposed on the entire community.[41] Depending on circumstances, it could be limited to one particular town or church, or observed simultaneously in every church and town throughout the land. On such days normal activities would cease and communities would come together at the meetinghouse to implore God's mercy and inquire into the meaning of events that bore on their collective well- being. Sometimes the precipitating causes were happy, as in the founding of a congregation or the dedication of a meetinghouse. More often, however, they were disasters such as drought, pestilence, earthquake, war, or internal division. Such events were always understood as divine messages signaling God's displeasure with the life of his people. By coming together in solemn assembly to hear God speak, the people expressed their dependence on God and their willingness to amend whatever evils had provoked the Lord's wrath.

As social guardians or "watchmen," ministers were responsible for being on the lookout for divine warnings and, when they appeared, for bringing the people together for a diagnosis of their spiritual ills and for corrective action. No matter what the particular calamity, fast sermons dwelt on the general underlying truth that "the sin of a people is the cause . . . of [God's] wrath against that people."[42] The only saving remedy was the elimination of sin through "repentance and reformation." Through the ritualized and highly repetitive formula of the fast sermon, inhabitants reminded themselves again and again that by their own solemn vows they confirmed God's special interest in them and their obligation to obey his law. If such obedience was not forthcoming, God could sever the national covenant and leave the people to their own devices in a hostile environment. Such a national desertion would not mean that all the inhabitants were damned—that was another story and another covenant—but it did mean that New England could no longer expect God's temporal blessings to them *as a nation.* By their sins and refusal to repent they had become one more profane nation in the wilderness of this world.

However somber and accusatory fast sermons were, they also conveyed hope and confidence in the knowledge that by gathering together for public "humiliation" and attendance on God's Word the people were taking the necessary first step toward deliverance. The ritual of the fast day served notice to the people and to God that desertion was "not yet" upon them. Invariably the trials passed, the enemy was vanquished, and the people heaved a collective sigh of relief. At such times of deliverance, another weekday sermon was called—a thanksgiving sermon—in which the minister reminded the people that it was God who delivered them and not they themselves. Thus in a thanksgiving sermon delivered after the Pequot Indians were defeated in 1637, Thomas Hooker insisted that "it was not ye army we sent into ye field it was not ye prayers that we mad[e] but it is ye lord that hath helped us hether to."[43] If the people forgot this for one moment the judgments would be even more severe. Just as fast days were cause for hope as well as lament, so thanksgiving days were moments for sober personal reflection as well as corporate celebration. In effect, the two occasions taught the same lesson: vows once taken lasted forever, and God would hold his people and their children to account for their commitment to his covenant.

Although Puritans preferred spontaneous fasts and thanksgivings to fixed religious holidays, they did allow themselves one civil holiday in May which, next to Sundays, was the most important day of the year. This was election day, when freemen throughout the New England colonies gathered to elect ~representatives to their assemblies and legislators met to nominate members of the Governor's Council.[44] Election day was important not only in confirming the covenant principles of consent and voluntary submission at the highest level of government but also in reminding the inhabitants that they were part of a larger experiment and mission. All the local covenants were bound in a larger unity comprising visible saints throughout the realm who, in addition to attaching themselves to churches, also bound their nation to the terms of God's law. For their sakes, God would bless the nation-as-a-whole and make it a beacon for lost humanity. They hoped—and this was the point of the New World mission—that England would take note of this decentralized but still coherent "nation" and imitate it. In the meantime, New Englanders would keep the covenant alive in their own corner of the New World and signify that fact on election day.

Beginning in 1634, and on an annual basis after 1640, provincial election days culminated in the delivery of an election sermon.[45] Other societies relied on elaborate traditions, rituals, and costume dramas of pomp and ceremony to confirm and legitimate political authority. New Englanders staged public dramas of a more austere sort: a political sermon delivered by one of the local ministers to all the assembled magistrates.[46] The setting of the election sermon, initially Boston's First Church and after 1658 the Boston Town House, reinforced the solemnity of the occasion. There, seated before the speaker in the principal building of the province, were the three orders of authority: the magistrates who represented the oligarchy, the deputies who represented the democracy, and the ministers who represented the theocracy. Each would be addressed in turn so that all aspects of government and authority would be illuminated by the Word of God. Unlike fasts and thanksgivings that were delivered irregularly in every town by a multitude of ministers, the election sermon was limited to a single day in the year and was spoken by only one minister. The communities would come together through their representatives and meet as one national assembly. With all the "tribes" gathered before him, the minister would speak and channel all the words of his peers into one voice of God to his New England people.

As the speaker entered the pulpit, the mood was expectant. What followed marked the moment of superb oratory in a culture that valued the spoken word above all other art forms. The speaker's goal was not to be innovative or entertaining, but to recall for his audience the vision that first impelled New England's mission. Terms like "covenant," "errand," "pilgrimage," "wilderness," "desert," "garden," or "controversy," recur frequently over the generations and seem never to have lost their power to stir souls. While the themes and images were constant, current events were not, and in the heat of controversy familiar terms took on new vigor and meaning. The wonder of election sermons, as A. W. Plumstead points out, is "not that there are as many poor sermons as there are, but that there are as many good ones."[47]

Beginning with John Cotton in 1634 and running through John Davenport in 1669, the pantheon of great founders all had their turn at the speaker's desk on election day. Their sermons initiated an ongoing drama that charted the epic quest of a peculiar people making their way in a strange new world filled with great dangers and great possibilities. Invariably, the election speakers reiterated the terms of God's national covenant with New England. They reminded the inhabitants and their leaders that they were not only bound in particular churches but were also part of a national "people of God" entrusted with a divine commission to let their light shine before the nations. New England's mission, they exulted, was glorious beyond anything that man could invent. But a sober warning was also sounded with contrapuntal regularity: while personal salvation was unconditional and irrevocable, national covenants required the ongoing condition of obedience; irresponsibility in leaders or followers, or a gross contempt for God's Word and messengers, would lead to their destruction. In time, these oft-repeated promises and warnings came to enjoy a sacramentlike significance. In the same way that baptism and communion were "signs and seals" of the individual covenant of grace, election sermons were a social sacrament signifying that for one more year New Englanders had kept the faith and were publicly and officially a peculiar people of God.

THE LIMITS OF OCCASIONAL SERMONS

Throughout all the changes that would take place in colonial New England, the occasional sermon would remain fixed at the center of public assembly. As time wore on, it became more and more significant; indeed by the Revolutionary era, occasional sermons rivaled regular Sunday sermons in importance. Yet, scarcely any of them were printed in the first generation.[48] As creators rather than preservers, the founders were preeminently men of speech, and all of their occasional sermons existed in one way or another to secure the place of the regular sermon spoken in weekly worship. Government, as Thomas Shepard explained in his unpublished election sermon notes for 1638, did not exist for its own sake or to uphold unlimited civil liberties but to "preserve our freedom which we have in this country . . . [to] cleave to the Lord and love his truth and ordinances."[49] For individual New Englanders, the saving sermons they had traveled three thousand miles to hear were not delivered on public occasions or read in print; these sermons were heard on Sundays. They had willingly risked life and property to come to the wilderness so they could sit on benches in drafty, gloomy barns for three to six hours on Sundays hearing the Word as it should be preached. It mattered little to them that their nation became great and powerful, if they or their families were damned. To them, if not to later historians, the most important sermons were the ones heard Sunday mornings and afternoons, for they held forth the keys to the kingdom of heaven and pointed the way to the salvation of the soul.

[2]

Regular Preaching and the Sequence of Salvation

Ultimately, the sermon was powerful because it offered guidance in the all-encompassing search for salvation that could not be obtained in any other way. Some scholars have emphasized independent "popular piety" bordering on autonomy among this Bible-reading people, but the more avidly people read their Bibles the more they depended for understanding and direction on the superior knowledge and resources of the minister, and therefore on the sermon.[1]

No seventeenth-century culture was more uniformly literate than New England. Empirical studies confirm that from highest born to lowest New Englanders were a "people of the Word" who could and, in most cases, did regularly read their Bibles from cover to cover. These same studies also reveal, however, that besides their Bibles these people read practically nothing else. The vernacular Bible was plain in grammar and syntax but also mysterious; a unique document "breathed by God, and therefore infallible and stamped with Gods own Authority."[2] To be understood correctly it had to be read in the original Hebrew and Greek, alongside textual commentaries accumulated over the centuries. Such sources were unavailable or unreadable for most people and therefore had to be summarized in the sermon. Instead of bringing a sense of independence and autonomy characteristic of "modern" literate societies, Puritan literacy enhanced the public respect for the sermon and for the minister who preached it.

The one exception to New England's literate but nearly bookless society was the minister's study. No matter how rustic the settlement, here were found most of the relevant texts bearing on the great and significant questions raised by the printed Word. On the minister's shelves lay the Greek and Hebrew texts of the Bible, commentaries in Latin and English indexed by chapter and verse, concordances of key words and metaphors in the original languages and in English, comprehensive systems of divinity from the church fathers to the English Puritans, natural histories to explain the imagery of the ancient Near East, encyclopedias of human knowledge, and a range of Protestant sermons dating back to the Reformation. Many of these sources were literally "Greek" to ordinary readers

32

whose only literary skills were in English, but for ministers having a "knowledge of Tongues and Arts" they were nothing less than the interpretive keys to the kingdom of heaven.[3] As the inhabitants struggled to carve out a living from rock-strewn soil, the ministers were called to the equally arduous task of tilling the pages of Holy Writ and sacred commentary so that on sabbath day they could plant in the hearts of their listeners seeds of eternity that would transform the untamed wilderness of the soul into the "Lord's garden."

The minister was expected to visit his congregation privately, tutor and catechize the youth and, when necessary, farm his own land. His chief responsibility, however, was preparing Sunday sermons. His books and many hours of preparation helped him project his listeners into the mysterious and sacred world of revelation where they might view their lives from a divine vantage point. This perspective had its own inviolate past, present, and future; it had a divinely conceived and executed chronology that charted the course of peoples and individuals from beginning to end, and that supplied purpose to an otherwise meaningless and uncontrollable flow of events. On weekday occasions, the minister examined New England's corporate meaning, but on Sundays his chief concern was the individual, personal pilgrimage from death in sin, to new life in Christ, to the hope of eternal life. It was not enough for people to understand divine direction and sacred history in its cosmic perspective, or even as it applied to their corporate experience in the New World; individuals had to understand it within the cycle of their own past, present, and future so that it would become a real force in their day-to-day lives.

REGULAR SERMON COMPOSITION

In a passage from 1 Corinthians 13 that Puritan ministers were fond of quoting, the sacred chronology of life-in-Christ is organized around the concepts of "faith, hope, and charity." Besides being three cardinal Christian virtues, these terms encapsulate main themes of regular preaching on salvation that will be summarized in this chapter. Faith for the Puritan was rooted in the past; it was the record in Scripture, and in the subsequent lives of God's elect, of his promises and saving accomplishments. Listeners accepted this generalized "historical faith" as their own personal promise and assurance of salvation, so that it became for them a "saving faith." In response to the gift of saving faith, God's law taught individuals how to live their lives in the present according to the rule of charity or love. For the Puritans, this divine love was less a feeling of closeness to Christ or deep gratitude for salvation (though these were important) than it was a practical commitment to obey God's law and teaching in all aspects of their life. Such "sanctified" obedience must not be motivated by self-righteousness but proceed from a deep sense of gratitude for what Christ had done on the cross. Finally, because God promised eternal life to the faithful and obedient, and because he fulfilled all his promises in the death and resurrection of Christ, believers could take hope for the future. Most generally this meant the "certain" hope of eternal life after death. But for some special few Christians living in the "end days," this hope would be more immediately centered on the moment when Christ would return to earth to inaugurate the "new heavens and new earth" when sin would be conquered and the saints would reign with Christ forever.

With this clear vision of the controlling themes and purposes of regular preaching, ministers selected their biblical texts and topics for maximum efficiency. To meet the demands of preaching at least two, one- to two-hour discourses weekly, they typically organized their sermons into larger blocks of thought to extend over many weeks or months in the form of "sermon series." Instead of selecting scattered texts that would vary widely in theme and subject matter from week to week, they preferred to take a chapter or book of Scripture for long-term study, a verse at a time. Sometimes a single verse could occupy their attention for many weeks.[4] By organizing their sermons rather like a modern college course, ministers could focus their collateral reading and simplify the process of sermon construction. At the same time, their immersion in single themes or texts facilitated the recall of ordinary listeners who relied on their memories rather than on books to store information and who needed to hear the same truths reiterated week after week.[5]

After careful textual study, ministers recorded their extensive sermon "notes" in leatherbound volumes that closely resembled printed treatises. The number of pages in sermon books varied between thirty and two hundred, and depending on their size could contain three to five hundred words per page. Generally each volume contained one or more series broken down into sermons of six to twelve pages each. In these extended sermon outlines, punctuation was scarce, but thoughts were developed fully in the distinctive text-doctrine-application formula of the plain style sermon. To conserve paper, margins were fully used to make note of scriptural cross-references that could be read during the sermon and to enter abbreviated rhetorical cues, like "doct," "reas," "use 1," that could lead the minister through the major "heads" or divisions of his discourse. The substance of the notes was almost exclusively scriptural exegesis and personal applications. Even when not quoting Scripture directly, ministers recorded phrases that borrowed freely from biblical terminology and indeed sounded like part of the Bible. Despite the wide reading in commentaries and concordances that went into preparing a sermon series, extrabiblical names rarely appeared in the notes. The ministers' intent in eliminating such references from the sermon was not to plagiarize their sources; strictly speaking, there was no human "original" to steal or copy. The only original was God's Word, and all commentaries were part of a derivative common enterprise. When people listened to the sermon they expected to hear God's Word—and only God's Word—made comprehensible to their limited capacities. As Dover's John Rayner warned, "If any minester will preach trash and toyes, traditions of men instead of the puer word of God, theire workes shall be burnt.'"[6]

SELF-EXAMINATION AS PRELUDE TO PREACHING

Ministers rarely talked about their own turmoils and uncertainties in their sermons; indeed, the pronoun *I* hardly ever appears in their notes. But such personal detachment was less a reflection of the minister's distance from his discourse than of his intent to create the impression that God himself was speaking through a human voice. In fact, ministers agonized over their sermons and recorded that agony in another staple of Puritan literature, the diary.[7] From these it is clear that, along with hours of biblical study and analysis, the ministers engaged in ceaseless self-examination and self-censure. Before calling the congregation to account to God for their lives, thoughts, and feelings, the minister first had to submit his own life to a withering divine scrutiny. Only then could he project that message outward and say to his congregation with the proper combination of humility and finality, "Thus saith the Lord."

The *Journal* of Thomas Shepard provides an especially complete and frank account of the interior struggles ministers faced in preparing their sermons. Not every minister spent as much time as Shepard "walking in my study musing on the sermon"; nor were others as eloquent in the pulpit. But all shared in Shepard's painstaking preparation. Of all the topics Shepard reflected upon in his diary, none was more engrossing or problematic than the course of his own soul's salvation. That course was not a smooth linear sequence from conviction of sin to conversion and unfailing assurance, but a ragged cycle of assurance and doubt, condemnation and "renewed conversion." He was plagued not only by his repeated failures to imitate Christ's "love and meekness" but even more by his consciousness of doing good for the wrong reasons; he was forever caught in the double bind of his own theology. Justification or salvation, he was certain, involved "nothing else but receiving God's kindness . . . and so was quite opposite to doing [meritorious works]."[8] Yet, at the same time, the "doing" of God's will was clearly required as a token of "thanksgiving." Faith required obedience, but obedience had to spring from the proper motive "in way of thankfulness." The enduring problem was how to do God's will in such a way that the doing never outweighed the sense of sheer gratitude for God's free gift of grace.

Nowhere was Shepard's dilemma more painfully focused than when he reflected on his preaching. Here was the one arena where he supposedly did the most good for God, but it was also the place where he saw most clearly "the hypocrisy of my heart" that "in my ministry I sought to comfort others and quicken others [so] that the glory might reflect on me as well as on God." In times when he felt "comfortably enlarged" in the pulpit he saw how easily he grew "puffed up" with pride. At other times, when restricted by a "straitened mouth," he grew downcast and discouraged. In both cases he erred by allowing his own natural feelings to take precedence over the gospel he proclaimed and by failing to recognize that it was the Holy Spirit who applied his words to listeners' hearts, not his own abilities. Unlike more mundane activities or "merely human acts," where a person might legitimately "have some respect to his own glory," the task of the ministry was "so wholly divine" that there was no room for "my own glory too."[9] Shepard imposed a double standard on his ministry that required him to be more self-denying and "emptied" than his hearers.

Like Anne Hutchinson, Shepard recognized from his own life that good works could lead as easily to pride as sincere thankfulness, and Christians must be ever careful "not [to] build their faith upon their life, but their life upon their faith and their faith upon God's free grace."[10] While it was necessary and proper to speak of obedience or "reformation" as a condition for divine favor in terms of God's national covenant with New England, this train of thought would be "as handwritings of death" if applied to the covenant of grace in regular preaching. At best, good works were an "evidence of reconciliation." But even there they were only a "mediate" evidence that had to rest self-consciously on the prior and more compelling "immediate evidence" of salvation impressed on the heart by the Holy Spirit through the hearing of God's Word in the sermon.[11]

Closely related in Shepard's thought to the problem of proper obedience and preaching was the question of personal assurance of salvation. This was less a question of correct theological understanding than of the "frame" of the heart or the "affections." Throughout the history of Christianity, churchmen have differed on the relative primacy of the "head" versus the "heart." For most first generation ministers, they were equal in importance. Historical faith required a minimal level of head knowledge about how God's promises worked, but saving faith involved the heart of the believer. Shepard was led "to see" that "the spirit of God's enlightening was firstly and chiefly a plain intuitive revelation of the truth, and afterward reason comes in to clear up to others what it reveals."[12] At the same time, however, the intuitive affections were, like good works, as apt to deceive as enlighten. Recognizing how easily his feelings vacillated from "sweet affections" to "slavish fears," Shepard learned why God did not use "private" feelings as the primary ground of faith any more than he used pure reason. The only reliable assurance of God's indwelling spirit was conveyed through the reading and hearing of God's Word:

> I saw that if any should look for a spirit without or beside the word, that they stood upon the precipice of all delusion, hence I saw this holy book of the scriptures is to be set before my eyes, and then the spirit prayed for to clear up the things of God's kingdom therein. And this I saw was evident, and I saw a wonderful wisdom in the Lord (1) that his spirit should not teach

but by the word, (2) that his word could not teach but by the spirit, that so I might not wander from him therein.[13]

Behind Shepard's interpretation of his own experience of saving faith and sanctified obedience was a structure of Calvinist theology that had evolved over generations and been codified in numerous confessions of faith and catechisms.[14] These confessions invariably followed a tripartite division of what was later tagged "sin-salvation-service" that placed faith, works, and assurance in a rigid sequence. Shepard instinctively applied this sequence both to his own experience and to his preaching: "The course I took in my preaching was (1) to show the people their misery [i.e., 'sin']; (2) the remedy, Christ Jesus [i.e., 'salvation']; (3) how they should walk answerable to this mercy, being redeemed by Christ [i.e., 'service']."[15] Unlike printed catechisms that developed Scripture teachings *seriatim*, one topic at a time, regular sermons like those of Shepard generally contained some mention of all three dimensions, differing only in the amount of emphasis given to each.[16] Each sermon not only had to present a complete sequence to avoid confusion or reductionism but also had to do so from the vantage point of a particular text. That text determined which dimension of the *ordo salutis* would receive the most attention.

The process by which Shepard translated his personal experiences and meditations into pulpit discourses is illustrated by a sermon series delivered to his Cambridge congregation in June 1644. Throughout the spring of that year, Shepard was again wrestling with the question of saving faith and assurance. He reminded himself that while obedience did not automatically "move the Lord" to save, an obedient will "made me capable and fit for to receive it and love it and be thankful for it" when it appeared. To "deny this preparation" would be to "shut out the communication of God's grace." Confirmation of this paradoxical truth came to Shepard when he comforted a dying member of his congregation and "saw that by [her] salvation Christ should be glorified." After this "a meditation came to my mind earnestly to desire men's conversion."[17] That meditation lay at the base of his June sermon series.

To provide clarity and focus to his recent experiences and determinations, Shepard selected Hebrews 10:22–23 as the text for his series, "for he is faithful that promised," and partitioned off two terms for special consideration: "faith" and "promise."[18] From personal experience Shepard knew how discomfiting the doctrine of free grace could be. It meant that people must look within themselves for evidence of their salvation *without* trusting solely in their feelings, even though "its marvelous naturall to every man never to beleeve untill hee feels." Shepard articulated the fears many in his congregation may have felt when they said to themselves, "I doe not feele the sence of the love of Christ in my Soul." Such fears, he went on, were baseless because God did not provide assurance through private raptures: "Doe not expect nor look for any settledness in your faith by any Personall Promice, That is that God should speak to thee by name. . . . Thers no such Promice." Contradicting "Antinomians" and "familists" who looked for the immediate inspiration of the Holy Spirit apart from the Word preached, he declared that "if you love your Dreams and fancies, know you that the Lord . . . will see you . . . burnt to ashes."

Instead of looking for "some good Dreame" or "some flash or some admirable rapture" to establish their faith, God's people must attend to the sermon, for God's spirit "speaks peace to you in and by a word only." When God's ministers repeated the simple promise of free grace contained in Scripture and charted the record of God's faithfulness in fulfilling his promises, the Holy Spirit worked in the soul of the listener to transform those words into a personal assurance that flooded the listener like "a light that falls down from the mountains of Eternity intoo the valeys of mens hearts." Though positive "feelings may bee a help to confirme a beleever in his faith," nevertheless "it is the Promice that is the ground of true faith." By repeating God's promise of deliverance and waiting on his Spirit, Shepard hoped that those in his congregation would be converted and drawn to a saving faith capable of withstanding the ebb and flow of human emotions.

SALVATION PREACHING

Not every founding minister left as complete a record of his private ruminations and public declarations as Shepard, but all of the surviving sermon notes from the first generation show an overriding concern with the salvation of the soul and stress the supernatural work of the Holy Spirit over human reason or emotion. At the same time that Shepard was leading his congregation to an understanding of saving faith, Thomas Allen delivered to the Charlestown church a sermon series on John 3:33 ("He that hath received his testimony hath set to his seal that God is true"). Allen's carefully thought-out sermon notes demonstrate that lesser known ministers were often as conscientious and technically accomplished as their more illustrious peers. They also confirm studies that correct Perry Miller's excessive emphasis on Puritan rationality.[19] Like Shepard, Allen was concerned with assurance. How did God's elect come to know and believe the promise of salvation in a personal sense? Was it by a sheer act of will that Abraham believed God's promises, or did some outside agency enable him to believe they were true? Here Allen's text was useful in describing the "sealing" activity of the Holy Spirit in convincing individual believers of God's promises. Before believers could will to "embrace" the gospel promises for their own, the Holy Spirit first had to "bend" the affections because "it is the frame of every naturall and carnall heart to reject a Promice, unless the Lord coms first with his effectual work."

Allen recognized that his hearers could be confused about the enabling work of the Holy Spirit because their conscious experience suggested that they did believe God's promise without any external assistance. This was because the self-conscious activity of the will to believe occurred simultaneously with the internal testimony of the Holy Spirit. As the Spirit persuaded the soul of the truths of God's promises, "in the same instant it is that the Soul Acts to receave." Yet—and this was the theological point of Allen's sermon—the people had to understand that although the work of the Holy Spirit and their will to believe might seem simultaneous the work of the Spirit came first in order of "nature." Allen likened the work of conversion to the creation of a soul: "As soon as [the infant is] created at that very instant of tyme the Soul's put intoo it, tho the Infant were created before in order of nature." Similarly, in conversion the Holy Spirit first enables the soul to believe. Otherwise, as John Cotton pointed out in a published sermon, "If our Faith be first active in laying hold on Christ for our righteousness, before God impute[s] it to us; then we doe justify God, before he doth justify us."[20] Such self-justification was nothing more than a "covenant of works" and was sure to result in the destruction of the individual soul.

To guide his listeners in a course of self-examination, Allen divided the sequence of salvation into a series of stages through which most souls passed in their spiritual pilgrimage from death-in-sin to life-in-Christ. Stages were, Allen recognized, an analytical construct and did not bind the work of the Holy Spirit. If God so chose he could collapse the stages of conversion into one shattering moment of self-revelation such as Paul experienced on the road to Damascus. But this was not God's usual practice: "The soul dos not ordinarily imediately receave [Christ] without any more adoo: without some Agitations too and froe . . . and this is Gods ordinary way." The saint might not be able to recall every stage in salvation, just as in reading one did not pause over every "letter and syllable." Yet the stages were there and discernable in retrospect if the saint looked closely enough at his or her spiritual experience.

Typically, the "agitations" of the soul began with a sense of deep "humiliation" when the saint discovered his sinful and lost condition. To ease his conscience and, in effect, to bribe God, the stricken but still unregenerate soul turned to pious works and "wilbee abundant in dutys and performances both towards God and man seeking how it may obtain that [which] it desires." Such a "legal obedience" or "covenant of works" proved unavailing and drove the soul into even deeper despair. At that point, when the soul was stripped of all its pretensions and stood in abject misery before God, the Spirit prepared to do his healing work. Only when the soul came to see all his good works as "dunge and loss" before a perfect God was the Spirit's seal of assurance "applied and set home." In those moments of deepest self-condemnation, the soul grasped the reality of God's grace and continued a life of obedience out of sheer gratitude and thanksgiving. Because of human pride and the persistence of the old sinful nature in regenerate saints, the process of self-condemnation was apt to recur and the whole sequence of salvation had to be reenacted. This was why Christians had to spend their whole lives under the tutelage of the sermon so that they might be reminded again and again of the differences between grace and works and never fall into the trap of relying on their own will and righteousness.

Under the methodical gospel preaching of their ministers, New England congregations internalized the language of sequence and learned to label every stage of their spiritual experience from humiliation, to saving faith, to true obedience. Such labeling gave them a vocabulary for self-examination and a basis for personal hope in the knowledge that guilt and anxiety were necessary prerequisites to the healing work of the Holy Spirit. In addition, the language of stages provided an objective standard by which ministers and congregations could judge the claims of aspiring members to visible sainthood and church membership. Before appearing for their public testimonies as adults, prospective members understood the mysterious order of salvation as it had been instilled over many years of Bible study, introspection, and gospel preaching.[21]

Thomas Shepard's transcriptions of the conversion narratives of his Cambridge congregation reveal how thoroughly ordinary men and women mastered the rigors of self-examination and applied the same terms to their spiritual experience that Shepard applied to his. A case in point is the anonymous "Katherine, Mrs. Russle's Maid."[22] Although she was obviously not part of the social elite, Katherine's narrative is remarkable for its articulateness and mastery of the vernacular Word. Her odyssey began with the influence of a pious aunt who spoke about "the misery of Christ" and prodded her "to see" the many sins in her own life that required Christ's sacrifice. Recognition of her sin created a profound sense of misery, for "I knew the Lord could [pardon sin], but yet I question would He [for me]? And hence I sought the Lord in public and private and I looked upon Manassah and upon the Scarlet sins of Isaiah made [as] white as snow. And so looking into the word, and finding some particular promises as—come to Me you that are laden. But yet I was under terror and I followed the word and loved saints dearly, yet I was doubtful of what would become of me."[23] Katherine's doubts continued for two years, "sometime thinking I might have mercy sometime not." Then came a moment of illumination in the time of the sermon when "I heard Mr. Rogers speaking—the just shall live by faith. And so I had abundance of comfort from the word and I blessed the Lord for that condition." Of course, comfort and assurance were two different things, and Katherine continued to agonize over "whether I was humble or no." Throughout this period she fell into satanic temptations and had "blasphemous thought[s] of slighting the Lord" and trusting in her own self-righteousness. Again a word of Scripture came to her assistance: "I searched for the word to oppose Satan, and so I remembered out of Zachary—the Lord rebuke these. . . . And so I sought the Lord in a way of humiliation, the name of the Lord be a strong tower . . . and I knew I should be armed like Jacob in all straights to have a promise."[24] Armed with the realization of her own frailties and the promise of God to triumph over all enemies, she was at last ready to "close with Christ in a promise. . . . As the rich man said—soul take thy rest—so I found Christ to me." This did not mean that doubts would never cross her mind again or that there would not be need for renewed conversion in time of the sermon and self-examination, but it did mean that she had crossed the threshold of visible sainthood and was ready to take her place as a full member of the church.

VISIBLE SAINTHOOD AS A LIFE OF THANKFUL OBEDIENCE

Much of the drama of Puritan preaching revolved around conviction and faith, or "law and gospel," but the theme of thankful obedience was never ignored and, if anything, occupied more of the ministers' attention from week to week than justification. The theme of obedience or "duty" invariably *followed* the message of free grace. Under the heading of thankful obedience, ministers would preach the duty of Christian living in church, family, commonwealth, and personal piety and devotion. No area of life fell outside God's Word, and for every human endeavor the Puritans discovered clear scriptural rules. This is exemplified in Shepard's long-running sermon series on the Ten Commandments. From the first two commandments to worship God purely he extracted several sermons on the virtues of the Congregational Way, which ensured that God's Word and name would be preeminent; from the commandment to honor the sabbath he extracted the duty of sermon attendance and worship; and from the commandment to honor parents he taught the duty of submission to "those who are our Superiours . . . both in church or commonwealth."[26] Throughout he asserted that these duties, although mandatory in the life of the Christian, were never meritorious; they were pleasing to God only to the extent that the heart was motivated by sincere gratitude and the realization that justification came by faith alone.

To sermon attenders who had not yet "closed with Christ in a promise," ministers also preached the duty of civil and spiritual obedience, but as a form of conviction and "humiliation" rather than thankfulness. "Legal" obedience, though not sanctified, was better than no obedience at all for, as John Cotton pointed out, "God never calleth any unto fellowship with himself in a Covenant of Grace, but ordinarily he first bringeth them into a Covenant of Works."[27] This kind of obedience would never "pacify" God's righteous anger at sin, but it served to convince people of their inability to obey God's law perfectly and of their utter dependence on a savior. Furthermore, as a major theme in occasional sermons, such "legal" or "outward" obedience and respect for God's Word helped preserve the nation in its federal covenant.

The theme of sin-salvation-service that dominated preaching on faith

and obedience also dominated printed sermons.[28] Whereas later generations employed the press primarily for occasional sermons, most of the
first generation's printed sermons were regular sermons drawn from long-
running series on the Christian pilgrimage. In *The Sincere Convert*, published from lay notes and destined to become one of the most frequently
reprinted of all New England sermons, Thomas Shepard outlined the way
of faith in three extended sermons that traced the path from sin and
remorse, to saving faith, to "true obedience."[29] Like their spoken counterparts, these printed sermons carefully distinguished godly living from
works righteousness. Christians were neither above the law (the Antinomian heresy), nor justified by the law or by their own self-will (the
Arminian heresy):

> That God the Father of our Lord Jesus Christ may be honored by the per-
> formance of these duties, therefore use them. Christ shed his blood that he
> might purchase unto himself a people zealous of good works, (Tit. 2.14),
> not to save our souls by them, but to honor him. O, let not the blood of
> Christ be shed in vain! Grace and good duties are a Christian's Crown; it is
> sin only makes a man base. Now, shall a king cast away his crown, because
> he bought not his kingdom by it? No; because it is his ornament and glory
> to wear it when he is made a king. So I say unto thee, It is better that Christ
> should be honored than thy soul saved; and therefore, perform duties,
> because they honor the Lord Jesus Christ.[30]

In an equally famous printed sermon series, Thomas Hooker developed
these same themes progressing from *The Soules Humiliation* (1638) to *The
Soules Preparation for Christ* (1632) to *The Soules Implantation* (1637) and
finally to *The Soules Exaltation* (1638). Norman Pettit has argued that of
all the first-generation ministers, Hooker came closest to identifying faith
with obedience.[31] But even Hooker dared not violate the Calvinist consensus in emphasizing the "enabling" activity of the Holy Spirit. In matters of salvation, "the word of the Gospel and the work of the Spirit
always go together. . . . They must first hear, then learn; hear by the word
and learn by the Spirit." Unless this unmerited supernatural assistance
applied the words of salvation to the heart of the believer, there could be
no saving faith. As to when these words were most clearly sounded and
acted upon by the Holy Spirit, Hooker was equally in step with his colleagues: "We preach the good Word of the Lord; and however [much]
ourselves have spoken this; if you oppose it, know it, that it is the Lord's
word [you oppose]."[32] Private Bible study, family devotions, and neighborhood discussions were all important activities, but they were not converting ordinances; the primary work of the Holy Spirit came in hearing
the sermon. Without that voice of guidance, an ordinary saint would drift
like a "ship without a compass."

It remained for Concord's Peter Bulkeley to publish the definitive work
on salvation in *The Gospel-Covenant*, first printed in 1646, but based on a

sermon series he had delivered during the Antinomian controversy a decade earlier. Bulkeley refuted the notion that sanctification was no evidence of salvation or that the elect existed somehow above the claims of God's law. All covenants, he pointed out, "have a condition." In the covenant of grace, the condition was faith freely dispensed through Christ's sacrifice. Nevertheless, God expected as a corollary condition that his elect would "walk according to the grace received" and that "as we desire to enjoy the blessed promise [of unmerited salvation], so we must see also what he requires of us" by way of response.[33] Obedience, Bulkeley said, marked the point at which the covenant of grace and federal covenant came together, albeit in different "manifestations." In both covenants righteous living was required if God's people were to discover evidences of their own personal salvation and if they were to enjoy the outward and temporal blessings of a professing nation. And in both cases, the terms and meaning of obedience were set forth through the sermon delivered on Sunday or during the week. Without that voice, God's people in New England would be deprived of the essential means of grace that God instituted for their personal salvation; and without the sermon there was no voice of national direction or deliverance.

METAPHOR AND TYPE IN REGULAR PREACHING

The sin-salvation-service formula was merely the skeleton around which the preacher crafted his discourse. To flesh out that skeleton, he had recourse to a broad range of tropes and metaphors drawn from Scripture and from the common experiences of his listeners. In metaphor or "similitude" all the latent extravagances of the preacher's imagination might find legitimate expression, as long as it was not at the expense of biblical truths or popular understanding. Similitude was, as Thomas Shepard explained, the "ground of love," and ministers would ransack the Scriptures for images and analogies that could hold up obscure spiritual truths to the apprehension and appreciation of their listeners. Moreover, since Scripture viewed all creation as a direct emanation of the divine mind, Puritan preachers also embraced nature as a means for clarifying and vivifying divine truth.

From their study of the arts curriculum—particularly grammar and rhetoric—ministers learned that different types of metaphor appealed to different audiences. For this reason they rejected all Latin and classical allusions in their preaching. However apt these figures might be, they existed outside the world of ordinary hearers and were as likely to confuse and frustrate as enlighten. From the same arts curriculum ministers also learned that different types of metaphors were better fitted to different "faculties" or compartments of the mind, including the "will," the "understanding," the "imagination," and the "affections."[34] Since all the faculties had to be addressed in the course of the sermon, ministers rarely dwelt exclusively on one metaphor but preferred to scatter a variety of figures of speech throughout the discourse, each calculated to engage different faculties. Diversity of speech and imagery best served the didactic and exhortatory function of metaphor in Puritan preaching. Ministers generally preferred similes and analogies to instruct the understanding and bring divine doctrines down to earth, and they employed metaphors drawn from Scripture and common experience to arouse and explain godly affections.[35]

While extrabiblical images like a "bee-hive" or "gilded post" with a rotten core were not absent from Puritan preaching, most imagery came from Scripture. To aid the minister in his selection of images, a variety of reference works were compiled that indexed all biblical metaphors and showed the context in which they were used. Such metaphors fell into several broad categories, including natural and domestic imagery.[36] In addition to these images, metaphors closest to the experiences of their hearers were maritime images to convey man's sin and passageway from death to life, and martial images to explain the Christian life of obedience and hope.[37] Maritime imagery was especially meaningful to the generation who crossed the Atlantic amidst great hardships and danger. Boston's John Mayo, for example, likened the human predicament to that of one who was cast forth "into the Sea in a little cork boate without oares or sails."[38] Without the "wind" of the Spirit and the "compasse" of the Word he would drift aimlessly forever, never reaching his heavenly destination. In another sermon, Thomas Allen asked his listeners to think of their duty to strip themselves of all pretensions to self-righteousness as "the throwing of all dutyes . . . and close walkings overboard" in time of great storms. The ship of a man's soul could not be saved until it was emptied of all excess baggage and self-righteousness.[39]

The first generation was directly involved in only one war—the Pequot War of 1637—but their brethren in England were constantly involved in civil wars or continental campaigns against "papist" nations that went back to the sixteenth-century religious wars. These experiences provided vital analogies to the Christian experience of spiritual warfare. Thus in a sermon series on the apostle Paul's martial imagery in Ephesians 6, John Warham explained that the saint "must behave himself like a man of war"; he must "provide armor, offensive [and] defensive."[40] Fortunately, the Christian warrior did not fight alone but marched under Christ, "your captain [who] will train you in marshall discipline." Because of what their captain had already done, Christ's army could march into battle boldly, confident that the mortal blow had already been struck on the cross and "our enemies are conquered already . . . [because] Christ hath overcome the world." In the same way that maritime imagery was ideally suited to feelings of fear and misery, martial imagery supplied terms for joy and exultation among those who were delivered from the raging seas and outfitted to march triumphantly against their captain's enemies. Throughout the first generation, those enemies were spiritual; in the second generation amidst war and carnage these same metaphors would assume a more literal meaning.

Closely related to metaphor in Puritan preaching, but also clearly distinct, was the use of "typology," in which Old Testament events, ritual objects, and historical experiences stood for or prefigured Jesus Christ and the Christian church.[41] Like metaphors, literary types involved multiple meanings, but unlike metaphors they were limited exclusively to Scripture and referred to God's providence rather than his pedagogy. According to typological theory, God planned events in the lives of his chosen people so that they would have both a present and a future significance. While the Old Testament people of Israel did not know how their messiah would be manifest in the world, God knew; and he supplied prophetic clues or "types" of Christ, whose full significance could be understood only in retrospect, after the Incarnation. Thus, for example, the ark of the covenant was a type of Christ's redemption, the sacrificial lamb was a type of Christ's death, Jonah's three days in the whale's belly was a type of Christ in the grave, and the rebuilt temple at Jerusalem was a type of Christ's resurrection. On a national level, the civil, political, and ecclesiastical experiences of Israel were a type of the temporal experiences God's "New Israel" would share as they prepared the way for Christ's Second Coming.

Of the two levels of typology referring to the person and work of Christ in an eternal setting and to the redemptive mission of New Israel in a temporal setting, the first was far less controversial and dominated regular preaching on Old Testament texts. In these sermons ministers seldom referred to the nation of Israel but focused on individuals like Adam, Melchizedek, Abraham, or David, or on ritual objects like the ark, the mercy seat, the brazen altar, or the sacrificial lamb as Christ-types that prefigured aspects of Christ's life and ministry.[42] By applying double meanings to persons and objects ministers were able to establish unity between both testaments that was essential for covenant preaching.

Frequent references to biblical types and metaphors taught ordinary audiences to view Scripture on multiple levels of significance and so to become rudimentary literary critics. Beyond that, it encouraged them to become sensible to spiritual nuance in the natural world and in history, and to insert themselves directly into the world of biblical promise and prophecy, believing that, like ancient Israel, the full significance of their New World churches would only become clearly evident in retrospect. From the vantage point of eternity there was a massive coherence to God's plan of redemption that bound past and future into one "everlasting present" grounded in the Incarnation.[43] For the most part, the typological meanings extracted in regular preaching were eternal and spiritual; more temporal and literal typological readings (for example, the promised land of Canaan as prefiguring the promised land of New England) were reserved for occasional sermons reflecting on the corporate experience of God's "American Israel."[44]

THE ANCHOR OF HOPE

As important as faith and love (obedience) were in establishing terms of
salvation and social conformity, they were incomplete without hope. True
faith had to be accompanied by a hope in the truth of God's promises and
an eager expectancy that one day soon they all would be fulfilled. Like
faith, hope was a gift of the Holy Spirit that came in conjunction with
hearing God's promises. And like faith, hope was not understood as a
wishful feeling or dream but as a certainty rooted as much in the reason
as the affections, resistant to all temptations of unbelief and despair.
There is, John Davenport explained in *The Saint's Anchor Hold*, an "inse-
parable connection of hope with faith," such that "what faith believes,
hope expects."[45] In both cases the ground of hope was "good and strong
reasons." While it was true that "reason of itself . . . cannot teach men to
hope in god," the Holy Spirit worked as a "convincing light" through the
preaching of the sermon and "causeth the soul to yield, as overcome by
the evidence and authority of the light and truth brought into it." No
external threat or evil could blot out the rays of hope: "This light is abiding in the renewed soul. Thus the Church, in my Text [Lamentations
3:24], was convinced and comforted, in their great distress, by the spirit
and word of God, so they could hold forth good and strong reasons,
whereupon their hope was strengthened, and their hearts were comforted
in sad hours." So too in Christ's New England churches, "faith is put to
use Arguments, and reasons to quicken and strengthen hope. Accordingly
study the grounds of hope, and improve them for your help."[46]

Both in Scripture and in preaching, the primary metaphors used to
describe hope were nautical.[47] Davenport had titled his sermon on hope
The Saint's Anchor Hold, and George Moxon used like imagery in an
unpublished sermon on Hebrews 6:19 ("which hope we have as an
anchor of the soule").[48] Considered typologically, the anchor was used in
Scripture as "a type of heaven." After defining hope as the "vertue
whereby we are Inclined to the expectation of those things from god that
he hath promised," Moxon located that promise chiefly with respect to
eternal life: "Its center is in heaven, Our hope is in heaven. We are saved
by hope." The anchor of hope could be considered in a metaphorical
sense as holding the Christian's faith secure in a world "exercised with
tossings and tremblings both outward and inward." Just as "a ship hath
nothing to hold it by in a storme if its anchor be gone," so also "in many
trobles many tryalls and tempt[ations] the child of god hath nothing but
hope to hold by." No matter what trials God's elect might face, they could
sustain themselves with the abiding hope that there "is never . . . any
danger while he doth depend on god, and while he doth waite on god."[49]

Along with the personal hope of salvation that comforted all Christians,
New England's first generation was urged to keep before them the hope
of the "end days" when Christ returned to earth. On that day, Shepard
declared:

Christ shall break out of the third heaven, and be seen in the aire . . . and this shall be with an admirable shout. . . . Then shall the dead arise: the bodies of them that have died in the Lord, shall *rise first.* . . . Then shall the guilty prisoners be brought forth, and come out of their Graves like filthy Toads against this terrible storm. Then shall all the wicked that ever were or ever shall be, stand quaking before the glorious Judge, with their same bodies, feet, hands, to receive their doom.[50]

Because the time of Christ's return was uncertain, congregations were urged to wait constantly on God's promise of salvation. Even those who foresaw a long lifetime ahead of them could not be certain that Christ would not return to earth and discover them in their sins and unbelief. Such a prospect encouraged both expectancy for the saints and fear for those not yet committed. In a sermon on 2 Timothy 4:5 ("watch thou in all things"), John Mayo manipulated both emotions to good effect: "You should shine as lights. We have little tyme and much work. You are called to the knowledge of god to the work of Christ, the more weighty the work the more carefull should you be. God threatens those that doe not watch. *I will come on them as a Thief in the night.* Our danger is greate. . . . I say to all watch."[51] That attitude had characterized the apostolic church and God expected it to persist through all ages. Faith and obedience marked the boundaries of the saint's life on earth, but hope instilled the confidence to stare unblinkingly into the future where a new heaven and a new earth awaited all God's children.

Christians in all ages were commanded to look for Christ's return, but they must not presume to know exactly when that moment might come. Millennial predictions based on biblical prophecies were admittedly speculative, and ministers rarely engaged in any precise dating or extended discussion of the millennium in their regular preaching. In his meditations, Thomas Shepard concluded that "a man that is bold to prophesy future events with certainty is a deceiver unless he be extraordinarily and infallibly assisted as in former times, because it secretly steals away the hearts of men to rest upon the fancy of a man and so fall off from resting upon the word."[52] The Word, unlike man's fancy, spoke of the end of time in veiled language that did not admit of a precise date. Ministers could and did speculate that they were living in the end days, but of the exact moment none could be sure. For this reason every generation of Christians had to be constantly watching so they would not be caught unawares.

THE THURSDAY LECTURE

The main reason Puritans rejected exact prophecies of the Second Coming was Christ's warning that he would return at a time when no one expected him. The ministers realized, moreover, how often God's people of old misread the times and prophecies of their age, teaching the lesson that God's calendar of sacred history was unknowable in exact detail.

Still, there were prophetic texts in Daniel and Revelation that required explication like any other portion of Scripture; the only stipulation was that sermons on these texts be preached in a proper spirit of humility and uncertainty. In practice, few ministers felt sufficiently knowledgeable in ancient languages and cultures to undertake a systematic study of these texts, and most preferred to cite the opinions of other trustworthy exegetes who labored through millennial texts.

Those gifted few who felt equipped to examine such texts generally preferred occasions other than the sabbath to air their views. One such occasion long favored for millennial commentary was the Thursday lecture, initiated shortly after the first arrival in New England and continued throughout the colonial era. The lecture was a midway point between regular and occasional preaching. At times it was used as a fast or thanksgiving day, but more often it was devoted to extended sermon disquisitions on technical or speculative questions deemed too abstract for sabbath worship. Besides providing congregations with an opportunity to hear systematic theology, the lecture provided ministers with a rare opportunity to hear other ministers preach on difficult topics.[53]

Of all the first-generation ministers, John Cotton was most respected for his skill in opening millennial prophecies. He was, his grandson Cotton Mather later recalled, a "walking library" who could discourse in Greek and Hebrew as in his native tongue. In an unguarded moment, Cotton himself once confided "that he knew not of any difficult place in all the Bible, which he [had] not weighed, some what unto his satisfaction."[54] Between 1639 and 1640, Cotton devoted his Thursday lectures to the most difficult place in all of Scripture: *An Exposition Upon the Thirteenth Chapter of the Revelation.* Cotton noted that the central figures in Revelation were the "lamb" who represented Christ, a pregnant woman "cloathed with the sun, and moon under her feet" who represented the church, and a serpent or "beast with seven heads and ten horns" who represented Satan, the Antichrist. The final days, he went on, were characterized by a mortal struggle between the serpent and the woman "in a place called in the Hebrew tongue Armageddon." To prepare the woman to give birth to a deliverer—the lamb of God—God provided "two wings of a great eagle, that she might fly into the wilderness, unto her place where she is nourished for a time." During this time a great many people would worship the beast and fall down before him—all, that is, but the elect whose names were registered in the "lambs book of life." Power would be given to the beast "to continue forty and two months." At that time Christ would return to earth on a "white horse," smiting the nations with the sword of the spirit, binding Satan, and inaugurating a new heaven and a new earth.

Few Puritans doubted that the figures and dates recorded in Revelation contained a veiled timetable for the last days, if the figures of speech could be properly matched to historical events and the dates decoded. Like all Protestants, Cotton identified the beast with the Roman Catholic

Church, "the Mother of Harlots and Abominations of the earth."[55] Having identified the beast, it remained to understand the temporal duration represented by "fourty and two months" to determine exactly when the final confrontation would begin. From Old Testament exegesis and cabalistic speculation, Cotton determined that the prophets used "day" as a synonym for year; as forty-two months represented 1,260 days, so Christ would return in 1,260 years from the birth of the beast.[56] Cotton dated those stirrings to A.D. 395, when the Pope was elevated to supreme status in the Church of Rome. If this was so, then the first triumphs over the beast would begin in 1570 and his final destruction would be sealed in 1655—the very year Cotton's lectures were published in London!

Although Cotton was careful to couch his predictions in speculative terms, the prospects were dazzling and could not help but add incentive and urgency to New England's special mission. The beast raged in Europe, and that was where the climactic battles would take place when "Christian Princes, and States shall powre out the wrath of God, upon Popish Superstition, and Idolatry."[57] But New England had a crucial role to play by setting forth a model of pure churches and faithful preaching such that "if you be corrupt in New-England . . . believe it one of these two will unavoidable follow, either all *England* will judge your Reformation but a delusion and an invention of your magistrates, or Elders, or otherwise looke at you, as not sincere but counterfeit."[58] In either event, failure in New England would jeopardize the entire Protestant cause and incur the wrath of God. Fortunately, at the time Cotton penned his thoughts, New England was succeeding in its mission. England was watching them closely as they persevered in their peculiar way of gospel liberty. When the final day arrived, New England would be found vigilant, ready to play its part in guiding European Protestants to their final triumph.

[3]

"Sion's Out-Casts"

CIVIL WAR IN ENGLAND

When John Cotton penned his thoughts on the approaching millennium, events on both sides of the Atlantic seemed to confirm the rising strength of Christ's true churches and army. By 1640, New England's population had swelled to twenty thousand inhabitants, and over forty meeting-houses had been built.[1] Even more portentous than New England's growth were developments in England. The conflict between the crown and Parliament finally erupted into a civil war that pitted Puritan against Anglican and led to the creation of the short-lived (1649 to 1660) Puritan Commonwealth and Protectorate.[2] With Cromwell's New Model Army controlling the field and Parliament running the state, it seemed to many in New England that all the pieces in the eschatological puzzle were fall-ing into place. New England's pure Way was complete and England was freed to copy that example. In light of the rapid growth of "New Churches and a new Common-wealth" in New England, together with the Puritan triumphs in England, the Woburn joiner, militia captain, and chronicler Edward Johnson speculated whether "these poore New England People be not the forerunners of Christ's Army."[3]

Though they lived in the New World, most of the founders still iden-tified themselves as Englishmen whose cultural identities and millennial hopes were deeply rooted in the homeland. Taunton's William Hooke spoke for all: "There is no land that claimes our name, but *England*. . . . Brethren! Did we not there draw our first breath?. . . . Did not that land first beare us . . . but for sin, I would say, that Garden of the Lord, that paradise?"[4] Indeed, so strong was this attraction that nearly half of New England's university men would return to England to participate directly in the Commonwealth and Protectorate.[5] Many such returnees were younger second-generation graduates of the recently founded Harvard College in Cambridge (1636) who faced unemployment in the colonies once the immigration surge ended and new churches were no longer founded. But important founders like Hooke, Thomas Weld, Hugh Peter, Nathaniel Ward, or Thomas Allen also went back to England to occupy

50

key positions in church and state. The cause in England was so compelling that they were willing to leave New England's stewardship to others. Few of the returning founders would see New England again.

For most of the founders, however, and many of the best graduates of Harvard College, return to England was not possible or even desirable. Practically speaking, many were too old and established in the New World to consider another uprooting and perilous voyage. Thomas Hooker, for example, died in 1647, and John Cotton died five years later. Other considerations were equally important. The cause of ecclesiastical reform that first drove them to New England must be prosecuted until England's reformation was complete; otherwise there would be no model to implement in England. Even more importantly, as architects of the New England Way the founders were bound both by a creator's sense of pride and by their covenantal pledges to remain with their congregations. Those congregations still needed their wisdom and guidance; already a new generation of native-born children was coming of age and starting families of their own. The needs and aspirations of these children were clearly different from those of their parents and required the special attention of their elders. Perhaps most importantly, by the 1650s most founders were in fact less English than they thought. In a nostalgic sense England would always be their home, but by imperceptible degrees they had changed in their cultural orientation and their millennial hope. By the 1650s and 1660s they had begun to have a past and tradition of their own.[6] The founders had arrived in the New World as English wayfarers and reformers, but those who survived to witness the collapse of the Protectorate and the rise of a New World generation would die as *American* Puritans.

A PLATFORM FOR ENGLISH REFORM

For most of the leading founders return to England was impossible, but they could and did supply other kinds of aid to the Puritan cause in England. Of these, the most important were prayers and publications that explained and defended the virtues of the New England Way. The number of fasts for England peaked during the 1640s and 1650s, when congregations met regularly to implore God's blessings on his people in England.[7] In one fast sermon, William Hooke enjoined his congregation to pray for England, decrying the selfishness of those who would ask, "How are we concerned in the miseries of other men, so long as we are free?" The "affections" binding English saints "stand firme from one end of the World to the other," such that "if we forbeare to deliver them that are drawne unto death, and those that are ready to be slaine; if we say, *we knew it not,* or *what did it concerne us? He that pondereth the heart considereth it, and hee will render unto us according to our workes.*" John Warham employed a fast in Windsor to remind his congregation in similar terms that "our own welfare lies in England's welfare." If the situations were reversed, "would not they pray for you?" New England must pray for God's cause in England so that "it may save us in a time of danger."[8] For reasons of political expediency New England did not publicly and officially endorse the parliamentary cause, but in their prayers and fasts the Puritan brethren received their "constant sympathy."[9]

Besides their prayers, the founders offered England the benefit of their New World experience in the form of a series of closely reasoned defenses and explanations of the New England Way. Leading ministers like John Cotton, Thomas Hooker, Richard Mather, Thomas Shepard, and John Davenport prepared ecclesiastical treatises, virtually all of which were published in London for English audiences. With the exception of a political tract by John Eliot that was subsequently censured by the General Court, these writings did not presume to offer political guidance or even a systematic theology like that of the confession prepared by the Westminster Assembly of Divines. Rather they dealt with more limited questions of church order and discipline. This was the mission that had drawn them to the New World twenty years earlier, and which they had accomplished, creating pure churches and a Bible commonwealth. If their reading of biblical prophecy was correct, England would appropriate New England's creation and complete the reformation that was prerequisite to the final triumph over the beast.

The most important document to emerge in these years was *The Cambridge Platform*, prepared by a ministerial synod in Cambridge in 1649. In 1646 the General Court had requested a synod to compose a summary statement of Congregational church practice in New England. They hoped in this way to resolve differences between the Congregational majority in New England and the small but influential "presbyterian" minority led by James Noyes, Thomas Parker, Peter Hobart, and Dr. Robert Child. More importantly, however, they hoped that such a detailed description of Congregational practices would serve as a model for the Puritan reformers coming to power in England.[10] Unlike most of the summaries of church order produced in Europe, *The Cambridge Platform* enjoyed no juridical status that could "bind" particular churches to each of its provisions. But church members *did* vote to endorse it, and insofar as it captured the essential "balance" and limitations on power that characterized Congregational theory, it enjoyed a symbolic importance in New England for generations.[11]

THE PLATFORM REJECTED

Disappointingly, *The Cambridge Platform* had little influence on reform in England. It did nothing to reconcile tensions between Presbyterians and Independents. If anything, it exacerbated their debates and highlighted the inability of the European churches to fuse purity and power. Presbyterians endorsed the unitary ideal of the *Platform* with its state-enforced orthodoxy and a national church but refused the principles of congregational autonomy and the requirement of visible sainthood for church membership. Independents preserved the Congregational Way but undermined the unitary ideal of a Christian nation by tolerating such "heretical" schismatics as Baptists, Quakers, and a host of "Antinomian" sects.[12]

For the founders who were witnessing the widening divisions between Presbyterians and Independents in England nothing was more frustrating than the knowledge that their successful "Middle Way" was not gaining acceptance. In a thanksgiving sermon in 1651, John Cotton celebrated Cromwell's victories and the institution of the Commonwealth, but openly wondered where it would all lead. In years past, he recalled, the nation was deeply divided over episcopacy, liturgy, and doctrine:

> But Now though these matters of Contention Be Removed yet the Like Contention still continuith aboute presbitterie and Independencye, yet Caried with Such Distaste one Against another, that A man would wonder that those that have gotten Victorie over popery, and the image of it should Be Soe transported with Bitterness and outrage Against theire well Approved Brethren and yet Both stand in a Sea of glass And See the face of god in christ, and yet Cannot Looke one another in the face with any Concord and mutuall Love.[13]

At the very time when hopes burned brightest in New England, a dark cloud threatened to blot out the dawning light of millennial glory in England and render the Puritan revolt meaningless. It threatened as well the integrity of the New England mission. If England would not learn from her New World laboratory, then what purpose could that laboratory possibly retain?[14]

Cotton's death in 1652 prevented him from seeing how well grounded were his fears. The long-awaited Christian commonwealth never materialized under the Lord Protector. Presbyterians and Independents, parliamentary republicans and leaders of the New Model Army became hopelessly fragmented and were incapable of sustaining national leadership. With Cromwell's death in 1658 and the restoration of monarchy in 1660, New England's dream for Old England's glory came to an end. England's failure to reform created a crisis of corporate identity in New England. The founders' meticulously constructed laboratory had produced a workable, even thriving, operation, but they now realized that no one in Europe would imitate them, or even cared about their creation. The questions concerning pure churches and a Bible commonwealth that brought the Puritans to the New World were no longer being asked in England. New England had discovered the answers to these questions, but their historical moment had passed.

TYPOLOGY AND AMERICA'S NEW ISRAEL

By 1660, besides Cotton, leading founders like Thomas Hooker, Thomas Shepard, John Winthrop, Nathaniel Rogers, Ralph Partridge, and Peter Bulkeley had all died, leaving only a handful of the original founders to interpret the meaning of England's refusal to follow New England's example. For guidance, the surviving founders turned to the Scriptures. From the start, the Bible and its record of providential design had supplied the terms of their New World settlement and the key to understanding contemporary events. Looking around them, the founders realized that despite England's failure to heed their example, there was no evidence that God had forsaken his covenant with New England, or that he no longer intended to use it for his glory. The way of salvation could still be seen in their pure independent churches protected by the coercive arm of the civil magistrates and dedicated to the sovereignty of God's Word. Instead of bending to the breeze of religious toleration, New England's ministers and magistrates stiffened their resolve to root out heresy and preserve a pure orthodoxy.[15] Clearly, they were still a covenant people; their only mistake was that instead of looking backwards to England they should have been looking forward to the New World their children would inhabit. The mission would live on for the sake of New England, and the founders would serve as models for the rising generation who would grow up to enact in America that which was impossible to achieve in Europe. The founders now needed new sources for cultural identity and found them in two places: in the experiences of ancient Israel and in their own brief but thoroughly recorded New World history. The memorialization of the founders that would occupy so much subsequent occasional preaching actually began with those founders who survived beyond 1660.[16] Israel had always been New England's typological model in corporate commentary, but after 1660 this theme became an obsession and was now reserved exclusively for New England. God's New World people were in fact less a New *England* than a New *Israel*; genealogy tied them to the Old World, but providence linked them to ancient Israel so thoroughly and explicitly that words in the Old Testament could be taken as if literally intended for New England.

As the founders studied again Israel's pilgrimage from Egypt to Canaan, the parallels between their own isolation and Israel's sojourn in the wilderness were too compelling to ignore. This was not simply a coincidence but a providentially controlled reenactment. Just as Israel was spurned by the world and forced to wander aimlessly for forty years before entering the promised land, so also was New England consigned to brief cultural oblivion in the eyes of surrounding nations. The extremity of their isolation was cause not for despair but for hope and expectancy. The biblical image of the woman in the wilderness nursing her strength before giving birth to a deliverer was meant as a reference to America. The American environment was the place where God would purify his churches through adversity and neglect until, in the fullness of time, they would emerge triumphant. In the meantime, they had only to keep faith in themselves and their covenant.

While regular preaching remained the same after 1660, occasional sermons changed dramatically. Such sermons defined the corporate sense of New England's experiment, and they had to articulate the country's new identity and redirect the mission of their covenant from England to America. The election sermon was the most auspicious occasion, and never was one more important than that delivered by John Norton in 1661 on *Sion the Out-cast Healed of her Wounds*. It was the first election sermon published in New England, and that for good reason. Norton was one of the few remaining founders. He had arrived in the New World with Thomas Shepard in 1635 and lived long enough to succeed John Cotton at Boston's First Church. Now, on the eve of his departure for England on a mission to preserve New England's charter with the new monarch Charles II, he spoke on the meaning of New England as seen from the vantage point of divine providence.

Unlike later election sermons that exceeded thirty pages and were clearly intended for print, Norton's sermon notes were relatively brief (sixteen pages) and to the point. His text from Jeremiah 30:17 supplied both the title and main theme of his discourse—a theme which, he pointed out, was as applicable to New England as it was to Israel: "For I will restore health unto thee, and I will heal thee of thy wounds, saith the Lord; because they called thee an Out-cast, saying, This is Sion, whom no man seeketh after." From this text, Norton isolated two terms for analysis: "Out-cast" and "Sion." He began by noting that Israel's rejection, like New England's, was total. They were not only "cast out of the[ir] Country" but "out of the hearts and affections of others." The world either ignored them or heaped abuse on them, affixing them with the derisive label "Sion," meaning in Hebrew "a dry, withered, sapless thing; a barren, and forsaken, and undesirable place and society." Yet there was a paradox here, Norton continued, for the Hebrew word for Sion had a double meaning: it signified not only rejected by man but also chosen of God. Israel could take comfort in this paradox and so could New England. As with Israel, New England's rejection was not a sign of divine desertion but of their ongoing covenant with God. New England's equivalent to a national constitution was *The Cambridge Platform*, which England had repudiated: "'Tis that for which we are Out-casts at this day; that . . . is it that sheweth what *New-England* is." They were, Norton explained, "A People, none neglected like them; a People none beloved like them: Neglected, if you look at men; beloved if you look at God."[17]

Norton urged his listeners to take courage from Jeremiah's promise and take his words for their own. Adversity, as Richard Mather had explained earlier, was a prerequisite to glory: "For can a child be born, where there was never any travailing paines? Can there be a crop of corn at harvest, where the ground was never plowed or broken up? Is not the way to Canaan through the wilderness?"[18] So too in 1661, Norton did not attempt to minimize the afflictions that came with England's derision, but neither did he neglect to mention the "healing Plaister," which was the very gospel order for the sake of which New Englanders were labeled outcasts and "fanaticks." Better to absorb the barbs of English ridicule than to forget the glorious commission still in effect: "That our polity may be a Gospel polity, and may be compleat according to the Scriptures, answering fully the word of God.''[19] As long as that commission was honored, New Englanders could accept their rejection and live secure in the conviction that they were still a chosen people.

A HEROIC PAST FOR THE CHILDREN

If Norton was correct in identifying New England with Israel then the time of New England's glory had not yet begun. Like Moses and his wandering generation, none of the founders would live to see the new promised land complete, but could only view it from afar. The heady visions of millennial triumph that so occupied the founders in the 1650s and 1660s were replaced by formal recollections of New England's brief but heroic past that could be passed on to the children. Now that the day of reckoning was postponed indefinitely and the central theater switched from Old World to New, it was the children who must see the experiment through according to the terms of initial settlement. The all-important question for the founders in their last days was no longer whether a model covenant Way could be devised—that was already settled and codified in *The Cambridge Platform*—but whether it could be preserved and perpetuated by the New World generation.

The founders were not without hope in the face of this problem. Their attachments to England and millennial expectations were never so strong that their own future was ignored. The very language of covenant pledges and privileges implied a binding continuity from generation to generation. From infancy the children heard about the covenant in sermons, catechisms, and family devotions, and learned that they were automatically part of its promises and conditions. Indeed they did not hear much of anything else. By controlling the children's world of communications in both reading and speech, the parents spared them from the corrupting influences of places like England where, as Thomas Shepard complained, "much sin and evil was abounding and where children might be polluted." Although the children were not expected to undergo conversion before adulthood, they were thoroughly indoctrinated in the precepts of God's law both for the evangelical purpose of "conviction" that was antecedent to conversion, and for the social purpose of instilling civic loyalty. With knowledge came self-discipline and submission for, as George Moxon pointed out in a message to young people, "how can a man be a judge if he be not acquainted with the law?"[20]

Along with instructing the children in the terms of the covenant, the founders attended to the problem of supplying a self-perpetuating core of native-trained civic and spiritual leaders. Nowhere were the long-range intentions of the founders more clearly expressed than in the early founding of Harvard College. In a commemorative sermon delivered in 1643, the college's second president, Charles Chauncy, recalled how

> after God had carried us safe to NE, and wee had builded our houses . . .
> rear'd convenient places for Gods worship, and setled the civill Govern-

ment: One of the next things we longed for, and looked after was to advance
Learning and perpetuate it to Posterity; dreading to leave an illiterate Ministry to the Churches, when our present Ministers shall lie in the Dust.[21]

The primary purpose of the college was to train ministers in the New
England Way and avoid dependence on England. As Thomas Shepard's
successor at Cambridge, Jonathan Mitchell, pointed out, "It sufficeth not
to Have Supplyes for the ministry, for time will shew that unless we
Have the Helps of Learning and education [in New England] . . . things
will languish and goe to decay among us."[22] Spiritual sincerity, natural
wisdom, and the "ability to read English" were, Richard Mather insisted,
insufficient to the high calling of opening and explaining the mysteries of
God's Word. When in 1654 Boston's Second Church sought to ordain
their ruling elder, Michael Powell—a pious man but "illiterate as to aca-
demical education"—as their pastor, the General Court refused on the
grounds that "if such men intrude themselves into the sacred functions
[of the ministry], there is danger of bringing the profession into contempt."[23] Like Jonathan Mitchell, the General Court recognized that if the
ministry ever lost its high social and academic standing it would also lose
authority to speak as the sole representative of Christ. And once that happened the sermon would lose its distinctive power to order and organize
a coherent way of life. The result would be civil and ecclesiastical chaos.

In the decentralized institutional setting of the New England Way, Harvard College played an indispensable role in supplying cultural cohesion
and hierarchical control. The college collected a common cultural core
which, through the ministers, would be exported to every settlement in
the land. By 1660, there were 135 college-trained leaders among the second generation, of whom 116 were Harvard graduates. The vast majority
(85 percent) of these early graduates could not remain in Boston and had
to attach themselves to local congregations.[24] Whenever a new town was
incorporated there was an accompanying settled minister who was
trained at Harvard and entrusted with applying God's Word to his community. Inevitably, these ministers' words were similar in matters of personal salvation and the meaning of New England because they emerged
from a common education in Cambridge. Harvard College was as much
a cultural and political institution as an academic one. As long as it continued to produce leaders with a common background, training, and
vision for New England, there was no need for centralized political institutions imposing a common culture and identity on the inhabitants from
without. That function was delegated to the sermon, and through the college the founders ensured that the sermon would survive in its original
form and meaning.

If the founders had anything to fear from the rising generation it was
not the abilities or trustworthiness of their Harvard-trained successors
(over half of whom were their own sons) but lack of piety and strength
of will among the general inhabitants. Careful study of the Old Testament
led them to believe that periods of revival were always followed by

decline, and New England was no exception.[25] When Thomas Shepard condemned England's failures in his 1645 fast sermon, he also censured New England's "Divisions and Distractions" and general "hankerings after the Whoredomes of the World" that were "the cause of the Lord's hand against us."[26]

By the 1660s, the signs of spiritual decay and diabolical hindrances were even more ominous and called into question the suitability of the children to succeed their parents. As the second generation came of age and began raising families of their own, they were not experiencing conversion and joining the church as their parents expected. Whereas children were not expected to join the church, young adults were; yet this was not happening. Church membership rates declined in the 1650s to one in two inhabitants in settled towns like Dedham and were even lower in Boston.[27] Although these not-yet-converted children still fell under the discipline and direction of the church by virtue of their baptism, their eternal souls were in mortal danger. Equally disturbing to the founders was that since the children had not "owned" the church covenant, *their* children (the third generation) could not, according to the provisions of *The Cambridge Platform,* be baptized. This meant that, technically speaking, they did not fall under church discipline at all; there was no covenant— either through baptism or personal confession of faith—to bind them to the church. For the New England Way to survive, the churches had to be pure, but they also had to represent a core of the society large enough to exert power and influence over all its operations. Clearly, the delicate balance of purity and power that worked so well for the first generation would have to be readjusted for the second and third generations. Otherwise, purity would stifle power and become self- defeating; the churches would remain pure—and empty.

THE HALF-WAY COVENANT

As their legacy to the rising generation, in 1662 the surviving founders buttressed the institutional foundations of the New England churches by modifying and expanding the provisions for church membership (and discipline) to include third-generation children whose parents were still only "outward" church members by virtue of their baptism. This "Half-way Covenant" was founded on a proposal, first suggested by Richard Mather, that third-generation grandchildren could be baptized if their parents agreed to two requirements. First they had to assent to the churches' "historical faith" in the hope that one day it would become their personal saving faith. And second, they had to live lives in outward conformity to God's Word.[28] This innovation, Mather insisted, would not dilute the purity of gathered churches by introducing unregenerate members. Neither the baptized grandchildren nor their unconverted parents would be entitled to participate in the Lord's Supper or allowed to vote in church meetings. These privileges would be reserved for confessing members. At the same time, however, the children and grandchildren would be bound in an outward covenant to particular congregations, which meant they would continue to fall under church discipline. They would, in brief, have all the responsibilities of covenant keeping without the attendant privileges.

The intensity of clerical and congregational debate for and against this Half-way Covenant demonstrates the fact that by 1662 everyone's attention had turned inward. The most important question was no longer how might New England best serve the cause of reform in Europe, but how could their abandoned Way be preserved in the American wilderness until such time as Christ returned to earth. Not all agreed that the Half-way Covenant was the appropriate strategy for retaining New England's privileged status as an elect nation, but enough did for the idea to be recommended to the particular churches.

The Half-way Covenant would stand as the crowning achievement of the founders. It not only marked the formal shift in emphasis from the European brethren to the children of New England but also reinterpreted New England's mission in a way that showed subsequent generations how to alter particular details in church (and later state) administration, for the sake of preserving Independent churches in a society that acknowledged no sovereign but *Sola Scriptura*.

By the mid-1650s, when church membership rates were at their nadir, many ministers considered expanding membership along the lines suggested by Richard Mather and Thomas Shepard.[29] Mather's own Dorchester congregation balked at the idea of diluting pure church membership, but at least two churches—Ipswich and Chelmsford—accepted the new recommendations and went ahead to extend baptism to the children of baptized members. Such diverse practices were permissible in Congregational church government but they were not desirable. To provide some general guidance, the General Court called an assembly of teaching and ruling elders to meet in June 1657 and resolve the issue of "church members and their children" with reference to baptism. The ministers at this conference could not agree any more than the congregations, but a majority, led by Mather, declared that on the basis of covenant logic and "the People of *Israel*" baptized children were "external" or "outward" members of the church organism.[30] This identification, in turn, led the majority to the practical suggestion that children of external members could also be baptized if their parents "understand the grounds of Religion, are not scandalous, and Solemnly own the Covenant in their own persons, wherein they give up both themselves and their children unto the Lord, and desire Baptism for them." This, the majority insisted, did not compromise the covenant of grace because in allowing baptism they were not claiming that the infants were saved. Just as in Israel "many were in that [external] Covenant, which never were in saving state of grace," so in New England external members might not all be saved, and for that reason could not vote or take communion until their conversion. But they were incorporated into external church fellowship with their congregations, where they enjoyed the special benefits of covenant care and attention. Equally important, these external members were, by their own pledge, obliged to "subjection to Ecclesiastical Discipline."[31]

Having settled among themselves the permissibility, if not the necessity, of comprehensive baptism, the elders met again in a synod in 1662 to prepare a general statement for the churches. Again the debates were sharp with a strong minority, led by Richard Mather's precocious son Increase and New Haven's John Davenport, opposing the new measures. But again a majority—led by most of the surviving founders—endorsed the principle of comprehensive baptism.[32]

In recommending the Half-way Covenant, the majority was aware that their audience was limited solely to New England. The document was printed in Cambridge for internal circulation; it made no reference to European Protestants who had ignored the light of New England's Way. Instead it sought to reconcile the new measures with New England's own brief past as recorded in *The Cambridge Platform*. Already in 1662 the *Platform* had assumed an almost canonical status among congregations who saw in it a written guarantee of their congregational liberties. Such reverence, the majority now reminded them, should be reserved exclusively for the Scriptures. The writers of the *Platform* were not infallibly inspired, nor should their pronouncements be considered as engraved in stone. Some of the original writers had lived long enough to revise their own past, recognizing that "defects in practice" were inevitable in any human document. One such defect was in the area of church membership where, in 1648, "we had . . . no occasion to determine what to judge or practise in that matter."[33] By 1662 the evidence was in and pointed to the need to modify existing practice. The only absolute principle was that God's Word must remain sovereign over the churches and towns of New England; that was God's "one end" in "leading so many of his poor people into this Wilderness." If the present rules of church membership and discipline limited the number of obedient listeners to a tiny and impotent fraction of the larger community, then the rules must change, so that God's Word could remain sovereign and binding over all.

In codifying the new measures and recommending them to the churches, the elders recognized that their declaration could not bind local congregations any more than could *The Cambridge Platform*, and that disagreements were inevitable. Such was the course of Protestantism from its origins. As Jonathan Mitchell observed in defense of the synod's formulations, "Every Stage of Truth's progress, since the first dawning of the Reformation, hath been accompanied with sharp Debates, even among the godly Professors of it, and so it was foretold [in] Rev. 15."[34] This was especially true in New England where, as John Norton pointed out in another defense, congregational liberties allowed the churches to join in the debates with their ministers and determine their own policy of church membership. Still, Norton went on, congregations should consider the advice of synods very carefully: "When a Controversie ariseth in a Church, (differences must not alwayes continue) what shall resolve the same, if a Ministerial judge[ment] be not admitted?"[35]

The surviving founders who spearheaded church membership reform emerged from the debates battered but triumphant. The Half-way Covenant came to be accepted in most churches by the last quarter of the seventeenth century, and in time many half-way members in fact experienced conversion and became full members.[36] Despite international isolation, waning church membership, and the dissent of a vocal minority who opposed the new arrangements, the founders adapted successfully to the challenge of perpetuating the New England Way and preserving the bonds of covenant discipline that made them a special people of God. Their dying concern was with the children of New England. In the conclusion to their preface, as in the main body of their recommendation, the synod ignored the Old World and directed their exhortation to the new hope of God's Israel, "the Youth of the Country":

> Take heed therefore unto your selves, when owned as the people of the Lord your God, (Deut. 27. 9, 10). Lest there should be among you any root that beareth gall and wormwood. . . . Remember, that all Relations to God and to his people, do come loaden with Duty; and all Gospel-duty must be done in humility. . . . Learn subjection to Christs holy Government in all the parts and wayes thereof. Be subject to your godly Parents: Be subject to your spiritual Fathers and Pastors, and to all their Instructions, Admonitions and Exhortations. . . . Let it not be said, that when the first and best generation in New-England were gathered to their fathers, there arose another generation after them that knew not the Lord.[37]

THE FOUNDERS' DYING CHARGE

The Synod of 1662's closing exhortation contained three injunctions that encapsulated the essential elements of Puritan preaching for generations thereafter: the memorialization of the founders—the "first and best generation in New-England"; the duty of "subjection to Christs holy government in all the parts and wayes thereof"; and the dire consequences (the "gall and wormwood") that would accrue to "another generation . . . that knew not the Lord." Some of these themes were more conspicuous in occasional preaching, others in regular. But taken together the three provided New England with its own independent and self-contained past (the founders), and an ongoing mission in the present—to preserve the founders' covenant. That ongoing mission, moreover, was fraught with constant danger: not the danger that England would ignore their reforms, but the danger of divine desertion if the covenant was forsaken by the children.

As the end of their lives drew near, the surviving founders reiterated the meaning of New England. John Wilson's dying charge to his Boston congregation was to remember the mission of his generation: "But consider, what came you into this Wilderness for? did you come to gaze upon one another? No, you came to see, and hear the great Prophet, even the Lord Jesus in his Ministers, that you might have the Ordinances of God in his Churches rightly gathered, and the holy Sacraments rightly administered." Above all, Wilson warned, the children must remember to honor the words of their ministers when speaking in the pulpit, or face the avenging wrath of God:

> God will tell you one day you had your *Cotton* and your *Norton*, and your *Hooker*, and your *Shepard*, and your *Rogers* . . . you had my Ministers, and there is never a Minister that God hath sent, but the time will come, when as, if you have heard them, and obeyed them, O what a sweet meeting that will be, and then may they say, Lord, here we are, and the Children thou hast given us. But otherwise God will say, Why did you not receive them? When they come to despise the Prophets . . . the wrath of the Lord rose against his people, so that there was no remedy.[38]

For John Davenport, who resisted the Half-way Covenant to his dying day, New England continued to be the hope of "God's Israel." He concluded his 1669 election sermon by recalling the words John Cotton had written him in Holland thirty years earlier, "that the Order of the Churches and of the Commonwealth was so settled, by common consent; that it brought to his mind, the New Heaven and New Earth." That vision, though to Davenport's mind strained by an overly innovative synod, was still intact. Now it was up to the children. They must

> take heed and beware . . . lest he remove the golden Candlesticks, and the burning and shining Lights in them, as he hath already done [to] many eminent Lights; and wo to them for whom the Gospel is spurned, for their abusing it, and the messangers of it. . . . And see that your fruitfulness is good, answereth the cost and pains that God hath been at with you in his Vineyard, lest the Lord be provoked to deal with us, as he did with his ancient Vineyard.[39]

The stern warnings uttered by the founders in their final sermons were no mere hyperbole or distant fears. They had redefined the children's mission from England to New England, but they feared the eventual outcome. And they made sure their listeners shared that fear; without it there was no incentive to corporate covenant keeping. Human pride was such that people would conform and reform only if they were conscious of grave shortcomings in their present lives that brought them dangerously close to divine desertion. And shortcomings the founders found aplenty. At the same time that John Wilson reiterated New England's mission, he bemoaned the fact that "I have known *New-England* about thirty-six years, and I never knew such a time as this is that we live in." The cause, he went on, was spiritual decay and waning resolve.[40]

In sounding the rhetoric of failure—what Perry Miller termed the "jeremiad"—the founders and their children discovered a far better rhetorical strategy than words of fulsome praise. Such denunciations underscored the theological point that God was sovereign and merciful, and the giver of all things. Socially, the rhetoric impelled an earnest effort to conform to the teachings of God's Word before it was "too late," while it affirmed New England's special corporate status.

For all its negations the language of condemnation inspired hope and confidence.[41] God only chastised those whom he loved and his punishments were signs of concern, not desertion. The tendency of Puritan ministers to lambast their congregations for their sins and evil ways has been well noted by historians. Less noted, but equally significant, however, is the fact that no minister ever dared insinuate that New England was so evil that God had abandoned the country and annulled its covenant. The very fact of the sermon's existence ensured that desertion was "not yet." As long as God's Word sounded in the pulpits, the people could be certain that "*Sions* recovery by [way of] repentance from her backsliding, is an effect of grace, and a fore-runner of the set time of *Sions* mercy."[42]

Even as pessimism and fear dominated the final remarks of the founders in their occasional sermons, they carefully reminded their successors that regular preaching should be less concerned with the state of New England's federal covenant than with instilling in their congregations what John Davenport termed a "serious and fixed apprehension of Eternal life and death, in relation to God."[43] To commemorate that message of salvation and keep it emblazoned in the records of New England's past, congregations often published the final regular sermon of their pastor. The printed funeral sermon would not be invented in New England for another generation. In the meantime, the memory of the founding ministers as gospel heralds would be preserved in their own words.

In the town of Dedham, John Allin hotly debated the Half-way Covenant with his more conservative congregation right down to the day of his death in 1671. But in all of the heat, his listeners never turned him out of the pulpit or challenged his preaching office.[44] Following his death the grief-stricken congregation collected the manuscript notes of his final sermon and printed them at the press at Cambridge, "for the better keeping alive the memory of him whom we so much loved and honored." The sermon appeared, according to the foreword, in Allin's seventy-fifth year in the "ordinary course" of his preaching. Though a typical sabbath performance, with no particular occasion in mind, it seemed to the congregation to be providentially suited to posterity.

For his text, Allin selected "the farewell speech of Jesus Christ" in John 14:27: "Peace I leave with you, my peace I give unto you: not as the world giveth, give I unto you. Let not your heart be troubled, neither let it be afraid." The times, Allin began, were perilous. In Europe, "bloody wars," "persecutions," and "trials" abounded and plagued true churches everywhere. In New England, internal peace was upset by church disputes over the Half-way Covenant, "ill neighbors," and "disquiet in the families." Talk of peace was illusory, "more in words than realities." No sooner did tranquility appear "then suddenly destruction comes upon them as a whirlwind." Even in moments of external repose when all seemed to be well with the world, the individual soul remained troubled at the prospect of death. No earthly scheme of happiness could illuminate the darkness of the soul in its contemplation of eternity. In such times there was only one hope, which Allin extracted as the doctrinal lesson of his text: "That the peace which Jesus Christ hath purchased, and given to his true disciples, is such as may strengthen them against all distracting troubles and feares in this world."[45] Such a peace, Allin went on, could not be earned; it could only be "received" as the "great and wonderful gift of Christ." Dedham's covenant children must not rest content until they found such a peace; they must "breathe after it" and "labor for it" through prayer and attendance on the Word. Once received, they must hold onto it as a fixed and certain hope:

> Let nothing dismay or disquiet the hearts of those that Christ hath given this peace unto, whatever you hear of in the world; we hear of many troubles and disquiets abroad in the world, and the cause of God suffers much, we should lay it to heart, but not to be troubled, disquieted, or dismayed in the sorest troubles; in a word, Faint not, for we look not at things present, which are temporary, but at things to come, which are eternal.[46]

In this sermon, Allin's congregation found the words of hope and courage that had brought them to the New World and sustained them when Europe stopped listening. By printing them they ensured that New England's mission would live, if only in the memories of their children.

PART II

ARRANGEMENT, 1666–1700

[4]

Days of Trouble and Thankful Remembrances

At the same time that congregations were printing the final sermons of the founders, Northampton's Eleazar Mather (HC, 1656) delivered a sermon series on 1 Kings 8:57: "The Lord our God be with us, as he was with our fathers: let him not leave us or forsake us." These sermons were a son's tribute to his recently deceased father, whose dying charge was to "seek the good of the Rising generation." Unknown to Eleazar those sermons would also be his last. Within weeks, he contracted a fever and died at the age of thirty-two.

Using the manuscript notes of Eleazar's series, his brother Increase created a composite sermon that he entitled *A Serious Exhortation*. The sermon was printed at the Cambridge press in 1671 and reprinted seven years later, by which time it had come to stand as a statement of the second generation's purpose and mission. Unlike the final sermons of the founders, Eleazar's sermon embodied a sense of hopeful mission and eagerness to get on with the work of his generation. The words of his text were taken from Solomon's prayer of dedication at the temple in Jerusalem when Israel was at the apex of her power and influence. As Solomon completed the work of his father David and inherited God's covenant promise of blessing, so too would the children of New England be blessed, for in the words of Mather's doctrine, "The Continuance of the Lords gracious Presence with a People, from fathers to children after them, is a special favor of God, and much to be desired by all that are cordial to the weal of the Israel of God."[1]

The "special favor" of which Eleazar spoke was God's covenant with New England that by his grace the children inherited. Thus divine "continuance" came in recognition of the founders' unswerving faith and loyalty; for their sakes the children would be blessed. But what were the children expected to do with their legacy? From Solomon's case, Mather determined that just as covenants were continuous from generation to generation, so also were they cumulative and progressive. Solomon was not superior or even equal to his father in piety, but he stood on his father's shoulders and so had a foundation on which to build and make Israel even more powerful and glorious in the eyes of the surrounding

67

nations. So too in New England, the founders had advanced Europe's
Reformation through their invention of the "Congregational Way," and
the children, having their "pattern and example," were in a unique position to advance God's kingdom even further. For each generation that the
covenant survived, expectations grew higher: "You will be instrumental
(above what your fathers have been) either to the advantage or disadvantage of Religion." The children had to remember their parents' covenant,
but even more important they had to remember that

> you are a generation of great hopes and great fears. The Lord expects much
> from you, that you will do much for the glory of his Name; *He said, Surely
> they are children that will not lie;* he hath been expecting a long time. And
> your predecessors, those that have been before you, all their expectations
> under God himself, are in you.[2]

Mather's challenge to the rising generation was not an easy one. If they
succeeded in keeping the covenant, they praised only the founders; to
warrant praise in their own right the children must somehow outdo the
founders, a near-impossible task. And if they failed, they had no one to
blame but themselves. From birth to death they would be a generation of
"great hopes and great fears."

At the time that Mather spoke, the "great fears" were a more pressing
consideration than the "great hopes." Many in his congregation were not
yet full church members and were prone to considering the things of this
world in preference to the state of their eternal souls. That worldly interest, in turn, led to selfish dissembling. Whatever New England's ultimate
hope and destiny, the present was not bright:

> The dayes wherein you live are backsliding times, *evil dayes*, times of great
> degeneracy and Apostacy. Alas! little humble walking now, little self-denial,
> little holiness; Oh how weighty and difficult is their work, that are now
> called out to stand up for Christ. . . . How hard it is to keep up an House
> when it's falling down, to keep the Ship from sinking, when the leak that
> is sprung hath almost filled it with water.

To keep the ship afloat all must strive to draw nearer to God and to one
another in Christian love: "Labour therefore for a Publick Spirit, let all
your own interest give way to his; Oh let nothing be dear in comparison
of Christ and his interest. . . . To be of a private Spirit is not to be for
God."[3] Similar words had been uttered before, but now they must be
addressed to another generation; the whole process had to begin anew.
Charity, unlike the covenant, was not inherited; it would take many bitter
trials and disappointments before its truth would be set home and applied
to the hearts of a "degenerate" people.

MAINTAINING THE FOUNDERS' ARRANGEMENT

Mather's sermon to the rising generation contained all the central themes
that would occupy the second wave of ministers in their occasional

preaching on the providential meaning of New England. The children's mission was set from infancy on maintaining in thought and deed the "church-state" created by their parents. As Dorchester's William Stoughton (HC, 1650) explained in his 1668 election sermon: "The solemn work of this day is *Foundation-work*; not to lay a new Foundation, but to continue and strengthen, and beautifie, and build upon that which hath been laid." New England's foundation, Stoughton went on, was their inherited covenant, which distinguished them from all other New World inhabitants, including their parents who had been born in England. Only the children could claim God's special corporate promises by way of inheritance:

> God had his *Creatures* in this Wilderness before we came, and his *Rational Creatures* too, a multitude of them; but as to *Sons* and *Children* that are Covenant-born unto God, Are not we the *first* in such a Relation? In this respect we are surely the Lords *first-born* in this Wilderness.

By virtue of their parents' "Vows and Promises" the children received a special blessing; they had only to keep the covenant, secure in the knowledge that "a people in Covenant, are a people of many Advantages, and the Lord builds his Expectations upon these."[4]

Stoughton, like Eleazar Mather, recognized that the children were a different people from the founders. The cumulative principle of covenanting described by Mather was important not only because it promised "special favors" but also because it made divine revelation from biblical times applicable to their own immediate past. When the founders had spoken of "patterns" they meant Israel and the New Testament apostolic church. They did not speak of their own Old World parents as a corporate pattern because their parents had not founded a new way of life. The children, however, had the benefit of forty years of covenant keeping to guide them, and they attached a revelatory significance to those experiences as well. When Eleazar spoke of "patterns" he meant his immediate predecessors in New England whose record of faithfulness, charity, and hope was like that of God's people of old. Stoughton too, in recalling the founding of New England, observed how "God sifted a whole Nation that he might send Choice Grain over into this Wilderness." By blessing them with "mercy and kindness" God signified his approval of their covenant and his expectations that the children would do the same.[5] In thus elevating the founders to brotherhood with the patriarchs of old, the children transformed their New World history into sacred mythology and harnessed that myth to the task of cultural preservation and continuity. For them, the history of New England could be read as an extension of Holy Writ.

As we have seen, the legend of the founders actually began with those founders who survived beyond 1660. But the children brought the genre to a high art. They had no Old World "homeland" to call their own and invested all their hopes and identity in New England. The primary mission of their generation was recall and preservation, and the appropriate vehicle for such corporate commemoration was the occasional sermon. Unlike the founders, who published few occasional sermons, the children devoted the old press at Cambridge largely to the task of printing occasional sermons, and they accorded them a significance they had never enjoyed with the founders.[6] These printed products were not intended to encompass the main themes of regular preaching, nor were they exact replicas of the speeches at the time of their delivery. Their purpose was literary and historical; they were revised and expanded for print and intended to serve as sacred commentaries on the history of God's covenant people in New England. They served notice that New England now had a history of its own that did not depend upon Europe for its origins or legitimacy and which, by divine promise, would continue as long as the children kept the covenant of their parents and honored their ministers.

ELECTION SERMONS AND THE MYTH OF NEW ENGLAND

Of the seventy-nine occasional sermons printed at Cambridge before 1690, the most important (and numerous) were election sermons.[7] The ritual significance of election day had already been fixed by the founders as the time when God instructed the nation-as-a-whole on federal covenants, reminding the people how they had come into being as an elect nation and pointing out what they must do to preserve their privileged status. Beginning in 1663, and on a regular basis after 1667, these sermons were published so that they could be distributed to the ministers and summarized from every pulpit in the land. Instead of the abbreviated headnotes that characterized the surviving election sermon outlines of first-generation preachers, second-generation election speakers prepared fully written treatises, expanded after initial delivery to comprise fifty pages or more of printed text. These elaborate publications—more pamphlet essays than sermon outlines—testified that for one more year New Englanders had kept the faith and the legacy of their parents.

As literary products whose purpose was to restate New England's historical mission and rehearse its progress down to the present, election sermons quickly became standardized and assumed a stereotypical form. They invariably included a discussion of human government as seen from the divine vantage point. From the divine perspective, the form of government was less important than its end in promoting what Jonathan Mitchell termed "the welfare of the people." This end, Mitchell went on, was affirmed both by "the Light of *Nature*" and the "Law of God." Whatever form government assumed, rulers must govern "for the people . . . they are to make it their main business, and the scope of all their Actions, Laws and Motions, to seek the welfare of the people."[8] When Mitchell and other election speakers spoke of welfare or the "common good," they meant the covenant. God did not specify how a people should organize authority, but he required that they honor him in their lives and in their public institutions. Covenanted societies had to erect governments that preserved internal peace and protected their citizens from outside enemies, but their governments must also establish orthodox religion and suppress rank heresy and immorality. Any other concept of government would threaten the covenant and, for that reason, defeat the common good.

Of all the functions of government, none received greater attention in the 1660s than the suppression of heresy. Religious intolerance, like Congregational polity, was a badge of New England's covenant fidelity. It was essential to the preservation of the country's privileged status. In his 1663 election sermon, Salem's John Higginson declared that England's policy of religious toleration encouraged the worship of false gods. Religious tolerance, he said, using terms remarkably similar to those of the founders, was not a valid deduction from Christian liberty: "That which is contrary to the Gospel hath *no right*, and therefore should have *no liberty*."[9]

Election speakers spent less time on the mechanics of government than on the mission of New England. Frequently, election sermons were grand epics that took audiences away from local concerns and personal crises and into the great drama of providential history.[10] For struggling settlements whose only distinction was the Congregational Way for which England belittled them as "persecutors" or "fanatics," the rhetorical world of providential history was preferable to the brute facts of profane history. From the profane viewpoint New Englanders were bit players, scorned on the larger stage of English history; but in sacred history—the history election speakers never forgot—these same people were heroic, possessed of a historic meaning that placed them above every other nation.

Second-generation election speakers signaled their entry into providential history by locating their text in ancient Israel and then, through typology, extending the message to the children of New England. The children came to understand the history of Israel as well—perhaps better—than their parents knew the history of England. To solidify this identification the speaker assumed the persona of the Old Testament prophet he quoted in his text and encouraged his audience to identify with the tribes of Israel. In his 1663 election sermon, for example, John Higginson began by speaking in the character of Solomon, using the same text Eleazar Mather had chosen six years earlier:

> Me thinks I look upon this present Assembly . . . [as] resembling the great assembly of the People of Israel mentioned in the text. . . . And I am perswaded you are affected to this Cause, as that Assembly was, your desire is to see *Religion flourish*, and the Cause of God and his people be maintained amongst us.

Higginson then turned to the present situation which, not surprisingly, was very similar to that of Israel. The causes of ancient Israel and New England were so closely allied as to be virtually interchangeable:

> The *cause of his people Israel* was right from God, and liberty from God, to keep Gods Commandments in matters of Religion. This was the cause of

God and Israel then, and I hope it will appear anon, that the very same is the cause of God and his people now. . . . It was not for worldly wealth, or a better livelyhood here for the outward man . . . it was another thing and a better thing that we followed the Lord into the wilderness for. My Fathers and Brethren, this is never to be forgotten, that *New-England is originally a plantation of Religion, not a plantation of Trade.*[11]

Second-generation election speakers also included frequent references to the founders, to underscore their position as the keepers of an inherited covenant. Often they would silently incorporate key phrases or biblical texts from the founders' sermons into their own. In his 1670 address to the General Court, Samuel Danforth used the text of John Wilson's final sermon (Matthew 11:7–9) to describe New England's "errand into the wilderness." That errand was the perpetuation of "your Liberty to walk in the Faith of the Gospel with all good Conscience according to the Order of the Gospel." The founders had not employed the term "errand" to describe their mission, but the children found it useful; it supplied not only continuity with their past but a sense of their own generation's superiority over the other colonies and nations in preserving "gospel liberty." To confirm that superiority, Danforth again returned to the founders, not only by direct reference but by paraphrasing the text of John Cotton's farewell sermon to the Winthrop fleet in 1630:

We left our Country, Kindred and Fathers houses, and came into these wilde Woods and Deserts where the Lord hath planted us, and made us *dwell in a place of our own, that we might move no more, and that the Children of wickedness might afflict us not any more,* 2 Sam. 7.10. What is it that *distinguisheth New-England* from other Colonies and Plantations in *America*? Not our transportation over the *Atlantick* Ocean, but the *Ministry* of God's faithful Prophets, and the fruition of his holy *Ordinances.*[12]

This text from 2 Samuel—originally given to Israel but appropriated by the children to refer to "America"—would recur in Puritan preaching down to the Revolution. It conveyed a divine right to the land ("a place of our own") that no other colonies could claim, and it conveyed the mission to maintain the "ministry of God's faithful prophets" according to the pure Congregational Way.

Like the founders, the children discovered that the occasional sermon's power to encourage social and spiritual conformity lay not in the promise of success but rather in the threat of failure. Election speakers repeatedly claimed that federal covenants were probational and entailed a set of conditions. In William Stoughton's words, "When the Lord enters into Covenant with any people, this Covenant of his is a Covenant with Conditions. . . . Hence there are the *Laws,* as well as the *Promises* of the Covenant. As the Lord *obligeth* himself *to us* so he *requires* something *from us,* and thus the *Commandments* and *Statutes* of God are frequently called his Covenant." For proof he turned to sacred history, which confirmed that federal or "external political Covenant[s]" were "frequently *broken and made void.''* The children, like their parents, must recognize that they were on trial for their lives; they must "look upon our selves as under a *solemn divine Probation.''*[13] Proportionally, as ministers portrayed their society as nearer and nearer to the edge of disaster, their words gained in power.

The evolution of the election sermon into a specialized essay of recorded remembrances, hopeful errands, and dire fears was complete by 1673. In that year Urian Oakes (HC, 1649), pastor at Cambridge and soon to be president of Harvard College, prepared a sixty-four-page treatise that covered the span of providential history from the creation of the world to the founding of New England. His text—which would frequently be cited in subsequent occasional sermons—was taken from Moses' "farewell sermon" in Deuteronomy 32:29: "O that they were wise, that they understood this, that they would consider their latter end.''[14] These words, Oakes began, appeared at a time in Israel's history when they were done wandering in the wilderness and preparing to enter Canaan, "a Land of rest, and liberty, and glorious enjoyments." Unknown to them, God had set this land aside from the beginning of time, "in the first division of the habitable parts of the World, that there might be an Inheritance laid out for the Children of *Israel.''* For many generations thereafter Israel enjoyed the bounties of the land and the protection of their covenant God. Then they broke the covenant, ignored God's "Laws and Commandments," and suffered the fate of divine withdrawal. Their experience was a prototype for subsequent "peculiar peoples."

From the case of Israel, Oakes turned immediately to New England, whose "place of rest" was also fixed from the beginning of time:

As when there was a *Division* made of the *habitable parts of the Earth in the sons of Adam*, there was an Assignation of *that good Land of Canaan* in the purpose of God to the Children of Israel . . . so was there an Allotment, in the Counsel of God, of these *Ends of the Earth* unto this part of our Nation for the *Bounds of their Habitation*. This *wilderness* was the place which God decreed to make a *Canaan* to you. And *what he thought in his heart, he hath fulfilled with his hand, in bringing you to this good Land,* and providing wonderfully for your well-being here.[15]

Such a destiny, Oakes went on, could only be seen in retrospect from the vantage point of the second generation. First came the Reformation, begun by Luther and advanced by "Geneva and Scotland." This was brought to its "highest step" in the "Congregational Way." By transporting the founders to a New World set aside for them from the Creation and overseeing their unique way, God ensured that a people would grow strong in him. In retrospect the children could see how they were repeating Israel's errand: *"You have had Moses. Men, I mean of the same spirit, to lead and go before you.''*[16] If these deliverances were to continue, the children must honor the conditions of their covenant.

Oakes closed by unveiling the millennial destiny of New England, hidden from the world (and even from the founders), but inescapably clear to the children of New England:

> So, *we are Abraham's Children,* a people in Covenant with God. . . . You have been *as a City upon an hill* (though in a remote and obscure Wilderness) *as a Candle in the Candlestick that gives light to the whole House* (world I mean) as to the pattern of God's House, the Form and Fashion and Outgoings and Incomings thereof: convinced and helped many [by your example], and left others, that shut their eyes against the Light of your Profession and Practice, without excuse. God hath been doing (in my Apprehension) the same thing for the substance of it here, that shall be done more universally and gloriously, when *Israel shall blossom and bud and fill the face of the World with fruit.* You have been though an handfull of people separate from the greatest part of the Christian World (as it is prophesied of *Jacobs* remnant that it should be in the midst of many people.) *as a Dew from the Lord, and as the showers upon the grass.* God hath priviledged and honoured you greatly in this respect.[17]

From words like these the second generation learned to celebrate their isolation and fix on New England a sacred significance that would grow stronger as time went on.

FAST SERMONS AND THE
RHETORIC OF ANCESTRAL DECLENSION

Though the road to New England's glory was sure, the journey would not be easy. Divine providence, ministers repeatedly preached, was not a substitute for human exertion and conformity to the demands of God's law; nor did it assure an easy time for the elect. On the contrary, Scripture prophecies and past experience warned of unceasing trials, tribulations, and fallings away from faith. As John Higginson pointed out in his election sermon, "The History of the Church in all ages hath informed us of this, that after a time of *peace,* comes a time of *trouble.*"[18] The primary occasion for publicly recognizing these times of trouble was the fast day— the time when ministers integrated the theory of federal covenants into the public life of their particular communities. The election sermon was limited to one pronouncement a year and necessarily spoke in more general, cosmic terms of New England's sacred birthright. The fast sermon, however, could be finely tuned to particular local sins and applied with a chilling directness to the specific calamities that occasioned the fast. Few common inhabitants personally witnessed the ceremonial of the election day sermon, but all experienced the fast and heard its relentless cry to return to the Lord before it was "too late."

Throughout the 1670s and 1680s, more fast day sermons (fourteen) were printed at Cambridge than any other type of sermon except election sermons.[19] To understand this publishing pattern, one must recognize that in New England print functioned primarily as a historical rather than evangelistic tool. It was not intended to represent regular preaching but to chart the children's location in providential history. All of the salient facts regarding covenant theory, church order, and personal salvation had already been published by the founders and reiterated weekly by their successors. The children did not need the press to reprint these familiar teachings so much as they needed it to chart the performance of their generation in transforming theory into practice. Performance, not invention, would be the standard by which they would be judged in sacred history. Printed fast sermons, like printed election sermons, served the function of recording the ways in which the children had conformed to their inherited mission and the ways in which they had fallen short, only to be saved by providential mercy.

For every fast sermon that was published, scores more were delivered in towns throughout the land.[20] The overwhelming majority of these sermons dealt with corporate sin. In sounding the rhetoric of failure, ministers echoed the jeremiads of the founders but added an emphasis distinctive to their generation. Pointing to the lives of their parents, they would show how far short of that pattern the children had fallen. To the founders' rhetoric of failure, native-born generations would add their own mythology of ancestral declension. The fears of the first generation were as nothing compared to those of their wayward children who stood even closer to divine desertion.[21]

Throughout the 1660s and 1670s, natural disasters seemed to occur with greater frequency than at any time in the lives of the first generation. No sooner did one calamity end than another occurred: in 1662 and 1666 there were severe droughts; in 1664, 1665, and 1668 the wheat crops were "blasted" by mildew and invaded by an "Army of Caterpillars"; in 1666 there were fires and a smallpox epidemic; in 1664 an "avenging comet"; and in 1667 an ominous display of "zodiacal" light appeared in the heavens, shaped like a spear and aimed at the heart of New England. When these events were piled one on top of another, the ministers were led to the inescapable conclusion that something was particularly amiss with their generation. And who knew how long God would continue to send these warnings before "utterly rejecting" New England? After describing the peculiar pattern of "the Late Comet or Blazing Star" that appeared over New England in 1664, Samuel Danforth said that it portended death and revealed "what a jealous eye the Lord hath upon us."[22] New England's fears of divine desertion were brought home in particularly graphic fashion in Michael Wigglesworth's best-selling poem, *God's Controversy with New-England*, one stanza of which read:

> For think not, O Backsliders, in your heart,
>   That I shall still your evill manners beare:
> Your sinns me press as sheaves do load a cart,
>   And therefore I will plague you for this geare
> Except you seriously, and soon, repent,
>   Ile not delay your pain and heavy punishment.[23]

Such fears dominated print in the 1660s and after, not because ministers preached no other sentiments in these years but because they were the most appropriate to understanding the current status of God's ongoing covenant (and controversy) with New England.

SOCIAL CHANGE AND DECLINING MINISTERIAL STATUS

If there was anything that bothered ministers more than the displays of God's wrath in natural calamities it was the fact that, although in many other outward respects New England seemed to prosper, the people seemed loathe to humble themselves before their benefactor. The early days of subsistence farming in small agricultural villages were beginning to pass. Immigration to New England all but stopped after 1640, but the internal growth rate was explosive, doubling the population every twenty-seven years and making it the largest English region in the New World.[24] Along with growth came economic diversification and greater institutional complexity. Merchant firms and shipbuilding industries proliferated in port cities like Boston, Salem, and New London; foodstuffs, fish, and timber products were traded up and down the North American coast, in the Caribbean islands, and across the Atlantic.[25] Inland, small tradesmen and farmers entered the dynamic commercial system by marketing surplus goods and produce through a network of strategically located "central places," which linked agricultural village and port city. In hurly-burly, unpredictable fashion, individuals amassed fortunes which, though modest by Old World standards, far exceeded those of the first generation. All of these changes threatened traditional patterns of life and communal solidarity. It was not clear how traditional theories of deference, social rank, and corporate cohesion would operate in a dynamic economy whose ranks were fluid and constantly changing. Rapid social change gave rise to social tensions which, for the ministers, were evidence of spiritual decline.

Nowhere did these social tensions appear more clearly to the ministers than on what they perceived as their own loss of social status. In a pattern that was to recur in each succeeding generation, ministers became convinced that they were denied the respect that had been given their predecessors. And in part their perceptions were correct. The automatic deference the founders seemed to enjoy in their churches was no longer forthcoming. When young ministers assumed the pulpits of their venerated predecessors, they encountered resistance from all sides: merchants, magistrates, and ordinary townspeople all seemed less disposed to honor their social position. In many new communities established on the peripheries of old towns, ministers were not settled immediately and, when called, were not provided with a decent living befitting their rank.[26] Looking for explanations, the ministers bypassed "natural" causes and seized instead upon declining spirituality. They did not consider the fact that they were not patriarchs but young men—often in their twenties and early thirties—ministering to other young people who had grown up with them and who, from infancy, had internalized their fathers' language of gospel liberty and limitations on all authority. Neither did they understand that their New World environment was inherently unstable and that, relative to other New World societies to the south, they were in fact still a model of stability and social cohesion. Instead they saw only a deterioration of Christian love and piety. By identifying their spiritual prerogatives as God's prophets with social deference they began equating social disrespect with spiritual disrespect and a contempt for God's Word. For New England, this meant trouble.

Sooner or later fast day denunciations and lamentations came back to the subject of disrespect for God's "watchmen." If the sins of pride and envy showed themselves in land acquisitiveness, usury, presumptuous apparel, and petty bickering between neighbors, they were even more apparent when congregations challenged the status and authority of their ministers, particularly in matters of salaries and synodical pronouncements. Matters worsened continually. Fast days came and went with distressing regularity but the tensions persisted. Taking their rhetoric of failure and ancestral declension seriously, the ministers reasoned that God was getting angrier and angrier—as they themselves were. When the children of Israel refused to amend their ways and honor God's prophets, their miseries grew progressively more severe. By the 1670s, most ministers were predicting a similar time of dread for New England.

At a church fast in 1674, Increase Mather made known his prediction that, in the words of Ezekiel 7:7, New England's "day of trouble is at hand." To support his prophecy Mather invoked divine inspiration: "God by a secret Providence is wont to move upon the hearts of his faithful Servants, that they should speak according to what is in the Lords heart to do. Therefore ever observe it . . . that if the Lords Watchmen do with one voice cry, *The day of trouble is near* . . . it is so indeed." Special powers of prediction had not been claimed with such conviction by the founders (particularly after Anne Hutchinson). But by the 1670s, the situation had changed. Faced with declining respect, ministers emphasized their superior prophetic powers in strong words intended to set them apart from the pious rank and file.[27] Dire predictions like Mather's were certainly sobering and apt to make even the most hardened New England sinner pause; they were also risky. With such claims of special prophetic powers, the ministers preached themselves into a corner. For their own credibility and legitimacy, they needed a disaster even more than they needed success. Either their diagnosis was correct and would be confirmed by "dismal and calamitous days," or they were wrong and New England would continue to flourish. It was a time for ministers and their congregations to wait and see.

NEW ENGLAND'S DAY OF TROUBLE

In 1674, when Mather issued his prophecy of impending doom, the evidence was not forthcoming. There were "yearly judgments" to be sure—

what Boston's Thomas Thacher termed prodding "reprieves"—but nothing to suggest unprecedented calamities.[28] Then, in the summer of 1675, something dreadful happened. It began on Sunday, June 20, when a tribe of Wampanoag Indians led by Chief Metacom or "King Philip" attacked the neighboring town of Swansea, burning and looting deserted homes while the townspeople were at church. Four days later, a day on which Plymouth had declared an emergency public fast to avert disaster, Philip attacked Swansea again in force, killing nine and wounding several others. New England's long-standing peace with the surrounding Indians came to an abrupt end. In war, the ministers found the evidence they needed to confirm their prophecies and document the extent of God's nerve-shattering and bloody controversy with his wayward New England children.

Once begun, there seemed to be no stopping the great Indian offensive.[29] In mid-August 1675, the exposed outlying settlements in the upper Connecticut Valley were attacked, as were the western Massachusetts towns of Lancaster, Hadley, Northfield, and Deerfield. By then Philip had been joined by the powerful Narragansetts and Nipmucks who banded together in a great and general war for national and cultural survival. Everywhere, on both sides, there was devastation and dislocation. Philip had the advantages of surprise and guerrilla tactics. The New England Confederation—including Rhode Island, Plymouth, Connecticut, Massachusetts, and New Hampshire—had superior manpower and firepower. As in America's Civil War two centuries later, surprise and tactics won the early battles but they could not sustain a protracted war. In the summer of 1676, Philip's troops hammered their way to within ten miles of Boston, but they could not manage the final push. By then attrition had begun to take its toll and the tide turned. In August 1676, Philip was isolated in a swamp, captured, and executed. His people were either killed in battle, confined in "praying villages," or sold into slavery in the West Indies. The devastation wrought on the colonists was also severe. Half the towns were attacked and twelve completely destroyed. Women and children were killed or carried into captivity. One in every sixteen men of fighting age died in what would stand as the costliest (in deaths per capita) war in American history. Economic growth and frontier settlement stopped and would not recover for a generation. Never in their brief history had New Englanders experienced "so dreadful a judgement."

Coming after ministerial prophecies of doom, the devastation of King Philip's War strengthened the sermon's place in New England society. It gained in power and in solemnity. Such destruction was, after all, exactly what the ministers had predicted in their fast day sermons. The people were too familiar with the history of Israel's defeats to risk offending God further. They flocked to the meetinghouses to discover the meaning of their tragedy and the way to deliverance. From the opening battles they were taught to perceive the war in providential terms as a rebuke from God for their failures. Military defeats, Edward Bulkeley pointed out in a fast sermon on October 21, 1675, supplied the "ground of *humbling and abasing our selves*, in the Consideration of our great neglect of serious observation of Gods favours towards us, and also our short returns we have made to him for them."[30] While militia captains and magistrates raised an expeditionary force and gathered to plot military strategies, the ministers and churches turned to days of prayer and fasting. Connecticut towns fasted weekly on a rotating basis, averaging twelve fasts per county during the year of war. Plymouth and Massachusetts Bay were similarly occupied, so that in any given week particular churches in every colony were meeting during the week and collectively imploring God's mercy.[31]

In the early phases of the war, churches were shocked to discover their fasts were unavailing. This time God was not satisfied with outward shows of humiliation, and he signaled his continuing anger by inflicting defeats on the very days set aside for fasting: Mendon was assaulted on July 13 as the church at Dorchester fasted; Captain Hutchinson's defeat at Quaboag on August 5 coincided with fasts in Boston; and Deerfield burned to the ground as Hadley gathered for repentance. The reasons for these bitterly disappointing setbacks were clear and had nothing to do with military strategy. By inflicting defeats in time of fasting God made plain that it was not enough for the people to repent of their sins; they must also reform their hearts and lives. To encourage such a reformation, the civil magistrates intervened and sought ways to change the outward behavior of their citizens. In October 1675, the Massachusetts General Court appointed a ministerial committee to implement moral reform, and following the ministers' recommendations, passed laws to combat immorality in the army and society. Connecticut passed similar laws at its January and May sessions. Such measures were intended to lend substance to outward shows of humiliation and avert the avenging hand of God. And, much to the relief of the ministers and magistrates, the new measures seemed to work.

When King Philip was finally overcome, the people celebrated their deliverance in public thanksgivings held in every church throughout the land. In victory as in defeat, the offical explanation was God's sovereign control over his people. To make certain the people would never forget this cardinal point, the ministers rushed into print with histories and narratives of the war that shared the common theme of providential deliverance.[32]

As the trials of defeat represented, in William Hubbard's account, "a day of great rebuke and trouble to the poor people sojourning in this wilderness," so deliverance came, as Increase Mather calculated, the instant true repentance was followed by moral reformation: "From that day when there was a vote passed for the Suppression and Reformation of those manifest evils . . . The Lord gave success to our Forces."[33] All of these accounts subordinated military history to prophecy, confirming New England's probationary status as an elect nation whose blessings and trials were commensurate with their observance of covenant conditions.

Instead of seeing the Indians as national rivals, Puritan writers portrayed them impersonally as God's instrument of correction. In stamping out the Indian threat the colonists were stamping out their own sins and signaling their return to corporate grace.[34] The whole affair was a stunning confirmation of ministerial inspiration and God's continuing covenant interest in his New England people.

The urgency with which thanksgiving sermons and providential histories of King Philip's War were issued shows how determined the children were not to let tragedy break into their belief in New England's ongoing mission. In other, less cohesive societies, the devastation wrought in time of war could weaken faith in the old verities and perhaps lead to chaos and revolution. Indeed this was exactly what happened in Virginia in 1675, when a similar (though far less destructive) Indian war exacerbated pre-existent strains within white Virginia society and precipitated a civil war between the Tidewater and frontier that had little to do with the Indians. Before it was over, the frontier "rebel" Nathaniel Bacon seized power from Governor Berkeley and ruled most of Virginia. Bacon's premature death prevented his followers from sustaining their civil war and, in October 1676, twenty-three rebel leaders were rounded up by Berkeley and executed for treason.[35] In New England there were no insurrections, and church membership actually increased to record highs during and immediately following the war.[36]

King Philip's War, rather than undermining New England's faith, reinforced traditional beliefs, thus confirming that the New England Way was equally compatible with failure and success. Where other experimental societies would uphold corporate morale through promises of paradise on earth, the New Englanders' experiment would thrive on its failures. Theirs was not the perfect society but the model less-than-perfect society. When events turned sour, whether in war or natural calamity, it merely confirmed the ministers' dark warnings of impending doom for a degenerate people who refused to acknowledge God's providential deliverances and care. As long as the society was not utterly destroyed or vanquished, ministers could accommodate calamity to their social and historical vision for New England. By always living in the *fear* of desertion without ever conceding the *fact* of desertion, the clergy could rein in a wayward people carried along by the centrifugal pulls of the wilderness. The language of "almost" destruction turned out, in King Philip's War, to be a powerful incentive to renewed corporate solidarity and covenant loyalty.

King Philip's War confirmed that the children were a covenant people whether they liked it or not. It confirmed as well the prophetic gifts of the ministers. So charged was this experience with revelatory significance that ministers preached from it as if from a Scripture text. In closing his history of the war, Increase Mather prepared a forty-page "exhortation" that was no different in style and organization from the many occasional sermons he had published. The difference was that this exhortation had no formal Bible text heading the discourse. Instead, the "text" was the preceding history, which taught the doctrinal lesson that God's people must "hearken to the voice of God in his late and present dispensations." As in all fast sermons, he began by listing the procuring sins that had prompted divine retribution: "contention," "sensuality," "Drunkenness," "pride," and, worst of all, "an Ill entertainment of the Ministry."[37] Then came the parallel with Israel. New England's judgments were likened to the time "when the like hand of God was upon the Land of Israel." Drawing from Josephus's *Jewish Wars* (in many respects a model for Mather's New England wars), Mather noted how "*Pompey* seized upon the Temple, when it was the Jews solemn Fasting-day; and after that *Sosius* took *Jerusalem* upon a day of solemn Humiliation." In both cases, the reasons for defeat were the same: "The Jews were then exceedingly degenerated having the form of these duties, but little of the power of them: hath it not been so with us in a sad degree?"[38]

Having fixed New England's guilt, Mather then supplied the grounds for New England's hope. Times had changed dramatically since his fast sermon in 1674, when the warnings and rebukes could not be too severe. Although victorious, God's people were badly wounded. They had learned their lesson the hard way, and too much guilt could "run into extreams" just like too much pride. They must be reminded that they were not utterly destroyed. In unusually comforting tones Mather implored his readers that they "not now faint when we are rebuked of him. . . . Do not think that God will utterly destroy *New-England* as yet." Despite their rebuke the people were still special: "The Lord hath a great Interest in this Land which he will not easily part with." Because there were still "many Churches of Christ here" with pious ministers and a strong core of believers, God's aim in bringing war was corrective, not destructive: "The Lord then sheweth, that his design, in bringing this Calamity on us, is not to destroy us, but to humble us, and reform us, and to do us good in the latter end."[39] As long as God's Word survived at the center of corporate assembly, the myth of New England exceptionalism would live on and draw strength as easily from disappointment as success.

In concluding his exhortation Mather turned to the subject of ministerial authority. For all his words of comfort and assurance he could not resist adding a "we told you so" reminder that New England's miseries resulted from failure to take the ministers' warnings seriously. He hoped the people would now concede that their ministers had special prophetic powers just like the prophets of old and honor them accordingly:

> *Hearken to the voice of God in the Ministry of his word,* mind what the Messengers of God speak in his name, *for surely the Lord will do nothing, but he revealeth his secrets to his Servants the Prophets.* If I were to give Counsel to N. E. for my life, it should be the same that Jehosophat gave to the people of God in his time, when circumstanced in respect of a Combination of heathen Enemies, against them, as we are this day: *Believe in the Lord your God, so shall you be established, believe his Prophets so shall you prosper.* What

though in these dayes Ministers are not infallible? yet they are in respect of Office *Watchmen* and *Seers,* and therefore you may expect that God will communicate Light to you by them, yea they told you of these dayes before they came. Do not say that the Ministers of God cannot tell you why this Judgment is come, how then could they give you faithfull warning therof long enough before it came? I pray you consider this one thing, What were the sins which the Messengers of God declared would certainly bring A *day of Trouble* upon this Land? And hath the Lord confirmed the word of his Servants? Then you may without danger conclude, it is for those sins that the Lord is now contending. And truly if we refuse to hearken to the voice of God not only in the *former Prophets,* but also by those who are still speaking in his name, why should we marvel that the Lord doth not incline his ear to our voice when we pray and humble our Souls before him? God cryeth to us by his Messengers, and we will not hear; therefore it is that though we cry to God he will not hear.[40]

Few readers could miss the self-legitimating apologia contained in these words; nor could they miss the lesson that if there were failures in the second generation—above and beyond those of the founders—it was the people who were at fault. It remained to be seen if the people would heed the warnings and submit to their prophets.

A PEOPLE OF WAR

Besides confirming ministerial authority, King Philip's War had the extremely important effect of establishing New England's identity as a people of war. Apart from a brief and limited engagement with the Pequots in 1637, the founders had had little direct experience with war. While upholding the traditional Calvinist doctrine of just (defensive) wars, and supporting their countrymen in Europe's wars of religion, they did not perceive themselves as an active military outpost. Their martial terminology tended to be employed metaphorically in illustration of the "church militant," whose battlefield was lodged in the soul and whose common enemy was Satan and death.[41] From the second generation onward this would all change. After 1675, the saints' battleground expanded to include external enemies who made war on God's New World saints. The children learned from bitter experience that they must be not only spiritually armed but literally armed as well; they must be adept in the art of war and ready to shed blood for the survival of Christ's kingdom.

The transformation in the use of martial terminology is dramatically reflected in the occasional artillery election sermons which, beginning in 1659, were delivered annually before the Boston militia and their new officers.[42] Initially these sermons were largely ceremonial and continued the first generation's practice of "spiritualizing" Christian "souldiery" (the spelling was deliberate) whereby, as Urian Oakes explained in the first printed artillery election sermon, "every Believer is a Souldier in a spiritual Consideration."[43]

Beginning in 1675 however, a new note was sounded in artillery election sermons. In that year, Newbury's John Richardson explored the practical lessons taught in 2 Samuel 1:18: "Also he made them teach the Children of Judah the use of the Bow." The text referred to David's military prowess and underscored the truth that while God's people must trust in providence they must also hone their military skills. In a phrase that would recur in subsequent artillery election and militia sermons, Richardson told his listeners that Israel's God was a self-proclaimed "man of War," and therefore *"Martial Weapons and Military skill and Exercise do well become and truely belong to a Christian Commonwealth."*[44] The children learned they must be prepared to fight not only on the interior battleground of the self but also against external enemies who were constantly lying in wait, eager to destroy and plunder what God had set apart: "The Church of God upon Earth is Militant, in a Civill as well as in a Spirituall sense. . . . While the Church hath her Enemies in the World, men ought to be in readiness, not only to Pray with their hearts and tongues, but to fight with their hands for the *Peace of Jerusalem*." In artillery election sermons audiences were instructed to chop and hack their way to the New Jerusalem over the bodies of diabolical enemies:

> You may be called to be in good earnest; thou knowest not how soon Orders may come from the Lord of Hosts for thy Sudden March, and then there will be no time to get any Skill to defend thy self. You are now as it were in *Garison*, but you may very quickly be in the Field, not in a naked field, but in a field of Warr, yea perhaps in Aceldema, a field of blood.[45]

During King Philip's War, the ministers discovered how effective the artillery election sermon and sermons before local militia musters were as instruments to mobilize the people for war. That function dictated a tone and method of argument very different from the rhetorical strategies employed in fast or election sermons. Instead of fear and guilt, the engrossing themes were righteous anger and unlimited confidence. Artillery election sermons contained some of the most radical and violent sentiments in all Puritan preaching, and some of the most self-assured statements about New England as a superior people who need fear no mortal enemy. Often historians have looked at second-generation occasional preaching solely from the vantage point of fast and election sermons, and have drawn the false conclusion that ministers did little more than rail against the people for their sins. In times of war or rumors of war, soldiers had to be prepared for battle and they had to be confident. The artillery election sermons after 1675 were designed to fulfill both these requirements.

Following the hard-won, bloody victory over the Indians, the colonial army's chaplain, Samuel Nowell (HC, 1653), delivered and published an artillery election sermon on *Abraham in Arms* that would lay down the main lines of martial preaching in time of war for the century to follow. Nowell's title was taken from his text in Genesis 14:14: "And when Abram heard that his Brother was taken captive, he armed his trained

Servants." Nowell's doctrine, like Richardson's a year earlier, was "that the Training of Souldiers to be fit for War, is a commendable practice, yea a Duty of Great Consequence." And, like Richardson, he took as his motto the refrain from Exodus 15:3: "The Lord is a Man of War."[46] Instead of recalling Israel's sins in the manner of a fast, Nowell preached that God would bless the military exploits of his people in any "lawfull war" they prosecuted. It is, Nowell went on in obvious reference to Quakers and other pacifist sects, "a strange piece of dotage befallen this crazy-headed age, that men should not use the sword." On the contrary, when God granted lands and liberties to a people (as in the case of New England who had "as fair a title as any ever had since Israel's title to Canaan"), he expected them to be defended. In words that would recur in time of danger down through the Revolution, Nowell declared that

> these are our Rights both as Men, and as Christians, our civil Rights and libertyes as Men and our religious Liberties and Rights as Christians; both which we are to defend with the Sword, as far as we are able.... There is such a thing as Liberty and Property given us, both by the Laws of God and Men[;] when they are invaded, we may defend ourselves.[47]

Since God would not ordinarily intervene directly to deliver his people, they must be prepared to defend themselves: "God's vineyard hath no other walls, but only our Souldiery." As earlier artillery election speakers had used martial imagery as a metaphor for spiritual warfare, Nowell used the enthusiasm of vital piety as a metaphor for war. In the same way that individual Christians had to be active in maintaining their spiritual armor and always looking out for enemies of their souls, a Christian nation must learn to be "vigilant" and "expert for War." Military preparedness was not optional; it was a sacred duty, and they are "greatly to blame that do neglect it."[48]

On days of fasting and humiliation, ministers were expected to look inward and focus on the sins of the people. But when facing outward threats, ministers praised the country's virtue; the sin-sick people of the fast became the unconquerable army of the Lord. In scores of local militia assemblies, soldiers were reminded that whatever the shortcomings of the people in comparison to the founders there was still enough piety and courage in the land to set them apart from all other peoples and warrant the blessings and favor of God. As an eyewitness to the campaigns of King Philip's War, Nowell could say with complete confidence that "there hath rather been an excess of Courage then defect or want of it.... You have been men full of activity and Courage, forward enough, notwithstanding danger. You have a People bred up in this Country, that have the heart of Lions."[49] As the children discovered their sin in military defeat so they discovered their faith and God-given courage in time of victory. No other colony came to their aid. Their courage could not have stemmed from any source but the assurance that God was still on the side of New England.

In the immediate afterglow of victory it occurred to Nowell that God may have had additional purposes in mind, beyond repentance, in afflicting his people with war. That brutal experience also served to harden them for yet more horrible encounters to come. New England's season of war had not ended with the death of Philip. As God's New Israel, the children could be sure they would play an active and bloody role in the final destruction of Antichrist as foretold in Revelation. Unlike the founders, they located the battles with Antichrist in America, rather than Europe. Already, Nowell observed, "*Rome's* Agents are abroad at work" in the New World and "there is not a small Island in *America,* but the Princes or States of Europe are striving for it." New England was faced with a simple choice: "We must either learn to defend ourselves, or resolve to be vassals."[50] King Philip's War was both a warning and a testing ground for New England's martial resolve. It taught them the enduring lesson—confirmed in every subsequent militia sermon—that New England's God was not simply a loving savior but a "Man of War." It also taught them that, however dark the day, as long as they acknowledged Christ as their "general" they would never be destroyed.

THE FLEXIBILITY OF OCCASIONAL PREACHING

Taken together, election, fast, and artillery sermons show how flexible and comprehensive occasional preaching had become in the second-generation pulpit. Although all occasional sermons dealt with the concerns of this world and the state of New England's ongoing federal covenant, no single category of occasional preaching adequately encompasses the full range of concepts and emotions ministers employed to adjust New England's mission to rapidly changing New World circumstances. Those sermons that addressed internal problems like leadership turnover, materialism, instability, and contention invoked the rhetoric of failure and impending doom for New England's native-born generation. Other sermons directed against external enemies celebrated the superior piety and unconquerable faith of the same generation. It is necessary to look at the entire picture in order to grasp the full import of the occasional sermon as a multifaceted institution that served both political and religious purposes, and explained history and society to the inhabitants.

Yet, for all the importance that occasional preaching came to enjoy in the second generation, its real strength derived from the presumption that regular preaching continued to define the primary end of the sermon. The themes and concerns of occasional sermons varied from year to year as circumstances and perceived problems changed. Regular preaching, however, remained constantly attuned to the question of the soul's salvation. In the regular pulpit, second-generation ministers demonstrated, over careers that completed the seventeenth century, that they were indeed the equals of the founders.

[5]

Returning unto God: The Conversion of the Children

Even as the second-generation ministers expanded the range, frequency, and publication of weekday occasional sermons to remind the children of their national privileges, martial duties, and covenant engagements, they continued to acknowledge personal salvation and Christian service as their primary ministerial calling. National blessings could be expected only if the Word was being rightly proclaimed by converted ministers and faithfully received by a core of visible saints. A federal covenant did not demand that all inhabitants be converted, but it did require those who lacked saving grace to remain silent before the Word preached—no matter what their inner feelings, to conform outwardly to its teachings and acknowledge its sovereignty whatever their station in life, and to wait on the Lord in the hope of eventual salvation. All these things presupposed ongoing evangelistic preaching in regular worship.

While prosecuting their New World ministries, the founders delivered a multitude of sermons, something on the order of twenty-eight thousand regular sermons. But their immediate successors, second-generation ministers graduating from Harvard College between 1642 and 1675 and continuing their ministries into the early eighteenth century, would deliver upwards of three hundred thousand regular sermons before their careers ended.[1] Few of these regular sermons were published, but in the society of colonial communities, they dominated public communications. Printed occasional sermons can give the impression that few people continued to revere the Word proclaimed or to join the churches. The corpus of occasional sermons suggests that the gospels received but a passing nod in the pulpit, and that the sermon itself lost its power to stir the soul, becoming instead a cold instrument of social control. But when regular sermons are laid alongside the corporate commentaries of the occasional sermon, a very different impression emerges. Here it becomes apparent, when preaching is considered as a weekly event in public communications, that the sermon was as powerful a cultural and spiritual influence on the children as it had been on the founders—perhaps even more so.

REGULAR PREACHING
AND THE CIRCULATION OF INFORMATION

Unlike their parents, the second generation matured in an insulated theocratic environment; from infancy they heard or read about little save the New England Way. Despite the region's impressive growth in trade and commerce, most of the population remained concentrated in small towns consisting mainly of interlocking "quasi-extended" families.[2] In these rural villages, life was still organized around the institutions of church and family. These powerful, patriarchal institutions transmitted to the children a culture defined in terms of religion, the Bible, and personal salvation. Parents sought to "break" the selfish wills of their children, so that ministers could "bend" their hearts to God. The long-lived parents, because they controlled the land until the time of their death, retained an influence and authority unrivaled in other "traditional" societies in which people tended to die young, or in "modern" societies where the nuclear family prevails. Their authority was not always accepted gratefully, but it was so successfully inculcated that, when the children began to raise families of their own, they would replicate the same patterns and perpetuate the inherited culture, and even name their children from the Old Testament.[3]

In the larger society, as in the family, behavior was closely monitored; corporate assembly, public speech, and the diffusion of information were strictly controlled. Small group activities were limited to (male) tavern going. The only fully inclusive associations were weekly worship services, which became the time for broadcasting news of interest to the community. At church meetings, rules of rank and order were scrupulously observed both in "seating" people according to their social position in the town hierarchy and in limiting public address to the minister. Literacy rates among the second generation were exceptionally high, but the range of available information excluded anything that did not coincide with the mission of New England. Popular reading remained limited to catechisms, religion-oriented primers, psalters, almanacs, sermons, and the Bible.[4] The Cambridge Press was censored by a board of ministers and the president of Harvard College, and its publications were limited largely to devotional manuals, legislative summaries, sermons, and systems of divinity. Some imported books of poetry, drama, science, and the classics entered New England through the Boston book market, but in small numbers and for an audience of mostly college graduates. Folk legends and superstitions were not entirely absent, but the second generation's symbolic universe began and ended with the Bible, whose teachings were interpreted and updated in the weekly sermon.[5]

By limiting the circulation of information and the public expression of acceptable ideas, Puritan leaders created a social system that somewhat paradoxically encouraged both unquestioning lay piety and unending conflict. The authority of parents in the household and of ministers in the church was so uncompromisingly defined that confrontations were inevitable. At the same time, however, the range of available ideas was limited, so that debates proceeded from a common foundation. When the founders rebelled against English authorities, they created a set of alternative ideas and values. But when the children rebelled against *their* authorities—the founders—they found no alternative ideas, only alternative emphases. Heated controversies over church membership, synodical authority, ministerial support, or new church formation were circumscribed by a shared circle of knowledge.[6] Ministers and dissidents within their congregations attacked each other with the same arguments from covenant logic, biblical warrant, and from the Congregational "Middle Way" first formulated in *The Cambridge Platform*. That "way" was designed to ensure that neither ministers nor congregations could ever dominate the churches. Both ministers and congregations endorsed that balance, but were continually casting jealous eyes on one another, on the lookout for "anarchy" or "encroachments" on their respective liberties.

Ministers would complain that their flocks had declined in piety and respect for God's Word, even as congregations complained that their ministers were usurping powers not granted them in *The Cambridge Platform*. In fact, neither charge was true. The sermon was, perhaps, too successful in training an intelligent laity, well versed in the biblical world of providential design, ever-mindful of their inherited Congregational liberties (and duties) and capable of taking issue with the ministers on their own terms. Though the sermon may have been challenged more often after 1670, it became more powerful in molding a public identity that was never exposed to competing ideologies. The second generation might complain about the founders and the clergy, but they were too well trained ever to leave the household of faith, or to alter its foundation set in the English Bible.

HARVARD COLLEGE AND MINISTERIAL TRAINING

The same constraints that molded the second generation's attitudes toward authority and fixed their loyalty to the Congregational Way were felt equally by the ministers. Nearly half of all second-generation ministers were themselves children of ministers who had observed their fathers in the household and the meetinghouse, and well understood the demeanor and responsibilities of their office. Others, as sons of merchants or magistrates, were equally imbued with the habit of superiority, and would begin their careers as junior colleagues to aging pastors and observe their predecessors' workings firsthand.[7] Most importantly, before attaining the pulpit, almost all second-generation ministers would attend Harvard College where they would be exposed to the social discipline and formal arts that defined their office and set them apart as the watchmen and prophets of their generation.

Besides training ministers to preach, Harvard College prepared its students for a life of leadership in all aspects of society. Students entering the college differed from the other youth in the colonies in that they experienced a period in life analogous to "adolescence," where their primary relationships were with their peers.[8] Upon entering the college somewhere around the age of thirteen, all students were assigned a class rank based on academic merit and on their parents' social status. As underclassmen they were taught the rules of submission both by the senior "tutors" and by upperclassmen. Discipline was strict, and students who broke the rules or acted out of their place were punished by fine, loss of class rank, or, in the most serious cases, public whipping.[9] At a time when others their age were being apprenticed out to countinghouses or to neighboring farms to learn a trade, Harvard's undergraduates were serving their apprenticeships in the art of leadership. Each year they would be given added responsibilities and liberties until, by the time of their graduation, they were prepared to assume social leadership in local communities.

In addition to their social indoctrination, Harvard students spent hours in the classroom preparing for the work to follow. For aspiring ministers, who constituted over half of Harvard's seventeenth-century graduates, the arts curriculum and training in systematic divinity were important not only for their particular contents but also because they instilled a habit of mind constantly attuned to the invisible realities and metaphysical principles around which the visible universe revolved.[10] From youth, students were taught to look beyond the material world to the unseen spiritual forces and immaterial rules that governed the universe. These rules, called "technologia," were not *invented* by man, but *discovered* by him through reason, revelation, and "Ramist" method.[11] Both art and doctrine originated in the mind of God, and by mastering them students acquired a special access to the divine mind that uniquely fit them for the demanding tasks of prophecy, social leadership, and cultural preservation that lay ahead. When ordinary people inquired into the meaning of events in nature or history, the ministers could draw on their training to supply the necessary understanding that was prerequisite to right action or "eupraxia."

Harvard's curriculum was organized around the mind and understanding, but the hearts of its students were not ignored. Godly preaching required piety as well as understanding, and Bible devotions were an important part of the students' collegiate experience. The college was as much a "spiritual nursery" as a social and academic training center, and most students experienced conversion at a younger-than-average age.[12] A chief concern of college life was "the practice of Piety," and this meant frequent Bible study and attention to sermons. Chapel attendance was required of all students "twice daily" as well as on Sunday. In addition, daily periods were set aside during which, according to the college laws, "all students shall read the Old Testament in some portion of it out of Hebrew into Greeke, and all shall turne the New Testament out of English into Greeke, after which one of the Bachelors or Sophisters shall in his course Logically analyze that which is read, by which meanes both theire scill in Logicke, and the Scriptures and the Scriptures originall language may be increased." Of all seventeenth-century colleges, only Harvard required Hebrew of all its graduates, because that tongue was thought most reliably to communicate the mind of God for his new American Israel.[13]

On Sundays students attended local churches, particularly the church at Cambridge, where they heard the best preaching in the land, which they later recited for practice. Surviving student notebooks contain complete collections of sermon notes that no doubt were invaluable when the young ministers came to fashion their own sermons.[14] To complete their biblical and homiletical training, the president of the college and master's students delivered biweekly declamations that defended "commonplaces" drawn from "divinity" rather than the classical *loci communes*. These speaking performances taught students how to combine logic and Scripture for the purpose of "avoiding and refuting" heretical teachings that might crop up in their reading or in the course of their parish ministries.

In addition to tutorial duties, recitations, and devotional activities, students began at Harvard a life-long process of assembling the libraries and reference systems that would accompany them to the rural villages they served. Although classroom instruction and examination were almost exclusively oral (in preparation for life in an aural society), students "contained" what they heard by assembling "commonplace books" of notes and textual summaries. These books—really hand-sewn leaves of paper—represented crude information retrieval systems that indexed the "scope and manner of handling" of their lectures and reading, and served as "repositoryes for the matters referrible to each of them."[15] Any number of topics could be summarized in these notebooks, though in practice they tended to concentrate on the main "heads" of divinity.

Insofar as they were able, students augmented their compilation of notebooks with the purchase of books that would be useful throughout their careers. The size of these libraries varied greatly, ranging from a single shelf to hundreds of volumes. Library size was the single clearest index of ministerial status and influence. Those who published the most and served the largest congregations possessed the largest libraries.[16] But all ministers possessed a stock of basic reference tools including concordances, Bible dictionaries, indexes to types and metaphors, Greek and Hebrew grammars and Bibles, commentaries, and catechisms. They also collected sermons which, by the second generation, included as many New England authors as European. One typical country library was that of Thomas Weld III of Dunstable who, at the time of his death in 1702, possessed a collection of 170 reference sources. The sermons were divided equally between English Puritan worthies like Richard Baxter, John Owen, and Thomas Cartwright, and New England ministers of both generations like Hooker, Cotton, Norton, Willard, Increase Mather, and Solomon Stoddard. To update their understanding of the state-of-the-covenant in New England, ministers throughout their careers purchased or received as gifts occasional sermons, particularly election sermons.[17] No doubt works by Puritan ministers were at best modest contributions to the grand sweep of Western literature, but in local libraries they represented the hub around which all true knowledge revolved.

THE ONGOING TRUTHS OF CONVERSION

Like the founders, second-generation ministers spent as much time in their studies as possible and defined their vocation primarily in terms of the regular sermon. There were other responsibilities to be sure—catechizing, visitations, and for country clergy, farming—but these were perceived as interruptions and breaks in their primary calling. Increase Mather, who took the emphasis on preaching to an extreme even by colonial standards, immersed himself in his study and invariably regretted "Time lost by visitants" who came to see him apart from his posted hours. Weekdays were given to Bible study and the arrangement of extensive notes for sermon series. Often this task would occupy Mather until late in the evening long after the household had retired. Weekends were no less given over to the sermon. Saturdays were spent "imprint[ing the] sermon in my memory," and Sundays given entirely to meditation and the delivery of two sermons.[18] The length of the sermon could vary with the seasons of the year (summers yielding longer sermons and winter briefer ones), but every minister's calendar revolved around those moments on the sabbath when the entire community gathered together to hear God speak.

In terms of subject matter, second-generation regular preaching was nearly an exact reproduction of sermons the children had heard in their youth and studied at Harvard College. Despite differences in tone and emphasis, the overall framework of interpretation and doctrine remained unchanged. Invariably the children began from the assumption of *Sola Scriptura*; as John Allin's successor at Dedham, William Adams (HC, 1671) explained, the Bible's "original was not from man but God." The prophets and apostles recorded the words of Scripture to be sure, "but it was the Lord's Word . . . brought to [the writers] by inspiration from God."[19] *Sola Scriptura* actually strengthened ministerial authority, for, as Allin went on, since Bible times "God does not chuse to speak immediately from heaven himselfe, nor to speak by Angels, but he raises up instruments of the sons of men whom he fits and qualifies by furnishing them with a suitable measure of the gifts and graces of his Spirit and by them he finds and speaks his mind to other men." As long as the minister based his message on Bible truths, the people could assume that his "Authority was not humane, but divine."

For the most part, second-generation ministers observed the rules of Bible preaching and did not use the sabbath to comment on politics, complain about salaries, or dwell on themes and issues more properly reserved for town meetings or weekday occasions. In the vast majority of regular sermon notes, it is impossible to determine from an internal analysis of the text alone whether the minister was enjoying good or bad relations with his congregation, or whether some particular event inspired the particular theme of the day. For the second generation no less than the first, Sunday worship was the time for imparting the grand truths of eternity, which stood above other more immediate questions of place and time that might be addressed after the sermon. The same sequence of sin-salvation-service that organized the founders' regular preaching characterized the children as well. Their authority depended on faithfulness to this framework. Any other scheme of preaching was, to the well-tuned ears of the congregation, extrabiblical and not to be trusted.

While regular preaching had to proceed from a Scripture text and follow the sequence of sin-salvation-service, a wide range of topics could be brought in under this rubric. Over the course of thirty weeks in 1678, for example, William Hubbard included under the topic of "sin" such diverse doctrines as original sin (James 1:15), repentance (Revelation 2:5), divine afflictions (Psalm 94:12), the unforgivable sin of unbelief (John 6:30), the Last Judgment (Matthew 15:14), and God's hatred of sin (Jeremiah 14:9). Under the topic of "salvation" he examined the meaning of eternal life (1 John 5:11–12), the parable of the ten virgins (Matthew 25:2–14), the hearts of believers (Romans 17:22), the duty of watchfulness (Revelation 3:2), the substitutionary atonement of Christ (Psalm 49:8), the saints' exaltation (Psalm 30:1), divine providence (Philippians 2:13), the glory of Christ (Hebrews 1:1–2), and the means of salvation through the preaching of the Word (Revelation 2:7). Finally, "service" was treated in sermons on the duty of meekness (Psalm 37:11), the duty of gratitude and godly living (Luke 17:17), the duty of fasting (Zechariah 7:5–6), the responsibility of church discipline (Revelation 2:2–4), and support for the poor and needy (Luke 6:20). The following year, John Leverett (HC, 1680), then a student at Harvard, recorded sermons by president Urian Oakes on such topics as divine submission (Job 1:21), Christ's sacrificial atonement (Isaiah 53:4), self-denial (Matthew 10:25), the uses of divine affliction (Psalm 119:67), the extension of covenant promises to future generations (Psalm 90:16), the duty of prayer (Psalm 122:6), and justification by faith alone (Psalm 116:12).[20] All of these sermons were less concerned with New England's national errand than with the state of the individual soul and the life of godly submission to the Word of God. They were drawn as much from New Testament texts as from Old and addressed their audiences less as an American "second generation" than as members of a single, vast generation predestined from eternity and stretching from Adam to the end of time.[21]

Along with delivering two or more sermons on a particular text, second-generation ministers continued the founders' practice of preparing longer-running series that could extend months and even years. In one of his earlier sermon notebooks, Thomas Shepard II inserted a note on how he came to select the upcoming year's Scripture texts for his Charlestown congregation: "Having through Gods assistance finished the Last Lord's Day that exercise on the 14th chapter of *Hosea* (which this first month is two years since we began) and after many struggles and looking up to heaven for another text, it pleased God to resolve the question using this portion of Scripture: those fifteen Psalmes, called Songs of Ascents [Psalms 120–135]." For the first two months Shepard lingered over Psalm 120:1 ("In my distress I cried unto the Lord, and he heard me"). Because this was part of a regular sermon series rather than a fast, Shepard focused less on prayer as a response to "temporall distress" than on prayer as an ongoing response to "spiritual distress" because "The Lord loves to have his people draw near to him often by prayer." Two years later, Shepard had only reached Psalm 124![22] All of Shepard's sermons, like his father's, paid close attention to the sequence of salvation, "in the way which Christ hath prescribed."[23] Such obedience was difficult, but "this strait narrow, difficult, very very hard way is the only true way to [eternal] life." Only by participating in the "beautiful union" with Christ could the individual escape the terrors of hell and inherit the "crown of great glory" that awaited him in heaven.

With the text for long-running sermon series set far in advance of delivery, ministers could not always match up doctrines with weekly events. But in times of protracted crisis the parallels between events and exegesis were not neglected. During the year of King Philip's War, Joshua Moodey delivered a sermon series on Revelation 2 that dealt with only eight verses.[24] Of particular concern to Moodey was the seventh verse, which employed martial imagery to convey the promise that "to him who overcometh will I give to eat of the tree of life." Throughout the series, Moodey's own terminology was thoroughly militaristic, as he enjoined his congregation to "Be Couragious" and to "Be Watchfull of your enemies." Although ostensibly concerned with spiritual warfare, none in his congregation could miss the parallels with the military struggle around them. Nor could they miss the double meaning contained in the apocalyptic promise at the end of the chapter: "And he that overcometh, and keepeth my works unto the end, to him I will give power over the nations." Thus when calamities were severe enough and dangers loomed large, even regular sermon series could be enlisted for service in the cause of New England.

By the 1680s, the Cambridge Press's board of censors commissioned the publication of regular sermon series drawn primarily from the sermons of Boston's finest ministers. In addition to running Harvard College and meeting often with Boston's magistrates, Increase Mather spent many days in his study doing "little besides Transcribing" regular sermons for the press.[25] Unlike the first wave of printed fast and election sermons that came from the second-generation press, these sermon treatises were as evangelical and conversionist as the manuscript notes of less notable ministers and provided a necessary balance to the preoccupation of the occasional sermons with corporate guilt and legal obedience. In *Some Important Truths About Conversion*, for example, published in 1684, Mather strung together a 151-page "manual" of four Sunday sermons (morning and afternoon) that cautioned against reliance on mere "external performance of duties" and warned that "a sound and Thorough Conversion, Is of Absolute Necessity in Order to the Souls Entrance into the Kingdome of Heaven." Typically, said Mather, the soul progressed toward salvation through stages. First came "conviction of sin" and "self-denial": "This is the first, and indeed one of the hardest lessons in Christianity, that a man must *deny himself*. A natural man, maketh not only the World, but *self* his God. He maketh *himself* his own *Last end*." Only when the reality of sin was experienced could the believer turn to Christ in utter dependence and begin the life-long process of conversion and thankful living to God: "Sin is a departure from God: So *Conversion* is a going to him again. Hence the converting Prodigal said, he would *go to his Father* . . . by these two parts . . . is the whole nature of Conversion described."[26]

Mather's allusion to the parable of the prodigal son became the subject for a seven-month sermon series by Samuel Willard at Boston's Old South Church in 1684. After Mather, Willard was the most prolific writer of his generation, and his regular sermons, like Mather's, centered on the theme of salvation. From his sermon notes on the prodigal son, Willard prepared a 391-page treatise designed to show "those secret wayes wherein God carries his Decree of Election under ground a great while, before it rise and break out in effectual calling."[27] Each sermon in the treatise took a different episode in the prodigal son's odyssey, from his despair in a "far Countrey," to the welcome return in his father's home, and finally to his elder brother's hypocritical resentment. In the end the elder brother's hypocrisy turns out to be greater than the prodigal son's sin, thus teaching the covenant children of New England to "beware that we rely not upon our selves and our duties, but to renounce all, and fly to the Grace of God in Christ, that is the only way to come by, and be partakers in special and soul refreshing grace."[28] In most of these regular sermons—printed and manuscript—there is none of the external legalism that governed occasional pronouncements on New England's federal covenant. Historians have seen a decisive shift from piety to moralism in second-generation preaching. But these sermons reveal an enduring concern with the doctrines of conversion and unconditional election that conforms closely to the pietistic preaching of the founders.

THE NEW TONE OF REGULAR PREACHING

Though second-generation regular preaching remained constant in doctrine and conversionist in orientation, it was not without variations that set it apart from that of the founders. Just as occasional sermons reiterated traditional formulas at the same time that they added their own distinctive twists, so regular preaching differed in ways that reflected the ministers' perceptions of their generation and the unique needs of their congregations. The most immediate difference was a movement away from the founders' tendency to dichotomize their points according to a rigid Ramist format. The arrangement of Scripture teachings in paired opposites was far more characteristic of the English-bred Puritans than of their American-born children. In England such "methodizing" was necessary to distinguish Puritan preaching from the rival Anglican-Ciceronian rhetoric. In seventeenth-century New England, however, there were no rival rhetorics, and ministers were free to adopt a more relaxed construction. The "plain style" remained, to be sure, with its myriad of points and subpoints and its emphatic rejection of Latin tags and extrabiblical authorities. But the brackets gradually disappeared, and with them the obsession to organize Scripture doctrines in geometric patterns in imitation of the Ramist arts curriculum.

Beyond mechanical differences in note construction, second-generation regular sermons also displayed differences in tone and emphasis that reflected the children's sense of inherited covenant and their perception of a declension in popular piety. The founders' preaching style was molded in England where they had addressed adults from many different backgrounds who were bound only by a common opposition to the established church. They could make no assumptions about the faith of their hearers' parents, the authenticity of their ecclesiastical backgrounds, or the coercive support of the state. They had to assume ignorance on the part of their audience and begin their ministries as elementary teachers rather than advanced tutors. Second-generation ministers, however, labored under no such disadvantage. They addressed audiences who had been schooled in the basic truths of Scripture from infancy, and who fell under the coercive discipline of church and state. Yet these same audiences—educated, disciplined, and meticulously organized in particular Congregational churches—also seemed far more prone to challenge the prerogatives of their ministers and resist conversion.

In response to these new circumstances, second-generation preachers adopted a tone that was less cajoling and more authoritative. Native-born ministers did not have to win friends or persuade strangers; they had to remind wayward children to own up to their duties and seek the Lord.

The covenant children could be sure that God's "line of election" ran, in Increase Mather's words, "through the loins of [their] Parents." But that line could never be taken for granted. Converting grace, Mather went on, "is of absolute necessity in order to Salvation, and that as to the Children of godly Parents as well as others."[29] The children were without excuse in matters of personal salvation and corporate blessing. Left without excuse, they were all too easily left without sympathy. Even as second-generation clergy repeated the conversionist truths of the founders, they sharpened the goad of rebuke when conversions were not forthcoming.

As they worked through the Bible, second-generation ministers came upon texts for regular sermons that invited corporate condemnation in the manner of a fast sermon. Thus, in a sermon series on Joel 1, William Adams applied the warning in verse 2 ("Hath this [evil] been in your days") to the children of Dedham: "The Scope of this prophecy is to awaken a stupid people to a serious and awful consideration of the hand of God set against them in his judgments . . . and to draw them to repentance and reformation of those sins which were the cause of their calamityes."[30] With verse 3 ("Tell ye your Children of it, and let your Children tell their children, and their children another generation"), Adams (then only thirty-three years old) called upon the elderly in his congregation to recount the sacred history of Dedham as both a corporate and personal incentive for the children:

> Old men are here called upon to recite what they could remember of things done before many others now living were born. . . . We should labor to know and be able to give account of what speciall things have been [done] not only in our own, but also in our fathers dayes. . . . Marvilous and strange works must not be lightly passed over. . . . Let it put us in mind of our duty. . . . The bringing over such a people over the great ocean, planting them and making them to thrive in a wilderness . . . [is] call for our special notice.

In these sermons the text clearly called for rebuke, condemnation, and corporate recall. Such jeremiads thus were not wholly absent in regular preaching. But they could not be repeated every week without distorting the biblical balance of consolation alongside condemnation. In general, the jeremiad remained a convention reserved for occasional fast and election sermons.

COVENANT RENEWAL AS A CONVERTING ORDINANCE

The trauma of King Philip's War, together with low membership rates of churches in the early 1670s, convinced the ministers that they needed to take more positive steps to encourage moral reform and conversion. In a covenanted society where God promised to save the children unless through positive unbelief they rejected him, such aggressive strategies were not out of line. The problem of moral reform was addressed at a

Boston synod convoked in 1679 to determine "what are the Evils that have provoked the Lord" and "what is to be done so these Evils may be Reformed?" The first question posed by the "Reforming Synod" was easily answered: pride, vain apparel, intemperance, idleness, contention in congregations, disrespect for ministers, sabbath breaking, erosion of family discipline, lying, and usury all contributed to God's anger with New England. These evils could be traced back to the people's failure to take God's Word seriously and honor its teachings.[31] To deal with these evils the ministers turned first to the magistrates and, repeating their requests of 1676, urged stricter enforcement of moral and sumptuary legislation. Magistrates could not coerce conversion or church membership, but they could enforce a closer outward compliance with the laws—compliance that would protect New England's national covenant.

Increased civil suppression of evil was important, but was not adequate to cure New England's woes. To encourage spiritual revival, the Reforming Synod added to their requests for civil reform the recommendation that individual churches gather for a time of "covenant renewal," when they would reenact the first church covenants of the parents and affix their own names to those terms and promises. Such ceremonies were in a sense redundant, since the children were already "implicitly" bound to the covenant by virtue of their baptism. Nevertheless, they could personalize covenant reflections and lead eventually to conversion. In the meantime, they would further the cause of outward reform on which the national covenant depended. Covenant renewals required public vows which, as the synod recognized, were rarely made and not apt to be taken lightly:

> There is an Awe of God upon the Consciences of men when so obliged. As it is in respect of Oaths, they that have any Conscience in them, when under such Bonds, are afraid to violate them. Some [there be] that are but Legalists and Hypocrites, yet solemn Covenants with God, have such an Awe upon Conscience, as to enforce them unto an outward Reformation, and that doth divert temporal Judgements.[32]

From the start Puritans relied on internal sanctions as the chief means of preserving order and piety. Covenant renewal, they hoped, could succeed where civil prosecution could not because the enforcement agency was lodged within the self, at the core of "conscience."

In examining the corrective measures set forth in the Reforming Synod's report, historians from Perry Miller onward have emphasized the reformers' concern with external civil reform and "outward" ritual to the virtual exclusion of their pietistic concern with covenant renewal and revival.[33] From this one-sided examination, they have concluded that the synod's "preoccupation" with external morality signaled a dilution of Puritan thought and piety; having lost their parents' piety, the children settled for outward shows of morality that preserved the husk of religiosity without the nourishing kernel of inner spirituality. This interpretation parallels the view that emerges from sermon studies that rely exclusively on printed occasional sermons. Like those studies, it misses the enduring concern with personal piety on which the synod's report rested. Of the two programs of action recommended by the Reforming Synod, covenant renewal was more important to the framers and far more effective at the local level.

The magistrates did not sustain increased moral supervision, but by the 1680s most churches had accepted covenant renewal as a valid means of encouraging conversion and church membership, and the ministers saw that social and spiritual commitment could survive without active state supervision. To be sure, most ministers continued to accept the idea of a theocratic state and religious intolerance, but without the urgency and dependence of the founders. The churches could exert moral influence with or without the active support of the magistrates because the children continued to take their covenant vows seriously. Civil laws might impart fear to the inhabitants, but not the all-consuming "awe" that came with covenant renewal and public oaths.

Like the Half-way Covenant, covenant renewal ceremonies functioned more as recruiting devices to draw the rising generation into the churches on Sunday than as engines of conversion. On these occasions parents collectively rose and pledged to bring up their children in the fear of the Lord.[34] But covenant renewal did not end with corporate pledges. Rather, ministers employed the occasion to inaugurate a period of intensely conversionist preaching whose goal was "revival"—a time when large numbers of the rising generation would come into full church membership at once. All regular preaching treated salvation themes, but in periods of revival the "New Birth" received concentrated attention. These periods were a "season" of weeks and even months during which time many adult "children" and half-way members were converted and became full church members. Most ministers could count on such dramatic returns only once or twice in their preaching careers, when the combined factors of covenant renewal, conversionist preaching, and a large pool of eligible candidates (adult children in the mid- to late-twenties) converged to produce an influx of new members. As early as 1678, Increase Mather reported a "shower of converting grace" in Roger Newton's congregation in Milford, Connecticut, and noted how in his own Boston congregation "fourscore persons . . . have come before the Church, and declared what God hath done for their Souls, and in that way subscribed their names to the God of *Israel*."[35] These revivals would soon be repeated in other churches throughout New England, so that by the 1680s church membership rates in Massachusetts, Plymouth, and Connecticut would rival those of the first decades of New World settlement. Through these second-generation revivals the ministers came to understand that declension was not the irreversible slide into apostasy they had once feared but a cyclical phenomenon that corresponded to a new generation's coming of age.[36]

SOLOMON STODDARD AND THE ART OF REVIVAL

While Increase Mather was the moving force behind the Reforming Synod's proposals and one of the first to lead his church in covenant renewal, he was not the leading revivalist of his generation. That honor belonged to his western counterpart, Solomon Stoddard (HC, 1662), who served in the "frontier" parish of Northampton. At the time Stoddard began his ministry as successor to Eleazar Mather, there were only fourteen adult church members. To bring in larger audiences, Stoddard revised established practices and assumptions regarding church admission and the sacraments. In what surely were meant as fighting words to Mather and the Boston clergy he averred that "it is commendable for us to Examine the practices of our Fathers; [but] we have no sufficient reason to take practices upon trust from them. Let them have as high a character as belongs to them, yet we may not look upon their principles as [infallible] Oracles."[37] To back these words, Stoddard published treatises recommending the creation of a national ("instituted" or presbyterian) church system. Within his own congregation, moreover, he instituted an "open communion" where half-way church members could receive the sacrament of the Lord's Supper as a "converting ordinance."[38] Few ministers accepted Stoddard's iconoclastic innovations, but none denied his success in building Northampton into the largest, most influential church in the Connecticut River Valley.

Despite their ecclesiastical differences, Mather and Stoddard agreed on the importance of conversion preaching. Ultimately, all of Stoddard's innovations were designed to bring people into the church and under his powerful ministry. As a gospel preacher and winner of souls, he was without equal. In the course of his long ministry (1669–1729) he presided over five seasons of revival "harvests" in 1679, 1683, 1696, 1712, and 1718, during which large numbers of people experienced the New Birth and entered the church as full members.[39] So effective was Stoddard's conversionist preaching that in 1714 Mather interrupted his war over ecclesiology to commend his adversary's ninety-six-page treatise on preaching—*A Guide to Christ*—to all students of the ministry.[40] In that treatise, Stoddard reiterated many traditional assumptions regarding the manner and importance of gospel preaching. Like his peers and predecessors, he adopted the tenets of the faculty psychology in which "the Will always follows the last dictates of the Understanding. The Understanding is the guide of the Will; the will always follows its direction." Equally traditional was the paradoxical emphasis on the heart and the insistence that conversion required the supernatural activity of the Holy Spirit on the soul, dispensed without regard to natural capacity or moral goodness: "The only reason why God sets his love on one man and not upon another is, because he pleases. He acts the sovereignty of his own will in it."[41] Nevertheless, skill in sermon delivery was important as "an Antecedent to Conversion," because ordinarily the Holy Spirit worked to convince people's hearts in time of regular worship. None of these concepts was new, but Stoddard's remarkable successes lent special authority and significance to his words.

If Stoddard's preaching was distinguished from that of his contemporaries by anything besides raw talent, it was the single-mindedness with which he pursued the New Birth. He sounded more like first-generation ministers in England whose regular sermons were simple and direct in language, homely in metaphor, and taken up with the joys of supernatural conversion.[42] Fear ("law") and hope ("gospel") were the themes of his sermons and were never far apart. Passages depicting the horrors of hell were invariably followed by "calls" to the blessed hope of Christ for, as Stoddard explained in his *Guide*, "God leads men through the whole work of *preparation* partly by *fear*, and partly by *hope*. If [sermons] run into either extream, to have fear without hope, or hope without fear, they are like a Ship that goes beside the Channel, and is in danger to be broken to pieces; a mixture of fear and hope makes men diligent."[43] Thus "channeled" between the emotions of misery and hope, Stoddard pressed his hearers for an immediate personal commitment. His was less a gradualist message centered on life-long covenant duties and proper obedience (though these were not ignored) than an invitation to emotional catharsis, intended to drive sinners to their knees, then raise them up to new life in Christ.

A good example of Stoddard's early revival preaching appears in a volume of unpublished sermon notes dating back to his first harvest in 1679.[44] Upon returning from the Reforming Synod, he led his congregation in a covenant renewal ceremony and then preached for the next twenty-three weeks on Joshua's renewal of the covenant at Shechem (Joshua 24:14–24). From covenant renewal he turned to conversion in a series on Psalm 23:3 ("He restoreth my soul: he leadeth me in the paths of righteousness for his name's sake"). Rather than the *persona* of a fiery prophet, he adopted the Christ-like pose of a spiritual physician holding forth the only cure for a "heart sick" people incapable of curing themselves. Sin, he explained, was like a terminal disease that rendered the stricken conscience unable to function:

> [As] in the body there are the seeds of all naturall diseases, so in the souls are the seeds of all spiritual diseases . . . as it is with a man that has consumption, he is not laid up but walks to work a little. But he is in a very pining condition. So sometimes is the soul of a godly man. He is in a withering estate . . . his distemper may prevaile so dreadfully that he can't make an acceptable prayer, can't sanctify a Sabbath, can't doe any such service as he was wont to do in an acceptable manner unto God. His corruption may have such power over him as to render him unservicable.

The harder a troubled soul tried to cure itself, the worse it felt: "Men can't heal it: the land lies bleeding under heavy sins and miseries."

Having driven his hearers to the depths of despair, Stoddard turned with textbook simplicity to their only cure. In such pitiable circumstances, when life was darkest, Christ "becomes a physician" to his covenant elect. If they would open their hearts to him in utter dependence, they would discover that their lost condition was not permanent but a necessary precondition to healing: "He will also heal your conscience . . . the Lord Jesus will pour oil into the wounds: he will take away the guilt, rebuke the accuser, [and] dispell your darkness." Through Christ, fear was transformed into hope, and with hope came healing:

> He causes the souls of his decayed people to recover their strength again, they shall not lie allways in such a heartless frame, but he will restore spirituall strength, putting them into a growing, thriving condition, they shall not allways languish and fall but he will put them into a flourishing pasture, that they that were in a pining way shall flourish, be fat and flourishing. 32 Ps[alm]13: He will create a clean heart in you.

Such words—simple in diction, graphic in imagery, and filled with emotional overtones—were ideally suited to revival and the needs of Stoddard's congregation. They were the rhetorical nucleus around which he, and the other New England ministers, would weave more complex themes of sanctified duty and chosen peoplehood.

MONTHLY LECTURES

Beyond their regular preaching, second-generation ministers continued the practice of delivering weekly or monthly lectures. The primary function of these weekday sermons was "teaching" rather than "preaching," and they assumed a greater importance for the children than they had for the founders. Most early churches had two ministers—a pastor and a teacher—who concentrated on different aspects of the church's ministry; the preacher focused mainly on questions of salvation and the teacher on more systematic theology. By the second generation, economic factors, together with the rapid growth and dispersion of the population, limited most churches to one pastor who combined both functions.[45] This was dealt with in part by devoting Sundays to salvation preaching and lecture days to systematic theology or topics too speculative for regular sermon series. As before, lecture days could be converted into fast or thanksgiving days, but their primary function remained pedagogic. Because the day of the lecture sermon varied from town to town and because most ministers did not prepare lectures every week, the lecture also offered ministers the opportunity to come together and hear one another preach. Solomon Stoddard, for example, frequently traveled to Boston to attend lecture sermons and, on occasion, to deliver them.[46] More often, ministers in a particular locale lectured on a rotating basis so that their colleagues could attend. Weekday lectures, together with printed sermons, association meetings, and circulating sermon notes, were important channels for the exchange of information that tied ministers together as a self-conscious "semiprofessional" group.[47]

Of all the speculative themes treated in lecture sermons, none was more intriguing than the millennium, and of all the millennial commentators, none was more respected than Increase Mather, who enjoyed in the second generation a prophetic status comparable to that of John Cotton in the first. Ever since his prophecy of impending doom was confirmed by King Philip's War, Mather was fascinated with the providential meaning of New England and its eschatological implications. In a lecture on August 31, 1682, he pointed out that in covenanted societies like New England "*the* [natural] *Works of God have a Voice in them, as well as his Word.*"[48] These natural signs and portents not only confirmed the doctrine of providence but also were tools for predicting the future "glory of the heavenly world" which, he believed, was about to descend on New England.

As the chief seer of his generation, Mather devoted considerable lecture attention to the coming end times. Though they shared many of the millennial assumptions of the founders, Mather and his generation differed in their chief interest, which lay less with the convulsive wars in Europe that would precede the millennium than with the shape of the future kingdom.[49] First-generation commentators said little about this because, apart from ancient Israel, there were no earthly analogies from which to draw valid inferences about the coming kingdom. That was not true, however, for the children of New England. Their identity as a New Israel and their unique church-state pattern supplied new insights into God's millennial designs for his elect: "Some of us are under special advantage to understand these mysterious truths *of God*; that is to say, such of us as are in an exiled condition in this Wilderness."[50] By laying millennial prophecies alongside New England's providential experience, Mather believed he could speak with unprecedented confidence about the social and spiritual landscape of the New Jerusalem.

In 1687, Mather unveiled the shape of New Jerusalem in a lecture series on Revelation 3:12: "The name of the Citty of my god new Jerusalem which comes downe out of heaven from my god." From the phrase "comes downe out of heaven," Mather concluded that the New Jerusalem would be located "down" on earth rather than "up" in heaven, and that it would appear after Christ's Second Coming. To Mather this "premillennial" view of the end meant that the millennium would not be something wholly alien to human experience, rather it would be an enlargement and perfection of godly societies already existing on earth.[51] Chief among these earthly "types" or "figures" of the New Jerusalem were the nations of Israel and New England, because both were governed by the "written word of god" and "the word preached." The new heavens and new earth would differ in degree only, not in kind. In Mather's hands, millennial prophecies served the same double function as natural portents: they both confirmed New England's messianic status and were powerful calls to convert before it was too late:

> Oh! *you whose feet stand within thy gates O Jerusalem*, look to yourselves, you dwell where god himself Dwells, and therefore are concerned to look well to your feet, and hence the ground wheron you stand is holy ground. You that are church members, there is a speci[al] presence of god, and of Jesus christ the son of god, where you are. Then are you not concerned to look well to it, that you may be not only of the visible but of the Invisible Church of God? That being of the visible you may be also of the invisible and heavenly Jerusalem.[52]

In seeking to identify signs of the coming time when "the whole world shall be astonished to see, new Jerusalem coming downe from heaven when the son of god shall appear," Mather and his contemporaries fixed on the prophesied return of the Jews to Canaan and their conversion to Christ. The children's identity was so caught up in ancient Israel that speculation on the "Mystery of Israel's salvation" superceded interest in the European Reformation. Although unwilling to set the exact date when this miracle would occur, Mather was encouraged by reports of Jewish conversions in Hamburg and drew from them the breathtaking intuition "that the Lord *is coming, is coming, is coming*, the great and terrible day of the Lord, it is near, it is near wherein the mighty man shall cry bitterly."[53] Until that time, God's saints in New England must labor to protect their "little Jerusalem" which, blurred and imperfect as it was, still represented the closest approximation yet to the glorious kingdom to follow.

Besides millennial speculations, lecture sermons were also ideally suited to indoctrination in systematic theology. No lecture sermons were more ambitious than the monthly disquisitions of Boston's Samuel Willard on the Westminster Assembly's *Shorter Catechism*. They were delivered in Boston and spanned nineteen years, from 1688 through his presidency of Harvard to his death in 1707, by which time Willard had completed 226 lectures that carried him through the first hundred questions of the catechism. Month by month and piece by piece he dissected the body of Reformed doctrine and set forth in painstaking detail the relationship and consistency of each dogmatic principle with the whole "analogy of faith." These lectures to the clergy were so memorable that in 1726 the massive collection of notes was published posthumously under the title, *A Compleat Body of Divinity*. This not only represented the largest project yet undertaken by the American press but also would stand as New England's only systematic theology until the publication of Samuel Hopkins's *Systems of Doctrine* in 1793.[54] Unless the distinction from regular preaching is understood, Willard's lectures will seem to represent an arid scholasticism snuffing out the life of piety and emotion in second-generation preaching.[55] But viewed in their proper light as weekday lectures, they demonstrate the impressive fund of Reformed doctrine that survived unchanged into the second generation and underlay regular preaching on the life of piety and conversion.

From the technical detail and sophistication of Willard's lectures it can be seen that the laity were not the only, or even the primary, audience for lecture sermons. The presence of other ministers not only encouraged lecturers to pitch their message a cut above the usual plain style but also led them to speak on matters of common concern, most notably the status and high calling of their ministerial office. On two occasions Joshua Moodey employed the lecture to speak on the sermon and warn the people not to "let . . . any Ordinary Business divert you from a Sermon. . . . You shall be [held] accountable not only for all the sermons you *have* heard, but also for those you *might* have heard." "If you refuse to hear," Moodey went on, "God may justly refuse to speak. *Ezekiel* shall be made dumb to a rebellious people."[56] With such words, the ministers confirmed to one another their office as watchmen for their country and anticipated the spate of self-justifying ordination and convention sermons that would be preached in subsequent generations. In lectures as in fasts, the ministers portrayed themselves as an endangered species who, if not protected by the state and properly respected by their congregations, would soon become extinct. And if that were allowed to happen, the flame of New England's radiant candle would be extinguished forever.

AN ONGOING PIETY

When regular sermons, whether in print or manuscript, are examined alongside printed occasional sermons, they confirm the enduring power of the sermon to mold corporate values and personal piety in the second generation. Too often, histories of this period emphasize the themes of moral reform and waning piety as they were featured in fast sermons, election sermons, and synodical pronouncements, and ignore the hundreds of thousands of Sunday sermons on the salvation of the soul and the life of sanctified obedience. Through hearing regular sermons, joining the churches, and renewing covenant oaths, many colonists found the inner resources and cohesion that enabled them to face corporate crises as a united front. When the second generation would face their greatest crisis with the revocation of Massachusetts' charter in 1684, many institutions would be changed, but the regular sermon remained unchanged and fixed at the center of local public assembly. And, for that reason, New Englanders would retain their inherited identity as "children of the kingdom" entrusted with a unique messianic destiny.

[6]

Perpetuating the Covenant in Uncertain Times: The Sermon at Century's End

In spite of victory in war, covenant renewal, revived church membership, and economic prosperity, Increase Mather feared that the country was in danger of divine desertion. Though there might be a constant supply of faithful ministers, material blessings, and converted souls, these blessings could not disguise the ominous truth that *"the present Generation in New-England is lamentably degenerate. . . .* The first Generation of Christians in New-England is in a manner gone off the Stage, and there is another and more sinful generation risen up in their stead." Other ministers agreed. In his final fast sermon in 1682, Urian Oakes conceded that "the Lord Jesus Christ hath a very glorious interest among us," but insisted that that interest was "very little beholding to us, that have weakened and disparaged it exceedingly by our great miscarriages." Oakes used the inclusive "us" and "ours" to describe New England's sins, but the chief culprits were the people whose "miscarriages" were most grievously displayed in their lack of deference towards superiors in church and state. Such insubordination threatened to rend the fabric of corporate hierarchy on which the covenant depended. The wonder of New England, Oakes concluded, was not the country's undeniable "growth and prosperity," but that God "hath waited and spared so long such an unworthy People."[1]

For Mather and Oakes to decry the sins of declension, even while acknowledging New England's material blessings and glorious destiny, was a confession that neither they nor their colleagues could reconcile the dynamic and inherently unstable circumstances of New World settlement with traditional habits of thought. For all their reverence to Bible supremacy and the principle that all human authority be limited, the second-generation ministers could not shed the accompanying Old World view of the good society as a hierarchy of superior and inferior in which every individual knew his or her place and acted accordingly. But in the New World, their claims to superiority would not go unchallenged. Unlike the founders, the children were reared three thousand miles from aristocratic controls, and had repeatedly been admonished to subordinate all authority to the Word of God. While willing to concede their ministers' superiority in the pulpit, they were not prepared to acknowledge clerical superiority in every aspect of faith and life. The lay-clerical divisions of the second generation were caused less by a decline in piety, as the ministers believed, than by the strict application of Congregational piety to all social arrangements, including those binding ministers and their communities.

THE ENDANGERED RULE OF HIERARCHY

Social order survived in the second generation, but there were stresses and strains attributable to the unique circumstances of New World settlement. The unitary ideal could be maintained only in stable, fully settled societies in which the social and economic gaps separating leaders and followers were clearly defined and enduring, and where new settlements could not be constantly emerging to challenge the old. In New England, as in other parts of North America, this situation could not be obtained. By Old World standards, the social, economic, and intellectual boundaries separating leaders and followers were blurred; they were not built upon generations of hierarchy or powerful, hereditary aristocratic institutions. Access to open lands and new markets gave scope for expansionist energies that enabled the transformation of dependent children into independent yeomen and merchants, and disrupted the lines of order and subordination. In these fluid circumstances, clear-cut distinctions were impossible to sustain, despite increasingly stringent sumptuary legislation. Contention and confrontation—even revolution—were inevitable. This contentious atmosphere was made more frightening to colonial leaders by the realization that once popular insurrections began the leaders had no way to contain them. When, in his 1676 election sermon, William Hubbard referred to the "heap of confusion" attendant on democratic notions of "parity" in society, he was not merely speaking metaphorically; in the decentralized setting of New World institutions, these were very real fears.[2]

Studies of New England towns in the seventeenth century show that controversies occurred in particular communities as an unforeseen consequence of unprecedented population growth and cheap land.[3] As record numbers of children survived infancy, grew up, and moved out from the old town centers, conflicts followed. Second-generation "outlivers" resented taxation for churches, roads, bridges, or schools far removed from their farms; and they petitioned the General Court for independent status. Selectmen and ministers in the town center resisted such independence because it threatened to diminish their tax base and reduce their influence over the second and third generations.[4] In Salem, Massachusetts, where differences between the trade-oriented townsmen and the outlying farmers in "Salem Village" were extreme, the conflict was particularly acute. Most often the disputes centered around the issue of new meetinghouses and ministers. In 1672, after frequent and acrimonious disputes and petitions, the farmers of Salem Village were authorized to build a "parish" meetinghouse of their own, while remaining under the discipline and sacramental control of the parent church in Salem Town. The uncertain status of Salem Village parish led to even more bitter disputes between townsmen and outliers, which would not be resolved until long after the witch hysteria had passed.[5] In other towns, the strains were similar, if not always as intense. These conflicts led ministers to conclude that their generation was spiritually apathetic and perverse.

Among all the issues that sharpened the ministers' sense of declension and anticlerical sentiments, the payment of clerical salaries loomed largest. As social superiors, ministers believed they were entitled to superior salaries. Many in their congregations, however, believed that a modest salary was more appropriate to their emulation of Christ's humility. Since it was the congregation's right to fix and collect salaries, ministerial payments were kept low and, in time of contention or economic difficulty, went unpaid. In Dedham, for example, William Adams complained repeatedly about salary arrears that kept him at a bare subsistence level. Not every minister suffered as much as Adams (most were at or not far above the median income of their community), but all were acutely conscious of the power congregations held over their finances. By the 1670s, salary disputes had become so common that incoming ministers routinely demanded written contracts with fixed salaries as a precondition to the "peace and comfort" of their settlement.[6]

The ministers did not enumerate the different types of contention they witnessed in their communities perhaps because, in their eyes, any breakdown in deference and subordination was symptomatic of religious decline. But historians have discovered that most lay-clerical disputes were peripheral to the pulpit or Scripture doctrine, and instead involved social issues of ministerial status and economic support.[7] In view of the high levels of church membership, conversion, and other indexes of enduring popular piety, these cases suggest that lay-clerical divisions were less an index of declining lay spirituality, as the ministers feared, than of a crisis of authority in a volatile, rapidly growing society. Interestingly, in the cases where debates over Scripture doctrine did occur, as in the case of the Half-way Covenant or, later, psalm singing by note, it was the congregations who sought to preserve the old purity while their ministers pushed for innovation.

To counter what they sincerely believed was a loss of piety, the second-generation ministers took both institutional and rhetorical action. On the institutional level, they moved to protect the sanctity of Word and order (and their own preeminence). In a move that David D. Hall has described as "resurgent sacerdotalism," ministers redefined their office as devolving as much from apostolic succession as from the call of a particular congregation. Such a definition left them freer to regulate themselves. To allow themselves greater control in matters of church admission, the Reforming Synod approved the practice (already common in many churches) of having prospective members relate their testimony of saving grace privately to the minister, and also of having ministers ordain themselves rather than being ordained by their congregations.[8]

In addition, ministers sought to uphold the sanctity of their office by claiming increased authority for their regional associations and provincial synods. One leader in this regard was "Pope" Solomon Stoddard whose Hampshire Association of ministers was a prototype for similar associations throughout New England.[9] These "presbyterian" associations were intended as self-protective regulatory agencies to arbitrate local disputes between ministers and congregations, and approve new candidates for the ministry. More informally, but perhaps more importantly, associations offered the ministers opportunities to share common problems and discuss issues of doctrine or discipline that arose in their ministries. Finally, ministers sought further to solemnize their office by increased emphasis on the sacraments, which only they could administer. They could and did withhold the sacraments from feuding congregations, suspending a "means" of grace until such time as "order" was restored.[10]

No such institutional modifications could achieve the intended end of domination of congregations, however, simply because the ministers' deliberations were not binding on particular churches. Congregations continued to view their liberties as both a right and a sacred duty, and successfully blocked movements in presbyterian directions by refusing to acknowledge the ministers' sovereignty. The state was an effective ally of the clergy in matters of church establishment and college support. But beyond church founding and maintenance, magistrates emphasized the functional distinctions between church and state, and chose not to meddle in ecclesiastical affairs. After 1690, the Massachusetts assembly refused to convene a province-wide synod of ministers. In Connecticut, consociations were established by law for purposes of ministerial licensing and arbitration, but they were so hampered by resistant congregations that they were never able to function as intended.[11] Change, it was clear, could not be arbitrarily imposed on the churches from the top down. The people would have to be persuaded, and persuasion would be accomplished through changed circumstances or effective speech, not institutional fiat.

MINISTERIAL AUTHORITY
AND THE RHETORIC OF DISCOVENANTING

From the start of colonization, rhetoric had been the ministers' most powerful weapon. Pious congregations might deny the claims of ministerial synods and associations, but they could not even think of silencing their ministers without bringing the very Word of God into contempt. In the pulpits, the ministers' voices remained sovereign and unchallenged, and there they would promulgate their most powerful claims to authority and deference.

As always, the most potent weapon in the ministers' arsenal was fear and the specter of divine desertion. Whereas King Philip's War provided a stunning confirmation of the ministers' prophetic powers, it did not put an end to strife in the churches. The words of consolation offered in the immediate aftermath of the war soon gave place to familiar words of warning. Though it should not be thought that ministerial accusations and laments were the prevailing note in second-generation preaching, they nevertheless cast a pall over the pulpit. In occasional fast and election sermons, one can discover little joy or celebration of accomplishment; only a mournful, at times querulous, pondering of spiritual hardening that seemed to grow worse as prosperity increased. Any change in social relationships became, by definition, change for the worse and cause for divine punishment.

Throughout the late 1670s and 1680s, pulpit warnings grew more graphic as ministers outdid one another describing the horrors of desertion. To the familiar history of covenanting they added their own fully developed, terrifying history of "discovenanting," occasions when, as Increase Mather explained, God had "excommunicated" chosen nations for their apostasy.[12] Ministers began using the occasional sermon to trace the thread of discovenanting throughout human history, and to define it as the time when God's probation period expired. The list of broken covenants was, as John Norton pointed out in his election sermon, distressingly long:

> God may bear long, wait long; but not always . . . God hath so done. He hath oft done it. He will so do [again]. He is the same God. He is Unchangeably Just and Holy. God hath so done to *Shiloh*, where the House of God was continued almost four hundred years. To *Jerusalem*, once called, *The perfection of beauty, the joy of the whole Earth*. To the Churches in *Asia*, once glorious, planted by the Apostles. These Candlesticks have been removed for a long time out of their places, not one remaining. To many Thousand Churches in *Africa*. Many Churches in *Europe*, since the Reformation. In *Saxony, Bohemia, Hungaria, Poland, France*, and other Places, Unchurched and Dissipated. To the Churches among the ancient *Britains*, in the Land of our Fathers Sepulchres. When other Judgments would not Reform them, God at last brought the *Saxons* upon them, who rooted them out of the Land. There is a day of Gods Patience, a set time, with some longer, some shorter; when that time is once expired, there is no place for Repentance, either on Gods part, or on Man's part.[13]

In all of these cases (save Israel), the desertion was final and easily distinguished from the merciful "reprieves" of ordinary afflictions and difficulties. As Joseph Rowlandson explained in a 1682 fast sermon on *The Possibility of Gods Forsaking a People*: "An evil whilst God is present, may have much good in it, the Lord may sanctifie it for abundance of blessing. There is hopes of this whilst the Lord continues amongst them; but if he be gone, it is an only evil, and the evils that come upon them are such, they have nothing but evil in them."[14]

How far could God's patience be pushed before it was "too late"? Was there a single common sin that previous discovenanted peoples had shared? In researching the history of discovenanting, ministers made the self-validating discovery that the perpetuation of the covenant depended on the survival of God's true prophets. In a sermon on apostasy, Increase Mather explained that God's prophets were the covenant's lifeline, and no matter what else a people did, they must respect the Word preached.[15] Many sins could provoke God's anger, but the one unpardonable corporate sin was to reject him by silencing his messengers. Happily, in New England there was still an abundance of faithful ministers by whose agency as William Adams explained, "the Word of the Lord hath been to us, precept upon precept, line upon line; We have in that respect been planted in the house of the Lord." For the sake of his prophets, God would not abandon his New England people, but would continue to chastise them as a call to repentance and as a confirmation of his prophets' authority.[16]

In the history of discovenanting, ministers found a variation on the rhetoric of failure that served both to incite popular repentance and to reinforce their own self-image as the unappreciated saviors of New England. Increasingly they used occasional sermons to expand upon their own indispensability to New England's covenant and to console one another for the necessity of laboring among this ungrateful generation. For typological identification, they turned to the Hebrew prophets whose words of warning were not appreciated by the children of Israel. In his 1682 election sermon, Samuel Willard considered Jeremiah and his strained relationship with the people of Israel. The people failed to honor the prophet's divinely commissioned ministry, and Jeremiah framed an apologia for his office, which Willard used as his text. This "apology," Willard observed, was equally applicable to the present generation of ministers who shouldered the "unthankful errand" of ministering to a headstrong people who would not heed the warnings of their watchmen. In language at once scathing and self-pitying he inveighed:

> The fouler the stomach, the more nauseous is the physic. . . . He that will undertake to lay open the true state of [a] degenerous people by ripping up their sins, displaying their impenitencies, and applying the threatenings of divine displeasure, shall expose himself to the hatred and injurious usage of those for whom he doth this kindness.[17]

In the same year Willard also published a fast sermon with the same apologetic theme. This time his type was Ezekiel who, like Jeremiah, was commissioned by God but spurned by his people. When the Israelites refused to acknowledge the divine origin of Ezekiel's foreboding vision of the four wheels, God punished them. He did this, Willard explained, not only to correct his people but also to confirm the office of his prophet. The double lesson contained in Israel's punishment also applied to New England. If the children had not yet repudiated their ministers, neither did they accord them the dignity due their office; this alone was sufficient to incur God's wrath: "If therefore God should withdraw from us, and leave our publick affairs to miscarry in our hands, I would say it is of the Lord, *that he might fulfil the words of his Ministers*, that told and warned us of dayes of great calamity approaching."[18]

Harsh words of warning and self-justification did not restore congregations to perfect harmony. Ministers hoped, however, that they would prevent further deterioration. As familiar as the warnings were, they still had power as words spoken from "on high" and because they were supported by chilling examples from covenant history—history the children knew even better than that of their parents' homeland. The ministers' self-justifying logic about discovenanting secured their place in the pulpits and ensured that in times of crisis the people would turn to them for perspective and interpretation, just as they had in King Philip's War.

THE REVOCATION OF THE
MASSACHUSETTS BAY CHARTER

Such a time of crisis appeared in October 1684, when Massachusetts Bay lost its charter—its political badge of distinction. Until then the second generation had lived in isolation from other colonies and from England. That all changed when the lords of Trade, acting on the advice of their colonial agent, Edward Randolph, annulled the Bay charter. In its place they incorporated all the New England colonies into a new administrative system, the "Dominion of New England," that would be governed by the crown and its representatives. In one bold stroke, self-government was replaced by a royal governor and his council. The new government was charged with enforcing all of England's laws, including religious toleration as it came to be codified in the Act of Toleration (1689). In addition it claimed all title to New England lands and instructed its rulers to reissue land titles in the king's name and attach them to a quitrent.[19] Almost overnight, New England ceased to be a society of self-governing Bible commonwealths and became a royal colony whose laws and operations were formulated and enforced by outside agencies. English law replaced *Sola Scriptura* as New England's sovereign authority, at least nominally.

In the early months of administration, there hardly seemed to be a crisis. Most of the ministers initially chose *not* to portray the loss of the charter as a calamity or a judgment for New England's sins. Although sudden, the new government was not entirely unanticipated and, in view of the strained relations between leaders and followers in the colonies, not entirely unwelcome. For many "moderate" (pro-English) merchants, magistrates, and ministers—like William Stoughton, Samuel Willard, or Gershom Bulkeley—the dominion seemed to offer a needed external source of stability in the New World's "anarchic" environment.[20] This was particularly plausible during the interim presidency of Joseph Dudley, scion of the early governor, Massachusetts native, and former assistant under the old charter. Dudley refused to exercise many of his broad discretionary powers (particularly the power to order new taxes and qui-

trents), and he assured the ministers and people he would do nothing to
threaten the Congregational churches. With their churches intact and
their properties safe from arbitrary seizure, the new government
seemed—to the leaders anyway—more a blessing than a trial.

All of this began to change when, on December 20, 1686, the lords of
Trade, again acting on the advice of the meddlesome Randolph, replaced
Dudley with the former governor of New York Colony (now annexed to
the dominion), Sir Edmund Andros. Unlike Dudley, Andros was a
stranger to New England who alienated his subjects immediately. His
overbearing, arrogant military style offended the plainer sensibilities of
the region, and his policies imposed a strict, unyielding order on the recal-
citrant inhabitants.[21] With obvious relish, Andros demanded the use of
Boston's Old South Church to institute Anglican services—the first to
appear in the Bay Colony. Even more threatening was his willingness to
suppress civil liberties through crown-appointed vice-admiralty courts
and his decision to expropriate the common lands in and around Boston
for his own use. It did not take long for the frightened inhabitants to realize that if Andros could seize common lands he could also seize properties
granted under the old charter, or at least tax those properties without
common consent. To back up his claims and policies, Andros appeared
frequently at the head of a long regiment of British redcoats—the first that
living New Englanders had ever seen. Until then, *tyranny* had been a
word the children associated with the founders and Charles I. Suddenly,
the term assumed chilling immediacy.

Left with no means of institutional redress such as that previously provided for in the General Court and town meetings, many colonists
responded to Andros's regime in unlawful ways. Merchants, who initially
welcomed the new government because it promised to weaken the ministers' powerful control of local affairs, raised smuggling to a fine art in
open defiance of the navigation acts. Many towns refused to recognize
the sovereignty of the dominion and continued to govern themselves
through the town meeting. Under the influence of their doughty minister,
John Wise, the Ipswich town meeting went so far as to refuse to pay any
taxes Andros might levy. They based their resistance on ancient English
rights which, in their reading, provided that "*no taxes shall be levied on
the subjects* without consent of a [popular] assembly chosen by the free-
holders for assessing the same."[22] Such sentiments were radically "democratic" by seventeenth-century standards and not widely encouraged by
other ministers in other towns. Wise himself was imprisoned for several
months for his civil disobedience and would not become a popular hero
until the Revolutionary generation.

Instead of choosing words calculated to arouse confrontation and rebellion, most ministers avoided pointed pulpit commentary and focused
their preaching on eternity and the conversion of the children. Ministers
sought, with some success, to channel frustration and uncertainty into a
pattern of revival and covenant renewal. In Boston, for example, where

the weight of the Andros regime pressed heaviest, church membership at Samuel Willard's Third Church grew at a rate nearly equal to that of the great revival of 1680, when ninety-one new communicants owned the covenant. In the towns of Milford and New Haven, Connecticut, new admissions between 1685 and 1690 exceeded any other period in the towns' history.[23] With renewed fervor, ministers urged parents to seek the salvation of the children. No political treatises or election sermons were printed (or delivered) in the years 1687–1689, but more regular (conversionist) sermons were printed than at any other time in the second generation's ministry.[24] All of these sermons assumed that, though gravely imperiled, New England's covenant endured and would stay in effect so long as the people heard the Word and sought the Lord through repentance, reformation, and conversion. The children would demonstrate how "peculiar" they really were by continuing to cleave to the covenant without the supporting apparatus of a sympathetic—and coercive—government.

Throughout 1686, Cotton Mather kept a notebook of sermons delivered by his father and other Boston clergymen that had as their primary theme the covenant of grace and the children's salvation. At a morning fast sermon on March 25, for example, Nathaniel Gookin (HC, 1675) reminded the parents that the new laws of religious toleration did not "exempt" them from the duty of preserving the founders' faith. The dismantling of the Puritan state did not change the fact that "the Children of Covenant parents are members of [Christ's] Body." More than ever before, parents must teach their children to preserve "such good things as our Fathers came into this Wilderness for."[25] Samuel Willard pursued the same theme in the afternoon sermon on Joshua 22:24–25: "In time to come your children might speak to our children, saying, what have ye to do with the Lord God of Israel?" Willard's chief concern was that in the furor over "rights and titles" the people might forget their first priority, which was "to secure the Rights and Titles of their Children, to the visible worship of God." The children of New England, Willard went on, were still in the "same covenant of grace" as Israel and must never forget that "true faith engages the people of God in Duty. . . . When men cast off their duty about the children of the covenant, tis a woeful sign that God is about to cast off those Children." Only by setting the children's "spiritual good above all others," could New England remain a special "people of God" and continue to enjoy divine protection and mercy.[26]

Sermons like Gookin's and Willard's show how carefully ministers avoided pulpit commentary on explosive political issues, concentrating instead on the salvation of the soul. By selecting texts that spiritualized adversity and focused attention on eternity, ministers hoped to direct the people's immediate fears into programs of personal and family revival rather than rebellious political programs or hysterical crusades. In delivering a Boston lecture in 1686, Joshua Moodey departed from the customary disquisitions to deliver a simple message on Luke 12:4–5: "Be not afraid of them that kill the body, and after that have no more that they can do. But I will forewarn you whom ye shall fear: Fear him which after he hath killed hath power to cast into hell; yea, I say unto you, Fear him." Moodey began by noting how in his text "the Greek Name for Fear comes from a verb that signifies to fly." Many in his audience feared for their properties and rights, but such fears were misdirected. The covenant-keeping Christian need "fear God only." Once the fear of the Lord was implanted in the soul, the fear of death and deprivation vanished and was replaced by a pious fear of sin: "Truly, it makes a man fly from the evil feared . . . to Duty." Having died to the world and the concerns of the world, death itself ceased to frighten for "no man ever truly closed with Christ, but hee was in Heart a Martyr." It was "a brave Thing to be able to suffer," Moodey concluded, because the hope of final vindication was sure. Christ "will not let [you] loose a crown for want of bearing a cross."[27]

While ministerial caution was the rule for pulpit commentary in the late 1680s and 1690s, there were exceptions. The most notorious such exception to ministerial restraint, indeed the most notorious episode in all New England history, occurred in Salem Village where the new parish pastor, Samuel Parris, identified evil happenings with witchcraft. Parris had not enjoyed a moment's peace since the commencement of his ministry in 1689, when he found himself caught between warring factions in Salem Town and Salem Village. Instead of confining and channeling social fears and tensions into revival and covenant renewal as his colleagues were seeking to do, Parris inflamed local rivalries by declaring that "if ever there were witches, Men and Women in covenant with the Devil, here are Multitudes in New-England."[28] By March 1692, he was convinced that witches had infiltrated the churches, including his own Salem congregation. In a sermon on Judas Iscariot he declared that "as in our text [John 6:10] there was one [devil] among the 12 [disciples] . . . so in our churches God knows how many Devils there are." Such preaching offered a powerful and dangerous release for social and political tensions that had been brewing throughout the previous decades. It encouraged the villagers to purge their feelings of frustration and guilt by locating and destroying the "witches" in their midst. In many cases these witches were individuals who had run afoul of Parris and his key clan of supporters, the Putnam family.[29] Before the panic subsided and the neighboring ministers intervened to halt the judicial proceedings, over 150 suspected witches had been imprisoned and nineteen hanged at "Witches' Hill" on the western side of the town.

As might be deduced from its notoriety, the witchcraft episode was an exceptional response to social change and political insecurity. In their analysis of the social bases of witchcraft, Paul Boyer and Stephen Nissenbaum point out that the social tensions at Salem *could* have been channeled into revival. As evidence they point to the Great Awakening of 1740, when ministers turned guilt and anxiety to mass conversions.[30] What Boyer and Nissenbaum do not say, however, is that this was precisely what most ministers did in 1690 as well. The 1690 revivals were not as dramatic as those in 1740, but the pattern was basically the same. Indeed, when the neighboring ministers perceived how the accusations at Salem had gotten out of hand, they played the leading role in halting the prosecutions. As a study in social pathology and moral cowardice that also confirms ministerial influence for good and evil, the witchcraft hysteria deserves the rich attention it has received. But its anomalousness must be stressed as well; most ministers used their influence to minimize conflict and maintain social equilibrium.[31]

NEW ENGLAND'S GLORIOUS REVOLUTION

Regular and occasional preaching helped to quiet popular fears by reinforcing the confidence that New England was still a covenant people. It did not, however, dampen popular outrage against Andros's "tyranny." With his cavalier disregard for property rights and the public happiness, Andros confirmed that he was a civil tyrant who ought to be resisted. All that was needed was a pretext. When unconfirmed reports of Parliament's expulsion of James II from the English throne reached Boston in April 1688, the people found the excuse they needed. Despite efforts by Andros to suppress news of the "Glorious Revolution," accounts of the ascension of William of Orange ran "like Lightning through the Town." On April 18, thousands of Bostonians mobilized to the beat of militia drums, "driving and furious" to redeem their government from "the *worst of Treasons*." The next day, "some Thousands on Horse and Foot were come in from the Towns Adjacent, to express the unanimous content they took in the *Action*, and offer their utmost Assistance in what yet remained for the compleating of it." Assembled en masse, the people discovered they were indomitable.[32] After imprisoning Andros, Randolph, and Dudley, and abolishing their "arbitrary" government, the people established self-appointed "Committees for the Conservation of Peace" to preserve internal order. To a remarkable extent the committees worked. There was no violence or civil war. From the start, the goal was to eliminate tyranny only, not responsible self-government.

The new popular assertiveness evidenced in the Committees for Peace extended to the formation of an interim government. At a special convention of town delegates in May 1689, the people rejected the advice of the "old magistrates," who wished to retain a twenty-two member "Council of Safety" with oligarchic powers, and voted instead to reestablish a representative government modeled on the old charter with the significant difference that all landowners and taxpayers could now vote in provincial elections regardless of church membership status. This government restored those rights of consent and representation that New Englanders were conditioned to identify with their public happiness and security. Old leaders feared that the interim government was dangerously popular and democratic, but they could not change it.

The Committees for Peace and self-appointed popular legislatures were only the first in a long line of experiments in popular liberty and power that would occupy New Englanders for the next century. These experiments affected both church and state, and the results showed that in the New World no force and no individual could control the people against their will. With the Glorious Revolution, New Englanders had discovered the awesome powers they commanded in a New World setting, where there were no aristocratic controls and no large standing armies. When they had driven the Andros regime to its knees and reinstated representative government, the populace resolved never again to allow a government—either of "strangers" or their own countrymen—to deprive them of civil and property rights which, since King Philip's War, they had been taught to reverence as much as their right to worship.

Besides discovering their power, the people had also discovered that revolution against established rules and rulers need not lead to anarchy and mass confusion. In the vacuum left by the overthrow of traditional authority, social order did not disappear. Ordinary men and women did not expend their potent energies in hysterical crusades and random rioting; they discovered something far more tantalizing to occupy their attention in mass assembly—the possibility of seizing power and promoting social order at the same time. Drawing on their New World experience, the people created a social order that their "betters" had claimed was impossible to achieve without aristocratic controls. The full implications of New England's interim experiment in self-rule would not be developed for another seventy-five years, but once discovered, the idea would never disappear.

For New England's tradition-minded civil and religious leaders, however, the tumultuous events of 1688 and 1689 marked a time of great confusion and uncertainty. On the one hand, they rejoiced to see the oppressive burden of tyranny lifted from them and few disputed their countrymen's right to revolt against Andros. On the other hand, events after the revolt planted fears of a runaway popular assertiveness that would throw all authority overboard in churches and governments. There was also the problem of placating the new monarchs, William and Mary. If New England was to retain its civil and religious liberties, the new monarchs had to be convinced that New England was capable of responsible self-government. New England's leaders had to condemn insubordination and anarchy when addressing their own people at home, and at the same time persuade English audiences that New England's revolution was just, and the people restrained and submissive.

Immediately after the insurrection, Increase Mather set out for England on a self-appointed mission to present the colony's case to the English court and, if possible, recover the old charter.[33] Meanwhile, publicists at home—civil and ministerial—broke their pattern of silence and issued a torrent of self-justifying tracts and pamphlets which, as T. H. Breen demonstrates, represented "the first sustained discussion of political beliefs to take place in the Puritan colonies since Winthrop's death."[34] These documents were clearly intended to be read by English audiences—particularly the crown and lords of Trade. The writers evidently knew that they had to satisfy a royal audience who would not be impressed by appeals to divine commissions, Congregational liberties, the evils of Anglicanism, or covenant theology—all the terms that dominated political discourse during New England's period of cultural and political autonomy. Therefore they limited their discussion to constitutional questions of English rights and liberties guaranteed by the Magna Carta and confirmed by the recent ouster of James II. New England's covenant mission is conspicuously absent from these treatises, certainly not because it had ceased to figure in their political thought but because the writers knew it was peripheral to the interests of their present audience. If the mission was to be preserved, it would be indirectly through a general defense of New England's rights and liberties as English subjects.

Before New England's leaders could plead their rights of property and conscience, however, they had to demonstrate their loyalty to the new monarchs. To that end, the interim governor, Simon Bradstreet, and his advisors launched a hastily assembled and poorly planned expedition against French fortresses in Canada. From the start the uncoordinated planning provoked severe criticism both from the soldiers and from observers like the chaplain, John Wise. Before the defeated and demoralized troops returned home, one thousand men would die in battle, shipwreck, or from disease, leaving behind a new class of widows and dependent poor who would be placed in the public care. With no captured enemy treasure to defray the expense of the expedition, New England's debt, already high as a consequence of King Philip's War, soared; to compensate, provincial taxes rose, outstripping those of any other North American colony. To further compound the region's fiscal difficulties, the interim government issued paper currency, which set in motion a depreciatory trend that would continue for the next two generations.[35] In the end, everyone but the enterprising merchants lost in "King William's War." New England troops may have demonstrated their loyalty to the new monarchs but certainly not their competence or dependability. At home, the ignominy of defeat and the burden of unprecedented taxes provoked a wave of public criticism and hostility that rivaled earlier criticism of the dominion. So violent was this criticism that many leaders came to believe their old charters were simply too democratic and lacking in external coercive controls. They hoped for a new government with what Gershom Bulkeley termed a "Supreame Power" capable of preserving hierarchy and deference at the same time it protected property and rights of self-government.[36]

In May 1692, Increase Mather returned to Boston with a new royal charter that abolished the interim government and created in its place the royal province of Massachusetts, expanded to include Plymouth and Maine. (Connecticut was allowed to retain its old charter.) Heading Massachusetts's new government was a crown-appointed royal governor, William Phips, together with a popularly elected assembly empowered to pay the governor's salary and appoint his advisory council. The new government would survive to 1774, but whatever divisions had existed under the old charter were minor in comparison to the divisions growing out of the new charter. Many commoners who had tasted power in the Glorious Revolution and interim government were bitterly disappointed in the new government, despite the fact that it guaranteed property rights, representative government, religious toleration, and an expanded franchise based on property rather than Congregational church membership. The nonelected governor and accompanying appointive offices, they believed, claimed arbitrary powers that would be resisted at every opportunity. Other, more established elites, including merchants, ministers, and major landowners, heartily endorsed the aristocratic controls included in the new charter but resented both the new governor and Increase Mather, who recommended him. They soon divided into factions that contested bitterly for a voice on the Governor's Council, for seats in the popular assembly, and for control of Harvard College. The underlying cause of all this contention was clear. As long as government was tied to the churches and covenant consent, there was some measure of stability. Once that connection was severed, and the magistrate transformed into a secular functionary bound to tolerate all Protestant sects, political harmony dissolved and the theocratic state came to an end.[37]

PRESERVING THE COVENANT THROUGH A NEW MYTHOLOGY

Though the theocratic state was gone, New England's self-identification as a unique people of the Word persisted, and in this sense the new charter brought about no "secularization." The formal dismantling of a coercive Congregational establishment—already completed in the dominion—in no way diminished the power of the Word preached in local assemblies. Habits of thought and worship were too deeply ingrained. Because the Congregational churches were tolerated, if no longer exclusive, ministers could compete for and win the loyalty of the populace through the well-established means of persuasion at their disposal. No town experienced a large-scale exodus of alienated church members chafing under the yoke of an oppressive Congregational establishment. If anything, the churches *gained* in public respect, for they alone retained the full measure of gospel liberties meted out by the founders. Life still revolved around self-contained local communities, and within those communities, the ministers retained their exalted positions as gospel heralds and cultural guardians. The persistence of Congregational loyalty marked the second generation's coming of age. Instead of annulling New England's covenant, the new charter confirmed it. God continued to bless or chastise his people in direct proportion to their covenant keeping.

While such divine continuance was gratifying, it was also bewildering. According to the old orthodoxy, covenant keeping was not supposed to survive in an atmosphere of religious toleration and externally appointed magistrates. For over fifty years, ministers had routinely identified New England's covenant with an exclusive state-enforced orthodoxy. But the new government accorded with none of the inherited verities. Its origins lay in London, far removed from the body of the faithful; its laws were derived from the English "constitution," not Scripture; and its rulers were answerable to the crown, not the visible saints. To all outward appearances, New England had become just one more appendage to a vast and sprawling imperial network. Why then were they still a peculiar people?

Confronted with the fact of continued popular loyalty to the Congregational churches, the ministers could draw only one conclusion: the original supposition that a theocratic state was essential to covenant keeping was wrong. This was the religious lesson learned from the Glorious Revolution in New England. If pure worship and voluntary submission to God's Word were achieved through the new charter—as they apparently were—then the theocratic state could disappear without detriment to the federal covenant. Within a period of time so short that it tended to obscure the profundity of the transformation, the leaders came to accept that the old charter was not as essential to New England's mission as had originally been supposed. The Congregational church-state may have been necessary at first to establish patterns of action and habits of thought. But after fifty years of indoctrination, those patterns were indelibly fixed and the New England Way would perpetuate itself as long as the people were at liberty to organize their social and spiritual lives according to their conscience. As the founders pointed the way to change in the Half-way Covenant, so the children modified the original orthodoxy concerning government and the covenant. Concurrently they rewrote the history of New England to be compatible with the new realities. New England's mission would continue even though the Puritan state did not.

Far from bemoaning the new charter as a divine judgment, ministers employed printed tracts and special occasions to celebrate the new order as a signal interposition of providential mercy, coming at a time when the colonies were badly in need of internal stability and external protection. The anti-Anglican rhetoric that had fueled political discourse in the Winthrop era disappeared. Now the ministers praised religious toleration as the liberty to continue in their special covenant without passing judgment on other Protestant traditions. Similarly, the founders' record of persecution was passed over in silence. Henceforth, the founders would be officially remembered not for their intolerance (now an embarrassing episode of misguided zeal) but for their heroic defense of religious and civil liberty. The Great Migration was redefined as an act of desperation which, like the Glorious Revolution, was necessitated by a tyrannical regime unwilling to grant the Puritans their natural-born rights as Englishmen.[38]

Had the tolerant laws of 1688 been in effect in 1630, there would have been no migration because there would have been no persecution. It was tyranny the founders fled, not wholesome English laws and protection.

The new mythology was officially ratified in the 1692 election sermon delivered by Increase Mather's precocious son, colleague, and staunchest ally, Cotton Mather. In form and language, Mather's sermon marked a sharp departure from earlier election sermons, reflecting the new royal audience it addressed, as well as the young pastor's proclivity for ornate prose. It also reflected the recognition that if the New England Way was to survive the new imperial system its defenders must reason with the governor on his own terms; they would have to carve out a place for their sacred offices and institutions from the bedrock of English constitutional law. These new rhetorical requirements pushed the vocabulary and style of provincial oratory (and public knowledge) in a more secular direction, even as it was invoked to defend traditional religious goals and practices.

Mather did not begin his sermon with Israel and then make the typological identification with New England; he began by establishing New England's loyalty to the crown and submission to its lawful dictates. In words redolent of loyalty and veneration, he declared that "the Nearness of our Dependence on the *Crown*, which does now so sensibly protect us, will be found one of our most glorious Advantages." Such dependence and loyalty, he went on, transcended words and could be seen in New England's honorable, if futile, expedition to Canada and in the leaders' eagerness to accept the new royal government. The people of Massachusetts did not expect their royal governors to be visible (Congregational) saints (though they should be God-fearing men who "prefer the Interest of God, above all secular Considerations"). The people only expected that the ruler act to uphold every person's "Right unto his Life, his Estate, his Liberty, and his Family."[39] Among those liberties was the liberty of worship, now expanded to protect all Protestants. While "old charter" purists complained that Mather's endorsement of English toleration compromised the founders' ideals by opening the door to heretical sects, Mather was astute enough to recognize that the new political circumstances did more to protect the ministers' place in the Congregational churches than to threaten them. As long as the Congregational churches represented an overwhelming majority of the population, they would remain, in effect, the established church of New England.

Mather and other ministers worked with the new government because, in matters of religious jurisdiction, it claimed less for itself rather than more. Even as Mather commended the expansion of royal influence and stability in New England government, he specified the limits of its range of influence. Government need not worry about anything beyond the maintenance of external social order and the suppression of public vices "which disturb the good order and repose of *Humane Society*." The new government, he explained, existed outside of the churches, so that "when a man sins in his *Political Capacity*, let Political Societies animadvert upon him; but when he sins only in a *Religious Capacity*, Societies more purely Religious, are the fittest then to deal with him."[40] Under this definition, ministers and congregations were free to organize and police themselves as they had always done.

Recognizing that many inhabitants still felt betrayed by the new charter his father had negotiated, Mather turned from the responsibilities of the royal governor to the people's duty to submit to the new government. While the new government was not directly commissioned by God to stand as the coercive arm of the Congregational churches, it did protect the lives, liberties, and properties of its subjects and so must be honored. Nothing positive could come of constantly contrasting the new government with the old, because the old would never be reinstated. For perspective, the people should look to the more recent horrors of the Andros regime and remember their deliverance from tyranny. In contrast to the dominion, Mather pointed out, the new charter protected the people's right to self-government in the popular assembly. Furthermore, Massachusetts alone among royal colonies in the New World enjoyed the privilege of electing the Governor's Council through their representatives. There were no "strangers" exacting oppressive quitrents for "what they had before possess'd as their *Free-holds*," nor was there any law or tax "imposed upon them, except what their own Acts [assemblies] concurr'd unto."[41] Most importantly, there was no "disturbance in the *worship* of God." The new rulers were simply upholding social order according to the tolerant laws and liberties of England's constitution, and for that reason the people owed them deference, obedience, and gratitude.

Having explained the governor's right to rule and the people's duty to submit in essentially secular and self-interested terms, Mather returned to conventional themes and concluded his sermon with a word concerning the churches of New England and their ongoing federal covenant. Many things had changed in a short period of time, but the covenant continued to define New England's identity at the deepest social and cultural levels. The language of rights and liberties continued to be understood mainly in an instrumental sense as the liberty to preserve New England's covenant.[42] God was the ultimate source of New England's charter rights and economic prosperity, and he blessed them to confirm his covenant: "If any one ask, unto what the Sudden and Matchless thriving of *New-England* may be ascribed? It is the Blessing of God upon the *Church-Order*, for the sake whereof . . . this Plantation was first Erected." The new charter did not change the terms of God's covenant with New England, and if the people forgot that, no nation on earth could protect them from the avenging hand of God: "If we don't go *Leaning* upon God, every step, we shall *go wrong*, and nothing will go *well* in our Hands."[43]

For the next seventy-five years, election speakers would organize their messages around the fusion of English law and covenant logic as set forth in Mather's oration. As we will see, the ministers could support the royal government so enthusiastically because it confirmed and protected hierarchical principles that they had been defending against an assertive populace, without jeopardizing the original covenant. In the past, ministers based their claims to superiority on the "light of nature" and revelation. Henceforth, they would add to these pillars of liberty the laws of England which, as Samuel Willard pointed out in his 1694 election sermon, upheld the principle of hierarchy and the divinely ordained balance between "Orders of Superiority and Inferiority among men." The added support of English rule represented, in Willard's view, a vast improvement over "the short *Anarchy* accompanying our late *Revolution*."[44] That "anarchy" was more frightening than the tyranny that preceded it. Without English law, the people might forget their limitations. The absence of formal aristocratic controls in the New World encouraged the people to move in excessively democratic directions and to forget the fact that, as Joseph Easterbrook explained in a later election sermon, they were "not competent judges of the actions of Magistrates: it is a usual saying, that there are . . . Mysteries of State, to the bottom of which, People are not able to dive."[45] English law would remind them of this and prevent the people from taking a headlong "dive" into anarchy. At the same time—and more importantly—English laws and manners would reinforce deferential habits of mind the ministers hoped to inculcate in their churches—habits which, they believed, were essential to the preservation of New England's covenant and their own preeminence.

CHILDREN OF THE COVENANT

The second generation had come into early adulthood convinced that they were a lapsed people. But by century's end this sentiment disappeared. A lifetime's commitment to the Word sustained through trying circumstances qualified them to claim the title "children of the covenant." The rhetoric of failure and impending doom continued, to be sure, but now it was directed to the third generation. After shaky beginnings the children had proved themselves worthy successors to the founders. Although they were not the giants of piety their parents had been (their location in sacred history deprived them of that position), they had honored God's Word in their communities, renewed the covenant of their parents, and joined the churches. They had survived the horrors of King Philip's War and seen how the loss of their charter was, in reality, a divine deliverance. Their record of achievements, deliverances, and modifications of inherited theory could be engrafted onto the history of the founders so that the third generation would have two generations to emulate.

To commemorate the faith of New England's first native-born generation, ministers began printing funeral sermons, which had as their overriding theme the enduring piety of the deceased. In the 1690s, examples of this genre of sermon constituted the most numerous printed sermons in New England.[46] Like the printed final sermons of the founders, funeral sermons used death to underscore the passage of generations and the covenant's continuity. Above all, they urged the rising generation to remember their predecessors and imitate their piety. Most of the subjects of funeral sermons were second-generation ministers or their wives, but prominent lay leaders were also remembered. At a funeral for the wealthy Boston merchant and magistrate John Hull, Samuel Willard explained the purpose of printed funeral sermons in terms of the specific history they preserved:

> We should embalm the memory of the Saints with the sweet smelling Spices that grew in their own Gardens, and pick the chiefest Flowers out of those Beds to strew their Graves withal; we should remember and make mention of them with honourable thoughts and words. And though it be now grown a Nick-name of contempt among wicked and prophane Men, yet count it the most orient Jewel in their Crown, the most odoriferous and pleasant Flower in their Garland, that we can say of them that they lived and died Saints; all other Eschutcheons will either wear away, or be taken down, every other monument will become old, and grow over with the Moss of time, and their Titles, though cut in Brass, will be Canker-eaten and illegible. This onely will endure and be fresh and Flourishing, when Marble it self shall be turned into common dust.[47]

Through sermons like these, New England's history would survive and, at the hands of third-generation ministers like Cotton Mather, be elevated to a status nearly equal with that of the founders.

Along with the children's changing perceptions of their own generation came a changed perception of England. For most of their lives the second generation labored in relative obscurity and isolation as "Sion's Outcasts." They had fashioned an independent identity for themselves that largely ignored England and drew instead from the ancient model of Israel and Scripture promises of a New Israel in a New World. Only at the end of their lives, amidst revolution and royal government, did circumstances force them to take into account the Old World their parents had left behind. Clearly the third generation would enjoy no such isolation. They would be thrust into a larger world where, at every turn, the faces of English institutions, customs, and officials would have to be recognized and reconciled to the original mission of New England. If, in the new atmosphere of liberal toleration and imitation of things English, the grandchildren forgot their legacy and were, in Cotton Mather's words, "permitted to run wild in our woods," they would "soon be forsaken by that God whom our fathers followed hither." But if churches and families used their liberties to continue nurturing the youth who were already "very sharp and early ripe in their capacities, above most in the world," then mankind could expect that "our little New England may soon produce them that shall be commanders of the greatest glories that America can pretend unto."[48] New England's period of isolation, Mather was certain, was over. It would be up to the grandchildren to preserve the covenant in a new century and in an increasingly anglicized provincial society.

PART III

STYLE, 1701–1730

[7]

Anglicization

At the close of the seventeenth century, a third generation of ministers completed their studies at Harvard College and entered pulpits throughout the land. Many, like Nathaniel and Cotton Mather, Urian Oakes, Jr., Samuel Danforth, Jr., Thomas Shepard III, John Cotton III, or Grindall Rawson, had grown up as the sons and grandsons of illustrious ministers and magistrates, and were virtually commissioned to lead in their generation as their fathers and grandfathers before them. Other ministers who came to maturity in these years shared with their well-connected contemporaries a cohesive set of experiences: Harvard College, English rule, religious toleration, and wars with France. These experiences would shape their perceptions of New England's mission-in-the-world in new and more tolerant directions. Marcus Hansen's three-generation model of the immigrant experience, according to which the first generation preserves their Old World identity, the second generation casts off their parents' culture, and the third generation acts to reclaim Old World customs and traditions, may not apply to all immigrant groups, but it certainly describes the English colonial experience in New England.[1] The founders and their children, because of English persecution or imperial indifference, grew up in relatively isolated, self-contained circumstances. The third generation, however, was thrust into a larger Anglo-American world where they discovered, much to their "delight" (a term which came to enjoy unprecedented popularity in pulpit usage), that they could enjoy the benefits of England's culture *without* sacrificing their commitment to the covenant. They were Congregational "liberals" who would enjoy the best of both worlds.

Historians have described this early eighteenth-century receptivity to British influence and ideas as "anglicization."[2] The causes of anglicization were diverse and included the presence of English ruling officials and English laws of toleration, increased trade, military cooperation, and widespread reading in English letters. Added to these influences was the new English influence particularly apparent among educated and mercantile elites in the coastal cities. Most obviously, anglicization operated as a political force reshaping institutions of law and government to conform to English practice. Less immediately, but more pervasively, it was a cultural force, transforming ideas about nature, design, and beauty. At the same time New England reestablished its cultural ties with the mother country, England was experiencing an intellectual revolution that was redefining its universe and expanding the boundaries of natural knowledge in all directions. The age of Cotton Mather, Urian Oakes, Jr., and Thomas Shepard III was also the age of Newton, Locke, Addison, and Tillotson. No well-read provincial could escape the excitement these luminaries were generating in science, literature, epistemology, and ethics; nor could they resist English influence in dress, speech, literary style, or architecture. For New England elites, England supplied standards of urbanity, sophistication, and broad-mindedness to be emulated for both intellectual and social reasons.

Yet there was still another set of standards that derived from the covenant and weighed heavily on the New England conscience, limiting the extent of cultural borrowing. Alongside celebrations of England's Enlightenment, the covenant continued to give New Englanders a sense of common purpose and corporate identity that set them apart from other peoples. In matters of government, science, literature, wealth, and taste they knew themselves to be imitators and parvenus; but in the all-important matter of world redemption they were still a chosen people second to none. Ministers might clothe old truths in new styles and vocabularies, but they did not abandon the original terms of settlement. The people's future depended on English attention and protection, but even more it depended on their willingness to keep the covenant. Sooner or later that message came through in virtually every occasional pronouncement in the eighteenth century. Anglicization, in short, gilded the face of New England society but did not transform its soul.

THE REDEFINED ERRAND

The Revolutionary settlement did not affect the Congregational churches' position as the center of communal activity. It did, however, require that people view the mission of their churches in a different light. The first two generations had grown up believing that the Congregational Way was not simply a religious preference but a sacred commandment from which no deviations were permitted. *The Cambridge Platform* was what distinguished them from all other churches as the true church of Christ. New England colonists coming of age in the eighteenth century would define the true church by different criteria. They continued to believe the Congregational Way was scripturally defensible, and they *knew* it was best for New England's well-trained laity, but they no longer insisted that it was the only valid mode of order for Christ's church, or that a shared Congregational polity was the sine qua non of Christian union. For the more ecumenical third generation, a true church was defined by the degree to which church members and ministers incorporated values of

Christian piety (conversion) and moral rectitude into their society. Church governments, like civil governments, were "humane inventions" that were right or wrong only insofar as they promoted or discouraged pious faith and good works.[3] If New Englanders were to remain a spiritual *exemplum* for the world, it would not be so much for their Congregational design as for the enduring monuments of "piety and virtue" they exported to a sin-sick world.

The terms "piety," "virtue," and "union" were certainly not original to the third generation. But the frequency of their usage and expanded application to non-Congregational Protestants was new and a sign that a silent revolution had taken place in New England's corporate mission. With remarkably little fanfare or internal debate, the grandchildren altered the major categories of New England's ongoing errand just as they had altered their past to fit the new circumstances. Many historians see in their new emphases on morality and ecumenical union a betrayal or secularization of the theocratic Puritan state. But this view underrates the ways in which the third generation acted to retain as much of the original Puritan errand as possible; their new terms and emphases were not intended to belittle the world of the founders but to preserve it in terms an enlightened century could understand and embrace.

Cotton Mather understood the implications of English rule and religious toleration as clearly as anyone in his generation, and he set out to redefine New England's errand in terms that European Protestants of a Reformed persuasion could admire and emulate. Because of Mather's family name and his stupendous output of over four hundred publications he was *the* voice of New England Puritanism to the outside world. Mather remained a strict Congregationalist to his dying day, but this was not the platform from which he trumpeted New England's glory. Rather, New England's virtue, as in other Protestant churches and nations, was measured by its willingness to forge an "evangelical" union of "piety and morality" that would confront the powers of darkness and speed the course of God's coming millennial kingdom. To be part of this united front, people did not have to be Congregationalists, but they did have to be zealous for "well-doing": "Let no man pretend unto the name of *a Christian*, who does not approve the proposal of *a perpetual endeavor to do good in the world.*" Without a commitment to sanctified obedience and goodness, the millennial kingdom would not dawn. But through well-doing, God would make his presence known and return to earth in power and glory.[4]

As the third generation has been maligned for its betrayal of Puritan piety and inept imitation of England, so its greatest spokesman has been ridiculed as a pedantic—even neurotic—moralist. Beginning with the young Benjamin Franklin's satirical essays on "Silence Do Good," students of eighteenth-century Puritanism have interpreted Mather's preoccupation with "piety and morality" as symptomatic of a shift from piety to moralism that marked the end of the authentic New England Way.[5]

These studies emphasize Mather's teachings on doing good at the expense of his equally forthright (and traditional) emphasis on supernatural conversion as the necessary precondition to God-pleasing works. In fact, Mather used the terms "piety" and "morality" in exactly the same way as his predecessors. Like previous covenant theologians, he insisted that for good works to please God "the *first* thing, and indeed the One thing, that is *needful*, is, a glorious work of GRACE on the soul, renewing and quickening of it, and *purifying* of the sinner, and rendering him *Zealous of good works*: a *workmanship* of God upon us, creating us over again, by Jesus Christ, *for good works*."[6] Mather's words (and those of third-generation preaching generally) were distinguished not by the emphasis on right living but by the careful avoidance of any intimation that non-Congregationalists were counterfeit Christians incapable of true virtue.

By emphasizing piety and good works over proper polity, third-generation ministers made possible an anglicization of preaching and religion alongside that of politics and culture. The limits of religious borrowing and rapprochement varied from minister to minister and from congregation to congregation. But in their theological reading and in their preaching, all demonstrated a new willingness to accommodate outside influences. Mather's ecumenicity was limited largely to English Presbyterians, although Baptists and Anglicans of a "Reformed" persuasion were not excluded. If these diverse traditions could not agree on common patterns of worship and church order, they could band together in voluntary "Reforming societies" that would work for "the execution of wholesome *laws*, whereby *vice* is to be discouraged." Such societies, he observed, already existed in England and incorporated "virtuous men of diverse qualities and persuasions": "persons high and low, con[forming] and non-con[forming], united; the union become formidable to the Kingdom of Darkness."[7] By prescribing a realm of ecumenical cooperation that did not affect local preferences in worship, Mather hoped to free the New England churches to participate in a union with English "brethren" without sacrificing traditional commitments to Congregational polity. His terms were chosen carefully with an eye to international recognition and respectability, at the same time as they preserved New England's right to keep their distinctive Congregational heritage.

Other New England ministers went further in accommodating themselves to non-Congregational ideas and practices. Chief among these more extreme innovators was a group of anti-Mather Boston ministers and laymen led by Harvard tutor (later president) John Leverett, Cambridge pastor William Brattle, and his merchant brother Thomas. These gentlemen shared a commitment to traditional Calvinism but combined it with a tolerance for diverse traditions, including the Church of England. As a group, they "did not place Religion so much in *particular Forms*, and modes of Worship, or Discipline, as in those substantial and *weighty matters* of the Gospel, *Righteousness, Faith and* Charity."[8] Together they formed the Brattle Street Church in Boston whose "catholic spirit" drew deeply from the Church of England as well as from Presbyterianism. In 1699, they installed Benjamin Colman as their pastor without benefit of a local ordination. Under Colman's ministry, tests for saving grace were abandoned and communion was open to all. The liturgy was substantially anglicized to include Scripture readings without commentary and public recitations of the Lord's Prayer—practices long identified with the Church of England.[9] While their extreme adaptation of Anglican forms was never widely adopted, they were accepted by the other churches in New England and wielded considerable influence on their society and on the college at Cambridge.

THE NEW LEARNING AT HARVARD
AND OCCASIONAL PREACHING

The influence of the Brattle group at Harvard College was especially significant. Next to the provincial government, no institution was more threatened by the new government or underwent more sweeping changes than Harvard. For some time the status and direction of the college was in doubt. The first question was who would control it once the original charter was revoked. Within the college there was a contest for control between the Mather faction (father and son) and the anti-Mather faction led by John Leverett and Thomas Brattle, and their "liberal" ministerial allies. These issues were not resolved until 1707, when Governor Joseph Dudley restored the college's charter of 1650 on condition that John Leverett—not Increase Mather—would succeed Samuel Willard as president.[10] Leverett was the only nonminister president before the nineteenth century, and under his long tenure (1708–1724) the college changed in subtle but far-reaching ways. By 1718, enrollment jumped to 124 students, including many who were preparing for vocations other than the ministry. Ministerial students continued to be the largest group at the college, but they were no longer the hub around which the college revolved. Alongside them were future judges, merchants, magistrates, and royal officers who, Leverett realized, must be prepared to participate in the expanding Anglo-American world on its own terms. Many of these students came, in Samuel Eliot Morison's words, "to be made gentlemen, not to study [divinity]."[11] Leverett's challenge (and accomplishment) was to retain the college's historic mission of supplying learned and orthodox prophets, without impeding its progress into an enlightened age.

In order to blunt the criticisms of archconservatives like Boston's leading magistrate, Samuel Sewall, or the Mathers, who were constantly on the lookout for excessively tolerant (and nonorthodox) Anglican "highflyers," Leverett introduced no sweeping changes in the college curriculum or in the laws governing student piety.[12] But he did assign more importance to natural science and history, and deemphasized rhetoric. Just as science supplied lessons about God's vastness and sense of design, history taught great and enduring moral lessons with a sciencelike precision. Alongside sacred history, which had always occupied a central place in colonial thought, students began absorbing the "Whig" history of liberty as it came to be articulated in the aftermath of the Glorious Revolution. Of particular note to informed colonial New Englanders was a radical group of "country" theorists or "commonwealthmen" who championed popular liberties and the commons over against the crown and aristocracy.[13] These histories of liberty were never widely endorsed by English elites, but by the mid-eighteenth century they were being read almost as thoroughly as the sacred history of New England. Together, sacred and Whig histories supplied lessons that would guide ecclesiastical and political thought throughout the century.

Even more important than the new emphases in classroom instruction were the changes Leverett encouraged in general student reading. By the eighteenth century, both Harvard and the newly founded Yale College in New Haven (1701) made additions to their libraries that embodied the substance and spirit of the New Learning.[14] Many of the new names appearing on library shelves were Anglican writers and ministers who were admired partly for their open-minded tolerance of different religious practices (including Puritan nonconformity) but even more for their brilliant style and clear thought. The New Learning supplied not only breathtaking discoveries in science but also new canons of literary style and philosophical taste, and even a new vocabulary that was assimilated into colonial speech and writing. Moral essays like Addison's *Pleasures of the Imagination* (1707) circulated widely at the colleges and encouraged student ventures into the literary realm of belles lettres. A student periodical, *The Telltale*, appeared at Harvard in direct imitation of the *London Spectator* and *London Magazine*. Even Cotton Mather tried his hand at satire and allegorization in a series of four *Political Fables* aimed at rival political factions in Boston. None of these compositions were literary classics but, as Perry Miller recognized, "they tried to be; they aimed at, if they did not quite attain, wit and urbanity, and deliberately sought to be amusing. They were an effort to bring the manners of London to solid Boston."[15]

Inevitably, exposure to new ideas and literary styles influenced ministerial students at the colleges. Anglican authors had been ignored in the first two generations. But a new generation of more tolerant Anglican preachers and essayists came to be widely read and admired for their pleasing style. According to the new liberal spirit, these authors could no longer be ignored simply because they endorsed a different polity. Truth and "elegance" (a new value) came from many sources and had to be taken wherever they appeared. Printed sermons continued to dominate the personal libraries of eighteenth-century colonials, but new voices appeared alongside the old. Among Anglican preachers, none was more widely read or admired than Archbishop John Tillotson. Part of his appeal could be traced to his Puritan upbringing and enduring friendliness to nonconformists, but more important was his literary style, which showed a preference for plain style and "natural" syntax, and shunned the bitter invective that treated every divergent point of view as "heretical," "Antinomian," or "Arminian."[16] Tillotson exemplified a polite style of elegance, grace, and ease that New England ministers could integrate with their own preaching heritage.

To express the sense of mechanical order and cosmic vastness common to the age, preachers like Tillotson adapted a new "aesthetics of the infinite" to their pulpits. The object of this new style was to stretch the imagination and overwhelm the soul with a sense of divine beauty and the "natural sublime."[17] Terms like "stupendous," "great," "sublime," "vast," "unlimited," "spacious," or "unbounded," recurred in descriptions of the visible universe to instill an intellectualized emotional response (or "sentiment") of "happiness," "pleasure," "joy," or, most frequently, "delight." God himself came to be referred to by such extrabiblical, mechanistic titles as "the Almighty Being," the "Father of Lights," the "Great Governor of the Universe," the "Almighty Hand," or the "Supreme Architect"—epithets that rarely appeared in seventeenth-century preaching. Along with scientific discoveries and the enoblement of reason came a more approachable, manlike God who could be imagined as "smiling" or "frowning" on his creation, and "overseeing" its operations according to flawless designs of structure that proceeded from self-perpetuating laws and principles. Assuming a "natural and easy" manner, preachers like Tillotson sought to capture the "essential truths of Christianity" that all Christians held in common and which could be deduced from nature as clearly as from Scripture.

The new vocabulary and style of English literature affected all colonial preaching, as we shall see, but its impact was most direct in election sermons at which royal audiences were present and speakers demonstrated, as clearly as their theology allowed, that they belonged in the eighteenth century. Like the student literary enterprises, most election sermons fell short of the studied ease and eloquence of a Tillotson or Barrow, but it was not for want of trying. Like the English stylists they admired, election speakers adopted the new language for social as well as aesthetic reasons. The study of English essayists and preachers not only introduced New England's leaders to the language and speech forms they would need to deal with royal agents; it supplied a style and cultural sensibility that set them apart from the rank and file at a time when their authority was increasingly called into question.

Accompanying the new discoveries and styles were social assumptions that confirmed the hierarchical attitudes of most New England civil and ecclesiastical leaders.[18] With Newtonian precision, essayists and preachers moved from nature to society and argued that the same God-ordained laws of greater and lesser, balance and proportion, which governed the pulls and orbits of the planets, also governed relations of superior and inferior social beings. The difference was that as volitional creatures, people could choose to break the laws governing society and upset godly order; they could destroy the very laws of hierarchy ordained for their welfare. Such "anarchy" was to be avoided as an affront both to nature and to nature's God.

As useful as such deferential principles seemed to leading ministers and magistrates, they were not eagerly endorsed by the populace, whose experience in the Glorious Revolution had taught them to question imposed authorities of all sorts. Aristocratic claims to superiority had been resisted before whenever they conflicted with popular liberties. Many ordinary inhabitants, and some leaders, believed that New England had conceded too much to aristocracy in its recovery of English rules and values, and they resisted the new pretensions at every turn. These conflicts were most dramatically apparent in politics, but they continued to plague the churches as well. Earlier in-house disputes paled in comparison to the factional contention that began once New England's political culture and institutions were formally severed from the Congregational churches. In Boston (where confrontations were most heated), a popular or "country" faction emerged under the leadership of the Elisha Cooke family. They asserted that government originated and continued as a voluntary covenant between all citizens. Stressing the popular basis of civil and ecclesiastical authority, they challenged aristocratic presumptions and urged the people of New England to oversee their rulers' policies and instruct them in the courses they preferred. Popular theories of authority equated "government" with the popular assemblies to the virtual exclusion of the executive branch and its "placemen" who lived on crown patronage.[19] Such theories were partly an outgrowth of the logic of Congregationalism as it had been internalized over three generations. Primarily, however, they reflected English Whig theories, which celebrated representative government and had begun to surface in New England. Thus, they too were an index of anglicization, but an index that most colonial leaders preferred to ignore.

Opposing the popular party was a "court" faction made up of successful merchants, crown appointees, cultural anglophiles, and many ministers, who feared mass participation in government and clung to the crown as a necessary source of stability and order.[20] While conceding—even demanding—the peoples' right to election in their popular assemblies and congregations, they feared an excess of "democracy" in which ordinary people would presume to instruct their betters. The central theme running throughout court writings and occasional sermons was the need for order. As the popular party looked to elective privileges under the old charter, so the court faction held fast to the traditional image of society as a hierarchy of mutually exclusive superior and inferior orders. Such a hierarchy, they believed, required a single authority at the top (the crown and its appointees), which no persons (including the popular assemblies) could touch. Having witnessed the unending bickering and insubordination to which the "giddy People" were prone, court ministers believed, with Benjamin Wadsworth, that "Tho' *Tyranny* is burdensome and *hateful*, yet it's counted a *smaller evil* than meer *Anarchy*, and confusion."[21]

New England needed the strong central authority of the English crown, both for internal stability and for external protection from rampaging French and Indian enemies who, by 1702, were engaged in yet another war for New World dominion. Better to ally with a crown who promised protection and religious liberty than with a people who seemed bent on reducing all to chaos. Anarchy had not yet destroyed New England society, and ministers worked with their oratorical styles and institutional arrangements to ensure that it never would.

THE LIMITS OF NEW LEARNING

There were limitations to New England's anglicization, especially in terms of preaching and the dissemination of an official cultural identity. To a much greater extent than their second-generation predecessors, third-generation ministers were in an ambiguous position, their identity as intellectuals and cultural guardians at odds with their identity as preachers of the Word. As intellectuals, they participated in the Anglo-American "Republic of Letters" and, on occasion, sought to make their own modest contributions to the rising fund of knowledge. But as Congregational ministers answerable to Bible-reading congregations, they were obliged to shed their provincial preoccupations and proclaim the inherited truths of revelation as they had been taught from childhood. The effect of these conflicting impulses was that ministers would borrow the polite style of their English models but apply it to a restatement of New England's inherited covenant and ongoing errand into the wilderness.

To the extent that refined English pulpit oratory could reconcile divine revelation with the new sciences and reaffirm traditional assertions of God's orderliness in nature and society it was a welcome support for New England ministers. In England, however, natural theology and the light of reason threatened not to augment revelation but to displace it, and that was something no Congregational minister in New England was prepared (or allowed) to do. English theology and preaching (particularly Anglican) was, to most Puritan sensibilities, moving dangerously close to "deism"—a natural theology that minimized *Sola Scriptura* and elevated natural reason to equal or superior status in the discovery and implementation of divine truth. Seeking a common ground for all Protestant Christians, English latitudinarians reduced religion to a system of morality or "virtue" upon which all could agree. Salvation was presented less as a supernatural infusion of grace than as a leap of the aesthetic imagination into the divine wonders of the universe.[22]

On two counts, a purely natural theology was unacceptable even to the most liberal and open-minded New England ministers. First, it ignored the familiar Scripture teachings on sin and supernatural grace that congregations knew by heart. It was a truism of New England pulpit teaching that the natural man—no matter how wise and enlightened—was incapable of reconciling himself to God. This reconciliation could be accomplished only through the intervention of the Holy Spirit, often in time of the sermon. Second, natural theology threatened New England's original mission. The inevitable tendency of natural theology was to move God so far to the periphery of human action that the concept of an active divine providence lost all historical meaning; natural laws and causal forces explained all. Neither ministers nor congregations were willing to exchange their sacred birthright and ongoing cultural identity for the heady stuff of membership in the Republic of Letters. However much they might admire English culture and draw from its storehouse of new discoveries and luminous prose, there were limits to their provincial mentality—limits that would become clear wherever English reason and pretensions threatened to undermine their sacred destiny.

Ironically, New England's anglicized generation was also a generation with an unrivaled determination to preserve its own past. Instead of sacrificing the founders' messianic mission for England's enlightened present, third-generation ministers combined their cultural borrowing with an ambitious effort to collect and print everything in their past that confirmed their identity as a covenant people. For them, New England's history represented the extension of Holy Writ into the eighteenth century. The tendency of third-generation ministers to record and "idealize" their past in virtually every tract and occasional sermon cannot be accounted for solely in terms of disillusionment with the present or nostalgic yearning for a simpler past.[23] Something far more powerful was at work in their ancestor worship: a deep-seated conviction, nurtured over three New England generations, that if they did not know their history they did not know God. Reason could deduce certain conclusions about God's nature, and Scripture could add knowledge about God's special plan of redemption for all humanity; but only the history of New England could verify the continued applicability of federal covenants and document God's continued involvement in the affairs of men and of nations. Without New England's history, revelation would be anachronistic and incomplete. The colonists' record of covenant making, church formation, and remarkable deliverances contained lessons about God's dealing with nations not duplicated anywhere else—lessons every bit as revealing of God's will and providential oversight as the Old Testament books of Moses, the New Testament book of Acts, or Foxe's *Book of Martyrs*.

The seeds of the third generation's fascination with their unique sacred history had been sown by their parents. Increase Mather had pointed out that much of the Old Testament comprised nothing more than a series of "chronicles" recording the experiences of God's people over time. Because New England was the New Israel, Mather went on, their own experiences should be "faithfully recorded and transmitted to posterity" to bring the history of redemption up to date.[24] These chronicles would be more important to New Englanders' self-identity than the royal charter; they would demonstrate that God continued to be involved and interested in their affairs above those of any other nation on earth. Increase Mather's own chronicle of King Philip's War and his subsequent *An Essay for the Recording of Illustrious Providences* were models for the sort of history he had in mind: an account of the inspired leaders and supernatural deliverances that confirmed New England's identity as a peculiar people of God.

By the eighteenth century, with the aid of the technologically improved printing presses at Cambridge, Boston, Hartford, and New London, ministers were producing a torrent of fast, thanksgiving, funeral, and election sermons that set forth the record of God's stupendous providences in New England. And indeed, on days of fasting and thanksgiving every minister rehearsed the general and local history of New England.

COTTON MATHER AND THE PROVIDENTIAL MEANING OF NEW ENGLAND

Cotton Mather's was the most remarkable history of New England ever produced: the *Magnalia Christi Americana*. Of all the third-generation ministers, he was best equipped for such a work. He had the living memories of his father to draw from as well as a prodigious memory of his own. Moreover, he possessed an enormous library handed down from two generations, collections of published and unpublished documents that were the envy of New England.[25] Perhaps most important, however, was Mather's indefatigable zeal for the glory of New England and almost mystical faith in the power of writing to supply meaning and direction to his own life. To an extraordinary degree, Mather lived his life for posterity. A piece of advice from his preaching manual for young ministers was, in reality, his own personal creed:

> If they persecute you with *Libels*, 'tis a notable Hint, that *Le Clerc* has given you. Instead of answering them, write such learned and useful *Books*, as will be of *perpetual Service* to Mankind. . . . These *Books* will be durable Monuments of your Valuable and Honourable Character, when the Libels of these poor *Animalculicuncles* will perish among the *Wast-Paper*, which the *Haberdashers of small Wares* have occasion for.[26]

No founder expressed such a faith in print or would have done so in such a stilted literary style, but by the third generation, New England had a remarkable history that needed to be told and preserved in Scripture-like chronicles. And Mather was the man to tell it. The *Magnalia* would be his "monument" to the "New English Jerusalem" and would ensure that in the new age, "whether *New-England* may *live* any where else or no, it must *live* in our *History!*"

Mather wrote his epic church history during the tumultuous years between 1694 and 1698, and published it in England in 1702. At the time of its publication the *Magnalia* failed to win the fame he craved—both for New England and for himself. But it *did* live on among later historians.

They mocked its baroque style but depended upon it as an unequaled mine of anecdotal and documentary evidence that survived nowhere else.[27] Indeed, without the *Magnalia* much of New England's civil and ecclesiastical history would be lost.

Apart from its broad scope and ponderous style, Mather's work was distinguished by its rhetorical appeal. Many parts of the history originated as commemorative or funeral sermons, and these set the tone for the entire work. Throughout, Mather remained the preacher-historian who invited his readers—both American and European—to view America from the vantage point of sacred history. When addressing royal audiences, no one celebrated New England's legacy of civil liberties or loyalty to the crown more avidly than Mather. But when it came to unveiling the innermost meaning of New England for world history, crown loyalties disappeared and the theme of providence dominated all. The most important question he asked the reader to consider was, "What can I see of the Glorious GOD in these ocurrences?" What he saw in the unfolding saga of New England was the calling of an elect nation and a history that was nothing short of miraculous. The Great Migration, in which thousands survived shipwreck and scurvy and made it "as upon eagels' wings" to the New World, was only the beginning of a remarkable story that had no living counterpart:

> If we were able to recount the singular workings of divine providence, for the bringing on this work, to what it is come unto, it would stop the mouths of all. . . . Look from one end of the heaven unto another, whether the Lord hath assayed to do such a work as this, in any nation! *to carry out a people of his own, from so flourishing a state, to a wilderness so far distant, for such ends, and for such a work; yea, and in few years hath done for them, as he hath here done, for his poor despised people.*[28]

In Mather's hands, New England's history was not that of a provincial colony condemned to live out its existence as an obscure appendage to the great London metropolis but rather the story of a great nation whose experiences ought to "stop the mouths of all."

The only historical precedent was Israel. Like every preacher before him, Mather interwove the history of New England with the history of Israel so completely that it became one integrated narrative.[29] Instead of likening the Great Migration to the Exodus, as the first two generations did (identifying England with Egypt), Mather went back to Noah's experience after the flood. He combined that narrative with the equally familiar metaphor of an "errand," which had symbolized New England's mission in famous sermons by John Wilson and Samuel Danforth:

> The people in the fleet that arrived at *New-England*, in the year 1630 left the fleet almost, as the *family* of *Noah* did the ark, having a whole world before them to be peopled. . . . Where-ever they sat down, they were so mindful of their *errand* into the wilderness, that still one of their *first works* was to gather a church into the covenant and order of the gospel.

In tracing the course of settlement, Mather moved from the churches to the first ministers and magistrates, and he assigned to each a typological parallel to the patriarchs of old. Most dramatic was Mather's depiction of Governor Winthrop who "did as our *New-English Nehemiah*, the part of a *Ruler* in managing the public affairs of our *American Jerusalem*." Through his faith, wisdom, and generosity, Winthrop made himself (and was made by providence) "an exacter *parallel* unto that governor of Israel."[30] Through typology, Mather infused New England's history with the strongest possible sacred significance in terms lifted directly from Scripture records. As in Puritan sermons, the use of this language was not a literary device but was seen as appropriate to part of a single revelation of light and guidance to a lost creation.

A subordinate theme in the *Magnalia* was human faith working itself out in loving obedience or waning in misdirected disobedience. God's providence was remarkable, but so too was the faith of the founders who, despite their "*natural affections* to our dear country," risked all "in the hopes of enjoying Christ in his ordinances, in the fellowship of his people." For Mather, it was axiomatic that God would only work his miracles among a people he had first "*redeemed* and *purified* unto himself."[31] God was the author and finisher of New England's faith, and Mather could trace his history from the pious founders to the backslidden third generation in the confidence that New England's destruction was "not yet." Mather concluded by returning to the mercy and patience of God that sustained New England in times of shaky faith. Such times, alas, marked the present. To the present generation of New Englanders and to English observers he would exclaim:

> Above all, we must acknowledge the singular pity and mercies of our God, that hath done all this, and much more, for a people so *unworthy*, so sinful, that by *murmurings* of many, *unfaithfulness in promises, oppressions*, and other *evils* . . . that the Lord should yet own us, and rather correct us in mercy, than cast us off in displeasure and scatter us in this wilderness; which gives us cause to say, "*Who is a God like our God, that pardons iniquities, and passes by the transgressions of the remnant of his heritage; even because he delighteth in mercy!*"[32]

By looking into their past even as they marched into an uncharted future, New Englanders retained an identity that supplied continuity and cohesion in all circumstances.

A MULTIVALENT LANGUAGE

The *Magnalia* was unique in its scope and style, but it embodied assumptions about God's active governance of the universe and special regard for New England that were as common to third-generation Congregationalists as gravity and heliocentric theories of planetary motion.

In rhetorical practice, third-generation ministers adjusted to eighteenth-century cultural and political realities by adopting a multivalent vocabulary that deliberately conveyed different messages to different audiences through a single vocabulary. English latitudinarians like Henry More, John Trenchard, or the third earl of Shaftesbury could clothe seventeenth-century concepts of the covenant, eupraxia, or the "heart" in secular garb to elaborate new systems of ethics, psychology, and politics. New England ministers did the same in reverse.[33] They embraced new terminologies that enjoyed secular meanings in England but which in New England were turned to a traditional defense of inherited religious beliefs and values that would hold New England to the covenant.

The new rhetoric was especially evident in election sermons where speakers sequentially addressed external royal authorities and the country-as-a-whole. When addressing crown representatives they would expropriate the language and style of polite English culture and celebrate the "light of nature" and the secular genius of England's constitution that upheld the people's "liberty" to enjoy "peace" and "happiness." But when addressing popular audiences or their elected representatives, they specified exactly what "liberty," "peace," and "happiness" meant in terms of New England's covenant with God. For protecting New England's constitutional liberties (and property), the good ruler deserved the highest loyalties of the people. But only by observing the terms of the covenant could the people be assured of possessing churches and properties for their good governors to protect. And rulers had to understand that they must tolerate New England's covenant or find themselves with nothing to rule. Finally, English rights and liberties came to mean nothing more than the old covenant duties of obedience and submission to the dictates of *Sola Scriptura*.

Studies of eighteenth-century election sermons have often focused only on those sections of sermons directed to royal audiences and have defined government solely in terms of liberty and property. These studies point to numerous instances where entire paragraphs of election sermons were devoted to considerations of rights, property, and social rank that had no foundation in Scripture but relied instead on English law and the light of reason. They have noted, furthermore, how the style and terminology of election sermons moved in more literary, urbane directions, complete with sententious sayings, extra commas and italics, Latin quotations, and classical allusions—all qualities having more in common with secular pamphlets than with sacred oratory. Such passages, they conclude, show the birth pangs of a "secular state" in which "Yankee" elites "needed English constitutional rulers, not Christian magistrates," and where "the threat of a broken covenant or an angry Lord no longer affected New Englanders as it had in former days."[34] Such observations do show how rapidly third-generation ministers absorbed new styles of speech and new vocabularies drawn from English constitutional theory, but they pass over the sacred portions of election sermons, which were addressed primarily to New England audiences and used to convey theology. Nor do these studies consider the fact that election orators could speak of government in such secular terms because they had separated "government" from its earlier theocratic identification with "society." Because government was no longer the coercive arm of the Congregational churches, ministers could describe it as a neutral referee or secular creation without minimizing the continuing importance of the churches to New England's well-being. Government no longer had to enforce piety, but this did not release New England society from covenant obligations that would be observed and enforced through the churches, colleges, and families. Election speakers made sure that New Englanders had ample cause to fear an angry God, and there is no evidence to suggest that their threats carried any less weight than before.

The persistence of covenant prescriptions and historical recall in election sermons is particularly evident in Connecticut, where speakers did not have to address a royal governor. But even in Massachusetts, providential themes and biblical allusions continued to dominate the discourse in terms that could be distinguished from earlier election sermons only by their more expansive literary style.[35] This fusion of old and new can be seen to best advantage in Samuel Danforth, Jr.'s, election sermon of 1714, which for sheer artistry ranks near the top of sermons written in his generation. Danforth's prose reads less like the seventeenth-century style epitomized by his own father's 1670 address on New England's "errand into the wilderness" than the more naturalistic preaching that attained its peak in the pulpit artistry of Jonathan Edwards (then an eleven-year-old prodigy in East Windsor, Connecticut). And, just as Edwards later would, Danforth brought that style to a defense of traditional themes in Puritan preaching.

One of Danforth's most apparent stylistic innovations is the sustained use of a single metaphor, in this instance the "vineyard," throughout his discourse.[36] The image was derived from Psalm 80:14–15, where the writer implored God to "look down from heaven, and behold, and visit this vine." Before turning to his doctrine, Danforth observed that Scripture frequently used "similitudes from things common and obvious" to point out supernatural truths. Such was also the purpose of his sermon, whose simple metaphor was meant to show how God cultivated nations to "become plants of renown among whom Christ loves to walk. . . . He delights himself with the observation of the flourishing of this his vineyard." Danforth turned his metaphor quickly to traditional themes. Israel was the first sacred vineyard to enjoy God's attention and "delight." They enjoyed the fruits of peace, liberty, and property "on condition that they kept his precepts." When Israel, "out of carnal policy," imitated their neighbors in false worship, God "made their friends turn to be their enemies" and transformed nature from an ally to an enemy such that "one frown of God's face was . . . sufficient to blast, wither, and dry up the tender plants of his vineyard."[37] God's "frowns," like his delight, were bestowed in direct proportion to the obedience of his people.

Like earlier election speakers, Danforth traced the vine of sacred history through successive gentile nations whom God "visited" with special privileges and blessings. These visitations were selective and governed by the same condition of obedience that applied to Israel. New England was another such "religious people by a visible profession" who were planted to give "vision" to the world. Despite predictable "great decays and declensions," the churches remained healthy, giving the people cause "to bless God who gives some revivals of his work, sometimes in one church and sometimes in another; and from thence should [all] be encouraged to plead with God for a more general effusion of his Spirit upon all his Churches, that all parts of his vineyard may flourish."[38]

Turning his attention to the royal governor, Joseph Dudley, Danforth sustained his metaphor in a properly respectful manner. If New England encountered times of trouble, the fault could not be laid at the feet a good civil ruler who succeeded so well

> in managing the civil affairs of this Province so . . . that the vineyard of the Lord of hosts therein hath enjoyed tranquility hitherto; and in giving forth proclamations and exhortations to your people here from time to time to excite and encourage them to set about the work of reformation; and in countenancing and encouraging the propagation of religion, the planting of it in the dark corners of our land, and the upholding of it where it was planted.

Rather, the blame for calamities belonged to a headstrong people who, given the liberty to worship according to their consciences, ignored the words of their ministers. Those ministers were the covenant's lifeline, and thanks to royal support they continued to overspread the land:

> This success of the laborers in God's vineyard consists in the upholding of religion where it is set up and in planting and propagating of it to other places. It is the good hand of God working for his people which provides pastors after his own heart for his Church successively from age to age. . . . Again, it is a gracious visit from heaven that causes this vine to propagate, so that as people are multiplied, churches also should be multiplied and more ministerial vineyards and gardens enclosed for our Lord Jesus to take delight in and to walk in the midst of.[39]

God's vineyard was defined by his churches and ministers and not by civil rulers who were more like "managers" than custodians. The errand of New England society was the same in 1714 as it was in 1670, but custody now was given—temporarily at least—solely to the churches.

If election sermons preserved the original mission alongside their royal encomiums, fast and thanksgiving sermons did so to an even greater extent. Unlike election sermons, which addressed multiple audiences, fast sermons were local and internal, and so required fewer rhetorical adjustments. Ministers could deliver them using a form and terms that were virtually unchanged from prior generations. The rhetoric of failure continued to dominate, and with it the specter of an avenging God whose patience was nearly spent. In words that might easily have been heard fifty years earlier, Grindal Rawson warned in 1709 that "a dark and black day is hastening on you; it is coming; it is coming apace, but through the wonderful and astonishing Patience of God, it is not yet come; Nothing can prevent its coming but your Repentance, and Reformation." Even in Brattle Street's more liberal atmosphere, fast day warnings were equally harsh. As William Brattle pointed out, "It is our Reformation God aims at in his punishing us. . . . Consider that God is angry with us for our neglect of our duty. . . . Consider that if we continue and go in the neglect of our duty . . . his anger will be increased and his judgments multiplied upon us."[40] As before, the fast was the time when the people contemplated the fearful magnitude of God's anger and found the incentive to confess their sins and amend their evil ways.

Of all the "procuring evils" in need of reformation, popular insubordination and the pursuit of wealth ranked highest. Success was cause for grave alarm because it gave rise to pride and inordinate attachment to "the world," especially for eighteenth-century provincials whose opportunities for profit making were unexcelled. In a fast sermon to his Hatfield congregation, William Williams lingered over the sin of acquisitiveness: "Men often wrong their Souls, and wound their Consciences, as well as blast their Reputation, when they take any unrighteous ways of gain; defraud, oppress, and overreach in their dealings; dont deal truly and honestly; or neglect paying of just debts; or necessary acts of Charity." Such individuals "dare not depend upon Divine Providence, or the encouragement of the Promise [of success]." Too many farmers, tradesmen, and land speculators were caught in what Samuel Danforth, Jr.'s, brother John termed "This *Sheba*, SELF"—the all-out pursuit of self-aggrandizement that came at the expense of corporate loyalty and mutual commitment. Material aspirations were insidious; they were like a deafening "Trumpet of Rebellion" in which "*Self* is the *Idol*, and the *Oracle* [so] that men will hear nothing against it, tho' spoken by the LORD Himself." By charging excessive interest, speculating, or exploiting wartime contracts at the public's expense, such entrepreneurs endangered the covenant, and this for no other purpose than "*to take their Ease and to Eat and Drink, and be Merry*."[41] While English law allowed such transactions to take place, God's law did not, and that was the law New Englanders heard at the fast.

For the most part, fast sermons pointed to public sins that could not be blamed on an unfaithful ministry. "We live in a land of *Light*," Williams confidently proclaimed in the same fast sermon, and "it is not the want of *Light*, but the want of *Improving* and *Submitting* to the Light that we have, that retards the Reformation, which hath so long been called for."[42] Third-generation ministers saw clearly how the increase in trade and introduction of English manners and dress threatened to inject sinful pride into the lives of modest tradesmen and wealthy merchants. They saw less clearly, however, that anglicization affected their own ministries in equally direct fashion. The ministers had in fact become as caught up in court manners as merchants and magistrates. Immediately after inveighing against the "vile prophanations of prosperity," for example, Danforth followed with a collection of witty aphorisms and turgid prose which reflected the very anglicization of literary style that he bemoaned in mercantile life styles:

> As *Selfishness* is their *Disease*, so Temporal *Prosperity* is the *Diet*, that is perverted to nourish that *Disease*. The Fatter the Soil, the Ranker the Weeds; The more Drink, the more Dropsie; the more Gunpowder, the fiercer Blast. A Sword in the Hands of a Murderous Villain, not only Arms the Man, but also Arms his Vice. Prosperity Equips and mounts a proud man; affords Idols to the Covetous, and furnishes the Drunkard and Sensual Epicure to fill up his measure: *Vessels* excessively and most richly Laden, do often sink with over-much *Weight*. The Spider doth not draw more nourishment for her *Poison* from the *wholesome Flowers*, than *Self-Idolizers* do from their Temporal *Prosperity*.[43]

Again New England society was changing, and again the ministers were bound by the long-standing rhetorical form of the fast to separate themselves from the process and to blame New England's woes on a lapsed generation.

THE SWORD OF THE COVENANT

Third-generation ministers, like their predecessors, found no shortage of natural and man-made calamities to document God's controversy with his people and call for fasting. In addition to the familiar summer droughts, bone-chilling winters, and harvest blasts, came a new wave of smallpox epidemics and raging fires that were especially severe in urban areas where, as the ministers noted, the commercial economy was most active.[44] Most ominous, however, was the specter of war and foreign invasion that repeatedly haunted New England. No sooner was King William's War ended than Queen Anne's War began (1702–1713), bringing new military defeats in Canada and the northern frontier, unprecedented debts, the highest taxes in North America, and a growing class of war widows and orphans to burden already overstrained charity rolls.[45] Added to this were even more serious losses in manpower as battle casualties, malnutrition, and shipboard disease took their toll. At any given time in the war years up to one-fifth of the region's able-bodied men were drawn into frontier expeditions or naval assaults, and many never returned home. No other colony suffered losses comparable to those of New England, and war did not occupy a central place in their thought as it did in New England. So ominous was the threat of war in New England that court-country tensions in government were temporarily laid aside as the governor and assembly worked together to strengthen internal defenses and prosecute the ambitious (if futile) expeditions to Canada.[46]

At no time did ministers sound the supportive themes of transcendent hope and corporate rebuke more dramatically than in times of war. In one sense, war was a judgment for New England's sins. Following a failed expedition to Port Royal in 1709, Grindal Rawson inquired whether "the Lord [hath] drawn out the Sword of the Covenant against us? Has it not for almost four and thirty years, with little Intermission devoured much Flesh, and increased the number of the Lord's slain in the Land? . . . Has not the Stink of our Camps been sent into our Nostrils, and our hopefulest Expeditions frowned upon and disappointed [us], so that our Enemies laugh amongst themselves, and those that hate us clap their hands?"[47] Yet in another sense, war was necessary to their identity as a nation of war, commissioned to engage the forces of Antichrist wherever they appeared. Ministers were faced with the problem of separating that aspect of war which was a judgment for New England's sins from that aspect which was a necessary consequence of their righteous identity as Christ's army. Typically, ministers approached the problem in pragmatic fashion: general discussions of war or actual victories were couched in optimistic, assured terms, whereas defeats were interpreted as judgments for sin. Defeat, not war, was the punishment New Englanders could expect if they turned away from the covenant.

In practice, the occasions for proclamations of judgment on the one hand and optimistic hope on the other followed the division of rhetorical labor as fixed by the second generation. Fast sermons typically employed harsh Old Testament texts to concentrate on themes of rebuke and judgment, whereas militia sermons employed triumphant passages to arouse sentiments of hope and supremacy. In both cases, themes of military strategy or logistical support were subordinated to providence and covenant keeping. In an unpublished fast sermon to his Windsor, Connecticut, congregation in 1709, following "Our fatal disappointment in our expedition against our French and Indian Enemies," Timothy Edwards (father of Jonathan) explained that defeat was a corrective affliction, not a sign of divine desertion. When God's people failed to acknowledge the messages contained in divine mercies, then God "trys afflictions and the Rods of anger. He makes use of many angry frowning dispensations." The remedy for divine rebukes was painfully familiar, even if the afflictions were new: "Sincere Repentance and hearty and Real returning unto God is the proper voice and Loude call of the Judgments of God . . . the Judgments of God do with a Loud voice call upon a Sinfull and disobedient people to Repent and Return unto the Lord."[48] Only through repentance could New England hope for victory. Only then, as William Williams explained in characteristically eighteenth-century prose, would "God . . . bless Our Sovereign, and our Nation; smile upon their Warlike Preparations; still honor them with Success and Victory . . . preserve our Land from the incursions of Adversaries . . . bless, guide and prosper our Military Forces; [and] remember and restore our distressed captives."[49]

Artillery election and militia sermons represented, as Cotton Mather noted, "things of considerable Observation" in the land, and invariably they commented on New England's martial destiny in more hopeful and glorious terms than in the dismal and self-condemnatory fast sermon.[50] As in second-generation artillery election days, sermons in times of peace spiritualized warfare, whereas in times of war they spoke of foreign enemies and the duty of military preparedness.[51] In his 1704 artillery election sermon on Psalm 44:6 ("And I will not trust in my Bow: neither shall my sword save."), Henry Gibbs of Watertown began by defending the just war as the inevitable lot of God's people in the latter days. Besides the truism that "bloody Wars . . . have been carry'd on, from the first Ages of the World," there was the more particular truth that "the Church hath always had Enemies combining and conspiring for its Ruin." This was nowhere more true than for Christ's churches in New England. When faced with diabolical enemies, God's people were bound both by the "Law of Nature" and the "Revelation of the Mind and Will of God in his Word" to fight: "'Tis lawful, warrantable, and a duty for the People of God, to employ Military Weapons, in order to their own Safety." Despite God's sovereignty, the people of New England must learn the "art" of war: "What will Stores and Magazines signify, without men of Skill and Spirit to apply and manage them?" Without due regard for self-defense and a firm resolve to fight, "all Civil and Sacred Liberty would soon be ravished by Unreasonable men." Such mortal deprivations had "not yet" happened to New England because "by a chain of Memorable Providences . . . the Divine Favour [hath] been manifested in the Preservation and Establishment of our Civil and Religious Liberties." Recent defeats were to be seen as correctives whereby "God designs to make us thoroughly sensible, of our absolute dependence upon himself."[52] Once that divine sensibility was established through attendance on the Word, victory and deliverance would follow.

In the following year's artillery election sermon, Boston's Thomas Bridge urged the military company to understand their wars and battles in the largest possible providential perspective. None could doubt, he began, that God's New England people were being summoned to war: "The consideration of the state of things in *Europe,* calls upon us both to be Expert for *War,* and to be Ready for Service. . . . The state of things in *this Land* also calls for being always ready." When war came it would be part of a great apocalyptic struggle between the forces of Christ and Antichrist. To "encourage ourselves" in such ominous times, Bridge turned to Daniel 11:32, where the prophet promised that in the end times "the people that do know their God shall be strong, and do *exploits.*" Those times seemed to be dawning. In the speculative terminology common to millennial themes, Bridge enjoined the troops to augment their martial training with Bible study so they would know why they were fighting and what was at stake. Ignorant troops were ineffective troops. Therefore:

> *Study the Scripture Prophecies.* Tho there are *Depths* therein we cannot find out . . . Yet as far as he hath Revealed [them], we should Read, and Pray

that we may so understand the times, *as to know what we ought to do.* It seems as if the time to Execute the Judgments written on *Antichrist* were at hand; the time when the *Kings of the Earth shall hate the Whore, and burn her Flesh as it were with fire;* when the Lamb shall Overcome. . . . Who knows what the present Commotions may issue in?[53]

Bridge's words help to explain why, despite all their suffering and losses, New Englanders never questioned their identity as the preeminent people of war in North America and their willingness to enlist in endless campaigns that left the region broken and bleeding.[54] By treating each campaign *as if* it might be the commencement of the last apocalyptic struggle, New Englanders could be sure that when the real finale came they would be ready to meet the dreaded enemy in whatever guise he assumed.

ENGLISH COLONY AND REDEEMER NATION

Besides arousing millennial expectations, Queen Anne's War confirmed New England's sense of dependence on English rule and protection. None were fooled by the Peace of Utrecht (1713) into thinking hostilities had ended, or that there would not later come a great conflict for control of North America. As long as the French and Indian menace persisted, and internal tensions threatened aristocratic pretensions, ministers—like magistrates—would actively court English assistance and celebrate the enlightened rationalism of English rule. But alongside this anglicization, ministers would continue to articulate New England's historic identity as a chosen people destined to be the chief actors in the final chapter of sacred history. New England could be both a loyal provincial colony and an incipient redeemer nation as long as England protected civil and religious liberties, and the ministers continued to preach the covenant. Nothing short of the silencing of God's ministers through apostasy, conquest, or tyranny could indicate a divine desertion and an end to the covenant.

From first settlement, the genius of Puritan rhetoric and corporate identity was its imperviousness to contrary facts, whether waning church membership or revoked charters. As long as the sermon prevailed as the dominant ritual of social order, the orthodox were confident that the covenant prevailed; and as long as the covenant prevailed, any event could be absorbed into its providential framework. The immediate facts of New England history were irrelevant to New England's ongoing mission: self-rule or English rule, political stability or instability, summer harvest or summer drought, military victory or military defeat—all these diverse and contradictory signs confirmed the covenant and, with it, the authority of the ministers to decipher providential messages and point the way to temporal prosperity and eternal salvation.

[8]

Regular Preaching
and the New Pietism

As important a political and cultural force as anglicization was, its immediate effects were felt mainly in the provincial capitals among the ruling elite. Most New England inhabitants (perhaps 90 percent) continued to live in and around self-contained villages of one hundred families or fewer, where the minister was the only member of the community who was at all urbane or educated. There were no postal lines connecting inland towns and few newspapers or periodicals to consolidate audiences and to assist in the forging of a centralized, imperial network. Royal officials enjoyed few coercive controls over New England towns, which were so detached from provincial affairs (except in times of crisis) that many neglected their constitutional right to send deputies to the General Court. Rather than furthering the imperial goal of centralization, the new government accentuated the seventeenth-century tendency toward "persistent localism" in which political, cultural, and religious life were defined within the particular community.[1]

In view of this enduring localism, it seems surprising that historians of eighteenth-century religion have concentrated on printed occasional sermons originating in Boston virtually to the exclusion of the handwritten notes ministers carried with them into local pulpits. If there was a secularization of the Puritan ethic, as some suggest, it would be reflected in the regular sermon notes that defined religious culture in the New England towns. Yet, on examination, these sources reveal no such secularization. Congregational ministers continued to monopolize public communications in New England towns, and their message echoed the salvation-oriented preaching heard since first settlement. In their regular preaching, ministers took the old message of salvation, adorned it with new terminology, and developed it in the context of a new pietism of love and toleration. The sequence of sin-salvation-service remained unchanged throughout.

THE PERSISTENCE OF THE CONGREGATIONAL WAY

As the Mathers predicted, the new laws of toleration did little to alter popular loyalty to the Congregational Way. According to the Religious

Act of 1692, New England inhabitants were free to practice their own form of church government and to settle a "learned, able, and orthodox" minister of their choice who would be supported by public taxes. "Dissenters" like Baptists, Quakers, and Anglicans were free to worship as they pleased, but until 1727 they were still required to pay religious tithes to support the majority church and minister. This meant that every town maintained a Congregational church and, almost always, a Harvard- or Yale-trained Congregational minister. On the basis of available statistics, William G. McLoughlin estimates that as late as 1735 less than 4 percent of New England inhabitants were attached to dissenting congregations. In Massachusetts and Connecticut, few provincial leaders came from the dissenting churches, and their ministers were never upheld by the courts as entitled to full public support.[2] Congregational churches, however, continued to expand with the population. From the low point in church membership at the turn of the century, the numbers rose in the decade 1710–1720 (when the third generation came of age) to percentages comparable to those of the second generation.[3] Whether supported by theocratic law or majority rule, Congregational sermons continued to be the primary medium for shaping corporate identity. In all, third-generation ministers educated between 1676 and 1710 would deliver roughly one-half million sermonic messages in the first four decades of the eighteenth century to a population totaling less than 150,000.[4]

The continuing social and ritual power of the sermon in New England communities derived from the unique qualities of that Congregational polity which, though no longer conceived of as the essence of Christian faith, was still the rule for most ministers and congregations. The militantly localistic and voluntaristic basis of Congregational order fit naturally with New England social realities, and there seemed little need to search for alternatives. More particularly, ministers and congregations continued to rally around the sermon as the symbolic expression of unity and corporate purpose in their community. Clergy and laity alike continued to affirm *Sola Scriptura* and to perceive themselves as joint custodians of the sermon. Only ministers could preach, but their authority derived from the voluntary pledges and promises of their congregations, who reserved the right to dismiss them for heresy or immorality. If anything, churches became even more voluntaristic in the eighteenth century because inhabitants were freed to embrace other alternatives. Both ministers and their congregations were aware of this new reality, and together they infused the sermon with the power to create and enhance corporate solidarity and internal order.

With so much authority devolving on the local congregations, great care was taken to preserve the binding commitments of members and ministers. As in the seventeenth century, members could remove to new parishes only if they obtained letters of dismissal from their old congregations; ministers likewise first had to obtain the consent of their parishes before they could transfer to other pulpits. Ministers and (where they survived) ruling elders continued to oversee their congregations, but the congregations retained the right to elect officers, fix clerical salaries, and dismiss unorthodox ministers. Through these inherited binding and counterbalancing mechanisms, each congregation maintained an "enclosed orthodoxy of its own" with a balance of power that protected the interest of all and perpetuated the third generation's identity as a uniquely gathered and providentially led people of the Word.[5]

From the midst of the congregation came the only voice New Englanders recognized as sovereign in their lives, and behind that voice was the Bible. As always, church members agreed to honor their minister's voice only if it conformed to the "Scripture rule" as codified in the doctrines of the Westminster Confession of Faith and the polity of *The Cambridge Platform*. Eighteenth-century congregations studied that Word and honored its precepts as closely as their parents had. In addition to aggregate membership statistics and literacy rates, evidence of enduring lay piety abounds in ministerial observations, funeral sermons, catechism classes, school primers, lay sermon notes, journals of "meditations and self-examinations," and devout lay resistance to any "innovations" in doctrine or polity that diverged from inherited standards. A case in point is Timothy Edwards's transcript of "relations for church membership," which in style and substance is remarkably similar to the accounts recorded by Thomas Shepard in the first generation. New members described their sin and "self-righteous Spirit"; the "discouragement" of their hearts; and the assurance of pardon, which meant, for one Esther Bissell, "that my heart was opened to Christ, and I saw him to be a lovely excellent and Glorious Saviour."[6]

Like their parents, children born in the eighteenth century internalized the language of the Bible and instantly recognized discrepancies or departures from their Scripture orthodoxy. If a minister deviated from the biblical foundation or substituted extrabiblical authorities in regular preaching, his voice ceased to be authoritative and he was removed from office.[7] For the grandchildren, scriptural language alone shaped their understanding of the peculiar genius of their past and expressed the triumphant hope of their future.

THE WAY OF SALVATION

However attracted eighteenth-century ministers were to the discoveries of natural reason, their regular sermons dwelt on the primacy of special revelation (the Bible) and the way of salvation it contained. After extolling in his best Latinate prose the merits of a liberal education to ministerial students, Cotton Mather went on to define the essential subject matter of the sermon in terms much like those used by William Perkins a century earlier. The minister's primary responsibility was to preach not on the wonders of natural theology or the duty of social hierarchy but on Christ:

> And shall they who call themselves *Christians*, and would be honoured as *Ministers of the Christian Religion*, preach as if they were ashamed of making

the *Glories* of JESUS, the *Subject* of their *Sermons;* and so rarely introduce Him, as if it were an *Indecent Stoup* to speak of Him! God forbid! I make no Doubt of it, that the almost Epidemical Extinction of True *Christianity* . . . in the Nations that profess it, is very much owing to the inexcuseable *Impiety* of overlooking a Glorious CHRIST, so much in the *Empty Harangues,* which often pass for *Sermons.*

While allowing more room than Perkins did for experiments in literary style, Mather shared with his predecessor the conviction that christocentric preaching was the minister's main "exhibit."[8]

In preparing their sermons, third-generation ministers continued to follow a strict regimen of intensive Bible study and private self-examination. Ministers, Mather cautioned, must look first to their own conversion before they could reach out to others: "Your *Conversion* to GOD, must be accomplished, or else you will have no *Heart,* nor *Skill,* nor *Strength,* for that Life of *PIETY,* which must be laid in the *Foundation* of all the Good, that is to be expected by you, or from you."[9] Mather's own detailed diary reveals the pattern of renewed conversion shown by prior generations of ministers. Frequently, he set aside days for "personal Fasting and humiliation" when he would "cry Mightily unto God" for forgiveness and a renewed assurance of salvation. On February 7, 1707, he prepared himself for a sermon on "the Sacrifice of a Glorious Christ" by fasting and contemplating "my horrible Corruptions and Miscarriages." To appreciate the merciful sacrifice of a "Glorious Christ" in his sermon, he first had to focus on his own unworthiness in private meditation. Throughout the day, he noted:

> I loathed and judged myself before the Lord exceedingly. The Victories which Temptation had obtained over me, filled me with unspeakable Confusion. I thought, that as vile as I was, yet it was my Duty to look still unto the Lord, for Pardon and Healing. So I pleaded the *Great Sacrifice.* I cried unto a Glorious *Christ,* that He would be my *Advocate.* I begg'd I begg'd, that an holy Heart might be bestowed upon me; because a Glorious *Christ* had purchased it for me, and by His Death purchased the Death of my Sin. I begg'd, that the dreadful wrath of Heaven, might not break forth against me, nor against my Flock, nor against my poor Family, for my sin.

From self-examination, Mather turned to the sermon and preached to himself the same message he would bring to his congregation on Sunday: "I pondered my own Discourse, about *Falls into Sins* [Hebrews 10:26]; and my Spirit actually conformed unto every one of the Articles in it, that propose how a Recovery out of the *Falls* may be attended with special Revenues of Glory and Service to God."[10] Having "conformed" to his own preaching, Mather was at last ready to bring the message to his "flock" and hope for the same uplifting response.

Once the minister prepared his heart and fixed on a text, he turned to the standard commentaries and concordances employed since the first generation.[11] The sermons continued to be drafted in the form of essaylike notes of twelve pages or more that could either be followed in the pulpit or memorized in advance. The founders' penchant for Ramist dichotomies had largely disappeared, but not their habit of constructing numerous divisions and subdivisions of sermon "heads." Unlike occasional sermons prepared for print in the manner of periodical essays replete with completed transitions, regular sermon notes employed simply numbered points and subpoints recorded in phrases that could be expanded during delivery.[12] Theories of sermon delivery also remained constant and required a demeanor of gravity and solemn deliberation. Nowhere was there a hint of humor or ease in the pulpit. As summed up by Mather:

> A *well prepared* Sermon should be a *well pronounced* one. Wherefore, Avoid forever, all *Inanes sine Mente Sonos* [empty sounds without intelligence]; and all Indecencies, every thing that is *Ridiculous*. Be sure to speak *Deliberately*. Strike the *Accent* always upon that *Word* in the Sentence which it properly belongs unto. . . . Don't *Begin* too High. Ever *Conclude* with Vigour. If you must have your *Notes* before you in your Preaching . . . let there be with you a Distinction between the *Neat using* of Notes, and the *dull Reading* of them. . . . Finally; Let your *Perorations* often be, lively *Expostulations* with the *Conscience* of the *Hearer*.[13]

So constant and inflexible were the rules of delivery that they did not begin to change until the mid-eighteenth century, and then amidst great confusion and dispute.

Not every minister paid as careful attention to sermon composition as Cotton Mather, nor did all follow his practice of composing sermons while on his knees.[14] But in general, patterns of composition, memorization, and delivery were standard. In describing his ministerial training at Harvard College in 1700, Marblehead's John Barnard revealed how little outlines of preparation had changed from the first generation. While in college, he recalled, "I gave myself to the study of the Biblical Hebrew, turned the Lord's prayer, the creed, and part of the Assembly's Catechism into Hebrew (for which I had Dr. Cotton Mather for my corrector), and entered on the task of finding the radix of every Hebrew word in the Bible, with design to form a Hebrew Concordance." From biblical languages he moved to divinity: "The pulpit being my great design, and divinity my chief study, I read all sorts of authors, and as I read, compared their sentiments with the sacred writings and formed my judgment of the doctrines of Christianity by that only and infallible standard of truth; which led me insensibly into what is called the Calvinistical scheme."[15] Elsewhere Barnard noted his appreciation for the New Learning he absorbed at Harvard, but the focus of his thought and study was traditional, because these were the materials he would need for the pulpit.

After completing the broad course of linguistic and theological study required of ministerial students, Barnard began preparing his own sermons according to the tried and true method of his predecessors:

> Having, in a proper manner, fixed upon the subject I designed to preach upon, I sought a text of Scripture most naturally including it; then I read

such practical discourses as treated upon the subject . . . sometimes having ten or a dozen folios and other books lying open around me. . . . After having spent some time (perhaps two or three days) in thus reading and meditating upon my subject, I then applied myself to my Bible, the only standard of truth, and examined how far my authors agreed or disagreed with it. Having settled my mind as to the truth of the doctrine I had under consideration, I then set myself to the closest meditation upon the most plain and natural method I could think of for the handling of the subject. Sometimes, not always, I penned the heads of the discourse. Then I took the first head, and thought over what appeared to me most proper to confirm and illustrate it, laying it up in my mind; so I went through the several heads; and when I had thus gone over the whole, in its several parts, then I went over all in my meditation, generally walking in my study or in my father's garden.

Once the basic structure and verification of sermon heads was completed, Barnard turned to composition in preparation for delivery:

I sat down to writing, and being a swift penman, I could finish an hour and a quarter's discourse, with rapid speaking, in about four hours' time. This manner of studying sermons cost me, 'tis true, a great deal of time, perhaps a week or fortnight for a sermon, and sometimes more; but I had this advantage by it, there was a greater stock laid up in my memory for future use, and I found it easy to deliver my discourses memoriter; and by the full and clear view I had of my subject, I could correct the phraseology in my delivery. I kept indeed my notes open, and turned over the leaves as though I had read them, yet rarely casting my eye upon my notes, unless for the chapter and verse of a text which I quoted.

Barnard penned his recollections of early sermon preparation late in life, at a time when the topic of sermon reading was in great dispute, and he was at pains to point out the distinction in his own preaching between the *appearance* of reading and the *actual* reading of sermons verbatim. In fact, minister's notes were seldom complete discourses that could be read from the pulpit, but were instead extended outlines that could be "corrected" and enlivened during delivery.

Also apparent in Barnard's recollections was the importance of age and experience in the pulpit. Once he established a "stock" of phrases and doctrines through careful preparation, he dispensed with the elaborate process of his youth and composed sermons more rapidly, "only penning head by head as I meditated on them." This was especially true for regular preaching; occasional sermons continued to require the full, formal preparation: "When I was settled in the ministry, I found this [formal] method too operose, yet when called to special public services, if I had time, I practised it." By the third generation, the form of the occasional sermon was determined by the corpus of printed sermons that existed in every minister's study and, in preparing their own, ministers instinctively thought in terms of a literary essay and historical memorial—terms generally not applied when preparing regular sermons.

SOLA SCRIPTURA AND THE WAY OF SALVATION

The corpus of regular sermon manuscript notes surviving from the third generation is much more extensive than that of earlier generations. The notes reveal how closely ministers followed the themes and procedures outlined by Mather and Barnard, and also how little regular preaching had changed over seventy-five years. Apart from stylistic changes and more standardized spelling and punctuation, third-generation sermons can hardly be distinguished from their predecessors. One is left with a distinct impression of deliberate repetitiveness and studied unoriginality. One generation's notes meld into the next with few changes in biblical foundation, theological focus, social orientation, or thematic organization from Scripture text to doctrine to application.

As tedious as the repetition in a broad sampling of colonial preaching can be, it is an essential aspect of the New England minister's art. The unadorned notes, neither witty nor pompous nor filled with flights of personal imagination, signaled the enduring loyalty to *Sola Scriptura*. Such a loyalty was not simply a matter of personal conviction, formal training, or aesthetic preference; it was the New England minister's badge of entry into the Congregational churches. Thus in preaching to his Boston congregation, Benjamin Wadsworth (future president of Harvard College) frequently urged his hearers "to be constant and diligent in reading God's word. That should be the light of our foot and the lamp of our paths."[16] That word, as Joseph Lord reminded his Chatham congregation, was unique. Contradicting the European deists and rationalists who believed reason supplied access to all truth, he pointed out how "many appendices of the law are unknown by the light of nature." Where nature revealed attributes of God in general terms—his "beauty," "order," "omniscience," "omnipotence"—it did not reveal the personal love of God or teach sinners how to "Get an interest in Christ." Nor did nature unveil the providential meaning of New England as a covenant people. New England's "peculiarity," like salvation, could only be discovered from Scripture. In light of its promises, Lord exhorted his congregation to "consider [that] we are all peculiarly the Lords people. Tho we are not all in the same manner the Lords, yet we are of that people that the Lord has taken for his having set up his peculiar kingdom among us."[17]

Occasionally ministers devoted entire sermons to the sovereignty of God's Word, but more often they preached about the salvation of the soul. As before, in preaching salvation the place to begin was conviction of sin. "Saving faith hath Humiliation laid for its Foundation," Jeremiah Shepard warned, and ministers could not neglect sin and condemnation as the prelude to grace.[18] Medfield's Joseph Baxter (HC, 1693) set the age-old condition in eighteenth-century theatrical prose, beginning a sermon on grace with the observation that "man having by his Sin brought a curse upon the whole creation, all his posterity as soon as they make their appearance on the Stage of Being doe launch forth into a sea of troubles."

In equally forthright terms, Samuel Moodey (HC, 1697) reminded his York congregation that church membership did not guarantee salvation: "Many that enjoy the Means of Grace, with the People of God, here; shall be thrust out of Heaven into Hell, hereafter."[19] The eighteenth-century confidence in human potential and celebration of sentiment were not without influence in regular preaching, but ministers carefully pointed out what happened to a people who were so caught up in the cares of the world that they neglected to look to the care of their eternal souls.

Although sin and damnation were not ignored in regular preaching, neither were they used to dominate and terrorize congregations—at least not before 1740. Much more conspicuous were the themes of salvation and service considered under the heading of the covenant of grace. To communicate the message of salvation, ministers adopted a more conciliatory tone in their regular preaching than in occasional sermons. While the concepts of condemnation (law) and salvation (gospel) always appeared together, sermons varied widely in emphasis and orientation. "Hell-fire and brimstone" sermons fit most closely with fasts, funerals, and most dramatically, executions; dire calamities demanded explanations and a list of procuring sins. But such denunciations could not bear repetition week after week. More common was the theme of God's love, patience, and mercy to ailing sinners. Beyond the example of their predecessors who frequently preached on God's goodness, third-generation ministers were encouraged by the eighteenth-century Age of Discovery to stress God's love for humanity. God became a more beneficent, "good natured" being who sympathized with the sufferings of his image-bearing creation.[20] This changed orientation did not entail denial of the doctrines of original sin or hell, but it placed them in a broader perspective of hope and deliverance.

Themes of love and reconciliation were especially prominent in the preaching of Boston's "liberal" clergy because they were doctrines held in common by all Protestants. Though none of these preachers denied traditional teachings of sin and condemnation, they did not dwell on them; their focus was christocentric and optimistic. In a sermon on 2 Corinthians 1:20 ("all the promises of God are yea, and in him Amen"), for example, William Brattle proclaimed hope for all his listeners because Scripture promises were "absolutely firm and unchanging in and thro Christ Jesus."[21] From the same text, Wadsworth drew the "healing" advice that "God will be your God. This in general comprehends all other promises . . . tis only by the knowledge of Christ, that persons come to be interested in God as your Covenant God."[22] True knowledge, Wadsworth continued, required the transforming powers of the Holy Spirit in effecting supernatural conversion. There were "many who profess to be children of God, but yet never had a regenerating change wrought in their souls."[23]

In preaching "regeneration," ministers continued to emphasize both the "head" and the "heart." Jeremiah Shepard stressed the importance of both when he pointed out in a published sermon series on Luke 8:12 (the parable of the sower) how "in the day of Grace when the Spirit, by its powerful operations, works Saving Faith in the Soul; it doth it by opening the eyes of the understanding, to see Christ revealed and freely offered in the Gospel, and letting in the sweetness and favour of it to the Heart and Will."[24] By keeping head and heart in tension, ministers avoided the heresies of Antinomianism and Arminianism that threatened from opposite poles. When faced with Antinomian appeals to soul-ravaging experiences, ministers agreed with John Barnard that

> the Soul is capable of *understanding*, the Nature of other things, the Dependance and Connexion of Causes and Effects; tis capable of Retiring within it self . . . taking a view of its own Essence, and reflecting upon its own Actions. . . . Tis capable of knowing God and Jesus Christ, whom He hath sent; whom to know is Life Eternal. . . . It acts by Counsel, and is able to *Determine its choice*, and always Acts as a *Free* and Spontaneous Agent . . . Even in the work of Conversion, the *Will* is not forced, but guided and directed."[25]

In responding to pure rationalism, ministers turned to the heart and emphasized, with the popular English nonconformist, John Flavell (1627–1691), that "an Honest well-experienced Heart, is a singular help to a weak Head, such a Heart will serve you instead of a *Commentary* upon a great part of the Scriptures." This balance was preserved until 1740, when ministers divided into rival camps championing one faculty or the other.[26]

Unlike the new academic theories studied at college that pitted the head against the heart, preaching required that the two be held in tension because Scripture itself alternately emphasized first one and then the other. Depending on the particular text, the same minister could address the primacy either of the intellect or the affections.[27] The occasion was also important in determining which faculty would be stressed. Insofar as occasional preaching flowed from a covenant logic of rewards and punishments it tended to emphasize the understanding. Regular preaching—particularly that on conversion and the New Birth—spoke to the heart. Discussions of eighteenth-century preaching that claim to find a shift toward "rationalistic" and "moralistic" themes are based largely on printed occasional sermons in which the logic of federal covenants encouraged emphasis on conditions and corporate morality.[28] Alongside these pleas to do good, however, there appeared in regular preaching an important counterbalancing theme that emphasized the heart or affections and explained conversion by analogy to the aesthetic experience. Indeed, this was the prevailing emphasis in regular preaching.

If New England ministers could not identify aesthetic enjoyment or intellectual delight as the end of spiritual experience in the manner of English sentimentalists like John Dennis, the third earl of Shaftesbury, or Joseph Addison, they could employ the eighteenth-century vocabulary of "natural sublimes" as a metaphor for supernatural grace. In the same way that English essayists used mountaintop views, oceans, or planetary vistas to excite a sense of "joy," "wonderment," or "delight," ministers described the ways in which the Holy Spirit worked through the sermon and sacraments to enlighten the mind, ravish the heart, and overwhelm the soul with a sense of divine love and majesty. In his sacrament sermons, Westfield's poet-pastor Edward Taylor frequently invoked natural imagery to explain salvation. Just as a clove tree "yields the pleasentest Smell in the World" when its leaves change, so in Christ's death on the cross "we have the tree of Life that yields the most pleasentest fruits that ever were born under the Canopy of Heaven."[29]

To a greater extent than their predecessors, third generation ministers preached that an "experimental" knowledge of God was not only reasonable but exhilarating—an experience that demanded extravagance and hyperbole. As Nehemiah Walter (HC, 1684) exulted in a sermon series on Isaiah 9:6 ("His Name shall be called Wonderful"):

> No knowledge is so excellent, none so necessary as the knowledge of Christ. A sight and knowledge of his Wonderfulness will be of singular advantage to us, to strengthen our faith and dependence on Him, our love to Him, delight in Him, admiration of Him, and longing desires to be with Him. . . . In Heaven and Earth there is nothing *Superiour* to Him, nothing *Equal* to Him, but every thing is *infinitely inferiour* to him. There is none that is like unto the Lord, none that may be compared with Him for wonderful excellencies. In Jesus Christ there is a *Collection* of all ravishing excellencies in an *All-fulness* of Perfection.[30]

For Walter's Harvard classmate and pastor at Marshfield, Edward Tompson, conversion was a "soul-satisfying Enjoyment" of heavenly things in which "our heads will be so full of knowledge and our hearts with joy, that we shall say Lord we have enough!" The prospect of union with Christ in heaven so enraptured Samuel Moodey that language itself broke down: "But oh! the Joys and Delights, the Ravishing Delights and Overflowing Joys, that every moment of that Endless Duration will give us fresh and new experience of. No Tongue of Man or Angel can Express them. They will be a Thousand, Thousand fold higher and Sweeter than we can now imagine."[31] These salvation sermons confirm the influence of new vocabularies, even as the themes themselves remained supernatural and otherworldly.

Since in Puritan theory God authored and finished salvation, ministers continued to remind their congregations that while works of service and morality were necessary in the Christian life they could not be performed to display moral rectitude or for self-justification. God's intention in saving souls and prompting them to good works was not, Nathaniel Stone cautioned, to puff up human pride, but to enhance his glory: "Christ came into the world to redeem sinners, that God might be glorified. For as Gods end in makeing all beings was his own Glory so his end in redeeming sinners was the same."[32] While these words were familiar, they took on an added significance in response to rationalistic equations of morality or "virtue" with grace. As Eleazer Mather's son Warham Mather (HC, 1685) warned, "Morality is a fine Ornament and Praise worthy, but these concessions notwithstanding, it is certain that onely those that are in an estate of Grace do any *actions that are good*."[33] For Mather and his peers, true morality was the product of salvation, not the means to it. When New England congregations heard abstract terms like "virtue," "morality," or "duty," they understood them in the traditional context of salvation and service.

THE PROBLEM OF WORSHIP AND DEFERENCE IN A TOLERANT AGE

Of all the duties of godly service, none were more frequently enjoined than worship and deference to the Word preached.[34] Earlier generations also preached frequently on worship but, as church attendance was required by law, they could take that for granted and concentrate on questions of polity or sabbath observance. Third-generation ministers, however, had to persuade their listeners to attend public worship by pricking their consciences and reminding them that civil liberties did not exempt them from religious duties. They encouraged attendance by asserting that the only way to salvation was through the assembly of God's people on Sunday. Ministers backed their claims with the sober reminder that those in New England who ignored church services would be held more accountable than persons in countries where true churches did not abound. Following a meeting of the Windsor Consociation in 1712 that resolved to "carefully watch [for] Irreverence in the Worship of God," Timothy Edwards preached a sermon on Psalm 89:7 ("God is greatly to be feared in the assembly of his Saints") whose main theme was that "it is our duty to draw nigh to God in the duties of his worship with Great seriousness, solemnity and Reverence." In the last days, when "men must give an account to God" for their actions, those who stayed away from worship would "Judge and Condemn yourselves before God."[35]

Closely related to the themes of worship and accountability was deference to the word preached, and to the minister who preached it. Obedience to God's laws required, in William Brattle's words, that listeners "shew forth our love to Christ's Ambassadors not by sleeping at Sermon, not by carping at them, but by improving them to your spiritual good. This will provoke not only the joy of Christ's Ambassadors but [also will work] to your good in this life and also in the day of the Lord." While the sabbath was a day of rest for God's people, Benjamin Wadsworth warned that "tis not a Day of rest with the Devil. . . . When the minister is speaking to your ears, the devil is often very busy with your hearts. He's ready to shoot in his firy Darts, to suggest a thousand diverting thoughts." Apparently, the effect of one of the devil's most powerful "darts" was sleeping in church, which prompted Timothy Edwards to complain (after developing three doctrines with five propositions each) of those who had "often allowed yourselves and sinfully yielded to a drowsy sleepy Frame in the time of Divine worship."[36]

The frequent enjoinders to worship and sermon attendance in regular preaching are revealing in several ways. Besides reflecting the new circumstances of Congregational churches in eighteenth-century New England, they register ministerial insecurities stemming from the new voluntaristic rules of church affiliation. Despite the continued growth of Congregational churches, ministers perceived themselves as an embattled remnant whose misfortune it was to labor at a time when popular respect for God's ministers had sadly declined. As evidence, they pointed to low salaries that steadily lost ground to inflation and, at least in urban areas, placed them far beneath the wealthier members of their congregations. Tight-fisted parishioners continued to argue that low salaries were good for clerical humility—and so they were. But too much humility, ministers complained, could bring their high office into contempt. As evidence, they cited instances of "excessive" congregational assertiveness over questions of church rule such as the appointment of ruling lay elders (which most eighteenth-century ministers resisted) or the ministers' right to a negative voice in church meetings (of which they approved).[37] Perhaps the most dramatic division between ministers and their congregations came about when ministers sought to introduce "regular singing" or singing by note in worship according to the "method" set forth in John Tuft's *Introduction to the Singing of Psalm-Tunes*. As in earlier debates over the Half-way Covenant, church members resisted the "innovations" as trespasses upon their congregational liberties, while the ministers insisted that "custom . . . is no sufficient Reason for the continuance of old Practices that need to be Reformed." In most churches, the congregations won out, refusing the new style of singing.[38]

The trust between ministers and congregations was not broken by disputes like the psalm-singing issue, but the social relationships between them were strained to the point where ministers began to renew their efforts to establish stronger associations with presbyterianlike powers. In 1704, a ministerial "convention" (there were no longer synods in Massachusetts) met in Boston and recommended to the government that "standing councils" of ministers be appointed with powers to arbitrate congregational disputes, screen candidates for the ministry, and issue binding statements on controversial issues. Their proposal never got past Governor Joseph Dudley who, because of his Anglican loyalties and his hatred for Cotton Mather (whom he held personally responsible for his own arrest during the Glorious Revolution), was not about to invest Congregational ministers with any more power than they already possessed.[39] But in Connecticut, where there was no hostile governor, the Boston proposals were put into law through the *Saybrook Platform* (1708), which provided for the establishment of clerical "consociations" to overlook local congregations and screen ministerial candidates.[40] Churches that resisted the decisions of consociations would be shunned or placed under a "Sentence of Non-Communion," which, in theory, isolated them from neighboring churches.

Although impressive on paper, the *Saybrook Platform* never won for the ministers the binding powers they sought. Congregations continued to stand on their autonomy as guaranteed under the old *Cambridge Platform* and refused to acknowledge as sovereign and binding any external authority, whether in church or state.[41] Thus in Massachusetts and Connecticut, ministerial ambitions were thwarted, and the contest for control within congregations was conducted in accordance with the original balance of power.

When institutional modifications proved largely ineffective in buttressing clerical status and authority, ministers turned to rhetoric using the sermon—which they continued to monopolize—to assert their claims to authority. The sermon remained a powerful force against assertive congregations. Election sermons continued to thunder against the sin of insubordination and urged submission to civil magistrates.[42] Other occasional sermons were employed to uphold ministerial authority. If they could not silence lay disputes, they could prevent widespread insubordination. Equally important, sermons served to encourage and unify the ministers themselves. This was particularly true of lecture sermons, funeral sermons, and ordination sermons, which were intended for an audience composed as much or more of the fellow ministers as of the laity. Many of these sermons were printed and distributed to ministers. Indeed, in the early decades of the eighteenth century, printed lecture, funeral, and ordination sermons outstripped fast, election, artillery election, and thanksgiving sermons by a ratio of two to one.[43]

LECTURE SERMONS, FUNERAL SERMONS, AND MINISTERIAL AUTHORITY

While lecture sermons had been delivered regularly since the first years of settlement, public interest in them had steadily waned as the subject matter and social focus of these addresses coalesced more and more around the ministry. By the third generation, ministers were routinely complaining about slack attendance at lectures, not recognizing that the occasion had become primarily directed to themselves. This was particularly true of printed lecture sermons which, in the first decade of the eighteenth century, constituted the single largest category of printed sermons.[44] In contrast to the more eclectic subject matter of spoken lectures, those lectures selected for print centered on the themes of ministerial authority, worship, and the duty of social submission.[45] In words certain to please the ministers, if not the laity, Ebenezer Pemberton (HC, 1691) lectured on 1 Thessalonians 4:11 ("Study . . . to do your Own Business"), reaffirming the principle of social inequality in which "superiour and Inferiour, publick and private Orders of men; are distinctions which

Divine Providence has made necessary." By the laws of nature and the covenant, everyone in New England was obliged to "observe the whole body of *Social duties*, according to the Relation he stands in." These duties stipulated that rulers in church and state "are to study the *Publick Good*," whereas all others should "study to be *quiet*." Failure to do so would result in a loss of temporal privileges: "Know it, God expects it of you; the dark Cloude of Providence hovering over our Land, which seems charged with Storm and Thunder, calls aloud for [submission]." Other lectures echoed the same themes.[46] If these and similar sentiments did not reach large public audiences, they did reassure the ministers in attendance and confirm them in their unthankful errand.

Printed funeral sermons were also well suited to the task of ministerial enoblement. By the eighteenth century, the practice of solemnizing death with elaborate ceremonies, rituals, and gravestones had become common, representing one more instance of cultural anglicization.[47] This formalization brought standardized funeral sermons that served the dual purpose of evangelistic preaching and social commentary. Often the contemplation of death prompted the utterance of some of the most conversionist sentiments outside of the regular pulpit.[48] But besides evangelistic preaching, funeral sermons were ideally suited to social commentary—particularly when the deceased was a minister. The eulogization of the deceased occupied an increasingly central position in the sermon, serving as a reminder of respect for superiors. By 1720, funeral sermons surpassed lectures as the type of sermon most frequently printed, reminding all that God's messengers were a gift that could be withdrawn.[49] God would not allow his ministers to be removed unless the people ceased to honor their words and position at the center of society.

Printed funeral sermons' power to encourage public deference to the ministry is illustrated in Benjamin Colman's funeral sermon for Increase Mather, whose long life extended into the second decade of the eighteenth century. Although the two had been spirited rivals in life, they shared a vocational bond that transcended differences in style and temperament and brought forth from Colman sentiments of highest praise. Mather's accomplishments in the public realm, said Colman, entitled him to be honored as "the Father of his Country, and a Father to the Standing Ministry."[50] Most significant, however, Colman went on, was his contribution to the spiritual condition of New England, which he shared with every other minister in the country. To make this point, Colman used as his text Isaiah 3:1, 2, in which "the prophet" warned the tribes of Judah that if they did not respect their prophets calamities would come upon them. The Hebrew word for prophet was, Colman noted, "no small Name in the Israel of God," nor should it be in New England. When ministers died the people should reflect on their great use and importance, and respond with deep lamentations: "God accuses his people, and charges it upon them as Contempt of Him and his Judgments, when the Righteous perish and no man lays it to heart. Isa. 57.1 They are no common Deaths, but are to be lamented as a publick and common loss." Nor ought the "Aarons" of New England to "be only murmur'd at while [they] live, and *wept* for when [they] die." Rather the people must "let our Regards to God and his Servants be *Uniform* and of a piece." Ministers must be respected and deferred to as the country's primary line of defense. Without them, Colman concluded, New England would be left "naked and exposed to temporal and Spiritual Enemies."[51] Funeral sermons were important not only for personal reflection but also for corporate reflection on the security of New England—particularly when the deceased was a minister.

THE ORDINATION SERMON AND GOD'S "AMBASSADORS"

To ensure respect for ministers in life as in death, third-generation ministers inaugurated the practice of printing ordination sermons for circulation among themselves. While ministers could not rule over their congregations in all matters as they wished, they did win control over their own ordinations on the premise that God "appointed other spiritual rulers to represent him in this Authoritative work of ordination."[52] The revised procedure reinforced the trend toward sacerdotalism and had the effect of shifting the ritual locus of ministerial power from the popular election of the congregation (which never ceased) to the act of clerical fraternity. By printing the sermons delivered on these occasions, ministers formalized the ritual as yet another "memorial" to their high calling and unique standing before God.[53]

For the most part, ordination speakers devoted little time to rehearsing the formal rules of pulpit oratory in their charge to the new minister. That preachers were "to observe the modest grave Decorum of an Orator" in their pulpit speech was so commonplace that it required no elaboration.[54] Instead they concentrated on the place of ministers in church and society. As election sermons confirmed the superior place of the magistrate in the civil life of society, so ordination sermons confirmed the superior place of ministers in the churches. In both cases, public respect and deference were equated with future prosperity and societal peace. The importance of the minister's office came to loom so large in clerical self-conceptions that in 1726 William Shurtleff would apply Winthrop's image of a city upon a hill specifically (and almost exclusively) to the ministry: "The ministers of Christ should remember that they are in a peculiar manner *The Lights of the World* . . . they are as a *city set upon a Hill, which cannot be hid.*" With equal conviction, Nathaniel Eells asserted that ministers "officially stand nearer to God than others do."[55] These expressions, common in ordination sermons, show how ministers used the occasion to trumpet their authority. If such words did not necessarily convince congregations, they did convince the ministers that, in Azariah Mather's words, they were "to be looked upon as Sacred Persons, Men Representing the King of Glory."[56]

To confirm the identification of ministers as Christ's peculiar agents, ordination sermons diverged from the general practice of citing Old Testament texts for occasional preaching and instead drew their Scripture lessons almost exclusively from the New Testament. Of all the ministerial images contained in the New Testament, that most frequently cited by third-generation ministers was "ambassador." While the Old Testament term "watchman" was well suited to the prophetic warnings of fast days, it did not capture the regal quality that ordination speakers wished to convey. They were a generation accustomed to the language of royalty, and they did not hesitate to apply it to their office. In explaining why the term "ambassador" fit the minister's vocation so well, Ebenezer Thayer focused on the "royal dignity" it conferred in the thinking of New Testament writers. Nor could any miss the contemporary parallels with New England's royal government and the high calling of the magistrates.[57] In submitting to ministers, congregations were submitting to Christ, their executive "officer."

Solomon Stoddard lived long enough into the careers of third-generation ministers to publish many ordination sermons. While discoursing on the office of the ministry, he could barely conceal his disdain for assertive congregations who held on to liberties granted in "ancient platforms" as if they "were the Pattern in the Mount." Underlying his unrealized hope for a national (presbyterian) church governed solely by teaching elders was the conviction that "the Spiritual power of governing the church . . . doth belong entirely to the [teaching] Elders." If individual members or congregations resisted the rulings of Christ's ambassadors, then those rulers "have a Coercive power to execute Censures on them that are obstinate." By temperament and training Stoddard was incapable of making the leap, as his grandson would later do, from preaching revival to granting greater privileges and authority to the laity. He was certain that if church government was shared by the laity "they will be carried head long by a tumultuous cry. If the multitude were to be judges . . . things would quickly be turned up-side down."[58] Order could be preserved only to the extent that rulers and judges were separate and superior to a "quiet" populace.

Of all the disorderly threats posed by a noisy laity, none was more frightening than the prospect of ordinary people taking it upon themselves to preach the gospel. Although the incidence of itinerant preaching or "lay exhorting" was slight in the early eighteenth century, and confined largely to Baptist "pietists," ministers rightly saw in lay speech a grave threat to their own authority.[59] And, by implication, anything that threatened their authority threatened the continuation of the New England Way. The status of the clergy depended on the monopoly of speech they enjoyed; that more than anything else counterbalanced the lay majority's claims to power. Lay "usurpers," the ministers believed, were certain to doom the covenant. Piety was an important qualification for the preaching office but social qualifications were also important. Ministers were required to have a formal education and be screened by committees comprised of established ministers. In opposition to Baptists, who used the uneducated New Testament apostles as models for their own lack of formal training, Samuel Wigglesworth insisted that

> ministers are, or ought to be, Persons of an elevated Education and Accomplishments. . . . Our Lord saw cause by immediate Inspiration to confer ministerial Gifts on Persons wholly illiterate; yet none may now reasonably expect, that unsought Accomplishments will be infused into him. Education, Study, and Prayer are now the Method, whereby the Candidates of the Evangelical Ministry must be fitted for their charge.[60]

Such arguments undoubtedly flowed from biblical as well as social considerations, but it is the social considerations that require our attention. New charters that permitted liberty of worship could not threaten the New England Way or the ministers' positions of local preeminence. But an ignorant, illiterate ministry did pose such a threat because it challenged all distinctions between superior and inferior—distinctions that were most clear in social conventions regarding who could speak and who must remain quiet.

Besides Scripture arguments on a learned ministry, ordination speakers turned to history. From the example of radical sectarians in the English Revolution of 1640, John Hancock concluded that "an ignorant, unlearned, unskilful injudicious Ministry is the bane of the Church; Christ looks upon such as no Ministers." It was for this reason, Benjamin Colman added, that the New England colleges in Cambridge and New Haven had to be reverenced as "immortal Mothers" of the churches. They stood between order and chaos, and trained ministers to preserve the covenant balance demanded by New England's providential status. In addition to training ministers in theology, the colleges provided the grounding in ancient languages that every modern minister had to possess. "Altho' we have [Bibles] excellently translated unto, and expounded in familiar languages," Thomas Paine noted, "yet doubtless *it is better drinking at the Fountain.*" Despite the spectacular gains in eighteenth-century vernaculars, third-generation ministers defended the superiority of classical languages for social and spiritual reasons. Knowledge of the ancient tongues continued to separate the clergy from the rank and file. Besides that, Edward Tompson noted, these were the languages that would be spoken in heaven: "The Hebrew, a language that Christ himself spoke in this world and the most ancient. . . . The next thereto is greek as most rich, then the Latine most copious." Without an acquaintance with these superior tongues, Isaac Chauncy argued, no person should dare to be "God's Mouth unto the People."[61]

A PERSISTENT PIETY

The full potential of clerical pretentiousness to provoke lay revolts would not be realized for another generation. In part this was because traditional habits of deference and subordination to the Word preached still ran strong. The populace had not declined in piety as much as the ministers claimed, nor were they immune to the power of threats like Joseph Belcher's: "How long have you liv'd under the Ministry of the Word, How many Years He that has planted you in this Vineyard, has come, and sought fruit, but found none. . . . The worst of Heathen will fare better in the Day of Judgment, than such as these."[62] In fact, much of the lay resistance that ministers decried as spiritual decay grew from a vibrant strain of lay piety that reflected deep atavistic yearnings to preserve the divinely mandated congregational liberties of their parents and grandparents. In part also, popular resistance to clerical pretensions was limited by the ministers' own common sense. Funeral and ordination sermons—like fast sermons at an earlier date—may have dominated the printed literature of the early eighteenth century, but their occurrence in the life of any particular congregation was rare. Ministers had other things on their minds besides their ambassadorial relationship to their congregations. As "shepherds" they were responsible for feeding the souls of their flock with comforting, evangelistic preaching. As "watchmen" they were responsible for spying trouble on the horizon—particularly the ever-present French menace—and supplying appropriate remedies. And as "prophets" and intellectuals they were responsible for reconciling their culture's anglicized present to its theocratic past and for fashioning a coherent vision for the future that all New Englanders could share. Unlike clerical status or congregational liberties, questions of salvation, protection, and corporate destiny promoted harmony and postponed, for a time, the convulsive divisions that would rock congregations by the mid-eighteenth century.

[9]

Israel's Constitution

In the thirty-year period of formal peace that followed the Treaty of Utrecht (1713–1745), third-generation ministers completed the cultural and intellectual transition to a new Anglo-American world that began with the new charter. This transition required a reinterpretation of New England's past that emphasized the founders' love of civil and religious liberty, and wrote off their intolerance as an error common to all respectable seventeenth-century societies. As the eighteenth century wore on, however, it became more apparent that their own past was not the only past in need of revision. Because of the enduring hold of *Sola Scriptura* on New England's self-consciousness, anglicization became as much an exegetical as an historical problem; one that involved rereading the Old Testament in light of current social and political realities. Just as ministers recalled aspects of their own past selectively to coincide with present circumstances and orthodoxies, so they now switched their emphasis in Old Testament preaching from Israel's "theocracy," where God spoke directly through his inspired prophets and miraculously intervened in the course of nature, to "Israel's constitution" or the civil laws and human instruments that God used to uphold his people without recourse to miraculous interventions. Considered as a civil and political tract, the Old Testament yielded a multitude of social and political doctrines compatible with English law but independent of it. If their new constitutional rights and liberties could be presented as *sacred* principles, enjoined by Scripture as well as by their own past, New Englanders could retain their historic identity as a unique people of the Word who did not depend exclusively on England for guidance and direction. The anglicization of Israel's history allowed ministers to complete New England's entry into the eighteenth century as a now enlightened but still-chosen people.

A PEOPLE LEFT TO THEIR OWN METHODS

The transition to an enlightened reading of the Old Testament was one that eighteenth-century ministers *had* to make, but it was done so gradually that the issue was never joined in major controversy. And because the exegetical transition was gradual, historians have missed its revolutionary significance or confused biblical reinterpretation with secularization.[1] There were many aspects of Israel's Old Testament experience that no longered paralleled New England's experience that had to be explained if the people were to retain their identity as a New Israel. Chief among these discontinuities was Israel's record of divinely sanctioned intolerance and persecution, which New England no longer practiced actively, at least against other Protestants. But persecution was merely the most obvious reminder of how the two chosen peoples differed. Equally conspicuous was Israel's record of miraculous deliverances, when God had interrupted the course of nature to deliver his people. These differences raised the question of whether theocratic rule or miraculous interventions were necessary to support the claim of peculiar peoplehood.

The answer, as it emerged in the early decades of eighteenth-century occasional preaching, was that theocratic governments and miraculous interventions were incidental to the claim of peculiar peoplehood, not essential. In an enlightened age, God could as easily uphold his people through natural means and human agencies. In fact, third-generation ministers concluded from a close reading of the Old Testament, those were exactly the means that God had used to guide Israel through most of its history. What made Israel peculiar was its covenant, not theocratic rule or miraculous deliverances. In rereading the ancient chronicles, the most startling feature of divine providence was the fact that God required his people to rely on their own natural wisdom in governing and protecting themselves. More important than the Old Testament miracles were the general principles of government and social order that upheld Hebrew life on a day-to-day basis and were confirmed by the law of nature so that they applied equally to all nations.

The anglicization of Old Testament teachings regarding government and society can be seen most clearly in election sermons delivered after the Treaty of Utrecht. These sermons were less concerned with describing the details of Israel's government at different points in time than with establishing the general attitudes and expectations toward government and society that God required of his people. In general, election speakers taught that God did not expect his people to wait passively on him either for miraculous deliverances or for direct instructions, but to look to themselves in dependence on him. This did not invalidate the principle of providential leading on which New England's identity depended. Though God, in Thomas Buckingham's words, "leaves his People to their own Methods of Chusing and Electing their Rulers, yet his Providence is to be seen and acknowledged in all their Preferments."[2] Just as churchgoers need not rely on mystical raptures to confirm their eternal election, so these same citizens need not look for miracles to know that God had singled them out as a peculiar people. God's providential leading could be inferred from society so long as government protected the Word and churches, and upheld the people's liberty to worship God freely.

The new interest in "Israel's Constitution and Rulers" was evident in Peter Thacher's 1726 address to the Massachusetts General Court. With his text from Psalm 77:20 ("Thou leadest thy People like a Flock, by the hand of Moses and Aaron"), Thacher underscored the point that as the "universal *First Cause*" of all creation God was capable of ruling his people through "immediate inspiration," but this was not the "ordinary agency" he employed. Moses was a perfect case in point. True, God spoke directly to Moses in the burning bush, but this was less important than the ways in which he prepared Moses for leadership through natural means. Moses' early training in the court of the pharaoh and his "extended knowledge of Men and Things; and particularly the Methods of Government" supplied him with the skills he displayed later as Israel's leader.[3] For his skills, Moses was granted coercive powers over his people, and he applied those powers for their welfare in conformity to the law of God.

From Moses, Thacher extracted the general truth that "'tis for the People's sake, not their own, that Rulers must exhibit this Coercive Power, and use the Sword of the Revenger; and not willingly suffer the Lawless at home, or Enemies abroad, to despise and trample on them." As long as God's people submitted to "a Constitution of Government formed to the just Liberties, and best interests of human Nature, in Civil and Religious Affairs," and as long as leaders preserved constitutional liberties, it was "as if declared by a voice from heaven." Because Israel's constitution was established in conformity to the "great Ends of Society and Government"—liberty and order—it was providential and God inspired: "When in the Ordinary ways of Education, Experience, etc. Men are qualified for, spirited to, and introduced into the proper Stations and Opportunities to employ them for the publick Good; it is really *GOD's* work as if they were Inspired, and called out extraordinarily, by Name, to the honourable Business." This was equally true in New England. Looking back to New England's deliverance from Andros's tyranny, Thacher saw that "when the Designs of subtle and powerful Tyrants against a People's just Liberties are dashed, and their valuable Rights are preserved and restored, it's GOD's glorious Work and precious Gifts when done by Ordinary, as well as Extraordinary methods."[4] By choosing leaders like Moses, New Englanders could be as certain of their providential leading "as if" God had spoken to them directly.

As election speakers looked beyond Moses to subsequent rulers of Israel they found the same lessons again and again. After outlining the wise and public-spirited deportment of "Governor Nehemiah" as he supervised the rebuilding of Jerusalem's walls after the Babylonian captivity, William Burnham urged Connecticut's leaders to "let the Characters given of Nehemiah and Mordecai hold true of you; make it manifest that you seek the wealth of your people, and that you are men come to seek the good of our Israel."[5] God expected rulers to use their natural skills and formal training to enhance the public good, not to further their private gain. Benjamin Colman's election sermon also examined the character of Nehemiah and emphasized how he had sacrificed a life of "Ease and Pleasure" at the court of Artexerxes to serve God's people in Jerusalem: "He preferred the very dust of *Zion* to the Gardens of *Persia*, the broken Walls and Gates of *Jerusalem* to the Palaces of Shushan." The same was true of Solomon, who employed his God-given wisdom for the glory of his subjects. The careers of both leaders brought home the general lesson that "NO man is made only for *himself*, and his own private affairs, but to serve and benefit others. . . . IF a man receive *Wisdom* (and largeness of heart like *Solomon*) from the Father of light, he must be liberal and communicative thereof for the benefit of the world; as men do not light a candle and put it under a bushel, but set it on a Candlestic[k] and it giveth light to all that are in the room."[6] In all of these cases, God's leadership "exhibits truths which Nature confirms."

As before, election speakers were obliged to make Israel's past a typological parallel to their own situation. The history of Israel under the kings was especially important because it offered the closest analogy to New England's eighteenth-century status as colonies ruled by a constitutional monarchy. Of all Israel's kings, David was most important. Earlier ministers had emphasized David the outcast poet-in-the-wilderness, but third-generation ministers studied David the triumphant warrior and king. In his 1731 election sermon, Salem's Samuel Fiske (HC, 1708) traced David's career as king of Israel and drew from it many general lessons in "sagaciousness" and a public spirit that all rulers in all times must embody. Besides the obvious lessons, Fiske went on to infer other qualities of David's rule that fit with eighteenth-century assumptions about the good ruler. Chief among these qualities was the fact that David, like his successors, was a native son of Israel according to "the ancient Law [of Israel] . . . [which] forbid Strangers ruling over his People." From this precedent Fiske extracted the universal principle ("which is but the agreed sense of mankind") that rulers—whether appointed or elected—should be "*Natives* and *Inhabitants of the Land*; Born, Educated, Principled and Settled in it; and so have a right by Birth and common Inheritance, to be Chief and Rulers among the People, their Brethren."[7] Only native-born rulers possessed the "exact Knowledge of the civil and religious Constitution of their own Country" that was necessary for effective leadership.

Beyond David's nativity and natural qualifications for leadership, Fiske noted his piety. Rulers need not be Congregationalists, but they must acknowledge and promote gospel morality, and be "as sensitive of their entire Dependence on the Almighty, as they would have others [depend] on them, and infinitely more." God's "great design" in allowing kings to rule was to "promote religion": "Nor did any People ever yet flourish, however happy their Constitution was, but by this Care and fidelity." Fortunately, Fiske concluded, such care and fidelity were observed in New

England, "who made this Rule of King *David's* their own," and whose constitution embodied principles of piety and morality whose origins were sacred and unchanging.[8]

For Fiske and other election speakers, David's piety was as important as his statecraft; in this sense, the model of Israel had not changed. If rulers had regard for their souls they would seek God and not depend on their earthly office to save them. Timothy Edwards made this point forcefully in his 1732 election sermon, *All the Living Must Surely Die, and Go to Judgment*. From the Old Testament example of "that great Ruler in and over Israel, King *David*," Edwards reminded rulers that they must "set their Affection to the House of their God." On the day of judgment, "when the Monarchs of the world, with the Meanest of the People . . . must stand at Christ's Bar," there would pass "that final and definitive Sentence, that will unalterably settle them in their Everlasting State." Therefore, Edwards went on, "that you may not, when you die, go to Hell, and there be in dispair, Horrour and Torment . . . get a saving Interest in Christ, by Faith get your Hearts renewed, and Lives reformed . . . that so your Peace may be made with your Judge before Death comes."[9]

The state was no longer the coercive "sword" of the Congregational churches. It was, however, as John Barnard explained, responsible for providing a "shield" to protect "true religion" and to enforce outward compliance to the rules of morality taught in Scripture. The shielding function of the state involved not only the maintenance of established churches but also support for God's ministers and the colleges that produced them. It was, Barnard went on, "but just in the civil ruler to show a decent respect to the ministers of Christ and remember the honor that belongs to him in his place and encourage him to do his work."[10] Because of their classical education and local preeminence, ministers were—in their proper "place"—as entitled to "honor" as magistrates and equally responsible for maintaining social order and hence public submission to authority. Religious leaders were to civil leaders what religious liberties were to civil liberties: remove one and the other was certain to suffer; both must work together if social order and divine protection were to continue.

By selectively reinterpreting Israel's past in tandem with their own, election speakers brought eighteenth-century New England into line with their typological identity as the New Israel and were able to retain a sense of continuity in the midst of change. This continuity justified not only the retention of covenant logic in local oratory but also the extrapolation from Scripture of enlightened political lessons not entirely dependent on English rule or on England's interpretation of the law of nature. Read aright, sacred history yielded civil and political precepts identical to conclusions derived from natural reason. Before Saul and David were anointed as kings, John Barnard concluded, "they were first presented to the choice of the people, and their right to take power into their hands and administer in the affairs of government was by no means thought good until they had obtained the suffrages of their brethren—as is very clear from the sacred History [of Israel]." From this precedent, Barnard concluded that "'tis apparent the right to rule . . . is founded in compact." Any other system of government was bound to break down: "The State will become giddy with a continual whirl and all things run into such confusion as oversets the foundation of government." While Scripture did not specify "which form and scheme" of government by consent was "best," or how far consent ought to be taken in terms of the rights of the governed to instruct their betters, some popular covenanting or compacting was clearly required for government to be just. That England fulfilled the requirements of consent was clear from experience. Indeed, in Barnard's view and that of his peers, England came closer to realizing scriptural requirements for a just government than any other nation because "God hath blessed [them] above all people upon the face of the earth, in the felicity of their Constitution."[11]

Once rulers were chosen by popular consent they had to govern according to fixed laws. Any other standard of rule was bound to be "arbitrary" and "tyranical." England's standards were not recorded in any single statement but were contained in a bundle of documents and precedents running from Magna Carta to the Glorious Revolution. But England's "constitution" was illustrative, not determinative, of political thought in the New England pulpit. Its provisions duplicated and clarified truths already established in ancient Israel and practiced in seventeenth-century New England. As Barnard went on to explain:

> [I]t is the demand of righteousness that these powers and privileges be preserved in their proper channels, without the use of any secret craft or open violence to dam up the current or divert its course another way. That is to say that rulers are to govern according to law. Hence when the Kingdom was founded in Israel, Samuel wrote the manner of the kingdom in a book and laid it up before the Lord (1 Sam. 10.25), that it might be their Magna Carta, the fundamental constitution of the Kingdom and the standing rule of their government for the future.[12]

Israel's constitution was if anything more binding than England's because it was written. From the case of the "Kings of *Israel*," Thomas Buckingham deduced the necessity of a written "*constitution of Good Laws*":

> This is absolutely needful for the well Ordering and Governing of any People. It is not fit they should be left to do what is right in their own eyes; they need a rule to guide them and to bind them to their good Behaviour. Nor is it safe for Rulers to act Arbitrarily, and to make their Wills and Passions a Law to themselves and others. *There should be some fixed Rules of Government, and these duely Published,* that the subject might know what Terms he stands upon, and how to escape the lash of the Laws.[13]

In the long run, written laws and restrictions on rulers were even more important than the precedent of constitutional monarchy. When New Englanders eventually rose up against their sovereign, it was because he claimed powers that transgressed his constitutional limitations, trampling on the laws of men and the law of God.

NEW ENGLAND'S CENTURY OF COVENANT KEEPING

The historical analyses of Old Testament lawmakers and constitutions set forth in eighteenth-century election sermons are not profound political treatises, but they do show what happened to the typology of Israel in the third generation. By 1730 historical revision was virtually complete. In that year, Boston's Thomas Prince delivered the centennial election sermon. With Cotton Mather's death in 1728, Prince had emerged as New England's leading historian and the logical candidate to speak on the meaning of New World settlement. After extensive travel and study in England, Prince returned to New England and began collecting documents for a projected history or *Chronology* of New England that would bring Mather's earlier history up to the present.[14] By 1730 that work was far enough along for Prince to incorporate its main themes into his election sermon. The finished product combined New England's revised past with Israel's revised past so adroitly that it stood as a model for subsequent treatises on the transcendent meaning of New England.

In familiar fashion, Prince signaled his entry into New England's providential meaning with an extensive summary of the setting and content of Samuel's address to the people of Israel after they selected Saul as their first king. That setting, he went on, was not so different from the present. There, on that "great occasion" of confirming their ruler, God's prophet addressed the people arranged before him in a "vast and attentive audience." Those people differed from the surrounding nations in two ways that defined their identity as a peculiar nation. First, in matters of faith they were "free from all those human inventions and superstitious customs which were then the establish'd . . . way of worship in that ancient kingdom." They were a people called into being by the Word of God and confirmed in that identity by special promises and covenants. Second, in their civil arrangements they were governed by "excellent constitutions" whereby their leaders were "not merely rulers over the people but their representatives also." Instead of ruling the people directly by his voice, God allowed the tribes of Israel to select elders "who were men of chief renown and esteem among them for their singular abilities and public virtues." These elders chose from their midst a council of "seventy" who, with Moses and Aaron, "seem to be form'd into a supreme court of judicature over all the tribes—not destructive of the other orders but superior only to them."[15] Those arrangements bore remarkable similarities to the forms of government prescribed by the governor and legislature of Massachusetts, and it was thus eminently possible to reconcile English rule with peculiar peoplehood.

From the setting of Samuel's historical address and the nature of the government of the Israelites, Prince turned to the substance of Samuel's address, noting how "this wise and great master of assemblies first leads them back to the fountainhead of their present state and happiness." That fountainhead was divine providence. But—and this was the crucial point for Prince—God made his "divine appearance" known to Israel indirectly by "raising up such superior persons as Moses and Aaron as their distinguish'd heads and leaders, and by these renowned men conducting them out of the land of their oppressions and thro' all the difficult and hideous scenes of their progress thro' the wilderness to their desired country." The miracles that accompanied the Israelites in their odyssey to the promised land were, Prince concluded, incidental to their privileged status as a peculiar people. To clinch this point Prince asked his audience to consider whether Israel would have been any less a chosen people if they had arrived in Canaan without obvious interruptions of the course of nature like the parting of the Red Sea or the pillar of fire to guide them by night: "Wou'd not their deliverance out of Egypt and their entrance into Canaan be as truly the works of the Lord and as happy to Israel as if they were accomplished in a way beside the usual way of acting?" The answer was yes and underscored the general principle—essential to the providential meaning of New England—that, while "the works of the Lord for [Israel] were of a miraculous nature," among other professing peoples God's "righteous acts are done in a more veiled way by his invisible tho' real influence on material and intellectual agents, according to the course of nature, which is nothing else but his usual manner of acting and ruling in the world."[16]

If New England's century-long experience was not identical to Israel's in the matter of miracles, it was in other regards and, for Prince, these other considerations were the only ones that mattered in confirming peculiar peoplehood. Turning from Israel's past to New England's past, he could not conceal his delight in the obvious parallels:

> And here I cannot forbear observing that there never was any people on earth so parallel in their general history to that of the ancient Israelites as this of New England. . . . Excepting [the] miracles and changing names, one wou'd be ready to think the greater part of the Old Testament were written about us, or that we, tho' in a lower degree, were the particular antitypes of that primitive people.

Like Israel, New England was delivered from a land of persecution to a land of promise, and though their settlement was accomplished through natural means, in retrospect God's hand could be seen. The founders could not see that their persecution in England was in fact a means of mercy, any more than the Israelites could appreciate their sufferings in Egypt. But Prince could see that both were preludes to later good:

> It was well for our fathers, and for us in the end, that they were thus afflicted. For had there been then a succession of such indulgent princes and bishops in England as there have [been] since the Prince of Orange ascended the throne, there never had been such a country as this for religion, good

order, liberty, learning, and flourishing towns and churches, which have given us a distinguishing name in the world and have reflected a singular honor to the persons and principles of its original settlers for this hundred years.

Clearly, New England's growth and glory could not be ascribed to the environment or to chance. Had God not been behind the migration—and even the persecution—New England would have been "in no better condition" than the struggling "bordering plantations" in Nova Scotia and the South.[17]

After describing the providential circumstances of New England settlement, Prince traced God's continuing protection and blessing in the form of plentiful harvests, a robust maritime trade, college-trained leaders, military victories, and most recently, "the happy advancement and Succession of the illustrious House of Hanover to the British throne in which alone under God, we trust to preserve our constitution, laws, and liberties, and desire nothing but the continuance of all these things." Prince desired the continuation of British rule because it did not interfere with New England's "solemn covenant" with God. While the state no longer determined and enforced Puritan orthodoxy (at least in Massachusetts), neither did it seek to impose heterodoxy. If the current generation of New Englanders failed to retain the covenant, it could not be blamed on their rulers but on their own failure to maintain the "belief and practice" of their predecessors.

Because the covenant continued, Prince could still use the rhetoric of failure both as a warning to heed the voice of God's prophets and as a confirmation of New England's chosen status. While eighteenth-century occasional rhetoric minimalized Israel's miracles and persecutions, it retained the familiar litany of Israel's sins and judgments, meant as a solemn warning and mirror of New England's own endangered status. Even in the excitement of centennial celebration, the people must not forget the sobering truth that they had "done worse and worse in every generation," and thus stood even closer to divine desertion. This, Prince need hardly add, was in spite of the fact that the "faithful ministers" had not flagged in their proclamation of the will of God. The warning was harsh, but in a twist of logic perfected by his predecessors, Prince turned it into a ringing affirmation of New England's greatness. Despite fallings-away in the faith, there was a core of faithful ministers and pious church members who ensured the continuation of covenant protections. Prince's benediction radiated the confidence that New England was still special:

May we be Emmanuel's land, the people of the holy One of Israel; and may the Lord make us an eternal excellency, a joy of many generations. May our righteousness go forth as brightness and our salvation as a lamp that burneth; may the nations see our righteousness and all Kings our glory, and may the Lord delight in us and rejoice over us, and make us a praise in the earth.[18]

RENEWING THE COVENANT IN AN EXPANDING POPULATION

In preserving New England's place as "Emmanuel's land," third-generation ministers faced many obstacles in addition to the political and cultural adjustments made necessary by English rule. The chief threats to the congregational establishment were internal and social; excessive decentralization and widespread migration could do far more than royal government to undermine local discipline. As before, the underlying cause of social strain and dispersion was unprecedented population growth through natural increase. By 1700, New England's population had grown to nearly one hundred thousand, making it the wealthiest and most populous English region in North America.[19] Within particular towns the pattern of "enclosed orthodoxy" continued, but the towns themselves did not remain stable. The partitioning off of new subdivisions accelerated at an alarming rate as families grew up and pushed town boundaries to the outermost limits. What began as a trickle of new parish formations in the last quarter of the seventeenth century had swelled to a flood tide in the opening decades of the eighteenth century. In Dedham, Massachusetts, for example, the original town grant was subdivided into five parishes by 1720, each with its own minister and meetinghouse. In Connecticut, new parishes were partitioned off at an average rate of seventeen per decade throughout the eighteenth century, with a high point of twenty-three new societies incorporated in the decade 1721–1730.[20] With every new division churches faced anew the problem of settling orthodox pastors with binding Congregational covenants.

Even more threatening than constant parish subdivisions was the creation of new towns in previously unsettled "frontier" territories. As land ran out in the original towns, children of the third and fourth generations were forced to relocate in substantial numbers. With King Philip's War safely behind and an uneasy peace with France, New England entered a period of regional expansion. In 1715 new tracts of land were available in Worcester County in what marked the start of a major push inland. Nine townships were granted in 1727 to the heirs of New England militiamen who served in wars with the French and Indians, and thirty-three more townships were added in the next ten years.[21] These towns were very different from the first corporate settlements of preexistent congregations. For the first time, land speculation became common as inland buyers and militia claimants bought and sold land for a profit, with no intention of residing in the towns where they owned land.[22] The actual settlers came from different places as private owners, and thus these towns lacked the strong corporate impulse that had marked the first New England towns. For the most part, these settlers were young people, detached from their places of birth and strangers to one another. They were slow to organize churches and schools, and too poor to support orthodox ministers with even a minimal living. Ministers who eventually settled in these communities encountered a populace whose literacy and doctrinal skills were meager in comparison to settled towns, and who often valued their minister more for his skills in crop cultivation and animal husbandry than in divinity.[23] Somehow they too had to be incorporated into local church discipline if the Congregational Way was to survive the pressures of inexorable growth.

In confronting the problems of their generation, ministers found that no single strategy suited the diverse situations of urban, rural, and frontier settlement. But in general they emphasized either covenant renewal or revival, depending on local circumstances. Of these two time-honored strategies for church renewal, covenant renewal proved especially effective in long-settled communities, whereas revivals were emphasized on the frontier.

Covenant renewal was especially well suited to older towns and their newer subdivided parishes where there was a foundation of corporate familiarity on which to build. For the most part, young people in these communities had grown up in churches where they knew one another's families and where they had been indoctrinated since youth in the importance of local covenant keeping. They understood salvation less as a sudden conversion experience than as a gradual process that coincided with their coming-of-age as parents and landowners. And they were prepared to think of their local church in corporate rather than individual terms. In such communities, ministers (who themselves had grown up in settled towns) were constantly on the lookout for events or ceremonial occasions that could serve as a pretext for a season of covenant renewal and consequently increased church membership.

When possible, ministers organized covenant renewals around joyous events such as the incorporation of a new parish or the dedication of a new meetinghouse. In Andover, Massachusetts, where a new South Parish was incorporated in 1709, the children and grandchildren of the original settlers renewed their covenant bonds by setting aside a special fast day on which they pledged to "give ourselves one to another in the Lord, covenanting to walk together as a Church of Christ, in all the ways of his worship, according to the holy Rules of his Word." Included in the ceremony were both full and half-way members who further promised to "submit ourselves to the discipline and power of Christ in his Church," thereby fulfilling the minimum prerequisite for continued Congregational order.[24]

Where new parishes were not established, existing meetinghouses were enlarged to accommodate the larger population. The small, plain structures that served seventeenth-century towns gave way to larger, more imposing buildings that testified to the increase in prosperity and population, and to the influence of English architecture on eighteenth-century sensibilities.[25] New structures were dedicated with a day of fasting and covenant renewal. Sermons on these occasions reminded the present generation of vows made long before on the same spot and urged them to remember their obligations to keep the covenant alive.[26] Full members were enjoined to hold fast to their faith, and half-way members were pressed not to rest content until they could participate in the sacrament of the Lord's Supper.

A less pleasant but more common incentive for covenant renewal was the sort of calamitous event associated with fast days. If the crisis was serious enough, fast days could be turned to the double purpose of corporate repentance and covenant renewal. The increasing incidence of epidemics, fires, wars, and natural disasters convinced the ministers that "the Lord hath of late years been marching thro' the Land in Indignation, and by the Sword, and Sickness, and many other ways, [has] been dropping down his anger." Smallpox epidemics and fires had become so grave a menace to Boston's concentrated population that throughout the early 1720s the churches met to renew their covenant vows and "to ask [for] the Effusion of the spirit of Grace on their *children*; and on the children of the Town."[27] For the most part these rituals were locally observed and did not involve large numbers of churches. Then, in 1727, an event occurred that brought the whole country to its knees.

For some time ministers had been predicting a great day of trouble, just as their predecessors had done in the early 1670s. So palpable had these fears become that on Sunday morning, October 29, Hampton's Nathaniel Gookin ventured into the realm of prophecy. Earlier that week in preparing for his sermon on Ezekiel 7:7 ("The Day of Trouble is Near") he had experienced a premonition that he shared with his congregation:

> I don't pretend to a Gift of foretelling future things; But the Impression that these Words have made upon my mind in the week past, so that I cou'd not bend my tho'ts to prepare a Discourse on any other Subject.... I say, It being thus, I *know not* but there may be a *particular Warning* design'd by God of some Day of Trouble near, Perhaps to *me*, Perhaps to *you*, Perhaps to *all of us*.[28]

That night, townspeople throughout New England awoke to the most convulsive earthquake in living memory. It began, according to several accounts, with "a flash of Light," which was then followed by a "horrid rumbling" and "weighty shaking" that continued to reverberate throughout the evening. Weymouth's Thomas Paine recalled how "the motion of the Earth was very great, like the waves of the sea.... The strongest Houses shook prodigiously and the tops of some Chimnies were thrown down.... It affected the People of N-E, especially those near the Center of it, with more Fear Amazement than ever is thought to have befallen the Land since it had that Name." Awakened sleepers huddled in groups in the streets, certain that the day of judgment had come. The aftershocks continued for nine days which, Paine observed, "mightily kept up the Terror of it in the People, and drove them to all possible means of Reformation."[29]

Unlike other calamitous events that were limited to one locale or spread out over a number of weeks and months, the earthquake of 1727 was felt throughout New England and served to bring the whole country to the churches. Fasts were called spontaneously throughout the land on the day after the earthquake and repeatedly during the ensuing weeks. Over seventeen of these fast sermons were published, and throughout that year, the printing of the fasts overwhelmed the presses. Although no lives had been lost, ministers and people alike interpreted the event as a portentous sign of God's anger with his people and his demand for their reformation and renewal of covenant pledges.

Ministers brought to their interpretations of the earthquake the same fusion of natural knowledge and providential doctrine that characterized their response to the New Learning generally. They drew from the Royal Academy and recent scientific literature to demystify the event by explaining its natural causes. Earthquakes, John Barnard explained, were not miracles but natural convulsions that occurred when bodies of water met with "subteraneous Fires" in underground caverns to produce rumblings at ground level. In like manner, Brooklyn's John Allin explained the flashes of lightning that preceded the earthquake as a natural "mixture of Sulphurous and Nitrous Particles extracted from the Earth by the Sun." Nor were earthquakes especially rare. From accounts of convulsions both in Scripture and in profane history, Thomas Prince constructed a typology classifying earthquakes according to their intensity, duration, and spiritual significance.[30] All of these explanations reflected the best learning of the age and were invoked by ministers attuned to the natural laws of the universe. Pulpit commentary on the earthquake portrayed it as a perfectly understandable phenomenon that followed a predictable cause-effect sequence.

While science provided a proximate understanding of earthquakes as natural phenomena, it could not supply the last word—at least not in New England. The laws of science, Prince observed, provided no assurance that earthquakes were anything other than random, "fatal Things that move and act of themselves . . . without Design or Reason."[31] This rubbed against the grain of providential theory, and so alongside natural explanations, ministers deduced a more important providential explanation. From the history of professing peoples, third-generation ministers had already extracted the principle that God worked as actively through natural or "second" causes as he did through miracles as such. In the same way that God used the natural skills of human leaders to guide his people he used the regular course of nature to convey his providential care. While a chain of natural events precipitated earthquakes, God—as "First Cause"—still had to "permit" them to run their course. Such permission would not have been granted had his people honored him. Who could tell how many potential earthquakes of much greater devastation were preempted by God because the people had kept the covenant? As James Allin explained, "God is the cause of this [natural] cause. . . . And it is certain the *Second Causes* could produce no such *Effect* without leave from him."[32] Therefore, ministers concluded, the appropriate response of congregations was not resigned paralysis but active—even frenetic—reformation. If the people reformed, the next time cauldrons boiled they would not destroy the land. Fear of earthquakes was, John Cotton said, perfectly natural; indeed, it was precisely God's intention to evoke such fear in allowing the earthquake to proceed. But to serve its providential purpose, the fear had to be channeled into a reform of those "procuring" evils that were as well known to eighteenth-century audiences as to their predecessors: "oppression, Injustice, Cozning and Deceit, Falsehood and Evil Speaking, Pride and Contention, Intemperance, Drunkenness, Unchastity, or Excessive love to the World, and I may add the Rudeness and Profaneness of Young People?"[33] Only through a fusion of natural science and providential history could the surrounding chaos yield meaning that would do justice both to science and religion and, at the same time, incite the course of reformation charted by the ministers.

The success of the Great Earthquake in promoting reform and renewal was spectacular. In Haverhill as in numerous other communities, all the inhabitants gathered to hear the covenant read and offer their collective assent, "the Women by now arising From their seats and *Standing* up. And all the Males by standing up and openly *lifting up our Hands*, to the most High God, 'till 'tis ended."[34] Along with covenant renewal came mass conversions. While all were affected by the "solemn" occasion, ministers directed their pleas especially to the youth. In Andover, John Barnard concluded with the plea that "our *Young People*, who seem to be much affected with GOD's awful Providence, [might] bitterly think of their *sinful Omission*, I mean their neglecting to lay themselves under more strict *Engagements* to GOD, by Renewing their *Baptismal Covenant* and coming to the *Lord's Table*."[35] Such invitations were not without effect in bringing new members into the church. In a letter to John Cotton, John Brown of Haverhill noted how in the first week after the earthquake and covenant renewal ceremony thirty new converts were added to full communion: "The next Sabbath we had propounded 84 persons; and again yesterday Nov 19 (for my hands were full the third week), 39. And People are still coming to me. So that now, since the *Earthquakes*, I have admitted and propounded 154 Persons; 87 for the Lords Table, the rest for Baptism, or the Renewing the Baptismal Covenant. The number of Men and Women pretty near equal; mostly younger people, from 15 to 30."[36] Elsewhere the results were similar. In Andover's North Parish, 158 new members were added in the year following the earthquake, while in Hingham, Ebenezer Gay admitted more new members (34) than in any other year of his long ministry.[37] More than any other event, the Great Earthquake convinced ministers of the potential for mass revival.

REVIVALS IN A NEW KEY

The calls for conversion heard in the earthquake fasts were part of a larger campaign for revival that had begun over a decade earlier. While revivals were viewed as especially useful preaching strategies in frontier settlements that lacked the supporting institutions of churches, schools, and well-entrenched families, ministers elsewhere began issuing the same call for evangelical harvests where "great Numbers" of the churches and communities would experience conversion simultaneously. Already in 1716, Cotton Mather urged province-wide revivals at a Boston lecture, pointing out how Reformed pastors in Europe were inaugurating a great "Growth of churches" that promised the eventual triumph of "The Protestant Religion" over its Roman Catholic enemies.[38] Similarly, at a thanksgiving sermon in Windham, Connecticut, in 1721, New London's Eliphalet Adams rejoiced at how "many have been awakened" under the conversionist preaching of the local minister Samuel Whiting: "There had been a greater *stirring* than Ordinary among the *dry bones*, Many have been Awakened to Consider and Enquire with a great deal of Earnestness, *What they should do to be Saved*?" Windham was only part of a regional revival that also included the neighboring communities of Windsor and Norwich.[39] None of these towns were frontier communities, but they were reached by ministerial calls to be "awakened."

After the model of Solomon Stoddard, forty years earlier, revivalistic preaching differed from regular preaching in limiting the range of subject matter to the first two stages of the sin-salvation-service sequence, often summarized as "law" and "gospel." Unlike regular preaching in covenanted communities, which devoted extensive attention to "sanctification" and the more advanced "head" knowledge of Reformed doctrine, revivalistic preaching aimed at the "heart" of the listener, first by "convicting" him or her of sin, and then holding forth the "reprieve" of the gospel. While this was admittedly a limited fare of "spiritual milk" without the "meat" of advanced doctrine, it was, many ministers believed, the necessary precondition to meaningful moral and corporate reform. Without a strong core of converted families, the corporate covenant would lose all meaning.

Increasingly ministers called upon each other to concentrate on laying a foundation of personal faith and spirituality through a return to the simple gospel message of the "New Birth." Covenant renewal was not a sufficient antidote to New England's ills; it had to be supplemented with calls to conversion. In his Massachusetts election sermon, Ipswich's Samuel Wigglesworth urged his colleagues to substitute evangelical preaching for empty calls to corporate morality:

> And then as to our *Preaching*, Let us not labour to build up a *Shell*, to form a meer *Carcase of Godliness*, by furnishing our Auditors with *Moral Virtues* only, void of *Internal Vital Principles*; but *Travail in birth* with them until *Christ be formed in them*, and they are become holy in Heart, as well as blameless of Life. I know not how we can begin with our Flocks better, than the *Great Prophet and Teacher* did with *Nicodemus, Except a man be born again, he cannot see the Kingdom of God.*

In similar terms, Boston's John Webb employed Habakkuk 3:2 ("O Lord, revive thy work in the Midst of the years") to urge his congregation to "adopt this Prayer of the Prophet to our own case." Such exhortations recurred frequently in regular preaching.[40] They did not reflect a radical shift in belief but rather a more general application of rhetorical strategies first heard in Stoddard's Northampton parish.

Much more than before, eighteenth-century calls for revival were directed particularly to young people. The quasi-extended New England family, long the primary carrier of religious faith from one generation of church members to the next, was changing as a result of population growth, urbanization, and geographic mobility. With so many children no longer living under the direct control and supervision of their parents, ministers recognized that they must encourage conversion at an earlier age. Increasingly, they spoke of "the time of Youth" as "the Accepted time with the most that are Converted."[41] Addressing the "religious societies" of Boston youth, for example, Benjamin Colman implored them to "show that they have given their Hearts to God by coming into full Communion; and by continuing stedfastly (all their Life) in the Fellowship of the Saints. Give your hearts to God and it will bring you to the *Table* of Christ, and make you welcome there."[42] The tendency of revivalistic preaching to aim at the "heart" became even more pronounced in sermons directed to the youth. In a sermon delivered to the young people two weeks before the Great Earthquake, Samuel Wigglesworth emphasized the "affections," because "the motives drawn from these are of all the most persuasive." Only through a changed heart could the believer enjoy "ravishing discoveries of the Divine excellencies; and his Redeemer's allsufficency, Beauty, and Goodness."[43]

By the third decade of the eighteenth century, New England's political, cultural, and exegetical adaptation to English rule and the cultural environment of the Enlightenment era was virtually complete. By a mighty intellectual effort, third-generation ministers had opened their pulpits to an enlightened age; at the same time they held fast to covenant assumptions and their identity as the New Israel. These cultural achievements were accompanied by geographic expansion and a substantial growth in population and wealth—all of which meant more power confronting the French menace to the north. But this was not enough. Along with power came a social and economic complexity that threatened to diffract and dim the beacon of religious purity. New England was in danger of being swallowed up by its own successes. What the rising generation clearly needed was a revival of popular piety. But it seemed that the people's hearts could not be moved by the sublime cadences of Joseph Addison or John Tillotson. New speakers, new voices and styles were needed to penetrate the darkness of ordinary souls with divine and supernatural light. Such speakers would soon appear from the rising generation and from abroad; they would bring down on the parched ground of New England piety showers of converting grace such as the region had never before seen; and they would spread their message of the New Birth with such a transforming intensity that the New England pulpit and New England society would never again be the same.

PART IV

DELIVERY, 1731–1763

[10]

Awakening

The task of promoting revival and preserving corporate loyalty to the New England Way was inherited by a fourth generation of ministers who completed their studies at eighteenth-century Harvard and Yale in an atmosphere of cosmopolitan learning and polite culture. They were confident of their ability to maintain the inherited reins of leadership in an enlightened age. But inherited principles, no matter how familiar and enlightened, would not survive their generation. The formal continuities of their office and the old habits of superiority that linked ministers to their venerable predecessors could not conceal a complex web of internal tensions and anxieties in church and state. Leaders were pitted against followers in endless contests for control that grew more bitter as time went on. Confrontation and conflict had been a constant but manageable fact of life in New England's decentralized and inherently unstable institutions for a century. But never before were there so many changes, on so many fronts, in so contentious an atmosphere. Traditional social categories were about to explode and splinter in many directions. Instead of peace and continuity, this generation would be forced to create from the fragments of a once-coherent hierarchical social ethic a more democratic configuration that their predecessors would barely have recognized—or endorsed. The trigger, oddly enough, would not be internal insurrections or mob violence, but George Whitefield, the young English itinerant whose stated intention in visiting New England was the salvation of the people's souls.

SOCIAL TENSIONS AND THE LOSS OF UNIFORMITY

A generation of "new" social historians has convincingly identified the middle decades of the eighteenth century as a critical "takeoff" period in the American colonies' evolution from a "traditional" to a "modern" society.[1] But few contemporaries were aware of profound change in their society or the strains that such change placed on institutions and social assumptions. Unlike wars, earthquakes, or political upheavals that were explosive and highly visible events, the two prime movers in effecting

185

New England's social transformation—demographic growth and economic development—were far less perceptible, though they were the products of trends set in motion decades and even generations earlier. New England's ministers, like elites in other eighteenth-century cultures, were not attuned to explaining change through impersonal historical forces like demography or economics.[2] They looked for personal and providential causes, and in so doing failed to recognize the new forces that were reshaping their society. New England's clerical watchmen were adept at spying trouble in the form of immorality, godlessness, diabolical agents of Satan, tyrannical rulers, or a giddy people, but no minister thought to proclaim a fast in response to runaway population growth or a thanksgiving for the vertical integration of government and economy.

New England provincials may not have understood the cause of all their woes, but they did recognize that their society was now different; it was much larger, more scattered, and displayed greater structural differentiation and complexity. Increases in "overcrowding," inequality of wealth, and geographic mobility were so significant that no institution was left unchanged.[3] New England's culture remained religious in its orientation, but tensions also increased in the churches—tensions that lay at the heart of the colonists' social world. Disputes between parents and their children in the outlands over new meetinghouses and religious taxes—old issues to be sure—were more intense than ever before. The effects of the laws of toleration finally began to be felt as rising numbers of dissatisfied inhabitants—both wealthy and poor—applied for dissenter status as Baptists, Quakers, "Rogerenes," and Anglicans. Although these dissenting churches never included more than a small fraction of the population, they did promote controversy over religious taxes and served as popular and, in the case of Anglicans, elite alternatives to the Congregational establishment.[4] Within the Congregational churches crises of authority were manifested in increased disputes between ministers and their congregations over clerical authority, ministerial salaries, and theological orthodoxy.[5] Instead of ameliorating tensions, the churches were racked by problems that defied simple solutions.

Added to discord within churches were divisions among the fourth-generation clergy. By 1740 the number of Congregational ministers had grown to 420, scattered over a wide area and drawn from different social and regional backgrounds.[6] Whether considered in sheer numbers, geographic range, social composition, or personal temperament, they were a far less homogenous group than their predecessors and much more likely to disagree on crucial questions of church order and preaching style. The arrogance of some ministers, together with the successes of competing Anglican churches, forced many younger ministers to redefine the limits of clerical authority in terms that accorded greater recognition to lay liberties, and even many staunch Congregational ministers began to fear the drift of their own sacerdotalism. Clerical presumption at the expense of congregational liberties was, as Gloucester's John White explained, "arbitrary" and squinted toward "tyranny." Others, however, were of a different mind. Singling out the Baptist pietists and exhorters, ministers complained that some congregations had grown too powerful and autonomous, and must be curbed by stronger clerical associations. Some ministers, like Stratford's Samuel Johnson, went so far as to take orders in the Church of England, believing that Congregationalism represented "a way so entirely popular [that it] could but very poorly . . . answer any ends of government; but must from the nature of it crumble to pieces, as every individual seems to think himself infallible."[7] What had once been differences in emphasis within the ministry were fast becoming opposing "schools" or "sides" that preferred to publicize their differences than stress their commonalities.

Different attitudes toward clerical authority correlated with different preaching styles. Congregational preaching had traditionally struck a middle ground between ornate Anglican discourse and impassioned lay exhorting, or between the "head" and the "heart." But by 1730 that balance was giving way to extremes, as ministers stressed one faculty or the other. In part these alternative preferences stemmed from diverse social backgrounds, childhood experiences, and personal "temperaments."[8] More immediate causes were the preaching tastes of particular congregations and the rival academic theories taught in the colleges. By the eighteenth century, the old theories of Aristotle and Ramus had been largely discredited, but there was no agreement on appropriate substitute theories, especially in the areas of "moral philosophy" (ethics), "psychology" (a subsection of physics), and rhetoric. European luminaries like Descartes, Locke, Hume, the third earl of Shaftesbury, Francis Hutcheson, and Bishop Joseph Butler were read avidly and aroused strong controversy. Earlier generations integrated rival "intellectualist" and "voluntarist" theories of will, intellect, and emotions into their preaching. Fourth-generation ministers began taking sides: some advanced the new "sentimentalist" theories of Shaftesbury or Hutcheson, which underlined the "affections" as the seat of virtue and conversion, while others retained a more traditional emphasis on the "understanding" and discounted the "passions" altogether.[9]

Debates over the problem of the will and the question of moral responsibility followed ministers into their pulpits. A minister's own model of human psychology and ethical action determined whether sermons would be constructed to reach the head or the heart and influenced their delivery as well. But in promoting one style or the other, ministers could not ignore lay preferences. In considering pulpit candidates, congregations expressed clear preferences which, like the ministry itself, reflected diverse social and regional differences. In general, well-established, urban congregations desired polished, literary discourses, whereas country and frontier churches preferred a more popular, emotional style.[10] These factors ensured that ministers could no longer speak with any degree of uniformity on the burning issues of their day.

RUMBLINGS IN NORTHAMPTON

Discord in the churches, dissension among the clergy, and heightened political and social tensions convinced fourth-generation ministers of the need for revival. In view of the laws of toleration and the Baptist and Anglican alternatives, ministers could prevent widespread defections and unrest only insofar as the people continued to identify the words of the ministers with the Word of God. This required a united clerical front. Once divisions within the ministry over revival became public, congregations would be forced to determine the truth for themselves. At that moment, revivals would promote the opposite of what the ministers intended: discord instead of harmony, and a general weakening of clerical authority. This is exactly what happened during New England's "Great Awakening."[11]

The first major rumblings of revival to attract international attention came from the Connecticut River Valley in 1734. The center of revival activity was Northampton, where Solomon Stoddard's brilliant grandson, Jonathan Edwards, preached a series of conversion sermons that brought over three hundred new converts into full church membership in one year. Edwards rejoiced at how the revival saved sinners and "immediately put an end to differences between ministers and people." The healing effects, he went on, were nearly universal, so that "All seemed to be seized with a deep concern about their eternal salvation; all the talk in all companies, and upon [all] occasions was upon the things of religion, and no other talk was anywhere relished; and scarcely a single person in the whole town was left unconcerned about the great things of the eternal world."[12]

In many respects this published account of mass conversions and heightened religiosity was similar to reports issued in earlier generations. But two features of Northampton's revival diverged from past patterns and boded ill for the future of the Congregational clergy. First was the regional rather than local character of the event. Word of Northampton's revival immediately "filled the neighboring towns with talk," and before all was said and done more than thirty surrounding towns in the valley participated in a common revival. Gone were the days when revivals were local affairs conducted by the resident pastor. The same social and economic forces that drew eighteenth-century towns into widening webs of interdependence and intercommunication paved the way for religious movements that could transcend local boundaries and mobilize groups from neighboring communities into a united revival. Edwards was well aware of this difference in scale and scope, and hoped that what happened in the valley would presage an even broader revival that would incorporate the entire country.

Related to the regional character of the Valley revivals was the equally novel fact that local ministers were not the prime movers. Instead, according to Edwards's account, once the call for conversion was sounded, the primary momentum was generated from beneath, among people "in all companies" (though "the youth" were especially active) who met in their "neighborhoods" and who, through lay "testifyings" of the "great things of religion," produced a "great noise" that could be heard throughout the region. In the course of identifying the towns where revivals took root and flourished, Edwards seldom even mentioned the local ministers' names and focused instead on the primary human "instruments," the people. Because of the "meanness and weakness" of these popular instruments, more respectable observers did not always appreciate the "noise" they produced. Some ministers, both within the valley and outside, were cool toward the event. Edwards noted that "there were many that scoffed at and ridiculed it; and some compared what we called conversion to certain distempers." Nevertheless, the movement continued to thrive for some months and its friends hoped that it would "soon become universal."[13]

Such hopes were not realized. At the time Edwards penned his narrative in 1735 the revival had already passed its zenith.[14] The "late" work of God, though dramatic, proved ephemeral; it was not able to sustain its momentum. By late May 1734, it was clear to Edwards "that the Spirit of God was gradually withdrawing from us," and "the instances of conversion were rare here in comparison of what they had before been." Revivals either continued to grow in intensity and expand across space, or they died; there was no standing still. Despite its promising beginnings and the "extraordinariness of the thing," revivalism waned and disappeared. Edwards's narrative remained more a guide book for future possibilities than a record of national revival.

THE GRAND ITINERANT

While revivals continued to appear in local congregations throughout New England, nothing dramatic happened to fulfill Edwards's universal hopes until 1740. Then the most sensational event in the history of New England preaching occurred. The catalyst was a twenty-four-year-old English evangelist named George Whitefield who, despite his youth and the fact that he had never had his own church, attracted crowds of such unprecedented size and enthusiasm that he became known as the "Grand Itinerant." First in the fields of England and then in 1738 in the Middle and Southern Colonies, crowds materialized out of nowhere to hear him speak in the most stirring terms about the "New Birth." Although nominally an Anglican, Whitefield deliberately minimized his connections to that church (arousing in turn the ire of the Anglican hierarchy) and spoke in the most general terms of his hopes "for a revival of true and undefiled religion in all sects whatsoever!"[15] Promote revival he would, though in a "catholic spirit" that was decidedly Calvinist in tone and aimed especially at listeners who would be moved by the rhetoric of total depravity and supernatural grace. Such listeners existed in the Southern and, to a greater extent, in the Middle Colonies (especially among the Presbyterians in Pennsylvania), but nowhere were they more concentrated or receptive than in New England. There, in 1740, Whitefield would realize his greatest triumph as an itinerant preacher.

By the time Whitefield arrived in Newport in September, word of extraordinary crowds and conversions in Philadelphia preceded him, preparing the region for his exciting and novel brand of mass evangelism. For his part, Whitefield was equally enthused. Despite sad declensions (which, Whitefield exulted, would soon improve under his ministrations), New England's piety was renowned and "certainly excels all other provinces in America; and, for the establishment of religion, perhaps all other parts of the world." These were the sort of words New Englanders desperately wanted to hear. In a whirlwind forty-five-day tour of central places in Massachusetts and Connecticut, Whitefield delivered over 175 sermons to thousands of hearers, "besides exhorting very frequently in private."[16] Before he was finished, most inhabitants heard him preach at least once. He generated such excitement that audiences appeared out of control as they "elbowed, shoved, and trampled over themselves to hear of 'divine things' from the famed Whitefield."[17] Whitefield himself was equally impressed. It was, he rejoiced in his *Journal*, like "putting fire to tinder." Elsewhere he concluded, "my heaven is begun indeed. I feast on the fatted calf."[18] Never had he or his audiences been part of an event so consuming as to hold an entire region captive to his oratory.

Any explanation of Whitefield's success as an itinerant preacher must begin with a comment on his sheer oratorical ability, discovered in childhood and nurtured throughout his career. By all accounts Whitefield's elocution was remarkable. The great power, timbre, and sonority of his voice excited attention wherever he spoke. Not only was his voice easily heard over great distances (Benjamin Franklin estimated it could reach thirty thousand hearers) but his words flowed without hesitation or uncertainty. Listeners were carried along a fixating stream of discourse filled with dramatic illustrations and heart-rending confrontations with the terrors of damnation and the joys of conversion. Whitefield straddled the line separating drama and melodrama to near perfection. So finely honed was his sense of timing (formed in part by a childhood exposure to the stage) that he frequently departed from his intended words to make some dramatic improvement on the moment. In one sermon, for example, he used a passing thunder storm to evoke the voice of God among the heavens:

> "See there!" said he, pointing to the lightning, which played on the corner of the pulpit—"'Tis a glance from the angry eye of Jehovah! Hark!" continued he, raising his finger in a listening attitude, as the distant thunder grew louder and louder, and broke in one tremendous crash over the building. "It was the voice of the Almighty as he passed by in his anger!" As the sound died away, he covered his face with his hands, and knelt beside his pulpit, apparently lost in inward and intense prayer. The storm passed rap-

idly away, and the sun bursting forth in his [its] might, threw across the heavens a magnificent arch of peace. Rising and pointing to the beautiful object, he exclaimed, "Look upon the rainbow, and praise him that made it. Very beautiful it is in the brightness thereof. It compasseth the heavens about with glory; and the hands of the Most High have bended it."[19]

These words, conveyed by Whitefield's early biographer John Gillies, show how Whitefield played on the events of the moment. The dramatic gestures—pointed finger, covered face, exclamatory voice—were undoubtedly contrived, but their effectiveness depended on an acute sensitivity to the immediate setting that no other eighteenth-century preacher could match.

To sustain a sense of vital engagement, Whitefield generally selected texts for their dramatic setting rather than doctrinal depth or polemical reference. Instead of preparing sermon series—the stock-in-trade of regular preachers—he fixed on the dramatic phrase or sentence, lifted from a larger historical or dogmatic context and capable of speaking on its own. The "opening" of technical doctrines occupied little of his attention because all his sermons came back sooner or later to the call for a New Birth. Of particular use were Scripture narratives structured around a dialogue that Whitefield could expand through the powers of his imagination. Old Testament texts were as useful as New, although more for their typological references to Christ than for the social and political lessons they contained. One favorite text was the Old Testament story in which God commanded Abraham to sacrifice his son Isaac. Earlier, God had promised Abraham that Isaac would preside over a great people; now he was asking for his life. What could this mean? Here the text did not elaborate, so Whitefield openly imagined the thoughts that might have passed through Abraham's mind, or someone else's mind if they were in a similar situation. Men of lesser faith than Abraham's would have rationalized the command away. In words that sounded remarkably like they could have originated in New England, Whitefield imagined the man of weak faith asking: "If I murder him, what will become of God's promise? Besides I am now like a city Upon a hill; I shine a light in the world, in the midst of a crooked and perverse generation: How then shall I cause God's name to be blasphemed, how shall I become a bye-word among the Heathen, if they hear that I have committed a crime which they abhor!" But this was not, Whitefield continued, Abraham's response. Despite his love for Isaac he prepared to sacrifice him until, at the last moment, God stopped his hand. Contained in this story, Whitefield concluded, was a double lesson that not only illustrated Abraham's faith but also pointed to a second sacrifice that would not be stopped:

Behold, I shew you a mystery hid under the sacrifice of Abraham's only son, which, unless your hearts are hardened, must cause you to weep tears of love, and that plentifully too. I would willingly hope you even prevent me here, and are ready to say, "it is the love of God in giving Jesus Christ to die for our sins." . . . For, if you admire Abraham offering up his Isaac, how much more ought you to extol, magnify, and adore the love of God, who so loved the world, as to give his only begotten Son, Christ Jesus our Lord.[20]

Sentiments like these had been proclaimed from New England's pulpits for a century but never with such dramatic flair or piercing pathos.

Whitefield's novel dramatizations stemmed from his habit of speaking "extemporaneously"—without notes. This method had never been practiced by Congregational ministers or taught at the colleges, and of all his innovations it attracted the greatest comment. Throughout his journeys, Whitefield urged ministers and aspiring ministers to "preach without notes," and criticized recorded sermons as a deficiency in faith: "I think the ministers preaching almost universally by note, is a mark that they have, in great measure, lost the old spirit of preaching. Though they are not to be condemned who use notes, yet it is a symptom of the decay of religion, when reading sermons becomes fashionable where *extempore* preaching did once almost universally prevail." While mistaken about the "almost universal" practice of earlier Puritans speaking without notes of any sort, Whitefield was correct in observing how many New England ministers ceased to depend on extensive notes or sermons memorized in advance and instead exhibited the influence of the Anglican tradition of reading sermons verbatim in the manner of a prepared essay rather than a living speech.[21] Such sermons, Whitefield recognized, could not reach popular audiences. Whatever the liabilities of extemporaneous speech in terms of literary cohesion and orderly progression, it had the immense advantage of channeling the full heart and soul of the speaker into the actual moment of delivery and fusing a unique bond between speaker, audience, and the immediate situation. Extemporaneous speech conveyed spontaneity and enthusiasm that extensive outlines or fully recorded sermon texts seemed unable to match.

THE ORALITY OF WHITEFIELD'S MESSAGE

For all intents and purposes, Whitefield's ministry was exclusively oral. He adamantly refused to use written notes and sometimes even failed to select a Scripture text before entering the pulpit.[22] When he prepared sermons for print they were inelegant and hurried. Typically they were written while on board ships to and from the New World. So pale were these texts alongside his actual performances that his friend and admirer (though never kindred spirit) Benjamin Franklin believed that "if he had never written anything . . . his reputation might in that case have still been growing, even after his death, as [there] being nothing of his writing on which to found a censure and give him a lower character."[23]

Whitefield's failings as a writer merely highlight his success as a speaker and confirm the insights of cultural studies that examine the medium of historical records alongside their message. In gathering his large and unfamiliar audiences, Whitefield employed the only form of communication that would surely impress all hearers: the spoken word proclaimed extemporaneously in everyday language. Recognition of the powerful social and psychological imperatives of direct oral address has led Walter Ong to observe that "writing commits the word to space. But to do so, it makes words less real, pretends they are something they are not: quiescent marks." Print and typographic culture create highly visual, sequential, and analytic patterns of thought that popular cultures, attuned to easily remembered forms of speech, cannot readily appreciate.[24] Popular culture in New England was literate to be sure, but it was limited largely to the vernacular Word, not the periodical essay. Whitefield recognized this and insisted that effective preaching depended more on delivery than composition. Proper method and sequence were secondary to zeal; and zeal depended on the minister's ability to speak from the heart without the props and constraints of prepared notes.

The impact of Whitefield's extemporaneous sermons was made possible by his career as an *itinerant* evangelist. Since he never had to give the same message in the same place twice, he could weave variations around simple gospel themes which, if delivered weekly to the same audience, would soon have become dull and repetitious. As a "planter" rather than "waterer," he could structure his sermons around the mnemonic device of "law-gospel" and the New Birth, then move on to the next audience. Settled ministers did not ignore this theme, but neither could they make it the sum and substance of their preaching. Along with supernatural conversion, they had to preach doctrine and social duty, and these required a technical attention to exegetical detail, moral philosophy, and orderly sequence that was not as well suited to immediate inspiration or as apt to move the emotion.

Itinerancy not only facilitated extemporaneous speech but also placed the minister in a unique social context of far greater significance for eighteenth-century audiences than we might suspect.[25] Immensely significant was the itinerant's unfamiliarity with his audience and his lack of personal connection to local authority figures. The itinerant speaker—neither employed by nor in authority over a particular congregation—was freed to establish a special rapport with his audience that dramatically altered the flow of authority in public communications. Whitefield spoke as one whose success depended entirely on his ability to persuade audiences to listen of their own free will. With his itinerancy, there blossomed an innovative style of public speaking that redefined the social context of homiletics. In his revivals the power to speak was dispensed from beneath, in the voluntary initiative of the people assembling in extrainstitutional settings, thereby creating new models of authority and social order. Gone were seated meetinghouses and every other distinction that reinforced the ministry's aristocratic claims. A new form of mass communications appeared in which people were encouraged—even commanded—to speak out concerning the great work of grace in their souls. What Whitefield lacked in theological subtlety and polite audiences he made up for in sheer audience size. That audience thrilled not only to the gospel message they heard but also to their own great power visibly manifested in mass assembly. Local authorities could either applaud or condemn his revivals, but they could not stop them.

AN INVERTED JEREMIAD

With all Whitefield's social and homiletical innovations it would be easy to lose sight of his message, which in certain key regards was equally novel. While Whitefield's gospel was traditional in its Calvinist emphasis on total depravity and unconditional election, it veered from the traditional by distributing the barbs of guilt and condemnation to the clergy as well as their followers. For over a century lay audiences had heard of failure and declension in terms that placed the onus of guilt primarily on their own shoulders. With Whitefield, the rhetoric of failure was inverted; in the new picture, the ministers and the colleges that trained them were the primary culprits. If there were troubles in the land, Whitefield cried, it was the fault of "lukewarm" ministers who "have only a name to live." The colleges were no better. They rested too securely on "head-knowledge" and ignored the gospel. Of Harvard he noted that it was "scarce as big as one of our least colleges at Oxford; and, as far as I could gather . . . not far Superior to our Universities in piety." Sentiments like these appeared frequently, not only in his *Journal* but also in his preaching. On one occasion he charged that

> many ministers are so sadly degenerated from their pious ancestors, that the doctrine of grace, especially the all-sufficient righteousness of Jesus, is but too seldom, too slightly mentioned. Hence the love of many waxeth cold; and I have often thought, was it possible, that this simple consideration would be sufficient to raise our venerable Forefathers again from their graves; who would thunder in their ears their fatal error.[26]

Here was the familiar language of failure and declension laid against the equally familiar standard of "pious ancestors," but this time it was the ministers in particular who came up short, not the people.

In explaining why so many ministers failed their congregations, Whitefield cited the frightening possibility that some were unconverted. Nothing prompted these accusations so much as those times when many ministers were in attendance with the mass of people. In speaking at the Old South Church in Boston, for example, he noted in his journal how

> when I got into the pulpit, I saw a great number of ministers sitting around and before me. Coming to these words, "art thou a master in Israel, and knowest not these things?" the Lord enabled me to open my mouth boldly against unconverted ministers; for, I am persuaded, the generality of preachers talk of an unknown and unfelt Christ. *The reason why congregations have been dead is, because they have dead men preaching to them. . . . How can dead men beget living children?*[27]

These strong words could not help but impress popular audiences. If Whitefield's charges were true, then New England was in far graver danger than even the ministers imagined; indeed, *they* were the root of the problem. Ordinary saints were liberated from shouldering the burden of New England's failings; far from being culprits, they were incipient saviors of New England. By meeting in mass revivals they were taking the first active steps in restoring piety to the land.

When confronted with Whitefield's electrifying manner of preaching, many ministers began to wonder if their own preaching had indeed grown too "cold" and "formal" in this most heated of revival seasons. After hearing Whitefield preach on the portentous Scripture phrase, "old things are passed away; behold, all things are become new" (2 Corinthians 5:17), Hartford's Daniel Wadsworth recorded in his diary: "What to think of the man and his Itinerant preachings I scarcely know. The things which I know not I pray god to teach me, wherein I am in error I pray god to discover it to me, wherein I have embraced the truth I pray god that I might hold it fast to the end." Apparently he decided to imitate the itinerant, for the next Sunday he preached on Ephesians 5:14 ("Awake thou that sleepest, and arise from the dead, and Christ shall give thee light"), praying that God would "bless the word that I have spoken on that some one at least might be awakened and some edified by it."[28] In Hingham, Ebenezer Gay—destined to become New England's "Arminian patriarch"—initially welcomed Whitefield's revivalism and joined the hue and cry against unconverted ministers who were "a Stench to the Nostrils of His Holiness." Whitefield had begun a season of "preparatory Convictions," which ministers like Gay hoped to nurture into "saving Conversion." Elsewhere the same expectations prevailed.[29] In all this renewed piety only a few voices dared demur—most notably Thomas Foxcroft's junior colleague at Boston's First Church, Charles Chauncy, who suspected from the start that Whitefield's methods and message could have devastating effects on the standing order of ministers.

LOCAL REVIVALS AND NEW CONVERTS

So great was Whitefield's influence that local revivals sprang up throughout New England. As in the Northampton revivals earlier, new converts flocked into the churches. Many of the elderly were "confirmed" in their faith, but the youth were especially moved. They organized "religious societies" for the purposes of "Prayer and reading Books of Piety." To document this surge in popular piety, Boston's chronicler Thomas Prince began America's first religious magazine—*The Christian History*—which collected and transmitted ministerial reports of revival as they occurred throughout the Christian world. In Boston, popular demand for "affective" preaching and spiritual counseling prompted Benjamin Colman to devote his Thursday lecture to the topic of *Souls Flying to Jesus Christ*, in which he marveled at the "many greatly affected" by conversionist preaching.[30] For a brief time, weekday lectures and sabbath sermons were given over entirely to the subject of the New Birth. But even that was not enough. Lyme's Jonathan Parsons was so inundated by townspeople clamoring after the state of their souls that he added "frequent lectures" on conversion to an already full schedule of weekly lectures and regular sermons. To meet these insatiable demands, he composed three new sermons a week and reclaimed others from his file of "old Notes," remarking with some regret that this was necessary because he had not yet mastered Whitefield's art of preaching "without writing."[31] Everywhere people were caught up in the whirl of revival and were asking the same question—"What must I do to be saved?" And everywhere ministers were repeating the same message in sermon after sermon: you must acknowledge your sin, humble yourself before Christ, and be born again through his Spirit.

The continuity of questions raised and answers given in 1740 reveals how, on the level of doctrine, these revivals shared much with their predecessors. Despite Whitefield's novel methods and itinerancy, the local revivals that followed in his wake were not new in kind so much as in degree; they accelerated patterns that began decades before Whitefield's arrival. In most towns the growth in church membership built on steady increases that began in the late 1720s and 1730s as a new generation came of age. But there were also differences in these revivals. Instead of continuing this gradual buildup in typically cyclical fashion, Whitefield inspired a huge influx in many communities that threw the cycles out of rhythm and brought "pools" of new converts into the church at once. So dramatic was the increase in the early 1740s that following these years many churches experienced record low rates of admission that would continue through the 1750s until a new generation came of age.[32]

By correlating lists of new converts in the years 1740–1743 with other economic and demographic variables, social historians have been able to reconstruct patterns of revival in particular towns. These "microcosmic" or community studies reveal that while the range of converts in revived towns was "great and general," embracing all levels and regions of New England society, revival activity was most heated in areas and among individuals experiencing the greatest changes in their lives; areas that the clergy most desperately wanted to reach. Besides the frontier, the new revivals spread to slightly older "second-generation" towns settled between 1691 and 1715, and to urban areas where diversity, mobility, and instability were highest. The oldest towns and villages settled between 1630 and 1690 seemed most immune to the upsurge in new church admissions—probably because covenant renewal and gradual conversion had worked effectively all along in these areas, minimizing the need for concentrated revival.[33] Mass revivals flourished best in areas where the forces of mobility and uprooting were the strongest, and where the numbers of unchurched were greatest.

Just as some regions were more susceptible to revivals than others, so also were individuals variously affected. In understanding who was most receptive to the calls for revival, social historians have found that economic or class variables were not as significant as demographic factors relating to age, sex, family, and childhood experience. While all ages could be found in the new membership lists, the most heavily represented were young people below the age of twenty who entered the church at an earlier age than their parents. Included among the influx of youth was a rising proportion (roughly half) of males, again reversing earlier patterns in which females generally outnumbered males.[34]

Most often, the young men and women converted in the revivals were themselves the children of full church members, thus confirming family influence as the primary carrier of religious piety in New England.[35] In frontier communities, revived churches represented para-families of uprooted young people who found in the churches a stability that was lacking when they moved away from the well-established communities of closely knit families their parents inhabited.[36] Once these towns and individuals were revived, ministers assumed that reform would follow, and with reform there would be a return to stability.

NATIVE ITINERANTS AND RELIGIOUS DISCORD

In late 1740 and 1741, when religious excitement peaked, most ministers expected the revivals to secure the religious foundation of communal life—and their own preeminence. Oftentimes they were correct. By adopting the Grand Itinerant's impassioned pulpit style and issuing their own fervent pleas for conversion, many ministers enlarged their church membership, restoring some measure of order and harmony to communal life. Other ministers had a very different experience. Instead of restoring harmony, the revivals exacerbated tensions and drove an even deeper wedge of contention into the heart of their communities. Many ministers discovered that this "Great Awakening," in frightening contrast to earlier revivals, was different; it could not be contained within their churches. Instead it often became a revival *against* their established churches.[37]

The novelty of the revivals in the decade 1734–1744 reflects the social changes taking place in those years. Demographic growth and overcrowding, social complexity, academic divisions among the ministry, and a spirit of religious toleration were all important and necessary preconditions to the ferment. But they are not sufficient explanations for heightened conflict. Another force—equally necessary and far more direct—was the sudden appearance of native itinerant speakers who, in the course of presenting genuinely religious concerns, ignited smoldering social tensions by calling into question the authority of local ministers and, in the process, challenging their monopoly on the Word. Initial clerical support for the revivals was premised on the assumption that Whitefield's late itinerancy would also be the last. For the revivals to foster corporate unity and stabilize internal tensions local ministers would have to retain their singular, unitary voice in the pulpit. But when competing speakers appeared presenting their own schemes for "true religion," unity broke down, placing established ministers in the position of defending their right to speak alone for God in public assembly.

The first hint of difficulty appeared as early as December 1740, when the Pennsylvania itinerant Gilbert Tennent received a commission from Whitefield to follow up the work of revival with a speaking tour of his own. Tennent was trained to lead revivals at his father's "Log College" in Neshaminy, Pennsylvania, and supplemented that education by following Whitefield on his tour of the Middle Colonies. In a letter to Massachusetts's Governor Belcher, Whitefield held forth the high hopes that he had invested in his first native imitator:

> This week Mr. G[ilbert] T[ennent] purposes to set out for *Boston*, in order to blow up the divine fire lately kindled there. I recommend him to your excellency as a solid, judicious, and zealous minister of the *Lord Jesus Christ*. He will be ready to preach daily. I suppose his brethren [the New England ministry] will readily open their doors [to him]: May the Lord at the same time open the people's hearts, that they may diligently attend to the things that shall be spoken.[38]

For the most part New England's ministers complied with Whitefield's request, and from December 13 to March 2, 1741, Tennent traveled throughout New England, concentrating on the areas that Whitefield had missed. As a speaker, he lacked Whitefield's dramatic delivery, but what he lacked in skill he made up for in sheer intensity. Thomas Prince observed him in practice and marveled how

> he was to have no regard to please the eyes of his hearers with agreeable gestures, nor their ears with delivery, nor their fancy with language; but to aim directly at their hearts and consciences, to lay open their ruinous delusions . . . and drive them out of every deceitful refuge wherin they made themselves easy.[39]

Despite his rhetorical limitations, Tennent reaped enormous harvests that were equal to or greater than Whitefield's. Clearly there was more to this awakening than Whitefield's oratorical genius. Wherever Tennent went, he found his preaching "sealed" by "surprizing and manifold Successes," and discovered that natural ability and formal knowledge were not the determining factors of success in the new revivals. The novel setting of itinerancy and the voluntary participation of large crowds of ordinary people were themselves inner accelerators of religious zeal and enthusiasm that counted far more than pulpit eloquence.[40] Quite simply, the itinerants conceded to their popular audiences an unprecedented importance in determining whether they would be revived or not.

Tennent's "searching" style succeeded in blowing the coals of popular piety to a white-hot intensity, but he also began to disturb many of his brethren in the established ministry who had never been ones to endure aspersions quietly. Under Whitefield's prodding and example, many ministers had already begun to cultivate a more emotional, evangelical tone in their regular preaching, but to hear Tennent speak, it was as if nothing had changed and they were still "unconverted." Many began to suspect that such charges were not so much reflections of the actual condition of their ministry based on personal familiarity as they were rhetorical ploys reflexively invoked by itinerants to elicit a mass response. And none could deny that they *did* effect a response. Tennent, even more than Whitefield, discovered that attacks on an unconverted ministry were extremely powerful incentives to popular revival. While such preaching succeeded in arousing popular enthusiasm, it inevitably eroded public trust in the local minister and pitted the itinerant and his message *against* the ministry of the local pastor. By 1741, in the midst of rapid social change, public contention, and heightened personal anxiety (intensified by ministerial denunciations), the accusations of the itinerants were messages New England audiences were prepared to endorse.

The clearest surviving specimen of Tennent's adversarial style is a sermon on *The Danger of an Unconverted Ministry*, delivered in Nottingham, Pennsylvania, on the eve of his New England tour and reprinted in Boston. That sermon served as a primer and party platform for itinerant preachers who believed the greatest enemy was not popular apathy and declension but "blind, unregenerate, carnal, lukewarm, and unskilled guides." From his text in Matthew 6:34 ("And Jesus . . . was moved with compassion towards them, because they were as Sheep not having a Shepherd"), Tennent extracted the doctrine that "as a faithful Ministry is a great Ornament, Blessing, and Comfort to the Church of God . . . So, on the contrary, an ungodly Ministry is a great curse and Judgment."[41] From start to finish the sermon was an attack on ministers who opposed his itinerancy and questioned his methods. Such opponents were, in his judgment, necessarily unconverted and little more than predatory "caterpillars" who "labour to devour every green thing." Instead of supporting the itinerants' simple proclamation of the New Birth, they muddied the waters of grace by preaching on works and morality, and constantly "Driving, Driving, to Duty, Duty." Such terms were painfully familiar to New England congregations and almost certain to meet with sympathetic nods. Since ministers could no longer be trusted as a class, it was up to the people to judge their ministers' preaching for themselves, and when it was deficient in gospel purity, to separate from their churches and "hear over parish line[s]." The only clear way to judge ministers' piety was by their willingness to welcome itinerant exhorters into their parish.

Tennent's intent in justifying lay separations was not to encourage mass defections from the established churches. Such extreme actions were, he made plain, only a last resort. Nevertheless, where appropriate, such courses were not only countenanced in Scripture but positively commanded. Popular removals from "carnal hypocrites" were, Tennent explained, not automatically evil; they could be a response to prior evils, and in that case they were not unlawful. Indeed, the greater sin would be in *failing* to resist, a principle that Tennent documented from Old and New Testament precedents: "Blessed Paul was accounted a Disturber of the Peace, as well as *Elijah* before him; And yet he left not off Preaching for all that. Yea, our blessed *Lord* informs us, that he came not to send Peace on Earth, but rather a Sword, Variance, Fire, and Division, and that even among Relations." Here, in a religious context, was the same rationale for resistance to established authority that the Revolutionary clergy would later articulate in political contexts against undeserving leaders who demanded unlimited popular submission to authority.

Whatever misgivings established ministers had about Tennent's preaching were not shared by large segments of the populace, whose appetite for itinerant speech appeared insatiable. Following Tennent's departure in March 1741, a swarm of native-born New England itinerants crisscrossed the region, reaching nearly every parish along the line with their extemporaneous proclamation of the New Birth. This first wave of itinerant speakers were young, recent graduates of Harvard and Yale seeking to restore religion's preeminence to their generation. For a brief moment, primary attention shifted from the civil magistrates and senior pastors in large urban pulpits to young itinerants like Eleazar Wheelock (YC, 1733), Benjamin Pomeroy (YC, 1733), Samuel Buell (YC, 1741), Joseph Bellamy (YC, 1735), Philemon Robbins (HC, 1729), Daniel Rogers (HC, 1725), Joseph Emerson (HC, 1743), Nathaniel Rogers (HC, 1721), Jedediah Mills (YC, 1722), or, most ominously, James Davenport (YC, 1732), Andrew Croswell (HC, 1728), and Timothy Allen (YC, 1736). Throughout 1741 and 1742 each of these men left his home parish (if he had one), traveled extensively, preached incessantly, and corresponded among the itinerants in support of the movement.[42] Through them Whitefield's methods lived on, promising to become a permanent fixture in New England's religious life.

In the course of promoting revival, the recently graduated itinerants discovered that much of what they had learned in college had to be unlearned. The new ideas, attitudes, and articles of reasonable faith that came with Enlightenment had to be left behind, as did carefully reasoned written discourses that could be read from the pulpit in a properly grave manner. Instead they had to learn to speak without substantial notes, and they had to deliver their message in a more animated, "heart-felt" style. They had to speak, in other words, as if they had no formal training at all. This new form of speech could only be learned on tour through imitation and practice. Before preaching on his own, the aspiring itinerant accompanied a more experienced revivalist, observing him closely, and then practiced in small group settings that preceded or followed the revival. Such was the experience of Daniel Rogers, grandson of President John Rogers and tutor at Harvard College. Beginning in 1740, Rogers followed Whitefield from Connecticut to New York and observed the master closely. From New York, he accompanied Tennent to New England and began delivering brief extemporaneous "exhortations" following Tennent's sermons. Finally, in December 1741 he preached his first extemporaneous sermon from Isaiah 55:6 ("Seek the Lord while he may be found; call upon him while he is near"). After a rough beginning Rogers discovered that "God was graciously pleased in Answer to Prayer to assist me much. I was greatly Enlarged toward the latter part of the sermon." Thus encouraged, Rogers began his own two-month tour of New England, where he spoke "freely and feelingly" without notes and witnessed many conversions that were "a great Encouragement to me to go on in this [extemporaneous] type of preaching." Rogers's experience would be duplicated by other young ministers who, following their apprenticeship, would inaugurate speaking tours of their own with nothing but Bible in hand and a raging desire to keep the coals of revival burning brightly.[43]

For the most part, these young itinerants discovered that the rigors of travel and daily preaching were so intense that they could not endure more than one tour. Despite his successes Rogers was left "much tired" after his two-month travels and could not go on. Similarly, Tennent recalled how, after returning from New England, "I never underwent such hardships by Reason of the intense Cold, frequent Travel, and continual Labours as there. So that I am like to feels the Effects thereof to my Death, having thereby contracted a hardness of hearing, with other bodily Disorders."[44] Only Whitefield was able to sustain a career in itinerancy throughout his life. In retrospect, his stamina may have been his most remarkable quality. Nevertheless, within the span of two or three months, the excitement these itinerants generated became significant enough to represent a more popular alternative to regular preaching that reached every man, woman, and child who wanted to hear. Instead of augmenting regular preaching, the itinerancies of young evangelists like Tennent, Croswell, and Davenport threatened to displace it.[45]

Even before James Davenport led a group of New London Separatists in the burning of a set of Puritan classics in a large bonfire, many established ministers of moderate or genteel sensibilities had moved from a position of tentative support for the new revivals and itinerancy to overt hostility. Daniel Wadsworth backed off from his early support of the revivals when he learned that an itinerant preacher said, "I preached nothing but myself." At the Connecticut General assembly in the winter of 1742 a group of "Old Light" critics of the revival passed legislation forbidding itinerancy. They assumed (erroneously) that the Saybrook system was binding on particular congregations. Many opposed the Assembly's legislation, thus dividing the clergy into two contending camps.[46] In Massachusetts, where there was no machinery for restrictive legislation, Charles Chauncy began an exhausting tour of his own to visit churches exposed to the revivals and to demonstrate how revivalists replaced reasonable Christianity with a blind "enthusiasm"—literally, madness. Following the publication of Whitefield's *Journal* in 1741, with its blunt criticisms of the colleges, the faculties of Harvard and Yale joined forces with Chauncy. In an extended critique of itinerant homiletics (and Whitefield in particular), the Harvard professors pointed out how *"extempore* Preachers give us almost always the same Things in the applicatory Part of their Sermons, so that [it] is very little akin to their Text, which is just open'd in a cursory, and not seldom perverted Manner, and then comes the same kind of Harangue which they have often used before, as an *Application."* Whitefield and his imitators could get away with such simplistic preaching because they were never in the same place long enough for their artless repetitions to catch up with them. Yet—and this was the insidious thing about the revivals—the settled minister who concentrated on meaty doctrines always appeared less exciting in contrast to the itinerant, with the result that he "will always be in the utmost Danger of his People's quarreling with [him], if not departing from him, shou'd he not consent to their impetuous Desires. . . . No Man will find [so] much Business as an *Itinerant* Preacher, who hath something in his Manner, that is . . . very taking and agreeable to the People."[47]

By 1743 the open warfare among New England's ministers began to attract more attention than the revivals themselves. The pointed accusations and theatrical antics of intinerants like Davenport or Croswell did not instigate these divisions so much as they fixed them into opposing camps. While both sides opposed the "extremes" for promoting lay itinerancy and open separation, they did so for very different reasons. Old Lights detected symptoms of enthusiasm throughout the ranks of their opponents, which Davenport and Croswell exhibited in acute form. Crowd behavior in New London showed them how people caught up in the revivals inevitably turned against established order and authority. Instead of bringing peace and harmony, the new revivals promoted censoriousness and a spirit of rebellion against the established churches. New Lights, led by Jonathan Edwards and Davenport's cousin Eleazar Wheelock, thought Davenport was peculiarly afflicted and were deeply embarrassed ("at a loss how to conduct themselves") at the whole affair.[48] The revivals, they insisted, did not have to lead to separations, nor was extemporaneous speech (when delivered by an ordained minister) necessarily a form of madness or hysteria.

THE CHAUNCY-EDWARDS DEBATES

Davenport's removal to New Jersey in 1744 did little to alleviate contention within the ministry. The damage was done and ministers battled openly with one another. Whatever reservations many ministers may have felt towards open bickering gave way to a steady barrage of sermons, pamphlets, petitions, and subscriptions, all stated in the most extreme terms: itinerancy, extemporaneous speech, lay testifying, and intensely emotional conversion experiences were a work either of God or the devil. The clerical associations and consociations—long valued as forums for quiet debate—broke down amidst bitter arguments and disbanded meetings. The middle ground of conciliation and compromise temporarily gave way to extreme voices on both sides of the revivals.

In this polemical atmosphere of confrontation and accusation, two familiar voices emerged to champion their respective sides. Charles Chauncy had opposed the revivals from Whitefield's first visit, and over the course of three years of travel had accumulated a wide body of evidence confirming the pernicious effects of the revivals. In his opinion, and the opinion of a growing body of supporters, the state of religion and the Congregational churches had never been worse. Jonathan Edwards, speaking for the other side, had an even longer experience observing the revivals closely and came to quite different conclusions. Despite errors in practice and regrettable extremes like Davenport, the revivals were clearly a work of God and piety had never been stronger. Their debates were not only an issue of "enlightenment" versus "piety," as some historians have maintained, but also a clash of rival academic theories and social orientations that had been building for generations.[49] Chauncy represented an extreme aspect of the intellectualist tradition that emphasized the "understanding" and strict clerical control over congregations. Edwards spoke for the voluntarist tradition that emphasized the "affections" and favored more active lay involvement in church affairs. For four generations these rival impulses had coexisted in the colonial pulpit, but under the press of the new revivals they separated into opposite and irreconcilable positions.

In presenting his intellectualist and aristocratic arguments against the revivals, Chauncy drew from current writings on "Reasonable Christianity." He drew even more, however, from the founders who, in rebutting "Antinomianism," had set forth a sequence of the stages in salvation that emphasized understanding over passions. In Chauncy's opinion, eighteenth-century New Lights were no different from "familists" and "Antinomians." There was no rational arguing with these people, he complained: "You had as good reason with the wind." They could talk about the passions, immediate conversion, and mystical assurance as much as they wanted, but "the plain Truth is, an enlightened *Mind*, and not raised *Affections*, ought always to be the Guide of those who call themselves Men."[50] That truth, he went on, was not simply a deduction from traditional faculty psychology but a scriptural dictate. Chauncy, no less than Edwards, viewed Scripture as the ultimate arbiter of debate and piled on text after text to demonstrate that "the arguments the SPIRIT uses are suited to the Reason of Men. . . . The Method he uses in Conversion is a rational Method." This principle was manifested not only in the Old Testament, where God addressed his people as rational creatures, but also in the New: "The Gospel doth not destroy *Reason* and *rational Proceeding*—the working of the SPIRIT is according to the Nature of Man, [and] moves not in contradiction to it, but in an Elevation of *Reason*."[51]

A corollary to Chauncy's emphasis on reason was the principle that conversion was more a matter of duty than emotion. Above all else, he insisted, "Salvation by *Grace*, through *Christ*, is in the *Way of Obedience*."

By "obedience," Chauncy meant not only personal piety but submission to social and ecclesiastical order and hierarchy. True faith, he observed, never worked to upset godly order in the churches or society, yet that was exactly what itinerants and lay exhorters accomplished through their wild censures and accusations. Besides disrupting the settled churches, they upset social order by encouraging laborers to "continue abroad 'till late in the Night, and so as to unfit themselves for the Services of the following day." Even worse, the revivals encouraged lay exhorters to abandon their proper calling and usurp the role of the minister. By taking "upon them[selves] the *Business* that is *assign'd to others*," such interlopers inevitably "throw the *Body of CHRIST* into great Disorder."[52] Particularly offensive in this regard were reports, gathered by Chauncy from many towns, of women testifying publicly in church services. Citing St. Paul's injunction to good order in 1 Corinthians 14 he exclaimed: "It is a shame: for WOMEN to speak in the church . . . 'Tis a plain case, these FEMALE EXHORTERS are condemned by the apostle." That responsible ministers would countenance such a perversion of gospel order was proof that they were afflicted by enthusiasm which, Chauncy speculated, had its sources in a "bad temperament of the blood and spirits." Unless saner minds prevailed, the contagion would spread and New England would be lost, for "there is no telling how high it may rise or what it may end in."[53]

The terms Chauncy used to oppose the revivals were, in characteristic eighteenth-century fashion, inflated with fears and forebodings. But they were no more extreme than the terms Jonathan Edwards would use to endorse the same phenomenon. Like Chauncy, Edwards wondered how the revivals would end, but unlike Chauncy his eyes turned to millennial glory. In contemplating the full flowering of revival zeal, he drew on traditional apocalyptic rhetoric to predict that "the work that is now begun in New England, is . . . eminently glorious, and if it shall go on and prevail, would make New England a kind of heaven upon earth . . . it gives more abundant reason to hope that what is now seen in America, and especially in New England, may prove the dawn of that glorious day."[54] Such a vision could lead to only one conclusion: instead of attacking the revivals for regrettable excesses, ministers should defend and encourage them as New England's salvation, and from there, as the salvation of the world.

Edwards augmented his speculative, millennial defense of the revivals with biblical and philosophical arguments that culminated in his massive *Treatise on the Religious Affection*, written originally as a sermon series on conversion and published in 1746. In his pamphlets Edwards followed Chauncy's tactic of citing the writings of Puritan worthies—especially Thomas Shepard and his grandfather Solomon Stoddard—but he turned them to very different uses. Instead of emphasizing the founders' warnings on Antinomianism and their corrective emphases on preparation and sanctification, he stressed their evangelical concern with supernatural conversion. That event—whether immediate or gradual—marked the beginnings of a "new creation" (one of Edwards's favorite terms), conceived through the work of the Holy Spirit and carried out through the "affections" of the heart rather than the enlightenment of the mind. In extraordinary times of revival the Spirit used the testimonies of ordinary men and women to effect the end of conversion. When ministers unequivocably condemned such popular "means" of grace, they limited the transforming power of the Holy Spirit; such restrictions, Edwards chided, tended "too much for the *clay* to take upon it[self] with respect to the *potter*." In evaluating the revivals, the proper procedure was not simply to question who leads but to examine the end accomplished by the revivals:

> If God is pleased to convince the consciences of persons, so that they can't avoid great outward manifestations, even to interrupting and breaking off those public means they were attending, I don't think this is confusion, or an unhappy interruption. . . . We need not be sorry for breaking the [usual] order of means, by obtaining the end to which the order is directed.[55]

In philosophical terms, Edwards continued, Chauncy and other Old Light ministers erred by opposing the revivals a priori from means, rather than a posteriori from the ends they achieved.

To illustrate the inadequacy of means as a criterion for judgment, Edwards cited numerous instances from Scripture in which God used "private persons" to effect his ongoing plan of redemption. Whereas Chauncy had singled out for particular denunciation women who testified, Edwards turned to the Old Testament prophet Deborah who led the Hebrew men to victory over the Canaanites. Most but not all of the men of Israel followed her leadership: it seemed the inhabitants of Meroz were unwilling to follow her and so they were cursed by God. Like the Old Lights, Edwards explained, the men of Meroz mistakenly argued from means; "They did not like the beginning of it, it being a woman that first led the way, and had the chief conduct in the affair." By arguing from means such critics set themselves up as gods. In typically direct language Edwards likened the men of Meroz and later-day Old Light critics to self-justifying worms: "If one worm be a little exalted above another, by having more dust or a bigger dunghill, how much does he make of himself! What a distance does he keep from those that are below him! Christ condescends to wash our feet; but how would great men (or rather the bigger worms) account themselves debased by acts of far less condescension!" If the Holy Spirit changed people's hearts and lives through the words of ordinary people, then those words must be a work of God. The people were not so unenlightened as the Old Lights thought; nor could their voices be so easily silenced. Without giving up on the high calling of the educated ministry, it was equally clear to Edwards that there could no longer be a silent democracy: "Not only magistrates and ministers, but every living soul, is now obliged to arise and acknowledge God in this work, and put his hand to promote it."[56]

Besides grounding his defense of the revivals in Scripture, Edwards turned to philosophy. As scriptural exegetes, Chauncy and Edwards were equals, but in bringing the external supports of philosophy to conversion, Edwards proved himself a master without peer. Considered as a philosophical problem, conversion was primarily a question of language and epistemology. Edwards believed that one reason so many people responded to the revivals through nonverbal "outward" seizures and fits was because their ministers had not adequately prepared them for conversion, or provided them with a vocabulary to explain their experiences.[57] In place of the rigidly segmented faculty psychology, he proposed a model of the mind that stressed the interconnections of thought and emotion so that neither existed prior to or without the other. For every word that signified an idea, there was an accompanying sentiment of love or hatred, so that it was impossible to think of reaching the head before the heart: "All acts of the affections of the soul are in some sense acts of the will, and all acts of the will are acts of the affections. All exercises of the will are in some degree or other, exercises of the soul's appetition or aversion; or which is the same thing, of its love or hatred." For Edwards, ethical and religious ideas were never emotionally neutral but laden with a range of feelings and sentiments that either attracted or repulsed the individual. This substratum of feelings and affections—what Edwards termed the "sense of the heart"—was the real "spring" of conversion because individuals invariably justified or rationalized what they already knew in their hearts to be true. Conversion then, was primarily a matter of the affections.[58]

To describe the new sense of the heart wrought by the Holy Spirit in conversion, Edwards lifted a page from the moral essayists and used the sense of beauty as an analogy to the conversion experience.[59] In *The Moralists* (which Edwards had read during his student years at Yale), the third earl of Shaftesbury defended "true enthusiasm" in positive terms as a form of "divine love" or as "being itself." Such love, he said, was disinterested and involuntary. It came from a mountaintop view, a vast ocean, or a starry night, when the beauty of the creator exhibited itself to the discerning eye. At such moments the emotional impact was sublime; it was "simple, pure, and unmixed . . . [it] has no other object than merely the excellency of that being itself, nor admits of any other thought of happiness, than on its single fruition." For Shaftesbury, such moments of aesthetic wonder contained the meaning of true religion: "Shall I be ashamed of this diviner love and of an object of love so far excelling all those [other] objects in dignity, majesty, grace, beauty, and amiableness? Is this enthusiasm? Be it: and so may I ever be an enthusiast." In similar terms Edwards described conversion as a form of enthusiasm, but one that came from the supernatural activity of the Holy Spirit transforming the heart from love of self to a disinterested love of "divine excellency," or "Being in general." And, like Shaftesbury's, Edwards's response to such a transformation was beatific and enraptured: "Now if such things are enthusiasm, and the fruits of a distempered brain, let my brain be evermore possessed of that happy distemper!"[60]

Shaftesbury and other sentimentalist writers provided Edwards with a vocabulary to distinguish the work of reason and emotion in conversion—and the knowledge of "true virtue" generally. But, as Norman Fiering points out, at the same time that Edwards expropriated their vocabulary he turned their meanings inside out by reassigning the transforming agent in true enthusiasm from the natural self to the Holy Spirit.[61] True enthusiasm, Edwards argued, could never be achieved solely through the "common improvement" of natural abilities. Human sinfulness was total to the extent that the affections were oriented to love of self rather than to love of God. They could only be transformed through the direct, experimental "knowledge of the loveliness of divine things" implanted by the Holy Spirit. Such knowledge, moreover, was not perceived through reason; it depended on the sense of the heart.

The social and spiritual implications of Edwards's treatises on the affections were momentous. As long as the sources of true enthusiasm lay within the grasp of natural man, then the true enthusiast was the person of superior breeding and refined sensibilites. But if the source of true enthusiasm came from without—as Edwards insisted it did—then *anyone* was a potential candidate for remaking, and distinctions of learning or breeding lost their significance. Thus in a brilliant but convoluted series of shifts and turns, Edwards used the sentimentalists against Chauncy and the intellectualists, only to turn the sentimentalists upside down by establishing an external basis for enthusiasm that allowed for a *popular* enthusiasm not dependent on formal ethical and aesthetic sensibilities. In a theological sense Edwards had simply reclothed the old Calvinist teachings of sin and grace in a new rhetoric of sentiment. But in a social sense he accomplished far more: he cut a doorway to an assertive lay piety that would open far wider than he ever imagined and that would permanently alter the relations between pastors and congregations in more democratic directions.

A NEW CLASS OF SPEAKERS

By stating their cases for and against the revivals in such extreme, polemical terms, Chauncy and Edwards made it nearly impossible for their supporters to speak with each other. Earlier generations of ministers had had their debates and personality conflicts, but never before had they become the public spectacle they now were as a result of their petitions, declarations, and subscriptions for and against the revivals. To survive, the New England Way's principle of *Sola Scriptura* required a rough clerical concord. If the ministers could not achieve perfect harmony to save the Way, they would at least have to agree upon a common set of assumptions large enough to accommodate divergent emphases and orientations; opposing points of view could not be stated in extreme terms of salvation or damnation. But in 1743 the long record of accommodation that had existed before the revivals was broken, and the results were cataclysmic.

By refusing to recognize the legitimacy of opposing views, the ministry as a whole temporarily lost the public trust. Once substantial numbers of ministers were labeled "unconverted" or "Antinomian," congregations everywhere faced the terrifying prospect that their ministers—historically the prime bulwark against divine desertion—might indeed be wolves in sheep's clothing. With these developments in mind, the decade 1735–1745 may be designated the most critical period in colonial New England's intellectual and religious history. Nothing in the Glorious Revolution came close to wreaking the internal havoc created by the ministers themselves in the midst of their raging debates. Nor would any event tip the balance of Congregational authority so firmly and decisively in the laity's direction. Suddenly it was the people—guided by their self-made leaders—who had to take responsibility for their religious lives to retain God's special favor for New England. What neither Old Light nor New Light ministers recognized was that in publicly dividing themselves the decision for or against the revivals was no longer theirs to make. In the vacuum of leadership created by clerical discord, congregations and their lay officers made decisions for themselves. Never before in New England's religious history were so many ministers censured by their congregations or removed from office. More frequently, New Light congregations removed Old Light ministers; but the recriminations cut both ways, as some Old Light congregations removed ministers who they found too tainted by enthusiasm to suit their taste.[62] Congregations joined ministers in circulating petitions of their own that set one faction in the church against another. More ominously, some factions departed entirely from ministerial rule and formed Separate churches with lay ministers of their own choosing. Between 1742 and 1745, Massachusetts had thirteen illegal separations and Connecticut nineteen. In the next five years there were twenty-one additional separations in Connecticut and twenty-four in Massachusetts. While assembly laws and clerical associations were effective in isolating and silencing individuals like James Davenport, they were unable to prevent *groups* of lay people from standing on their Congregational liberties and forming churches of their own creation.[63] Thus began another experiment in liberty—this one in the churches—as New Englanders discovered the power they possessed when united against authority.

Like the revivals generally, local separations tended to occur in areas experiencing the greatest diversity and change from the well-ordered seventeenth-century communities. In Connecticut they occurred most frequently in the densely settled eastern portion of the colony. Norwich, which in 1745 was the commercial center of the east, had four separations modeled on the pattern of neighboring New London. In Massachusetts the separations were most frequent in the southeastern portion of the province where Old Plymouth had a long tradition of Separatism; but they were also conspicuous in rural areas like Chebacco (Ipswich) parish in Essex county and in urban Boston. For the most part, the Separatists or, as they preferred, "strict Congregationalists," were young, interrelated, and drawn from the lower and middle rungs of the socioeconomic ladder; they were among the earliest self-made, popularly appointed "leaders" in New England history. Few, if any, college graduates or provincial political leaders participated in separations, but neither were the ranks of Separatists comprised solely of the lower classes, "walking poor," women, or the emotionally unstable.[64]

The major organizing device for Separate church formation was the local revival conducted by lay exhorters rather than ordained ministers. It is impossible to determine exactly how many such exhorters were active in the years 1743 to 1750, though something of their considerable range and influence can be inferred from the number of Separate churches they spawned and the many court proceedings against their itinerancy.[65] In most cases the lay itinerants borrowed their vocabulary from Jonathan Edwards and their rhetorical techniques from the earlier revivals led by ordained itinerants, particularly James Davenport. The indefatigable itinerant and pastor of the Preston Separate Church, Paul Parke, recalled how his own ministry began:

> When I heard Mr. Davenport and others preaching the way of Salvation for Sinfull mankind: and numbers of Common brethren Exhorting praying and Carrying on in publick meetings: as well as privat Confessions I said this is a Good Work [and] that these were labourours that God Imployed, in Carrying on the Greate and Glorious work of his Grace turning the people from Darkness to light.

Like other lay exhorters Parke determined not "to Sit under the Stupid and Deceiving performances of unconverted ministers," and he felt called to take his untutored message of rebirth throughout New England, "in the City and in the Country: in the field: in barns: wigwams and private houses, and also in Meeting houses of all Denominations, and upon almost all Ocations." In the span of his fifty-year ministry Parke estimated that he had preached "ten or twelve thousand sermons . . . nor Did I ever more than once prepare Notes and Use them nor Could I ever remember to repeat one." Throughout these strenuous endeavors he was aided by "Spiritual Illuminations and Grace."[66]

Unlike the ordained, college-educated itinerants, there was nothing these lay exhorters had to unlearn. The beauty of extemporaneous speech was that it lay within the possession of every pious Bible reader who discovered a gift for public speaking. In a letter to his wife the lay itinerant Elisha Paine described his simple, but compelling call to the ministry: "I felt the Spirit of the Lord come upon me. I rose up and exhorted and persuaded them to come to Christ; and immediately there was a screeching and groaning all over the multitude, and hath ever since been very powerful."[67] Such experience was typical of a new class of speakers in

New England who no longer trusted the preaching of ordained ministers and therefore embarked on untutored, extemporaneous itinerancies of their own.

In breaking away from the established churches, the Separatists employed revolutionary methods such as anticlerical rhetoric and lay exhorting, but the gospel they preached was nothing other than the old covenant of grace radically revived and purified. Theirs was at base a conservative religious movement whose ideals hearkened back to an earlier age of supposedly pure church membership and active lay involvement. Local leadership was taken over by deacons in the standing churches or, where they still survived, lay elders. Indeed, one of the more significant achievements of Separate Congregational churches was the revival of lay officers.[68] The character of Separate protest is preserved in scores of petitions and declarations that repudiate the demise of ruling elders, mandatory taxes for the established ministry, the practice of half-way membership, the failure of settled ministers to preach the New Birth "feelingly," and the attempts of civil authorities to suppress itinerancy and lay exhorting. At Norwich, Connecticut, for example, the Separatist Jedediah Hide justified his removal from the Congregational church first because "The Church [is] not making Conversion a term of Communion," and second "because it hath not Ruling Elders." Other Separatists enumerated additional reasons in their own words. William Lothrop opposed the established pastor Benjamin Lord because he was "Not a friend to Lowly Preaching and Preachers." Mary Lathrop stood firmly and simply on her Congregational liberties: "By Covenant I am not held here any longer than I am edified." In these and other cases, the justification for removal was individual "conscience," and that conscience was ultimately religious in character.[69]

Taken as a whole, the Separate petitions, pamphlets, and confessions reveal how deeply embedded Puritan piety had become in the mind of the eighteenth-century laity. They also reveal the new terminology of Jonathan Edwards and other New Light apologists that had such an impact on the people. Ordinary people never did master or respond to the cadences of polite literature, whose impact depended on wide reading and formal study, but the terminology of "affections," "holy ardours," "new creation," and "sensation" took root and blossomed in popular expression. In a process the clergy could not fully understand, their legacy of regular preaching had not failed the fourth generation but had succeeded too well in inculcating a popular culture of the Word in which ordinary men and women were able to formulate theological positions, defend them from Scripture, record them in their own words, and express them publicly in religious meetings. Even so stalwart an opponent of Separatism as Yale's future president Ezra Stiles conceded that the polemical writings of lay Separatists like Samuel Hyde, Isaac Backus, or Israel Holly represented an impressive "specimen of the Abilities of the Illiterate Men of New England even in writings as well as Things of Religion."[70] The writings to which Stiles referred clearly grew out of New England's Congregational heritage and the conviction, expressed by Framingham's Separate deacon Edward Goddard, that "every Man has a Right of judging for himself, of trying Doctrines by the inspired Scriptures, and of the Worshipping according to his Apprehension of the Meaning of them."[71] They grew as well from the works of Jonathan Edwards, whose defense of the revivals had the unanticipated consequence of liberating theology and the Word from the control of the ministry, and extending spiritual responsibility to the laity. Ironically, in the same way that Edwards had turned the secular moralists to his evangelical purposes, lay exhorters would take his logic to defend their "pure" churches. The noted Separate minister Isaac Backus, for example, boasted that he was "much better acquainted" with Edwards's thought than any of his Yale-educated pupils. Edwards taught Backus and others that while all did not enjoy the benefits of a classical education and refined understanding, all had a sense of the heart and must openly testify concerning its workings. If ministers renounced that voice then, as the Separate Lydia Kelly explained in justifying her removal from the established church, "the Church was as much Separate as I, and had gone off from the Settlement."[72]

THE LAITY PREVAILS

The real winners in the debates over the new revivals were neither the Old Light nor the New Light ministers but the laity. As censures grew and separations proliferated, ministers on both sides learned that in the New World their strength did not lie in the formal sanctity of their office, in the support of civil government, or in their associations; their authority depended on the trust and voluntary support of their congregations. That trust required that ministers respect the rights and liberties of their congregations to speak out on matters of great public concern. It required as well that they not encourage schism and lay separations by fostering the fear that many in their midst were "pharisees," "formalists," "enthusiasts," or "familists." Only after conceding these New World realities would ministers regain the loyalties of their congregations and come to see that the real enemy threatening New England's mission was not excessive democracy but tyranny.

[11]

A New Balance

While ministerial disagreements over the revivals continued to rage, New England's "Great Awakening" did not. By late 1743 and 1744, revival excitement had passed. When George Whitefield returned for a second tour in the fall of 1744 he found that "a chill" had come over the churches' work and that many pastors had closed their pulpits to his ministry. Others expressed similar regrets. In a letter to Thomas Prince, Taunton's Josiah Crocker lamented that "in the general, people have been growing more cold, dull, and lifeless in religion. There have been but few hopeful conversions since my ordination [in 1742]. . . . So that generally speaking there has been an awful withdrawal of the Divine influence both from saints and sinners."[1] Unlike Crocker, not every minister regretted the divine "withdrawal," but all agreed that New England's most intense period of revival enthusiasm had passed. This social and spiritual fervor simply could not be sustained indefinitely. Sooner or later, in one community after another, the mundane tasks of life in the world again took precedence.

But if the cyclical pattern of revivals was familiar, the lingering problems created by the recent revivals were not, confirming that this awakening was different from its predecessors. The most conspicuous institutional legacy of the new revivals was the survival and growth of "dissenting" Anglican and Separate congregations. Although the Separate churches never rivaled the established churches in size or influence, they did endure, and in the decade between 1745 and 1755 moved in new "Separate-Baptist" directions.[2] At the other extreme were Anglican and "Arminian" Congregational ministers like Charles Chauncy, Jonathan Mayhew, Ebenezer Gay, Lemuel Briant, or Robert Breck, who liberalized Old Light, head-centered preaching, identifying Christian faith with morality and emphasizing natural theology over divine revelation. By the 1750s this small but influential group of free thinkers was solidly established in wealthy commercial congregations along Boston's north and south shores and, like the Separate Baptists, showed no signs of disappearing.[3]

Though the Congregational ministers could not eliminate rival orders and suppress controversial theologies they could contain them, but that required concessions both to one another and to the laity. Efforts at coercion through licensing laws and imprisonments were clearly unavailing, as they merely seemed to stoke the fires of lay resistance. Connecticut's anti-itinerancy laws were strictest, but they could not overcome "New Light" political alignments in the lower house bent on removing those laws and thus safeguarding the rights of congregations to their independence.[4] Clearly more positive acts were needed, and they had to be initiated by the ministers themselves. Already in 1743 Nathaniel Eells, in his election sermon, urged his brethren to "be at Peace among our selves." The stakes were too large to permit internecine disputes: "We are not made for our selves alone, but we are made to help in making the World better; and if the Age we live in is not the better for us, it will be the worse."[5] Eells's message was clear. Before Old Lights and New Lights could improve the world they had to heal internal divisions, erase the stigma of their petition wars, and forgive the bad feelings left by their debates.

MINISTERIAL REUNION

When Eells spoke of clerical union he reiterated a basic principle of survival that had been temporarily forgotten during the revival debates. From the start of settlement, accommodation and disagreement-within-limits were built into Puritan theology and were essential to clerical success. Added to these traditional values was the eighteenth-century spirit of philosophical and theological latitudinarianism inculcated at Harvard and Yale. America's "enlightenment" was, as Henry May points out, a "moderate" and conciliatory cosmology that stressed balance, order, and religious compromise.[6] Thus, when division reared its ugly head in 1743, many ministers—perhaps most—were reluctant participants and longed for calmer days. For a time these "moderate" or "neutral" Congregationalists lost their voice to the extremes, but with the threat of Separatism and Arminian-Anglicanism so great they soon acted to reclaim the middle ground and establish mechanisms for peaceful conciliation rather than confrontation. The reconciliation they sought did not come overnight, nor was it ever as complete as in earlier generations, but it did provide a patchwork *modus vivendi* that most ministers could use to regain their spiritual leadership for another generation.

The primary mechanism ministers used to restore harmony among themselves was the clerical association. By 1745 consociations existed in every county of Connecticut by order of the *Saybrook Platform* and in most regions of Massachusetts on a voluntary basis. Although these organizations never achieved the power over individual congregations that some ministers hoped for, they were extremely effective conciliatory agencies for the ministers themselves. Indeed, as David Harlan suggests, the very *lack* of binding, coercive powers worked to the ministers' benefit by fostering an atmosphere of informal dialogue and mutual advice instead of open politicking.[7]

By 1744 many ministers began moving toward reconciliation in their associations by creating a common ground for dialogue. In particular they had to distinguish differences in opinion from doctrinal heresy. While all ministers agreed that heresy could not be tolerated, many believed the label had been applied too rashly in the debates over the revivals. Differences in orientation and style had become blown out of proportion, concealing fundamental principles that Old and New Lights held in common. One leader in this reassessment was, ironically, Gilbert Tennent, whose earlier sermon on *The Danger of an Unconverted Ministry* had done much to undermine clerical unity. Shaken by New Light separations in New England and by rising popular defections to pietistic sects in the Middle Colonies, Tennent reversed his earlier censures and made a plea for a new spirit of "Christian Union" among established ministers. When ministers become "unreasonably alienated from each other, not upon the Account of Differences in Essentials of *Doctrine, Worship, or Discipline*, but *circumstantial Matters*," Tennent confessed, they bring Christ into contempt and "Marr the publick *Good*."[8] In retrospect, that was what had happened in the "late revival," when matters of "finite opinion" like rival theories of mind and the affections were treated as infallible doctrines and imposed "upon others as a *Term of Communion*, either Ministerial or Christian." The practice of judging other ministers' spiritual estate according to their stand on the revivals was similarly reprehensible: "It is cruel and censorious Judging . . . to condemn positively and openly the spiritual *states* of such as are sound in *fundamental Doctrines*, and *regular in life*." If the churches were not to be rent asunder, ministers had to concede the principle that "good Men are apt to be of contrary sentiments because of their different Degrees of *Knowledge*, different *Experiences* in some Things, different *Tryals, Byasses*, and natural *Tempers*." Now that the church had returned to a more ordinary "calm," Tennent concluded, it was "high Time to forget" the rash censures of "many Years agone" and restore clerical unity.

Tennent's powerful plea for reunion would not bear fruit in the Presbyterian church until 1758. But in New England, where the Congregational associations were more flexible than Presbyterian synods, neighboring ministers came together for reconciliation. With the revivals safely behind and the threat of dissenters looming ahead, they no longer asked the divisive question of whether the revivals were a work of God or the devil, but sought instead to determine *what* in the revivals had been godly and *what* had created the disorder in the established churches.[9] By framing their discussion in both/and terms rather than either/or, ministers discovered that they still retained much in common. New Lights like Tennent—and even James Davenport—saw in lay itinerancy and separations how in the flush of enthusiasm the revivals had gone too far. Old Lights were asked to reconsider their unqualified rejection of the revivals and their tendency to romanticize the "peace" that existed before Whitefield's arrival. In an open letter to his colleagues, William Shurtleff asked: "Were those such glorious and happy Days, that you should earnestly wish . . . for their Return?" Those days, he went on, were filled with public apathy, and the established ministers were not entirely without blame. In a critical concession, Shurtleff acknowledged that "we who took upon us to be *Masters of Assemblies*, upon Reflection may find occasion to charge our selves with being too dull and sluggish, careless and negligent in our public Ministrations. . . . Tho' we saw but little Fruit of our labours in those Times . . . how many ways did we find to satisfy our selves, and how easy were we in [explaining away] our want of Success?" Besides the dangers of romanticizing the past were considerations of a more practical nature. One lay writer expressed these practical considerations well when he urged ministers on both sides "not to Quarrel with nor to publish any thing against each other, nor expose your Weakness and Foibles, lest you thereby bring your selves into Contempt with the Populace, for a House divided against itself shall not stand."[10]

Given such encouragements for reunion, or at least reconciliation, many ministers responded positively. Even as New Lights admitted that true religion required, in Tennent's words, a "right Reason" that governed "our own fickle and often partial and byass'd *Fancies* and *Humours*," so Old Lights conceded that reason alone, "without *Revelation*, and the *Assistances of God's Spirit*," was "not sufficient" to transform the soul. Braintree's Samuel Niles, one of the leading Old Light members of the Weymouth Association, reminded his colleagues that their differences were largely over "style" and "method," not substantial points of divinity or Scripture doctrine:

> If I have a true Idea of things, our present Controversy is not about the fundamental Points of Religion. All agree in the Doctrine of Original Sin, the Necessity of Conversion or the New Birth, of Justification by Faith in the Merits of CHRIST, the Imputation of CHRIST'S Righteousness received by Faith, and good Works or an holy Obedience as a Fruit and Evidence of true Faith. All my Brethren in the Ministry, that I am acquainted with, assent to these Doctrines, and preach them to their Hearers.[11]

In addition to Niles's list of common doctrines were two other assumptions so generally accepted by the ministers that they hardly required comment. Those were the primacy of *Sola Scriptura* over all human authorities and systems of belief, and the doctrine of divine providence with its federal corollary that made New England a peculiar covenant people. On all these cardinal principles the vast majority of ministers agreed, and on that basis they urged one another to restore the "beautiful Harmony of Ministers" that had long been New England's "distinguishing Glory."[12]

Ministerial pleas for moderation and tolerance did not eliminate substantial differences over preaching style as we will see, nor did polemical attacks on "formalism" and "enthusiasm" disappear. But for many, these issues were relegated to nonessential or "circumstantial" differences that could be resolved at the local level. Clerical divisions, while strongly felt, lost their image of schism and disunion and instead were treated like issues of debate before the revivals: as questions of conscience and congregational preference, not salvation or damnation. By 1760, Newport's Ezra Stiles could say on the basis of his "considerable acquaintance" with New England's Congregational ministers, that "I cannot perceive any very essential real difference in their opinions respecting the fundamental points of religion. I may be mistaken—but their different manner and phraseology in explaining the same principles appears to me to be their chief difference." For the most part, Stiles went on, ministers were willing "to forbear real differences in love, where there appears a sincere love of truth, candor and piety."[13]

COMMON CHRISTIANS AS GOOD JUDGES

Renewing ministerial unity was only half the problem ministers faced in 1745 and thereafter; the other half was reconciling themselves to an informed and assertive laity. Although brief in duration, the new revivals were a compelling reminder that in New England ministers had to satisfy the demands and honor the liberties of their congregations. Through a host of activities, including voluntary mass assemblies, "concerts" of prayer, street singing, ministerial dismissals, lay exhorting, or lay separations, the people spoke and made their presence felt. The underlying message was one of incontrovertible power. Whatever pretenses to sacerdotal authority and independence ministers might once have harbored were irretrievably shattered in the turmoil of the 1740s. For ministers to regain the trust and loyalty of their congregations and prevent them from organizing independent churches of their own, they had to trust them in return; they had to concede and even celebrate the "*unlimited, absolute,* and *self-determining* power" of each congregation to elect and supervise their leaders; and they had to acknowledge that "every individual church has the *sole power of judging and determining its own controversies.*"[14] No longer could ministers maintain the fiction of a speaking aristocracy directing a silent democracy. They would not relinquish the aristocratic prerogatives of their preaching office to be sure, but neither could they infer from that unilateral powers to silence congregations or impose ruling synods. The contest for control in the churches had moved in a decidedly popular or democratic direction. As Malden's Joseph Emerson (HC, 1717) exclaimed in an "exhortation" to Christian liberty: "If any should attempt to deprive you of this your Christian Priviledge, they are guilty of *Robbery.* They rob you of a very great Priviledge which your Lord has purchased for you with the dearest Rate."[15]

Clerical acknowledgments of lay liberties necessarily brought a new rhetorical image of "the people" as well. No longer could ministers routinely fix the blame for various judgments and calamities solely on a degenerate people. Nor could they place themselves above blame. Henceforth ministers had to recognize public virtues alongside public sins and ascribe New England's glory to those virtues. In a momentous departure from past conventions, fourth-generation ministers would emphasize that while New Englanders sinned like other peoples they also retained more general knowledge and piety than any other people on earth. Thus in his 1746 election sermon, Andover's John Barnard dismissed the old accusation that God was about to forsake New England for the sins of the rising generation as "highly *blasphemous.*" While the land was hardly perfect, even so, "thanks be to GOD . . . our Degeneracy hath not proceeded to this Degree and Pitch of *Atheism.* We yet believe there is a glorious Providence [for New England]." Congregational liberties of election and self-regulation were considerable but, as Ezra Stiles exulted, the children of New England could be trusted with them: "They have sense and ability to chuse their own pastors, especially since the revival of learning among the laity and the vernacular translations of the scriptures, [which] have rendered common christians good judges of pastoral qualifications."[16]

Stiles's reference to "pastoral qualifications" signaled one other concession begun during the revivals that continued through the Revolution: the requirement that ministers be converted and preach the New Birth in their regular sermons. Widespread charges of an unconverted ministry were not easily refuted or quickly forgotten. Henceforth congregations would be more active "watchmen" over their ministers' souls, again reversing the role ministers previously claimed as monitors of their profession. Ministers, in turn, had to redouble their efforts from the pulpit to reclaim lost souls, thereby confirming their legitimacy. They would not all preach the New Birth in the same style and manner, but they *did* preach the necessity of supernatural conversion and the duty of all (beginning with themselves) to look to the state of their souls.[17] The Old Light drift toward natural theology ceased, not to resume again on a broad scale until after the Revolution.

The end result of clerical reunion, celebrations of congregational liberties, and conversionist preaching was to reaffirm the churches and ministers as the center of New England society. The established ministers had met the Separatist challenge by coopting its message. Separatist strength, as we have seen, derived less from common social identities or common political and economic grievances than from traditional religious concerns with the New Birth, Congregational autonomy, and active lay participation. Once those themes were taken over by the majority of established ministers, the occasion for removal disappeared; there was no social, political, or economic program on which the Separatists could build a movement. Of the 77 Separate churches founded between 1742 and 1750, only 23 survived beyond 1765. While the Separate-Baptist churches stood as a permanent popular alternative (and a reminder of what could happen should ministers depart from the standards of their congregations), they never again threatened to engulf the country. Similarly, the initial spurt of new Anglican churches continued within modest limits.[18] Few New Englanders were willing to sacrifice their considerable ruling liberties for the "order" of episcopal hierarchy. Thus, in a remarkably short period of time, fourth-generation ministers successfully adapted to the new internal circumstances and turned what could have been a popular rebellion against the established churches into a confirmation of the traditional New England Way and the people who embodied it.

RATIONALIST AND EVANGELICAL PREACHING STYLES

While ministers learned to avoid formal schism through accommodation, differences in pulpit style and delivery still remained on the local level and extended beyond the ministers to their congregations. Although the new revivals marked the general ascendancy of the laity in running their churches, it would be a mistake to lump all congregations together in one "democratic" mold. In fact, congregations differed in their tastes and sensibilities just as their ministers did, and in large measure the story of preaching in the mid-eighteenth century is one of stylistically minded ministers and congregations attempting to match themselves to one another. Ministers and congregations no longer thought of the ties binding them as inviolable marriage vows. Instead, as in government, they thought more in contractual terms where both parties were free to disengage themselves from obligations that did not satisfy their consciences. Indeed, the growing acceptance of contractualism was the churches' most important institutional acknowledgment of the voluntary underpinnings of New England's religious life and the limitations on all authority. This acknowledgment benefited congregations and ministers alike for, as Ebenezer Devotion pointed out, "Where one of the Parties is left at Liberty [to remove], there is the other Part at Liberty also." In this contractual atmosphere, differences in homiletical theory assumed more than an academic significance; they often determined whether or not a minister survived in a particular congregation.[19]

Despite the many differences of opinion that characterized mid-eighteenth-century religion in New England, there were, rhetorically speaking, two styles or orientations that Alan Heimert labels "rational" and "evangelical."[20] These contrasting styles stemmed from the Edwards-Chauncy debates, and before them to the rival intellectualist and voluntarist traditions emanating from the colleges. While they were no longer considered grounds for censure or schism in the minds of most ministers, they continued to fix the sermon in very different molds that appealed to very different sensibilities. In effect, both sides agreed to disagree on the question of pulpit decorum and expressed their preferences clearly from their own pulpits.

Because most ministers refused to acknowledge stylistic differences as fundamental articles of faith, there are no comprehensive subscription lists or petitions to distinguish one school from the other after 1745. Fortunately, however, fourth-generation ministers have left other important clues to their orientation in their regular sermon notes. Unlike preaching notes from earlier generations that were uniformly six to twelve closely written pages, fourth-generation sermon manuscripts fell into two distinct categories. One group (the rationalists) prepared extensive sermon manuscripts that were longer and more completely written out than the notes of their predecessors. Included in this group were most former Old Light opponents of Whitefield and the Arminian-Anglicans. In contrast to these were the notes of evangelicals (New Lights, "New Divinity" men, Separates), which were often less than three pages in length. These differences do not appear in printed sermons for reasons that will become clear later. But when regular sermon notes are viewed inclusively, the differences are so striking as to constitute homiletical badges.

The practice of preparing extensive sermon notes began in the third generation when ministers expanded their notes in imitation of English literary essays. But the composition of verbatim sermon texts, replete with paragraphs and complete sentences, did not become common until after the new revivals. Skeletal sermon outlines, in contrast, had a considerably shorter ancestry, dating back to Whitefield's first preaching tour of New England. After hearing Whitefield preach, for example, Jonathan Edwards sought to reduce his sermon notes to briefer outlines—though he never succeeded in dispensing with them altogether.[21] Other New Lights similarly sought to keep their notes to a minimum and, when the occasion warranted, departed from their text entirely and spoke spontaneously. In a letter to Thomas Prince, Josiah Crocker expressed the balance that New Lights sought between preparation and spontaneity:

> I think, indeed, it is my duty to study my sermons as well as I am able, and to labour to feel the power of them upon my own heart before I deliver them to the people; yet I believe ministers may sometimes be called in Providence to preach when they had not had an opportunity for such preparatory studies as might be their duty at other times, and then they may humbly look up to the Holy Spirit for, and expect his gracious assistance answerable to their necessities.

One example of evangelically oriented preaching notes is a sermon Daniel Rogers preached in 1749. The full sermon was contained in one duodecimo leaf. First came the text from 2 Peter 3:3, and with it the opening lead: "This Doct. Speaks Terror to all Impenitent Sinners." The application and exhortation were equally brief: "If you continue such [impenitencies] you will be sealed in flaming Fire. Let such [sinners] be exhorted to make their Peace with God and get into favor with their Judge." From notes like these, Rogers would preach for one hour or longer, echoing themes associated with condemnation ("flaming Fire") and salvation (divine "favor"). Few New Light preachers' notes were as brief as Rogers's, but all relied on memory and the inspiration of the moment to a far greater extent than their rationalist counterparts.[22]

When alternative types of sermon notes are correlated with the ministers' place of formal education, a fascinating pattern emerges. To a remarkable degree, students trained at Harvard preferred sermon essays, whereas those trained at Yale generally favored extemporaneous outlines.[23] Yale's president and faculty objected to Whitefield's censoriousness as strenuously as their counterparts at Harvard, but the spiritual and intellectual atmosphere of the two schools differed markedly, especially in regard to the question of evangelical preaching. From its founding in 1701, Yale was intended to be a more pietistic or "orthodox" alternative to Harvard's latitudinarian and urbane bearing. By 1745 the different philosophical and theological orientations of the schools did not appear in matters of curriculum requirements or general reading, but they did persist among graduates entering the ministry. Yale's student body was drawn largely from Connecticut and western Massachusetts, and welcomed itinerant speakers during the revivals. Thereafter the college became the major training ground for the "New Divinity" followers of Jonathan Edwards and "moderate" Calvinists like the college presidents Thomas Clap and Ezra Stiles. From Yale, evangelical pastors entered the homes of New Light pastors for postgraduate study in the new methods of preaching, and from there they poured into the Connecticut countryside and the towns along the Connecticut River Valley. Conversely, Harvard graduates dominated the northeastern corner of Connecticut and eastern Massachusetts.[24] Virtually all the "Arminian" pastors graduated from Harvard, as did many moderates with an Old Light orientation. Of course there were notable exceptions to this pattern, but in general the correlations are strong and confirm that differences in pulpit style were quite literally the product of two different "schools" of thought.

On an individual level, different preaching styles were also the product of personal temperament and social background. Rationalist ministers tended to be drawn from higher socioeconomic ranks than their evangelical counterparts and retained a more elitist view of their calling. In an ordination sermon preached at the installation of Nathaniel Huntington, for example, Windham's Ebenezer Devotion emphasized the traditional image of the minister as a speaking aristocrat addressing a silent democracy: "The duty of one to *Speak*, and of the other to *Hear* the Word of the Lord, will remain in force to Ministers and People respectively throughout all Ages." If popular audiences did not thrill to sentiments like Devotion's, that was of scant consideration for, as Boston's Andrew Eliot pointed out, the minister's calling was not "to take his scheme of divinity from his hearers, and to alter and change as they do. . . . We are to look into the BIBLE for principles."[25] In the rhetorical world of the rationalists, the speaker did not exist for the sake of the audience, but the audience existed to be edified and enlightened by the minister.

The social orientation and personal temperament of evangelical ministers were very different. They defined their calling by the popular audience and the moment of delivery. As rationalist essays were geared to the understanding and appreciation of informed audiences, evangelical notes were aimed at public arousal and the inspiration of the moment. They were best when neither speaker nor audience knew what was coming next. Many ministers were uncomfortable with a style that placed such demand on recall and immediate inspiration, but those evangelicals who excelled in this manner of preaching emerged as the most popular speakers in urban centers and villages throughout New England.[26]

When rationalists and evangelicals defended their particular deliveries—and the importance of delivery generally—they applied different rhetorical standards. Until the 1740s and 1750s ministers paid little attention to the portion of rhetoric devoted to "delivery" or "elocution." Instead they devoted their energies to adapting the categories of invention, arrangement, and style to the needs of sacred oratory. All of these categories were concerned more with composition than the actual moment of speech. This changed in the wake of the new revivals, as both rationalists and evangelicals rushed to defend their particular methods. No longer did all agree with classical rhetoricians like Cicero and Quintillian that delivery should be "studied" and "grave." Different theories appeared—particularly in ordination sermons—both as to the appropriate manner of delivery and the role of the speaker in the speech act.

In general, rationalist preaching theories echoed traditional themes set forth in rhetoric texts and the classic Puritan manuals on preaching. At the ordination of Joseph Roberts, Andrew Eliot conceded that the topic of delivery had been "too much neglected" in the past, but then went on to develop that topic in traditional fashion. First he urged careful composition, warning that "they who neglect to prepare their sermons, are in danger of delivering many things, that are crude and indigested." From there he turned to delivery and issued a standard list of classical maxims: ministers should "deliver themselves with *decency*"; they should avoid "everything that is low and groveling in Language; and everything that is uncouth and affected in their *pronunciation*." In general, they should labor "after a good elocution, and an agreeable behaviour in the Pulpit."[27] The highest praises rationalists gave one another were drawn from classical sources and registered elitist conceptions of the speaker and "refined" audience. Thus at the funeral of Haverhill's Edward Barnard, Benjamin Parker drew his praises straight from classical rhetoric and polite literary conventions:

> His invention was most fruitful indeed, and his thoughts sublime. His stile was elevated, polite, nervous, and abounded with flowers. His voice was not strong, yet he was a graceful speaker; no man read his sermons to better advantage, or acceptance; and with a greater fluency of speech. And the gravity which set upon his brow, and that fervour of mind which appeared

to actuate and influence him, in the time of his delivery, gave a cadency to his heavenly rhetorick.[28]

As the preceding examples suggest, rationalist theories of delivery valued "stile," "gravity," restrained "reading," and a literary "cadency" over the new evangelical proclivities for "affected tones," "theatrical" gestures, or "inspired" spontaneity. Equally clear was the rationalists' penchant for "refined" and "polite" audiences. This traditional conception of sermon delivery coincided with a cultural and theological orientation that emphasized sanctified works and godly "order" over impassioned individual conversion experiences. Terms like "obedience," "fruits," "virtue," "unity," and, most importantly, "duty" punctuate rationalist rhetoric, revealing how closely their preaching was tied to New England's continuing corporate mission and the question of "external" public morality. Their message was especially well received in older, well-organized communities and among urbane congregations who perceived themselves as more refined and polite than their countrymen. They were communities and congregations whose piety found expression in corporate covenant renewal and a healthy respect for the moral demands of God's federal covenant with New England.[29]

PERSISTENT ORTHODOXY IN RATIONALIST PREACHING

Along with morality and duty, rationalist preachers valued balance in their discourses. Thus they carefully grounded their teaching of moral duty and reform in revelation as well as reason, and insisted that true obedience or virtue must flow as a consequence of grace, not as a means. Indeed, it was their emphasis on *Sola Scriptura* and the covenant of grace that established common bonds with educated evangelicals and prevented schism. While rationalists were receptive to the essays of secular moralists and eager to explore the dictates of natural reason, few believed they could establish a basis for moral obligation and true virtue solely through the understanding or philosophical description. For them, as for evangelicals, the light of nature was incomplete without the additional light of revelation that revealed man's original sin and need for supernatural grace. The question on which rationalists and evangelicals diverged was not original sin and supernatural grace but *how* the Holy Spirit worked to reconcile sinners and through *what* faculties this was accomplished.

The persistence of orthodox Puritan doctrines in rationalist preaching can best be seen in Old Light responses to "Arminian" rationalists who crossed the line of liberal theology and openly repudiated the inherited doctrines of original sin, divine election, supernatural conversion, and the primacy of *Sola Scriptura*. As Conrad Wright demonstrates, Arminian thought in New England occurred at least partly in response to the new revivals.[30] Socially, the Arminians represented an elitist response to the democratic tendencies of the revivals and evangelical preaching. In this, they were not so far removed from many moderate rationalists or Old Lights, who retained as much of the old theories of deference and hierarchy as they could. More disturbing to Old Lights, however, was the Arminians' rejection of traditional Calvinist theology, particularly the doctrines of original sin and imputation. From the Arminian point of view, the doctrine of original sin was unacceptable partly because it was offensive to refined sensibilities and partly because it seemed incompatible with principles of equity and justice. The Arminian-Anglican Edward Bass (HC, 1744) reasoned that since natural laws of justice and reciprocity corresponded to the divine mind, God "will not punish any man for the sins of another . . . whereof he is [in] no way accessary." Rather, men were judged only "thro their own personal guilt and transgressions."[31] Any other criterion for justice was arbitrary and unacceptable to enlightened minds.

In 1749, Braintree's Arminian-Congregationalist Lemuel Briant issued the most controversial blast against orthodox Calvinism when he declared, in a sermon from Jonathan Mayhew's pulpit at Boston's West Church, that the "true Sense of Revelation" and "perfect Religion of Jesus" was nothing other than a "refined System of morality." This system considered people "moral Agents" who were free to choose the good and capable of practicing the ways of *personal* good Behaviour" that would reconcile them to God and cause His grace to shine upon them.[32] In Briant's view, Scripture confirmed the ways of morality taught in nature. Christ's mission on earth was less to atone for man's guilt or operate as a "charm to work up our hearers to a warm pitch of enthusiasm" than to exemplify and enact the system of morality taught in nature. In contrast to both Old and New Light theology, Briant argued that man's faculties were not so distorted by sin that his reason could not discern the true and right, and guide the soul in the "Practice of Christian Morality."

In working towards a more reasonable Christianity, Briant and his small circle of friends perceived themselves as part of a select few who transcended the "error" and "superstition" of Calvinist glosses on primitive Christianity and thought for themselves. They were optimistic about man's true condition, and the source of that optimism was man's reason—or at least the reason of an educated man: "There always was and always will be some in the World (alas that their Number is so few) that have Sense eno' and dare trust in their own Faculties so far, as to *judge in themselves what is right*."[33] The majority's failure to see inherited superstitions for what they were merely confirmed their lack of understanding and blind zeal. As Briant's admirer Jonathan Mayhew pointed out, in terms not calculated to win popular approval, "Those of the lower class can go but a little way with their inquiries into the natural and moral constitution of the world."[34] It was for this reason, Mayhew went on, that the people must submit to the wisdom and understanding of their superiors who alone had the gifts to perceive the nature of true virtue.

In contrast to the conventional identification of man's chief end with "the glory of God," the general principle Arminians invoked to organize their religious and ethical teachings was human happiness. Since the third generation, election preachers had reflexively identified the end of civil government with the promotion of human happiness. But Arminians took this one crucial step further by identifying religion itself with human happiness. As far as Lemuel Briant was concerned, Christian faith could be measured "exactly to it's Tendency" to "promote the moral Rectitude and Happiness of his Creatures." Jonathan Mayhew was even more explicit. For him, the ends of civil government and religion were virtually identical. True virtue was not a state of being attendant on supernatural grace, or a "speculative" knowledge of creedal doctrines, but simply "what we are under obligation to practice, without the consideration of the being of a God, or of a future state, [but] barely from its apparent tendency to make mankind happy at present."[35] Such a formula "simplified" Christianity and purified it of superstitions that had accumulated over the centuries. Human happiness was something that all good men could agree upon and the only principle capable of transcending sectarian disputes and restoring unity of purpose.

Ebenezer Gay completed the Arminian assault on orthodox Puritanism with his 1759 Dudleian lecture on *Natural Religion as Distinguished from Revealed*. By that time, Gay had seen enough of the excesses of revived religion to outline a basis for Christian morality that did not depend upon *Sola Scriptura*. In words that would ring out as New England's "manifesto" or "*locus classicus*" of natural theology, he inverted the traditional primacy of revelation over natural reason: "Revealed Religion is an *Additional* to Natural; built, not on the Ruins, but on the strong and everlasting Foundations of it."[36] Orthodox New Englanders could not perceive reason's capacity to draw men into a "state of grace," Gay continued, because they exaggerated the debilitating power of sin and confused innate evil with simple ignorance. God's mercy did not allow for innate sin. To the contrary, God implanted an inner moral sense which, when properly enlightened and cultivated, would draw people to Him. In terms that reversed standard preaching themes, Gay asserted that mankind was "naturally disposed toward Religion," in the same way that planets were attracted to one another in the material universe. If properly guided, man's reason would naturally choose good over evil and be "designed and framed for the practice of virtue." Of course there would be some lingering imperfections even in the most enlightened moralists, but God in his mercy would overlook these shortcomings and "grant the Succours of his Grace, enabling them to do the same [moral virtues], and other things to better Acceptance, and to the obtaining a greater Reward, even that which the Christian Revelation proposes."[37] Revelation, it was clear, existed to ratify and elucidate truths that nature already taught.

Much to the dismay of Ebenezer Gay and his small circle of Arminian colleagues and students, their call to Christian Enlightenment attracted few marchers. The opposition of evangelicals like Jonathan Edwards and his New Divinity disciples was predictable. But more disturbing was the fact that *rationalist* ministers who had earlier denied Whitefield their pulpits led the initial assault on Arminianism and vigorously defended orthodox Calvinism in pulpit, print, and clerical association. Jonathan Mayhew, for example, was ordained without benefit of neighboring ministers and never participated in the Boston association of ministers. In the case of Briant, an association of Old Light ministers met in Braintree in 1753 and, under the leadership of Samuel Niles, condemned his sermon on natural religion as "unscriptural" and tending to undermine the foundations of the Congregational churches. Although Briant was not formally removed from office, the criticism of his peers was so harsh that he was forced to resign his pulpit and died a year later—a "martyr" to the Arminian cause.[38]

On other fronts, the rationalist clergy moved with equal dispatch to distance themselves from the taint of Arminianism and confirm their orthodoxy, both to their peers and their congregations. A chagrined Samuel Niles, who had earlier denied the existence of Arminianism in New England, issued a massive rejoinder to Briant's sermon that concentrated on the issue of moral entitlement and salvation. From start to finish the discourse set out to "reject all Pretenses of Justification in God's sight by our *Moral virtues*" and to uphold the traditional doctrine that "the whole and sole Matter of our Justification before God . . . is the *Righteousness* of Christ, graciously given to us in a way of *Imputation*, and received by Faith alone." Certainly, Niles went on, happiness on earth was important, but Briant and other Arminians failed to address the more important question of "final happiness."[39] Niles was careful to point out that teachings like Briant's by no means encompassed "the whole Body" of ministers, but they did influence some and therefore had to be addressed if the country was to remain pure.

Niles and other rationalists believed that the evil genius behind New England heterodoxy was the English Arminian John Taylor, whose treatise attacking *The Scripture-Doctrine of Original Sin* was widely read. Taylor's denial of original sin was the subject of vigorous attack by Jonathan Edwards in *The Great Christian Doctrine of Original Sin . . .* , published in Boston in 1758. But before that, Niles issued his own rejoinder, which anticipated many of the points that Edwards would later raise. Niles's central premise was simple: all doctrinal issues must be settled by appeal to Scripture, not logic. From Scripture, he found "plainly revealed" in both "the Old Testament and the New," the doctrine that "*Adam* being the natural and moral Head of Mankind, so *we* sinned *in him*, in his first Transgression. . . . The Guilt of his Transgression is imputed, and from him a depraved Nature is derived." The Arminians' denial of original sin, Niles shrewdly pointed out, not only contradicted numerous Scripture texts but also threatened to displace most of the major themes in regular preaching. By denying the imputation of sin through the "first Adam,"

Arminians could not exploit the sublime symmetry of the imputation of righteousness through Christ, the "second Adam." "Their want of a thorow Conviction of the *Sinfulness* of that State they were *born* in, makes the Gospel-Doctrine of the *New-Birth* such a Mystery to them, that they *Marvel*, when it's said to them, *Ye must be born again*."[40] Without the doctrine of original sin, in other words, ministers would be unable to proclaim the doctrine of the New Birth that their congregations demanded.

Throughout the 1750s, other leading rationalists were equally direct in their defense of original sin and the accompanying doctrine of supernatural grace. In a sermon delivered to Harvard students and later published at their request, Cambridge's Nathaniel Appleton repeated the familiar principle that when Adam "broke the law and covenant he was under; neither he nor any of his natural Descendants could ever be justified according to that Law." God's justice demanded an atonement for Adam's sin that could only come from the outside, "by Faith in Jesus Christ who alone has satisfied the Demands of the Law in the Sinner's Stead." Like Niles, Appleton reminded aspiring ministers in his audience that the Arminian denial of original sin and divine election left unexplained the meaning of Christ's suffering and undermined the Protestant doctrine of free grace: "The more there is of a legal Temper in Men, the less need they will see of Christ, and the more indifferent will they be about accepting of him and trusting in him." In similar terms, Boston's Andrew Eliot reminded his fellow ministers that: "When we press *morality* ... we should do it by motives fetched from the Gospel of Christ." Such motives included the doctrine of original sin and the performance of moral duties as a response to the "acquittal" from guilt freely dispensed through Christ's sacrifice.[41]

Despite Old Light attachments to a rational preaching style, they proclaimed the New Birth their congregations demanded. In 1766, Marblehead's "liberal" pastor John Barnard looked back over a long career of preaching and concluded that, "I can truly say, that in the course of my ministry, I have endeavored to preach Jesus Christ and his laws, and not vain philosophy or the traditions of men; to set forth Christ, as the promised Messiah, the son of God, and the alone Saviour of a guilty world, and the Judge of the quick and the dead."[42] The surviving sermon notes of rationalist or moderate ministers are even more revealing. On August 12, 1744, after the sudden death of a parishioner "whose cart wheel ran over his neck and killed him on the spot," Westboro's Ebenezer Parkman pled with his congregation to consider their final happiness: "Are you regenerate and converted? Let me exhort you all to get Ready and keep ever ready because you are so continuously exposed [to death]." In the same year, Samuel Checkley (HC, 1715) reminded his New South congregation in the starkest terms that "*There is a Hell.*" In harsh detail he described the destination of unbelievers who trusted in their own righteousness: they were headed for a "place of torments" and a "lake of fire" whose consuming flames could "never be quenched." Were the congre-

gation allowed a "messenger from the dead," they would discover the
horror of living eternally "in torment, in exquisite pain and misery, misery
beyond what tongue can express or heart conceive." In Wrentham, Henry
Messenger painted a similarly bleak picture and pointed to only one
escape: "Come to Christ that ye may be Saved, even every one of you!"[43]
Sentiments like these were a far cry from the optimism of Arminian liberals and confirm the orthodox response of New England rationalists to
the threat of "enlightened" Christianity.

In summarizing religious thought in eighteenth-century New England,
historians have too often ignored the enduring primacy of *Sola Scriptura*
on the rationalist mind. Perry Miller's apt characterization of seventeenth-
century priorities in which "reason does not make clear the sense of Scripture, but the clear sense of scripture creates the reason" held true for most
eighteenth-century ministers as well.[44] Brattle Street's Samuel Cooper
(HC, 1743)—destined to become a leading preacher in the Revolution—
declared his primary allegiance in no uncertain terms: "It is our Privilege . . . that we have the Bible in our own Hands, and in a Language that
we understand. That we may read and judge it for ourselves. That our
Faith may not stand in the wisdom and authority of men, but in the Power
and veracity of God." Nature and reason, as Thaddeus Maccarty
expounded in a sermon from Charles Chauncy's pulpit, were invaluable
in confirming the existence of "a Supreme Being who is the author of the
whole," but they could not lead a fallen humanity to salvation. Or, as
Andrew Eliot declared, "Reason alone in our fallen state, is not sufficient
to guide us to happiness; and therefore God has favored us with a revelation of his will. The great design of the Scriptures is, to make us wise to
Salvation."[45] Continuing appeals to *Sola Scriptura* served as a declaration
of independence from current European thought and "human" authorities, and a confirmation of the ministers' trustworthiness to congregations
whose only acknowledged sovereign was the Word of God.

Although most Anglican ministers endorsed Arminian conclusions,
there were exceptions like Stratford's Samuel Johnson (later president of
King's College in New York), who held fast to traditional doctrines of sin
and regeneration. In a sermon on "The Necessity of Revealed Religion,"
Johnson employed Proverbs 29:18 ("where there is no vision the people
perish") to remind his parish "that the people that are destitute of any
vision, or supernatural divine revelation . . . are in a wretched, broken,
scattered, wandering, and therefore perishing condition." The reason was
simple: the "mere" light of nature, based as it was on the natural senses,
could not bridge the gap between the visible and invisible world. Salvation, Johnson declared elsewhere, could not be found in the "cobwebs of
metaphysical philosophy" whose light in matters of the world to come
was "very dark and obscure." Rather it could only be discovered in the
Scriptures, by believers "having a strong appetite for them, and delight
in them, and in tasting the sweetness and suitableness of them."[46] Terms
like Johnson's sound very much like those used by Jonathan Edwards and

confirm that ministerial divisions—at least in terms of pulpit utterance—were not as extreme as their debates over polity, the freedom of the will, and the affections might suggest.

EVANGELICAL HOMILETICS

Evangelicalism's popular orientation and theological rigor fused in one towering intellectual figure, Jonathan Edwards. Though none of his followers ever matched his brilliance, they claimed him as their role model, both in the study and in the pulpit. In his lifetime, Edwards's sermons were as influential as his philosophical treatises in fixing the tone and substance of evangelical preaching. Beyond preaching, he invited many students like Joseph Bellamy and Samuel Hopkins into his home for postgraduate training. These students, in turn, began their own "schools of prophets" that spread Edwards's "New Divinity" throughout the countryside.[47] Other ministers in New England's long line of clerics exerted far greater political influence than Edwards, but no single minister did so much to alter preaching or set the tone for pulpit discourse as Jonathan Edwards.

For all of his influence on the pulpit, Edwards never prepared a formal preaching manual in the tradition of William Ames, Solomon Stoddard, or Cotton Mather. His most systematic statements on the role of a minister appeared in his frequently printed ordination sermons—virtually the only occasional sermons he published. In intellectual terms, these sermons remained true to the cause of revival and defined the minister's vocation primarily in terms of the New Birth. In social terms, Edwards's ordination sermons diverged dramatically from rationalist sermons in his steadfast refusal to dwell on exalted claims to social preeminence. Instead of describing ministers as ambassadors, he preferred to describe their role "as that of servants, to wash and cleanse the souls of men." The terms "condescension" and "love" dominated his charges to new ministers, while superiority and duty were consciously downplayed. From the New Testament example of Christ he warned ministers that, "as love to men's souls in Christ was far above any regard he had to his temporal interest, his ease, his honour, his meat and drink . . . so it should be with ministers." Elsewhere, he likened the relationship of a minister to his congregation "as a young man to a virgin that he marries."[48] Such imagery was not unknown to earlier Puritan preachers, but it did not dominate their descriptions of the preaching office as it did for Edwards.

As rhetorician, Edwards emphasized above all else the moment of delivery in preaching.[49] Careful preparation and study were important, but the Holy Spirit was most active through the sermon, and the minister had to prepare himself for maximum concentration in that time. To aid in this endeavor, Edwards recommended brief sermon outlines "to show earnestness." While Edwards's own delivery lacked the drama of a Whitefield or Tennent, his use of language was unexcelled. More than anyone else, he supplied a stock of images and metaphors that evangelical ministers could draw from to engage their listeners' affections. Certainly the most notorious of these images were ones related to death and judgment. In his most famous revival sermon on *Sinners in the Hands of an Angry God*, preached at Enfield, Connecticut, on July 8, 1741, Edwards likened the precariousness of the human condition to a falling weight and spider's web:

> Your wickedness makes you as it were heavy as lead, and to tend downwards with great weight and pressure towards hell; and if God should let you go, you would immediately sink and swiftly descend and plunge into the bottomless gulf, and your healthy constitution, and your own care and prudence, and best contrivance, and all your righteousness, would have no more influence to uphold you and keep you out of hell, than a spider's web would have to stop a fallen rock.

In artful—even contrived—fashion Edwards locked his listeners into the horrors of hell and eternal damnation: a "world of misery," a "lake of burning brimstone," and a "dreadful pit of glowing flames of the wrath of God." Without God's grace, mankind could do nothing to stop its plunging descent "into the fire."[50]

Edwards's depiction of hell and damnation was certainly dramatic and led rationalist critics like Samuel Johnson to complain that evangelicals said "all the most frightening things they could think of about the devil, hell, and damnation, so as to scare people out of their wits."[51] But such macabre themes were not the only or even the major images Edwards evoked to bring sinners to repentance. Like his grandfather, Edwards dwelt on the terrors of sin and judgment only as a prelude to the joy of salvation: "It is God's manner . . . [first] to lead them into a wilderness, before he speaks comfortably to them." For the most part, Edwards preached "so as to discover the motions of his own heart," and what he found there were thoughts "much taken up with heaven." The fears and terrors in his thought and preaching were offset by longings for a future world "where there is fulness of joy; where reigns heavenly, sweet, calm and delightful love without alloy; where there are continually the dearest expressions of this [divine] love. Where there is the enjoyment of persons loved, without ever parting. Where those persons, who appear so lovely in this world, will really be inexpressibly more lovely, and full of love to us."[52] Repeatedly he reminded his listeners that "happiness" was a function of their "future state": "We are pilgrims and strangers here, and are principally designed for a future world." That world was reached only through death. But, he added in comforting tones, death need hold no fear for the regenerate: "Death to the saint is always a passage or avenue, leading out of a world of vanity, and sin, and misery, into a world of life, light, and glory. . . . The darkness all vanishes away, and the light shines out of that glorious city in which they are entering."[53] Evangelical preaching in Edwards's hands was neither obsessed with terror nor with questions of happiness and duty in this world. It was, instead, a vision of heaven that strained his formidable powers of description and imagination to their outermost limits.

To vivify the word and confront his listeners with the wonders of the invisible world, Edwards relied heavily upon natural imagery as a type or "shadow of the spiritual world." Where earlier preachers had been careful to draw a strict distinction between natural "tropes" and biblical "types," Edwards conflated the two into one massive revelation of the will of God. No longer were natural metaphors limited to embellishing doctrinal truths; they were themselves a doctrine or "representation" of divine grace.[54] Seen in this context, Edwards believed that God created trees to flower by water intentionally so that mankind could understand the internal operations of the Holy Spirit in causing the soul to flower and produce noble fruits. Likewise, planets revolved around the sun to illustrate the dependence of Christians on Christ, the "Sun of Righteousness." What others perceived as a mechanical universe was, to Edwards, a representation of the spiritual principles underlying and upholding all of creation, moment by moment. As all rivers eventually empty into oceans, so "all things tend to one, even to God, the boundless ocean."[55]

Of all the natural imagery that Edwards employed to represent the central truths of redemption, the most important were images related to light and sun. In Edwards's view, other natural metaphors—heat, cold, water, wind, wilderness—elicited multiple meanings, positive and negative. Only light invariably produced a positive image, and that image was reserved exclusively to convey the truths of another, spiritual world.[56] Light, of course, was the master symbol of the Enlightenment, but Edwards related it less to reason than to the new sense of the heart. For example, in describing the religious experience of his wife, Sarah, he wrote how in times of acute communion with God her soul "remained in a kind of heavenly Elysium, and did as it were swim in the rays of Christ's love, like a little mote swimming in the beams of the Sun, or Streams of his light that come in at a window; and the heart was swallowed up in a kind of glow of Christ's love, coming down from Christ's heart in heaven, as a constant stream of sweet light." Similarly, at Robert Abercrombie's ordination Edwards preached from John 5:35 ("He was a burning and shining light"), and likened ministers to "the stars that encompass the glorious fountain of light."[57]

Ultimately, the light of which Edwards spoke was not available through reason but was dispensed from God to people regardless of social class, gender, or vocation. In *A Divine and Supernatural Light*, delivered six years before Whitefield's arrival, Edwards explained how the New Birth differed from other forms of knowledge contained in the "human arts and sciences," in that the Holy Spirit "imparts this knowledge immediately, not making use of any intermediate natural causes." Instead of a continuum between nature and grace there was an irreconcilable break; grace and light were gifts that could be acquired only in faith. In social terms, this meant that ordinary people need feel no disadvantage in acquiring this knowledge, nor should they feel timid about proclaiming it publicly:

> [P]ersons with an ordinary degree of knowledge . . . are capable of being taught by the Spirit of God, as well as learned men. The evidence that is this way obtained, is vastly better and more satisfying, than all that can be obtained by the arguings of those that are the most learned, and greatest masters of reason. And babes are as capable of knowing these things, as the wise and prudent.

The benefits of supernatural knowledge were infinitely preferable to mere human knowledge taught in the schools because conversion brought with it a vision of heaven that Edwards described elsewhere in dazzling terms as the beginning of eternity:

> [I]t is eternal life begun; and therefore, they that have it, can never die. It is the dawning of the light of glory. It is the day-star risen in the heart, that is a sure forerunner of that Sun's rising which will bring on an everlasting day. . . . It is something from heaven. And those that have it, however they may now wander in a wilderness, or be tossed to and fro on a tempestuous ocean, shall certainly arrive in heaven at last, where this heavenly spark shall be increased and perfected, and the souls of the saints all be transformed into a bright and pure flame, and they shall shine forth as the sun in the kingdom of their Father.[58]

Through his printed sermons and the school of prophets established in his household Edwards taught a generation of evangelical ministers how to articulate their extemporaneous sermons in glowing terms that warmed the hearts of their listeners. His two most famous students—Samuel Hopkins and Joseph Bellamy—remained lifelong adherents of the "Edwardean" theology and transmitted it to their postgraduate students, who in turn filled pulpits throughout Connecticut and western New England. All were concerned with the "new creature," and a "Disinterested Supream Regard to God the Attendant of True Grace."[59] The most important quality of this new creature was a direct "Experimental, Saving Knowledge" of God imparted by the Holy Spirit through evangelical preaching. Such knowledge was available to all and brought with it the responsibility to speak and testify.

A COMMON ENEMY

In looking back at rationalist and evangelical sermons delivered in the aftermath of the new revivals, one wonders how two such contrasting styles could have coexisted through the remainder of the eighteenth century. Clearly, style was important to these Congregationalists in defining their social and theological preferences, but not so important that it was worth open division or schism. Other mitigating factors were more important, and in closing this chapter it would be helpful to review them.

As we have seen, doctrinal agreement on Congregational polity, original sin, supernatural grace, and New England's federal covenant were important considerations in holding Congregational ministers together in a common tradition. Looking solely at printed sermons, it is easy to overlook this continuity because rationalists and evangelicals published different types of sermons. Because of their literary inclinations and refined congregations, rationalist ministers produced most of the printed occasional sermons. Election sermons and Dudleian lectures were exclusively products of rationalist pens together with many printed fast sermons. All of these centered on themes of corporate morality and ethical duties derived from the law of nature as well as revelation.[60] Evangelicals did not ignore these themes on days of fasting or election, but they generally were not published. Conversely, rationalist ministers published few regular conversionist sermons, in contrast to evangelicals who preferred to write out and expand upon their regular sermon notes for publication. Not since the first generation did so many ministers prefer to publish regular sermons as the mid-eighteenth-century evangelicals. Because of these divergent publishing preferences the differences between rationalist and evangelical oratory become exaggerated. When unpublished sermon notes are added to the analysis it becomes apparent that rationalists did not ignore biblical themes of sin and rebirth in their regular preaching, nor did evangelicals neglect to invoke the federal covenant on occasional days of distress.

As important as Bible-centered preaching, orthodox doctrine, and a common allegiance to Congregational polity were in holding the ministry together in an uneasy truce, it is doubtful that unity could have been maintained had it not been for one other external, unifying factor that was so important that it will occupy the next chapter. That factor was renewed war with France and the possibility of national extinction. For more than thirty years following the Treaty of Utrecht, New England colonists lived in formal peace. A generation came of age who knew nothing of the traumas of total war and who were free to disagree without fear of foreign reprisal. In 1745, that happy period of external peace came to an abrupt end. Never again would New England's colonists rest easy. Internal religious disputes dimmed in significance as ministers on both sides of the debate came to the realization that their programs for national regeneration meant nothing if the country did not survive. In war with France, rationalists and evangelicals discovered a common enemy so powerful and a cause so glorious that it demanded their total collective commitment both on the battlefield and in the pulpit. They would also learn anew the ancient lesson that New England's God was a "Man of War" and their enemies nothing less than the minions of Satan posed to extinguish the true church in the wilderness.

[12]

War

In May 1744 controversy over Whitefield's second visit to New England was cut short by news of renewed war with France. Almost overnight, energies were channeled from revivals to defense. Divisions between Old Lights and New Lights that had threatened to split the churches now lost their edge as both sides contemplated the specter of a French invasion. From earlier experiences in King William's War (1689–1697) and Queen Anne's War (1702–1713), New Englanders knew that international war would inevitably spill over into their borders.[1] If France was ever to gain control of North America, the first and most important region to conquer was New England. Conversely, if England was to prevail, the French would have to be driven from their Canadian strongholds in Louisbourg, Quebec, and Montreal. In either case New England soldiers, sailors, and shipbuilders would play a vital role in effecting the final outcome. On all sides the stakes were high. But nowhere were they higher than in New England, where every man, woman, and child faced armed resistance or foreign subjugation.

THE LOUISBOURG CAMPAIGN

The center of New England fears was the French fortress at Louisbourg on Cape Breton Island that defended the entrance to the St. Lawrence River. The fort had been the site of earlier encounters between the French and English, and assumed symbolic as well as strategic importance. If it could be taken communications between France and Canada could be cut off, and the French garrisons at Quebec and Montreal isolated for follow-up attacks. But the obstacles were forbidding. While New England had allowed its defenses to lapse during the interlude of peace, the French had refortified their fortress with four thousand regulars and a powerful naval fleet. This, together with the fort's location on the rugged highlands and steep bluffs of the eastern edge of the island, rendered it nearly impregnable. A Connecticut soldier recorded in his journal how

> the royal battery [at Louisbourg] . . . is a fort scarcely matchable in the French king's dominions; towards the sea it is strong and regular, about

twelve feet high to the embrazures, it mounts 30 large cannon and from the bastions the cannon sweep the whole face of the walls. . . . [I]t was judged 200 defendants would be more than a match against 5,000 that should attempt it without cannon, and cannon could not be brought against it without drawing them four miles in a very bad way.[2]

Few New Englanders believed they were ready for a massive military campaign against Louisbourg, but they would soon learn otherwise.

Despite the reluctance of the Massachusetts Assembly to prosecute a Canadian expedition without the aid of British troops and financing, Governor William Shirley initiated plans for an all-colonial assault on the French citadel. Ground forces would be supplied by New England volunteers led by the popular Maine merchant William Pepperell, while naval support would be under the command of the New Yorker, Commodore Peter Warren. From the start, Shirley and Pepperell recognized that success depended on the active support of New England's ministry, some 450 strong and scattered through every settlement in the region. Not only were the ministers needed for moral justification, but more immediately as recruiters who could help build enlistments to the required troop levels. No one was more important in this regard than the ever-popular George Whitefield. Despite ministerial opposition, Whitefield retained a wide following and could do more to move popular passions than any other speaker, civil or ecclesiastical. With Pepperell's urging, Whitefield interrupted his preaching tour to help build enlistments for the coming campaign. He supplied the troops with their motto, *Nil Desperandum, Christo Duce* ("Christ leads, never despair!"), and with his encouragement "great numbers enlisted."[3] Other ministers, both Old and New Light, were similarly effective in their role as martial exhorters and recruiters. By February 1745, thirty-five hundred Massachusetts and Connecticut soldiers and one thousand seamen streamed into Boston to form the largest colonial expeditionary force ever assembled in North America.

Besides serving as recruiters and later chaplains to the colonial forces, New England's ministers were active on the home front, putting party divisions behind and mobilizing public opinion for the coming campaign. The people had to be convinced that their cause was just in the eyes of God and that victory was possible. If past experience was any guide, the prospects for victory were not bright. One-fifth of New England's able-bodied males participated in the earlier campaigns of Queen Anne's War, and the results were disastrous: expeditions never sailed, ships were diverted off course, and unsuccessful and mismanaged battles seemed only to issue in high casualty rates and unrecoverable war debts.[4] To achieve victory, New England would have to depend on their special covenant with God and the promise of divine assistance that came with it. In 1745 the old corporate themes of repentance and success sounded with renewed urgency and provided New Englanders with the margin of hope they needed to prosecute the upcoming war.

To bolster military and civilian resolve, Governor Shirley proclaimed a series of local fasts that would culminate on April 4, when all the churches would assemble at once, confess their sins, and humbly implore God's blessing on the coming engagement.[5] For many ministers this would be their first wartime fast. On the eve of his fast sermon, Ebenezer Parkman could scarce contain his anticipation: "I earnestly desire and request a Suitable Preparation for the Extraordinary Fast approaching! May the Lord prepare us all, this whole people to Sanctifie it!" Similarly, Daniel Wadsworth, who two months earlier was defending himself against lay itinerants and organizing a "Testimony against Mr. Whitefield," turned his thoughts to the "Expedition against Cape Breton" and the sermons he would preach. On April 3 he delivered a fast sermon to his Hartford congregation on Deuteronomy 23:9 ("When the host goeth forth against thine enemies, then keep thee from every wicked thing"). The following day he met with Captain James Church's company of Hartford volunteers to "pray ye Lord of hosts go with them."[6] Elsewhere the situation was similar. Local contentions disappeared as ministers and congregations contemplated their common enemy and called upon their covenant God for deliverance.

NEW ENGLAND'S FEDERAL COVENANT CONFIRMED

In articulating the terms of victory, New Lights proved to be as quick to claim federal promises as their Old Light counterparts. Jonathan Edwards is often cited for his rejection of the old covenant theology.[7] But that was in matters of sacraments, not national identity. While rejecting the Halfway Covenant and "mere" external morality as means of grace, Edwards never questioned New England's corporate identity as a special people bound in an external national covenant. For Edwards, no less than the rationalists, New England was a "visible People of God"; a "city set on a hill" that was under great obligations to their covenant God. On the eve of the Louisbourg expedition he delivered a series of sermons on Leviticus 26:3–13 that had as their overriding theme the message that "temporal blessings" accrue to a people of God. Included in those blessings were martial promises; God's people could depend upon "safety . . . with reference to enemies," and eventually they would inherit "the blessings of peace." Edwards's April 4 "fast for success in [the] expedition against Cape Breton" followed the traditional formula exactly. From 1 Kings 8:44 he demonstrated how "a people of God may be called to go forth to war" and that such action was "lawful and a duty." With flawless logic he insisted that "if it be lawful for a particular person to defend himself with force, Then it is lawful for a nation of People made up of particular persons." In situations where God's people were threatened, they must look to Him for deliverance and, in dependence upon him, claim the victory: "God is ready in such a case to Hear the prayer of his People and give them success."[8] Unlike his regular sermons, Edwards's unpublished fasts were unoriginal; they offered nothing new in terminology or logic. There was nothing aesthetic about war; it was terrifying. When facing outward enemies Edwards, like his peers, instinctively fell back on federal promises in their simplest, most elemental form.

Throughout the spring of 1745 all ears anxiously awaited news from Louisbourg. On May 21, following another series of fast sermons, Daniel Wadsworth rejoiced to learn "news from Cape Breton that ye royal Battery is taken [and] ye english army encamped before ye Town."[9] Through a fortuitous set of circumstances including good sailing weather and French miscalculations, the New England troops had been able to set in a siege and wait out the outnumbered and undersupplied French. Finally, on June 17, the unthinkable happened: pressed by dwindling food and constant bombardment, the "Gibraltar of the New World" fell and passed to the command of William Pepperell. The impossible had been achieved. With no assistance from England, New England troops had humbled one of the most powerful French fortresses in the New World and fixed their self-image as a divinely assisted people of war.

News of the surrender did not reach Boston until July 3, at the same time that many ministers were convening there for the annual college commencement. The ensuing celebration was unrestrained. Ebenezer Parkman witnessed "all manner of Joy thereat. . . . The Bells were rung, Guns fired etc. Commencement was rendered the most gladsome Day." Thomas Prince later recalled how "when the Tydings came . . . we were like them that dream. Our mouth was fill'd with Laughter, and our Tongue with Singing." Throughout the evening the sky over Boston was illuminated by bonfires and fireworks. Religious controversies, which as recently as April 6 had been, in Parkman's words, "hotter than ever," melted away as all New England joined to celebrate the victory. Over the next two weeks, towns and churches throughout New England gathered for thanksgiving sermons and services of celebration.[10]

Like the earlier fast sermons, thanksgiving sermons portrayed the victory in apocalyptic terms and ascribed success to God's historic covenant with New England. No other explanation seemed adequate to explain the "train of providences" accompanying the New England troops on their feared expedition. Again, differences between rationalists and evangelicals disappeared in the occasional pulpit. Following news of the surrender, Edwards turned to history for comparable achievements. So magnificent a victory, he concluded, came "the nearest to a parallel with God's wonderful work of old, in Moses', Joshua's, and Hezekiah's time, of any that have been in these latter ages of the world."[11] Other ministers throughout New England voiced themes similar to Edwards's. None of their sermons offered original interpretations of the war; all invoked the standard themes of divine sovereignty and human faith.[12]

As in the aftermath of King Philip's War, many accounts of the Louisbourg campaign were published as Scripture-like revelations of continuing divine providence. In his 1746 election sermon, Andover's John Barnard concluded that God orchestrated the war to create "a Sense of our Dependence." While civil leaders must employ their own talents and wisdom in prosecuting battles, they must also recognize how "God is able to guide the *Guides* of a People, to lead their *Leaders*. . . . We need not doubt, that He . . . influenced our Honourable Rulers to form and prosecute this wonderful Scheme." In a printed thanksgiving sermon, Thomas Prince reiterated the claim he made earlier in his centennial election sermon that miracles were not essential to confirm divine intervention. The hand of God could be discerned as clearly through "ordinary means," when there appeared a "wonderful continued Train and timely *coincidence* of innumerable varieties of Means, both in the *material* and *moral* world together." Such a "coincidence," Prince went on, was plain at Louisbourg, where victory was obtained "by means of so small a Number, as about four thousand Landmen, unus'd to War, undisciplined, and that had never seen a Siege in their lives." The only possible conclusion was that "it is the Lord's Doing! It is marvellous in our Eyes." For Charles Chauncy, who had little in common with Prince over the question of revivals, Louisbourg taught the same lesson. Like Prince, he traced the hand of God in the "*ordinary* course of Providence" that arranged "second Causes" like sea winds and weather patterns to further the New Englanders' cause. The colonists' victory "in this part of the dominion of Antichrist" was so stupendous that the only historical precedent for it, according to Chauncy (and to Edwards), was ancient Israel: "I scarce know of a conquest, since the days of *Joshua* and the *Judges*, wherin the finger of God is more visible. . . . Let the inspired language of *Moses*, and the *whole Body of the Jewish Nation*, be ours upon this memorable occasion."[13]

Along with themes of providential deliverance, printed accounts of the expedition included as a subsidiary theme discussion of the role New England's people and troops would play in the coming millennium. Just as New Lights like Edwards saw in the earlier revivals a precursor of the end days, so all ministers saw in victory over France a hint of millennial triumphs when Antichrist would be finally vanquished. The most pointed millennial commentary appeared in a thanksgiving sermon by Joseph Sewall on Revelation 5:11, 12 ("worthy is the Lamb that was slain to receive power"). When the events at Louisbourg were laid alongside this prophecy of Christ's return to earth, it appeared that the end days could be approaching. While acknowledging that several prophecies had yet to be fulfilled—most notably the return of the Jews to Israel—Sewall nevertheless believed that "this glorious victory [may] be an Earnest of our Lords taking to himself the entire Possession of this *New World*. . . . May Antichrist be utterly destroyed by the Brightness of our Lords Coming; the *seventh Angel* found, and the kingdoms of this world become the kingdoms of our Lord."[14] In this account and others, the message was the same. By calling upon their covenant God, New Englanders not only confirmed their special status but also brought God's millennial kingdom closer to its glorious fulfillment.

A FRUSTRATED PEACE

In theory, the victory at Louisbourg should have been the first step in entirely routing the French forces from North America; in practice, however, this was not to be the case. At about the same time that many thanksgiving sermons were being published, the country was again plunged into despair as New England's untrained soldiers learned that taking a fortress was one thing, while holding it and prosecuting the war to other garrisons was something altogether different. No sooner had the colonial forces taken the fortress than disease struck their camps, killing ten times the number of troops lost in battle. With the first flush of battle passed, enlistments slowed to a trickle and casualties could not be replaced. Compounding the colonists' difficulties were the eastern Indian tribes. On August 23, 1745, war was declared on these tribes after they staged a series of hit-and-run attacks that set the frontier ablaze and reduced garrisons in Maine, Vermont, and western Massachusetts to ashes. These circumstances forced the colonists to abort their plans for a follow-up assault on the French fortress at Quebec. Thereafter the war bogged down into a series of inconclusive attacks and counterattacks, with neither side able to obtain an advantage. By 1748, when peace was formally declared, nothing substantial had been accomplished, leaving New England with unprecedented debts and a casualty rate that exceeded, in per capita terms, subsequent American losses in the American Revolution and Civil War.[15]

Already by 1746 it was clear that, however spectacular the victory at Louisbourg, the French could not be completely dislodged without British assistance. Yet that assistance was not forthcoming, causing many to suspect England's intentions towards her New World colonies. Two events in particular convinced New Englanders that France was not their only enemy. In an effort to fill quotas for the royal navy, Commodore Charles Knowles sent press gangs into Boston to muscle unsuspecting young men into service. This infuriated New Englanders—particularly lower-class Bostonians—who ever since 1741 had fiercely resisted British impressment. In November 1747 an "outrageious mob" of several thousand Bostonians took to the streets, forcing a startled Governor Shirley to evacuate to Castle William. For four days they ruled the streets and defied the highest authorities in the colony, acquiring a renewed sense of their power in mass assembly. The "rioters" dispersed only after the impressed Bostonians were released. The second factor straining Anglo-American relations was the Treaty of Aix-la-Chapelle, which ended the European war of the Austrian Succession in 1748. As part of the settlement, England agreed to return the Louisbourg fortress to the French in return for concessions elsewhere. For New Englanders who had fought and suffered to capture the fort, the treaty signified insensitivity and betrayal.[16] Even more than the impressment riots, the return of Louisbourg created suspicions about English good will that would not disappear.

Invariably, tensions with England and battlefield discouragements altered the tone of occasional preaching. Again fourth-generation ministers fell back on traditional formulas, but this time in the language of judgment and suffering rather than joy and exaltation. And, as before, they discovered that typological parallels with Israel and millennial prophecies were as compatible with failure as with success. On the eve of the colonists' abortive assault on Quebec in July 1746, Ebenezer Parkman invoked Ezekiel's prophecy of affliction as if it had been written for New England all along. That prophecy, he explained, "points to us—as if it should say this is New England!—This is Massachusetts! Consider how sore the calamities may be which come upon us. . . . What *can* we do? Necessity drives us to our prayer to Cry to God as the Israelites of old." Despite reverses, New England—like Israel—could gain strength by recognizing God's continuing covenant mercies, "in separating and distinguishing us from many others, in guarding us against our many and different kinds of enemies; in supplying our wants . . . and in our valuable privileges and Libertys Civil and Religious."[17] Such blessings and liberties might be endangered, but as long as God's Word prevailed, they would never disappear.

Among New Light ministers, the signs of divine testing and chastisement were similarly plain. And, like the rationalists, New Lights explained their current situation by looking back to their own past and Israel's, and by looking forward to millennial prophecies. This time, however, the millennial prophecies examined were ones dealing with suffering and tribulation rather than triumphant glory. By 1746 the fiery itinerant, Daniel Rogers, had settled down in a small parish in Exeter, New Hampshire, from which vantage point he could survey the menacing French threat to the near north. In his thanksgiving sermon of 1746 he turned from the joy and celebration of 1745 to a consideration of testing and judgment. From his text in Romans 2:3–5 ("do you think you will escape God's judgment?"), Rogers warned of trouble ahead: "There is coming a day of wrath and Revelation of the Righteous judgement of God, against such hard hearted impenitent Sinners as despise the riches of God's goodness exercised towards them in the Day of his patience in this world." In the same year Samuel Hopkins preached a sermon series on the allied evil powers gathered together against the Lamb (Revelation 19:19–20). That prophecy, he explained, was being fulfilled in the alliance between "the Pope and his French adherents." In time the lamb would triumph, but not before suffering great tribulations.[18]

From millennial prophecies and events in Europe, New Englanders concluded that their season of war had only begun. No one saw the treaty with France as anything more than an armistice, postponing the dreaded struggle that was sure to follow. Formal peace did not solve the territorial disputes between France and England, nor did it ease the hatreds—both national and religious—that had been accumulating for a century. Rationalists and evangelicals continued to be divided over questions of pulpit style and the sequence of salvation, but the overriding concurrence over enemies in this world released energies for common action. All believed that, as God's covenant people, New England had a glorious mission to uphold in this world, and that mission required the preservation of their civil and religious liberties against all threats. These liberties were interconnected in New Englanders' minds, and both were essential to their corporate identity. It did not matter which was threatened: remove one and the other was sure to follow. When that happened, God's Word would cease to reign supreme and New England would relinquish its special covenant.

Throughout much of the second and third generations the greatest threat to New England's covenant was anarchy—an excessive popular liberty that would turn all order upside down. Those fears did not disappear in the fourth generation, but they were subordinated to the greater threat of tyranny imposed from the outside. Fourth-generation congregations learned that resistance to tyranny was both a moral virtue and a sacred duty of the highest order. They learned as well that God's wrath would be directed not only against tyrants but also against any people who passively accepted tyranny without resisting to death.

A CATECHISM OF RESISTANCE TO TYRANNY

Nowhere were the renewed themes of liberty and tyranny more powerfully stated than in two occasional sermons delivered by Jonathan Mayhew in the interwar years between 1749 and 1754. There are many ironies in the fact that Mayhew cast in print what John Adams would later term the "catechism" of armed resistance in the American Revolution.[19] It was surely a source of bitter irony to Mayhew himself that one of his sermons, spoken in the elitist setting of Boston's opulent West Church on election day 1754, would furnish the materials for popular assaults on provincial authorities a decade later; to Arminian-Anglicans it was ironic that this notable latitudinarian and hater of creeds should attack the "tyranny" of their polity so viciously; to rationalists it was ironic that this lover of natural reason would speak of politics in a manner so pointedly aimed at the passions of ordinary hearers; and to evangelicals it was ironic that this Arminian, whose views on theology were never accepted in his lifetime, should write so clearly and eloquently about political principles they all held dear. Yet the very breadth of irony attached to Mayhew's political sermons supplies important clues to his unparalleled success in setting forth a theology and ideology of resistance that all New England could endorse. Mayhew's exclusive concern with "the great *drama* of [this] world" did not win many friends in matters of the soul's salvation, but it did clarify questions of happiness in this world far in advance of his clerical peers.[20]

The groundwork for Mayhew's political theory was laid in his extensive reading of British Whigs—especially Bishop Benjamin Hoadley—and in his early sermons on Christian morality, where religion and government were virtually synonymous. In the same way that evangelicals thundered against the sin of popular apathy in matters of vital religious concern, Mayhew raged against the sin of political apathy in the face of tyranny. Earlier than most he seized upon the ethical principle that those who failed to resist tyranny were as sinful as those who acted tyrannically in the first place.[21] In an unpublished sermon on 1 John 3:3–4 ("Sin is the transgression of the law"), he extracted the doctrine that just as sin was a transgression of just laws, so also was it sinful *not* to resist unjust laws: "When Iniquity comes to be established by Law; it can not be any iniquity to transgress that law by which it is established. On the contrary, it is a sin not to transgress it." By way of example he speculated that "if the civil authority should forbid us to love God and our neighbour; or do any thing else which god has plainly enjoined; it would be our duty to disobey."[22]

Mayhew's first opportunity to develop, in print, the principle of limited submission to authority came in 1750, on a day that most Congregational ministers preferred to let pass silently—the Anglican commemoration of Charles I's "martyrdom" at the hands of Puritan rebels. While Anglican clerics in England and North America joined in grieving Charles's execution, Mayhew took the opportunity to deliver an occasional sermon *defending* the Puritan's actions according to the libertarian imperatives he had worked out earlier. To further aggravate the situation he selected his text from Romans 13:1 ("Let every soul be subject unto the higher powers")—a passage that Anglicans had long employed to justify their claims to absolute submission to political authority. Mayhew began by observing that Paul's use of the term "subject" was never intended to be understood in an "absolute and unlimited" sense.[23] When rulers abused their powers and trampled on the liberties of their subjects, then "government" (defined in terms of the "general welfare") ceased to exist; it was a government in name only and did not deserve the respect and obedience of its subjects. Such tyranny, Mayhew hastened to point out, was not true of George II's administration, which allowed "all the liberty that is proper and expedient for us." But it *was* true of Charles I, who got what he deserved. New Englanders should celebrate his execution in the same way they celebrated the Glorious Revolution, "which has been so fruitful of happy consequences to Great Britain." The real sinners were those who passively allowed tyranny to flourish, not only in Laudian England but everywhere tyrants were accepted: "Those nations which are now groaning under the iron sceptre of tyranny were once free; so they might probably have remained, by a seasonable precaution against despotic measures."[24] The true saints were those who vigilantly protected their liberties and promoted the general good of their society. Resistance to tyranny was, like prayer and church attendance, a religious act of sanctification that separated triumphant saints from helpless sinners.

Despite its historical subject matter, Mayhew's *Discourse on Unlimited Submission* carried contemporary applications that elicited strong responses. Copies were reprinted immediately and sparked newspaper controversies in New England and England. Anglicans condemned the essay as an inept piece of plagiarism, citing Hoadley's earlier work, and marveled "how great a Matter a little Fire kindleth."[25] Congregationalists, however, praised the essay as the most spirited and enlightened defense of liberty to appear in their generation.

Four years later in his election sermon of 1754, Mayhew returned to the themes of tyranny and civil resistance in terms that were even harsher. By then, renewed war with France was looming on the horizon and the colonists had to be reminded of their duty to defend their civil and religious privileges. If the *Discourse on Unlimited Submission* was a model of libertarian logic and Scripture precedent, the 1754 election sermon transformed that logic into an enraged language that patriot ministers would later imitate in fomenting revolution against England. Together, these sermons would stand as the apotheosis of Revolutionary preaching in New England.

From start to finish Mayhew's election sermon aimed to pierce his listeners' hearts. In his own version of political hell-fire and damnation he reminded his audience that leaders who abused their powers and trampled the rights of their subjects would suffer extraordinary reprisals at the last judgment: "You will then see many of those who made the world tremble and stoop before them, in vain attempting to 'hide themselves in the dens and in the rocks of the mountains.'" In language more notable for its harshness than measured wisdom he blasted the sycophants and court flatterers—those "servile adorers of princes"—who "conceit themselves almost literally gods, and . . . think their subjects scarce better than brutes made only for their service." Such tyrants, Mayhew went on, would not find a home in New England. From its origins New England had been animated by a rhetoric of liberty that sounded loudly into the fourth generation. In opposition to nay-sayers who derided the declension in piety and virtue of eighteenth-century New Englanders, he insisted that the people were still "peculiar" and would fight to preserve their God-given liberties, both civil and religious:

Nor can I think we are so far degenerated from the laudable spirit of our ancestors as to despise and abuse what they procured for us at so dear a rate. I am not willing to believe we are running so fast into the evil practices and customs of other places, or so fond of imitating the fashionable follies and vices of any, even of those whom decency may perhaps require to call "our betters," as some would insinuate that we are, and from hence prognasticate our destruction. No, I will not believe but that we fear God, reverence the memory of our forefathers, love our country and ourselves, more than to do thus; and that God will still give to see the good of his chosen.[26]

Events in the revivals and impressment riots had taught public speakers not to demean popular audiences. Though no friend to revival, Mayhew showed in this sermon how completely the image of the people had changed by mid-eighteenth century; the real threat to New England's covenant status was not popular anarchy but civil tyranny.

Beyond upholding and dramatizing New England's libertarian heritage in his election sermon, Mayhew expressed concern about mobilization for war readiness. Intelligence reports that France was massing troops on New England's northern border signaled the inevitable conflagration to follow: "We must meet at length, which cannot be without a violent concussion, and the time seems not far off. . . . The continent is not wide enough for us both, and they are resolved to have the whole." For confidence and resolve, Mayhew turned in conventional fashion to "the tribes of Israel, surrounded and harassed by their common enemies." Though they valued peace, "yet we know very well that God's ancient people were not wont to be fighted out of their possessions, nor patiently to endure the incursions and ravages of their neighbors." Would Americans prove equally determined in the face of war? Mayhew was sure they would: "There is not a true New England man whose heart is not already engaged in this contest, and whose purse, and his arm also if need be, is not ready to be employed in it; in a cause so just in the sight of God and man, a cause so necessary for our own self-defense, a cause wherein our liberties, our religion, our lives, our bodies, our souls, are all so nearly concerned."[27]

To portray the horrors of French victory, Mayhew employed a rhetorical technique that would be imitated widely by colonial patriots in the Revolution. He asked his hearers to imagine their country enslaved to a tyrant because they refused to resist; through "restless, roving fancy," he asked them to picture a defeated Boston:

Do I see Christianity banished for popery! the Bible, for the mass-book! the oracles of truth, for fabulous legends! . . . Instead of a train of Christ's faithful, laborious ministers do I behold an herd of lazy monks, and Jesuits, and exorcists, and inquisitors, and cowled and uncowled imposters! . . . Do I see all liberty, property, religion, happiness, changed, or rather transubstantiated, into slavery, poverty, superstition, wretchedness! . . . O dishonest! profane! execrable sight! O piercing sound! that "entereth into the ears of the Lord of Sabaoth"! Where! in what region! in what world am I! Is this imagination (its own busy tormentor)? Or is it something more divine? I will not, I cannot believe 'tis [a] prophetic vision, or that God has so far abandoned us![28]

By modern standards, Mayhew's visionary ploy seems so transparently sensational and hysterical that it could not possibly have been sincere.

Yet, in Mayhew's mind and the minds of his readers these were not extreme sentiments; they were the terms that reflected so clearly the realities of life among an embattled people who faced the prospect of war and foreign "enslavement." Mayhew vivified and dramatized these fears in ways other speakers could imitate. Few ministers would agree with Mayhew's virtual identification of civic virtue and religion, but all would come to see that, next to their salvation, their liberties were their dearest possession; a possession worth fighting and dying to protect.

THE FRENCH AND INDIAN WAR: YEARS OF DEFEAT

Within one year of Mayhew's election sermon, New England's "day of darkness" had begun. In July 1755, before war was formally declared in Europe, General Edward Braddock and his British regulars were decisively defeated on the banks of the Monongahela River by a combined force of French and Indian allies. Thus began the fourth and final war for North American hegemony. In New England, one out of every three men able to bear arms was enlisted for service—a figure far exceeding other regions and colonies. Before the Seven Years' War (or "French and Indian War") was over, virtually every New England family had one member engaged in what would become the largest war fought to that time on North American soil.[29]

In keeping with previous wartime experiences, New Englanders were brought together by war, and the chief instrument of cohesion was the local sermon sounded on days of fasting and troop musterings. From the commencement of hostilities, the clergy was united in stirring martial resolve and specifying the terms and nature of divine assistance. In this war, as others, they encouraged armed conflict for nationalistic and prophetic reasons. Their rhetorical task on weekday fasts and artillery addresses was twofold. First, they had to establish the justness and necessity of war with France in terms drawn both from secular writings on civil liberties and property rights, and from Scripture prophecies foretelling terrible wars between God's new Israel and the forces of Antichrist. Second, they had to prepare their people for the possibility of short-term defeats and great sufferings before victory would be ultimately won. Defeats signaled the need for repentance and dependence on God; victories confirmed New England's chosen status as the unconquerable people of God. As before, fast days concentrated on New England's sins and the duty of repentance, whereas election sermons and artillery election sermons focused on New England's righteousness and invincibility as long as they trusted in God.

Of the righteousness of New England's cause there could be no doubt. Despite their many wars, ministers insisted, New England was not a militaristic culture that pursued armed conquest for the sake of vain glory. In an artillery election sermon, Jason Haven explained why wars had to be justified:

> The principles of [military] action must be taken into account, in order to determine the character truly good, or not so. Who, that is inspired with a generous love to mankind, can think with pleasure and approbation on a Pompey, a Caesar, or an Alexander who were mighty men, subdued people and cities not a few, and marked their steps in blood while they traversed the world! A man mighty in war, who is a stranger to humanity and the gentle spirit of the gospel, may force trembling crowds to yield a feigned submission; to "bow down their necks that he may go over;" but will never be a public blessing, nor enjoy sincere love and esteem.

God's Word did not condemn war, but it did specify that just wars were defensive in nature. Ebenezer Pemberton elaborated on those conditions in his address to the Ancient and Honorable Artillery Company in Boston:

> The Great God, condescends to wear the Title of a Man of War; and Princes, His Viceregents here below, are commanded not to bear the Sword in vain. When the Faith of Treaties is violated, the rights of a Community invaded, all Proposals of Accomodation obstinately rejected, it becomes the immediate Duty of the supreme Magistrate, to have Recourse to Arms; that he may establish Peace, protect Innocence, humble the Proud Oppressors of the Earth, and put a Stop to the Progress of Tyranny and Usurpation.[30]

Other ministers echoed Pemberton's sentiments. In his 1756 Connecticut election sermon George Beckwith explained how "the cause we are engaged in is most Just on our side; these [American] Governments never desired or attempted to cross the Line dividing the Claims between the two kingdoms in *North-America*." Notwithstanding America's self-containment, the French "openly make War upon us," such that "every thing that is dear to us [is] at stake; not only the Property of the Country, and our Enjoyments in it; but also our Liberties, Privileges, and the holy Religion we are blessed with." Because armed hostilities were unprovoked and in self-defense, "we [may] hope and expect that God will be for us, and on our side, and then we need not fear those perfidious Enemies."[31] In Beckwith's sermon as elsewhere, rights of property and self-defense were invoked more to secure the protection of New England's covenant God than for their own sake. Only then could troops be steeled to face the fears and sufferings of war.

While printed sermons like Pemberton's and Beckwith's were important for widespread distribution and unification, they had to be supplemented in speech by local ministers. The terms these ministers chose—whether evangelical or rationalist—were virtually identical to themes set in print. In a fast sermon following Braddock's defeat, Jonathan Edwards preached from Psalm 60:9–12 ("Give us help from trouble, for vain is the help of men"), to establish the doctrine that "it becomes a people after defeat in war to relinquish all other dependence and to look to him for help." On the same day, Framingham's Matthew Bridge delivered a fast sermon to the entire community on Psalm 79:9 ("help us O God of our Salvation"), "on the account of our enemies prevailing against us." After acknowledging that "perhaps there never has been so many slain in so short a time," Bridge went on to note the remedy: "How can we expect to be delivered from judgments, and afflictions, if the cause of them is not taken away? . . . Were it not for sin the Lord would be on our side and if God be for us who can be against us."[32]

In all of these local addresses the message of repentance and hope dominated. Defeats were not new to New Englanders and need not frighten them; they simply must repent of their sins and call upon God for deliverance. Genuine repentance and performance of covenant duties could not merit salvation but they could win battles. On this cardinal point, rationalists and evangelicals were in agreement. In a published address to the embattled people of New England, George Whitefield took time from his evangelistic message of free grace to declare that "solemn humiliations, whether performed by public communities in general, or individuals in particular, have always met with . . . a Divine acceptance. . . . Therefore, as a nation, we may boldly infer, that the righteous Lord, who delights to show himself strong in behalf of those who are of an upright heart, will favor, plead and vindicate our righteous cause."[33] Behind Whitefield's bold assertion was a theory of divine providence, familiar to all New Englanders, that promised God's direct or indirect intervention in time of war to save his people when they trusted solely in him. In this framework, military strategies and logistical considerations did not determine the outcome of battles; victory was ultimately won in the meeting-houses and household "closets."

Self-defense was the major justification of war, and the covenant supplied the essential terms for victory, but these were not the only themes invoked in weekday sermons. Millennial speculations and predictions also played a supporting role in arousing public support for war. While New England's present war was not directly with Rome, it fit with millennial predictions because France was a Roman Catholic nation. In reality, ministers explained, France's schemes of aggression and conquest were orchestrated by the diabolical hand of Antichrist, who hoped to achieve through national conquest what eluded him in the church after the Reformation. Whether the present war marked *the* climactic battle between the forces of Christ and Antichrist could not be known with certainty, nor could ministers initiate wars on millennial prediction.[34] Still, the *possibility* of Armageddon was there. The losses suffered in Braddock's defeat led Lynn's minister, Benjamin Adams, to wonder if "now is the time that the witnesses must be slain. And that Antichrist will return to his full power again; and that every one that will be religious must seal the truth with his Blood. Before such a prospect of war we never had, and [now] it seems as tho our Country would be the seat of it." While such a prospect was frightening, it was not a final sentence of doom because, as

Samuel Checkley comforted, the "downfall" of Antichrist was "clearly foretold" in Scripture and would be realized in America.[35]

Once establishing the double significance of war with France as a defensive right and a crusade against Antichrist, ministers could interpret the ongoing battles in covenantal and millennial categories that worked as well with failure as with success. Unlike Protestant denominations in the nineteenth century, there were no fixed schools of "premillennial" or "postmillennial" thought in New England that insisted things *had* to get better or worse before Christ's return; they could go either or both ways.[36] Since millennial prophecies mentioned great sufferings and great blessings in the end days, ministers could take either victory or defeat as a confirmation of their prophecies. In like manner, God's federal covenant with New England provided for chastisements and blessings according to the people's covenantkeeping; both confirmed New England's identity as a chosen people.

CONVERSION IN UNCERTAIN TIMES

Between 1755 and 1757 the signs of the times were mostly dark. Following the fall of Fort Oswego in August 1756 and Fort Henry a year later, all the northern colonies were exposed to direct invasion by the French and Indians. So devastating were the defeats suffered in the Ohio Valley that a shaken John Mellen declared in June 1756 that "Babylon the great, the Mother of harlots, and abominations of the earth, is not yet fallen. . . . Our enemies may yet triumph over us, and the gospel may be taken from us, instead of being by us transmitted to other nations."[37] Matthew Bridge was equally disconsolate. In a fast sermon on Lamentations 1:7 ("Jerusalem remembered in the days of her afflictions and of her miseries all her pleasant things that she had in the days of old"), he likened the present circumstances of New England to Israel's desolation during the Babylonian captivity: "They [could not] think of their former privileges and their present miseries and affliction without tears. [B]y the rivers of Babylon there we sat down, yea, we wept." So too in New England: "Many small towns [are] wholly broken up and most of the inhabitants slain by the enemy or carried into captivity. And no doubt there are many at this Day in captivity who now in their affliction and misery remember their pleasant things they once enjoyed. . . . [I]t seems to be as Dark a Day at present perhaps as ever New England saw. Our civil and religious privileges to appearance are in great Danger." Such perilous times demanded renewed attention to "the publick worship of God," where alone the people could discover hope and direction for their lives.[38]

In responding to the immediate crisis of defeat, ministers throughout New England invoked the same conversionist rhetoric their predecessors applied to the crises of King Philip's War and the revocation of Massachusetts's charter. Instead of submitting to apocalyptic resignation or dwelling on the agony of defeat, they sought to channel the fears of their listeners into conversion. Often their evangelical sermons grew from millennial texts. In February 1756 and on three later dates, Salem's James Diman (HC, 1730) delivered a sermon on "the time when this world shall come to an end." While cautioning his hearers against the dangers of exact predictions, and noting that some prophecies were yet to be fulfilled (notably "the downfall of Antichrist and the conversion of the Jews"), Diman noted that at least part of the prophecies *were* fulfilled in that "we are now 1700 years nearer the time and there are many things that were to be previous to it, fulfilled and accomplished that were not then." Because of this, God's people must "take care to prepare for that time and to be always ready to meet your Judge!" Like Diman, Lancaster's Timothy Harrington saw signs of apocalypse and urged his listeners to repent. Events in Europe and North America convinced him that "some considerable Event [is] near opening upon us. And whether the Time for slaying the Witnesses; and for their lying dead in the streets of the great City; and for the worshippers of the Beast to rejoyce over them, and to make merry, and to send Gifts to one another, is yet to come? I say to these Things, I know not what [is the] answer. . . . Repentance surely at this Day, and in this Situation of Affairs, may be urged with some Emphasis."[39]

Millennial prophecies were not the only texts ministers employed to proclaim the necessity of the New Birth in dangerous times. In a sermon to the Pomfret militia, James Cogswell urged the troops "to stand the Guardians of the Religion and Liberties of *America*; to oppose Anti-Christ, and prevent the barbarous Butchering of your fellow countrymen." But, he went on, "while you are engaged in this just and necessary War, be not unmindful of that Spiritual warfare, which it is of the greatest importance of all that you be engaged in." In the final analysis, Samuel Johnson concluded, it did not matter if the millennium came sooner or later because all must eventually die and face their maker: "For to us it matters little whether Christ's coming, in the sense of the prophesy, be nearer or further off, since it is certain that the time of every man's death is, to him, the time of Christ's coming; for after death comes judgment." The immediacy of war and the prospect of defeat and death "calls aloud upon us to search and try our ways, and turn to God with all our hearts."[40]

Throughout the 1750s rationalists and evangelicals continued to differ over the primacy of the head or the heart, but in the crucible of war all preached the necessity of conversion and charitably conceded that neither the understanding nor the affections could be emphasized to the exclusion of the other. Thus in a sermon on conversion preached five times from four different texts, Brookfield's rationalist Nathan Fiske (HC, 1754) warned that "a man whose Passions are not regulated by Judgment may be compared to a Ship, whose sails are spread, but her helm lost, and therefore cannot be steer'd to the proper Part: but is driven up and down by every wind." At the same time he insisted that besides the helm of reason, "God demands of us our heart, i.e. our Affections." Conversely, the evangelical Jonathan Parsons (YC, 1729) emphasized the heart in a sermon on conversion, but graciously allowed that "even good men differ with respect to the passionate part of religion."[41] In both of these cases there were alternative emphases to be sure, but equally apparent is the conciliatory tone of the argument and the recognition that head-centered and heart-centered New Englanders must come together against a perfidious enemy. Deliverance required moral reform *and* transformed hearts.

REFORM ALONGSIDE REPENTANCE

At the same time ministers spoke of conversion, they invoked the terms of New England's federal covenant and called for corporate repentance and external reform. While Antichrist was sure to win some battles through his own diabolical strength, military defeats and other calamities also registered New England's sin. Confirmation of God's controversy with New England appeared even before military defeats when, on November 18, 1755, the region was rocked by its largest earthquake in thirty years. Ebenezer Parkman recorded in his diary that "the shock seems to me to be as great and to last about as long as the great Earthquak Oct 29, 1727." Immediately ministers throughout New England delivered fast sermons that pointed to the divine warnings contained in earthquakes and military defeats.[42] In a fast sermon that he would later repeat and apply to military defeats in 1756 and 1757, Shutesbury's Abraham Hill (HC, 1737) pointed out that while earthquakes and wars had natural causes they also contained "moral" and "political" lessons when directed against the people of God. For New Englanders, both events manifested "the Power of the Great Governor of the Universe" and were "an indication of his anger against a sinful People." Ultimately, Hill speculated, "We may well suppose that an Earthquake will be the Harbinger of the last judgement." More immediately and certainly, the late earthquake confirmed how God "doth in some measure govern the moral by the natural world."[43]

In such perilous times of earthquakes and wars, ministers turned to standard outlines of covenant history and prescribed several courses of action for New England in addition to the obvious duty "to improve in every Art of Self-Defense." Corporately, the people must put away their outward sins and return to God. Along with this injunction came the old rhetoric of failure. For too long, Samuel Checkley bemoaned, New England had suffered from "abounding of drunkeness, prophaneness, uncleanness, covetousness, injustice, extortion, [and] oppression." The devastating defeats and earthquake were predictable, and their meaning was clear. As John Tucker declared in a sermon to his Newbury congregation: "May we conclude it is, that we are become a people very different from our Fathers. That we have fallen from their exemplary piety and virtue, and from their regard to God?"[44] Such words were not popular after the revival, but with so many defeats there was little alternative. Either the people (including leaders and followers) repented, or their calamities would become even more devastating.

VICTORY

News of William Pitt's appointment as secretary of state in 1757 did little to brighten colonial spirits. The strategic advantages ensuing from Pitt's decision to enlist the aid of twenty-four thousand additional British regulars would only be apparent in retrospect. More immediate was the trauma of yet another defeat, this one at Fort Ticonderoga, where a combined force of New England volunteers and British regulars failed miserably in their attempt to capture the fortress. A discouraged Ezra Stiles declared in his fast sermon that God permitted defeat, in order "to disappoint our best measures of Defense, by shewing us that the best Troops with experienced and Able commanders, do yet need the guidance and Aid of Jehovah to render their Arms successful." By the time of his sermon (April 6, 1758), word was passed of the arrival of additional British troops and plans to invade Canada. But Stiles was not reassured: "A yet larger Preparation is now making to carry the devastations of War into the very Bowels of our Enemies Country. But the Lord of Armies only knows whether we shall succeed in reducing *Louisbourg*, or *Quebec*, or close the year with another fruitless campaign."[45]

Happily for Stiles and all New England, the new campaigns of 1758 and 1759 proved gloriously successful. Fortified by fresh troops and brilliant young English commanders like Jeffrey Amherst and James Wolfe, the rejuvenated Anglo-American forces marched from victory to victory. First to fall was the citadel at Louisbourg. From there the armies moved inland in a three-pronged attack designed to encircle French fortresses. One army was set against Fort Niagara; another under General Amherst was to move down the St. Lawrence River and join forces with the third army under General Wolfe at Quebec. Amazingly, all three armies were successful, though delays to Amherst's forces compelled Wolfe to attack French forces at Quebec unassisted.[46] There, in the most renowned battle of the French wars, Wolfe led his force of forty-five hundred men onto the Plains of Abraham where they lured the French into open battle and took the fortress with modest casualties. With that victory, France's fate was sealed, and all looked forward to final triumph at Montreal.

The clergy understood the significance of the 1759 campaigns and, in their sermons, emphasized the dual themes of military readiness and divine dependence. On the eve of the battle of Quebec, John Tucker delivered a fast sermon urging his listeners to combine their prayers with active martial resolve; faith in God could not be an excuse for passivity in such crucial times. To spur them on, Tucker turned to sacred history and recounted the case of Israel during the rebuilding of the temple at Jerusalem:

> The Jews were now returned to their own land by the favor of the King of Persia. This powerful monarch had granted them liberty and offered to assist them in resettling them at Jerusalem. But had they now been intimidated by the threats of their Adversaries and neglected at this time with zeal and courage to prosecute the opportunity . . . [it] might never have returned again. Their enemies might have gained an Advantage over them, from which they might never have been able to recover themselves.

While Tucker addressed his Newbury congregation, Solomon Williams turned his Lebanon congregation's attention to the same period in Jewish history and cautioned them to continue trusting in God because "hopeful Beginnings often fail and disappoint our expectations." As New Englanders had nothing to blame for their defeats but their own sins, so in times of victory they must ascribe the glory to God or risk further devastations: "Boast not . . . for thou knowest not what a day may bring forth."[47] Neither of these sermons was printed, nor is there evidence that Tucker and Williams consulted over their text selection. But as in other critical moments in New England's corporate experience, ministers instinctively turned to parallel situations in the Old Testament where they discovered remedies and hopes for present circumstances.

When news of General Wolfe's heroic seizure of Quebec reached Boston in October 1759, congregations throughout the land met in thanksgiving services. Not since the fall of Louisbourg were so many of these sermons published, all acknowledging the success wrought by the combined forces of divine providence and American bravery. In language akin to evangelical descriptions of the New Birth, Samuel Cooper exulted, "I know not how to express the importance of that success and *yet I feel it*. . . . We have received a Salvation from Heaven, greater perhaps than any since the Foundation of the Country." In a thanksgiving sermon on Isaiah 35:9 ("No lion will be there . . . only the redeemed will walk there"), Edward Barnard explained that the "signal appearance of divine providence on our behalf" came because "there was a remnant according to the election of grace of those who feared the Lord and trembled at his word."[48] Cooper's sermon was published whereas Barnard's was not, but both wove the history of New England's deliverance around the theme of popular piety and dependence on God.

Besides the general theme of providence, thanksgiving sermons commended the people, often singling out the leaders or their followers for special praise. In a sermon on Exodus 32:11–12, Elias Smith examined the character of Moses the "Noble Patriot" and then paralleled him to a generation of American leaders raised in "our New-England Israel." Like Moses, New England's leaders combined "strict devotion" with "steady courage" and "perfect disinterestedness" so that God blessed their efforts.[49] But New England's leaders were not the only heroes: the ordinary farmer-soldiers were just as important. In a thanksgiving sermon, Thaddeus Maccarty extended the piety of the founders to the generations that followed:

> It is well known . . . that our renowned Ancestors left their pleasant habitations and fair inheritances on the other side of the Atlantic, and came into this howling wilderness, namely, that they might enjoy their Liberties and Priviledges, especially their Religious ones, and handed them down as the best legacy to those who came after them. . . . And what a fair and glorious Superstructure has been raised upon the foundation laid by them. . . . How have we grown and flourished and prospered . . . so that we are become great and respectable by [comparison to] other lands and peoples?[50]

Here the revised image of the people as pious and virtuous is clear, confirming the social lesson learned in the revivals that in the New World leaders depended on the voluntary support of their followers. With righteous popular support, leaders could establish strong churches and win mighty battles; without it, they would be left alone.

With the fall of Montreal in September 1760, the long contest for control of North America came to its conclusion. Despite enormous war debts that would soon lead to serious Anglo-American differences, the immediate response to victory was unrestrained joy and serene confidence. For New Englanders, victory over France signaled both an opening up of western lands and a restoration of self-confidence. In praising the New England people in his thanksgiving sermon, Thaddeus Maccarty exclaimed with unabashed pride how "North America has since the present War been more the object of Attention, at home, than ever before. Its importance to the Crown, more fully understood and known than ever before."[51] Just how clearly the crown understood America's importance was not clear even to Maccarty in 1760, but it soon would be.

Other thanksgiving sermons in the autumn of 1760 also echoed themes of joy and confidence.[52] The American people had legitimately and successfully defended their liberties, dealt Antichrist a mortal blow, and confirmed their status as an elect nation. With Anglo-American conflicts still in the future, it was a time to celebrate British rights and the enlightened constitution that upheld civil liberties and social order. There was, James Lockwood declared in his Connecticut election sermon, "no Nation now in Europe, [or] on the Earth, whose civil Government is like that of Great Britain."[53] Through the English constitution's balanced genius of monarchy, aristocracy, and commons, and through the might of England's armies, America's enemies had been removed and the inhabitants confirmed in a way of liberty and order.

Even as ministers praised England's army and constitution and celebrated America's status as English colonies, they did not forget their typological identification with Israel. Indeed, Israel remained as crucial to New England's self-identity in 1760 as it had been a century earlier. Ultimately,

Ezra Stiles explained, "God is now giving this land to us who in virtue of the ancient covenant are the Seed of Abraham. Nor are we to forget to thank old Father Abraham for these things—*for the Blessings of Abraham are come down upon the Gentiles.*" In his thanksgiving sermon, Simon Bradstreet IV also recalled God's ancient covenant with Israel and its enduring lessons for New England: "Now what was here spoken and ordered to the Jewish church and people is applicable to all Christian people and Societies. . . . God expects of his covenant people that they take a due and religious notice of his goodness, and rejoyce before him." English rights and colonial bravery were important, but they did not obscure God's providential leading and the covenant people's duty to honor his Word. This was especially true for New England: "We are brought up in a land of Light and knowledge where we have the gospel and the ministers of Christ to speak the gospel to us every Sabbath Day. So that no person can now plead ignorance of their duty."[54] New England's identification with Israel remained the chief focus of colonial preaching because it alone covered all contingencies. Israel's past and New England's past—fused in Christic unity—supplied a self-contained meaning for the present. Only God knew how or if the recent victory would figure in his eternal and unknowable plan of world redemption, but in the meantime New England would keep the covenant.

A MILITANT NEW ENGLAND

As it became apparent that the late war with France was not the climactic battle of Armageddon but one more skirmish in an ongoing campaign, millennial themes again receded into the background of colonial preaching. Millennial rhetoric was evanescent and event-centered; it could arouse in time of crisis, but it could not supply the terms for day-to-day living in time of peace. As the book of Revelation cast its prophecies in the tumultuous setting of sudden conversions and global wars, so also did New England preachers—tied to biblical texts—require spectacular events like revivals or wars to engage their apocalyptic sensibilities and mobilize a mass expectancy of imminent millennium. With peace, excited predictions and possibilities passed, and ministers warned their congregations that the millennium could be far off in the future. In the meantime, God's true churches were still in their "militant" phase and must be vigilant for human and spiritual enemies. This was especially true in New England, whose independent Congregational churches were, in Ezra Stiles's phrase, a "jewel of inestimable wealth." Like most of his colleagues Stiles believed the millennium might well be centuries away and, in the interim, "God has great things in design for this [American] vine which his irresistable arm has planted. . . . He purposes to make of us a great people and a pure and glorious church." To preserve New England's sacred jewel Stiles urged ministers and parents to teach their children history—particularly the sacred history of Israel and New England. Sacred history, unlike eschatology, was an exact science; a tried and true guide to the meaning of events, however bewildering or discouraging they might appear to the natural eye. History was of first importance if the children were to appreciate the value of their civil and religious liberties and the religious end to which those liberties were established:

> We should often relate to our posterity the history of the wonderful providences of God in the settlement of this Country; and remark [upon] the growth of our churches, and engage them by all the honorable motives of Christianity to steadfastness in the faith once delivered to the saints, and in the liberty wherewith the gospel has made us free. Let our children be often taught to read the sixth, seventh, eighth, and ninth verses of the twenty-sixth chapter of Deuteronomy with parallel application to the history of our ancestors. Let the great errand into America never be forgotten.[55]

While the secular history of liberty and tyranny was important to informed colonial readers, it was not the history ministers transmitted to their congregations. Much more important was the sacred history of Israel and New England. When days grew dark again, that would be the history New Englanders knew best, and the one they would draw upon for guidance and resolve.

Stiles's enjoinders would be echoed in hundreds of parishes throughout the land as ministers rehearsed again and again their predecessors' "great errand into America." A new generation was coming of age learning the same stories—updated through the wars with France—that their parents had learned before them. The values they absorbed—love of liberty, fear of Antichrist, covenant conditions, the duty of resistance to tyranny, and the certain hope of eventual triumph—would be tested far sooner than their elders expected against an enemy none could have anticipated in 1760.

In Lexington, Massachusetts, where the blood of the next struggle would first flow, the young pastor Jonas Clarke addressed a brief, unpublished sermon in 1763 "at night to [the] Young People." For some time Clarke had been concerned that the children who were born amidst the wars with France did not understand or appreciate the glorious legacy they inherited, or the price it extracted: "Has not God distinguished our Fathers and us, with peculiar Advantages? Yea, has he not done more for them and us than for any People under heaven? And have not we their children provoked him to anger [by forgetting]?" To underscore the importance of remembering and appreciating the sacred meaning of New England, Clarke applied the text of John Cotton's sermon on *God's Promise to his Plantation* ("Moreover I will appoint a place for my people Israel, and will plant them, that they may dwell in a place of their own, and move no more") to the eighteenth century. In words calculated to humble and inspire, he reminded the young people that they stood in the same relation to sacred history as Israel and their parents before them:

> Have we not forgotten the important Errand upon which our Fathers came into this Land? It was for the sake of God, Religion, Liberty of conscience

and the free Enjoyment of the Gospel in its simplicity. Now if we forget this . . . we defeat the blessed end of their coming into this Land, and provoke God. . . . The apostle puts the Hebrews in mind of their coming out of Egypt by Moses [in Hebrews 11]. . . . We also have heard with our ears, and our Fathers have told us what works God [did] for them, in Days and Times of old . . . that we might have a place for his holy name.[56]

At the time he spoke, Clarke had no idea how soon New England's sacred legacy would again be challenged by diabolical enemies, nor could he anticipate the role his young listeners would play as New England's "minutemen." But by instilling these values in them, he and other ministers made sure that wherever and whenever threats appeared, the rising generation would be prepared to take their turn in the long line of worthies who had defined and embodied New England's innermost meaning for over a century. When, in a few years, the mother country acted to deprive New Englanders of their God-given liberties and sacred calling, the ministers found that their preaching had not fallen on deaf ears. The young people had become adults and, with the encouragement of their civil and ecclesiastical leaders, they would lead America in its most glorious cause.

PART V

MEMORY, 1764–1776

[13]

Trust in God

Following war with France rationalist and evangelical ministers discovered anew the need to come together against common enemies in pursuit of a common cause. This time the common enemy was "tyranny," embodied in corrupt English officials, and the common cause was "liberty." After 1763, these two themes resounded in every settlement on an increasing variety of weekday occasions and eventually led to the conclusion that rebellion against the mother country was God-ordained. The patriot cry of "liberty or death" did not mark a secularization or politicization of the Puritan mission in the minds of most New England patriots so much as it represented a defense and continuation of themes first sounded by the founders. In political and constitutional terms, liberty came to assume far more democratic meanings than the founders could ever have imagined. But in religious terms—the terms New Englanders continued to hear most of the time—liberty had changed little. In 1776 as in 1630, it remained the liberty to submit to God's Word—and only God's Word—in all aspects of life and faith.

AN AGE OF ORATORY

That so many ministers discoursed so effectively on liberty was due largely to the classical and religious training they received at Harvard, Yale, and Princeton colleges. These schools continued to inculcate a common cultural core that could be popularized and transmitted by word of mouth to the surrounding settlements. Of all the skills taught at the colleges, speech remained the most important. On a formal level, student interest in *Theses Rhetoricae* rivaled the attention devoted to that subject during the heyday of Ramist reform at the seventeenth-century English colleges. Unlike earlier rhetorical instruction, however, new rhetoric manuals like Thomas Sheridan's *Course of Lectures on Elocution* or James Burgh's *The Art of Speaking* reflected the same recognition conceded earlier in the revivals that the moment of delivery defined the act of speech.[1] As early as the 1750s, Latin disputations were augmented by more practical training in "forensic" orations delivered in English and covering such subjects as law, religion, government, and ethics.[2] Besides formal instruction, students formed speaking societies in the 1760s and 1770s like the Speaking Club and Mercurian Club at Harvard College, which featured mock orations and debates on pressing political issues.[3] The effect of all this training and reading was to prepare large numbers of graduates, both ministers and nonministers, to speak effectively on matters of common concern. It taught them especially to be on the lookout for threats to civil or religious ' liberties that called for great oratory and popular mobilization.

Since ministers were entrusted with the responsibility of public speaking, rhetorical training served them especially well. Despite rapid population growth that exceeded one-half million inhabitants by 1760, the colleges produced enough trained ministers to fill every village pulpit. Of the sixteen hundred Congregational ministers who preached in New England throughout the colonial period, over one-third (six hundred) were alive and actively preaching during the decades of resistance and revolution. Unlike nonministerial graduates, who tended to cluster in urban areas where imperial bureaucratic positions proliferated and where the greatest concentration of wealth and professional services lay, educated ministers could be found wherever there was a meetinghouse.[4] The number of Congregational churches had grown to 530 by 1760 and, by Ezra Stiles's estimate, 85 percent of the population remained nominally Congregational. During the 1760s and 1770s many churches experienced revivals in full membership, allowing ministers to retain their dominance of public communications.[5] Pamphlets and newspapers were growing in importance—particularly in urban centers—but for sheer public exposure and influence, neither could match the sermon.[6]

Like all college graduates, the clergymen who began their ministries in the 1750s and 1760s augmented studies of divinity with reading in the literature of liberty and resistance to tyranny. Works by prominent Whigs such as Algernon Sidney, John Locke, James Harrington, John Trenchard, or Thomas Gordon appeared on their bookshelves beside conventional homiletical and doctrinal treatises. Added to these were works in sacred history from Israel to the present of which the most important was Josephus's history of the Jews (*Antiquities*), read since the first years of New World settlement.[7] These works convinced their readers that liberty was precarious and required constant vigilance. They also confirmed that without liberty sacred covenants would be revoked.

In 1760 few ministers feared that their covenant liberties were threatened under the balanced genius of England's constitution. But within five years that view changed. In an effort to pay a stupendous national debt, Britain taxed the colonies without granting them representation in Parliament. This led many to fear a British conspiracy against their liberties, and accordingly they drew on their sacred and secular reading to preach the duty of resistance and, ultimately, revolution.

THE STAMP ACT

In one way or another, virtually all of America's grievances with England grew from policies enacted in the aftermath of war with France. Word that England had allowed Quebec to retain a Roman Catholic bishop revived apocalyptic fears of a papal army coming out of the North and fed early suspicions of a conspiracy by highly placed British officials to extinguish New England's civil and religious liberties.[8] Further confirmation of conspiracy appeared in the Sugar or Revenue Act of 1764, designed by England's finance minister, George Grenville, to prevent smuggling and generate revenue for the crown. To ensure compliance, Grenville bolstered the colonial customs agency by creating search warrants or writs of assistance whereby British agents could try violations of trade or navigation acts in royally appointed vice-admiralty courts. Added to this judicial machinery was a stamp tax on legal forms, newspapers, and other documents that would go into effect in March 1765.[9] Grenville assumed that since "external" trade regulations always existed in theory, and since the proposed stamp tax was a model of leniency by English standards, the colonists would willingly comply in gratitude for England's assistance during war with France. He was sadly mistaken. The new legislation set in motion a chain of protest that would culminate in the Stamp Act riots of August 1765.

The initial protest to the Sugar and Stamp acts was led by a group of Boston radicals including the volatile representative James Otis, Jr.; lawyers John Adams, Josiah Quincy, and Oxenbridge Thacher; merchants Thomas Cushing and John Hancock; newspaper editor Benjamin Edes; and tax collector Samuel Adams. These individuals were part of the long-standing "country" opposition to the governor, Francis Bernard, and the Hutchinson family clan that ruled Massachusetts's royal branch of government. They were political "outs" who fastened on British legislation as a means of protesting royal prerogatives and multiple officeholding, while furthering their own careers in the process. As early as 1761, James Otis, Jr., delivered a vitriolic speech against the writs of assistance as an infringement on "English liberty and the fundamental principles of the constitution." Otis's speech won him a seat in the house at the same time that it aroused the bitter fury of Bernard and Thomas Hutchinson. Major treatises in 1764–1765 by John Adams, Oxenbridge Thacher, Stephen Hopkins, and James Otis outlined a comprehensive theory of constitutional rights with regard to taxes, the right of trial by jury, and the limits of parliamentary sovereignty. Also in 1765, Boston merchants, together with the popular assemblies of Massachusetts and Connecticut, issued declarations and instructions rejecting Parliament's right to tax the colonies without granting them representation in Parliament. To keep these matters before the public eye, the Boston radicals had newspapermen Benjamin Edes and John Gill of the *Boston Gazette* reprint portions of their polemical treatises together with critical letters condemning the revenue legislation on grounds of constitutional principle.[10] None of these early protests advised revolution but they did portray English legislation as an infringement on colonial rights which, if not resisted, could end in tyranny.

Much of this early protest came from civil elites in Boston. Ministers, for the most part, avoided public criticism of the recent legislation, though it was rumored that Charles Chauncy and Samuel Cooper had a hand in penning the libertarian letters pouring from the *Boston Gazette*. Throughout the spring and summer of 1765, most ministers cautioned restraint and submission. In his annual spring fast sermon, for example, Ezra Stiles chose to portray the Stamp Act as a punishment for New England's sins rather than as an occasion for outrage and resistance. Similarly, Andrew Eliot employed the annual election sermon to urge submission to British rule, even while reiterating the libertarian principle that "all power has its foundation in compact or mutual consent."[11] These were standard injunctions heard since the Glorious Revolution. Only after popular protests and insurrections mounted would New England's ministers portray parliamentary legislation as a threat to liberty and affirm the colonists' right of resistance. From that point on they would play a leading role in mobilizing their listeners to defend their God-given liberties.

RESISTANCE

In the summer of 1765, as colonists observed the zealous prosecutions of the vice-admiralty courts and waited for the stamp tax to go into effect, voices of protest grew louder and drew the support of many ministers.[12] In Boston, rising tensions were registered in the pages of the *Gazette* and in bitter political contests between the Bernard faction and their radical critics. Even more ominous was the emergence of protest groups called the "Sons of Liberty," comprised largely of ordinary laborers under the direction of self-appointed leaders like the Boston fireman Ebenezer MacIntosh.

On August 14, the Sons of Liberty attacked the home of the stamp collector, Andrew Oliver. Like earlier mass assemblies in the Glorious Revolution and revivals, the Sons of Liberty discovered that once assembled no force in the New World could overcome them; they *were* the law of the land. A frightened Governor Bernard took to his fortress at Castle William and complained in a letter to General Thomas Gage that "the mob was so general and so supported, that all civil power ceased in an instant, and I had not the least authority to oppose or quiet the Mob. You are sensible how extremely weak an American Governor is in regard to popular tumults. . . . In short, the Town of Boston is in the possession of an incensed and implacable Mob; I have no force to oppose them."[13]

Twelve days later, violence flared again, this time at least partly in response to an inflammatory sermon by Jonathan Mayhew on Galatians 1:7–9 ("I would they were even cut off which trouble you"). The sermon does not survive, but the hyperloyalist historian Peter Oliver recalled how Mayhew "preached so seditious a Sermon, that some of his Auditors, who were of the Mob, declared, whilst the Doctor was delivering it they could scarce contain themselves from going out of the Assembly and beginning their Work." The "work" to which Oliver referred began with an attack on the homes of William Story, deputy register of the vice-admiralty court, and Benjamin Hallowell, comptroller of customs. From there the mob turned on the home of Deputy Governor Thomas Hutchinson, leaving "nothing remaining but the bare walls and floors."[14] Mayhew deplored the violence done to Hutchinson's home and issued a public letter of apology. But by then the damage was done, giving Mayhew and others an unforgettable look at the popular power unleashed in part by their own libertarian rhetoric.

Similar outbursts occurred in other colonies, most notably in eastern Connecticut where Separatists and radical New Lights had long experience in challenging authority. To Connecticut's designated stamp collector, Jared Ingersoll (whose effigy could be seen dangling in the towns of New London, Norwich, Lebanon, and Windham), it seemed that "no one dares and few in power are disposed to punish any violences that are offered to the Authority of the [Stamp] Act; in short all the Springs of Government are broken and nothing but Anarchy and confusion appear in prospect."[15] While Ingersoll and other royal appointees were correct in describing the mobs' power to bring official government to a standstill, they were wrong about the "anarchy." These crowds, as recent historians have demonstrated, were ideologically charged, "extrainstitutional" assemblies whose actions were limited and calculated to protest a denial of their rights and liberties. No lives were lost in the riots, nor was property randomly destroyed. Instead, like the New London bonfire twenty years earlier, their actions represented highly ceremonial and ritualistic statements of public grievances that could not be expressed through any official channels.[16]

If the Stamp Act riots resembled earlier popular outbursts dating back to revival fervor in New London or the Glorious Revolution, the same could not be said of elite responses to popular protest. While no respectable civil or ecclesiastical leaders approved of the violence of August 26, neither did they issue blanket condemnations of popular assertiveness or counsel silence and passive submission, as many had done earlier in the revivals. Bitter experience taught elites the futility of seeking to silence the populace once they were aroused. Instead, many leaders outside the imperial network approved of popular initiatives in defense of liberties and endorsed Jonathan Mayhew's estimate that "the common people of New England . . . have all along been philosophers and divines in comparison of the common people in England."[17] These radical leaders sought to channel public protests into activities that would enhance their political power and influence. In speech and print they urged the people to draft local petitions and protests in town meetings, to elect "Whig" opponents of the Stamp Act to their colonial assemblies, and to support the inter-colonial gathering of a "Stamp Act Congress" (itself an illegal and extrain-stitutional gathering) meeting in New York in October 1765.

The radical voices did not go unheeded. In Boston, Samuel Adams was elected to replace the recently deceased Oxenbridge Thacher in the house where he took his seat alongside Thomas Cushing, James Otis, Jr., and John Hancock. Outside Boston the results were similar. In Windham, Connecticut, for example, the town inhabitants took the unusual step of electing one of their Whig pastors, Ebenezer Devotion, to a term as deputy to the Connecticut Assembly.[18] Town meetings in and around Boston drafted resolutions against the Stamp Act on the premise that government "originates from the consent of the people," according to the "Laws of Nature and of God," and that "it is the Duty of every person in the Col-onies, to oppose by every lawful Means, the Execution of those Acts imposed on them." Even more than the riots, these local resolutions instilled a taste for direct political action and self-expression that would not disappear.[19]

While few ministers followed Ebenezer Devotions's course of direct political participation in the assemblies, most participated enthusiastically at the local level in town meetings and in the occasional pulpit. By virtue of their diffuse locations and superior learning in law and morality, they were ideally placed to inspire and "catechize" the people on their political rights and sacred duties. Of these clerical catechizers, none was more effective or influential than Lyme's New Divinity pastor Stephen Johnson (YC, 1743). Johnson's covert role in organizing the Sons of Liberty in east-ern Connecticut was analagous to Charles Chauncy's and Samuel Coop-er's activities in Boston. During the autumn of 1765, Johnson made his political protests public in a series of anonymous newspaper articles in the *New London Gazette* and in a fast sermon delivered on December 18 and published anonymously the following March. For sheer intensity of expression and libertarian elan they are without equal among the early literature of resistance in New England.[20]

While deploring the "rash" activities of rioters who tended to "precip-itate into violences," Johnson went on in his articles to praise nonviolent resistance as a sacred duty. "If you tamely part with [your liberties]," he warned, "you are accessory to your own death, and entail slavery on your posterity." Parliament claimed there was no "enslavement" because the colonists were "virtually," if not "actually," represented in England. Their argument, Johnson chided, was absurd: "'Tis ridiculous to common sense that two millions of free people can be represented by a representative elected by no one of them." Worse yet was the fear that Parliament had lost its power to rule. Instead, decisions were being made by a coterie of nonelected "zealous, scribbling sycophants" who deceived Parliament into taxing the colonies unjustly. "Instead of hearing the cries and redressing the grievances of a most loyal and injured people, they are . . . for adding burden upon burden till they make the little finger of his present Majesty a thousand times heavier than the loins of his good grandfather, and would bind all fast with a military chain." No wonder the people reacted as they did. By November 1, when the stamp tax was due to go into effect, Johnson's pen grew even sharper. Unless measures were taken to redress the wrongs done the American colonists, he fulminated, "we have reason to fear very interesting and terrible consequences. . . . What an enraged, despairing people will do when they come to see and feel their ruin, time only can reveal."[21]

In the only printed fast sermon to appear in 1765, Johnson carried his polemic from press to pulpit and shifted his emphasis from constitutional law to scriptural precept. At the same time, his criticisms of England grew *more* harsh and provocative. Speaking as God's ambassador he introduced biblical arguments against tyranny that would become a staple of pulpit discourse in the decade to come. Johnson began by reminding his listeners and readers that New England's civil and religious liberties ultimately came through divine fiat, not natural right. Failure to preserve those liberties meant far more than a loss of political rights; it signaled the end of New England's special covenant with God. Earlier than most of his peers, Johnson employed covenant logic less as a rebuke for colonial sins (though this was not ignored) than as a somber warning to Great Britain. From the account of Egypt's sufferings during the Exodus he drew the lesson that "the enslaving [of] a free people, the covenant people of God, into a wretched state of bondage, is a very great iniquity, and high provocation in God's sight. Against the Egyptians his resentment is high and dreadful." England's constitutional government was certainly no Egypt, but dangerous individuals were grasping for power and undermining the integrity of English rule. They could be seen everywhere in the colonies among customs officials, vice-admiralty justices, royal appointees, and pensioners; men who were drunk with a "venal, covetous and arbitrary spirit of lawless ambition." Unless checked and resisted by the people, these "connivers" would undo in a moment the libertarian monument that took centuries for England to erect. Even now, Johnson feared, "the grand pillars of the state tremble, and are ready to fail."[22]

While the threats to colonial liberties were serious, Johnson believed there was still hope for reconciliation. If Parliament and the crown cleaned their house of vile placemen and repealed unjust laws like the stamp tax, the whole controversy with her loyal colonists would "soon blow over, and terminate in an unity, harmony, and love between Great-Britain and her colonies." But until that happy day, New Englanders must remain firm in their resistance and be ever jealous of their natural and God-given rights. Echoing the arguments of Jonathan Mayhew, Johnson insisted that the doctrine of unlimited submission was a "high breach of the great law of self-preservation"; a foolish notion "held only by high flying Churchmen." The New England colonists were as loyal to England's constitution as anyone and had no "temptation to independency." But neither, Johnson warned ominously, would they tamely sit by and watch their inherited liberties disappear: "If there be left in the colonies but this single, this dreadful alternative,—slavery or [in]dependency,—they will not want time to deliberate which to choose."[23] Printed assertions like this were strong by any standard. From this point on ministers would not mince words in the pulpit, and by preaching politics they would transform the occasional sermon into a most powerful engine for mobilization.

REPEAL

Much to New England's relief the choice for independence did not have to be made in 1766. In response to the wave of protests, Parliament repealed the stamp tax "totally," while retaining the Revenue Act and instituting the Declaratory Act, whereby it claimed sovereignty over the colonies in "all cases whatsoever." Royal sympathizers like Chief Justice Peter Oliver praised the Declaratory Act and regretted how the repeal seemed merely to fuel popular defiance of authority; it was, Oliver lamented, "vain to struggle against the Law of Otis, and the Gospel of his black Regiment."[24] But the majority of inhabitants, including the "black Regiment" of Congregational ministers, saw the repeal as a divine deliverance and ignored comment on the Declaratory Act. On one more occasion the people had discovered their overwhelming power en masse. In his Massachusetts election sermon of 1766, Edward Barnard departed from the careful language generally employed on that occasion to remind the General Court and royal governor that the best constitutions were "mixed" and that "it lays with rulers to preserve this balance." Rulers who sought the "happiness" and "welfare of communities" were entitled to all respect and deference. But when they transgressed the bounds placed upon them, "it is clear that unlimited submission,—submission in all cases, cannot be a duty." In such cases, it was the duty of the people to resist out of deference to the higher authority of God's Word and the liberties it proclaimed.[25]

In local contexts, inhabitants celebrated the repeal of the Stamp Act with unpublished thanksgiving sermons that were far more explicit about recent events and less restrained in their defense of colonial resistance. Shortly after his election sermon, Barnard preached a thanksgiving sermon to his Haverhill congregation on the familiar passage from Psalm 122 ("Jerusalem is builded as a city that is compact together"). From that text he turned to New England's "compact" and recalled the late stamp tax: "How were we alarm'd with a voice from home like thunder . . . commanding submission to a tax burdensome in itself and without the concurrence in any form of those who were to pay it, and ordering trials where we were not to be judged by our juries."[26] Liberty was essential to civil and ecclesiastical happiness, and its importance was confirmed in sacred and profane history. From the sacred history of Israel it was clear that God "gave them political laws as well as religious institutions whereby their liberty was secured beyond the possibility of reversal by any arbitrary monarch."

In England, Barnard continued, the same situation prevailed as lovers of liberty acted to preserve their rights of representation beginning with Magna Carta and moving through the revolutions of the seventeenth century that "formed the basis" for liberties enjoyed in the eighteenth century. The same was true in New England. In familiar terms Barnard recounted how "our fathers took their flight from the land of their nativity apprehending the importance of a purer worship than they found [in England]." When their charter privileges were revoked in 1684 "under a reign as infamous as it was shortlived," the people justifiably rebelled, and "upon the happy revolution we were reinstated in most of those privileges which we were then without." Happily, Barnard concluded, the same was true of New Englanders in 1765. Their resistance to an unjust law confirmed their place in history alongside the founders as lovers of liberty.

While the Stamp Act controversy did not inspire thoughts of independence or millennial outbursts directed against an English "Antichrist," sermons like Barnard's rekindled New Englanders' acute sense of their history and their own crucial place in the interrelated prophecies of universal liberty and redemption. Other speakers also recounted the history of liberty from Israel to New England and agreed that the popular tumults of 1765 should be added to the long train of providential deliverances that marked New England as a peculiar people. In his printed thanksgiving sermon, Joseph Emerson defended the popular protests of 1765 by analogy to the founders:

> And what is the great, the mighty deliverance we have experienced? Does it deserve a commemoration? Yes, if anything great and good ever did. Is it worthy to be handed down to posterity? Yes, to be printed in a book and preserved with sacred care as long as time shall last. . . . Acquaint yourselves as far as you have opportunity, with the history of our nation and land, and rehearse the wondrous things you meet with, in the ears of your children. . . . Tell them, that in the year 1765 the friends of liberty exerted themselves, combined together, with fixed resolution not to give up their liberty so far as to submit to a law which taxed them without their own consent.[27]

For Charles Chauncy, who twenty years earlier had nothing good to say about popular "enthusiasm," the events of 1765 were noble and praiseworthy. Indeed, "we should have been stupid had not a spirit been excited in us to apply, in all reasonable ways for the removal of so insupportable a burden [as the Stamp Act]." Popular protests, he claimed in a complete about-face from his 1743 declarations, were not cause for alarm; "nor is there any danger such a spirit should be encouraged or discovered, unless the people should be needlessly and unreasonably irritated." The people could be trusted to know their rights and not step beyond constituted bounds; their cause was just and therefore worth preserving in New

England's sacred history: "May the remembrance of this memorable appeal be preserved and handed down to future generations, in every province, in every city, and in every family, so as never to be forgotten."[28]

In all the thanksgiving sermons of 1766 the designation of ordinary people as heroes and libertarians rather than as enthusiasts and anarchists is clear, and illustrates the rhetorical grounds on which leaders and followers came together against a common threat. Fourth-and fifth-generation ministers reversed the teachings of their predecessors and taught that tyranny was a greater threat than anarchy. If the people should err on either side, it should be in the direction of liberty. While recognizing the "unhappy complication" that social divisions and confrontations were sure to ensue from "our great liberty," Barnard was unwilling to part with liberty. "The right of private judgment is too sacred to be given up." Though deeply regretting the mob violences associated with his sermon, Jonathan Mayhew, like Barnard, retained his libertarian credo:

> Having been initiated in youth, in the doctrines of civil liberty, as they were taught by such men as Plato, Demosthenes, Cicero and other renowned persons among the ancients; and such as Sidney and Milton, Locke and Hoadley, among the moderns. . . . Having, earlier still learnt from the holy scriptures, that wise, brave and virtuous men were always friends to liberty; that God gave the Israelites a king . . . in his anger, because they had not sense and virtue enough to like a free common-wealth. . . . I would not, I cannot now, tho' past middle age, relinquish the fair object of my youthful affections, *LIBERTY*; whose charms, instead of decaying with time in my eyes, have daily captivated me more and more.[29]

Mayhew's fusion of the sacred and profane history of liberty from ancient Greece and Israel to the "moderns," Locke and Hoadley, would be reiterated in countless occasional sermons. But more important were the citations to the Israelites' foolishness in seeking a king like the other nations. Those came from God's Word and could not be ignored by those who valued their salvation.

SALVATION IN REGULAR PREACHING: AN ONGOING THEME

Throughout the periods of crisis and calm, regular preaching retained its subject matter of salvation, self-examination, and godly living. Sundays remained the time to dwell on the life to come, and fifth-generation ministers labored to bring their distracted listeners into that world. Despite ongoing differences between England and the colonies over the Declaratory Act and Parliament's claim to unlimited sovereignty, most towns returned to more immediate local concerns after the repeal of the Stamp Act. Once again life revolved around internal questions of taxes, highways, ministerial settlement, schools, and new meetinghouses. When Parliament passed new revenue acts in 1767 and 1768, few towns did more than voice mild protests, and when those acts were repealed in 1770 (save for the tax on tea), the issues tended to be forgotten.[30]

While pulpits rang with weekday celebrations of the repeal of the Stamp Act, on Sunday ministers strove to remember their primary calling as physicians of the soul. Raynham's young pastor Perez Fobes (HC, 1762) had proved himself an eager patriot, but on Sunday he sought to confront his listeners with the necessity of conversion. Extraordinary times required unusual strategies if listeners' attentions were to be switched from the here-and-now to the world to come. In place of the traditional textual opening, Fobes began his sermon on conversion (Matthew 22:4) by playing on the imaginations of his listeners:

> Suppose while you have been rambling in the Fields, you should espy at a small Distance, a Number of Stout Men, furnished with . . . a large fishing net, and seemingly engaged in fishing for the wind. You ask them what they were Doing—and in Answer to your question [they] tell you that they were all hungry and were (attempting) to catch the East wind in the Nets. Would you not justly wonder at their Folly—in trying to obtain what was absolutely unatainable . . . I believe you would not hesitate to pronounce them Distracted and beside themselves at [the] least.[31]

The point of this fantasy soon became apparent, as Fobes likened the folly of men fishing for the east wind to those "fishing for happiness and salvation" without walking in the "fear of the gospel." Those who sought happiness in the terms of this world were bound to be disappointed. "All the Endeavors of Mortals are but a brittle (fragile) perforated net and all they can catch from the world will evaporate thro like fleeting air." Concern over temporal liberties was important but could never overshadow concern for the world to come. Eternal considerations dominated Fobes's concluding "invitation":

> Dost thou absolutely know that thy Life will not be required of thee before tomorrow, before this very Sun is set? Even before thou has heard the end of this, and the beginning of the next Sentence? . . . Will you see Christ stand (himself) at this great Day of the Feast and hear him cry saying if any man thirst let him Come unto Me and drink—will you hear him . . . and not comply with his Invitation?

In Dorchester, Jonathan Bowman occupied his congregation's minds with similar thoughts. From the same text that Fobes used to conclude his sermon (John 7:37), Bowman urged his listeners to spiritual awakening: "Awake thou, that sleeps, and arise from the dead, and Christ shall give thee light." Whatever trials or glories New Englanders experienced, they must never forget the power of sin or the need for personal regeneration. Speaking on Matthew 11:28 ("Come unto me all ye that labour and are heavy laden and I will give you rest"), Bradford's rationalist preacher, Samuel Williams (HC, 1761), insisted that "the true cause of all the infirmities to which we are subject is sin. . . . The rest therefore of which our Saviour speaks . . . consists very much in its purity and in being delivered from the power and dominion of sin." Such deliverance, West Springfield's Joseph Lathrop (YC, 1754) conceded, was freely dispensed, but carried with it the obligation of sanctified obedience:

> Tho we receive the Gospel, as a Dispensation of grace to Sinners, yet if we do not repent of our Sins, become new Creatures, and yield our selves to God in newness of life, we receive the grace of God in vain. We obtain no Benefit by it, and may in effect be said not to receive it, because we don't receive it according to the design of it.[32]

In all of these sermons by "liberal" or "rationalist" ministers the traditional order of sin-salvation-service prevailed and continued to organize their speech week in and week out.

Evangelical pastors, no less than rationalists, continued to occupy their sabbath preaching with questions of sin, supernatural grace, and grateful obedience. From his abbreviated notes, Hardwick's David White (YC, 1730) unraveled the meaning of salvation in Edwardean terms. True faith, he began, involved more than a head knowledge of God ("even devils believe in Christ"). Neither was it a "historical faith" that was "but a negative faith, one the person don't disbelieve." Nor was true faith a palliative for those who seek "after a Christ to give them present ease and when this fails them they don't like him." Such illusory faiths left their claimants "launching out of Time into Eternity in a confluence of imaginary horrour." Rather, White concluded in terms reminiscent of the best revival preaching thirty years earlier, true faith represented "a gracious principle wrought in the Soul by the Son of God . . . and therefore God and the things of God are real to the person; it being the new creature or new man, it has all the faculties of man and therefore becomes capable of discerning spiritual truth." The new creature saw the old self as "altogether vile and filthy," and viewed the new self through the cross: "The soul then is not beheld in himself, it does not stand naked before God in judgment but stands clothed and completely adorned . . . with the Righteousness of Jesus Christ and all his shame [is] covered." With such an eternal view in mind, White enjoined his listeners to "cry unto God to awaken and quicken you, and bring you unto himself through his own Son."[33]

However much social theories and political circumstances might change, the demands of the gospel remained fixed for fifth-generation ministers. To press this point, Milford's Samuel Wales (YC, 1767) concluded a sermon series on "The Great Commandment" of love (Matthew 22:37–38) with an eloquent exhortation confirming how New England's history continued to be invoked not only to confirm civil liberties but also to enjoin a life of personal piety:

> Love being, as our Saviour has told us, the sum and substance of Religion we may here infer that Religion is not, as some have been too ready to suppose, a variable, uncertain arbitrary matter; but is a constant, fixed, and immutable thing . . . Religion is not a fictitious or arbitrary thing; one thing

today and another tomorrow, one thing among this Denomination and another among that. . . . No, it is always has been and always will be essentially the same in kind and Substance tho not always the same in degree. . . . And the sum of it is *to love the Lord* and this was that Religion which the Patriarchs and all the pious men of old lived in and by.

Through terms like these congregations came in touch with their spiritual legacies and duties even more frequently than their civil obligations. However much themes of civil liberty and resistance to tyranny dominated the occasional pulpit, they did not come at the expense of personal salvation, nor did they signal a new "civil religion" replacing the old otherworldly religion.[34] After 1770 the topic of civil liberties and the British conspiracy to rob colonists of their rights consumed town meetings and the occasional pulpit. But throughout the critical years of 1770–1776 ministers carefully avoided celebrations of civil liberties for their own sakes. Rather, they were presented as necessary instruments for the preservation of the gospel and New England's ongoing covenant with God.

MASSACRE ORATORY

Only in Boston where the English presence was felt most directly did storm clouds continue to gather through the late 1760s and early 1770s. There, the bitter rivalry between the royalist faction headed by Governor Hutchinson and the country Whigs intensified, keeping issues of rights and liberties constantly before the public eye. Samuel Adams and his radical cohorts were particularly active in this period, exposing signs of a comprehensive conspiracy against colonial rights everywhere: in the gradual undermining of the judiciary and trial by jury through writs of assistance and the vice-admiralty courts; in the erosion of government by consent through plural officeholding, the dissolution of legally convened legislatures, and an ever-widening network of nonelected "placemen and pensioners"; in the suppression of civil liberties epitomized by the imprisonment of the English libertarian and colonial sympathizer John Wilkes; and, most ominously, in the garrisoning of four regiments of British regulars in Boston in September 1768.[35] All of these actions confirmed that the repeal of the Stamp Act was a ruse to disguise a deeper plot aimed at reducing the American colonies to a state of slavelike dependency. Therefore, Adams urged, "instead of sitting down satisfied with the efforts we have already made, *which is the wish of our enemies*, the necessity of the times, more than ever, calls for our utmost circumspection, deliberation, fortitude and perseverence."[36] The language of diabolical plots and conspiracies was nothing new to New Englanders; it was a message they were prepared to believe. While other country towns returned to life-as-usual, Boston's patriotic representatives and ministers stood vigilant, ready to raise the hue and cry at the next provocation.

On March 5, 1770, that provocation came. After three days of angry confrontations between Boston citizens and British regulars, the soldiers fired into a crowd, killing five colonials. Whig publicists immediately labeled the killings the "Boston Massacre" and called for revenge. Samuel Cooper expressed the general outrage in a letter to former governor Thomas Pownall: "Nothing we have ever seen has equal'd the Horrors of the Bloody Massacre . . . when a Party of Soldiers . . . fir'd upon the Inhabitants in King Street without [the command of] a civil Magistrate without the least Reason to justify so desperate a step and without any warning given to the People, who could have no apprehension of Danger." As massacres go, the violence at Boston was mild, but to a culture attuned to portents and signs, the "shocking and unexampled Scene of Barbarity" assumed vast symbolic proportions.[37] March 5, 1770, would stand as the most important commemorative date on the New England calendar until it was replaced by July 4, 1776.

Although the Boston Massacre did not lead to further bloodshed or mob violence, it provoked a torrent of sermons and outcries which, for their sheer fury and blood revenge, exceeded anything in the annals of New England oratory. Leading the way in this verbal fusilade were ministers like Charles Chauncy who concluded a sermon on the massacre by saying of the soldiers: "We heartily wish their repentance, that . . . they may escape the second death; though our eye is restrained from pitying them so as to wish their deliverance from the first death." English officials cried that instead of counseling restraint and forbearance the "black regiment" of ministers busied themselves with "blowing up the Coals of Sedition"; the loyalist Oliver was shocked at how "the Pulpits rung their Chimes upon blood Guiltiness, in Order to incite the people . . . to Revenge."[38] Oliver should not have been so surprised. As the chief seers and watchmen of their society, it was the ministers' responsibility to interpret the meaning of events. Having absorbed the history of endangered liberty since childhood, they naturally interpreted the shootings in the conspiratorial context of a plot against American lives and liberties. By so defining the shootings, ministers could use the event as a platform for moral outrage and as an opportunity to rehearse again the precarious history of liberty and the duty of resistance to tyranny.

In a rare (though not unprecedented) departure from usual custom, Boston's ministers interrupted regular sermon series on the first Sunday following the massacre to comment directly on the shootings. From his Old North pulpit, John Lathrop thundered forth God's condemnation of Cain in Genesis 3:10 ("The voice of thy brother's blood crieth unto me from the ground"). That reference to Cain's murder of his brother Abel paralleled the recent "gloomy time when our brethren were murdered before our eyes, and our most public streets were deeply dyed with innocent blood." For ministers to ignore this act of treachery would be "criminal," especially after Bostonians had warned England for years of the "infinite impropriety" of standing troops. If Britain did not change its policy of government by force and violence, it did not deserve to rule: "That *government* which, rejecting the foundation of the *law*, would establish itself by the *sword*, the sooner it falls to the ground the better." Nor, Lathrop concluded, could any doubt the righteousness of resistance to such a government: "If the essential parts of any system of civil government are found to be inconsistent with the general good, the end of government requires that such bad systems should be demolished, and a new one formed, by which the public weal shall be more effectually secured."[39]

Lathrop's printed sermon was the most famous address on the Sunday following the massacre, but it was not alone. An unsigned sermon manuscript survives from the same date and illustrates the many uses to which the massacre was put. Instead of directing his comments to the murders, the anonymous preacher addressed himself to the more general topic of endangered liberties.[40] He began in familiar fashion with New England's libertarian heritage. The "errand of our Fathers" he reminded his listeners, was to establish a place of religion and liberty without regard to comfort or safety:

> Men who know nothing of the power of Religion may wonder that they would venture so much in such a cause, but our Fathers knew not how to temporize, they . . . could not put on an appearance in Religion which was contrary to the sentiments of their hearts. They chose rather to venture among Savages and to encounter the harshness of a wilderness, than to live in ease at the expense of a good conscience or to give up those sacred liberties which they had a right to enjoy as men and as Christians.

Despite the "rapid progress" of vice introduced by godless British troops and corrupt officials, New Englanders remained unexcelled for "serious religion and virtue." In matters of legislation and political wisdom they even exceeded the founders who had "kept too near to the judicial law of Moses" and did not fully "understand the principles of toleration." Clearly this was a generation that would not sit idly by and watch their liberties disappear under the mere threat of armed rule.

In closing his sermon, this unidentified preacher turned from civil liberties to New England's covenant. Lest priorities become confused he reminded his listeners that while they guarded their civil liberties they must also uphold their covenant, otherwise their liberties meant nothing: "If we have lost religion it is hardly worth while to contend about [civil] liberties that are only appendages to it." In such trying times, resistance and outrage were called for, but so too was renewed dependence on God:

> Let us carry every difficulty to him, cast our burdens upon him and commit our cause to him. This need not prevent the use of all other means so far as they are consistent with religion. A just regard to our liberties and to the privileges of our fathers is so far from being displeasing to God that it would be ingratitude to him who has given them to us to despise them or tamely give them up. We are bound in conscience to stand fast in the liberty with which Christ has made us free. We deserve not the name of men much less of Christians if we are willing to be in bondage to any man. But while we contend for our civil liberties let us be more concerned to be the Lord's freemen. If the Lord shall make us free, then shall we be free indeed.

Outside of Boston, ministers employed a variety of occasions around the same time to reiterate the history of liberty in New England and its close connection to true religion. In an oration commemorating the centennial of Wallingford, Connecticut, James Dana traced the history of religion and liberty along a line that began with Israel and traveled straight to the founding of Wallingford in 1670. In the same vein, Litchfield's Judah Champion employed a fast sermon to "teach the children" of Litchfield how God constantly upheld the liberties of his covenant people in such events as King Philip's War, the Glorious Revolution, the Cape Breton expedition of 1745, and the repeal of the Stamp Act. This close-to-home history supplied reasons not to worry even under the threat of armed force and murder. Clearly, Champion concluded, God had established New England as "an asylum of liberty civil and religious." He would not allow his sanctuary to be chained unless the people abandoned the covenant: "The most high has gloriously owned the cause of liberty, in New-England, and will continue to own it, unless we so abuse, as to sin away our privileges."[41]

Through discourses like the massacre orations, the cause of liberty and the federal covenant became so closely intertwined that it was impossible for ministers to separate the two, or speak of one without mentioning the other. Though politically conscious and outraged, the ministers never lost their historical perspective; they never discussed New England's civil liberties in abstraction or as a simple deduction from constitutional and natural law. But neither did they believe for one moment that New England's special covenant could survive in an environment of tyranny and armed rule. In 1770 as in 1630 the covenant required that God's Word alone be sovereign and that God's people be at liberty to voluntarily commit themselves to its precepts. In entering into his covenant with New England, God simultaneously provided a place of liberty, which had to be maintained or the covenant would be annulled. Ministers who, in the name of the "holy scriptures," celebrated the "charms" and glories of liberty were no more secular than their forebearers who, in the name of Scripture, upheld the social prerogatives of a speaking aristocracy or the duty of submission to higher authority. But they *were* a changed body, giving expression to a new rhetoric of social order and political authority that upheld the people in their jealous defense of liberty and legitimated their resistance to unjust tyranny.

The conflation of resistance to tyranny and covenant keeping was sounded most clearly by Charles Chauncy in an unofficial election sermon preached on May 30, 1770. In an attempt to cool colonial tempers after the massacre, Governor Hutchinson removed the General Court to Cambridge, where the official election sermon was to take place. Not to be deterred, the Boston Sons of Liberty invited Chauncy to speak in Boston's First Church and keep the "antient custom" alive. Chauncy gladly complied and delivered a sermon entitled *Trust in God*. With no royal governor to address, Chauncy dispensed with the usual praise of England's constitution and rulers, and turned instead to New England's perennial model state, Israel. New England's long enjoyment of civil liberties and self-rule, he explained, was not owing to the English constitution or enlightened legislators but to God's sovereign protection. The cases of Israel and New England proved that as long as God's people trusted in him they would not be enslaved. As David could say, "Our fathers trusted in thee: they trusted and thou dist deliver them," so Chauncy went on, "There are no people, now dwelling on the face of the earth, who may, with greater pertinency, adopt the language of King David [for their own]."[42]

In familiar epic fashion that seemed to gain power with repetition, Chauncy traced the numerous occasions when God's New England people called on him and were saved. Whatever the threat, be it drought, war, earthquake, or tyranny, God delivered them as he had "his Israel of old." Although not "disposed to treason and rebellion," the people of New England operated under a higher law than England's, which required them to preserve their civil and ecclesiastical liberties. To confirm New England's sacred identity Chauncy employed the typological parallel with Israel and quoted the familiar words of Psalm 122, substituting "Boston" for "Jerusalem":

> Our feet shall stand within thy gates, O Boston. Boston is a city compact together, whither the tribes, throughout the province, by their representatives, the tribes of the Lord, assemble to give thanks to the name of the Lord, preparatory to the exercise of one of our important Charter-Rights, the Election of his Majesty's Council.[43]

By keeping the tradition of divine supplication alive in Boston, Chauncy demonstrated New England's still-chosen status to his listeners and affirmed the people's determination to continue such supplications despite contrary wishes of British officials and soldiers. At the same time, Chauncy's radical sermon illustrated how the New England ministry kept abreast of, or in the lead of, general unrest and resistance.

A NEW CLASS OF POLITICAL ORATORS

While many ministers had no qualms about leading a protest they deemed justified by the laws of England and the Word of God, others were timid about open defiance. Often they found themselves pushed by an assertive populace. At the autumn thanksgiving in 1771, Boston congregations prevailed on their ministers not to read the governor's annual Thanksgiving proclamation because it included a phrase thanking God "for the *Continuance of our Privileges.*" This phrase, Samuel Cooper explained, was "deem'd by the People an open Insult upon them, and a prophane Mockery of Heav'n." Cooper noted that most ministers refused to read the proclamation from their pulpits. Reluctant ministers were prodded by their congregations to ignore the proclamation: "Had the

Ministers inclined [to read it] it was not in their Power to read it, a circumstance w'ch never before [took] Place among us. It was read only in Dr. Pemberton's Church, of which the Governor is a Member. He did it with confusion, and Numbers turn'd their Backs upon him and left the Ch[urc]h in great indignation.'"[44] Experiences like Ebenezer Pemberton's were the exception not the rule. From 1770 on, differences between ministers and congregations faded, as both set themselves against a common threat to their liberties.

From the midst of congregations and the ranks of civil leaders a new class of lay speakers emerged alongside the ministers. Although lay orators were not unprecedented in New England, never before had they enjoyed the general approbation they did after 1770. The new (and still sparse) class of speakers were political, not religious, exhorters, and they emerged from the educated ranks of New England society. Beginning in March 1771, prominent patriot leaders delivered commemorative massacre orations that recounted the events of 1770 and urged the people to remain vigilant in the defense of their liberties.[45] Alongside these major events were local addresses delivered by leading members of the community. On May 18, 1772, for example, John Adams delivered a speech at Braintree on "the civil and religious rights and Priviledges of the people." Like countless election speakers before him, Adams began by reminding his listeners that government was "nothing more than the combined Force of Society, or the united Power, Order, Safety, Good and Happiness of the People." No matter what form governments might assume, the people were responsible for safeguarding their rights and happiness. Liberty was "always in Danger" and required constant public vigilance. "As long as knowledge and Virtue are diffused generally among the Body of a Nation, it is impossible they should be enslaved."[46] There was nothing new in sentiments like these, except the speaker himself. Most lay orations were distinctly sermonic in form. But by opening the words up to lay speakers, the bonds uniting people and their leaders were strengthened in the pursuit of a "common cause."

Besides speaking in town meetings, public assemblies, and commemorative occasions, patriot leaders put their pens to use. Between 1770 and 1772, when public interest waned, Samuel Adams alone contributed over forty articles and letters to the *Boston Gazette* urging vigilance and resistance to tyranny. Throughout, his terminology was strong and bordered on treason as illustrated in the following exhortation, based on the case of "Jeroboam's rebellion":

[T]he history of past ages will inform us, that even those civil institutions which have been best calculated for the safety and happiness of the people, have sooner or later degenerated into settled tyranny; which can no more be called civil government, and is in fact upon such accounts such a state much more to be deprecated than anarchy itself. It may be said of each, that it is a *state of war*.[47]

Meanwhile other lay leaders prepared more restrained pamphlets, intended primarily for elite audiences, that reiterated the constitutional bases of American resistance. Often these pamphlets were excerpted in newspapers where they enjoyed an even wider exposure. Lay and ministerial oratory reinforced one another, and together they laid the rhetorical foundation on which a revolutionary mentality would be built.[48]

THE BEAUTIES OF LIBERTY

As patriot leaders struggled to keep issues of liberty and tyranny before the public eye, the ministers were no less active. During the period that Samuel Adams composed his essays for the *Boston Gazette*, Ipswich's Separate pastor John Cleaveland authored a series of inflammatory essays for the *Essex Gazette* under the pseudonym "Johannis in Eremo" (John in the wilderness). Like Adams's, his essays were uncompromising in their attacks on British corruption and malfeasance. The Hutchinson government, he raged, was a "meer tool" of scheming members of Parliament plotting to enslave the colonies. Government and military activities had to be constantly monitored and resisted or all liberty would soon disappear.[49]

Even more important than the libertarian essays composed by ministers were sermons that were delivered and printed between 1770 and 1772. In village after village, ministers used days of fasting and commemoration to lecture their listeners on the ends of government, the fragility of liberty, and the sacred duty of resistance. In these sermons, Israel's past became as important as it was for second-generation ministers whose ties to England were tenuous.[50] Because God remained with them in a binding covenant, New Englanders could resist tyranny without fear of divine withdrawal or defeat. God's continued presence, ministers explained, was not threatened by resistance but by apathy and passive submission to tyranny.

Of all the sermons delivered in the early 1770s, the most widely read and reprinted was *An Oration Upon the Beauties of Liberty* delivered at Boston's Second Baptist Church in December 1772 by the Baptist lay exhorter John Allen. Allen had recently arrived in the colonies from England and like the other notable immigrant, Thomas Paine, he stated the case against Great Britain in the strongest possible terms. His text was drawn from the Old Testament "Son of Liberty" Micah who prophesied at a corrupt time in Israel's history when "the ruler demands gifts, the judge accepts bribes, the powerful dictate what they desire—they all conspire together (Micah 7:3)." That text was perfectly suited to contemporary applications and, with unprecedented fury and directness, Allen used it to broaden the attack on Parliament to include the king himself. Until then, the monarchy was virtually untouched by colonial protests. Observing that kings were "made for the people," Allen urged his listeners to "let not kings think too highly of themselves; for the God of heaven never intended they should be any more than the *servants* of the people." From the case of Israel's resistance to the tyranny of King Rehoboam, Allen justified resistance to unjust kings and their puppet judges. Citing the recent appointment of the Commissioners of Inquiry into the burning of the *Gaspee* in Newport Harbor, Allen noted that submission to those justices was tantamount to submission to tyranny: "It is in effect, giving up your *right* to all you have, to all that you, or your children can ever possess[. . . .] If the judges are wholly to be dependent upon the crown of England, for nomination and support, then you may easily judge whose servants and slaves you are to be."[51]

Once the colonists' right of resistance to English officials and the crown itself was explained, Allen challenged his listeners to defend themselves. While liberty was precarious and required constant vigilance, it could not be lost unless a people gave it away. To those timid souls who counseled restraint and submission to British officials, Allen replied that the colonies had already conceded too much; the time for active preservation was at hand. In stirring words that would be reprinted seven times in four cities between 1773 and 1775 he exclaimed:

> Has not the voice of your *fathers* blood cry'd loud enough in your ears, in your hearts? Have you not heard the voice of blood in your own streets, louder then that which reached to Heaven, that cry'd for vengeance, that was, saith the Lord to Cain, the voice of thy brother's blood, of only one, but this of many brethren? Therefore if there be any vein, any nerve, any soul, any life or spirit of liberty in the sons of America, shew your love for it, guard your freedom, prevent your chains; stand up as one man for your liberty; for none but those, who set a just value upon this blessing, are worthy [of] the enjoyment of it.[52]

Not until *Common Sense* would the colonists hear a more direct summons to action or find in the rhetoric of liberty so powerful a tonic to stiffen resolve in the face of a mighty antagonist.

THE RUBICON CROSSED

When, in 1772, Parliament announced that henceforth the Massachusetts governor's salary would be paid by the crown, Samuel Adams prepared to set in motion a system of "Committees of Correspondence" that would distribute information about British abuses to other towns and supply a network of communications for organized and collective resistance. By then it was clear that England was concentrating pressure on Boston, and equally clear that if Boston was to survive it must have the support of other towns and colonies. Confirmation of support from within New England appeared in the fall and winter of 1772–1773, when over a hundred Massachusetts towns endorsed an inflammatory pamphlet published by the town of Boston entitled *The Votes and Proceedings . . . of the*

Town of Boston.[53] In upholding Boston's course of outspoken resistance, these towns recognized that while the immediate battleground was limited to Boston the issues of government by consent, control of the judges' salaries, trial by jury, standing armies, or the possible establishment of an American bishopric concerned all and required a united front.

While Samuel Adams and other active patriots orchestrated the Committees of Correspondence in New England, others worked to spread the alarm south to other colonies. By 1773 Boston newspapers were openly discussing the possibility of independence, and their letters were picked up and published in other colonial newspapers.[54] For their part, ministers continued to preach the duty of resistance and began to print sermons intended for sympathetic audiences outside of New England. The 1773 election sermon was delivered by Charles Turner, and copies were distributed to the other colonies and to England. Like other sermons intended for broader audiences, Turner's downplayed the themes of New England's covenant privileges and independence, and concentrated instead on arguments from natural law and the English constitution that all "Americans" shared. In republican language that reinforced the messages transmitted in newspapers and pamphlets, he insisted that "it is incumbent on the people . . . to fix on certain regulations, which if we please we may call a *constitution*, as the standard measure of the proceedings of government." Once a constitution was established, the people were required to supervise their leaders, whether in church or state, to ensure compliance with its provisions. This, Turner recognized, "supposes the People have a right to judge of the conduct of government, and its tendency; and this again supposes them capable of judging in things of such a nature." Not all peoples had such a capability, but in America this was not a problem. While conceding that America was not Europe's equal in belles lettres, neither were Europe's common people equal to America's: "The common people in this land have had such advantages, and have so improved them, that they know as much as a like number of the common people, taken together, in any other part of the world, if not more."[55] In a twist of rhetoric that third-generation election speakers would have abhorred, the common people emerged in Turner's sermon as America's most distinctive asset; they were the incipient guardians and saviors of America's libertarian heritage.

The widespread broadcast of libertarian sentiments like Turner's placed the colonies, and New England in particular, in conflict with the crown. The first shock came in 1773 when Parliament passed the Tea Act granting the East India Company the exclusive right to sell tea in America, and granting that all sales of tea would be taxed. Almost immediately the towns of New England issued strong protests and met in mass assemblies to consider what further actions could be taken to protest the tax. The strongest steps were taken in Boston where, as Samuel Cooper explained in a letter to Benjamin Franklin, on the night of December 16, "two or three hundred persons, in dress and appearance like Indians," hastened to the town wharf where a consignment of tea was awaiting transfer and "soon emptied all the chests into the harbor." The destruction, Cooper hastened to add, was calculated and limited; it was "done without injury to any other property or to any man's person."[56] Nevertheless damage *had* been done, and this time Parliament would respond with force rather than conciliation.

In March 1774, Boston's port was blockaded until the East India Company was reimbursed for the tea. The blockade was followed by a succession of "Intolerable" or "Coercive" Acts in April and May and June that abolished representative government in Massachusetts and replaced Governor Hutchinson with the British-born General Thomas Gage, who was given vast powers, including the authority to requisition vacant private buildings to quarter English troops. With the legislative screws in place and tightened, England waited for Boston to buckle, confident that the issue of authority between Parliament and the wayward colonies would be settled once and for all.

News of the Coercive Acts soon spread throughout the colonies and prompted a profound transformation in colonial attitudes toward Great Britain. Until then most Americans assumed that while the issues of parliamentary authority were difficult they were not insoluble; independence was not at the forefront of their thought. All of this changed in the aftermath of the Coercive Acts. Instead of complying, Bostonians settled on a policy of open defiance. With that, as Peter Oliver told it, "the *Massachusetts* Faction found they had past the *Rubicon*; it was now Neck or Nothing."[57] Whether the end result would be wholesale executions for treason or independence depended in large measure on the collective resolve of the colonies. Samuel Cooper was satisfied that within New England "the people in the country have all along been equally zealous with their brethren in Boston, in the common cause." Confirmation of this appeared in the powder alarm in September, when thousands of armed New Englanders marched to the Cambridge common in response to a rumor of war.[58] But outside of New England many questions remained unanswered. Apart from a loose coalition during the last war with France, New England had gone its own way for one and one-half centuries. Now, if they were to survive, they would have to expand their loyalties and covenant promises to include all patriotic "Americans," and hope that other Americans would do the same for them.

As the painful alternative of independence or treason became increasingly clear, New England's Congregational clergy redoubled their patriotic and exegetical activities. Virtually to a man they had supported political resistance as both a political right and a sacred duty. Now they had to begin addressing the even more difficult assignment of justifying rebellion. As in 1690, the drastically altered political circumstances required a new exegesis. References to "Israel's constitution" would have to give way to a new orientation around the "Jewish Republic." And, as in 1690, the clergy had to perfect a speech that conveyed different messages to different audiences. Patriotic Americans outside of New England who might not understand or appreciate New England's exclusive covenant would have to be reached in more secular terms premised on self-interest and the rights of the governed. Audiences at home, however, had to understand the prophetic dimensions of independence in historical and millennial categories, and they had to understand that America's glorious struggle for liberty could never supersede questions of personal salvation and corporate covenant keeping, or the rebellion would be in vain. Throughout, time was of the essence. Never before had so much changed in so short a period of time. And never before had oratory and the sermon played a more pivotal role than when counseling and upholding New Englanders on their perilous road to revolution.

[14]

A Nation Born at Once

Much to the relief of Boston's embattled patriots, news of the Coercive Acts triggered an upsurge of organized protest and resistance on all levels of colonial society. In town meetings and local conventions throughout the colonies, "committees" of ordinary people and their local leaders assembled in extrainstitutional "congresses" modeled on the seventeenth-century popular assemblies. Finally, linking all the colonies, was a "Continental Congress" of patriot leaders appointed by their provincial congresses or popular conventions that met in Philadelphia in September 1774. Led by radical delegates like Samuel and John Adams of Massachusetts, or Patrick Henry and Richard Henry Lee of Virginia, the congress issued a stinging "Declaration of Rights and Grievances" that supported New England's resistance and approved the creation of an American-wide "Continental Association" of committees empowered to prohibit merchants and citizens from importing or consuming British goods until Parliament repealed the Coercive Acts. Instead of being isolated, Bostonians found themselves at the vanguard of a mounting intercolonial protest that was prepared to take colonial grievances to the brink of open rebellion.

In response to the declaration, George III declared Massachusetts to be in a "state of rebellion," hoping that if he could drive Boston's traitors to their knees the other colonies would retreat from their open defiance of parliamentary rule. This, however, was not to be the case. While General Gage occupied Boston, the patriots controlled the countryside, working frantically to inform the people of Boston's plight and raise popular support for the "common cause." With Boston's port blockaded, food and supplies poured in from all the colonies, and Bostonians never ate so well. Urban newspapers, led by the *Boston Gazette* and Isaiah Thomas's *Massachusetts Spy*, were filled with patriotic cries for solidarity and exposes of a British plot to rob Americans of their liberties. For the intellectually curious, the newspapers also printed excerpts from more learned treatises and pamphlets like John Adams's *Novangalus* essays that denied Parliament's jurisdiction over the American colonies and called for a separate "dominion" status under one king. Although no colonial newspaper ever achieved a truly mass circulation, they were often read publicly and kept colonial readers current on the subject of British tyranny.[1]

In America's predominantly "aural" culture, speech was even more important than print in mobilizing a revolutionary mentality.[2] Up and down the coast, lay orators and committeemen rose to defend the rights of Americans and elicit sympathy for Boston's plight. As in the earlier mass revivals and Stamp Act "mobs," established leaders found themselves unable to silence the new speakers; the more their voices were discounted, the louder they yelled. To Virginia's Anglican loyalist Jonathan Boucher, it was clear that the new speakers had won the contest for public loyalty before the battle was ever joined: "As though there were some irrefutable charm in all extemporaneous speaking, however rude, the orators of our committees and sub-committees, like those in higher spheres, *prevail with their tongues.*" The ability of public speakers to attract large sympathetic audiences signaled to Boucher the beginnings of a new, "invisible" government: "To public speakers alone is the government of our country now completely committed. . . . An empire is thus completely established within an empire; and a new system of government of great power erected, even before the old one is formally abolished."[3] In a remarkably short period of time things had gotten out of control and thoughts were moving irresistibly towards independence. This was most true in New England, and no one there saw this more clearly or trumpeted it more loudly than the ministerial "black regiment."

CLERICAL LEADERSHIP IN THE TRANSITION FROM RESISTANCE TO REVOLUTION

From the repeal of the Stamp Act on, New England's Congregational ministers played a leading role in fomenting sentiments of resistance and, after 1774, open rebellion. Historians who minimize the clergy's determinative role in shaping New England's revolutionary mentality, pointing out that they drafted no official resolutions in their associations, miss the points at which ministers made their vital contributions. Ministers' names pepper local records in a bewildering array of contexts: as town clerks, committee advisors, newspaper contributors, militia chaplains, and even militia commanders. Many ministers advocated a provincial nonconsumption of British goods through a "Solemn League and Covenant," over the objections of more cautious merchants and civil leaders. While the Solemn League and Covenant failed to receive popular endorsement, it did show that ministers were at the forefront of aggressive resistance tactics.[4]

As important as the ministers' political activities were, they were secondary to the crucial role ministers played as prophets entrusted with proclaiming God's will for his New World people. Patriot and British leaders alike realized the awesome fact that on any given fast or special occasion over six hundred authoritative voices could be raised simultaneously in over five hundred towns and churches, all imploring God's mercy and claiming the promises of a peculiar people. To the objections of Anglicans and loyalists that ministers had no business preaching politics, Congregational ministers replied that no topic was independent of God's Word and that political preaching had been part of their responsibilities since the first generation. In a fast sermon preached in defiance of General Gage's prohibition, Roxbury's William Gordon declared unequivocally that "there are special times and seasons when [the minister] may treat of politics."[5] Such times had clearly fallen on the colonies, and the clergy would be remiss if, as God's watchmen, they failed to sound the alarm.

In proclaiming the duty of resistance and ultimately rebellion, patriot ministers adopted the same pattern of bifurcated speech first seen in the Glorious Revolution, when royal audiences heard one thing and their own people another. In 1774, however, the outside audience was no longer England—or at least not primarily England—but other freedom-loving Americans outside of New England. When justifying resistance in orations intended for print and widespread dissemination, ministers emphasized the secular vocabulary of "rights and property" that all colonists shared in common. Like lay orators, pamphlet writers, and newspaper editors, they pointed to England's betrayal of her own constitutional heritage and said, as Joseph Perry did in his 1775 election sermon:

> A determined *plan* already pushed on, to the astonishment of all true Englishmen, calculated in its natural tendency to subvert the British constitution, which for ages has stood the guardian of the means of her subject's happiness, the envy of foreign nations, and the admiration of the whole world, and to substitute in the room thereof, *absolute despotism*, and as the certain consequence, *cruel tyranny*, and the *total slavery*, of all America.[6]

Words like these were calculated to arouse the largest possible number of colonial patriots. At the same time, however, they provide few clues to the message New Englanders routinely heard at home.

If outside audiences were unaware of how totally New Englanders understood the conflict with England in local covenantal terms stretching back to the first days of settlement, neither were New Englanders aware of the very different meanings resistance and revolution may have had for other colonists outside their region. Indeed, New Englanders did not hear much from the other colonies at all. As Richard Merritt demonstrates, New England directed the flow of intercolonial communications in the Revolutionary era so thoroughly that in almost all interchanges they were the "exporters" of information that other colonies received.[7] In local oratory, the message audiences heard most frequently was that the struggle with Parliament involved far more than questions of home rule or even, for that matter, who should rule at home; the issues involved nothing less than the preservation of *Sola Scriptura* and New England's privileged position at the center of redemptive history. Whatever the contrary facts of demography, wealth, or power, New Englanders would leave their meetinghouses confirmed in the idea that they were the spiritual core around which God's New World promises and blessings revolved; for their sakes, God had expanded the boundaries of peculiar peoplehood to include all patriotic Americans.

RESISTANCE AND REPENTANCE:
THE REVOLUTIONARY FAST SERMON

Political preaching, like all preaching, tended to be explanatory and exhortatory in nature. Preachers seldom sought to entertain their listeners but to enlighten them and exhort them to act. No single occasion embodied all the themes treated in the Revolutionary pulpit, but when all are examined together they reveal many layers of meaning that collectively made resistance to Parliament both intelligible and virtuous. Ministers drew on both sacred and secular ideas to present the struggle with England in the broadest possible context, both human and divine. Some ideas—the most important ones—reached all the way back to the founders and the principles of *Sola Scriptura,* covenant peoplehood, and the redemptive mission on which the New England Way was founded. Others could be traced to the more recent past of Glorious Revolution and "Real Whig" literature, while still others first appeared in the mass revivals of the 1730s and 1740s. All of these strains of thought and oratory were contained in New England's history, and history—both sacred and profane—remained the instrument ministers most relied upon for guidance, rebuke, and inspiration in time of crisis. Profane history was important because it taught the lesson that power corrupted, and absolute power corrupted absolutely. But sacred history was even more important because it showed how that power could be broken; it carried documented proof that God would never forsake his chosen people or allow their liberties to be forfeited, unless they first deserted him.

Of all occasional sermons, fast and thanksgiving sermons remained the most important. These sermons proliferated in the 1770s and, like their predecessors in earlier generations, described adversity as a punishment for sin.[8] England's tyranny was evil to be sure and would not go unpunished, but New England's woes came at least partly in response to their failure to honor the terms of the covenant. Thus in a fast sermon to his Barnstable congregation, Timothy Hilliard pointed out that "in seasons of great difficulty and distress we are very apt to look too much to second causes, and to forget that whatever evil or calamity is brought upon us, the hand of the Lord is in it." In looking at first causes New Englanders relearned the lesson, in Samuel Webster's words, that "it is for a people's sins, when God suffers this [evil] to come upon them." Clearly the present controversy involved far more than questions of taxes and representation; it meant nothing less than the reformation and reconstruction of American society.[9]

Through the fast sermon, New England audiences learned that the true cause of their trials was God. But they also learned that God was their ultimate savior because they were still a special people. New England's history taught the undeniable lesson that God always delivered his people when they trusted in him. As Samuel Webster told it, "*Our fathers trusted in God,* and he *did deliver them.* And the same Lord yet reigneth, therefore let New-England, yea let the *earth* rejoice!"[10] As always, pessimistic words of failure and judgment supplied the key to victory and optimism.

While criticizing the people for their sins, fast day preachers in the Revolutionary era were careful not to single them out as peculiarly degenerate or evil. Despite the usual sins and lapses in piety, William Gordon would say with complete confidence that relative to other peoples "the morals of this people, taken collectively, are superior to those of other places." Because of the people's virtue and piety, they could be trusted to oversee and participate in their governments. Elisha Fish defended the new image of the people when he distinguished the federal covenant from civil covenants between the rulers and the ruled. In the federal covenant, authority flowed from the sovereign to his subjects who owed him their unquestioning obedience. But in a civil covenant, the flow of authority and initiative was reversed, "and the breach of this covenant is greater on the side of the prince than the people, for it is against the whole body." The new orthodoxy that tyranny was more fearsome than anarchy had been in place for a generation when Fish uttered these words. It was a lesson that New Light ministers first broadcast in the revivals, and it supplied patriot ministers with the grounds they needed to ally with the people against their rulers in England.

Since the logic of repentance and deliverance was so familiar in occasional discourse, ministers invariably followed their prescriptions to moral reform and repentance with strong doses of New England history. This formulaic recounting was no mere ritual or ancestor worship but a necessary way of establishing a separate identity. Furthermore, the formulas imparted confidence. The formal recollections never appeared banal because New Englanders never lost the big battles. History showed one deliverance after another and, together with Scripture promises, proved that New England would be delivered from any foe, as long as they followed traditional remedies. The logic of the fast would only lose its force in the event of utter defeat, and that would not happen so long as God's warnings were repeated and his conditions honored.

Judging from the deprivations endured under the Coercive Acts, New England had little for which to be thankful in 1774. But from the divine vantage point, ministers saw otherwise and insisted on observing the annual fall thanksgiving and reiterating the terms of God's covenant with New England. In a thanksgiving sermon delivered in Boston and printed in two editions, William Gordon boldly urged his listeners and readers not to "disgrace our descent" by passively submitting to tyranny: "The important day is now arrived that must determine whether we shall remain free, or, alas! be brought into bondage, after having long enjoyed the sweets of liberty."[11] Even if it was "the awful determination of heaven, that we shall not retain liberties without fighting, let no one despair." Gordon concluded his sermon with the same formula of repentance and deliverance that appeared in the fasts:

> Do we join piety to our prudence and fortitude; do we confess and repent of our sins, justify God in his so trying us, accept . . . our punishment at his hands without murmuring and complaining; do we humble ourselves, amend our ways and doings, give up ourselves to God, become a holy People, and make the Most High our confidence? [Then] we may hope that he will be on our side; and "if the Lord is for us, what can men do unto us?" Have we the God of hosts for our ally, we might bid adieu to fear, though the world was united against us.[12]

ARTILLERY SERMONS AND THE RHETORIC OF WAR

While fast and thanksgiving sermons were ideal instruments for explanation, humiliation, and self-justification, they were also apt to be, along with election sermons, the most restrained in their hostility to the crown and in their discussion of war. Many fast sermons were printed for outside audiences and reflected the speakers' realization that if New England was to retain the sympathy of other respectable colonists they must portray themselves as victims not aggressors. Too often, historians have mistaken the restraint in these sermons for the whole of New England preaching, and they have therefore missed more radical sentiments that appeared on other, more local occasions and that reveal the full range of pulpit ideology. Of these, the most striking were the artillery election sermons and the local militia muster sermons. The traditional subject matter of these discourses was war. And in 1774 it was a topic that ministers almost relished.

In addressing militia musters, ministers publicized their assumption that open warfare was imminent. Already in January 1774, Zabdiel Adams (distant cousin to John) warned a muster of the Lunenburg militia that "an attack from that *power* to which we have been used heretofore to look for protection, seems now most immediate to threaten us." In such circumstances the oppressed had every right to fight back; war was not only permissible but necessary when rulers overstepped their bounds. In his 1774 artillery election sermon, John Lathrop reassured the troops, noting that "we may and ought, to resist, and even make war against those rulers who leap the bounds prescribed them by the constitution, and attempt to oppress and enslave the subjects." Such warfare, he went on, "is a principle on which alone the great revolutions which have taken place in our nation can be justified." Again history was enlisted, only this time the subject matter was not resistance but the "great revolutions" upending tyranny and arbitrary rule. If revolution came, New Englanders need not fear. Indeed, Lathrop exulted, "we may venture to say, our militia will soon be equal to any in the world."[13]

In locating particular targets of oppression, militia speakers concentrated on standing armies and the king who commanded them, rather than on corrupt civilian officials or members of Parliament. In an address to the Millbury militia in July 1774, Ebenezer Chaplin used the case of David's army of volunteers defeating Saul's regular soldiers to document the point that "a Standing Army of soulders arn't half so good Soulders in Battle against the Common Enemy, they haven't the incitement to Stand their ground." From the subject of standing armies, Chaplin turned to the king, observing that Israel enjoyed peace and prosperity for four hundred years under the "republic" of the judges, but then suffered grievously after "they asked [for] and insisted on a King like all the Nations." This argument, sounded earlier by Jonathan Mayhew, rapidly became the new reigning orthodoxy. In the new exegesis, the "Jewish Republic" clearly represented God's preference. Kings and standing armies typically led to exploitation and tyranny because they lay "out of the Reach of the people."[14] While Chaplin's aggressive sermon was never published, it *did* reach the people of Millbury and, like many other unpublished messages, prepared New Englanders to sever their ties with the mother country and eliminate monarchy from their government.

In March 1775, as word spread of the arrival of twelve thousand additional British regulars in Boston, ministers stepped up their rereading of Israel's past. Militia sermons in particular searched for Old Testament precedents to oppose kings and standing armies, and to justify civil insurrection. Arguments against the monarchy came from Israel's experience under the judges, while precedents for rebellion were taken from the period of the divided kingdoms in Israel. The partition of Israel occurred, ministers explained, when the people of Israel met to elect a successor to the recently deceased King Solomon. Normally, Solomon's son Rehoboam would have been elected but, as the historian Josephus explained, "contrarie to all reason," Rehoboam rejected the advice of his elders and promised the people he would tax them more harshly than his father.[15] In response, the ten northern tribes of Israel revolted and "took to their tents," and elected the Egyptian exile Jeroboam as their king. Rehoboam fled to Jerusalem where he established the rival southern kingdom of Judah. Neither ruler was distinguished, and both supplied the sacred precedents ministers needed to justify armed rebellion and supply hope for the outcome. Through his oppressive policies and disregard for the people, Rehoboam illustrated the evils of tyranny and the right of the northern tribes to revolt. Jeroboam was equally culpable. By introducing false gods in the north and engaging in an unsuccessful war with Judah (unsuccessful because he made war over the prohibitions of God's prophets), Jeroboam illustrated how a king with superior armies could not defeat his countrymen to the south because God would not allow it.

THE WAR BEGINS

During the strained days of March 1775 no minister studied the accounts of Israel's divided kingdom and the right of rebellion more closely than Concord's thirty-two-year-old minister, William Emerson. Till then, his world was dominated by local concerns and internal squabbles. All this changed in March and April of 1775, when the inhabitants of Concord were propelled into what Emerson termed "the greatest events taking place in the present Age." In those months, events would vault Emerson to the front ranks of New England clergymen and demonstrate just how extraordinary average ministers could be in extraordinary times.[16]

By March, Emerson and other Concord patriots knew that British spies had infiltrated their town and informed General Gage of hidden armory and munitions supplies. Many believed Gage was planning a preemptive strike on the military supplies and feared the outcome. At a muster of the Concord militia on March 13, Emerson preached a sermon on 2 Chronicles 13:12. In that text, God's prophet warned Jeroboam that if he attacked the smaller army of Judah, God would "sound the trumpet" for his defeat. With obvious agitation Emerson began his sermon with the somber note that recent intelligence warned of "an approaching Storm of War and Bloodshed." Many in attendance would soon be called upon for "real Service."[17] Were they ready? Real readiness, Emerson explained, depended not only on martial skill and weaponry but also on moral and spiritual resolve. To be successful, soldiers must believe in what they were fighting for, and they must trust in God's power to uphold them. Otherwise they would scatter in fear before the superior British redcoats.

To supply martial resolve, Emerson recalled the history of Israel and New England with particular reference to their military encounters. He reminded the soldiers that they were the descendants of "worthy Ancestors" who fought to establish and maintain their religious and civil liberties. By virtue of their trust in God, they were never defeated. Surely their descendants in the Concord militia would "dare not be guilty of such Edomitish Prophanity to sell, or rather to tamely resign our glorious Birthright into the bloody fangs of hungry Courtiers and greedy Placemen." In terms that had been uttered by other New England preachers before, Emerson employed the Old Testament account of Jeroboam's defeat at the hands of the smaller army of Judah as a warning to England: "It will be your unspeakable Damage to meddle with us, for we have an unconquered Leader that carries his people to Victory and Triumph."[18]

After describing New England's heritage and record of martial courage, Emerson restated the case for colonial resistance and military readiness. For standing by their constitutional liberties and trusting only in God, the people of New England were "cruelly charged with Rebellion and Sedition." That charge, Emerson cried, was a lie put forward by plotters against American liberty. With all the integrity of his sacred office behind him, Emerson took his stand before the Concord militia:

> For my own Part, the more I reflect upon the Movements of the British Nation . . . the more satisfied I am that our Military Preparation here for our own Defense is not only excusable but justified in the Eyes of the impartial World. Nay, for should we neglect to defend ourselves by military Preparation, we never could answer it to God and to our own Consciences or the rising [generations].

The road ahead would be difficult, Emerson cautioned, but the outcome was one preordained from the beginning of time. Accordingly, the soldiers could go forth to war assured that "the Lord will cover your head in the Day of Battle and carry you on from Victory to Victory." In the end, he concluded, the whole world would know "that there is a God in New England."[19]

Emerson's militia sermon was only the beginning of a nonstop pulpit campaign to prepare the towns surrounding Boston for war. Three days later he preached a fast sermon on Micah 7:1–4 ("the day of your Watchmen has come"), and on the following two sabbaths he preached a series on the triumphant theme, "ye Lord God Omnipotent reigneth." On Monday, March 27, he delivered yet another militia sermon, this one to the assembled troops in Acton who were "greatly alarmed by a Report that 1200 of the [British] Troops were on their March out of Boston. Under Apprehension [they are] coming to Concord."[20] Unlike the earlier rumors that drew thousands to Cambridge's common, these "apprehensions" were well grounded in a flurry of intelligence reports confirming Gage's intention to strike at "rebel" strongholds. Emerson's mission was not to counsel restraint or caution, but to arouse the citizenry for battles that were certain to come.

On April 19, the mounting apprehensions became fact as eight hundred British troops marched on Lexington and Concord in an effort to destroy the patriot munitions. At Lexington, Gage's troops were met by a small "army of observation" who were fired upon and sustained seventeen casualties. From there the British troops marched to Concord. Before their arrival the alarm had been sounded and militiamen rushed to the common. William Emerson was the first to arrive in the village, and he was soon joined by "minutemen" from nearby towns. Again a shot was fired—the famed "shot heard round the world"—and in the ensuing exchange three Americans and twelve British soldiers were killed or wounded. By then the American patriots had relocated much of their munitions, and the exhausted British troops faced the long march back to Boston. All along the way they encountered patriot surprise attacks organized in guerrilla fashion. Before the British reached Boston, 293 redcoats and 93 Americans had been killed or wounded.[21] New England's colonial war for independence had begun.

While tempers flared in New England and young men rushed to enlist for armed service, few colonists to the south desired a war with the most powerful nation in Europe. Yet war seemed inevitable.[22] In Philadelphia, delegates to the Second Continental Congress authorized the creation of a continental army under the command of the Virginian George Washington. Meanwhile armed hostilities continued. Battles at Fort Ticonderoga (May 1775), Bunker Hill (June 1775), and Quebec (December 1775) pointed toward independence. Any lingering hopes the colonists may have had for peaceful reconciliation were shattered in August, when George III rejected Congress's last-ditch "Olive Branch Petition" for peace and declared all the colonies to be in a state of rebellion. Henceforth British troops would be authorized to fire on patriot forces at will, and British warships were freed to seize American shipping.

A JUST REVOLUTION

As events unfolded at a bewildering pace, New England's ministers struggled desperately for insight and understanding. Explanation, interpretation, and balance had long been their chief responsibilities. But now everything seemed out of control. They had helped to lead the way into resistance convinced that they did so as loyal Englishmen seeking nothing more than the restoration of basic rights that all Englishmen accepted as self-evident. But as George's declaration made plain, this was not the case. Their radical perspective on the English constitution, with its stress on separate American legislatures and actual representation, lay outside the mainstream of British thought and never reached more than a handful of coffeehouse pamphleteers and "country" libertines. The Anglican loyalist Samuel Seabury (YC, 1748) was correct all along when he informed his patriotic countrymen that "the position that we are bound by no laws to which we have not consented, either by ourselves, or our representatives, is a novel position, unsupported by any authoritative record of the British constitution, ancient or modern. It is republican in its very nature, and tends to the utter subversion of the English monarchy."[23] Such "republican" sentiments subverted authority because they rejected the unitary ideal of one indivisible supreme authority (the crown-in-Parliament) and substituted for it the idea that the people were the best governors and judges of what laws they would obey. These ideas, Seabury concluded, could lead only to chaos, because if one person or colony "has a right to disregard the laws of the society to which he belongs, *all* have the *same* right; and *then* government is at an end."[24]

The logic of Seabury's argument was flawless, but American experience taught otherwise. In fact, Americans had defied Parliament's authority, but through their assemblies and congresses they had also governed and policed themselves *without* lapsing into a state of anarchy. And, at least in New England, colonists had governed themselves without crown or Parliament for two generations before English rule. When faced with the contradictions between the English constitutional law they had praised for three generations and their experience in liberty and self-government that spanned five generations, patriot leaders came down on the side of liberty. In a process that few could understand, ministers and people alike found themselves propelled down paths none had dared travel before to a destination none could clearly perceive. Their cause was undeniably just and confirmed by Scripture and experience. But it could no longer be justified by arguments from the British constitution or appeals to the crown. Other arguments would have to be invented to justify their experience. Where could the people turn for guidance? The answer was to their own covenant past and to Israel. Both had guided them unerringly before English rule, and they would continue to guide them after it came to an end. If England insisted that New England's conception of liberty and sovereignty was wrong, then the British constitution, not the ideas that had been fashioned from scriptural precept and covenant experience, would have to be removed.[25]

The persistence and even dominance of covenant themes in Congregational preaching alongside the secular ideology of republicanism reveals both the extent and limitations of revolutionary change in New England religious culture. The political chasm separating republican theories of power and government from the British constitution and theory of "mixed" government was immense. Republican ideas pointed to a new and revolutionary system of government where no authority existed independent of popular consent and where, through written constitutions, the people governed continually not only in the creation of their government but also in the moment-by-moment operation of that government through their actual representatives. On the issue of political sovereignty, colonial patriots departed from the traditional concept of a single supreme undivided authority with absolute and unlimited powers to a concept in which the people were the best rulers.[26] In ways that had yet to be worked out in concrete institutional form, and that would occupy the most creative minds in America throughout their lifetimes, the people in the independent American republic would be *both* the governors and the governed. But the finest political theorists and logicians of the age told Americans that a perfect identification of "government" and "society" was impossible; like John Cotton one and one-half centuries earlier, they asked, "If the people be the governors, then who shall be governed?"

That question would only be answered in practice as the violent encounters of 1775–1776 plunged the colonists ahead of theory. Almost overnight reflexive declarations of loyalty to the crown were replaced by harsh repudiations. One week after Lexington and Concord, John Cleaveland published his own declaration of independence:

Great Britian, adieu! No longer shall we honor you as our Mother; you are become cruel; you have not so much bowels [of compassion] as the sea monsters towards their young ones. . . . King George the Third, adieu! No more shall we cry to you for protection. . . . Your breach of covenant; your violation of faith . . . have DISSOLVED OUR ALLEGIANCE to your Crown and Government!—O my dear New England, hear thou the alarm of war! The call of Heaven is to arms! to arms![27]

In a militia sermon in June 1775, Nathan Perkins echoed the same theme and blamed New England's woes on the "accesion of the present king," who employed armed troops as "instruments of tyranny" and seized "every opportunity . . . to destroy those rights which have been purchased by the toil and blood of the most exalted individuals who ever adorned humanity."[28] In New England at least, the time for choosing between independence or "enslavement" had arrived. Circumstances compelled the people and their ministers to look in new directions, even as they looked back at a sacred past and mission that had never been annulled.

THE JEWISH REPUBLIC

Separation from the crown, though necessary, was not an easy psychological step for most Americans to take. There was something final and irrevocable about it that broke continuity with a long colonial past.[29] Earlier opposition to Parliament had been mere "resistance"; it aimed at reform rather than separation, and its guiding rationale was simply the recovery of supposed constitutional rights. But the repudiation of George III, and with it the very idea of monarchy, was a different story; this was rebellion not resistance, and in political terms it meant the creation of a new revolutionary order that required the strongest possible justification. The British constitution, founded on the bedrock of monarchy, was no longer of help: nor was the example of the Puritan Commonwealth widely invoked. New England's history before the Glorious Revolution was more amenable to the present change, but even that existed under a royal charter that claimed at least nominal loyalty to the crown. For justification New Englanders had to go back even further to Israel's history in the period before the introduction of monarchy. In a very real sense, the Old Testament had always served as New England's "ancient constitution," and each generation had read and interpreted it from their own unique vantage point. The first two generations focused on the "theocracy" of direct divine rule; the third and fourth on "Israel's Constitution" in its anglicized, "mixed" form under the Davidic dynasty. In 1775 New England's embattled ministers again returned to the Old Testament, but this time their attention was riveted on the premonarchic period of the "Jewish Republic." This was *the* Golden Age of mankind, and the one "America" was about to reenact (with New England's guidance) after millennia of quiescence.

The new political orthodoxy was formally announced on May 31, 1775, the time traditionally given to the election sermon. Despite the fact that Gage occupied Boston and disallowed both the election of counsellors and the election sermon, the provincial congress met in Watertown and called on President Langdon of Harvard College to deliver the sermon. In view of the college's role in providing cultural leadership and direction for five generations, the choice of Langdon to deliver the address was natural. For his text Langdon turned to the period of the divided kingdoms and quoted God's promise of deliverance in Isaiah 1:26: "And I will restore thy judges as at the first, and thy counsellors as at the beginning; afterwards thou shalt be called the city of Righteousness, the faithful city." This promise, Langdon began, came at a time in Israel's history when all was in a state of disarray. The nation's once vital piety had lapsed into "mere ceremony," and inept rulers ignored the needs of their subjects, regarding "the perquisites more than the duties of their office." As a result, the ten tribes of Israel had already fallen captive, and Judah stood perilously close to destruction. The reasons for this, it was now clear, were political as well as moral and spiritual. Once, the people of Israel had been united and at peace with one another; they governed themselves and lived solely in dependence on God. Then, against God's will, they demanded a king and began their steady descent into oppression and captivity.

Contained in Israel's political history was an invaluable lesson, hidden from earlier generations but now inescapably clear to the patriots of New England: Israel fell when they abandoned their "republic." As Langdon pointed out:

> The Jewish government, according to the original Constitution which was divinely established, if considered merely in a civil view, was a perfect republic. . . . And let them who cry up the divine right of Kings consider that the only form of government which had a proper claim to a divine establishment was so far from including the idea of a king, that it was a high crime for Israel to ask to be in this respect like other nations.[30]

So too, New Englanders had once governed themselves and created a pattern of government consistent in every regard with the laws of nature and of God. Now, when "British liberty is just ready to expire," they stood alone as the last bastion of freedom in an ever-darkening world. And their own liberties were in mortal danger. Strange names with "faces we never saw before" presumed to rule them and to "execute the most unrighteous decrees for high wages." Standing armies enforced arbitrary decrees at the point of a sword, all the while demanding "absolute submission to their unlimited claims of authority." Nor was the state of piety in New England what it might have been—a sad fact blamed in large measure not on a degenerate generation but on the introduction of corrupt English manners and Arminian ideas by which "the gospel is corrupted into a superficial system of moral philosophy, little better than ancient Platonism." The "many" who corrupted biblical Christianity with moral philosophy were, Langdon noted, not to be found in the Congregational churches. Rather they were to be found in England and the Anglican

Church. In New England the flame of "gospel liberty" continued to burn bright.

If patriots no longer defended their civil and religious liberties, America would soon be lost and all the world cast into darkness. Yet, and this was the point of Langdon's sad chronicle, things did not have to remain in such a sad state. Americans had the history of Israel to guide them; they did not have to make the same mistake in succumbing to monarchy. Instead they would fight to inaugurate a new era. Already they were at war with England and had severed their connections to the obnoxious idea of monarchy. But this, Langdon said, was not enough. Americans must reform their own society, ridding themselves of "corrupt" English practices and ideas: "Nothing but a general reformation can give good ground to hope that the public happiness will be restored." If armed resistance and spiritual reform were combined, New England's natal groanings would issue forth in a new creation; one that was "unexampled in any history" since Israel and that would complete the long "errand" embarked upon by the founders one and one-half centuries earlier. British troops might mock "our Solemn Fasts and every appearance of serious Christianity in the land," Langdon concluded, but that was to their great misfortune. The same God who could "command the stars in their courses to fight his battles" would intervene for his professing people. "In a variety of methods he can work salvation for us, as he did for his people in ancient days."[31]

Throughout the war-torn days of 1775–1776, ministers issued a steady barrage of fast sermons echoing the themes in Langdon's election sermon. They reminded their audiences that America's sense of peoplehood and destiny did not depend upon the British constitution but went back to a special covenant promise begun with Abraham and carried through to the founding of New England. Experience confirmed that independence and republican government need not provoke anarchy. In New England's first covenanted communities, republican forms existed in fact if not in theory, and the towns had never been more united or stable.

As Americans contemplated their perilous experiment in republicanism, they knew the greatest threats were anarchy and disunion. If order could not be maintained, America's novel stand for liberty would make them the laughing stock of the civilized world. To guard against anarchy and disunion, the Continental Congress took a cue from New England and appointed Sunday, July 20, 1775, as a national day of fasting and humiliation. On this day, and others like it in November and December, churches gathered so that "all the colonies should, as it were, make the case of suffering and oppressed Boston, their own." Besides solidarity they proclaimed the duty of covenant mutuality: "While we unite as brethren, let us also love as brethren, and as much as possible, study the things that make for peace and harmony, that if it be possible, we may preserve peace among ourselves."[32] Through the covenant and days of fasting, New Englanders discovered the essential means whereby they could come together with "countrymen" who, generations earlier, had stood outside of God's New World promises.

The covenant supplied New Englanders not only with the terms they needed for national union but also with the terms needed for understanding their present sufferings. This theme was especially prominent in unpublished fast sermons delivered in 1775 and 1776. In Millbury, Massachusetts, Ebenezer Chaplin employed abbreviated sermon notes (later transcribed and enlarged for posterity) to show how David's exile in the wilderness, like America's current straits, taught that God's people have "nothing else to trust or to take Courage in."[33] At Boston's Tenth Church, Samuel Mather preached a sermon on Isaiah 48:10 ("I have chosen thee in the furnace of affliction") to reiterate the same theme of covenant and affliction his great-grandfather, Richard Mather, stated a century earlier in his "farewell" sermon:

> Such is our Condition in this world, that we must at one time or another meet with afflictive things. And therefore beloved, we should not think it strange concerning the Fiery Trial, which is to tire us as though some strange thing had happened to us. The chosen people of God, who are bound for the Heavenly Jerusalem, do not certainly know what shall befall them. But this they may know, that Affliction abides them. . . . The *followers of Christ* therefore must go into the Furnace after Him.[34]

In Middletown, Connecticut, Elias Smith offered the same diagnosis of New England's ills, and with it the remedy: "Now are we the covenant people? Let us this day enter into a Solemn Covenant with God that we will put away all iniquity from our hearts. . . . Tho now it is a dark day with us, our light shall break forth in the morning . . . our righteousness shall go before us and the glory of the Lord shall be our reward."[35] In all these sermons, New Englanders viewed "America" as an extension of themselves: a covenanted society in which the people were bound by formal obligations to God and to one another. Instead of weakening their inherited vocabulary, the political crisis in pre-Revolutionary America strengthened covenant themes and extended them to the colonies-as-a-whole.

LIBERTY'S DOUBLE MEANING

Throughout the bewildering days of 1776, the one underlying principle, always insisted upon, was that New England remain a people of the Word. This meant a people who, along with their liberty and property, "owned" a special covenant with God; a people who confirmed that covenant by voluntarily gathering in autonomous local churches to hear the Word proclaimed; and a people who acknowledged no human authority (including a king) and no system of political ideas (including republican ideas) as equal in authority to that sovereign Word. So important was *Sola*

Scriptura in 1776 that in the annual Dudleian lecture of that year President Langdon interrupted his praise of natural theology to warn the attending students not to confuse moral philosophy with divine revelation: "Let us take heed of setting up natural religion too high, so as to vie with the honor of divine revelation. . . . [A]ll that are educated in this Seminary of learning, consider the excellency of the holy Scriptures above all the wisdom of this world."[36] Experience proved that God did not bless a people because of their political system, even if that system was republican. Rather his blessings came because the people continued to honor the terms of the covenant and to trust in him. If that cardinal fact was ever forgotten in the press of events, then the political revolution would be fought in vain and the experiment in liberty doomed to failure.

To make sure the lesson of covenant keeping was not forgotten, ministers augmented their political sermons with twice-weekly doses of regular preaching on the perennial themes of repentance and regeneration. Recognizing that the political language of "freedom," "union," "liberty," and "deliverance" sounded very much like the old gospel message of liberation from the bondage of sin, ministers took special pains to point out the differences. In no uncertain terms, the aged Nathaniel Niles declared that

> without spiritual liberty, the other will finally prove worse than nothing. It is in itself a great blessing, but by abusing it, we may, and shall be rendered much more miserable at last, than if we had never possessed it. . . . [B]y neglecting to embrace the gospel, we convert civil liberty, which is in itself, a delicious kind of food, into a slow poison which will render our death vastly more terrible than otherwise it would have been. . . . We boast of liberty, and value ourselves much on being free, when at the same time we are taken captive by satan at his pleasure. This is a much more shocking absurdity, than it would be for a man confined in a dungeon, to boast that he is at liberty, because he is not called on, in providence, to go into the field and labour.[37]

America's political redemption from bondage and tyranny was important and necessary, but not as important as personal, eternal redemption. Without spiritual redemption, ministers insisted, political redemption meant nothing.

By explaining their terms carefully and distinguishing regular sermons from occasional, ministers could praise both spiritual and political liberty. Depending on the subject matter and occasion, the same text could be made to elicit political or spiritual meanings in the same way earlier generations distinguished federal and personal covenants. Rather than substituting political for spiritual meanings, they retained both through the exegetical technique of extracting "double applications." Thus at a public fast in Norwich, Connecticut, on January 17, 1776, Andrew Lee (YC, 1766) selected his text from Isaiah 5:20 ("woe to them that call evil good, and good evil") because it contained a double meaning. The primary meaning of the text, he explained, referred to false teachers who perverted the gospel; but it could also be taken in a "moral" or "political" sense to condemn tyrants who passed evil laws and called themselves good. "They *call evil good*, who say it is good to submit to the will of tyrants, or tamely part with liberty at the summon of any *king* or *ministry* on earth."[38] From the beginning, Puritan preachers approached biblical language as plastic and multivalent. The cumulative and progressive nature of covenants, as well as the theory of typology, implied that later generations would see more in God's Word as they moved closer to realizing the full potential of its teachings and prophecies. Now, in the midst of Revolutionary fervor, moral and political applications that eluded earlier generations became inescapably clear.

Of all the terms enjoying a double meaning, the most reverenced in 1776 was *liberty*. That term was a familiar one to New Englanders in both political and civil contexts. It was, the loyalist Jonathan Sewall observed with caustic wit, "a Word, whose very Sound carries a Fascinating charm."[39] In the inherited Puritan grammar of meaning, liberty and life were interchangeable terms. Like food, water, or sunlight, liberty was a term for survival; the prospect of losing it triggered instinctual life or death responses. Samuel West summarized its importance at the conclusion of his Massachusetts election sermon delivered in Boston after the city's "liberation" by General Washington in March 1776:

> It is an indispensable duty, my brethren, which we owe to God and our country, to rouse up and bestir ourselves, and, being animated with a noble zeal for the sacred cause of liberty, to defend our lives and fortunes, even to the shedding of the last drop of blood. . . . To save our country from the hands of our oppressors ought to be dearer to us even than our own lives, and, next [to] the eternal salvation of our own souls, [it] is the thing of greatest importance,—a duty so sacred that it cannot justly be dispensed with for the sake of our secular concerns.[40]

Contained in West's oft-repeated declaration was both the importance of civil liberty (the "sacred cause") and its subordinate position, "next [to our] eternal salvation," the most dear. In fact, the two, while distinguished, were interrelated in the same way that federal covenants and covenants of grace were separate but interrelated. One sure sign of eternal salvation was an enthusiastic regard for the defense of civil and religious liberties. Tyrants, West explained, were "the ministers of Satan," and by resisting them Christians evidenced a concern with their spiritual as well as their temporal "estate." Saving grace, of course, was not guaranteed to lovers of liberty, and it *could* be granted in despotic societies. But, like children reared in "heathen" societies, enslaved peoples did not gain salvation through a "covenant promise."[41] Covenanted societies had to be free societies that acknowledged no sovereign authority besides the Word of God. By fighting to preserve their freedom, American patriots were fighting to secure inherited covenant promises for their posterity.

While scriptural references to "liberty" are relatively rare in comparison to terms like "law," "peace," or "love," patriot ministers seized on every instance of the term and extracted from it a double meaning which, they believed, was intended specifically for them. Of all the libertarian texts, the one invoked so frequently that it served as an American motto was St. Paul's enjoinder in Galatians 5:1: "Stand fast, therefore, in the liberty wherewith Christ hath made us free." This was a favorite text of the Boston patriot Joseph Warren and the text Litchfield's Judah Champion employed in his widely circulated Connecticut election sermon of May 1776, *Christian and Civil Liberty and Freedom Considered*. In a regular sermon, Champion began, this text would be interpreted in its "primary" spiritual sense to describe the Christian's liberty from the bondage of sin and the freedom that Christ bought through his death on the cross. But on that particular election day, when things were "gloomy and threatening" in the land, and when God's people faced political enslavement, the text also referred to civil liberties and the Christian's duty to stand fast in defense of the "outward" privileges on which covenant keeping depended.[42] Britain claimed that Americans' advocacy of republican liberty would inevitably lead to anarchy. But, Champion replied, "While our government is so popular; yet where are civil rulers and executive courts so truly revered as this colony? Where is so little of riotous and factious behavior?"

For five generations the inhabitants of Connecticut had governed themselves without internal eruptions. Experience showed that the people need not fear or seek protection against popular anarchy, but royal tyranny. America's path of liberty was true and divinely inspired, even if existing European constitutions allowed no room for such unchecked popular liberties. What Europe did not realize, Champion went on, New England's founders did; and they would have supported the cause of resistance and revolution. "Methinks we may this day, well nigh see the ghosts of our departed progenitors, and hear those blessed worthies, in solemn accents, through the vast Heaven, addressing us, saying, 'Stand fast in the liberty wherewith Christ hath made you free.'" Besides the founders, Champion continued, "God, angels and spirits in glory all look on" America's cause with approval. Therefore, none should speak evil of the current stand for liberty, nor fear the outcome:

> Under the Jewish Theocracy, God destroyed those who were intimidated and discouraged their brethren. We may be sorely chastised, but the righteous cause so dearly purchased will prevail. The Lord of Hosts will arm the whole creation—level the artillery of heaven—send all his angels, and martial all the elements in battle array, against his enemies, before his cause shall suffer.[43]

NEW OCCASIONS AND THE "GRAND QUESTION" OF INDEPENDENCE

Besides preaching provincial fast and election sermons, Congregational ministers promulgated the themes of liberty and providential deliverance in a wave of new occasions invented for the purpose of recalling New

England's libertarian heritage and keeping the present crisis in the public
eye. To commemorate George Washington's liberation of Boston in
March 1776, Samuel Cooper delivered an occasional sermon in the for-
merly occupied First Church of Boston on Sunday afternoon, April 7. All
who attended recognized that the moment was filled with deep historical
significance.[44] To signal that importance, Cooper employed the same text
John Cotton had used 150 years earlier to remind the departing Winthrop
fleet of *God's Promise to his Plantation*: "Moreover I will appoint a Place
for my People Israel, and will plant them that they may dwell in a place
of their own, and move no more." Cotton's famous sermon was first
printed in 1630 and reprinted in Boston in 1686 at the time of Massachu-
sett's loss of the charter, giving it a double significance to speakers like
Cooper. By 1776 many events stood between Boston's "America" and
Winthrop's Boston, but the underlying form and rhetorical strategies of
occasional preaching remained remarkably constant and furnished
Cooper with the main themes he would employ to prepare his listeners
for independence.

In his sermon to the Winthrop fleet, Cotton had compared Israel's
deliverance from Egypt to the Puritans' deliverance from English tyranny.
Through providential leadings, both were led to a "Land of Promise,"
where "they shall dwell . . . like Free-holders, in a place of their own. He
promiseth them firm and durable possession; they shall move no more."
In similar terms Cooper began with the observation that "there is, my
Hearers, [a] very striking Resemblance between the Condition of our
Country from the Beginning and that of antient Israel, so that many Passages in holy Writ referring to their particular Circumstances as a People,
may with peculiar Propriety be adopted by us." The point in Cotton's and
Cooper's sermons was that Americans' title to their land and liberty did
not come through ordinary means but through the providential leadings
and promises of God. Such a promise, Cotton explained, would remain
binding unless the people "wrong themselves" by turning away from
God and forfeiting their blessings.

After establishing the parallels between Canaan and the New World,
Cotton and Cooper employed the standard array of "reasons," "uses,"
and "observations" to engraft their own past onto Israel's. For Cotton,
speaking in 1630, the line of faith traveled from Israel in the time of the
divided kingdom to the Marian exiles: "When *Jeroboam* made a defection
from *Judah*, and set up golden Calves to worship, all that were well
affected, both Priests and People, sold their Possessions, and came to
Jerusalem for the Ordinances sake. This Case was of seasonable use to our
Fathers in the dayes of Queen *Mary*; who removed to *France* and *Germany*
in the beginning of her Reign, upon Proclamation of alteration of Religion, before any Persecution began." Cooper echoed the same theme, likening the Great Migration to Joseph: "This Country was born, it has been
nursed and educated amidst Alarms, Hazards, and great Conflicts. Like
Joseph, who was separated from his Brethren, we have been envied,

hated, calumniated, persecuted, and sold."[45] The cases of Joseph, the Jews returning to Jerusalem, and the Puritan founders were interrelated and confirmed a people of God who would remove and suffer rather than sacrifice their civil or religious liberties.

From New England's past, Cooper brought history to the present where an equally portentous struggle was taking place. The "grand Question" now before the American people concerned civil liberties and the "Fundamental Principle" that a subject should not be liable to taxes or laws, "but such as He himself has either personally, or by a Representative of his own free choice, publicly and Solemnly consented to." The defense of civil liberties was no less essential to preserving God's promise to his American plantation than the founders' defense of religious liberties. In both crusades God's Word reigned supreme, and God's people followed "the remarkable Footsteps of divine Providence." Like the bush Moses encountered in the wilderness, American libertarianism was "a Bush burning but not consumed."

In concluding his sermon of 1630, Cotton turned "for Consolation" to the surety of God's promises. "When he promiseth peace and safety, what Enemy shall be able to make the Promise of God of no effect? . . . Neglect not Walls, and Bulwarks, and Fortifications for your own defense; but ever let the Name of the Lord be your strong Tower; and the word of His Promise the rock of your Refuge." For consolation in 1776, Cooper turned to the same divine promises. Because of America's loyalty to Boston reflected in the recent deliverance wrought by "the illustrious Washington," all American patriots could appropriate the "sublime language" of Moses for their own: "Happy art thou, O Israel: who is like unto thee, O People saved of the Lord, who is the Shield of thy Help, and the Sword of thine Excellency. Thine Enemies will be found Liars unto Thee, and Thou shalt tread upon their high Places."[46] However much issues, events, and rhetoric separated Cotton and Cooper, their sermons were of a piece and together confirmed the righteousness of America's cause.

Throughout New England, ministers set aside an unprecedented number of weekdays to treat the themes of civil liberty and America's newfound union. On the day following Cooper's sermon, Enoch Huntington (YC, 1759) concluded a special assembly of the Middletown town meeting with a sermon on the importance of union. From Matthew 12:25 he established the principle, later immortalized by Abraham Lincoln, that "every Kingdom divided against itself is brought to desolation." England was already divided against herself because she employed "her power and force . . . against her interest and strength." Now a new set of ties existed among the American colonies and they would survive only so long as union prevailed:

We in this Country, at this present day, have everything to induce us to cultivate union, and guard against divisions among ourselves. Whatever is most dear and valuable in this world, to millions now living, and will be so

> to all the millions of their posterity after them, till this world shall be no
> more, is at stake. The prize contended for is the LIBERTY OF AMERICA.[47]

For five generations New Englanders had thought of themselves in exclusive terms as a peculiar people. Now they broadened their redemptive horizons to include all American patriots. Washington's liberation confirmed American unity, but success would continue only so long as the patriots remained one, a house united within itself.

While additional occasional sermons amplified the new theme of American union, they did not neglect the traditional refrain of divine providence. Historical occasions were especially well suited to the theme of providential deliverance because they confirmed over centuries the ways in which God saved his people. Samuel Baldwin underscored the continuing belief in providence when, in a sermon commemorating the first landing in Plymouth, he declared that "next to the belief of the being of a God . . . it is of the last importance to such creatures as we are, to be firmly persuaded of his providence." In his April 1776 commemoration of the Battle of Lexington and Concord, Jonas Clarke reiterated the same theme in almost the same words: "Next to the acknowledgement of the existence of a Deity, there is no one principle of greater importance in religion, than a realizing belief of the divine government of providence . . . in whatever happens to mankind, both as nations and kingdoms, and as individuals." When Clarke viewed tragic events like Lexington and Concord through the lens of providential history he understood them as loving reprieves, not final desertion: "Such dispensations, are so far from being an evidence, that God hath forsaken his people, given them up, or forgotten to be gracious, that they are rather to be considered as demonstrations of his paternal care and faithfulness towards them." From the vantage point of April 1776 and Washington's liberation of Boston, it was already apparent that God would eventually take his "vengeance" on English tyrants. At that time, he boasted, the world would see that "*America* shall dwell forever, and *this people* from generation to generation."[48]

By the spring and summer of 1776, events had escalated so dramatically that new weekday occasions were not enough. As in the violent days of King Philip's War, regular sermons were preached with a view to the present crisis. Throughout the summer and winter of 1776, Ebenezer Chaplin of Sutton, Massachusetts, delivered a topical sermon series on "what God has done . . . in the wilderness to and for his people." In all, he recounted eighteen providential deliverances ranging from "Deborah's War" and "Gideon's War" in the wilderness of Canaan, through the founding of New England, and "the success of our Forces thirty years ago against Cape Breton." By Sunday, July 28, 1776, Chaplin completed the series on a triumphant note by recalling the recent victory at Bunker Hill:

> It highly desires to be remembered what signal salvations God has wrought
> for us since the commencement of the present wars with Britain. How won-

derfully God wrought for us at the first when we were raw and naked as to Defense in the several battles on the Islands near Boston and even in the Bunker Hill fight. . . . How wonderfully did God fight for us by his strong wind the night after our People took possession of the Heights of Dorchester in all which the hand of God is most visible.[49]

Again the parallels to earlier sermons on great events are clear. Beneath the apparent natural causes and human agencies, ministers found the hand of God at work orchestrating events to fulfill his providential designs.

More sermons were preached in 1776 than in any previous year in New England's history. In many of these, confidence in divine providence was commingled with readiness for suffering. Alongside such traditional themes was a mounting certainty that all posterity was somehow caught up in the immediate struggle with England. In a sermon on Isaiah 31:1–3, Glastonbury's John Eells brought all these themes together:

Our days of sorrow still remain, and those who once were our friends continue to exert themselves against us without any relaxation of their measures. Deaf to all importunities to the Contrary, they seem inflexibly bent on desolation and war if we will not submit, and constrain us to open resistance for our own Safety. The consequences now—are exceeding great, and the issue thereof will undoubtedly be had in Remembrance to the end of time. Our expectations are big with Something important, we know not how nor when these things will terminate, nor what we have to endure thro' the dreadful Struggle.[50]

Eells's sermon was never published, but it is valuable nonetheless in suggesting how local ministers throughout New England struggled for understanding and prepared their listeners for the "dreadful Struggle" ahead. Words like his gave New Englanders a sense of importance that rivaled the founders. Indeed, the words told them that they too would be founders of a new order and that their actions would be remembered "to the end of time."

KINGLY GOVERNMENT IS NOT AGREEABLE
TO THE DIVINE WILL

When the Continental Congress declared the American colonies' independence from England in 1776, it officially recognized what New Englanders had known for over a year. That declaration did not create a new nation ("America" was now thirteen independent countries bound in a loose confederation), nor did it enjoy the dramatic significance then that it would later assume in American mythology. But it was welcome news to beleaguered New Englanders nonetheless.[51]

Throughout September the Declaration of Independence was read in pulpits across the land and commented on in occasional sermons. On Thursday, September 12, Peter Whitney devoted the public lecture to a reading of the document followed by a sermon on 1 Kings 12:16. By then, the scriptural text recounting the revolt of Israel's ten tribes against oppressive King Rehoboam was familiar to New England congregations throughout the region. Earlier, ministers had claimed that monarchy was not essential to good government. By 1776 they were prepared to say it was wrong. From his text Whitney exploded the old notion of divine right and declared the new political orthodoxy that "kingly government is not agreeable to the divine will, and is often a very great evil." Such was certainly true of George III, as it was of Rehoboam before him. The thirteen "tribes" of America had no choice but "to take to their tents." The verdict of Whig ideology, colonial experience, and scriptural precedent was unanimous: "Independency is, in every view, the interest of America."[52]

At the time Whitney remarked on Independence he did not know what shape the new nation would assume or how thirteen nations could become one. But of one thing he was certain. The new nation would require "new modes of civil government," unlike all European precedents, that would hearken back to the "Jewish Republic" and the early colonial experience of self-rule through popular assemblies. From these precedents he concluded that "the people ought to retain in their own hands a check upon the legislative powers, by having their elections very frequent, at least, once in a year." For further elaboration Whitney referred his listeners to "that incomparable pamphlet called *Common Sense*"—a "runaway best seller" that New England's clergy held in even higher esteem than did many patriot lawyers and statesmen, who were put off by the author's abusive language and faulty constitutional reasoning. It was natural for ministers to value this document more highly than many patriot leaders did because, as John Adams later explained, it undertook "to prove, that Monarchy is unlawful by the Old Testament."[53] Instead of relying on abstract constitutional arguments for republican rule, Paine traced in elaborate detail Israel's "national delusion" in requesting a king like other nations and God's subsequent displeasure at a "form of government which so impiously invades the prerogative of heaven." For all outward appearances, Paine (a deist) sounded like Congregational clergymen when he concluded his history of Israel with the following salvo against monarchy:

> These portions of scripture are direct and positive. They admit of no equivocal construction. That the Almighty hath here entered his protest against monarchical government, is true, or the scripture is false. And a man hath good reason to believe that there is as much of king-craft, as priest-craft, in withholding the scripture from the public in Popish countries. *For monarchy in every instance is the Popery of government.*

With unmitigated disdain Paine attacked the idolatrous "homage" paid to the "royal brute" of England: "How impious is the title of sacred majesty applied to a worm, who in the midst of his splendor is crumbling into dust!"[54] In 1776, Paine's words were even more important than the Declaration of Independence in rallying the American people around a single document that gave focus and hope to their ongoing struggle for independence.

Not surprisingly, militia sermons came the closest to matching the invective and disdain of *Common Sense*. In an unpublished address to the Massachusetts militia delivered after Independence, Malden's Peter Thacher (HC, 1769) attacked the "royal beast" of England in the harshest terms. Thacher had participated in the Battle of Bunker Hill and shared the outrage of New England's soldiery. In words that had quickly become commonplace he reminded the troops that "it was indeed in sore judgment to the Jewish nation that a king was given to them, for kings have been subject to them."[55] From sacred history, Thacher turned to profane history, noting with contempt how

> Alexander ridiculously called the great, in the fury of his ambition traversed the world, carried his army against princes and people who had never injured him and threw away the lives of thousands of his subjects, that, when he was done, he might sit down and *drivel* because he had no more worlds to conquer. What a contemptible opinion doth this give us of human greatness and ambition!

The case was no different in England when Charles I "was most righteously executed for his treason and murders against and upon the people of Great Britain." Nor could any in attendance doubt the righteousness of America's war against George III:

> If it is lawfull for mankind to defend and assert those unalienable rights which God hath given them; if it is lawfull to oppose the attempts of a perjured, faithless tyrant who hath added, with respect to this people, insult to treachery and murder to insult; if it is lawfull to oppose the designs of those who would deprive men of their religious as well as civil libertys; if it is fit to resist those who have slaughtered our friends in cold blood, who have brought ruin, desolation and destruction upon the abodes of peace and plenty; then it is lawfull for us to oppose the armys of George of Britain and then is our cause a just and a righteous cause.

Reports that George III was recruiting German mercenaries so outraged Thacher that his language nearly ran out of control:

> How much superior must American troops ... be to mercenary germans who like cattle are bartered from one prince to an other to serve the purposes of their ambition and who are come to fight for a foreign nation against a people who, never so much as in thought offended them; but it is scarcely worth our while to draw the comparison between freemen and these poor wretches who, speech and a few almost imperceptible senses excepted, scarcely rise in the scale of beings above a state of vegetation.

The prospect of war, Thacher said, was deeply unsettling. But far more horrible was the prospect of a failed revolution. In an updated version of

Jonathan Mayhew's visionary technique, Thacher imagined the scene of
an American defeat for the soldiers in attendance:

> But why doth busy imagination hurry me to a scene still more distressing,
> why doth it transport me to the field of blood, the place of execution for the
> friends of american liberty! Who doth it there call me to view led to the
> scaffold, with the dignity of *Cato*, the firmness of a *Brutus* and the gentleness
> of a *Cicero* in his countenance? It is the gallant *Washington* deserted by his
> countrymen and sacrificed because he loved his Country and fought in its
> defense! Of whom consists yonder group of heroes! It is an *Hancock*, an
> *Adams*, a *Franklin*, a *Lee*, an *Harrison* who—but I drop the curtain, I repress
> the bursting torment, my soul is bowed with unutterable grief!

Such a scene should animate even the most timid souls to fight: "Let us
spring to action, let us gird on the sword of the Lord and of Gideon, and
determine to conquer or die! . . . Do not let us hear of any of you who
behave like cowards."

Aware that his sermon had ranged far from his text, Thacher concluded
by returning to the theme of divine dependence and personal piety that
had been New England's strength for five generations:

> It becomes us all to remember that we depend . . . upon God alone. It is not
> our own sword nor our own bow which must get us the victory. God forbid
> that I should lead you to such a presumptuous confidence! God forbid that
> I should fail urging upon you that repentance and reformation, which, with
> the atonement of Jesus Christ, are necessary in order to avert the divine
> displeasure and secure his favor unto us. If we are saved God alone must
> save us.

Having returned to the ultimate ground of New England's hope, Thacher
closed his sermon with a triumphant benediction drawn from the words
of his text in 2 Samuel 10:12 ("Be of good courage, and let us play the
men for our people") and from New England's sacred legacy: "Can I conclude my address to you without solemnly blessing you in the name of
the god of the fathers of New England! May he be with you as he was
with those illustrious men! May he keep you at all times as in the hallow
of his hand! May he cover your heads in the day of battle and enable you
to play the men for your people and the citys of your God!"

THE BIRTHDAY OF A NEW WORLD

As Thacher's sermon illustrates, war required the strongest sentiments
language could provide and, in New England, this meant apocalyptic
rhetoric as well as lessons from Scripture, history, and experience.
Though moribund since the triumph over France, millennial rhetoric
returned in 1775–1776 as an additional source of incentive and hope.[56]
Prior to Lexington and Concord millennial speculations played no significant part in justifying resistance or in explaining the historic and constitutional grounds of protest; it was not a major topic in regular or occa-

sional preaching, nor was it conspicuous in print. With the onset of war, however, it played a vital role in affirming that the struggle was more than a constitutional dispute; it was part of a foreordained plan to establish a new order for the ages that would prevision, in civil and religious forms, the shape God's millennial kingdom would eventually assume in the fullness of time. The central focus of millennial rhetoric in the Revolution was less the attack on Antichrist than the actual shape of the coming kingdom. America was not the new heavens and the new earth—there were still sinners existing alongside the saints. But it came closer to approximating the future perfect state than any previous society.

Even in 1776, the best guide to the present was still the past, but the future could not be ignored. As ministers shifted the lens of providential history from past to future their thoughts turned to the dazzling possibility of transforming their new republic into a prototype of the new heavens and the new earth. Seen in this light, their revolution was fought not only *against* English tyranny but *for* a new world order. Thomas Paine sounded the heady note when he traced the shape of a republican government and its great promise of global regeneration:

> We have it in our power to begin the world over again. A situation, similar to the present, hath not happened since the days of Noah until now. The birthday of a new world is at hand, and a race of men, perhaps as numerous as all Europe contains are to receive their portion of freedom from the event of a few months. The Reflexion is awful—and in this point of view, How trifling, how ridiculous do the little, paltry cavillings, of a few weak or interested men appear, when weighed against the business of a world.[57]

Few readers—least of all New England's ministers—could ignore the thrilling promise contained in these words. Without the exactness of the first generation, and in a different rhetorical style, they suggested that America was about to inaugurate a millennial destiny prophesied in Scripture and nurtured over one and one-half centuries in the protective womb of New England.

One way for ministers to explain America's future destiny was to continue the pattern of applying double meanings to Scripture texts whose primary reference was to Christ's spiritual kingdom and the church. We have already seen the technique of double applications with terms like "covenant," "liberty," "freedom," or "union." In 1776 the practice was extended to the terms "nation" and "kingdom." In his Plymouth anniversary sermon in December 1776, for example, Sylvanus Conant focused on the word *nation*. Referring to Independence, he declared that

> the step that is taken hath the appearance of a literal accomplishment of one of those scripture prophecies which (if it is to be understood in a literal sense) must sooner or later take place. There is a prophetic query in Isaiah 66:8—*Shall the earth be made to bring forth in one day, or shall a nation be born at once?* If this passage is considered in a spiritual sense, no doubt it hath reference to the speedy, happy, and extraordinary effects of the plen-

tiful effusions of the Holy Spirit. But is there any thing that makes against a more literal fulfillment? If not, it is a question whether any thing has happened for these 1700 years past, that doth so literally and extensively answer this query, as when these thirteen united States, by the voice of their deputies in Congress assembled, were led to declare themselves free and independent of the jurisdiction of Great-Britain, and of all other powers on earth. By this act, we view these States as under no Civil government, laws or authority but their own; and if they Continue free and united, we may, with good propriety, consider them in their united capacity as *a nation born at once.*

For Conant and his listeners, the phrase "a nation born at once" implied far more for Independence than new constitution making. Because of its messianic context in Scripture, it meant that in some sense America, like the Christ foretold in Isaiah's prophecy, would be revelatory and meaning-bearing. To underscore the sense of America-as-revelation Conant, like Samuel Cooper eight months earlier, adopted Moses' encounter with God at the burning bush to describe the world's encounter with America: "Let all Europe, and the whole world turn their eyes this way, and behold, and wonder to see these young *American colonies* set on fire at both ends and the middle, and not consumed."[58]

Besides relying on double meanings, ministers confronted millennial prophecies directly and speculated that they referred to America. Such conjectures were always tentative and never replaced history and the covenant as the bedrock of America's revolution. But they were exhilarating. In contrasting the steady erosion of civil and religious liberties in Europe with the march of freedom in America, Danbury's youthful pastor Ebenezer Baldwin (YC, 1763) openly "conjectured" whether America might become "the Foundation of a great and mighty Empire; the largest the World ever saw." This new empire, Baldwin continued, would "be founded on such Principles of Liberty and Freedom, both civil and religious, as never before took place in the world." It seemed possible to Baldwin that in God's providence America may have been designated as "the principal Seat of that glorious kingdom, which Christ shall erect upon Earth in the latter Days." So admittedly speculative was this last conjecture that Baldwin confided he "had thoughts of suppressing this Conjecture in the Publication of the Sermon."[59] Finally he included it, but on the assumption that his readers recognized its tentative spirit.

The most explicitly millennial sermon to appear in 1776 was Samuel Sherwood's analysis of *The Churche's Flight into the Wilderness* (Revelation 12:14–17). From his text Sherwood speculated that the prophecy of the woman's escape to the wilderness on the wings of an eagle might "have reference to the state of Christ's church, in this American quarter of the globe." If this was so, then "the Beast" who was trying to destroy the woman referred not only to the Roman Catholic Church but also to all declared enemies of God's American people. The powers of Antichrist were "not confined to the boundaries of the Roman empire, nor strictly to the territory of the Pope's usurped authority." Rather, they extended to all enemies of Christ's church and people. In light of this prophecy England's monarchy "appears to have many of the features, and much of the temper and character of the image of the beast." The identification of George III with Antichrist, like resistance to tyranny, was a call to arms. The royal armies of the beast must be destroyed not only to protect liberty and property, but more importantly, to further the cause of Christ's kingdom. War with England, Sherwood hoped, "may possibly be some of the last efforts, and dying struggles of the man of sin."[60]

Millennial speculations like Baldwin's or Sherwood's were important because they completed and confirmed the providential outline of history in which America's revolution was ultimately justified. Unlike the radical Levellers or "Fifth Monarchy Men" in the English Commonwealth, or "Christian" sects in nineteenth-century America who dismissed their past as "dunge and losse," the Revolutionary clergy's millennial vision was built upon tradition and past authorities. When these ministers looked into the future they saw an enlargement and perfection of covenantal patterns they had inherited from their past. In their view, and the view of many of their listeners who took the fasts and covenant promises seriously, the past did not have to be eradicated before the millennium would come; it simply had to be preserved against the scheming designs of ungodly tyrants and antichrists until the end days arrived. It did not really matter to them if those days began in a year or in five hundred years. They could not read God's inscrutable designs, nor could they control the future. All they could do was make sure their way was preserved and passed down to the children. The constant references in Revolutionary sermons to past founders and future "posterity" do not reveal an apocalyptic sect constantly peering over the brink of eternity but a people living in history, by history, and for history. And history, whether considered in personal or national contexts, or whether articulated in civil or religious terms, was preeminently the history of redemption. "Redemption!" Boston's John Bacon exclaimed in 1775, "twas creation more sublime. Redemption!"[61]

NEW ENGLAND'S REVOLUTION AS
AMERICA'S SERMON TO THE WORLD

In tracing the long influence of the sermon on New England culture we have seen how piety, power, and liberty represented a sacred trinity of thought and action that oriented the people's identity and sense of mission over five generations. While each of these themes received major emphases at different times, none was ever emphasized to the exclusion of the others, and in this sense the *lack* of change is the major theme of preaching in Revolutionary New England. Just as the third generation could make the transition from theocratic government to mixed government with surprising ease, so the Revolutionary generation could shift with equal confidence from monarchy to republic because neither form of government demanded their ultimate allegiance. Republican governments, like earlier half-way covenants, religious toleration, and revivals, were merely means to the end of maintaining pure churches and a virtuous people of the Word. Temporal blessings and millennial triumphs would not necessarily come through theocracies, monarchies, or republics; success and power depended on keeping the covenant. After vindicating America's rebellion and extolling the merits of republican liberties, Peter Whitney returned to the question of religion and pure churches that defined New England's identity from the outset:

> Let us be careful to keep up among us, the religion of Jesus Christ pure and uncorrupted by human additions or mixtures, and the worship of God unadulterated, and then God in whom our fathers trusted and were delivered, will delight to build us up, and to plant us. . . . [F]or this vine which the Lord hath planted, shall extend her branches from sea to sea, and from the rivers to the end of the earth. Here shall we enjoy the most peaceful freedom and liberty, while we live, and transmit the same, as a good inheritance, to our children, and they to theirs, 'till time shalbe no more.

Revolution, republican ideology, pure churches, and future millennium all blended in New England preaching, supplying continuity in the midst of change and imparting to the transforming events of 1776 a familiar, atavistic quality.[62]

The religious underpinnings of Revolutionary rhetoric in the New England pulpit help to explain why the momentous shift from constitutional monarchy to republican government occurred as quickly and easily as it did. Other colonies also made the momentous transition but with much greater internal division.[63] New Englanders could take the giant and unprecedented leap from monarchy to republicanism because for them, it was not *that* great a leap; nor, for them, was the Revolution as discontinuous from their past as it seems to us. Throughout the controversy, New England audiences were taught to understand that the ultimate issue in the Revolution was not forms of government but the preservation of God's pure churches and their own piety. In these terms, the Revolutionary generation had more in common with their theocratic and aristocratic Puritan forebearers than with the pagan "republicans" of ancient Greece and Rome.[64] Instead of erasing their past, ministers invoked the founders constantly *as if* they were republicans all along without knowing it. New England's Congregational heritage and the model of Israel were, the ministers reasoned, far more consistent with republican principles than with monarchy.

For New England ministers and many in their congregations, this religious dimension of republicanism was precisely the point of revolution. Revolution and republican governments would enable New Englanders to continue doing what they had done all along. When ministers looked forward to the new republican order, they spent far less time on the constitutional shape of the new governments and considerably more time on the superior piety required of the American people. That faith, and not the "science of politics," would determine if the American republic would succeed where other republics had failed. "We are all thy people," Ebenezer Parkman declared in a fast sermon delivered in 1760 and repeated again in 1777 and 1780: "There is no other [people] that make an open Solemn profession of thy Name, and worship as we do." On that basis, he concluded, "we plead thou wouldst shew us peculiar Regards."[65] The formula was simple, familiar, and pat. Yet behind it was one hundred and fifty years of experience that proved God never deserted a loyal people of the Word. Nor would he fail them in 1776. America had God's promise on that, and soon the whole world would see that God's Word would prevail. New England's revolution would be nothing less than America's sermon to the world.

Epilogue

The transition to independent nationhood and republican government would not be nearly as smooth as the ministers predicted at the height of their Revolutionary fervor. Their "nation born at once" came so quickly that the birth pangs *followed* and led to complications that none could have foreseen. Like the first-generation Puritans, the patriots of 1776 were a new generation of "founders" who could only view the land of promise from afar. Some of the features of this new republican landscape were clear, especially the "sacred cause" of liberty with its political correlate of government by consent. Other, more troublesome implications were obscured by the newness of the territory and the patriots' inability to keep up with the ongoing rush of events. Revolutionary actions overtaxed the capacity of the colonial mind to adjust and committed the participants to a cause whose final destination was unplanned and unknown. In 1776, New England's Congregational ministers could not see much beyond the fact of war with England. The radical implications of republican government were just that—implications whose full meaning would only become apparent in retrospect.[1]

Not surprisingly, the chief source of strength within the new republic—its celebration of liberty—was also the chief source of internal strain and confrontation. The cry of "liberty or death," it soon became apparent, was lifted as easily against habits and traditions *within* American society as it was against outside threats. Like many abstract terms, "liberty" was expansive and contagious; a protean shape whose outline could never be fixed.[2] It threatened to contain as many meanings as there were speakers trumpeting its glories and invoking its protections. Without the restraining mechanisms of monarchies, aristocracies, standing armies, mercantile controls, or state churches, there was no telling how far Americans might go in reforming and restructuring their society, or where it would all end. Institutions which, on the surface, had no direct bearing on the issue of independence were vulnerable to libertarian criticism and condemned; social assumptions that once commanded respect were questioned and

312

replaced by more democratic principles. This revolution, it soon became apparent, involved even more than the widespread reformation envisioned by the ministers; it involved nothing less than a restructuring of institutions on all levels of society. Only gradually, and with great discomfort, did New England's ministers realize that they had helped create an engine for change and reformation that they ultimately could not control. Unwittingly, their libertarian rhetoric laid the basis for their own demise as the single voice of authority in their local communities.

For New England's clergy, the most frightening aspect of the internal revolution accompanying independence from England was a loss of mastery. In 1776 Congregational ministers still dominated public communications throughout New England and they continued to enjoy state support. But their hold was precarious. Belatedly they saw themselves threatened by other speakers in New England and in other "states" who held very different beliefs about the compatibility of established religion and republican ideology. In the middle states there was no single church that enjoyed the majority status of Congregational churches in New England and, by necessity, these citizens adopted laws and policies guaranteeing religious freedom long before Independence. In the South, the colonial Anglican Church enjoyed a privileged position similar to that of the New England Congregationalists, but it was so compromised by its loyalism in the Revolution that it would not recover for a generation. In neither region was there a group of clergymen even remotely comparable to the Congregational clergy in numbers, social prestige, education, and the ability to dominate public speech in local settings. Other, more powerful voices dominated in these regions and called for a complete separation of church and state. Through these cries for the disestablishment of religion, New England's ministers glimpsed a new social system that would deprive them of the exalted position they had hoped to preserve in first counseling resistance and revolution.

Even more threatening than voices outside of New England were voices for religious liberty within New England society. While a loose coalition of Quakers, Anglicans, Baptists, and Deists could not formally abolish religious taxes until the second decade of the nineteenth century, their criticisms of New England's Congregational "establishment" placed the ministers on notice that their days of privileged position were numbered. For these "dissenters," the Revolution had a "double aspect"; it meant an end to British "enslavement" and also an end to the special and "arbitrary" privileges enjoyed by the Congregational majority. Already in 1777 the Warren Association of Baptists employed the rhetoric of republicanism to condemn the idea of tax-supported churches:

> We are far from desiring to conceal or undervalue, the civil privileges which we have long enjoyed; but verily think they have been as great in New-England, as in any part of the world. And our denomination have as readily and vigorously joined of late in the general defense of them, as any others have. Yet how can any person lift up his head before God or man, in resist-

ing a power that would tax us where we are not represented, while himself doth the same thing![3]

Charges like these had been voiced for generations before in New England, but now they took on new meaning and urgency as Americans struggled to come to grips with the implications of their republican ideology. In justifying rebellion, the Congregational clergy had not intended to disestablish their churches or restrict their voices to matters of religion and the soul; yet that is exactly what happened as the logic of the Revolution pressed on in its relentless course of reform and reconstruction.

The internal criticism unleashed by republican rhetoric did not end with religious disestablishment. Other institutions and assumptions sustained equally harsh condemnation. Of these, the most important was the institution of slavery. While New England's ministers were a step behind most of their countrymen in questions of church and state, they pushed beyond most in their attacks on slavery. No single figure in New England did more in word and deed to attack the slave system and point out the inconsistencies of slavery and republican rhetoric than Samuel Hopkins. In a widely circulated address to the Continental Congress in 1776, he singled out the "very great and public sin" of slavery that "must be reformed before we can reasonably expect deliverance, or even sincerely ask for it." Failure to resist the sin of slavery was as sinful as slaveholding itself: "We, by refusing to break this yoke and let these injured captives go free, do practically justify and support this slavery in general, and make ourselves, in measure at least, answerable for the whole; and we have no way to exculpate ourselves from the guilt of the whole . . . but by freeing all our slaves." Ministers in particular were guilty of tyranny if they were silent about slavery because "they are commanded to lift up their voice, and cry aloud, and show the people their sins." Of these sins, Hopkins concluded, none were more "cruel" or "shocking" than slavery.[4]

While Hopkins was the most forthright and diligent in his opposition to slavery, he did not stand alone. As early as 1773 James Allen confronted his Boston listeners with the blatant contradictions between slavery and the liberties they sought for themselves:

> Blush ye pretended votaries of freedom! Ye trifling patriots! who are making a vain parade of being the advocates of your profession by trampling on the sacred natural rights and privileges of the *Africans*; for while you are fasting, praying, non-importing, and non-exporting, remonstrating, resolving, and pleading for a restoration of your charter rights, you at the same time are continuing this lawless, cruel, inhuman, and abominable practice of enslaving your fellow-creatures.

Nathaniel Niles underscored the same theme when he warned in a sermon on liberty that if America did not repent of the sin of slavery it might well suffer at the hands of a righteous God:

> God gave us liberty, and we have enslaved our fellow-men. May we not fear that the law of retaliation is about to be executed on us? What can we object against it? What excuse can we make for our conduct? What reason

can we urge why our oppression shall not be repaid in kind? Should the Africans see God Almighty subjecting us to all the evils we have brought on them, and should they cry to us, O daughter of America who art to be destroyed. . . . how could we object? How could we resent it? Would we enjoy liberty? Then we must grant it to others.[5]

Sermons like these illustrate the revolutionary power of libertarian rhetoric to call into question colonial institutions and to expose the gap between the ideal of freedom trumpeted in press and pulpit and the brute facts of life in American society. America's revolution, it became clear, had a long way to go before ever being complete.

Significantly, the ministers were defeated both in their efforts to avoid disestablishment and in their campaign to eradicate slavery. And herein lies a clue to what was perhaps the most radical and far-reaching transformation of all: the weakening of deference and the theory of fixed hierarchy on which it rested. Ministers, like other well-born patriot leaders, went into the Revolution and new republic persuaded that the people would continue to defer to their betters. They were mistaken. New groups with self-appointed "popular" spokesmen appeared everywhere in voluntary religious, civic, and political organizations, challenging and overturning the idea of rule by a traditional gentlemanly elite. Institutionalized deference, it soon became clear, required some external restraint or "mixed" constitution that could police the social order and preserve the "equipoise" of leaders and followers, superiors and inferiors. Once these centers of authority were removed and sovereignty relocated among the people, there was no limit to how often the people might change their minds, or whom they might elevate to positions of authority in church and state. With the end of the War for Independence came the beginning of America's "second revolution." As the radical patriot Benjamin Rush explained in 1787, "The American war is over: but this is far from being the case with the American revolution. On the contrary, nothing but the first act of the great drama is closed."[6]

In responding to attacks on traditional social order posed by republican rhetoric, New England's established clergy divided. The long truce between rationalists and evangelicals ended, and churches split into opposing and irreconcilable camps, each invoking their Congregational liberties. In the end, they both suffered. Rationalists sought futilely to turn back the tide of "democracy" by reiterating the duty of deference and moving closer to a religion of reason and enlightened order. Their Unitarian churches won the enthusiastic support of educated elites and control of Harvard College, but they failed to reach a larger audience.[7] Evangelical Congregationalists continued the themes of revival and New Birth that first won them public favor. But their enthusiastic regard for lay liberty, voluntary organization, and extemporaneous speech encouraged rival religious movements who, in the name of republicanism, severed all ties to the past and inaugurated new denominations whose only acknowledged authority was each individual's untutored reading of Scripture.

By the early decades of the nineteenth century, new "Christian move-

ments," proclaiming an "egalitarian religion," replaced Congregationalism as the driving force in the evangelical tradition.[8] Unlike their Puritan
predecessors, the new evangelicals had no colonial or European past they
wanted to emulate. Instead they incorporated into their theology and
sociology the new American gospel that change was, by definition,
change for the better. This transition to an antihistorical individualistic
faith was piecemeal and uneven, but it marked the start of "modernization" in religion that would be every bit as transforming as the changes
taking place in politics and society.

And what, in all this transformation and ferment, became of the sermon? On the level of regular salvation preaching, little had changed.
Revivals, awakenings, and programs for moral reform proliferated in the
new republic and gained strength from the voluntary ethos that suffused
all institutions. But on a civil and corporate level, much had changed. The
separation of church and state together with the new orthodoxy of inviolable individual rights meant that the sermon, in its occasional form as a
coercive ritual of social order, could not survive the transition to independent nationhood. In the colonial era election sermons were limited to
New England, and there they limped into the nineteenth century and
gradually disappeared, going the way of Oliver Wendell Holmes's "one
hoss shay." Fast sermons also survived for a time, but again as mere shadows of their former selves. The American people, it was clear, were bound
by ties of common ideology, not a common religious faith. In place of the
occasional sermon other, more secular rituals emerged to organize, direct,
and revitalize the collective ideals of the community and the nation.
Fourth of July orations, inaugural ceremonies, and Memorial Day observances did for the American republic what fast and election sermons had
done for colonial New England.

But even as the occasional sermon disappeared, its rhetoric lives on.
Whether they recognized it or not, new generations of civic orators, historians, writers, and poets inherited a vocabulary of mission and meaning
that drew heavily from the thousands of Puritan sermons that preceded
them and survived in print. Quite simply, there were no other distinc-
tively American rhetorical models to follow. The language of destiny, liberty, purity, desertion, and redemption lives on and testifies to the astonishing tenacity of the Puritan vision to shine before a world trembling in
darkness. The pews remain filled; there is no shortage of speakers; the
errand endures.

Notes

Introduction

1. For a sampling of research in modern communications theory, see *Daedalus*, 111 (1982).

2. That the terms *Puritan* and *New England* are often used interchangeably illustrates the power of Puritan ideas on New England society. In this book *Puritan* refers to those people organized in Congregational churches.

3. Statistics on church founding and ministers appear in Frederick Lewis Weis, *The Colonial Clergy and the Colonial Churches of New England* (Lancaster, Mass., 1936).

4. I have estimated the number of sermons preached in 17th-and 18th-century New England by computing the total number of years preached by all the Congregational ministers and multiplying by 100 (an average of two sermons per week). It might be helpful to compare these sermon attendance figures with the number of hours the modern college undergraduate spends in lectures. After four years of full-time course work, a college student will have sat through something like 1,500 hours of classroom instruction—a figure representing only 10 % of the total number of hours regular churchgoers sat through sermons in the course of their lifetimes.

5. See especially Perry Miller, *The New England Mind: From Colony to Province* (Boston, 1953), foreword. Miller's primary sources for *The New England Mind: The Seventeenth Century* (New York, 1939) were almost exclusively printed. They are reproduced in James Hoopes, ed., *Sources for the New England Mind: The Seventeenth Century* (Williamsburg, Va., 1981).

6. On the Revolutionary era, see chapter 14 in this study. Printed sermons were not automatically occasional sermons. Regular sermons were also printed with some regularity, especially before the Revolutionary era, and for ease of reference I have cited them wherever possible in my discussion of regular preaching.

7. The clearest indication that congregations understood sermons in terms that were similar to the ministers' appears in surviving lay sermon notes that correspond point for point with the manuscript notes of the minister. These lay sermon notes are cited throughout the text.

8. The reader will find some necessary overlapping in the following chapters, particularly among long-lived ministers whose careers spanned two generations, but in general I have followed this organizing sequence throughout the book.

9. For summaries of classical (Ciceronian) rhetoric see R. R. Bolgar, *The Classical Heritage and Its Beneficiaries* (Cambridge, Mass., 1954); Edward P. J. Corbett, *Classical Rhetoric for the Modern Reader* (New York, 1965); and George A. Kennedy, *Classical Rhetoric and Its Christian and Secular Tradition: From Ancient to Modern Times* (Chapel Hill, N.C., 1980).

10. The definitions are taken from Marcus Tullius Cicero, *De Inventione* (Cambridge, Mass., 1949), 19–21.

11. See chapter 13 in this study.

12. See, e.g., Bernard Bailyn, *The Ideological Origins of the American Revolution* (Cambridge, Mass., 1967); Nathan O. Hatch, *The Sacred Cause of Liberty: Republican Thought and the Millennium in Revolutionary New England* (New Haven, Conn., 1977); or Alfred F. Young, ed., *The American Revolution* (DeKalb, Ill., 1976).

13. For an analysis of New England's dominant role in the new nation in social, economic, and literary terms see Peter Dobkin Hall, *The Organization of American Culture, 1700–1900: Private Institutions, Elites, and the Origins of American Nationality* (New York, 1982).

Chapter 1

1. Winthrop's *Arabella* sermon, "A Modell of Christian Charity," is reprinted in *Winthrop Papers*, 4 vols., II (Boston, 1931), 282–95.

2. The process of erecting meetinghouses is described in Ola E. Winslow, *Meetinghouse Hill, 1630–1783* (New York, 1952), 50–65. Figures on church construction are compiled in Peter Benes and Phillip Zimmerman, *New England Meeting House and Church, 1630–1850* (Boston, 1979).

3. The Puritans' rejection of ornamented, "witty" preaching in the manner of "metaphysical" Anglican preachers like Lancelot Andrews or John Donne is well known. For descriptions of the Puritan "plain style" see William Haller, *The Rise of Puritanism* (New York, 1938), 128–72; and John F. Wilson, *Pulpit in Parliament: Puritanism during the English Civil Wars, 1640–1648* (Princeton, N.J., 1969), 137–65.

4. New England's mission to invent a way of "nonseparating Congregationalism" is developed extensively in Perry Miller, *Orthodoxy in Massachusetts, 1630–1650* (orig. publ. 1933; reprinted New York, 1970), 73–101. The millennial implications of national reform are traced in Katharine R. Firth, *The Apocalyptic Tradition in Reformation Britain, 1530–1645* (New York, 1979).

5. John Cotton, "Letter from Mr. Cotton to Lord Say and Sele in the Year 1636," reprinted in Perry Miller and Thomas H. Johnson, eds., *The Puritans: A Sourcebook of Their Writings*, rev. ed. in 2 vols. (New York, 1963), I, 209; and *God's Promise to His Plantation* (1630; reprinted Boston, 1686), 17. Cotton's famous sermon is summarized in Everett H. Emerson, *John Cotton* (New York, 1965), 52–53; and Alan Heimert and Andrew Delbanco, eds., *The Puritans in America: A Narrative Anthology* (Cambridge, Mass., 1985), 75–76.

6. John Cotton, *An exposition upon the 13th Chapter of the Revelation* (London, 1656), reprinted in Miller and Johnson, eds., *The Puritans*, I, 212–14. The political implications of this principle—especially in regard to theories of divine right monarchy—were, for reasons of expediency, ignored in official explanations of the New England Way.

7. John Winthrop, "Arbitrary Government Described" (1644), reprinted in Robert C. Winthrop, *Life and Letters of John Winthrop*, 2 vols. (Boston, 1866), II, 440.

8. *The Cambridge Platform* (1648), reprinted in Williston Walker, ed., *The Creeds and Platforms of Congregationalism* (New York, 1893), 234–37.

9. Thomas Hooker, *A Survey of the Summe of Church-Discipline* (London, 1648; reprinted New York, 1972), 79. The autonomy and "sufficiency" of Independent congregations, as Connecticut's magisterial founder, Thomas Hooker, explained, was never intended to issue in an exclusivistic "absolute supremacy" that arrogantly isolated one church from another. Though formally independent, Congregational churches were established in the New World as part of a common mission and depended upon one another for mutual support and "edification." In cases of irreconcilable divisions within a particular congregation or in cases of great mutual concern, the elders were authorized to assemble in collective "synods" to supply "direction and determinations" that individual congregations were to receive with "reverence and submission." *The Cambridge Platform* was itself the product of a synod called to draw up a general statement of Congregational polity that could guide individual congregations. At the same time, however, such synods were not empowered to "exercise Church-censures in way of discipline, nor any other act of church-authority or jurisdiction," for this would be to intrude on congregational autonomy. John Winthrop recorded numerous meetings between ministers and magistrates in the first years of settlement. See, e.g., James Kendall Hosmer, ed., *Winthrop's Journal "History of New England," 1630–1649*, 2 vols. (New York, 1908), I, 60, 66, 71, 74, 128. The evolution of clerical associations is described in Robert Scholz, "Clerical Consociation in Massachusetts Bay: Reassessing the New England Way and Its Origins," *William and Mary Quarterly*, 29 (1972), 391–414.

10. The Puritans' use of the covenant to explain salvation in the covenant of grace and social order in the federal covenant went back to John Calvin and the Marian exiles who studied at Geneva and transmitted Calvin's teachings back to England. For brief accounts of covenant theology in Puritan thought see Leonard J. Trinterud, "The Origins of Puritanism," *Church History*, 20 (1951), 37–57; Jens G. Møller, "The Beginnings of Puritan Covenant Theology," *Journal of Ecclesiastical History*, 14 (1963), 46–67; John von Rohr, "Covenant and Assurance in Early English Puritanism," *Church History*, 34 (1965), 195–203; and Richard L. Greaves, "The Origins and Early Development of English Covenant Thought," *Historian*, 31 (1968), 21–35. More recently, Michael McGiffert has clarified the linkages between Puritan covenant thought and John Calvin and the continental reformers in three important articles: "Covenant, Crown, and Commons in Elizabethan Puritanism," *Journal of British Studies*, 20 (1980), 32–52; "William Tyndale's Conception of Covenant," *Journal of Ecclesiastical History*, 32 (1981), 167–84; and "Grace and Works: The Rise and Division of Covenant Divinity in Elizabethan Puritanism," *Harvard Theological Review*, 75 (1982), 463–502.

11. Cotton's sermon is reprinted in Larzer Ziff, ed., *John Cotton on the Churches of New England* (Cambridge, Mass., 1968), 41–68. Richard Mather used the same text to defend covenanted churches in *Church-Government and Church-Covenant Discussed* (London, 1643).

12. John Winthrop, "Letter from Governor Winthrop to the Rev. Henry Painter" (1635), reprinted in Winthrop, *Life and Letters of John Winthrop*, II, 416–17.

13. The Salem covenant is reprinted in Walker, ed., *The Creeds and Platforms of Congregationalism*, 116. The Charlestown-Boston church covenant (reprinted *ibid.*,

131) was a more detailed version of Salem's: "In the Name of our Lord Jesus Christ, and in Obedience to His holy will and Divine Ordinance. Wee whose names are hereunder written, being by His most wise, and good Providence brought together into this part of America in the Bay of Massachusetts, and desirous to unite our selves into one Congregation, or Church, under the Lord Jesus Christ our Head, in such sort as becometh all those whom he hath Redeemed, and sanctifyed to Himselfe, do hereby solemnly, and religiously (as in His most holy Proesence) Promisse, and bind ourselves to walke in all our wayes according to the Rule of the Gospell, and in all sincere Conformity to His holy Ordinaunces, and in mutuall love, and respect each to other, so neere as God shall give us grace." The process of self-examination and mutual testimony that preceded public covenanting is described in great detail in the records kept by the first minister, John Allin. See Don Gleason Hill, ed., *Early Records of the Town of Dedham*, 6 vols. (Dedham, Mass., 1886–1936), II, 1–21. See also Kenneth Lockridge, *A New England Town: The First Hundred Years, Dedham, Massachusetts, 1636–1736* (New York, 1970), 24–30.

14. The extent to which Puritan ideas regarding Congregational polity and the requirement of regenerate membership accompanied the Puritans to the New World or were borrowed from Plymouth Colony after their arrival is a matter of some debate. Contrast, e.g., Miller, *Orthodoxy in Massachusetts* with Larzer Ziff, "The Salem Puritans in the 'Free Aire' of a New World," *Huntington Library Quarterly*, 20 (1957), 373–84. At least in the case of regenerate membership, the requirement seems to have been invented after the Puritans' arrival in the New World. See Edmund S. Morgan, *Visible Saints: The History of a Puritan Idea* (New York, 1963). For a general discussion see David D. Hall's introduction to Miller, *Orthodoxy in Massachusetts*.

15. *The Cambridge Platform*, 205–06. In a sermon on church order, Windsor's John Warham pointed out that the principle of leniency in matters of admission ought not to be "sertayne grace" but "charitable grace": "to expect eminency for admission is too much. The strong must beare with the weake. The house is a house and all Stones are not big ones." John Warham, "Sermon on 1 Corinthians 1:2," Aug. 15, 1647, in Jessie A. Parsons, trans., "Mathew Grant Diary," Manuscript Collections, 1 vol., Connecticut State Library, Hartford.

16. *The Cambridge Platform*, 210–14.

17. On the significance of print as an agent of change in 17th-century European and American contexts see: Elizabeth Eisenstein, *The Printing Press as an Agent of Change: Communications and Cultural Transformations in Early Modern Europe*, 2 vols. (Cambridge, Mass., 1979); and Harry S. Stout, "Word and Order in Colonial New England," in Nathan O. Hatch and Mark A. Noll, eds., *The Bible in America: Essays in Cultural History* (New York, 1982), 19–38.

18. John Cotton, *An exposition upon the 13th Chapter of the Revelation*, 212–14. In *The Keys of the Kingdom of Heaven* (1644), reprinted in Ziff, ed., *John Cotton on the Churches of New England*, 82, Cotton described the balancing and mutual limitation of power between ministers and congregations as a "mixed" government or "middle way" between a leveling "democracy," where congregations claimed all power for themselves, and an oligarchy, where all power belonged to the officers: "Thus by means of this due and golden balancing and poising of power and interest, in elders and brethren, this government might neither degenerate into lordliness and oppression in rulers over their flocks . . . nor yet into anarchy and confusion in the flock among themselves. "Cotton's writings on church doctrine

were considered by his colleagues to have the force of official statements. See James F. Cooper, " 'A Mixed Form': Church Government in Massachusetts Bay, 1629–1645" (M.A. thesis, University of Connecticut, 1983).

19. Similar objections were raised by a "presbyterian" faction in New England. See chapter 3 in this study.

20. *The Cambridge Platform,* 237.

21. The biblical context of New England law codes is discussed in George Lee Haskins, *Law and Authority in Early Massachusetts: A Study in Transition and Design* (New York, 1960); and Stephen Botein, *Early American Law and Society* (New York, 1983), 18–30.

22. Roger Williams, *The Bloudy Tenent of Persecution for Cause of Conscience* (1644), reprinted in Miller and Johnson, eds., *The Puritans,* I, 216; John Cotton, *The Bloudy Tenent, Washed, and made White in the bloud of the Lamb,* reprinted *ibid.,* 218.

23. "Reply to a Letter of Many Ministers in Old England, requesting the Judgement of their Reverend Brethren in New England, 1639," reprinted in Benjamin Hanbury, comp., *Historical Memorials Relating to the Independents or Congregationalists: From their Rise to the Restoration of the Monarchy,* 3 vols. (London, 1839–44), II, 20.

24. Edmund S. Morgan, *The Puritan Dilemma: The Story of John Winthrop* (Boston, 1958), 84–100.

25. "Thomas Shepard's Election Sermon in 1638," reprinted in *New England Historical and Genealogical Register,* 24 (1970), 363. See also John Winthrop, "Speech to the General Court" (1645), reprinted in Winthrop, *Life and Letters of John Winthrop,* II, 340: "It is yourselves who have called us to this office, and being called by you, we have our authority from God, in way of an ordinance, such as hath the image of God eminently stamped upon it, the contempt and violation whereof hath been vindicated with examples of divine vengeance."

26. The process of town formation is described in Lockridge, *A New England Town,* 3–22; Philip J. Greven, *Four Generations: Population, Land and Family in Colonial Andover, Massachusetts* (Ithaca, N.Y., 1970), 21–99; and Bruce C. Daniels, *The Connecticut Town: Growth and Development, 1635–1790* (Middletown, Conn., 1979), 64–93. An exception to the pattern of equitable distribution was Springfield, Mass., where the Pynchon family owned most of the best land. See Stephen Innes, *Labor in a New Land: Economy and Society in Seventeenth-Century Springfield* (Princeton, N.J., 1983).

27. On the importance of local government see T. H. Breen, "Persistent Localism: English Social Change and the Shaping of New England Institutions," *William and Mary Quarterly,* 32 (1975), 24–27; Kenneth Lockridge and Alan Kreider, "The Evolution of Massachusetts Town Government, 1640–1740," *ibid.,* 23 (1966), 560–65; David Grayson Allen, *In English Ways: The Movement of Societies and the Transferal of English Local Law and Custom to Massachusetts Bay in the Seventeenth Century* (Chapel Hill, N.C., 1981); and Daniels, *The Connecticut Town,* 64–93. All of these studies demonstrate the similarity of English town and county orientations and New England's local orientation. Left understated is the extent to which principles of local sovereignty flowed as much from covenant assumptions as they did from Old World familiarity. New Englanders copied English practices only to the extent that they conformed to covenant assumptions.

28. See T. H. Breen, "English Origins and New World Development: The Case

of the Covenanted Militia in Seventeenth-Century Massachusetts," *Past and Present*, 57 (1972), 74–96.

29. See Larzer Ziff, "The Social Bond of Church Covenant," *American Quarterly*, 10 (1958), 454–62.

30. See, e.g., John Winthrop, "Speech to the General Court," 341; or John Cotton, *The True Constitution of a Particular Visible Church* (London, 1642), reprinted in Handbury, comp., *Historical Memorials*, II, 182. Puritan conceptions of the family are summarized in Edmund Morgan, *The Puritan Family: Religion and Domestic Relations in Seventeenth-Century New England* (orig. publ. 1944; reprinted New York, 1966); and James T. Johnson, "The Covenant Idea and the Puritan View of Marriage," *Journal of the History of Ideas*, 32 (1971), 107–18.

31. See, especially, Philip J. Greven, *The Protestant Temperament: Patterns of Child-Rearing, Religious Experience, and the Self in Early America* (New York, 1977).

32. John Winthrop, "Letter from Governor Winthrop to the Rev. Henry Painter," 417.

33. On New England's social stability see T. H. Breen and Stephen Foster, "The Puritans' Greatest Achievement: A Study of Social Cohesion in Seventeenth-Century Massachusetts," *Journal of American History*, 60 (1973), 5–22. New England's low mobility rates are discussed in several demographic studies. In Andover, e.g., 78 % of second-generation settlers remained in the same town their fathers had settled. In Dedham, Kenneth Lockridge observes that "from 1648 to 1700, decade after decade the inflexible rule was continuity." See Greven, *Four Generations*, 39; and Kenneth A. Lockridge, "The Population of Dedham, Massachusetts, 1686–1736," *Economic History Review*, 19 (1966), 322–23.

34. The process by which English Puritans came to accept both covenant logics and to reconcile them to one another is described in McGiffert, "Grace and Works," 463–502.

35. For summaries of the Antinomian controversy see David D. Hall, ed., *The Antinomian Controversy, 1636–1638: A Documentary History* (Middletown, Conn., 1968), introduction; and Emery Battis, *Saints and Sectaries: Anne Hutchinson and the Antinomian Controversy in the Massachusetts Bay Colony* (Chapel Hill, N.C., 1962).

36. John Cotton, *A Treatise on the Covenant of Grace* (London, 1671), 37–38. For summary discussions of Cotton's emphasis on free grace in matters of conversion, see Norman Pettit, *The Heart Prepared: Grace and Conversion in Puritan Spiritual Life* (New Haven, Conn., 1966), 138; Jesper Rosenmeier, "New England's Perfection: The Image of Adam and the Image of Christ in the Antinomian Crisis, 1634 to 1638," *William and Mary Quarterly*, 27 (1970), 435–59; James Fulton Maclear "'The Heart of New England Rent': The Mystical Element in Early Puritan History," *Mississippi Valley Historical Review*, 42 (1956), 621–52; Larzer Ziff, *Puritanism in America: New Culture in a New World* (New York, 1973); and William B. K. Stoever, *"A Faire and Easie Way to Heaven": Covenant Theology and Antinomianism in Early Massachusetts* (Middletown, Conn., 1978). All of these studies point out Cotton's rejection of any covenant "conditions" prior to the covenant of grace. At the same time, however, Cotton never questioned the doctrines of sanctification or *Sola Scriptura*, and on that basis he made his peace with the New England Way.

37. Hosmer, ed., *Winthrop's Journal*, I, 234. The feminist implications of the Antinomian controversy are discussed in Lyle Koehler, "The Case of the American Jezebels: Anne Hutchinson and Female Agitation during the Years of the Antinomian Turmoil, 1636–1640," *William and Mary Quarterly* 31 (1974), 55–78. For

a discussion of Hutchinson's distinctive use of the Geneva Bible in her defense see Stout, "Word and Order in Colonial New England."

38. Hall, ed., *The Antinomian Controversy*, 57. Cotton later issued a formal disavowal of his involvement in Antinomianism in *The Way of the Congregational Churches Cleared* (London, 1648), reprinted in Ziff, ed., *John Cotton on the Churches of New England*, 234–57. On Cotton's "adjusted" outlook see Sacvan Bercovitch, *The Puritan Origins of the American Self* (New Haven, Conn., 1975), 93–94.

39. In general, historians like Emery Battis and Lyle Koehler have overstated the social impact of the Antinomian crisis. For the most part, the Hutchinsonian "contagion" never spread beyond the immediate Boston area, and once Cotton came out in opposition to Hutchinson it died out there as well. See Stephen Foster, "New England and the Challenge of Heresy, 1630–1660: The Puritan Crisis in Transatlantic Perspective," *William and Mary Quarterly*, 38 (1981), 624–60.

40. Peter Bulkeley, *The Gospel-Covenant; or the Covenant of Grace Opened*, 2d ed. (London, 1651), 16.

41. The evolution of fast and thanksgiving sermons in colonial New England is summarized in W. D. Love, *The Fast and Thanksgiving Days of New England* (Boston, 1895), 1–101.

42. John Warham, "Sermon on Numbers 16:44–50," Jan. 23, 1639, in Douglas H. Shepard, "The Wolcott Shorthand Notebooks Transcribed" (Ph.D. diss., Iowa State University, 1957), 131.

43. Thomas Hooker, "Sermon on 1 Samuel 7:12," Oct. 4, 1638, in Parsons, trans., "Mathew Grant Diary," 65.

44. The election day setting is described in A. W. Plumstead, ed., *The Wall and the Garden: Selected Massachusetts Election Sermons, 1670–1775* (Minneapolis, Minn., 1968), 3–37.

45. The first mention of an election sermon is John Cotton's 1634 address, for which there is no surviving manuscript. By 1637 the practice of delivering the sermon was well established. From 1634 to 1658 the Massachusetts election sermon was delivered at Boston's First Church and following that at the Boston Town House. The literature on election sermons is immense, but for general introductions see Plumstead, ed., *The Wall and the Garden*, 3–37; Lindsay Swift, "The Massachusetts Election Sermons," Colonial Society of Massachusetts, *Transactions*, 1 (1892–94), 388–451 (published Boston, 1895); Bernard C. Steiner, ed., "Statistics of the Connecticut Election Sermons," *New England Historical and Genealogical Register*, 46 (1892), 123–26; or Marvin X. Lesser, "All for Profit: The Plain Style and the Massachusetts Election Sermons in the Seventeenth Century" (Ph.D. diss., Columbia University, 1967), 80–148. For a listing of election sermon preachers and titles see Robert W. G. Vail, "A Check List of New England Election Sermons," American Antiquarian Society, *Publications*, 45 (1935), 233–66.

46. On the cultural significance of public dramas as enactments of social order and authority see Rhys Isaac, *The Transformation of Virginia, 1740–1790* (Chapel Hill, N.C., 1982); and Clifford Geertz, *The Interpretation of Cultures* (New York, 1973). Old world customs and pageantry are described in Sydney Anglo, *Pageantry and Early Tudor Policy* (Oxford, 1969).

47. Plumstead, ed., *The Wall and the Garden*, 35.

48. The first printed election sermons were John Norton's 1661 address, *Sion the Out-Cast healed of her Wounds* (Cambridge, 1664); and John Higginson's 1663 sermon, *The Cause of God and His People in New England* (Cambridge, 1663).

49. "Thomas Shepard's Election Sermon in 1638," 366.

Chapter 2

1. For examples of works that describe the overlap of lay and ministerial thought see, e.g.: David D. Hall, "The World of Print and Collective Mentality in Seventeenth-Century New England," in John Higham and Paul Conkin, eds., *New Directions in American Intellectual History* (Baltimore, 1979), 166–80; Charles Hambrick-Stowe, *The Practice of Piety: Puritan Devotional Literature in Seventeenth-Century New England* (Chapel Hill, N.C., 1982); George Selement, "The Meeting of Elite and Popular Minds at Cambridge, New England, 1638–1645," *William and Mary Quarterly*, 41 (1984), 32–48; and David D. Hall, "Toward a History of Popular Religion in Early New England," *ibid.*, 41 (1984), 49–55. In *The Practice of Piety*, Hambrick-Stowe confirms how the Puritan laity had a mind—and faith—of its own, but he understates how dependent popular faith was on years of weekly sermon hearing.

2. John Davenport, *God's Call to His People* (Cambridge, 1669), 7. On New England literacy, see Kenneth A. Lockridge, *Literacy in Colonial New England: An Enquiry into the Social Context of Literacy in the Early Modern West* (New York, 1974); and David D. Hall, "The Uses of Literacy in New England, 1600–1850," in William L. Joyce *et al.*, eds., *Printing and Society in Early America* (Worcester, Mass., 1983), 1–47.

3. For a listing of one first-generation minister's library, see Alfred C. Potter, "Catalogue of John Harvard's Library," Colonial Society of Massachusetts, *Transactions*, 21 (1919), 190–230; and the supplement to Potter, Henry J. Cadbury, "John Harvard's Library," *ibid.*, 34 (1943), 393–77.

4. In 1640, for example, Thomas Shepard began a sermon series on the Ten Commandments. At the end of a year he had only gotten through the first four. See Thomas Shepard, "Sermons on the Ten Commandments," 1640, Shepard Family Papers, oct. vol. I, AAS. In Boston, John Norton preached a sermon series on Canticles 2:9 to 5:1 that covered two and one-half years from 1657 to 1660. See John Hull, "Sermon Notes, 1657–1660," Gratz Collection, Box 1, HSP.

5. Recognition of high literacy rates in New England should not obscure the fact that the inhabitants occupied an "aural" world where most communications traveled by word of mouth in face-to-face social settings. What seems like endless repetition and tedious word splitting to modern readers was, to colonials, a necessary means of storing systematic doctrines in their memories.

6. John Rayner, "Sermon on 1 Corinthians 3:11," 1657, in Parsons, trans., "Mathew Grant Diary," 40.

7. On the significance of Puritan diaries and autobiographies, see Daniel B. Shay, Jr., *Spiritual Biography in Early America* (Princeton, N.J., 1968).

8. Thomas Shepard, *Journal*, in Michael McGiffert, ed., *God's Plot: The Paradoxes of Puritan Piety; Being the Autobiography and Journal of Thomas Shepard* (Amherst, Mass., 1972), 96. In his introduction, McGiffert describes the ongoing search for salvation as a process of "renewed conversions" (p. 26).

9. *Ibid.*, 104, 113.

10. *Ibid.*, 110, 111.

11. *Ibid*, 110.

12. *Ibid.*, 165. In *Moral Philosophy at Seventeenth-Century Harvard: A Discipline in Transition* (Chapel Hill, N.C., 1981), Norman Fiering traces the distinctions between a head-centered "intellectualist" tradition and a heart-centered "voluntarist" tradition. Both traditions appeared in 17th-century New England preaching and did not erupt into open divisions among the clergy until the 18th century.

(See chapter 10 in this book.) Besides Shepard, see John Warham, "Sermon on John 7:36–37," June 27, 1652, in Parsons, trans., "Mathew Grant Diary," 84, where Warham first describes "historical faith" and head-knowledge, and then moves to the work of the Holy Spirit: "No man can discover Christ to ye sowle [through reason], but God and Christ himsilfe. Christ must discover himsilfe Intuitously."

13. McGiffert, ed., *God's Plot*, 157, 166–67.

14. Reformed confessions of faith and catechisms are discussed in Philip Schaff, *The Creeds of Christendom*, 6th ed. (New York, 1931), I; T. F. Torrance, ed., *The School of Faith* (London, 1959); and James Axtell, *The School Upon a Hill: Education and Society in Colonial New England* (New Haven, Conn., 1974), 36–44. Thomas Shepard often preached through John Calvin's catechism, which was appended to the Geneva Bibles that most first-generation lay people owned. See Stout, "Word and Order in Colonial New England."

15. McGiffert, ed., *God's Plot*, 48.

16. For Hooker's close identification of faith and legal obedience see Norman Pettit, "Hooker's Doctrine of Assurance: A Critical Phase in New England Spiritual Thought," *New England Quarterly*, 47 (1974), 518–34; and Alfred Habegger, "Preparing the Soul for Christ: The Contrasting Sermon Forms of John Cotton and Thomas Hooker," *American Literature* 41 (1970), 342–54. Despite their different emphases, Hooker and Cotton preached essentially the same gospel, rooted in unquestioning allegiance to the principle of *Sola Fides* ("faith alone").

17. McGiffert, ed., *God's Plot*, 236.

18. Thomas Shepard, "Sermons on Hebrews 10:23," June 1644, trans. Charles Willoughby, in Shepard Family Papers, Folder 2.

19. Thomas Allen, "Sermons on John 3:33," June 1644, *ibid.* Despite his penetrating analysis of Puritan theology, Miller tended to overemphasize the legalistic and intellectualistic dimension of covenant theology. This was largely due to his heavy reliance on occasional sermons that discussed federal covenants and his imputing these constructs to Puritan theories of salvation whereby anxious saints "bargained" with God and demanded that he save them because they had prepared. For correctives that emphasize the role of the will and heart in Puritan preaching and theories of salvation see Norman Pettit, *The Heart Prepared: Grace and Conversion in Puritan Spiritual Life* (New Haven, Conn., 1966); Geoffrey F. Nuttall, *The Holy Spirit in Puritan Faith and Experience* (Oxford, 1947); James Fulton Maclear, "'The Heart of New England Rent'"; Hambrick-Stowe, *The Practice of Piety*; George Marsden, "Perry Miller's Rehabilitation of the Puritans: A Critique," *Church History*, 39 (1970), 91–105; or Robert Middlekauff, "Piety and Intellect in Puritanism," *William and Mary Quarterly*, 22 (1965), 457–70. For a summary of historiographical debates on will and intellect in Puritan theology see Michael McGiffert, "American Puritan Studies in the 1960's," *ibid.*, 27 (1970), 50–54.

20. John Cotton, *Gospel Conversion* (London, 1646), 41.

21. Edmund S. Morgan describes the Puritans' sequential understanding of conversion as the "morphology of conversion." For accounts see his *Visible Saints*, 66–73, 90–92.

22. Katherine's church confession is transcribed in George Selement and Bruce C. Wooley, eds., *Thomas Shepard's Confessions* (Boston, 1981), 99–101. For a general discussion of the confessions see Patricia Caldwell, *The Puritan Conversion Narrative: The Beginnings of American Expression* (Cambridge, Mass., and London, 1983).

23. Katherine's reference to "Manassah" is probably in reference to Genesis 41:51: "And Joseph called the name of the firstborn Manassah: For God, saith he, hath made me forget all my toil, and all my father's house." The reference to Isaiah is from Isaiah 1:18: "Though your sins be as scarlet, they shall be as white as snow; though they be red like crimson, they shall be as wool." The "promise" she found is from Matthew 11:28: "Come unto me all ye that labour and are heavy laden, and I will give you rest." In this confession and all the others that Shepard transcribed, the biblical citations and phraseology confirm the high level of biblical knowledge among ordinary New Englanders.

24. The reference to "Zachary" is from Zechariah 3:2: "And the Lord said unto Satan, The Lord rebuke thee, O Satan; even the Lord that hath chosen Jerusalem rebuke thee: is not this a brand plucked out of the fire?" The reference to a "strong tower" is from Psalm 61:3: "For thou hast been a shelter for me, and a strong tower from the enemy." The reference to Jacob is from Genesis 22:12–15, where in a dream the Lord appears at the top of a ladder to heaven and makes known his promise of salvation to Jacob (verse 15): "And, behold, I am with thee, and will keep thee in all places whither thou goest, and will bring thee again into this [promised] land; for I will not leave thee, until I have done that which I have spoken to thee of." Other examples of lay confessions appear in Robert G. Pope, ed., "The Notebook of the Reverend John Fiske, 1644–1675," Colonial Society of Massachusetts, *Publications*, 47 (1974).

25. McGiffert, ed., *God's Plot*, 108, 109. This same theme appears in John Norton, "Sermon on Ephesians 3:19," Feb. 17, 1656, in John Hull, "Sermon Notes, 1657–1660," Gratz Collection, Box 1, HSP.

26. Thomas Shepard, "Sermons on the Ten Commandments." On the social teachings of Congregational ministers see Stephen Foster, *Their Solitary Way: The Puritan Social Ethic in the First Century of Settlement in New England* (New Haven, Conn., 1971).

27. John Cotton, *A Treatise of the Covenant of Grace* (London, 1671), 33–34.

28. First-generation printed sermons were oriented largely around the question of personal salvation. See Phyllis M. and Nicholas R. Jones, eds., *Salvation in New England: Selections from the Sermons* (Austin, Tex., 1977), 17–22.

29. Thomas Shepard, *The Sincere Convert* (London, 1652). The popularity of this sermon continued well into the 18th century. See C. C. Goen, ed., *The Great Awakening* (New Haven, Conn., 1972), 26.

30. Thomas Shepard, *The Sincere Convert*, 126.

31. See Norman Pettit, "The Order of Salvation in Thomas Hooker's Thought," in George H. Williams *et al.*, *Thomas Hooker: Writings in England and Holland, 1626–1633* (Cambridge, Mass., 1975), 124–39.

32. For Hooker's traditional evangelical gospel appeal see, especially, *The Soul's Vocation or Effectual Calling to Christ* (1637–38), reprinted in Jones and Jones, eds., *Salvation in New England*, 82–83, 86.

33. Peter Bulkeley, *The Gospel-Covenant*, 101. Other printed sermons that outline the same sequence include John Norton, *The Orthodox Evangelist* (London, 1654); John Davenport, *The Knowledge of Christ Indispensable Required of all Men* (London, 1653); John Cotton, *The Way of Life* (London, 1641); Charles Chauncy, *The Plain Doctrine of the Justification of a Sinner* (London, 1659); and Richard Mather, *The Summe of Certain Sermons upon Genesis 15.6* (Cambridge, 1652).

34. For an extended discussion of faculty psychology and Puritan preaching see Miller, *The Seventeenth Century*, 240–41.

35. See Bonnie L. Strother, "The Imagery in the Sermons of Thomas Shepard," (Ph.D. diss., University of Tennessee, 1968), 83–86.

36. The most famous of these reference tools was Benjamin Keach, *Tropologia; A Key to Open Scripture Metaphors, together with Types of the Old Testament* (reprinted Grand Rapids, Mich., 1972). Also useful was Thomas Wilson, *A Christian Dictionary of the Chief Words in the Old and New Testament* (London, 1629).

37. On sermonic imagery see Babette May Levy, *Preaching in the First Half Century of New England History* (New York, 1945), 98–130; Strother, "The Imagery in the Sermons of Thomas Shepard," 112–29, 200–04; and David S. Shields, "Exploratory Narratives and the Development of the New England Passage Journal," *Essex Institute Historical Collections*, 120 (1984), 38–57.

38. John Mayo, "Sermon on 2 Timothy 4:5," Apr. 2, 1656, Gratz Collection, Box 1.

39. Thomas Allen, "Sermons on John 3:33." See also Thomas Shepard, "Sermon on Isaiah 51:12," 1644 in Shepard Family Papers, oct. vol. II.

40. John Warham, "Sermons on Ephesians 6," 1638 in Shepard, "The Wolcott Shorthand Notebooks," 62–90.

41. No subject has aroused greater interest in the past decade than that of typology and Puritan preaching and literature. For convenient summaries and bibliographies of this literature see Ursula Brumm, *American Thought and Religious Typology* (New Brunswick, N.J., 1970); and Sacvan Bercovitch, *Typology and Early American Literature* (Amherst, Mass., 1972). The use of typology in regular preaching was influenced by John Calvin. See, e.g., John Calvin, "Sermon on Genesis 14:13–17," in *Calvin Speaks*, vol. 2 (Waco, Tex., 1981), 8, where Calvin used the case of Melchizedek to show how the Old Testament represented "not only a history, but . . . [also] a lively image representing our Lord Jesus Christ." In the context of typology, Salo W. Baron observes that "it is small wonder . . . that the disciples of Calvin in many lands so eagerly turned for enlightenment to the Old Testament. . . . Calvinist divines and scholars in many lands became some of the foremost Christian Hebraists of the following two centuries." Leon A. Feldman, ed., *Ancient and Medieval Jewish History: Essays by Salo Whittmayer Baron* (New Brunswick, N.J., 1972), 350.

42. Many sermons employed Old Testament figures as Christ-types. See, e.g., Richard Blinman, "Sermon on Romans 5:15," 1649, in Richard Russell, "Sermon Notes," Russell Family Papers, AAS; John Pinch, "Sermon on Malachai 4:2," Dec. 13, 1640, Sermons Collection, Box 3, Folder 26, AAS; Thomas Allen, "Sermons on John 3:33"; John Norton, "Sermons on Canticles 3 and 4," Apr. 27, 1658, to Oct. 6, 1660, Gratz Collection, Box 1; or George Moxon, "Sermon on Hebrews 4:2," May 6, 1649, in "Notes by the Hon. John Pynchon," Gratz Collection, Box 9, vol. XXI, HSP. First-generation ministers frequently preached on Canticles for its rich typological significance. See Mason Lowance, *The Language of Canaan: Metaphor and Symbol in New England from the Puritans to the Transcendentalists* (Cambridge, Mass., 1980, 41–54.

43. See Bercovitch, *The Puritan Origins of the American Self*, 36.

44. The use of typology to refer to Christ as opposed to "New Israel" is discussed in Jean Danielou, *From Shadows to Reality: Studies in the Biblical Typology of the Fathers* (London, 1960).

45. John Davenport, *The Saint's Anchor Hold* (1658) reprinted in Jones and Jones, eds., *Salvation in New England*, 148.

46. *Ibid.*, 149, 151.

47. These figures of speech are summarized in Keach, *Tropologia*, 620–24.

48. George Moxon, "Sermon on Hebrews 6:19," Aug. 5, 1649, in Gratz Collection, Box 9, vol. XXI.

49. See also Thomas Hooker, "Sermon on Romans 1:18," June 29, 1647, in Parsons, trans., "Mathew Grant Diary," 1–11. Here Hooker showed that the true believer would rather be "caried with full saile to heaven, then bee tossed alwayes with feares and dobtes . . . the winds may tosse the ship wherein Christ is but not overturn it."

50. Thomas Shepard, *The Sincere Convert*, 85–86.

51. John Mayo, "Sermon on 2 Timothy 4:5." Mayo reiterated the theme of watchfulness in an 11-week sermon series on Revelation 3:2 in John Hull, "Sermon Notes, 1657–1660." See also Thomas Shepard, *The Parable of the Ten Virgins*, in John Albro, ed., *The Works of Thomas Shepard*, 3 vols. (Boston, 1853), II, 36.

52. McGiffert, ed., *God's Plot*, 164.

53. There has been little systematic work done on the Thursday lectures as a sermon genre despite the fact that numerous lectures are recorded in sermon notebooks and ministerial diaries.

54. Cotton Mather, *Magnalia Christi Americana*, 3 vols. (London, 1702), III, 249. See also Larzer Ziff, *The Career of John Cotton: Puritanism and the American Experience* (Princeton, N.J., 1962), 170–202; and Jesper Rosenmeier, " 'Clearing the Medium': A Reevaluation of the Puritan Plain Style in Light of John Cotton's *A Practicall Commentary Upon the First Epistle Generall of John*," *William and Mary Quarterly*, 37 (1980), 589–91.

55. John Cotton, *An exposition upon the 13th Chapter of the Revelation*, 214. On the standard identification of the beast and harlot with Rome see Keach, *Tropologia*, 862–93. In England, millennarian thought led to a division between "radical" lower class movements with "levelling" social goals and a more moderate "middle class" tradition. The radical traditions are traced in Christopher Hill, *The World Turned Upside Down: Radical Ideas During the English Revolution* (New York, 1972). The more moderate tradition, which also predominated among the New England clergy, is described in William Haller, *Foxe's Book of Martyrs and the Elect Nation* (London, 1963); and William M. Lamont, *Richard Baxter and the Millennium: Protestant Imperialism and the English Revolution* (Totowa, N. J., 1979).

56. The cabalistic influence on Cotton's calculations is described in Emerson, *John Cotton*, 97.

57. John Cotton, *The Powrring out of the Seven Vials . . .* , 7 vols. (London, 1645), VI, 22.

58. *Ibid.*, I, 23.

Chapter 3

1. See Weis, *The Colonial Clergy and the Colonial Churches of New England*, 238–80.

2. For convenient summary of the Puritan revolt and Interregnum see Ivan Roots, *The English Civil War and Its Aftermath* (New York, 1966).

3. J. Franklin Jameson, ed., *Johnson's Wonder-Working Providence, 1628–1651* (New York, 1910), 25.

4. William Hooke, *N Englands Teares for Old Englands Feares* (London, 1641), 16.

5. I have argued elsewhere that this "remigration" of university men between 1640 and 1660 reflected both the "pull" of events in England, where new positions opened up for Puritans, and a "push" out of New England, where new positions closed with the cessation of the Great Migration in 1640. Many of the returnees were first-generation malcontents at odds with the New England Way or second- generation Harvard graduates who could not find pulpits in New England after the Great Migration ceased. See Harry S. Stout, "University Men in New England, 1620–1660: A Demographic Analysis," *Journal of Interdisciplinary History*, 4 (1974), 375–400; and Harry S. Stout, "The Morphology of Remigration: New England University Men and Their Return to England, 1640–1660," *Journal of American Studies*, 10 (1975), 151–72.

6. The extent to which the founders were "English" or "American" in their cultural identity and millennial hopes is a matter of some debate. Contrast, e.g., Robert Middlekauff, *The Mathers: Three Generations of Puritan Intellectuals, 1596–1728* (New York, 1971), 32–34, 62; and Miller, *From Colony to Province*, 6–9, who both argue that the founders were "never to be Americanized," with Sacvan Bercovitch, *The American Jeremiad* (Madison, Wis., 1978), 93–131, who argues that the founders identified their millennial hope with the place, America, from the start of settlement. In the following section I argue that timing is crucial to this issue. Those founders who died before 1660, when the Commonwealth collapsed, never lost sight of their English homeland and resisted "Americanization." But those who survived beyond 1660 lived long enough to redefine New England's mission from Old World to New.

7. In 1644 there were 12 fast days for England in Massachusetts Bay that are recorded in church and commonwealth records. Since many records from the earliest period do not survive, this should be seen as a minimal figure. See Love, *Fast and Thanksgiving Days*, 111–12, 142–61. In Connecticut and New Hampshire the civil authorities set aside monthly fast days for events in England. See Francis J. Bremer, *The Puritan Experiment: New England Society from Bradford to Edwards* (New York, 1976), 109.

8. William Hooke, *New-Englands Sence, of Old-England and Irelands Sorrowes* (London, 1645), reprinted in Samuel H. Emery, *The Ministry of Taunton*, 2 vols. (Boston, 1853), I, 123, 124; and John Warham, "Sermon on Ezekiel 9:4," July 29, 1640, in Shepard, "The Wolcott Shorthand Notebooks," 306. Concern for England's reform was present from the start of New World settlement. In his sermon to the Winthrop fleet Cotton urged the travellers to *"Be not unmindful of our Jerusalem at home. . . . Forget not the womb that bare you, and the breast that gave you suck."* God's Promise to his Plantation, 18.

9. On New England's unofficial interest in and support for the parliamentary cause see Middlekauff, *The Mathers*, 31–33; and Francis J. Bremer, "Puritan Crisis: New England and the English Civil Wars, 1630–1670" (Ph.D. diss., Columbia University, 1972).

10. For discussions of *The Cambridge Platform* and its English audience see Miller, *From Colony to Province*, 6; Middlekauff, *The Mathers*, 41–57; David D. Hall, *The Faithful Shepherd; A History of the New England Ministry in the Seventeenth Century* (Chapel Hill, N.C., 1972), 83–120; and Henry Wilder Foote, "The Significance and Influence of the Cambridge Platform of 1648," Massachusetts Historical Society, *Proceedings*, 69 (1947–50), 81–101.

11. John Cotton, *An exposition upon the 13th Chapter of Revelation*, 212–14. The text of *The Cambridge Platform* is reprinted in Walker, ed., *The Creeds and Platforms*

of Congregationalism, 194–237. The concessions to synodical influence and author-ity were motivated both by the ministers' concern to consolidate and impose their authority over particular congregations and by their desire to placate English Pres-byterians. See Bremer, *The Puritan Experiment*, 120–21.

12. On toleration see Thomas Shepard, *Wine for Gospel Wantons* (Cambridge, 1668), 9. Elsewhere Shepard declared in a letter to Hugh Peter in England: "I feare greater sorrowes attend England if they do not seasonably suppresse and beare Publicke witnesse agaynst such delusions which fill the land like locusts without any king, and will certainly (if suffered) eat up the greene grasse of the land . . . but toleration of all upon the pretence of conscience I thank God my Soule abhors it." "Thomas Shepard to Hugh Peter, 1645," *American Historical Review*, 1 (1898), 106. John Norton defended New England's policy of intolerance in similarly strong terms in *The Heart of N-England Rent* (Cambridge, 1659).

13. John Cotton, "Sermon on Revelation 15:3," 1651, reprinted in Francis J. Bremer, ed., "In Defense of Regicide: John Cotton on the Execution of Charles I," *William and Mary Quarterly*, 37 (1980), 112.

14. Perry Miller developed this dilemma brilliantly in his essay *Errand Into the Wilderness* (Cambridge, Mass., 1956), 1–15.

15. In October 1659, the General Court executed three Quakers: William Rob-inson, Marmaduke Stephenson, and Mary Dyer. Following the Restoration, the death penalty for Quakers was rescinded, but coercive punishments in the "cart and whip Act" continued through the 1670s. See William G. McLoughlin, *New England Dissent, 1630–1833: The Baptists and the Separation of Church and State*, 2 vols. (Cambridge, 1971), I, 26–48; and Bremer, *The Puritan Experiment*, 138–142.

16. For descriptions of how the New England Puritans fused Israel, the early church, New England, and the millennium into a single historical narrative see Bercovitch, *The Puritan Origins of the American Self*, 35–71; and David M. Scobey, "Revising the Errand: New England's Ways and the Puritan Sense of the Past," *William and Mary Quarterly*, 41 (1984), 3–31. These fine studies combine Puritan histories from the first three generations. But, like the debates over "Americani-zation," they obscure exactly when the sense of *"America's* New Israel" began and why.

17. John Norton, *Three Choice and Profitable Sermons* (Cambridge, 1664), 2–3, 12.

18. Richard Mather, *A Farewel Exhortation* (Cambridge, 1657), 3.

19. John Norton, *Three Choice and Profitable Sermons*, 37.

20. McGiffert, ed., *God's Plot*, 121; and George Moxon, "Sermon on Romans 7:9," Apr. 1, 1649, in Gratz Collection, Box 9, vol. XXI.

21. Charles Chauncy, *New England's First Fruits* (London, 1643), reprinted in Samuel E. Morison, *Harvard College in the Seventeenth Century*, 2 vols. (Boston, 1936), II, 432.

22. Jonathan Mitchel, *A Model for the Maintaining of Students and Fellowes of Choisse Abilities of the Colledge in Cambridge* (1663), reprinted in Colonial Society of Massachusetts, *Publications*, 31 (1935), 321. For a similar defense see Nathaniel Ward's *Mercurius Anti-mechanicus* (London, 1648). In *The Founding of Harvard College* (Cambridge, 1935), Samuel E. Morison tended to exaggerate the secular ends of Harvard College and understate its primary function as a training ground for ministers. For more accurate descriptions of the motives in founding Harvard see Arthur O. Norton, "Harvard Text-Books and Reference Books of the Seven-teenth Century," Colonial Society of Massachusetts, *Publications*, 28 (*Transactions*,

1930–33), 361; and Winthrop S. Hudson, "The Morison Myth Concerning the Founding of Harvard College," *Church History*, 8 (1939), 148–59.

23. Richard Mather, *A Farewel Exhortation*, 8. The case of Michael Powell is reprinted in Chandler Robbins, *A History of the Second Church, or Old North, in Boston* (Boston, 1852), 8. In his "Sermon Notes, 1657–1660," John Hull recorded several sermons delivered by Powell after the decision of 1654. Lay elders could preach when the need arose but they could not be ordained as teaching elders.

24. For a listing of early Harvard graduates see Stout, "University Men in New England," appendix.

25. Because they were a covenant people—perhaps the only covenant people—they could be sure that Satan would be especially active in their corner of the world, working to undermine the faith and weaken the bonds of community among the native-born children. See Hosmer, ed., *Winthrop's Journal*, I, 121, 285. The language of diabolical evil and natural decay appeared in Boston as early as 1634, when John Winthrop observed that following John Cotton's revivalistic preaching "Satan hath bestirred himself to hinder the [further] progress of the gospel." Following the Antinomian crisis he was certain that "the devil would never cease to disturb our peace, and to raise up instruments one after another." Even when not directly assaulting the Puritan experiment, Satan was indirectly active through the ever-present temptations of worldliness and apathy towards the things of the spirit.

26. Thomas Shepard, *Wine for Gospel Wantons*, 13.

27. See Lockridge, *A New England Town*, 34; and Darrett B. Rutman, *Winthrop's Boston: A Portrait of a Puritan Town, 1630–1649* (orig. publ. 1965; reprinted New York, 1972), 147.

28. Mather's *Plea* is quoted in Increase Mather, *First Principles of New England* (Cambridge, 1675). See also Miller, *From Colony to Province*, 90; Robert G. Pope, *The Half-Way Covenant: Church Membership in Puritan New England* (Princeton, N.J., 1969), 13–42; E. Brooks Holifield, *The Covenant Sealed: The Development of Puritan Sacramental Theory in Old and New England, 1570–1720* (New Haven, Conn., 1974), 142–43; and McLoughlin, *New England Dissent*, I, 26–48.

29. Thomas Shepard's covenantal arguments were written in the 1650s and published in *The Church Membership of Children* (Cambridge, 1669), 4. On membership rates see Pope, *The Half-Way Covenant*, 206–38; and Gerald F. Moran, "The Puritan Saint: Religious Experience, Church Membership, and Piety in Connecticut, 1636–1776" (Ph.D. diss., Rutgers University, 1974), 102–39. Based on extensive analysis of records in Massachusetts and Connecticut, Pope and Moran demonstrate that while membership rates reached a low in the 1650s they surged in the following decades. Church membership patterns in New England were less a linear pattern of uninterrupted decline than a cyclical pattern that corresponded to the coming of age of new generations. See Gerald F. Moran, "Religious Renewal, Puritan Tribalism, and the Family in Seventeenth-Century Milford, Connecticut," *William and Mary Quarterly*, 36 (1979), 236–54.

30. The Ministerial Assembly and subsequent Synod of 1661 are discussed in Pope, *The Half-Way Covenant*, 13–74. For a study of the influence of Israel on Puritan sacramental thought see Rosemary K. Twomey, "From Pure Church to Pure Nation: Massachusetts Bay, 1630–1692" (Ph.D. diss., University of Rochester, 1971), 123–229.

31. The *Results of the Synod of 1657* are reprinted in Walker, ed., *The Creeds and Platforms of Congregationalism*, 296, 291, 294.

32. The dissenting view is represented in Charles Chauncy, *Anti-Synodalia Scripta Americana* (London, 1662); and John Davenport, *Another Essay for the Investigation of the Truth, In Answer to Two Questions* (Cambridge, 1663). These documents and others are described in Michael G. Hall and William L. Joyce, "The Half-Way Covenant of 1662: Some New Evidence," American Antiquarian Society, *Proceedings*, 87 (1977), 97–110.

33. *The Results of the Synod of 1662* are reprinted in Walker, ed., *The Creeds and Platforms of Congregationalism*, 302, 309–10.

34. Richard Mather and Jonathan Mitchell, *A Defense of the Answer of the Synod of 1662* (Cambridge, 1664), 1. See also Middlekauff, *The Mathers*, 55–57.

35. John Norton, *Three Choice and Profitable Sermons*, 8. In the same sermon Norton urged his listeners to "acknowledge the Order of the Eldership in our Churches . . . and the Order of Councils . . . without which, Experience will witness that these Churches cannot long consist." (13)

36. The gradual acceptance of the permissibility of the Half-way Covenant after 1670 is traced in Hall, *The Faithful Shepherd*, 199–207; and Pope, *The Half-Way Covenant*, 185–205. In "The Puritan Saint," 120, Gerald Moran notes that by the 1680s "control over church affairs had been assumed by second-generation saints." Moran goes on to point out that most of the second-generation members filling out the church rolls were full members and children of first generation saints. At no time did half-way members constitute a majority of the colonies' church members.

37. *Results of the Synod of 1662*, reprinted in Walker, ed., *The Creeds and Platforms of Congregationalism*, 311–12.

38. John Wilson, *A Seasonable Watch-Word* (Cambridge, 1677), 6, 7.

39. John Davenport, *A Sermon Preached at the Election* (Cambridge, 1670), 15, 16.

40. John Wilson, *A Seasonable Watch-Word*, 8. John Oxenbridge, *A Quickening Word* (Cambridge, 1670), 14; or John Davenport, *Gods Call to His People to Turn Unto Him* (Cambridge, 1669), 12. In *Power and the Pulpit in Puritan New England* (Princeton, N.J., 1975), 88–135, Emory Elliott describes an increasingly "angry" tone in (occasional) preaching that was directed against the increasing sinfulness of the rising generation. The extent to which a "decline" in piety was real or a rhetorical device is a matter of some debate. In *From Colony to Province*, Perry Miller described an actual "declension" (see especially Book I), as does Darrett B. Rutman in *Winthrop's Boston* and Ross W. Beales, "The Half-Way Covenant and Religious Scrupulosity: The First Church of Dorchester, Massachusetts, as a Test Case," *William and Mary Quarterly*, 31 (1974), 465–80. Other studies challenge this conclusion and speak instead of the "myth" of declension. See, e.g., Robert G. Pope, "New England Versus the New England Mind: The Myth of Declension," *Journal of Social History*, 3 (1969), 95–108; Greven, *The Protestant Temperament*, 5–12; or Gerald F. Moran and Maris A. Vinovskis, "The Puritan Family and Religion: A Critical Reappraisal," *William and Mary Quarterly*, 39 (1982), 29–63. This question is addressed more fully in Part II of this study.

41. Sacvan Bercovitch describes the ways in which the Puritans' rhetoric of failure was simultaneously pessimistic and optimistic in *The American Jeremiad* (Madison, 1978), 3–30.

42. John Norton, *Three Choice and Profitable Sermons*, 15, 6.

43. John Davenport, *Gods Call to His People*, 12–13.

44. Despite his congregation's resistance to the Half-way Covenant, John Allin

defended it in *Animadversions Upon the Antisynodalia Americana* (Cambridge, 1664). Following Allin's death his Dedham congregation reversed their position and accepted the Half-way Covenant. For a discussion of the debates in Dedham see Lockridge, *A New England Town*, 35.

45. John Allin, *Two Sermons* (Cambridge, 1672), reprinted in Ebenezer Burgess, comp., *The Dedham Pulpit* (Boston, 1840), 19.

46. *Ibid.*, 27.

Chapter 4

1. Eleazar Mather, *A Serious Exhortation* (Cambridge, 1671), 6. For additional background on this sermon see Philip F. Gura, "Preparing the Way for Stoddard: Eleazar Mather's *Serious Exhortation* to Northampton," *New England Quarterly*, 57 (1984), 240–49.

2. Eleazar Mather, *A Serious Exhortation*, 29.

3. *Ibid.*, 30, 24.

4. William Stoughton, *N-Englands True Interest Not to Lie* (Cambridge, 1670), 16, 17, 9.

5. *Ibid.*, 19.

6. The press at Cambridge began in 1638 but did not begin making a major contribution to New England print culture until the 1670s. See Sidney A. Kimber, *Cambridge Press Title-Pages, 1640–1665* (Baltimore, Md., 1954); Robert F. Roden, *The Cambridge Press, 1638–1692* (New York, 1905); and George P. Winship, *The Cambridge Press, 1638–1692: A Re-Examination* (Philadelphia, 1945).

7. By 1690 the Cambridge Press had printed 97 sermons of which 79 were occasional sermons. Of the first 56 sermons printed before 1680, the largest number (17) were election sermons. For sermon listings see Robert M. Benton, "An Annotated Check List of Puritan Sermons in America before 1700," *Bulletin of the New York Public Library*, 74 (1970), 286–337.

8. Jonathan Mitchel, *Nehemiah on the Wall in Troublesom Times* (Cambridge, 1671), reprinted in Miller and Johnson, eds., *The Puritans*, I, 237–42.

9. John Higginson, *The Cause of God and His People in New-England* (Cambridge, 1664), 12, 36.

10. For an extended description of the epic qualities of election sermons see Plumstead, ed., *The Wall and the Garden*, 3–37.

11. John Higginson, *The Cause of God and His People*, 4, 10–11.

12. Samuel Danforth, *A Brief Recognition of New- England's Errand Into the Wilderness* (Cambridge, 1671), 10, 17–18. On the children's invention of the term *errand* to refer to their generation see Middlekauff, *The Mathers*, 32.

13. William Stoughton, *N-Englands True Interest Not to Lie*, 10, 11, 16.

14. On the Puritans' use of Moses' Song see Richard Slotkin and James Folsom, eds., *So Dreadful a Judgment: Puritan Responses to King Philip's War, 1676–1677* (Middletown, Conn., 1978), 201. That text, as John Sherman and Thomas Shepard II explained in their preface to Oakes's sermon, was a historical summary of Israel's experience from Egypt through "the Vast and Howling Desert" to "the borders of Canaan." It also contained a prophecy of "what the Lord, the God of their Fathers, would do for that people of Israel in that good Land of *Canaan*; and of the manner of their demeanour and deportment of themselves there." See Urian Oakes, *New-England Pleaded With* (Cambridge, 1673), "To the Reader."

15. Urian Oakes, *New-England Pleaded With*, 2, 45, 17.

16. *Ibid.*, 17, 18. On the typological identification of the founders with Israel's patriarchs and of the nation of Israel with New England see Bercovitch, *The American Jeremiad*, 93–131.

17. Urian Oakes, *New-England Pleaded With*, 11, 21.

18. John Higginson, *The Cause of God and His People*, 8.

19. Between 1660 and 1680, 14 fast sermons were published. By 1700, the Cambridge Press had printed 30 election sermons and 30 fast sermons. See Benton, "An Annotated Check List of Puritan Sermons Before 1700."

20. Between 1620 and 1750, there are notices of 691 fast days and 374 thanksgiving days in surviving records. During the 1670s alone there were 113 fast days observed provincially or in particular churches. In the 1680s there were 87 fasts, and in the 1690s there were 79. These figures are computed in Ronald Bosco, ed., *The Puritan Sermon in America, 1630–1750*, 4 vols. (Delmar, Del., 1978), I, xxiii–xxiv. Because many church records do not survive from these decades, the figures must be taken as minimal.

21. Perry Miller describes the rhetoric of declension in *From Colony to Province*, 19–146.

22. Samuel Danforth, *An Astronomical Description of the Late Comet or Blazing Star* (Cambridge, 1665), reprinted in Miller and Johnson, eds., *The Puritans*, II, 739. The coincidence of natural calamities and fast warnings is traced in Karen O. Kupperman, "Climate and Mastery of the Wilderness in Seventeenth-Century New England," in David Grayson Allen and David D. Hall, eds., *Seventeenth-Century New-England* (Boston, 1985), 3–37.

23. Michael Wigglesworth, *God's Controversy with New-England* (1662), reprinted in Miller and Johnson, eds., *The Puritans*, II, 614.

24. New England's population growth is described in Daniel S. Smith, "The Demographic History of Colonial New England," *Journal of Economic History*, 32 (1972), 165–83.

25. For descriptions of New England's commercial economic growth see Bernard Bailyn, *The New England Merchants in the Seventeenth Century* (Boston, 1955); Carl Bridenbaugh, *Cities in the Wilderness: The First Century of Urban Life in America, 1625–1742* (New York, 1938); and Richard S. Dunn, *Puritans and Yankees: The Winthrop Dynasty of New England 1630–1717* (orig. publ., 1962; reprinted New York, 1971), 59–190. The larger Atlantic context of New England's economic growth is traced in Stuart Bruchey, *Roots of American Economic Growth, 1607–1861* (New York, 1965).

26. The settlement of "frontier" towns in 17th- and early 18th-century New England is described in Charles S. Grant, *Democracy in the Frontier Town of Kent, Connecticut* (New York, 1961); and Charles Clark, *The Eastern Frontier: The Settlement of Northern New England, 1610–1763* (New York, 1970).

27. Increase Mather, *The Day of Trouble is Near* (Cambridge, 1674), 22, 11. In the same year Mather published *Some Important Truths about Conversion* (London, 1674), and in the preface he issued the same warning: "It is most certain that there is a dark time coming on New-England; dismal calamitous dayes are at hand." For similar predictions see Samuel Willard, *Useful Instructions* (Cambridge, 1673), 47, 43.

28. Thomas Thacher, *A Fast of Gods Chusing Plainly Opened* (Boston, 1678), 24.

29. Detailed studies of King Philip's War have presented widely divergent views as to cause and blame. For accounts that are basically sympathetic to the Puritan cause see Douglas Edward Leach, *Flintlock and Tomahawk: New England*

in King-Philip's War (orig. publ. 1958; reprinted New York, 1966); and Alden Vaughan, *New England Frontier: Puritans and Indians, 1620–1675* (Boston, 1965). The best account from the native American Indians' perspective is Francis Jennings, *The Invasion of America: Indians, Colonialism, and the Cant of Conquest* (orig. publ. 1975; reprinted, New York, 1976). My intent here is not to assess blame but to reconstruct the "symbolic" or "mythological" meaning the war had for the Puritans.

30. Edward Bulkeley, "Sermon on Psalms 116:12," Oct. 21, 1675, published in Thomas Wheeler, *A Thankful Remembrance* (Cambridge, 1676), 13.

31. These fasts are compiled and summarized in Love, *The Fast and Thanksgiving Days of New England*, 196–204. There were more fasts in the years 1675–76 (23 in 1675 and 19 in 1676) than at any other time in the 17th century.

32. See especially Thomas Church, *Entertaining Passages Relating to Philip's War* (Boston, 1716); William Hubbard, *A Narrative of Troubles with the Indians in New-England* (Boston, 1677); William Hubbard, *The Present State of New-England* (London, 1677); Increase Mather, *A Brief History of the War with the Indians* (Boston and London, 1676); Increase Mather, *A Relation of the Troubles which have Hapned in New-England* (Boston, 1677); and Nathaniel Saltonstall, *The Present State of New-England with Respect to the Indian War* (London, 1675). Convenient collections of these histories appear in Charles H. Lincoln, ed., *Narratives of the Indian Wars* (New York, 1913); and Slotkin and Folsom, eds., *So Dreadful a Judgment*.

33. William Hubbard, *The Present State of New-England*, 114; and Increase Mather, *A Brief History*, 18.

34. For the Puritans' symbolic use of the Indians see the analysis in Slotkin and Folsom, eds., *So Dreadful a Judgment*, 35–39.

35. Bacon's Rebellion is discussed in Wilcomb E. Washburn, *The Governor and the Rebel: A History of Bacon's Rebellion in Virginia* (Chapel Hill, N. C., 1957). The contrasting effects of war on New England and Virginia society and the implications of this contrast for New England's cultural "cohesion" are discussed in Breen and Foster, "The Puritans' Greatest Achievement."

36. The pattern of rising church membership in the 1670s and 1680s is traced in Pope, *The Half-Way Covenant*, 236; and Moran, "The Puritan Saint," 102–39.

37. Increase Mather, *An Earnest Exhortation* (Boston, 1676), reprinted in Slotkin and Folsom, eds., *So Dreadful a Judgment*, 176–77.

38. *Ibid.*, 172, 179.

39. *Ibid.*, 191, 193.

40. *Ibid.*, 174.

41. A popular example of "souldiery spiritualized" on the shelves of many ministers was John Downame's *The Christian Warfare*, 2d ed. (London, 1609).

42. The history of artillery election sermons, like Thursday lectures, has received far less attention than fast or election sermons. Some preliminary observations on the origins, context, and delivery of militia sermons can be found in Levy, *Preaching in the First Half Century*, 87; Arthur Buffinton, "The Puritan View of War," Colonial Society of Massachusetts, *Publications*, 28 (1930–33), 67–86; and Rollo G. Silver, "Financing the Publication of Early New England Sermons," *Studies in Bibliography*, 11 (1958), 165–66. Publication of the artillery election sermons in Boston began in 1674 and was privately financed by the Ancient and Honorable Artillery Company of Boston. Other similar sermons were delivered at local militia musters, particularly in time of war.

43. Urian Oakes, *The Unconquerable, All-Conquering and More-then-Conquering*

Souldier (Cambridge, 1674), 1, 16. For a similar application see Joshua Moody, *Souldiery Spiritualized* (Cambridge, 1674), 6, 10.

44. John Richardson, *The Necessity of a Well Experienced Souldiery* (Cambridge, 1679), 4.

45. *Ibid.*, 15.

46. Samuel Nowell, *Abraham in Arms* (1678), reprinted in Slotkin and Folsom, eds., *So Dreadful a Judgment*, 277, 274.

47. *Ibid.*, 276, 278, 282.

48. *Ibid.*, 284–85. This theme was picked up in Urian Oakes's 1677 artillery election sermon: "Be not slothful, or neglective of Duty, because of the uncertainty of Events. Though you have not the issue in your own power, yet you are to do your utmost towards the compassing of your lawful Designs. Do your duty, or you cannot expect God's Blessing, and his determining Events on your side." *The Sovereign Efficacy of Divine Providence* (Boston, 1682), 29.

49. Slotkin and Folsom, eds., *So Dreadful a Judgment*, 290.

50. *Ibid.*, 287, 288.

Chapter 5

1. This minimal estimate of second-generation regular sermons is based on multiplying 2,928 (the total number of years preached by all ministers graduating from Harvard College between 1642 and 1675) by 100 (an average of two sermons per week).

2. The literature on New England town life in the second generation is rich in detail. On family networks and low geographic mobility see Greven, *Four Generations*, 103–72; Lockridge, *A New England Town*, 91–138; and Daniels, *The Connecticut Town*, 45–63.

3. On child-rearing patterns and Puritan religion see, especially, Greven, *The Protestant Temperament*; and Moran and Maris Vinovskis, "The Puritan Family and Religion," 29–63. On naming patterns see Daniel Scott Smith, "Child-Naming Patterns and Family Structure Change: Hingham, Massachusetts, 1640–1880," (Newberry Papers in Family and Community History, No. 76-5, Chicago, 1977).

4. New England literacy rates are discussed in Lockridge, *Literacy in Colonial New England*, 97–101. On general reading patterns in the second generation see Hall, "The Uses of Literacy in New England," 1–47.

5. The Cambridge Press is discussed in Roden, *The Cambridge Press, 1638–1692*; Winship, *The Cambridge Press, 1638–1692*; and George E. Littlefield, *The Early Massachusetts Press, 1638–1711*, 2 vols. (orig. publ. 1907; reprinted New York, 1969). The 17th-century book trade is discussed in Worthington Chauncey Ford, *The Boston Book Market, 1679–1700* (orig. publ. 1937; reprinted New York, 1972).

6. See the discussion in Hall, "The World of Print and Collective Mentality in Seventeenth-Century New England," 166–80.

7. The familial and residential backgrounds of second-generation Harvard graduates are discussed in Harry S. Stout, "Remigration and Revival: Two Case Studies in the Social and Intellectual History of New England, 1630–1745" (Ph.D. diss., Kent State University, 1974), 55–290.

8. On adolescence and Harvard College see Axtell, *The School Upon a Hill*, 207.

9. See Morison, *The Founding of Harvard College*; and *Harvard College in the Seventeenth Century*.

10. The original curriculum is reprinted in Morison, *The Founding of Harvard College*, 420–26. See also the course of study summarized and recommended in Samuel Willard, *Brief Directions to a Young Scholar* (Boston, 1735).

11. The term *Ramist method* refers to the method of binary division or dichotomy that was applied to the arts curriculum by the French educator and Protestant martyr Peter Ramus (1515–72). Ramus's logic and its relationship to Puritan thought and preaching was first outlined in Perry Miller's *The Seventeenth Century*. Since then, many works have clarified the connections between Ramist logic and Puritanism. See, e.g., Walter J. Ong, *Ramus: Method, and the Decay of Dialogue* (Cambridge, Mass., 1958), 35; Howard H. Martin, "Ramus, Ames, Perkins and Colonial Rhetoric," *Western Speech*, 23 (1959), 74–82; John G. Rechtien, "Logic in Puritan Sermons in the Late Sixteenth Century and Plain Style," *Style*, 13 (1979), 237–58; and Lee W. Gibbs, trans., *William Ames: Technometry* (Philadelphia, 1979), introduction, 22–30. The popular appeal of Ramist method is explained in Hugh Kearney, *Scholars and Gentlemen: Universities and Society in Pre-Industrial Britain, 1500–1700* (Ithaca, N.Y., 1970), 52.

12. Increase Mather dated his conversion to 1654, the year before his graduation at age 15. See Middlekauff, *The Mathers*, 82–83. Numerous accounts of students' wrestling with conversion are contained in Edmund S. Morgan, ed., *The Diary of Michael Wigglesworth* (New York, 1965). Most inhabitants did not experience conversion and join the church until after marriage in their late 20s. See Moran, "The Puritan Saint," 140–98.

13. The college laws are reprinted and discussed in Norton, "Harvard Text-Books and Reference Books of the Seventeenth Century," 361–438. Harvard's Hebrew requirements are discussed in Morison, *Harvard College in the Seventeenth Century*, I, 200–05.

14. See, e.g. Samuel Whiting (HC, 1653), "Sermon Notes," 1653, in Sermons Collection, 1 oct. vol., AAS; and John Leverett, "Sermon Notes," 1679, in Sermons Collection, 1 oct. vol., EI.

15. See Leonard Hoar's letter to his nephew Josiah Flynt, a beginning student at Harvard, Mar. 27, 1661, reprinted in Morison, *Harvard College in the Seventeenth Century*, II, 640–41. The contents of the original Harvard library were destroyed by fire, but for a reconstruction of their holdings see Potter, "Catalogue of John Harvard's Library," 190–230; and Norton, "Harvard Text-Books and Reference Books."

16. Not surprisingly, the largest ministerial library in the second generation belonged to Increase Mather. Charles Chauncy reckoned it to be the "largest by far of any private one in the continent." It grew from 1,000 volumes in 1664 to over 3,000 volumes at the time of his death. See Julius H. Tuttle, "The Libraries of the Mathers," American Antiquarian Society, *Proceedings*, 20 (1909–10), 268–356. At the other extreme, Leonard Hoar kept a library "in a little compasse: (scarce yet having more bookes than my self can carry in my arms at once[;] my paper bookes [sermons] only excepted." "Letter to Josiah Flynt," 641. For catalogues of early ministerial libraries somewhere in between these two extremes see Franklin B. Dexter, "Early Private Libraries in New England," American Antiquarian Society, *Proceedings*, 18 (1907), 135–47; Charles and Robin Robinson, "Three Early Massachusetts Libraries," Colonial Society of Massachusetts, *Publications*, 28 (1930–33), 107–75; Thomas G. Wright, *Literary Culture in Early New England, 1620–1730* (New Haven, Conn., 1920), 110–36; and Louis B. Wright, *The Cultural Life of the American Colonies 1607–1763* (New York, 1957), 126–53.

17. Thomas Weld's library is catalogued in Robinson and Robinson, "Three Early Massachusetts Libraries," 156–75. William Adams's library was similar to Weld's. In addition to standard texts and reference works it included 56 printed New England sermons indexed on a separate leaf by occasion and text. The catalogue is contained in William Adams, "Sermon Notes," in Sermons Collection, 1 oct. vol., EI.

18. Portions of Increase Mather's manuscript diary have been transcribed by Michael Hall in the Mather Family Papers, AAS. The entry is from Aug. 21, 1717.

19. William Adams, "Sermon on Joel 1:1," Aug. 21, 1679, in Sermons Collection, EI.

20. See William Hubbard, "Sermon Notes," in Sermons Collection, AAS; and John Leverett, "Sermon Notes," 1679.

21. In *Power and the Pulpit in Puritan New England*, 13–14, Emory Elliott classifies printed sermons according to date and Scripture text, and finds a transition from New Testament texts in the period 1630–50 to Old Testament texts in the period 1650–80. From this he deduces a shift in second-generation preaching from "mercy and grace" to an "angry and wrathful God." In fact such generational distinctions do not appear, and the pattern Elliott discovers is a simple reflection of which sermons happened to have been published in which years. In the period 1650–80 most of the printed sermons were occasional sermons which, as we have seen, drew heavily from Old Testament texts. But unpublished sermons from this same period reflect an ongoing concern with New Testament texts and a "protective Christ" in much the same terms as the first generation. In the period 1681–95, Elliott finds a return to New Testament texts, but again this is a reflection of publishing patterns, not pulpit oratory. During the last decades of the 17th century, the Cambridge Press printed more regular sermons, which had more New Testament texts.

22. Thomas Shepard II, "Sermon Notes," in The Shepard Family Papers, oct. vol. III, AAS; and "Sermons on Psalm 124," 1663, *ibid.* oct. vol. IV.

23. Thomas Shepard II, "Sermons on Matthew 7," 1668, *ibid.*, oct. vol. IV.

24. Joshua Moodey, "Sermons on Revelation 2," 1676–77 in Sermons Collection, 1 oct. vol., AAS.

25. Increase Mather, Diary, entry Nov. 1, 1717.

26. Increase Mather, *Some Important Truths About Conversion*, 5, 11, 13. Mather's conversionist preaching is summarized in Middlekauff, *The Mathers*, 164–70.

27. Samuel Willard, *Some Important Truths About Conversion* (Boston, 1684), "To the Reader."

28. *Ibid.*, 375. On Willard's conversionist preaching see Ernest B. Lowrie, *The Shape of the Puritan Mind: The Thought of Samuel Willard* (New Haven, Conn., 1974), 160–85.

29. Increase Mather, *Pray for the Rising Generation* (Boston, 1679), 14, 16.

30. William Adams, "Sermons on Joel 1."

31. *The Results of the Synod of 1679* are reprinted in Walker, ed., *The Creeds and Platforms of Congregationalism*, 423–37. For a general summary see Williston Walker, *A History of the Congregational Churches in the United States* (Boston, 1894), 185–90; and Breen, *The Character of the Good Ruler*, 106–10.

32. *The Results of the Synod of 1679*, 436. The importance of oaths in Puritan culture was summarized in Samuel Willard's *The Fear of an Oath* (Boston, 1701).

33. See the discussions in Miller, *From Colony to Province*, 33–39, 116–18.

34. The conversionist theory of covenant renewal is set forth in Increase Math-

er's *Renewal of Covenant* (Boston, 1677); *Pray for the Rising Generation; or Returning Unto God* (Boston, 1680). See also Samuel Willard's *The Duty of a People* (Boston, 1680); and *Covenant–Keeping the Way to Blessedness* (Boston, 1682).

35. Increase Mather, *Pray for the Rising Generation,* 18, 21. Figures supporting the revival at Milford are presented in Moran, "Religious Renewal, Puritan Tribalism, and the Family in Seventeenth-Century Milford, Connecticut," 236–54.

36. Pope, *The Half-Way Covenant,* 119–24, 242–46, 271; and Moran, "The Puritan Saint," 102–39. Moran points out that most converts were adult children 25 or over, and a slight majority were female (p. 140–98).

37. Solomon Stoddard, *The Inexcusableness of Neglecting the Worship of God* (Boston, 1708), preface. On church membership patterns in Northampton see Patricia J. Tracy, *Jonathan Edwards, Pastor: Religion and Society in Eighteenth-Century Northampton* (New York, 1979), 20–23.

38. Stoddard's position on admitting half-way members to communion is summarized in *The Doctrine of the Instituted Churches* (London, 1700), 22. Increase Mather led the attack on this view in *The Order of the Gospel* (Boston, 1700); *A Dissertation . . .* (Boston, 1708); and *Ichabod* (Boston, 1700). Stoddard's views were not accepted even by many of his fellow ministers in the Connecticut River Valley, and within the churches lay people generally resisted his "presbyterian" sentiments. See Paul R. Lucas, *Valley of Discord: Church and State Along the Connecticut River, 1636–1725* (Hanover, N.H., 1976), 169–88; and Thomas M. Davis and Jeff Jeske, eds., "Solomon Stoddard's 'Arguments' Concerning Admission to the Lord's Supper," American Antiquarian Society, *Proceedings,* 86 (1976), 75–111.

39. Stoddard's revivalistic preaching is discussed in Thomas G. Schafer, "Solomon Stoddard and the Theology of the Revival," in Stuart C. Henry, ed., *A Miscellany of American Christianity: Essays in Honor of H. Shelton Smith* (Durham, N.C., 1963), 328–61; and Perry Miller, "Solomon Stoddard, 1643–1729," *Harvard Theological Review,* 34 (1941), 227–320.

40. See Mather's preface to Solomon Stoddard, *A Guide to Christ* (Boston, 1714).

41. Solomon Stoddard, *A Treatise Concerning Conversion* (Boston, 1719), 35. See also Stoddard's *The Safety of Appearing at the Judgment* (Boston, 1687), 325. Stoddard's traditional (if not always consistent) use of faculty psychology in the intellectualist tradition is discussed in Eugene E. White, "Solomon Stoddard's Theories of Persuasion," *Speech Monographs,* 29 (1962), 235–59; and James G. Blight, "Solomon Stoddard's *Safety of Appearing* and the Dissolution of the Puritan Faculty Psychology," *Journal of the History of the Behavioral Sciences,* 10 (1974), 238–50.

42. White, "Theories of Persuasion," 244.

43. Solomon Stoddard, *A Guide to Christ,* 2.

44. These early sermons are recorded in Solomon Stoddard, Sermons Collection, 1 oct. vol., AAS. I am indebted to Thomas M. Davis for sharing his transcript of Stoddard's sermon on Psalm 23:3 from which the following quotations are taken.

45. See the extended discussion in Harold F. Worthley, "The Lay Officers of the Particular (Congregational) Churches of Massachusetts, 1620–1755: An Investigation of Practice and Theory," (Th.D. diss., Harvard University, 1970).

46. See, e.g., Stoddard's *The Necessity of Acknowledgment* (Boston, 1701); *The Danger of Speedy Degeneracy* (Boston, 1705); or *Those Taught by God the Father to Know God the Son* (Boston, 1712).

47. The theme of clerical "professionalization" has received substantial attention. See, e.g., John W. T. Youngs, *God's Messengers: Religious Leadership in Colonial New England, 1700–1750* (Baltimore, 1976); Hall, *The Faithful Shepherd*, 227–69; and James Schmotter, "Provincial Professionalism: The New England Ministry, 1692–1745" (Ph.D. diss., Northwestern University, 1973).

48. Increase Mather, *The Latter Sign Discoursed of* (Boston, 1682), 22. See also Mather's *Doctrine of Divine Providence* (Boston, 1684); *Kometographia, Or a Discourse Concerning Comets* (Boston, 1683); and *An Essay for the Recording of Illustrious Providences* (Boston, 1684). Mather's interest in the providential signs of everyday life was shared by many of the laity. See David D. Hall's discussion of the noted magistrate Samuel Sewall's diary in "The Mental World of Samuel Sewall," Massachusetts Historical Society, *Proceedings*, 92 (1980), 21–44; or, more generally, Jon Butler, "Magic, Astrology, and the Early American Religious Heritage, 1600–1760," *American Historical Review*, 84 (1979), 317–46.

49. Mather's millennial views are summarized in Mason I. Lowance and David Watters, eds., "Increase Mather's 'New Jerusalem': Millennialism in Late Seventeenth-Century New England," American Antiquarian Society, *Proceedings*, 87 (1977), introduction, 343–61; and Middlekauff, *The Mathers*, 179–87. Not all of Mather's views concerning particular events in the millennium were shared by his contemporaries. But all ministers shared a common interest in the shape of the New Jerusalem and the conversion of the Jews (discussed in the following paragraphs). See James West Davidson, *The Logic of Millennial Thought: Eighteenth-Century New England* (New Haven, Conn., 1977), 142.

50. Increase Mather, *The Mystery of Israel's Salvation* (London, 1669), 163.

51. Mather's treatise on Revelation 3 is reprinted in Lowance and Watters, eds., "Increase Mather's 'New Jerusalem'," 362–408. Although the term *premillennial* is used here to distinguish Mather's timing of the millennium and Christ's Second Coming it did not have the technical precision the term would later enjoy in the 19th century. See Bercovitch, *The American Jeremiad*, 77–80.

52. Lowance and Watters, eds., "Increase Mather's 'New Jerusalem'," 378.

53. Increase Mather, *The Mystery of Israel's Salvation*, 160. On second-generation preoccupations with Israel see Middlekauff, *The Mathers*, 181.

54. In *The Shape of the Puritan Mind*, 19, Ernest B. Lowrie characterizes *A Compleat Body* as "the fullest statement of the Puritan [theological] synthesis in American colonial history." Included in the subscription list to *A Compleat Body of Divinity* (Boston, 1726) were many prominent ministers together with what amounted to a social register of college-educated merchants and magistrates throughout Massachusetts and Connecticut.

55. In *From Colony to Province*, 30, Perry Miller mistakenly ascribed Willard's "*summa* of New England doctrine" to sermons delivered on "successive sabbaths," missing the crucial distinction between regular preaching and weekday lectures. This confusion, in turn, led him to conclude (p. 434) that by the 1690s, when Willard's lectures were delivered, the "logical structure of the [Puritan] mind" had become "detached from religion." That such an intellectualization of the Puritan faith had not occurred in second-generation preaching is clear from Willard's regular sermons which (unlike his lectures) were published in his lifetime for contemporary audiences. See, e.g., Willard's regular sermons on *The Barren Figtree's Doom* (Boston, 1691); or *A Brief Discourse of Justification* (Boston, 1686).

56. Joshua Moodey, *A Practical Discourse* (Boston, 1685), 93, 104–05. Two years later Moodey's Boston lecture reiterated the same theme in *The Great Sin of Formality in Worship* (Boston, 1691).

Chapter 6

1. Increase Mather, *A Discourse Concerning the Danger of Apostacy* (Boston, 1685), 87; and Urian Oakes, *A Seasonable Discourse* (Cambridge, 1682), 24, 32.

2. William Hubbard, *The Happiness of a People* (Boston, 1676), reprinted in Miller and Johnson, eds., *The Puritans*, I, 247, 249. Hubbard repeated this same theme in a fast sermon eight years later. See *The Benefit of a Well-Ordered Conversation* (Boston, 1684), 21, 23.

3. For summaries of scholarship on the New England town see John Murrin, "Review Essay," *History and Theory*, 11 (1972), 226–75; and James A. Henretta, "The Morphology of New England Society in the Colonial Period," *Journal of Interdisciplinary History*, 2 (1971), 379–98.

4. See, e.g., Lockridge, *A New England Town*, 93–118; and Greven, *Four Generations*, 103–72.

5. See Paul Boyer and Stephen Nissenbaum, *Salem Possessed: The Social Origins of Witchcraft* (Cambridge, Mass., 1974), 41–43.

6. David D. Hall describes the rise of written contracts in *The Faithful Shepherd*, 190–91. On the case of William Adams see Lockridge, *A New England Town*, 86. The only exception was Boston, where voluntary payments continued into the 18th century.

7. On the basis of available town and church records Clifford K. Shipton discovered that between 1680 and 1740 "the commonest cause of difficulty [between congregations and ministers] was financial." See "The New England Clergy of the 'Glacial Age'," Colonial Society of Massachusetts, *Publications*, 32 (*Transactions*, 1933–37), 50.

8. *The Results of the Synod of 1679*, 433. The permissibility of clerical ordination had been established in *The Cambridge Platform* (together with scattered early incidents), but the practice did not become widespread until the second generation. See Hall, *The Faithful Shepherd*, 220–221.

9. See Hall, *The Faithful Shepherd*, 220.

10. The "sacramental renaissance" that began in the second generation and continued down to the Great Awakening (1740) is traced in Holifield, *The Covenant Sealed*, 197–224.

11. Lucas, *Valley of Discord*, 191.

12. Increase Mather, *A Discourse Concerning Apostacy*, 62.

13. John Norton, *An Essay Tending to Promote Reformation* (Boston, 1708), 18. See also Urian Oakes, *A Seasonable Discourse*, 13.

14. Joseph Rowlandson, *The Possibility of Gods Forsaking a People* (Boston, 1682), 11.

15. Increase Mather, *A Discourse Concerning Apostacy*, 69.

16. William Adams, *The Necessity of the Pouring Out* (Boston, 1679), 32, 2, 6.

17. Samuel Willard, *The Only Sure Way* (Boston, 1682), reprinted in Plumstead, ed., *The Wall and the Garden*, 86. See also William Adams, *God's Eye on the Contrite* (Boston, 1685), reprinted in Burgess, comp., *The Dedham Pulpit*, 115.

18. Samuel Willard, *The Fiery Tryal No Strange Thing* (Boston, 1682), 18–19. Italics are mine. See also Samuel Torrey, *A Plea for the Life* (Boston, 1683), 28, 34, 40.

19. For accounts of Randolph and the Dominion of New England on which this narrative is based see Michael G. Hall, *Edward Randolph and the American Colonies, 1676–1703* (Chapel Hill, N.C., 1960); Viola F. Barnes, *The Dominion of New England: A Study in British Colonial Policy* (New Haven, Conn., 1923); and Breen, *The Character of the Good Ruler,* 134–79.

20. The term *moderate* is taken from T. H. Breen to describe the influential core of ministers, merchants, and magistrates who sought to establish closer economic, cultural, and political ties with the mother country. See *The Character of the Good Ruler,* 122–23. The moderate merchants are described in Bailyn, *The New England Merchants,* 112–68.

21. Andros's commission is reprinted in Michael G. Hall, Lawrence H. Leder, and Michael G. Kammen, eds., *The Glorious Revolution in America: Documents on the Colonial Crisis of 1689* (Chapel Hill, N.C., 1964), 25–26.

22. Quoted in Breen, *The Character of the Good Ruler,* 144. The best account of Wise's ecclesiastical and political theory is Miller, *From Colony to Province,* 155–59, 288–302.

23. On Boston see Pope, *The Half-Way Covenant,* 222, 284. On Milford and New Haven, see Moran, "The Puritan Saint," 125.

24. In the 20-year period from 1660–80 only 4 regular sermons were published at Cambridge, compared to 14 in the decade from 1681–90. In the later decade, only 6 election sermons were printed. See Benton, "An Annotated Check List of Puritan Sermons," 287–320.

25. Nathaniel Gookin, "Sermon on Ezra 8:21," 1686, in Cotton Mather, "Substance of Sermons Delivered by Several Ministers in Boston," 1 vol., Manuscripts Collection, HL.

26. Samuel Willard, "Sermon on Joshua 22:24–25," *ibid.* In the same year Willard published a similar sermon entitled *A Brief Discourse of Justification* (Boston, 1686). See also Increase Mather's "Sermon on Ephesians 6:14," 1686, in Cotton Mather, "Substance of Sermons Delivered"; and two published sermons: *The Greatest Sinners Exhorted* (Boston, 1686); and *The Mystery of Christ* (Boston, 1686).

27. Joshua Moodey, "Sermon on Luke 12:4–5," 1686, in Cotton Mather, "Substance of Sermons Delivered."

28. Samuel Parris, "Sermon on Revelation 17:14," Sept. 11, 1692, in Parris's sermons, 1689–1695, transcript, CHS. Parris's sermons on Satan followed a lecture series on witchcraft delivered by Parris's unordained predecessor Deodat Lawson. Like Parris, Lawson was born and educated in England where he imbibed European theories of witchcraft set forth by Joseph Glanvil and Henry More at Cambridge. See T. Wright, *Literary Culture in New England,* 107. For a description of Parris's preaching see Larry D. Cragg, "Samuel Parris: Portrait of a Puritan Clergyman," *Essex Institute Historical Collections,* 119 (1983), 209–37.

29. Samuel Parris, "Sermon on John 6:10," Mar. 27, 1692, Parris's Sermons, 1689–1695, transcript, CHS. The social and political tensions underlying the witchcraft hysteria and Parris's "psychopathology" are described in Boyer and Nissenbaum, *Salem Possessed,* 80–216.

30. Boyer and Nissenbaum, *Salem Possessed,* 27–30, 215–16.

31. On the ministers' role in halting the trials see *ibid.,* 9–21; and Richard Weisman, *Witchcraft, Magic, and Religion in Seventeenth-Century Massachusetts*

(Amherst, Mass., 1984), 160–83. In *Entertaining Satan: Witchcraft and the Culture of Early New England* (New York, 1982), 300–01, 401–09, John Demos shows that instances of witchcraft were not uncommon in 17th-century New England, but mass executions and "major panics" *were*.

32. The quotations are taken from contemporary accounts of the Glorious Revolution in Boston reprinted in Hall *et al.*, *The Glorious Revolution in America*, 39–53.

33. Mather's activities in London and his unappreciated diplomatic triumph are described in Kenneth B. Murdock, *Increase Mather: The Foremost American Puritan* (orig. publ. 1925; reprinted New York, 1966), 155–286.

34. Breen, *The Character of the Good Ruler*, 135.

35. The impact of King William's War on New England society is described in Gary B. Nash, *The Urban Crucible: Social Change, Political Consciousness, and the Origins of the American Revolution* (Cambridge, Mass., 1979), 54–65; and T. H. Breen, "War, Taxes, and Political Brokers: The Ordeal of Massachusetts Bay, 1675–1692," in Breen, ed., *Puritans and Adventurers: Change and Persistence in Early America* (New York, 1980), 81–105.

36. Gersholm Bulkeley, *The People's Right to Election* (Philadelphia, 1689), reprinted in Colonial Society of Massachusetts, *Collections*, 1 (1860), 71.

37. On divisions ensuing from the new charter see especially Breen, *The Character of the Good Ruler*, 180–269; and Richard R. Johnson, *Adjustment to Empire: The New England Colonies, 1675–1715* (New Brunswick, N.J., 1981), 242–305.

38. See Breen, *The Character of the Good Ruler*, 195–202; and Miller, *From Colony to Province*, 149–72.

39. Cotton Mather, *Optanda, Good Men Described and Good Things Propounded* (Boston, 1692), 87, 41, 43.

40. *Ibid.*, 46, 43.

41. *Ibid.*, 33.

42. In *From Colony to Province*, 171, Perry Miller interpreted Mather's language as a "shedding of the religious conception of the universe, a turning toward a way of life in which the secular state . . . has become central." This view, as Robert Middlekauff points out, exaggerates the religious changes posed by the revolutionary settlement. Mather and his ministerial colleagues retained a view of the universe that was every bit as religious (if not as intolerant) as their predecessors. See *The Mathers*, 214–15.

43. Cotton Mather, *Optanda*, 77, 83, 51–53.

44. Samuel Willard, *The Character of the Good Ruler* (Boston, 1694), reprinted in Miller and Johnson, eds., *The Puritans*, I, 250–56.

45. Joseph Easterbrook, *Abraham the Passenger* (Boston, 1705), 21. See also Samuel Belcher, *An Essay Tending to Promote the Kingdom* (Boston, 1707), 14–15.

46. Between 1691 and 1699, 23 funeral and execution sermons were published in comparison to 7 election sermons and 5 fast or thanksgiving sermons. See Benton, "An Annotated Check List of Puritan Sermons," 320–37. For a summary and discussion of funeral and election sermons see Lonna M. Malmsheimer, "New England Funeral Sermons and Changing Attitudes Toward Woman, 1672–1792" (Ph.D. diss., University of Minnesota, 1973), 1–132. On the Puritan theory of death contained in these sermons and the models of piety (funeral sermons) and apostasy (execution sermons) they contained, see David E. Stannard, *The Puritan Way of Death: A Study in Religion, Culture, and Social Change* (New York, 1977); Wayne C. Minnick, "The New England Execution Sermon, 1639–1899," *Speech*

Monographs, 35 (1968), 77–89; and Ronald A. Bosco, "Lectures at the Pillory: The Early American Execution Sermon," *American Quarterly*, 30 (1978), 156–76.

47. Samuel Willard, *The High Esteem* (Boston, 1683), 16.

48. Cotton Mather, *The Way to Prosperity* (Boston, 1690), reprinted in Plumstead, ed., *The Wall and the Garden*, 137.

Chapter 7

1. Marcus L. Hansen, "The Problem of the Third Generation Immigrant," Augustana Historical Society, *Publications*, 1938. See also Hansen's suggestive essay on "Immigration and Puritanism" in *The Immigrant in American History* (orig. publ. 1940; reprinted, New York, 1964), 97–128.

2. The theme of anglicization is most fully discussed in John M. Murrin, "Anglicizing an American Colony: The Transformation of Provincial Massachusetts" (Ph.D. diss., Yale University, 1966). See also John Clive and Bernard Bailyn, "England's Cultural Provinces: Scotland and America," *William and Mary Quarterly*, 11 (1954), 200–13; Dunn, *Puritans and Yankees*, 191–356; Breen, *The Character of a Good Ruler*, 210–26; and Kenneth Silverman, *The Life and Times of Cotton Mather* (New York, 1984), 138–90.

3. Cotton Mather's concept of church polity as a "humane invention" is discussed in Middlekauff, *The Mathers*, 209–30.

4. Cotton Mather, *Bonifacius: An Essay Upon the Good*, ed., David Levin (Cambridge, Mass., 1960), 18–19. Mather's millennialism was as intense (and cautious) as his father's, though identified less with Congregational polity than moral reform. See Middlekauff, *The Mathers*, 320–49; David Levin, *Cotton Mather: The Young Life of the Lord's Remembrancer* (Cambridge, Mass., 1978), 174–222; and Silverman, *The Life and Times of Cotton Mather*, 171.

5. This argument is most clearly represented in Perry Miller's discussion of *Bonifacius* as "a compensation for public failure." See *From Colony to Province*, 395–416 (quoted at 405).

6. Cotton Mather, *Manuductio ad Ministerium: Direction for a Candidate of the Ministry* (1726; reprinted New York, 1938), 28–29. See also Mather's 1713 fast sermon, *Advice From the Watch Tower*, reprinted in George H. Orians, ed., *Days of Humiliation* (Gainsville, Fla., 1970), 188, 198: "There will be no bringing of the Sinner to *Do Good*, if the Divine Grace be upheld from them. . . . Nothing but a *New Nature* will thoroughly Cure an *Old Custome* of doing Evil."

7. Cotton Mather, *Bonifacius*, 132–33, 137. The idea of voluntary reforming societies for the suppression of vice originated in England and was introduced to New England by Cotton Mather. See Middlekauff, *The Mathers*, 269–70; and Miller, *From Colony to Province*, 411.

8. Nathanael Appleton, *A Great Man Fallen in Israel* (Boston, 1724), 31.

9. The Brattle Street Church is described in Walker, *A History of the Congregational Churches*, 199–201.

10. See the discussion in Samuel Eliot Morison, *Three Centuries of Harvard, 1636–1936* (Cambridge, Mass., 1937), 46–75; and Hall, *The Organization of American Culture*, 102–04.

11. Morison, *Three Centuries*, 54. The percentage of ministerial students at Harvard College (and Yale College) declined from roughly 1 out of 2 in the 17th century to 1 out of 3 in the 18th. Fragmentary evidence further suggests that the

wealthiest students from the most prestigious New England families avoided the ministry in the 18th century, though this is easy to exaggerate as every graduating class included ministers drawn from the best-connected families. John W. T. Youngs, Jr., describes the shifting composition of the student body in *God's Messengers*, 12–14.

12. Despite his Anglican sympathies in matters of church membership and liturgy, Leverett remained orthodox (Calvinist) in matters of theology. See Arthur D. Kaledin, "The Mind of John Leverett" (Ph.D. diss., Harvard University, 1965), 182–87.

13. On the demise of Ramist rhetoric see Porter Gale Perrin, "The Teaching of Rhetoric in the American Colonies Before 1750" (Ph.D. diss., University of Chicago, 1936), 15. The importance of sacred history as a discipline is described in Edward T. Dunn, S. J., "Tutor Henry Flynt of Harvard College, 1675–1760" (Ph.D. diss., University of Rochester, 1968), 206. The two most popular "Real Whigs" in New England were Thomas Gordon and John Trenchard, whose articles in the radical weekly *The Independent Whig* (especially a series entitled *Cato's Letters*) were widely read as the 18th century wore on. The libertarian orientation of English Real Whig theory and its rising influence in the New World are summarized in Caroline Robbins, *The Eighteenth-Century Commonwealthman* (Cambridge, Mass., 1959), 115–25, 384–86; and Bernard Bailyn, *The Origins of American Politics* (New York, 1968), 3–58. For a more extended discussion of these themes see Part V of this book.

14. Bequests by Thomas Hollis to Harvard's library and by Jeremiah Dummer to Yale's were especially important in bringing current English writers to the attention of students. The increased flow of English literature to New England is described in T. Wright, *Literary Culture in New England*, 169–215; L. Wright, *The Cultural Life of the American Colonies*, 126–53; Ford, *The Boston Book Market*, 62–64, 163–82; and Norman Fiering, "Transatlantic Republic of Letters: A Note on the Circulation of Learned Periodicals to Early Eighteenth-Century America," *William and Mary Quarterly*, 33 (1976), 642–60.

15. Miller, *From Colony to Province*, 170.

16. Virtually every surviving student library inventory includes works by Tillotson. For accounts of his vogue see Youngs, *God's Messengers*, 65–68; and Norman Fiering, "The First American Enlightenment: Tillotson, Leverett, and Philosophical Anglicanism," *New England Quarterly*, 44 (1981), 307–44. For a complete discussion of Tillotson's life and work in the context of English Restoration preaching see Irene Simon, *Three Restoration Divines: Barrow, South, Tillotson: Selected Sermons*, 2 pts. in 3 vols (Paris, 1967–76), I, 1–300.

17. This literature is discussed generally in Marjorie H. Nicolson, *Mountain Gloom and Mountain Glory: The Development of the Aesthetics of the Infinite* (Ithaca, N.Y., 1959), 271–323.

18. On the interconnections of science, religion, and social order in 18th-century thought see Margaret C. Jacob, *The Newtonians and the English Revolution, 1689–1720* (Ithaca, N.Y., 1976).

19. For a discussion of "court" and "country" politics in the context of New England society see Breen, *The Character of the Good Ruler*, 206–09.

20. On the court sympathies of most third-generation ministers see Youngs, *God's Messengers*, 64; and Breen, *The Character of the Good Ruler*, 210.

21. Benjamin Wadsworth, *Rulers Feeding and Guiding their People* (Boston, 1716), 22. See also Ebenezer Pemberton, *A Sermon Preached in the Audience of the*

General Assembly (Boston, 1708), 25–28. Third-generation ministers routinely identified anarchy as a more frightening evil than tyranny. See Baldwin, *The New England Clergy* 36.

22. In *The Imagination as a Means of Grace: Locke and the Aesthetics of Romanticism* (Berkeley, Calif., 1960), 46, Ernest L. Tuveson points out how "once the mind has been absorbed into nature, it takes on characteristics of the natural world; and when the cosmic order appears as a marvelously and perfectly contrived machine, each part working precisely with every other part, the mind too must appear as natural. . . . The emphasis is on environment rather than on a hereditary tendency to disobey and forget God." For extended discussions of the impact of the New Science on liberal English religious thought see Roland N. Stromberg, *Religious Liberalism in Eighteenth Century England* (London, 1954); and G. R. Cragg, *From Puritanism to the Age of Reason: A Study of Changes in Religious Thought within the Church of England, 1660–1700* (Cambridge, England, 1950).

23. These explanations are set forth in Miller, *From Colony to Province*, 184, 189–90.

24. Increase Mather, *A Discourse Concerning the Danger of Apostasy*, 96.

25. See Tuttle, "The Libraries of the Mathers," 286–356.

26. Cotton Mather, *Manuductio ad Ministerium*, 141–42.

27. David Levin traces the contribution of the *Magnalia* to New England historiography in *Cotton Mather*, 250–69. For positive evaluations of Mather's work see also Richard F. Lovelace, *The American Pietism of Cotton Mather: Origins of American Evangelicalism* (Boston, 1979); and Silverman, *The Life and Times of Cotton Mather*.

28. Cotton Mather, *Magnalia*, I, 350.

29. Cf. Bercovitch, *The Puritan Origins of the American Self*, 39–41, and Middlekauff, *The Mathers*, 211, who argues that in Cotton Mather's writing "typology remained . . . a rhetorical device, not an instrument to be used in the analysis of history." In fact, typology was *both* a rhetorical device and an aid to understanding history.

30. *Magnalia*, I, 32, 111.

31. *Ibid.*, 350, 37.

32. *Ibid.*, 351.

33. In *Moral Philosophy at Seventeenth-Century Harvard*, Norman Fiering traces the intellectual ancestry of Cambridge Platonists and the 18th-century cult of sensibility to Puritan (and Augustinian) strains. The links of "Whig" political ideology to ideas emerging during the Puritan Commonwealth are discussed in Robbins, *The Eighteenth-Century Commonwealthman*, 4–5.

34. The term *secular state* is taken from Miller, *From Colony to Province*, 367–84, while the "ineffectiveness" of threats of a broken covenant is discussed in Breen, *The Character the Good Ruler*, 166. Both Miller and Breen correctly identify the secular themes appearing in election sermons, but they then extend those themes to an assumed secularization of New England society-as-a-whole. Evidence for such a transition is not forthcoming—at least in terms of New England's churches and ministries. See chapter 8 in this study.

35. For Massachusetts see, e.g., Grindal Rawson, *The Necessity of a Speedy and Thorough Reformation* (Boston, 1709), 27, 12–13; or Cotton Mather, *Things for a Distressed People to Think Upon* (Boston, 1696), reprinted in Orians, *Days of Humiliation*, 3, 15. Francis J. Bremer discusses Connecticut's political situation in *The Puritan Experiment*, 211. It would be easy to exaggerate Connecticut's isolation

from English rule and politics. The colony retained its charter on royal sufferance and, as the dominion demonstrated, it could be forfeited at any moment. Although Connecticut election speakers did not have to formally address a royal governor, they were careful not to give offense to the crown or ignore stylized celebrations of English liberties and court prerogatives. See, e.g.: John Bulkeley, *The Necessity of Religion in Societies* (Boston, 1713), 6; Timothy Cutler, *The Firm Union of People Represented* (New London, 1717), 8, 38–39; or Samuel Eastabrook, *A Sermon* (New London, 1718), 19–20. Between 1700 and 1710 only 1 Connecticut election sermon was published, compared to 10 in Massachusetts. For an analysis of Connecticut election sermons after Queen Anne's War see chapter 9 in this study.

36. Extended metaphors in Puritan sermons did not appear on a regular basis until the third generation. For an analysis of literary techniques in the context of 18th-century election sermons see Plumstead, ed., *The Wall and the Garden*, 145–47.

37. Samuel Danforth, Jr., *An Exhortation to All* (Boston, 1714) reprinted *ibid.*, 151, 153–54, 156–67.

38. *Ibid.*, 172, 176.

39. *Ibid.*, 163–64, 174–75.

40. Grindal Rawson, *The Necessity of a Speedy and Thorough Reformation*, 6; and John Leverett, "Sermon Notes, 1696–1710," 2 oct. vols., AAS.

41. William Williams, *The Danger of Not Reforming* (Boston, 1707), 17; and John Danforth, *The Vile Prophanations of Prosperity* (Boston, 1704), 35.

42. Williams, *The Danger of Not Reforming*, 17.

43. John Danforth, *The Vile Prophanations of Prosperity*, 36.

44. Benjamin Wadsworth preached a sermon series occasioned by the burning of the "Old Meeting House" in 1711 and published it in *Five Sermons* (Boston, 1714). The rising incidence of fires and epidemics attendant on increasing population concentration is discussed in G. B. Warden, *Boston, 1689–1776* (Boston, 1970), 13, 18, 66–67, 105.

45. William Pencak discusses New England's participation in Queen Anne's War in *Wars, Politics, and Revolution in Provincial Massachusetts* (Boston, 1981), 35–59. See also, Johnson, *Adjustment to Empire*, 375–80.

46. In *The Urban Crucible*, 55–73, Gary B. Nash describes how New England's greater involvement in the wars with France retarded its growth in numbers and wealth relative to other urban centers in New York and Philadelphia. For a discussion of how war with France minimized court-country tensions between the governor and legislature see Pencak, *War, Politics, and Revolution*, 36.

47. Grindal Rawson, *The Necessity*, 37. See also John Danforth, *The Vile Prophanations of Prosperity*, 44.

48. Edwards's sermon notes are printed in John A. Stoughton, *"Windsor Farmes": A Glimpse of an Old Parish* (Hartford, Conn., 1883), 143, 122, 126. Cotton Mather recorded similar themes for fast days in war years. See Worthington C. Ford, ed., *The Diary of Cotton Mather*, Massachusetts Historical Society, 2 vols., *Collections* (Boston, 1911–12), entries for Apr. 14, 1706; Apr. 18, 1706; May 5, 1706; May 19, 1706; or May 23, 1706.

49. William Williams, *The Danger of Not Reforming*, 29.

50. *The Diary of Cotton Mather*, I, 132.

51. A good example of peacetime martial oratory is Joseph Belcher's 1698 election sermon, *The Worst Enemy Conquered* (Boston, 1698), which described the

"many hazards, and hardships . . . every Christian must endeavor to endure as a good soldier of Jesus Christ."

52. Henry Gibbs, *The Right Method of Safety* (Boston, 1704), 7–9, 11, 37, 40–41.

53. Thomas Bridge, *The Knowledge of God* (Boston, 1705), 50, 54.

54. Gary Nash estimates that 1 out of 15 able-bodied Massachusetts males participated in the campaigns of King Williams's War and Queen Anne's War, and that "one-quarter never lived to tell the terrors of New England's first major experience with international warfare." Despite these "staggering" losses, New England towns invariably met enlistment quotas—particularly in the early phases of a war. See *The Urban Crucible*, 58–59.

Chapter 8

1. The term is taken from Breen, "Persistent Localism," 3–28. The continuation of localistic orientations into the eighteenth century is traced in Michael Zuckerman, *Peaceable Kingdoms: New England Towns in the Eighteenth Century* (New York, 1970), 10–45. Zuckerman's study was limited primarily to eleven Massachusetts towns. In Connecticut, where there was no royal government with centralizing ambitions, Bruce Daniels observes that "the locus of authority [moved] away from the center of the colony and towards the town and society or neighborhood." *The Connecticut Town*, 171–80 (quoted at 176).

2. William G. McLoughlin traces the evolution of toleration laws and the Anglican governor's inability to circumvent local Congregational establishments in *New England Dissent*, I, 114, 120–27, 200–04.

3. This cyclical membership pattern emerges from a study of 54 Connecticut towns; see Moran, "The Puritan Saint," 238–55.

4. This estimate is derived by multiplying 4,795 (the number of man-years of preaching by Harvard students graduating between 1676 and 1710) by 100 (the average number of sermons preached per year by each minister). Between 1690 and 1740, New England's population tripled from 50,000 to 150,000. See Nash, *The Urban Crucible*, 54. On the continued place of the ministers at the center of public communications see Richard D. Brown, "Spreading the Word: Rural Clergymen and the Communication Network of Eighteenth-Century New England," Massachusetts Historical Society, *Proceedings*, 94 (1982), 1–14.

5. The term *enclosed orthodoxy* is taken from Zuckerman, *Peaceable Kingdoms*, 111. Within particular towns, ministers remained with their congregations for long periods of time. John W. T. Youngs calculates that the average tenure of an 18th-century minister at any one congregation was about 25 years. See *God's Messengers*, 29.

6. Edwards's transcripts are included in "Sermon Box," 1 vol., Manuscript Collections, CHS. Kenneth Lockridge estimates that in the period 1710–60 lay literacy rates approached universality and that "the focus of literacy remains essentially religious." *Literacy in Colonial New England*, 57–71 (quoted at 69). Funeral sermons, like Cotton Mather's sermon for Jerusha Oliver, often included extracts from lay diaries and journals that reflected a continuing lay piety. See Cotton Mather, *Memorials of Early Piety* (Boston, 1711). John W. T. Youngs discusses 18th-century lay diaries generally in *God's Messengers*, 92–108. The religious orientation of 18th-century schools, primers, and readers is described in Axtell, *The School Upon a Hill*; and Hall, "The Uses of Literacy," 26, 45.

7. Ebenezer Parkman recorded 55 clerical dismissals in his early 18th-century diary. Most of these were, John W. T. Youngs observes, "commonly . . . based on piety rather than apathy." *God's Messengers*, 98, 104.

8. Cotton Mather, *Manductio ad Ministerium*, 94, 93.

9. *Ibid.*, 80, 16.

10. *The Diary of Cotton Mather*, I, 584, 592. Mather's meditations and devotions in preparation for preaching are described in Levin, *Cotton Mather*, 59–65.

11. To organize and contain theological doctrines, Cotton Mather recommended standard 17th-century reference works like Alstead, Wollebius, Calvin, Ames, Strong's Concordance, and the commentaries or "synopsis" of Poole and Matthew Henry. See *Manductio ad Ministerium*, 71–89.

12. In a typical sermon taken from Canticles 1:8 in 1722, Nathaniel Stone (HC, 1690) of Brewster, Mass., enumerated two doctrines, twelve propositions, and seven uses — all supported with copious scriptural cross- references. See "Sermon on Canticles 1:8," May 11, 1722, Sermons Collection, 1 vol., CL.

13. Cotton Mather, *Manductio ad Ministerium*, 105–06. Neither Mather nor Perkins devoted much attention to the topic of delivery, preferring to cite standard classical authorities. See Howard Martin, "Puritan Preachers on Rhetoric: Notes on American Colonial Rhetoric," *Quarterly Journal of Speech*, 50 (1964), 278–92.

14. See Levin, *Cotton Mather*, 114.

15. John Barnard, *Autobiography*, reprinted in Massachusetts Historical Society, *Collections*, 3d Ser., 5 (1836), 186–88.

16. Benjamin Wadsworth, "Sermon on 2 Samuel 11:5," Dec. 4, 1709, in "Sermons, 1709–1719," AAS.

17. Joseph Lord, "Sermon on Isaiah 33:22," 1721, in "Sermons, 1721–1755," 1 vol., AAS.

18. Jeremiah Shepard, *A Sort of Believers Never Saved* (Boston, 1711), 6.

19. Joseph Baxter, "Sermon on Isaiah 57:1," Dec. 24, 1727, in Sermons Collection, Box 1, Folder 5, AAS; and Samuel Moodey, *The Doleful State of the Damned* (Boston, 1710), 9.

20. See, e.g., Benjamin Wadsworth, *The Highest Dwelling with the Lowest* (Boston, 1711), 43–44.

21. William Brattle, "Sermon on 2 Corinthians 1:20," Apr. 19, 1696, in Leverett, "Sermon Notes, 1696–1710," I, AAS. See also Benjamin Colman, *Faith Victorious* (Boston, 1702), 11–13.

22. Benjamin Wadsworth, "Sermon on 2 Samuel 11:15." See also William Brattle, "Sermon on 1 Thessalonians 2:20," Apr. 5, 1696, in John Leverett, "Sermon Notes, 1696–1710," I.

23. Benjamin Wadsworth, "Sermon on 2 Samuel 11:15."

24. Jeremiah Shepard, *A Sort of Believers Never Saved*, 38.

25. John Barnard, *The Hazard and the Unprofitableness* (Boston, 1712), 27.

26. John Flavell, *Keeping the Heart* (Boston, 1720), 160. Prior to 1740, debates over the faculties seldom appeared in sermon notes. See William J. Scheick, *The Will and the Word: The Poetry of Edward Taylor* (Georgia, 1974), xii.

27. In *Moral Philosophy at Seventeenth-Century Harvard*, Norman Fiering traces ongoing academic debates over the head and heart that had begun in the first generation. However, these distinct emphases were not conspicuous in preaching before the fourth generation revivals of 1740. Both "voluntarist" and "intellectualist" sentiments can be found in the sermons of both "orthodox" and "liberal" ministers. Among the liberals, for example, compare Benjamin Colman's intellec-

tualist sermon on *God Deals with Us as Rational Creatures* (Boston, 1723) with his voluntarist sermon on *The Friend of Christ* (Boston, 1731). Among orthodox ministers compare Cotton Mather's *Reasonable Religion* (Boston, 1700) with *The Quickened Soul* (Boston, 1720).

28. The one-sided emphasis on 18th-century moralism is reflected in standard histories of preaching and theology. See, e.g., Haroutunian, *Piety to Moralism*; Levy, *Preaching in the First Half of the Eighteenth-Century*; and Miller, *From Colony to Province*, 417–36.

29. Edward Taylor, "Sermon on John 15:24," Oct. 1703, reprinted in Norman S. Grabo, ed., *Edward Taylor's Christographia* (New Haven, Conn., 1962), 439. On the English sentimentalist orientation to "natural sublimes," see Nicolson, *Mountain Gloom and Mountain Glory*, 271–323.

30. Nehemiah Walter, *A Discourse Concerning the Wonderfulness of Christ* (Boston, 1713), 4, 230.

31. Edward Tompson, "Sermon on Matthew 5:8," July 5, 1685, in Samuel Tompson, "Notebook, 1678–1695," 1 vol., Manuscript Collection, AAS; and Samuel Moodey, *The Doleful State of the Damned*, 171.

32. Nathaniel Stone, "Sermon on Canticles 1:8," Sept. 7, 1722, in Sermons Collection, CL.

33. Warham Mather, *A Short Discourse* (New London, Conn., 1716), 6. See also Thomas Bridge, *What Faith Can Do* (Boston, 1712), 12; and Nathaniel Stone's "Sermon on Canticles 1:8," Sept 7, 1722, whose central theme was that "God is not Glorified by what we do out of Christ."

34. See, e.g., Joshua Moodey, *The Great Sin of Formality*; Solomon Stoddard, *The Inexcusableness of Neglecting Worship*; Benjamin Wadsworth, *Assembling at the House of God* (Boston, 1711); and *Publick Worship* (Boston, 1704); William King, *A Discourse Concerning the Inventions of Men* (Boston, 1712); Benjamin Colman, *Four Sermons* (Boston, 1717); and Cotton Mather, *A Good Evening for the Best of Dayes* (Boston, 1708).

35. Timothy Edwards, "Sermon on Psalm 89:7," May 1712, recorded and transcribed in John A. Stoughton, "Windsor Farmes," 139, 143. See also Benjamin Wadsworth, *Assembling at the House of God*, 4.

36. William Brattle, "Sermon on 1 Thessalonians 2:20," Apr. 26, 1696, in John Leverett, "Sermon Notes, 1696–1710," I; Benjamin Wadsworth, "Sermon on Matthew 15:8," Oct. 16, 1709, in "Sermons, 1709–1719," AAS; and Timothy Edwards, "Sermon on Psalm 89:7."

37. These disputes are traced in Youngs, *God's Messengers*, 97–108.

38. John Danforth, Samuel Danforth, and Peter Thacher, *An Essay Preached by Several Ministers* (Boston, 1723), reprinted in Emery, ed., *The Ministry of Taunton*, I, 279, 284. For other works by ministers supporting the new method of psalm singing see Thomas Symmes, *The Reasonbleness of Regular Singing* (Boston, 1720); Cotton Mather, *The Accomplished Singer* (Boston, 1721); Timothy Woodbridge, *The Duty of God's Professing People* (New London, 1727); and Nathaniel Chauncy, *Regular Singing Defended* (New London, 1728). The initial refusal of congregations to accept the new measures is traced in Winslow, *Meetinghouse Hill*, 160; and Cyclone Covey, "Puritanism and Music in Colonial America," *William and Mary Quarterly*, 8 (1951), 378–88.

39. The Massachusetts clergy's proposals are recorded in Congregational Churches of Massachusetts, Convention of Ministers, "To Serve the Great Inten-

tions of Religion," June 1, 1704, Manuscripts Collection, HL; and Congregational Churches of Massachusetts, "Proposals in Reply to the Question," Sept. 13, 1705, *ibid.* Dudley's antipathy to the Mathers and his refusal to endorse the ministers' proposals is traced in Breen, *The Character of the Good Ruler*, 235–39. The rejection of standing ministerial councils in Massachusetts did not stop ministers from meeting in local and regional associations on an ad hoc basis. See Youngs, *God's Messengers*, 73–76.

40. The *Saybrook Platform* is reprinted in Walker, ed., *The Creeds and Platforms of Congregationalism*, 502–07.

41. Paul Lucas describes congregational opposition to the *Saybrook Platform* in *Valley of Discord*, 189–93. He observes that "the brethren [lay members] transformed the debate over the Platform into a test of lay Congregationalism. The issue was never in doubt. The associations were emasculated, stripped of their power to render binding decisions in either disputes or cases of discipline, and the clergy's carefully prepared counteroffensive collapsed like a sand castle." Quoted at 191.

42. See, e.g., Azariah Mather, *God's Rulers a Choice Blessing* (New London, 1725), 1–2, 20; Anthony Stoddard, *A Sermon Preached* (New London, 1716), 28; Timothy Cutler, *The Firm Union of a People Represented* (New London, 1717), 47; or Benjamin Wadsworth, *Rulers Feeding and Guiding Their People* (Boston, 1716), 59.

43. Between 1700 and 1730 there were 108 printed fast, election, artillery election, and thanksgiving sermons, compared to 217 printed funeral, ordination, and lecture sermons.

44. Between 1700 and 1730, 87 lecture sermons were published; they were surpassed in numbers only by funeral sermons, 96 of which were printed during the same period.

45. For a summary of the self-justifying apologias of lecture sermons in the 18th century see Youngs, *God's Messengers*, 67.

46. Ebenezer Pemberton, *A Christian Fixed in His Post* (Boston, 1704), 13–14, 20, 37. For similar pronouncements in lecture sermons see John Danforth, *The Right Christian Temper* (Boston, 1702); Benjamin Wadsworth, *Considerations to the Right of Christian Temper* (Boston, 1702); Benjamin Wadsworth, *Considerations to Prevent Murmurings* (Boston, 1706); John Williams, *God in the Camp* (Boston, 1707); Benjamin Colman, *The Piety and Duty of Rulers* (Boston, 1708); John Webb, *A Sermon Preached* (Boston, 1722); Thomas Bridge, *Jethro's Advice* (Boston, 1710); Cotton Mather, *The Day Which the Lord Hath Made* (Boston, 1703); Benjamin Colman, *Four Sermons Preached*; Benjamin Colman, *The Doctrine and Law of the Holy Sabbath* (Boston, 1725); John Barnard, *The Worship of God* (Boston, 1729); or Henry Flynt, *An Appeal to the Consciences of a Degenerate People* (Boston, 1729).

47. See Stannard, *The Puritan Way of Death*, 109–22.

48. See, e.g., Cotton Mather's focus on "the Invisible World" in *Hades Look'd Unto* (Boston, 1717), 32–33. Mather set the form for printed funeral sermons more than any other third-generation minister. Besides the *Magnalia*, he published over 50 funeral sermons in the course of his pulpit career. These sermons are discussed in their social and political contexts in William D. Andrews, "The Printed Funeral Sermons of Cotton Mather," *Early American Literature*, 5 (1970), 24–44.

49. In an analysis of nearly 500 printed funeral sermons delivered between 1672 (when the first funeral sermon was printed) and 1792, Lonna M. Malmsh-

eimer found that 65 % were for ministers and 25 % were for women. Of the women's funeral sermons, roughly half were wives or daughters of ministers. "New England Funeral Sermons and Changing Attitudes Toward Women," 32.

50. Benjamin Colman, *The Prophet's Death* (Boston, 1723), 35.

51. *Ibid.*, 11, 28.

52. Ebenezer Pemberton as quoted in Thomas Prince, *A Sermon Delivered* (Boston, 1718), appendix, p. 17. Other ordination sermons also defended the procedures of ministerial ordination. For example, at the ordination of Warham Williams in 1723, William Williams reminded the congregation that "meerly that such a thing [as lay ordination] hath been an ancient practice and usage of our Nation and Fathers is no Argument: for in matters of Religion it is no rule to do as men hath thought best, but we must inquire whether their Judgments have been regulated by the Word of God." William Williams, *The Great Concern of Christians* (Boston, 1723), 10.

53. The evolution of ordination rituals and sermons is traced in Youngs, *God's Messengers*, 30–39; Hall, *The Faithful Shepherd*, 220–22; and Martin, "Puritan Preachers on Rhetoric," 278–92. Between 1709, when the first ordination sermon was printed, and 1740, 78 ordination sermons were published. See Youngs, *God's Messengers*, 36.

54. Thomas Paine, *The Pastoral Charge* (Boston, 1720), 21.

55. William Shurtleff, *The Labour that Attends the Gospel-Ministry* (Boston, 1727), 30; and Nathaniel Eells, *The Ministers of Gods Word* (Boston, 1725), 8, 16.

56. Azariah Mather, *The Gospel-Minister Described* (New London, 1725), 12.

57. Ebenezer Thayer, *Ministers of the Gospel are Christ's Ambassadours* (Boston, 1727), 2. See also Benjamin Lord, *The Faithful and Approved Minister* (Boston, 1726), 27.

58. Solomon Stoddard, *The Duty of Gospel-Ministers* (Boston, 1718), 12, 20; and *The Presence of Christ* (Boston, 1718), 2, 4, 11.

59. William G. McLoughlin describes the early efforts of itinerant Baptist "pietists" in *The New England Dissent*, I, 134.

60. Samuel Wigglesworth, *The Excellency of the Gospel- Message* (Boston, 1727), 5, 13–14. The need for superior social and academic status (along with a superior life style) was also defended in Nathaniel Eells, *The Ministers of Gods Word*, 16; and Daniel Lewis, *Of Taking Heed to, and Fulfilling the Ministry* (Boston, 1720), 19.

61. John Hancock, *A Sermon Preached* (Boston, 1726), 14; Benjamin Colman, *Prayer to the Lord* (Boston, 1727), 13; Thomas Paine, *The Pastoral Charge*, 12; Samuel Tompson, "Notebook, 1678–1695;" and Isaac Chauncy, *The Faithful Evangelist* (Boston, 1726), 25.

62. Joseph Belcher, *God Giveth the Increase* (Boston, 1722), 31.

Chapter 9

1. The most important description of changes in 18th- century political thought to appear since Perry Miller's *Colony to Province* is T. H. Breen's analysis of *The Character of the Good Ruler*. Here Breen clarifies the new qualifications of provincial rulers, but fails to note how the clergy reconciled the altered situation to the analogy of Israel.

2. Thomas Buckingham, *Moses and Aaron* (New London, 1729), 25.

3. Peter Thacher, *Wise and Good Rulers* (Boston, 1726), 16–17. Thomas Buck-

ingham emphasized this same point in *Moses and Aaron*, 27: "He had a Liberal Education becoming the Son of *Pharaoh's* Daughter, by whom he was adopted in his Infancy. . . . He was learned in all the wisdom of the *Egyptians*, who were at this time perhaps the Politest People in the world."

4. Peter Thacher, *Wise and Good Rulers*, 20, 14–15.

5. William Burnham, *God's Providence in Placing Men* (New London, 1722), 27.

6. Benjamin Colman, *The Religious Regards We Owe to Our Country* (Boston, 1718), 3, 15, 17–18. Peter Thacher described the duty of public-minded leaders in similar terms in *Wise and Good Rulers*, 33: "A Private, narrow, Selfish Spirit in a Publick Person, is most loathsome to GOD and Man; [it] brings Infamy and a Curse upon the Guilty and innumerable Oppressions and Mischiefs upon the People."

7. Samuel Fiske, *The Character of the Candidate for Civil Office* (Boston, 1731), 10–11.

8. *Ibid.*, 13, 21, 36, 41. For similar analyses of David in election sermons see especially: Benjamin Colman, *David's Dying Charge* (Boston, 1723); Joseph Sewall, *Rulers Must be Just* (Boston, 1724); and Phineas Fiske, *The Good Subject's Wish* (New London, 1726).

9. Timothy Edwards, *All the living Must Surely Die* (New London, 1734), 9, 11–12, 20–21, 52. For similar pronouncements see Timothy Woodbridge, *Jesus Christ Doth Actually Reign* (New London, 1727), 32. The theme of piety and godliness in rulers was especially prominent in Connecticut election sermons. See also: Samuel Whitman, *Practical Godliness* (New London, 1714); Nathaniel Chauncey, *Honouring God the True Way to Heaven* (New London, 1719); Stephen Hosmer, *A Peoples Living in Appearance* (New London, 1720); Jonathan Marsh, *An Essay, To Prove the Thorough Reformation* (New London, 1721); and Samuel Woodbridge, *Obedience to the Divine Law* (New London, 1724).

10. John Barnard, *The Throne Established by Righteousness* (Boston, 1734), reprinted in Plumstead, ed., *The Wall and the Garden*, 265–66.

11. *Ibid.*, 243, 241, 240. The importance of typology for New England's political morality in the 18th-century pulpit has not been given sufficient attention in recent scholarship. Ministers invariably employed Israel as a civil model, agreeing with Joseph Moss that "the Scriptures containeth a Body of Political Statutes, which altho' they were instituted by God as the Civil Law of the Common Wealth of *Israel* only; yet many of them are of a general Nature, and are founded in Natural Equity; and so are suitable for other Nations." *The Discourse Sheweth* (New London, 1715), 17.

12. John Barnard, *The Throne Established by Righteousness*, 249.

13. Thomas Buckingham, *Moses and Aaron*, 43. Italics are mine.

14. The first volumes of Prince's history were published in *A Chronological History of New England*, 2 vols. (Boston, 1736–[55]).

15. Thomas Prince, *The People of New-England* (Boston, 1730), reprinted in Plumstead, ed., *The Wall and the Garden*, 184–85, 186.

16. *Ibid.*, 187, 196–98.

17. *Ibid.*, 199, 201, 205.

18. *Ibid.*, 211–12, 220.

19. Population estimates are taken from Evarts B. Greene and Virginia D. Harrington, *American Population Before the Federal Census of 1790* (1932; reprinted, Gloucester, Mass., 1966), 10. In Connecticut, population increased 58% from 1670 to 1700 and jumped to a 280% increase from 1700 to 1730. See Richard L. Bush-

man, *From Puritan to Yankee: Character and the Social Order in Connecticut, 1690–1765* (Cambridge, 1967), 83.

20. On Dedham, see Lockridge, *A New England Town*, 94–103. On Connecticut, see Daniels, *The Connecticut Town*, 96–97. Michael Zuckerman traced parish divisions in 5 of his 11 Massachusetts towns in *Peaceable Kingdoms*. J. M. Bumsted traces the creation of seven new societies in Norwich, Conn., between 1716 and 1761. See "Revivalism and Separatism in New England: The First Society of Norwich, Connecticut, as a Case Study," *William and Mary Quarterly*, 24 (1967), 591.

21. The movement west and north is described in Greven, *Four Generations*, 222–58; and Daniels, *The Connecticut Town*, 45–63. The creation of new townships in the early 18th century is described in Lois Kimball Mathews, *The Expansion of New England* (orig. publ. 1909; reprinted New York, 1962), 76–107; Roy H. Akagi, *The Town Proprietors of the New England Colonies* (orig. publ. 1924; reprinted Gloucester, Mass., 1963), 175–229; and Clark, *The Eastern Frontier*, 111–20, 169–79.

22. Altered patterns of land ownership and settlement in the 18th century are described in Grant, *Democracy in the Connecticut Frontier Town of Kent*, 1–65; and Bushman, *From Puritan to Yankee*, 73–82.

23. See, e.g., Timothy Walker's account of his parishioners in Rumford, N. H., summarized in Clark, *The Eastern Frontier*, 254–57.

24. The South Parish covenant is reprinted in George Mooar, *Historical Manual of the South Church in Andover, Massachusetts* (Andover, Mass., 1859), 61. Andover's population growth and expansion into the South Parish is described in Greven, *Four Generations*, 175–80.

25. On the process and design of new meetinghouse construction in the 18th century see Benes and Zimmerman, *New England Meeting House and Church*, 2. Generally speaking, the proportions of meetinghouses completed between 1700 and 1730 were double that of their 17th-century predecessors. For descriptions of the new meetinghouses and accompanying rituals of covenant making and renewal see, e.g. Henry A. Hazen, *History of Billerica Massachusetts with a Genealogical Register* (Boston, 1883), 4, 47; John Daggett, *A Sketch of the History of Attleborough* (Boston, 1894), 14, 61; or Abiel Abbot, *History of Andover from Its Settlement to 1829* (Andover, Mass., 1829), 36.

26. See, e.g., James Keith and Samuel Danforth, *Two Sermons* (Boston, 1717); Cotton Mather, *Zelotes* (Boston, 1717); Cotton Mather, *A Vision in the Temple* (Boston, 1721) or Benjamin Colman, *A Gospel Ministry the Rich Gift* (Boston, 1715). For one account of the "vast Auditory" at the dedication of the New South meetinghouse in Boston see *The Diary of Cotton Mather*, II, 393.

27. Thomas Cheever, *Two Sermons Preached at Malden* (Boston, 1726), 88; and Benjamin Colman and William Cooper, *Two Sermons* (Boston, 1723). The theme of failure and declension can be seen in many fast and election sermons in this period. See, e.g. Jonathan Townsend, *An Exhortation* (Boston, 1729); Eleazer Williams, *An Essay to Prove* (New London, 1723); Ebenezer Thayer, *Jerusalem Instructed and Warned* (Boston, 1725); or Cotton Mather, *Concio ad Populum* (Boston, 1719).

28. Nathaniel Gookin, *The Day of Trouble* (Boston, 1728), 2.

29. Thomas Paine, *The Doctrine of Earthquakes* (Boston, 1728), preface. The earthquake fasts and revivals are described in Love, *Fast and Thanksgiving Days*, 185–95; and Youngs, *God's Messengers*, 110–12.

30. John Barnard, *Two Discourses Addressed to Young Persons* (Boston, 1727), 78; James Allin, *Thunder and Earthquake* (Boston, 1727), 7; Thomas Prince, *Earthquakes the Works of God* (Boston, 1727), 6–10. The logic of earthquake sermons is summarized in Miller, *From Colony to Province*, 444–46; and Maxine Van De Wetering, "Moralizing in Puritan Natural Science: Mysteriousness in Earthquake Sermons," *Journal of the History of Ideas,* 43 (1982), 417–38.

31. Thomas Prince, *Earthquakes the Works of God,* 11.

32. James Allin, *Thunder and Earthquake,* 8. See also Nathaniel Gookin, *The Day of Trouble,* 39: "Threatened Judgments may be *averted.* . . . when *God threatens these,* for the most part, his Threatenings are *not absolute,* but *Conditional;* and the Design of God in *threatening* before he *strikes* is, that we may receive Warning and return to Him."

33. John Cotton, *A Holy Fear of God* (Boston, 1727), 12.

34. John Brown, *Solemn Covenanting* (Boston, 1728), 30. For an account of a similar renewal service in Andover's South Parish see Mooar, *Historical Manual of the South Church,* 62.

35. John Barnard, *Sin Testify'd Against* (Boston, 1727), 48. See also John Barnard, *Two Discourses Addressed to Young Persons; and Joseph Sewall, The Duty of a People* (Boston, 1727), 21–22.

36. Brown's letter is reprinted in the appendix to John Cotton, *A Holy Fear of God,* 4–5.

37. See Abbot, *History of Andover,* 131; and Robert J. Wilson, *The Benevolent Deity: Ebenezer Gay and the Rise of Rational Religion in New England, 1696–1787* (Philadelphia, 1984), appendix I, 293. In Boston, Cotton Mather recorded 71 new admissions in 1727—the largest admissions pool in his career. See Silverman, *The Life and Times of Cotton Mather,* 418–19.

38. Cotton Mather, *Menachem* (Boston, 1716), 39–42. Mather's emphasis on "experimental" or "evangelical" religion and revivals was heavily influenced by his correspondence with the European pietist August Hermann Francke. See Middlekauff, *The Mathers,* 305–19.

39. Eliphalet Adams, *A Sermon Preached at Windham* (New London, 1721), 22–24. On the regional pattern of revivals in the 1720s see Bushman, *From Puritan to Yankee,* 183.

40. Samuel Wigglesworth, *An Essay for Reviving Religion* (Boston, 1733), 31. Wigglesworth reiterated the need for revival in two other printed sermons: *The Excellency of the Gospel-Message; and The Pleasures of Religion* (Boston, 1728). See also John Webb, *The Duty of a Degenerate People* (Boston, 1734), 3. Among unpublished sermons calling for revival see, e.g., Henry Messinger, "Sermon on 1 Chronicles 28:9," Dec. 13, 1733, Sermons Collection, CHS; or Nathaniel Eells, "Sermon on Matthew 12:31," Aug. 19, 1739, *ibid.*

41. Joseph Sewall, *The Holy Spirit* (Boston, 1728), 31. The connections between youth and 18th-century revivals are discussed in chapter 10 of this study.

42. Benjamin Colman, *The Duty of Young People* (Boston, 1728), 83. For additional examples of revival sermons directed to young people see: Samuel Moodey, *The Vain Youth Summoned* (Boston, 1701); Cotton Mather, *The Young Man Spoken to* (Boston, 1712); Jeremiah Shepard, *Early Offerings Best Accepted* (Boston, 1712); Benjamin Colman, *The Warnings of God unto Young People* (Boston, 1716); William Cooper, *How and Why Young People should Cleanse their Way* (Boston, 1716); Israel Loring, *Sermon at Lexington* (Boston, 1718); John Webb, *The Young Man's Duty*

(Boston, 1718); Daniel Lewis, *The Sins of Youth* (Boston, 1725); and Daniel Baker, *Two Sermons* (Boston, 1728).

43. Samuel Wigglesworth, *The Pleasures of Religion*, 6–7, 9.

Chapter 10

1. For summaries of social change in the mid-18th century see Richard D. Brown, *Modernization: The Transformation of American Life, 1600–1865* (New York, 1976), 49–73; and James A. Henretta, *The Evolution of American Society, 1700–1815: An Interdisciplinary Analysis* (Lexington, Mass., 1973), 1–157.

2. For a description of the "personalistic and rationalistic modes of explanation" that dominated 18th-century discourse see Gordon S. Wood, "Conspiracy and the Paranoid Style: Causality and Deceit in the Eighteenth Century," *William and Mary Quarterly*, 39 (1982), 401–41. Historians agree that the key unacknowledged factor in social change was population growth. In Massachusetts, the population grew to 245,698 as reported in the census of 1764. In Connecticut, population increased at a rate of 58% from 1670 to 1700 and then jumped to 280% from 1700 to 1730. See Robert V. Wells, *The Population of the British Colonies in America before 1776: A Survey of Census Data* (Princeton, N.J., 1975), 79; and Bushman, *From Puritan to Yankee*, 83.

3. See, e.g., Robert A. Gross, *The Minutemen and Their World* (New York, 1976), 100; and Daniel Scott Smith and Michael S. Hindus, "Premarital Pregnancy in America, 1740–1971: An Overview and Interpretation," *Journal of Interdisciplinary History*, 5 (1975), 537–70. Philip J. Greven describes the movement of third- and fourth- generation children away from overcrowded towns in *Four Generations*, 222–38. Political tensions in Massachusetts and Connecticut are described in Breen, *The Character of the Good Ruler*, 203–76; Bushman, *From Puritan to Yankee*, 101–03; Pencak, *War, Politics, and Revolution*, 61–90; and Warden, *Boston*, 80–101. Social tensions are described in Nash, *The Urban Crucible*, 132–33; and John Lax and William Pencak, "The Knowles Riot and the Crisis of the 1740s in Massachusetts," *Perspectives in American History*, 10 (1976), 163–216.

4. William G. McLoughlin estimates that by 1740 there were 15 Baptist churches in Massachusetts and Connecticut with a combined membership of 800. *New England Dissent*, I, 279. After a slow start, Anglican church membership grew to 2,000 in Massachusetts and Connecticut in the same period. See Bushman, *From Puritan to Yankee*, 164–82.

5. Based on an examination of surviving church records, Clifford Shipton estimates that serious divisions between ministers and their congregations grew from 11 per decade in 1680–1720 to 37 per decade in 1721–40. "The New England Clergy of the 'Glacial Age,'" 50–51.

6. For a social description and collective biography of the Congregational clergy in 1740 see Harry S. Stout, "The Great Awakening in New England Reconsidered: The New England Clergy," *Journal of Social History*, 7 (1974), 21–47. The changing social backgrounds of many ministers is described in Donald M. Scott, *From Office to Profession: The New England Ministry, 1750–1850* (Philadelphia, 1978), 1–17.

7. John White, *New England's Lamentations* (Boston, 1734), 35; and Herbert and Carol Schneider, eds., *Samuel Johnson: His Career and Writings*, 3 vols. (orig. publ. 1929; reprinted New York, 1972), I, 12. Johnson's conversion to Anglicanism in

1722 was part of a larger defection of Yale tutors and ministers known as the "Great Apostacy."

8. In *The Protestant Temperament*, Philip J. Greven distinguishes an aristocratic, "genteel" style from "moderate" and "evangelical" styles.

9. In *Moral Philosophy at Seventeenth-Century Harvard*, Norman Fiering traces the long rivalry of these academic theories. Because his concern is with formal instruction at Harvard, however, he does not distinguish the different effects and influence these debates had on preaching in the 17th and 18th centuries.

10. The different regional and social backgrounds of ministers and the influence of these variations on subsequent "New Light" and "Old Light" schools of thought are summarized in Stout, "The Great Awakening in New England Reconsidered," 32–36.

11. Jon Butler points out in "Enthusiasm Described and Decried: The Great Awakening as Historical Fiction," *Journal of American History*, 69 (1982), 305–25, that the term *Great Awakening* (describing the revivals of 1730–45) is a misnomer if it is meant to imply that revivals per se were unique to the 18th century. At the same time, however, these were unique qualities to these 18th-century revivals that are described in the following sections of this chapter.

12. Jonathan Edwards, *A Faithful Narrative* in Goen, ed., *The Great Awakening*, 101, 103. Edwards's narrative has been reprinted over 60 times in 5 countries and 3 languages (see Goen, ed., *The Great Awakening*, introduction, 90), making it the most popular of all his printed works. For a description of the social context of the Northampton revivals and the participation of other neighboring communities see Tracy, *Jonathan Edwards, Pastor*, 109–22.

13. Jonathan Edwards, *A Faithful Narrative*, 161–53. On the popular impulse of the Northampton revivals see Goen, ed., *The Great Awakening*, introduction, 22–23.

14. Two factors that cooled the fervor for revival were clerical unrest, fostered by the settlement of the "Arminian" Robert Breck in Springfield, and the suicide of Edwards's uncle, Joseph Hawley.

15. George Whitefield, *Letters of George Whitefield, 1734–1742* (Carlisle, Pa, 1976), 66. William H. Kenney discusses the significance of Whitefield's Anglican affiliation in conjunction with his Calvinist theology in "George Whitefield, Dissenter Priest of the Great Awakening," *William and Mary Quarterly*, 26 (1969), 75–93. Whitefield's American career has yet to receive the attention it deserves in social and cultural contexts. Two general biographies of Whitefield's career are Stuart Henry, *George Whitefield: Wayfaring Witness* (New York, 1957); and Arnold Dallimore, *George Whitefield: The Life and Times of the Great Evangelist of the Eighteenth-Century Revival*, 2 vols. (London, 1970, 1979).

16. George Whitefield, *Journals* (London, 1960), 482, 499.

17. Quoted in Kenney, "George Whitefield," 85.

18. George Whitefield, *Journals*, 476; and *Letters*, 208.

19. Quoted in John Gillies, comp., *Memoirs of the Rev. George Whitefield* (New Haven, Conn., 1834), 267–68.

20. George Whitefield, *Abraham's Offering Up His Son Isaac*, first printed in *Fifteen Sermons Preached on Various Important Subjects* (Glasgow, 1744), 96–97, 105.

21. George Whitefield, *Letters*, 207; and *Journals*, 483. The practice of reading sermons, common among English court preachers, was imported to the colonies in the third generation. By the fourth generation the practice had become more

common, particularly on the part of Anglican ministers and genteel, urban pulpits. See Daniel Walker Howe, *The Unitarian Conscience: Harvard Moral Philosophy, 1805–1851* (Cambridge, Mass., 1970), 169–70.

22. While speaking in Philadelphia, for example, Whitefield recorded how: "At dinner I had not fixed upon a text. When I was going to preach, I was so ill that some of my friends advised me to go home. I thought it best to trust in God. I went on, began preaching, and found my heart somewhat refreshed; but, all on a sudden, my soul was so carried out to talk against depending on our natural reason, that my friends were astonished, and so was I too; for I felt the Holy Ghost come upon me, and never spoke on the wise before." *Journals*, 492.

23. Benjamin Franklin, *The Autobiography* (New York, 1964), 122. See Gillies, *Memoirs of the Rev. George Whitefield*, 263: "Had [Whitefield's sermons] been delivered from a written copy, one delivery would have been like the last; the paper would have operated like a spell, from which he could not depart—invention sleeping, while the utterance followed the eye. But when he had nothing before him except the audience whom he was addressing, the judgment and the imagination, as well as the memory, were called forth. . . . The salient points of his oratory were not prepared passages,—they were bursts of passion, like the jets from a Geyser, when the spring is in full play."

24. Walter J. Ong, *Why Talk? A Conversation about Language* (San Francisco, 1973), 17. On the connections of literacy and analytical thought see Jack Goody and Ian Watt, "The Consequences of Literacy," *Comparative Studies in Society and History*, 5 (1963), 304–45; and Jack Goody, "Evolution and Communication: The Domestication of the Savage Mind," *British Journal of Sociology*, 24 (1973), 1–12.

25. On the altered social context of 18th-century mass revivals see Harry S. Stout, "Religion, Communications, and the Ideological Origins of the American Revolution," *William and Mary Quarterly*, 34 (1977), 525–32.

26. George Whitefield, *Journals*, 473, 462; and *The Lord Our Righteousness* in *Fifteen Sermons*, 32.

27. George Whitefield, *Journals*, 470. Italics are mine.

28. G. L. Walker, ed., *Diary of Rev. Daniel Wadsworth, 1734–1747* (Hartford, Conn., 1894), 56. After hearing Whitefield preach, Lyme's Jonathan Parsons noted how it "had great Influence on my mind: God made use of frequent Accounts about him to awaken my Attention, to humble me for past Deadness, and rouse me up to see my own Standing, and sound an Alarm in Some poor sort, to a drowsy, careless People." See Parsons's "Account of the Revival at Lyme," reprinted in Alan Heimert and Perry Miller, eds., *The Great Awakening: Documents Illustrating the Crisis and Its Consequences* (Indianapolis, Ind., 1967), 40.

29. Ebenezer Gay, *Ministers' Insufficiency for their Important and Difficult Work* (Boston, 1742), 22, 31–32. On Gay's early endorsement of the revivals and later repudiation see Wilson, *The Benevolent Deity*, 90. See also Eastern Consociation, Fairfield County, *Invitation to the Rev. Mr. Whitefield . . . 7 Oct. 40* (Boston, 1745), reprinted in Richard L. Bushman, ed., *The Great Awakening: Documents on the Revival of Religion, 1740–1745* (New York, 1969), 23–25.

30. Thomas Prince, *The Christian History* (Boston, 1740), 26.

31. Jonathan Parsons, "Account of the Revival at Lyme," 198–99.

32. Connecticut and Massachusetts membership patterns are summarized in J. M. Bumsted and John E. Van de Wetering, *What Must I Do To Be Saved? The Great Awakening in Colonial America* (Hinsdale, Ill., 1976), 128–33.

33. The effects of the revivals on frontier areas is described in Clark, *The Eastern*

Frontier, 271–92; urban revivals are described in Nash, *The Urban Crucible,* 198–232; and "second-generation" towns in J. M. Bumsted, "Religion, Finance, and Democracy in Massachusetts: The Town of Norton as a Case Study," *Journal of American History,* 57 (1971), 830–31. On the "coolness" of the oldest towns to the revivals see Greven, *Four Generations,* 279.

34. This pattern of entering the church at an early age began, as we have seen, in the 1720s and would not be duplicated again in New England until the 19th century. On youth and 18th-century revivals see Bumsted and Van de Wetering, *What Must I Do To Be Saved?,* 133–38; Philip J. Greven, "Youth, Maturity, and Religious Conversion: A Note on the Ages of Converts in Andover, Massachusetts, 1711–1749," *Essex Institute Historical Collections,* 108 (1972), 119–34; Ross W. Beales, Jr., "In Search of the Historical Child: Miniature Adulthood and Youth in Colonial New England," *American Quarterly,* 27 (1975), 379–98; William Whittingham, "Religious Conversion in the Second Society of Windham, Connecticut, 1723–1743: A Case Study," *Societas,* 6 (1976), 109–19; and Tracy, *Jonathan Edwards, Pastor,* 109–22. On sex ratios among the new converts see Cedric Cowings, "Sex and Preaching in the Great Awakening," *American Quarterly,* 20 (1968), 635–40; and Moran, "The Puritan Saint," 326–30. Like the pattern of youthful conversions, the trend toward gender parity in church admissions ended when the revivals of 1740–42 subsided.

35. The centrality of the family in New England religion and church membership is described in Greven, *The Protestant Temperament;* Moran and Vinovskis, "The Puritan Family and Religion;"and James Walsh, "The Great Awakening in the First Congregational Church of Woodbury, Connecticut," *William and Mary Quarterly,* 28 (1971), 543–62.

36. It is worth noting that the data from community studies on church membership are statistical *generalizations* that conceal prominent deviations from town to town. While youth were the most conspicuous additions to church membership rolls, they still amounted to less then 40% of new converts and did not dominate in every community. In Hingham, for example, the average age at admission for new members between 1741 and 1742 was 31.7 years—a figure far closer to 17th-century norms (see Wilson, *The Benevolent Deity,* 92–93). Similarly, not every old town was immune to the contagion of revival, as evidenced by the case of Concord, Mass. (see Gross, *The Minutemen and Their World,* 19–21). Nor were youthful converts always the children of church members as the revival at New London illustrates (see Peter Onuf, "New Lights in New London: A Group Portrait of the Separatists," *William and Mary Quarterly,* 37 (1980), 627–43). All of these exceptions and variations point to the limitations of social variables as final explanations for the impact of revivals in New England.

37. Events after 1740 are traced in Edwin S. Gaustad, *The Great Awakening in New England* (New York, 1957), 61–79; and Eugene E. White, "The Decline of the Great Awakening in New England, 1741–1746," *New England Quarterly,* 24 (1961), 35–52.

38. George Whitefield, *Letters,* 221. Tennent's activities in New York and Pennsylvania are traced in Leonard J. Trinterud, *The Forming of an American Tradition: A Re-Examination of Colonial Presbyterianism* (Philadelphia, 1949), 86–108.

39. Quoted in Joseph Tracy, *The Great Awakening: A History of the Revival of Religion in the Time of Edwards and Whitefield* (Boston, 1845), 115.

40. For a contemporary account of Tennent's successes in Massachusetts which, at many points exceeded Whitefield's, see William Shurtleff, *A Letter to*

those of His Brethren (Boston, 1745), reprinted in Heimert and Miller, eds., *The Great Awakening*, 360. In Connecticut, both Tennent and James Davenport recorded more conversions than Whitefield. See Harry S. Stout and Peter Onuf, "James Davenport and the Great Awakening in New London," *Journal of American History*, 70 (1983), 573.

41. Gilbert Tennent, *The Danger of an Unconverted Ministry* (Boston, 1742). This sermon was originally delivered when Tennent was under censure of the "Old Side" Donegal presbytery. For a summary of the Old Side and New Side factions of Presbyterianism that paralleled Old Light and New Light divisions among the Congregationalists see Trinterud, *The Forming of an American Tradition*, 89.

42. Much of this correspondence survives in *The Papers of Eleazar Wheelock*, microfilm ed. (Dartmouth College, Hanover, N.H., 1971). See, e.g., entries 740276, 740322, 740356, 740419, 740555.

43. "The Diary of Rev. Daniel Rogers, 1740–1751," Manuscript Collection, NYHS. I am grateful to the society for making the microfilm of this diary available to me. See in addition to Rogers's diary, Samuel Hopkins's account of his early itinerancy in "A Journal," Gratz Collection, Box 18, vol. XVIII, HSP.

44. Quoted in Gaustad, *The Great Awakening in New England*, 34.

45. The social disruptions of itinerant preaching are discussed in Stout and Onuf, "James Davenport and the Great Awakening in New London."

46. Walker, ed., *The Diary of Daniel Wadsworth*, entry of Apr. 17, 1742, p. 82. On the assembly's legislation and the political divisions that ensued see Bushman, *From Puritan to Yankee*, 221–66.

47. *The Testimony of the President, Professors, Tutors, and Hebrew Instructors of Harvard College Against George Whitefield* (Boston, 1747), reprinted in Heimert and Miller, eds., *The Great Awakening*, 350–51. Yale College issued similar charges in *Declaration of the Rector and Tutors Against Whitefield* (Boston, 1745), reprinted in F. B. Dexter, ed., *Documentary History of Yale University* (New Haven, Conn., 1916), 369–70.

48. *Boston Evening Post*, Apr. 11, 1743.

49. These pamphlets and declarations are summarized in Gaustad, *The Great Awakening in New England*, 80–101. Here Gaustad identifies Chauncy with the forces of "reason" and Enlightenment, and Edwards with "medievalism" (p. 81). Such a view oversimplifies a more complex situation in which Edwards drew more heavily from the New Learning and extrabiblical sources than did Chauncy. Furthermore, in terms of the social significance of the debates, Edwards's argument pointed in more "radical" democratic directions. The philosophical context of Edwards's thought is traced in Norman Fiering, *Jonathan Edwards's Moral Thought and Its British Context* (Chapel Hill, N.C., 1981). Alan Heimert explores the social significance of Edwards's thought in *Religion and the American Mind: From the Great Awakening to the Revolution* (Cambridge, Mass., 1967), 95–158.

50. Charles Chauncy, *Seasonable Thoughts on the State of Religion in New England*, (Boston, 1743), 302.

51. *Ibid.*, 112–13.

52. *Ibid.*, 280, 370, 227.

53. Charles Chauncy, *Enthusiasm Described and Cautioned Against* (Boston, 1742).

54. Jonathan Edwards, *Some Thoughts Concerning the Present Revival* (Boston, 1742), reprinted in Goen, ed., *The Great Awakening*, 353–48. Edwards's millennial premonitions would not be so closely connected to America after 1743, but in the full flush of revival excitement it occurred to him that all American history led to

the revivals and from there to global redemption. In a notebook on spiritual typologies, he speculated that "the changing of the course of trade and the supplying of the world with its treasures from America is a type and forerunner of what is approaching in spiritual things, when the world shall be supplied with spiritual treasures from America." *Images or Shadows of Divine Things*, ed., Perry Miller (New Haven, Conn., 1948), entry 147, p. 102.

55. Jonathan Edwards, *Some Thoughts Concerning the Present Revival*, 294; and *The Distinguishing Marks of a Work of the Spirit of God* (Boston, 1741), reprinted in Goen, ed., *The Great Awakening*, 267.

56. Jonathan Edwards, *Some Thoughts Concerning the Present Revival*, 364, 379.

57. See Jonathan Edwards, *The Distinguishing Marks*, 276: "Some things that they are sensible of are altogether new to them, their ideas and inward sensations are new, and what they therefore knew not how to accomodate language to, or to find words to express."

58. Jonathan Edwards, *Some Thoughts Concerning the Present Revival*, 297; and *A Treatise Concerning the Religious Affections* (Boston, 1746), reprinted in John E. Smith, ed., *Religious Affections* (New Haven, Conn., 1959), 272. On Edwards's psychology see James Hoopes, "Jonathan Edwards's Religious Psychology," *Journal of American History*, 69 (1983), 849–65.

59. Edwards's use of aesthetics as an analogy of conversion is described in Paul Conkin, *Puritans and Pragmatists: Eight Eminent American Thinkers* (New York, 1968), 39–72; Sang Hyun Lee, "Mental Activity and the Perception of Beauty in Jonathan Edwards," *Harvard Theological Review*, 69 (1976), 369–96; and Roland Delattre, *Beauty Sensibility in the Thought of Jonathan Edwards* (New Haven, Conn., 1968). Norman Fiering cautions that the analogy of beauty in Edwards's thought can be taken too far. For Edwards, unlike the sentimentalists whose vocabulary he borrowed, "the discovery of the forming power [of natural forms], the highest order beauty, was possible only with the aid of grace, that is, by providential assistance. With this assistance, one can become an enthusiast of supernature, which is quite different from being merely an intellectual admirer of the natural order." *Jonathan Edwards's Moral Thought*, 110.

60. Shaftesbury, Anthony Ashley Cooper, *Characteristics of Men, Manners, Opinions, Times etc.*, ed. John M. Robertson, 2 vols. (London, 1900), "The Moralists: A Philosophical Rhapsody," II, 223; and Jonathan Edwards, *Some Thoughts Concerning the Present Revival*, 341. Edwards read Shaftesbury at an early age and evidenced a greater dependence on him than on Hutcheson or Locke. See Fiering, *Jonathan Edwards's Moral Thought*, 108–110; and Thomas H. Johnson, "Jonathan Edwards' Background of Reading," Colonial Society of Massachusetts, *Publications*, 28 (*Transactions*, 1930–33), 211–12.

61. Fiering, *Jonathan Edwards's Moral Thought*, 60, 106. Fiering here points out that Edwards could accomplish this reversal of meaning fairly easily because the naturalistic ethics of the 18th-century sentimentalists were themselves a secularization of 17th-century "voluntarist" thought.

62. See Stout, "The Great Awakening in New England Reconsidered," 27–28; and Gaustad, *The Great Awakening in New England*, 75. The most notorious instance of Old Light dismissals occurred in Northampton, where Edwards was dismissed in 1750 for refusing to continue "open" (Stoddardean) communion in the church.

63. See Gaustad, *The Great Awakening*, 75. In *New England Dissent*, I, 345–47, William G. McLoughlin identifies 125 separations between 1743 and 1755.

64. For general descriptions of the Separates' social backgrounds see C. C.

Goen, *Revivalism and Separatism in New England, 1740–1800* (New Haven, Conn., 1962), 188–93; McLoughlin, *New England Dissent*, I, 340–76. Local and regional analyses of Separatism appear in Bushman, *From Puritan to Yankee*, 191–95; John M. Bumsted, "The Pilgrim's Progress: The Ecclesiastical History of the Old Colony, 1620–1775" (Ph.D. diss., Brown University, 1965); Christopher Jedrey, *The World of John Cleaveland: Family and Community in Eighteenth Century New England* (New York, 1979), 46–57; Onuf, "New Lights in New London;" James H. and Esther D. Barnett, *On the Trail of a Legend: The Separatist Movement in Mansfield, Connecticut, 1745–1769* (Mansfield, Conn., 1978); Bumsted, "Revivalism and Separatism in New England"; and John W. Jeffries, "The Separation in the Canterbury Congregational Church: Religion, Family, and Politics in a Connecticut Town," *New England Quarterly*, 52 (1979), 522–49.

65. Included among the more conspicuous lay itinerants were Paul Parke, Nathaniel Shepard, Jedediah Dewey, Elisha Paine, Solomon Paine, Isaac Backus, Ebenezer Frothingham, Joseph Marshall, Thomas Denison, Joseph Meacham, John Stephens, Dyer Hyde, Joshua Morse, Noah Hammond, Matthew Smith, Wait Palmer, Shubal Stearns, John Merriman, Samuel Hovey, Joseph Adams, Jonathan Parsons, Richard Elvins, and Thomas Marsh.

66. Paul Parke, "Anniversary Sermon, July, 1797," reprinted in Elizabeth H. Ruppert, ed., *The Parke Scrapbook*, no. 2 (Baltimore, 1966).

67. Quoted in Goen, *Revivalism and Separatism*, 118.

68. On the backward-looking quality of Separate revolts see James Walsh, "The Pure Church in Eighteenth Century Connecticut" (Ph.D. diss., Columbia University, 1967); Goen, *Revivalism and Separatism*, 148–49; and Jedrey, *The World of John Cleaveland*, 55–57. On the revival of lay leadership see McLoughlin, *New England Dissent*, I, 347–48.

69. The Norwich petitions are reprinted in Bushman, ed., *The Great Awakening*, 102–03. See also three volumes of unpublished Separate petitions bound in the Manuscripts Collection, CHS; and Winslow, *Meetinghouse Hill*, 231–35. For two examples of Separate confessions see Michael J. Crawford, ed., "The Spiritual Travails of Nathan Cole," *William and Mary Quarterly*, 33 (1976), 89–126; and "The Self-Examination of Edward Goddard," is preserved among a bundle of papers in the Goddard Family Papers, Manuscripts Collection, AAS.

70. F. B. Dexter, ed., *The Literary Diary of Ezra Stiles*, 3 vols. (New York, 1901), I, 68. The writings of these and other Separate authors are assessed in McLoughlin, *New England Dissent*, I, 399–417. On the persistence of Awakening terms into the Revolutionary era see Bercovitch, *The American Jeremiad*, 130–31.

71. Edward Goddard, *A Brief Account of the Foundation of the Second Church in Framingham* (Boston, 1750), 4.

72. Backus is quoted in William G. McLoughlin, *Isaac Backus and the American Pietistic Tradition* (Boston, 1967), 184. Kelly is quoted in Bushman, ed., *The Great Awakening*, 103.

Chapter 11

1. George Whitefield, *Journal*, 529. Crocker's "Letter of 24 November 1744," is reprinted in Samuel E. Emery, *The Ministry of Taunton*, 2 vols. (Boston, 1853), I, 365. The demise of revival enthusiasm is described in Gaustad, *The Great Awakening in New England*, 61–79; and White, "The Decline of the Great Awakening in New England."

2. The growth of Anglican societies was especially pronounced in Connecticut where, between 1740 and 1750, 11 towns requested Anglican missionaries from the Society for the Propagation of the Gospel. See Joseph J. Ellis, *The New England Mind in Transition: Samuel Johnson of Connecticut, 1696-1772* (New Haven, Conn., 1973), 119-21. William G. McLoughlin describes the Separates' transition to Baptist principles in *Isaac Backus and the American Pietistic Tradition*, 57-88.

3. Two works have questioned the extent of Arminianism—and the accompanying denial of the doctrine of original sin—in pre-Revolutionary Congregationalism: Gerald J. Goodwin, "The Myth of 'Arminian-Calvinism' in Eighteenth Century New England," *New England Quarterly*, 41 (1968), 213-37; and Edmund S. Morgan, *The Gentle Puritan: A Life of Ezra Stiles, 1727-1795* (Chapel Hill, N.C., 1962), 16. This is not, however, to say that there were no Arminian preachers in the Anglican or Congregational churches around Boston. See Goen, ed., *The Great Awakening*, introduction, 8-10. For descriptions and biographical accounts of early Arminians see Conrad Wright, *The Beginnings of Unitarianism in America* (Boston, 1955), 281-91; Charles W. Akers, *Called Unto Liberty, A Life of Jonathan Mayhew, 1720-1766* (Cambridge, Mass., 1964); Edward M. Griffin, *Old Brick: Charles Chauncy of Boston, 1705-1787* (Minneapolis, Minn., 1980); Wilson, *The Benevolent Deity*; and James W. Jones, *The Shattered Synthesis: New England Puritanism before the Great Awakening* (New Haven, Conn., 1973), 131-98.

4. Richard L. Bushman describes "New Light politics" in *From Puritan to Yankee*, 235-66. In 1750, New Light forces succeeded in getting the anti-itinerancy laws dropped.

5. Nathaniel Eells, *Religion is the Life of God's People* (Boston, 1743), 29, 35.

6. Henry F. May, *The Enlightenment in America* (New York, 1976), 3-104.

7. Much of this paragraph is dependent on arguments and evidence set forth in David Harlan, *The Clergy and the Great Awakening in New England*, (Ann Arbor, Mich., 1980), 99-113.

8. Gilbert Tennent, *Irenicum Ecclesiasticum* (Philadelphia, 1749), reprinted in Heimert and Miller, eds., *The Great Awakening*, 367-75.

9. Even Jonathan Edwards's *A Treatise Concerning the Religious Affections* published in 1746 was notable for its attempt to balance the virtues of the revivals against their excesses. See also Joseph Bellamy, *True Religion Delineated* (Boston, 1750).

10. James Davenport, *The Reverend Mr. James Davenport's Confession and Retractions* (Boston, 1744); William Shurtleff, *A Letter to those of His Brethren in the Ministry . . .* ; and *The Testimony and Advice of a Number of Laymen respecting Religion and the Teachers of it* (Boston, 1743), 8.

11. Gilbert Tennent, *Irenicum Ecclesiasticum*, 369, 371; [Samuel Niles *et al.*], *The Sentiments and Resolutions of an Association of Ministers at Weymouth, Jan 15 1744-5* (Boston, 1745), 10-11; and Samuel Niles, *Tristialae Ecclesiarum . . .* (Boston, 1745), 15. On Niles's efforts to establish an orthodox consensus in Weymouth see Wilson, *The Benevolent Deity*, 149-50.

12. Samuel Niles, *Tristialae Ecclesiarum*, 3. This was a common theme in regular sermon manuscripts as well. See, e.g., Daniel Boardman, "Sermon on Psalm 68:13," June 13, 1742 (repeated thereafter), 1 vol., Sermons Collection, CHS.

13. Ezra Stiles, *A Discourse on the Christian Union* (Boston, 1761), 52, 55.

14. *Ibid.*, 43-44.

15. Joseph Emerson, *Mr. Emerson's Exhortation to his People* (Boston, 1742), 6.

16. John Barnard, *The Presence of the Great God* (Boston, 1746), 5, 6; and Ezra Stiles, *Discourse on Christian Union*, 43.

17. Regular sermon manuscripts after 1742 are filled with conversionist themes and warnings against works righteousness. See, e.g., Nathaniel Eells, "Sermon on 1 Timothy 1:16," May 24, 1744, Sermons Collection, CHS: "It is not our own dutys and performances, it is not all the good Works that we can possibly do, that can deliver us from the wrath to come [and that] purchases and procures for us the favour of God, and a right and title to eternal life . . . salvation can not be obtained any other Way than in the Way of Believing. . . . By faith alone."

18. On the Separates see McLoughlin, *New England Dissent;* I, 384–85. The impediments to Anglican growth are described in Ellis, *The New England Mind in Transition,* 119–21.

19. Ebenezer Devotion, *The Mutual Obligations Upon Ministers and People . . .* (New London, 1750), 15. Lay "dismissals," clerical "removals," and increased clerical mobility after 1740 are tabulated and described in Daniel H. Calhoun, *Professional Lives in America: Structure and Aspiration, 1750–1850* (Cambridge, Mass., 1965), 88–177; Stout, "The Great Awakening in New England," 34–36; James W. Schmotter, "Ministerial Careers in Eighteenth-Century New England: The Social Context, 1700–1760," *Journal of Social History,* 9 (1975), 256–66; and James W. Schmotter, "The Irony of Clerical Professionalism: New England's Congregational Ministers and the Great Awakening," *American Quarterly,* 31 (1979), 159.

20. In *Religion and the American Mind,* 159, Alan Heimert observes that "there were not in fact all that many varieties of preaching in mid-eighteenth-century America. The Great Awakening had brought a rhetorical division almost totally congruent with the doctrinal opposition of evangelical and rational religion." Heimert provides a brilliant description of these differences in his chapter on "The Danger of an Unconverted Ministry," 159–236.

21. Edwards was never fully able to preach extemporaneously, an inability he viewed as a regrettable weakness. In his biography of Edwards, Samuel Hopkins wrote that "though . . . he was wont to read so considerable part of what he delivered; yet he was far from thinking this the best way of preaching in general; and looked upon his using his notes so much as he did, [as] a deficiency and infirmity." *The Life and Character of Rev. Mr. Jonathan Edwards* (Boston, 1765), reprinted in David Levin, ed., *Jonathan Edwards: A Profile* (New York, 1969), 47–48. While unable to fully adopt extemporaneous notes, Edwards clearly shortened his sermon notes after hearing Whitefield preach. Wilson H. Kimnach traces Edwards's shift to abbreviated sermon outlines in "The Literary Techniques of Jonathan Edwards" (Ph.D. diss., University of Pennsylvania, 1971), 136, 176–77.

22. Josiah Crocker, "Letter of 24 November 1744," 355; and Daniel Rogers, "Sermon on 2 Peter 3:3," 1749 in Sermons Collection, 1 envelope, CL. John Cleaveland's and Samuel Hopkins's abbreviated sermon notes are described in Jedrey, *The World of John Cleaveland,* 107; and Joseph M. Conforti, *Samuel Hopkins and the New Divinity Movement* (Grand Rapids, Mich., 1981), 179–81.

23. For sermon notes that bear out the alternative Harvard and Yale patterns, see, e.g.: Jonathan Ashley (YC, 1730), Sermons Collection, HL; Samuel Langdon (HC, 1740), Sermons Collection, Box 2, Folder 1, AAS; Phillips Payson (HC, 1724), Sermons Collection, AAS; David Hall (HC, 1724), Sermons Collection, Box 1, Folder 38, AAS; Edward Dorr (YC, 1742), *ibid.,* Box 1, Folder 23; John Chandler (HC, 1743), *ibid.,* Box 1, Folder 13; Job Cushing (HC, 1714), *ibid.,* Box 1, Folder 18; Seth Storer (HC, 1720), *ibid.,* Box 2, Folder 34; Nathaniel Appleton (HC, 1712), 1 envelope, Sermons Collection, EI; Joseph Ashley (YC, 1730), 1 envelope, *ibid.;*

Ebenezer Bridge (HC, 1736), 1 envelope, *ibid.*; Peter Clark (HC, 1712), 1 envelope, *ibid.*; Daniel Bliss (YC, 1732), 1 envelope, *ibid.*; Isaiah Dunster (HC, 1741), 1 envelope, *ibid.*; Nathaniel Eells (HC, 1728), 1 envelope, *ibid.*; Elisha Williams (HC, 1711), 1 envelope, *ibid.*; Dudley Leavitt (HC, 1739), 2 envelopes, *ibid.*; Jonathan Marsh (YC, 1735), Sermons Collection, CSL; Adonijah Bidwell (YC, 1740), Sermons Collection, CHS; Nathaniel Eells (HC,1728), *ibid.*; John Trumbull (YC, 1735), *ibid.*; or William Hobby (HC, 1725), *ibid.*

24. For one account of an itinerant preacher's powerful influence on Yale ministerial students see Ross W. Beales, Jr., ed., "The Diary of John Cleaveland, January 15–May 11, 1742," *Essex Institute Historical Collections*, 107 (1971), 166. Yale's continuing evangelical orientation in the 18th century (both in "moderate" and "New Divinity" forms) is described in Louis L. Tucker, *Puritan Protagonist: President Thomas Clap of Yale College* (Chapel Hill, N.C., 1962), 78–79; Morgan, *The Gentle Puritan*, 314; and Bruce Kuklick, *Churchmen and Philosophers: From Jonathan Edwards to John Dewey* (New Haven, Conn., 1985), 5–111. In *The Beginnings of Unitarianism*, 258, Conrad Wright observes that "whereas Harvard students ranged from Arminian through moderate Calvinism, Yale graduates ranged from moderate Calvinism through Hopkinsinianism, and the popular image of the two colleges tended to be fixed by the more extreme types."

25. Ebenezer Devotion, *The Mutual Obligations Upon Ministers and People*, 1, 10; and Andrew Eliot, *A Sermon Preached* (Boston, 1750), 23. The diverse social backgrounds of rationalists and evangelicals are described in Stout, "The Great Awakening in New England;" C. Wright, *The Beginnings of Unitarianism*, 252–80; and Conforti, *Samuel Hopkins*, 9–22.

26. The social implications of diverse rhetorics are discussed in Stout, "Religion, Communications, and the Ideological Origins of the American Revolution," 519–41.

27. Andrew Eliot, *A Sermon Preached* (Boston, 1754), 22–23. For similar rationalist prescriptions see: Ebenezer Devotion, *The Mutual Obligations*, 11–12; Nathaniel Appleton, *The Great Apostle Paul Exhibited and Recommended* (Boston, 1751); William Rand, *Ministers Shall Have a Sincere and Ardent Love* (Boston, 1742); or Ebenezer Gay, *Ministers are Men of Like Passions with Others* (Boston, 1725).

28. Benjamin Parker, *The Excellent Spirit Described* (Salem, 1774), 11.

29. See Greven, *The Protestant Temperament*, 178–79; and Jones, *The Shattered Synthesis*, 158.

30. C. Wright, *The Beginnings of Unitarianism*, 28–58.

31. Edward Bass, "Sermon on Ezekiel 18:2–4," 1759, Sermons Collection, Box 1, Folder 4, AAS.

32. Lemuel Briant, *The Absurdity and Blasphemy of Depreciating Moral Virtue* (Boston, 1749), reprinted in Heimert and Miller, eds., *The Great Awakening*, 542.

33. *Ibid.*, 545. For discussions of the polemical importance of Briant's sermon see Gaustad, *The Great Awakening*, 130; and Jones, *The Shattered Synthesis*, 131–38.

34. Jonathan Mayhew, *Seven Sermons Upon the Following Subjects* (Boston, 1750), 30. These sermons were part of Mayhew's Thursday lecture series on moral Christianity.

35. Lemuel Briant, *The Absurdity and Blasphemy*, 545; Jonathan Mayhew, *Seven Sermons*, 11.

36. These descriptions of Gay's sermon on *Natural Religion* (Boston, 1759) are

taken from Heimert, *Religion and the American Mind*, 5–6; and Jones, *The Shattered Synthesis*, 133. The Dudleian lectures were endowed in 1751 at the bequest of Massachusetts's Chief Justice Paul Dudley. They were delivered at Harvard every third year and given over to the subject of "Natural and Revealed Religion." See Howe, *The Unitarian Conscience*, 70.

37. Ebenezer Gay, *Natural Religion*, 13, 19–20.

38. Briant's censure was printed in *The Result of a Late Ecclesiastical Council* (Boston, 1753).

39. Samuel Niles, *A Vindication of Divers Important Gospel Doctrines* (Boston, 1752), 12–13, 77.

40. Samuel Niles, *The True Scripture-Doctrine of Original Sin* (Boston, 1753), 41, 317. Taylor's influence on New England Arminianism is summarized in C. Wright, *The Beginnings of Unitarianism*, 73–84.

41. Nathaniel Appleton, *The Difference Between a Legal and an Evangelical Justification* (Boston, 1749), 10, 14–15; and Andrew Eliot, *A Sermon Preached* (Boston, 1754), 27.

42. John Barnard, "Autobiography," in Massachusetts Historical Society, *Collections*, 3d Ser., 5 (1836), 241. Barnard's recollection of orthodox preaching is confirmed in scattered sermon manuscripts preserved in the Sermons Collection of the Essex Institute. Throughout the 1740s, Barnard preached regularly on such orthodox topics as justification by faith alone (Psalm 119:9), the priesthood of all believers (Psalm 110:4), the necessity of converted ministers (2 Corinthians 11:14), divine providence (Psalm 105:40); prayer (Job 22:26), or eternal life and damnation (Matthew 12:40).

43. Ebenezer Parkman, "Sermon on John 1:7," Aug. 12, 1744, "Sermons, 1740–1749," Parkman Family Papers, Box 1, Folder 4, AAS; Samuel Checkley, "Sermon on 1 Peter 1:10," Dec. 30, 1744, Sermons Collection, Box 1, Folder 12, AAS; Henry Messenger, "Sermon on Matthew 3:13–17," Feb. 12, 1747, Sermons Collection, 1 envelope, CL.

44. Miller and Johnson, eds., *The Puritans*, I, 55.

45. Samuel Cooper, "Sermon on Psalm 11:7," 1748, Sermons Collections, HL; Thaddeus Maccarty, "Sermon on Daniel 4:35," June 1, 1755, Maccarty Family Papers, 1742–1863, 1 folder, AAS; and Andrew Eliot, *A Sermon Preached*, 10.

46. Schneider and Schneider, eds., *Samuel Johnson*, III, 369, 457, 453. Johnson's rationalist theology is summarized in Ellis, *The New England Mind in Transition*, 123–44.

47. The "schools of prophets" are described in Conforti, *Samuel Hopkins and the New Divinity*, 23–40; and Mary Latimer Gambrell, *Ministerial Training in Eighteenth-Century New England* (New York, 1937).

48. Jonathan Edwards, *Christ the Example of Ministers* (Boston, 1750), reprinted in Sereno E. Dwight, ed., *The Works of President Edwards*, 10 vols. (New York, 1829–30), VIII, 457, 459; and *The Church's Marriage* (Boston, 1746), reprinted *ibid.*, VI, 207.

49. This theme is developed in Ziff, *Puritanism in America*, 309; and Conrad Cherry, *The Theology of Jonathan Edwards: A Reappraisal* (New York, 1966), chapter 3.

50. Jonathan Edwards, *Sinners in the Hands of an Angry God* (1741), reprinted in Dwight, ed., *The Works of President Edwards*, VII, 169, 168.

51. Schneider and Schneider, eds., *Samuel Johnson*, I, 28. Other examples of Edwards's "hell-fire" preaching include his "Sermon on Romans 2:8–9" (date

unknown) reprinted in Dwight, ed., *The Works of President Edwards*, VIII, 195–226; "Sermon on Matthew 11: 16–19" (date unknown), *ibid.*, VIII, 320–54; "The Future Punishment of the Wicked Unavoidable," 1741, *ibid.*, VI, 89–105; or "The Eternity of Hell Torments," 1739, *ibid.*, VI, 106–24. While prominent, this theme did not dominate Edwards's preaching. The necessity of hell in Edwards's theory of divine justice is summarized in Fiering, *Jonathan Edwards's Moral Thought*, 200–60.

52. Jonathan Edwards, *A Treatise Concerning the Religious Affections*, 152; Samuel Hopkins, *The Life and Character*, 47–48, 16.

53. Jonathan Edwards, "Sermon on Acts 16:29–30" (date unknown), reprinted in Dwight, ed., *The Works of President Edwards*, VIII, 15. Edwards often expressed sentiments like this. See, e.g., *Treatise on the Religious Affections*, 114: "All who are truly religious are not of this world, they are strangers here, and belong to heaven; they are born from above, heaven is their native country, and the nature which they receive by this heavenly birth, is an heavenly nature, they receive an annointing from above; that principle of true religion which is in them, is a communication of the religion of heaven, their grace is the dawn of glory; and God fits them for that world by conforming them to it."

54. Miller, ed., *Images or Shadows of Divine Things by Jonathan Edwards*, entry 8, p. 44. Here, Edwards observes, "There is a great and remarkable analogy in God's works. . . . God does purposely make and order one thing to be in agreeableness with another. . . . We see that even in the material world, God makes one part of it strangely to agree with another, and why is it not reasonable to suppose He makes the whole as a shadow of the spiritual world?" On Edwards's use of nature as spiritual type see *ibid.*, introduction, 1–9; and Elizabeth Flower and Murray G. Murphy, *A History of Philosophy in America*, 2 vols. (New York, 1977), I, 166.

55. Miller, ed., *Images or Shadows of Divine Things*, entries 64, 77, pp. 67, 75. See also entry 26, p. 49: "Christ often makes use of representations of spiritual things in the constitution of the [world] for his argument, as thus: the tree is known by its fruit. These things are not merely mentioned as illustrations of his meaning, but as illustrations and evidences of the truth of what he says."

56. In general, English essayists preferred natural imagery from mountains and oceans to light. Joseph Addison, for example, commented that, "Of all the objects that I have ever seen, there is none which affects my imagination so much as the sea or ocean." *Spectator*, no. 489, in Joseph Addison, *Works*, ed. G. W. Greene (New York, 1857), 6. See also, Nicolson, *Mountain Gloom and Mountain Glory*, 271–323.

57. Jonathan Edwards, *Some Thoughts Concerning the Present State of Religion*, In Goen, ed., *The Great Awakening*, 332; *The True Excellency* (Boston, 1744) reprinted in Dwight, ed., *The Works of President Edwards*, VIII, 441–42. For descriptions of the new sense of the heart as a "spiritual light," or "light of the mind," wherein "a person is made to understand spiritual things in a new manner," see Miller, ed., *Images or Shadows of Divine Things*, entries 45, 50, 53, 54, 128, 152, 168, 186, or 209.

58. Jonathan Edwards, *A Divine and Supernatural Light* (Boston, 1734), reprinted in Dwight, ed., *The Works of President Edwards*, VI, 172–73; and Jonathan Edwards, *True Grace Distinguished . . .* (New York, 1753) reprinted, *ibid.*, VI, 261. For examples of light and conversion in Edwards's unpublished sermons at Beinecke Library, see "Sermon on John 18:12," Jan. 1742; "Sermon on John 5:35," Aug. 30, 1744; or "Sermon on Matthew 5:15–16," Dec. 1746, BL.

59. Samuel Hopkins, "Sermon on 2 Corinthians 5:17," Feb. 14, 1744, in Sermons Collection, HL; "Sermon on 1 Peter 5:11," Jan. 27, 1754, *ibid.* See also Joseph Bellamy, *The Great End of Sin* (Boston, 1753), 2, 10; and *Sermons Upon the Following Subjects* (Boston, 1758), 207. For a listing of 55 "Edwardean" ministers trained in the homes of Edwards, Hopkins, and Bellamy see Conforti, *Samuel Hopkins and the New Divinity*, appendix, 227–32.

60. Between 1740 and 1760 rationalist ministers like Isaac Stiles, Jonathan Todd, Ebenezer Devotion, and George Beckwith of Connecticut; or Nathaniel Eells, Ebenezer Gay, John Barnard, Charles Chauncy, Jonathan Mayhew, or Samuel Cooper of Massachusetts all delivered at least one election sermon. Prominent evangelicals like Edwards, Hopkins, Wheelock, or Croswell delivered none.

Chapter 12

1. For general discussions of the wars with France see Douglas Edward Leach, *Arms for Empire: A Military History of the British Colonies in North America, 1607–1763* (New York, 1973), 80–164; and Howard H. Peckham, *The Colonial Wars, 1689–1762* (Chicago, 1964), 25–76.

2. *Journal of Roger Wolcott* (1745), reprinted in Connecticut Historical Society, *Collections*, 1 (1860), 154–55. On the strategic importance of Louisbourg see Peckham, *The Colonial Wars*, 99–100; and Jack M. Sosin, "Louisbourg and the Peace of Aix-la-Chapelle, 1748," *William and Mary Quarterly*, 14 (1957), 506–35.

3. Whitefield's important role in stimulating New England enlistments is summarized in Arnold A. Dallimore, *George Whitefield*, II, 201–03.

4. On the "monumentally mismanaged" expeditions of Queen Anne's War see Nash, *The Urban Crucible*, 59–60.

5. The expeditionary fasts were announced in the *Boston Weekly News-Letter*, Mar. 28, 1745. Between Apr. 1744 and May 1745 there were 13 public fasts in Connecticut, Massachusetts, and New Hampshire. See Love, *Fast and Thanksgiving Days*, 299–302, 494.

6. Francis G. Walet, ed., *The Diary of Ebenezer Parkman, 1703–1782* (Worcester, Mass., 1974), 114; and Walker, ed., *The Diary of Daniel Wadsworth*, 120–22.

7. See, e.g., Perry Miller, "Jonathan Edwards and the Great Awakening," reprinted in *Errand Into the Wilderness*, 153–66; and Conrad Cherry, "The Puritan Notion of The Covenant in Jonathan Edwards' Doctrine of Faith," *Church History*, 34 (1965), 328–41.

8. Jonathan Edwards, "Sermon on Leviticus 26:3–13," Feb. 28, 1745; "Sermon on 1 Kings 8:44ff," Apr. 1, 1745 (repeated in 1755) Edwards Manuscripts, BL. See also Edwards's "Sermon on Matthew 5:14," July 1736; and "Sermon on Joshua 7:12," June 28, 1744, *ibid.*

9. Walker, ed., *The Diary of Daniel Wadsworth*, 123. The psychological and rhetorical importance of the Louisbourg conquest is summarized in S.E.D. Shortt, "Conflict and Identity in Massachusetts: The Louisbourg Expedition of 1745," *Social History (Histoire Sociale)*, 5 (1972), 165–85.

10. Walet, ed., *Diary of Ebenezer Parkman*, 120, 114; and Thomas Prince, *Extraordinary Events . . .* , 2d ed. (Boston, 1747), 34.

11. Jonathan Edwards, *An Humble Attempt*, reprinted in Stephen Stein, ed., *Apocalyptic Writings*, vol. 5, *The Works of Jonathan Edwards* (New Haven, Conn., 1977), 362. See also Jonathan Edwards, "Sermon on 2 Chronicles 20:27–29," Aug. 1745; and "Sermon on Psalm 111:5," Aug. 1745, Edwards Manuscripts, BL.

12. See, e.g., Nathaniel Tucker, "Sermon on Exodus 15:1–3," July 17, 1745, Sermons Collection, 1 envelope, EI; or Gillies, comp., *Memoirs of George Whitefield*, 105. For one soldier's account of Louisbourg in sermonic language see [Auth. unk.], *A Journal from New England to Cape Breton* (1745), Manuscripts Collection, HL. John Shy describes the Louisbourg campaign as a "Puritan crusade," in "A New Look at the Colonial Militia," *William and Mary Quarterly*, 20 (1963), 175–85.

13. John Barnard, *A Sermon Preached* (Boston, 1746), 6, 27–29; Thomas Prince, *Extraordinary Events*, 14, 20; and Charles Chauncy, *Marvelous Things* (Boston, 1745), 11, 20.

14. Joseph Sewall, *The Lamb Slain* (Boston, 1745), 6, 34. For similar pronouncements, see also Thomas Prince, *The Salvations of God in 1746* (Boston, 1746), 35; Thomas Prentice, *When the People . . .* (Boston, 1745), 8, 17, 39; and William McClenachan, *The Christian Warriour* (Boston, 1745), 15. For an extended discussion of millennial themes sounded during war with France see Hatch, *The Sacred Cause of Liberty*, 21–54; and Ruth H. Bloch, *Visionary Republic: Millennial Themes in American Thought, 1756–1800* (Cambridge, England, 1985), 22–50.

15. See Leach, *Arms for Empire*, 80–116; and Nash, *The Urban Crucible*, 172.

16. On urban riots and England's treaty with France see Richard Maxwell Brown, "Violence and the American Revolution," in Stephen G. Kurtz and James H. Hutson, eds., *Essays on the American Revolution* (Chapel Hill, N.C., 1973), 117–18; and Sosin, "Louisbourg and the Peace of Aix-la-Chapelle, 1748."

17. Ebenezer Parkman, "Sermon on Ezekiel 5:5," July 10, 1746, "Sermons, 1724–1781," Parkman Family Papers, Box 1, AAS. On preaching generally see Ronald F. Reid, "New England Rhetoric and the French War, 1754–1760: A Case Study in the Rhetoric of War," *Communication Monographs*, 43 (1976), 259–86.

18. Daniel Rogers, "Sermon on Romans 2:3–5," Nov. 27, 1746, "Sermons, 1739–1779," 1 envelope, EI; and Samuel Hopkins, "Sermon on Revelation 19:17–20," Mar. 12, 1746, Sermons Collection, HL. Hopkins reiterated this theme one week later in "Sermon on Revelation 7:12, *ibid.*"

19. Lester J. Cappon, ed., *The Adams-Jefferson Letters* (orig. publ. 1959; reprinted New York, 1971), 527. In presenting a copy of Mayhew's *Unlimited Submission* to Jefferson, Adams recalled how "It made a greater sensation in New England than Mr. [Patrick] Henry's Philipick against the Parsons did in Virginia."

20. Jonathan Mayhew, *Seven Sermons*, 91; and *A Sermon Preached . . .* (Boston, 1754) reprinted in Plumstead, ed., *The Wall and the Garden*, 294.

21. Mayhew's deep reading in British Whig writers, including Benjamin Hoadley, is described in Bernard Knollenberg, ed., "Thomas Hollis and Jonathan Mayhew: Their Correspondence, 1759–1766," Massachusetts Historical Society, *Proceedings*, 69 (1947–1950), 102–93.

22. Jonathan Mayhew, "Sermon on 1 John 3:3–4," Mar. 1749, Sermons Collections, HL. See also, Jonathan Mayhew, *Seven Sermons*, 88.

23. Jonathan Mayhew, *A Discourse Concerning Unlimited Submission* (Boston, 1750), reprinted in J. W. Thornton, *The Pulpit of the American Revolution* (Boston, 1860), 64.

24. *Ibid.*, 104, 50–51, 63.

25. Quoted in Charles Akers, *Called Unto Liberty: A Life of Jonathan Mayhew, 1720–1766* (Cambridge, Mass., 1964), 90–91.

26. Jonathan Mayhew, *A Sermon Preached*, 299, 297, 302.

27. *Ibid.*, 309–10.

28. *Ibid.*, 310–11.

29. In 1755, Massachusetts enlisted 8,000 soldiers and seamen for military service compared to 500 from New York and even fewer from Pennsylvania. Between 1758 and 1759, New England raised an additional 9,500 troops from a population of 195,000. See Nash, *The Urban Crucible*, 242–43; and Fred Anderson, "A People's Army: Provincial Military Service in Massachusetts during the Seven Years' War," *William and Mary Quarterly*, 40 (1983), 499–527. From an examination of troop rosters Anderson concludes that New England's troops were not the "cast-offs" of society but "Everyman's sons," such that "the Seven Years' War must have been an event of profound importance . . . in the lives of practically every family in every village in the colony" (quoted at 526).

30. Jason Haven, *A Sermon Preached . . .* (Boston, 1761) reprinted in Burgess, comp. *The Dedham Pulpit*, 304; and Ebenezer Pemberton, *A Sermon Preached to the Ancient and Honourable Artillery-Company* (Boston, 1756), 9.

31. George Beckwith, *That People* (New London, 1756), 34, 59–60.

32. Jonathan Edwards, "Sermon on Psalm 60:9–12," Aug. 28, 1755, Edwards Manuscripts, BL; and Matthew Bridge, "Sermon on Psalm 79:9," Sermons Collection, Box 3, Folder 35, AAS. See also Edward Barnard, "Sermon on Micah 6:6–8," Sept. 7, 1755, Sermons Collection, Folder 4, EI.

33. George Whitefield, *A Short Address* (Boston, 1756), reprinted in Gillies, *Memoirs of the Rev. George Whitefield*, 619.

34. The Puritan identification of Antichrist with the pope is summarized in Thomas M. Brown, "The Image of the Beast: Anti-Papal Rhetoric in Colonial America," in Richard O. Curry and Thomas M. Brown, eds., *Conspiracy: The Fear of Subversion in American History* (New York, 1972), 1–20.

35. Benjamin Adams, "Sermon on Jeremiah 8:20," Nov. 30, 1755, Sermons Collection, 1 envelope, EI; and Samuel Checkley, *The Duty of God's People* (Boston, 1755), 28–29. See also John Ballantine, *The Importance of God's Presence* (Boston, 1756), 18–19. Studies of millennial thought, e.g., Hatch, *The Sacred Cause of Liberty*; Davidson, *The Logic of Millennial Thought*; or Bloch, *Visionary Republic*, point to the vibrancy of millennial thought—especially in time of war—but fail to place apocalyptic themes in the larger context of occasional preaching. Furthermore, they tend to minimize the speculative qualifications that accompanied ministers' statements on the place and timing of the millennium. See Melvin B. Endy, "Just War, Holy War, and Millennialism in Revolutionary America," *William and Mary Quarterly*, 42 (1985), 16.

36. On the inapplicability of 19th-century "postmillennial" and "premillennial" categories to 18th- century millennial thought see Bercovitch, *The American Jeremiad*, 95; Davidson, *The Logic of Millennial Thought*, 75; and Donald G. Mathews, "Review Essay," *Religious Studies Review*, 5 (1979), 16.

37. John Mellen, *The Duty of All to be Ready* (Boston, 1756), 19. See also Thomas Barnard, *A Sermon Preached in Boston* (Boston, 1758), 11–12.

38. Matthew Bridge, "Sermon on Lamentations 1:7," Sept. 12, 1756, Sermons Collection, Box 3, Folder 35, AAS. For extended descriptions of the pessimistic themes that characterized occasional preaching between 1755 and 1758 see Kerry A. Trask, "In Pursuit of Shadows: A Study of the Collective Hope and Despair in Provincial Massachusetts During the Era of the Seven Years' War, 1748 to 1764" (Ph.D. diss., University of Minnesota, 1971); and Reid, "New England Rhetoric and the French War," 259–86.

39. James Diman, "Sermon on Mark 13:32–33," Feb. 8, 1756, Sermons Collection, 1 envelope, EI; and Timothy Harrington, *Prevailing Wickedness and Distress-*

ing Judgments (Boston, 1756), 23. See also Elnathan Wight, "Sermon on Revelation 2:5," Mar. 20, 1757, Sermons Collection, Box 3, Folder 35, AAS. The fear that New England might not be destined to survive the war with France was especially strong in 1756–57. See Trask, "In Pursuit of Shadows," 199.

40. James Cogswell, *God the Pious Soldier's Strength* (Boston, 1757), 26, 30; and Schneider and Schneider, eds., *Samuel Johnson*, III, 550, 551.

41. Nathan Fiske, "Sermon on Revelation 3:19," July 9, 1758, in Fiske Family Papers, 1750–1799, AAS; and Jonathan Parsons, "Sermon on Proverbs 9:6," Feb. 16, 1757, "Sermons, 1758–1774," Sermons Collection, 1 envelope, EI. See also Elias Smith, "Sermon on Mark 12:30," 1758, "Sermons, 1755–1784," I, *ibid.*

42. Walet, ed., *Diary of Ebenezer Parkman*, Nov. 18, 1755, p. 298. See also the account in *Boston Weekly News-Letter*, Nov. 20, 1755.

43. Abraham Hill, "Sermon on Jeremiah 10:10," Nov. 30, 1755, Sermons Collection, Box 1, Folder 41, AAS. John Winthrop outlined the natural causes of earthquakes in *A Lecture on Earthquakes* (Boston, 1755), but this explanation did not preclude additional moral and eschatological meanings when the quakes disrupted a "peculiar people." On the multiple meanings of earthquakes in 18th-century sermons see Heimert, *Religion and the American Mind*, 68–75; and Eleanor M. Tilton, "Lightning-Rods and the Earthquake of 1755," *New England Quarterly*, 13 (1940), 85–97. On the same day, Benjamin Adams delivered an unpublished sermon that reflected the same interpretation. See "Sermon on Jeremiah 8:20," Nov. 30, 1755, Sermons Collection, 1 envelope, EI. For similar pronouncements in print see Thomas Prince, *Earthquakes the Works of God* (Boston, 1727; reprinted 1755); Jonathan Parsons, *Good News from a Far Country* (Portsmouth, N.H., 1756); Jonathan Mayhew, *The Expected Dissolution of All Things* (Boston, 1755); Mather Byles, *Divine Power and Anger Displayed in Earthquakes* (Boston, 1755); or Charles Chauncy, *Earthquakes* (Boston, 1755).

44. Samuel Checkley, *A Day of Darkness* (Boston, 1755), 9; and John Tucker, "Sermon on Jeremiah 18:6–8," Apr. 29, 1756, "Sermons, 1746–1786," Sermons Collection, 1 envelope, EI. See also Jason Haven, *A Sermon Preached*, 312; Timothy Harrington, *Prevailing Wickedness and Distressing Judgments*; and Amos Adams, *The Expediency and Utility of War* (Boston, 1759), 24.

45. Ezra Stiles, "Sermon on Psalm 60:1," Apr. 6, 1758, Ezra Stiles Papers, *Sermons*, BL. See also Benjamin Throop's election sermon, *Religion and Loyalty* (New London, 1758), 22–25. The defeats of 1758 are summarized in Edward P. Hamilton, *The French and Indian Wars: The Story of Battles and Forts in the Wilderness* (New York, 1962), 226.

46. The campaigns of 1759 are described in Lawrence Henry Gibson, *The British Empire Before the American Revolution*, vol. 7, *The Victorious Years, 1758–1760* (New York, 1965); and Leach, *Arms for Empire*, 415–85.

47. John Tucker, "Sermon on Nehemiah 4:9 and 14," Apr. 5, 1759, "Sermons, 1746–1786," Sermons Collection, 1 envelope, EI; and Solomon Williams, "Sermon on Ezra 4:23–24," Aug. 5, 1759, Sermons Collection, Box 3, Folder 8, AAS.

48. Samuel Cooper, *A Sermon Preach'd October 16, 1759* (Boston, 1759), 38–39; and Edward Barnard, "Sermon on Isaiah 35:9," Oct. 14, 1759, Sermons Collection, 1 envelope, Folder 4, EI. See also: Nathaniel Appleton, *A Sermon Preached Oct 9* (Boston, 1760); Mather Byles, *A Sermon Delivered March 6th* (New London, 1760); Thomas Foxcroft, *Grateful Reflections on the Signal Appearances of Divine Providence* (Boston, 1760); Jonathan Townsend, *Sorrow Turned into Joy* (Boston, 1760); or Solomon Williams, *The Relations of God's People to Him* (New London,

1760). The optimistic millennial pronouncements following the victory at Quebec are described in Hatch, *The Sacred Cause of Liberty*, 41–42.

49. Elias Smith, "Sermon on Exodus 32:11–12," Oct. 14, 1759, Sermons Collection, EI.

50. Thaddeus Maccarty, "Sermon on Judges 8:28," Oct. 22, 1759, Sermons Collection, AAS. For similar sentiments see also Jonathan Parsons, "Sermon on Psalm 92:4," Oct. 17, 1759, 1 envelope, "Sermons, 1758–1774," Sermons Collections, EI.

51. Thaddeus Maccarty, "Sermon on Judges 8:28."

52. See, e.g., John Mellen, *A Sermon Preached at the West Parish in Lancaster* (Boston, 1760); Jonathan Mayhew, *Two Discourses Delivered Oct. 9, 1760* (Boston, 1760); or Samuel Haven, *Joy and Salvation by Christ* (Portsmouth, N.H., 1763).

53. James Lockwood, *The Worth and Excellence* (New London, 1759), 13. See also Samuel Frink's Massachusetts election sermon, *A King Reigning* (Boston, 1758), 13.

54. Ezra Stiles, "Sermon on 2 Chronicles 20:6–7," Sept. 25, 1760, Ezra Stiles Papers, BL; and Simon Bradstreet IV, "Sermon on Deuteronomy 12:7," Nov. 1760, "Sermons, 1743–1769," Sermons Collection, 1 envelope, EI.

55. Ezra Stiles, *Discourse on Christian Union*, 96, 108, 116.

56. Jonas Clarke, "Sermon on Hebrews 3:16," Mar. 13, 1763, Sermons Collection, Box 1, Folder 16, AAS.

Chapter 13

1. Between 1720 and 1750, Harvard and Yale colleges produced 421 *Theses Rhetoricae*, establishing a pattern that would continue throughout the 18th century and into the 19th. For summaries of the revival of interest in formal rhetoric at the colonial colleges see Perrin, "The Teaching of Rhetoric in the American Colleges before 1750," 106–24; and Warren Guthrie, "The Development of Rhetorical Theory in America," *Speech Monographs*, 13 (1946), 14–22; 14 (1947), 38–54; 15 (1948), 61–71. The elocutionary movement and its emphasis on delivery is discussed in Wilbur Samuel Howell, *Eighteenth-Century British Logic and Rhetoric* (Princeton, N.J., 1971), 147–51; W. Haberman, "English Sources of American Elocution," in Karl R. Wallace, ed., *History of Speech Education in America* (New York, 1954), 105–26; and Kennedy, *Classical Rhetoric and Its Christian and Secular Tradition from Ancient to Modern Times*, 227–29.

2. On the growth of the libraries at Harvard and Yale through the gifts of Thomas Hollis and Jeremiah Drummer see Joe W. Kraus, "The Book Collections of Five Colonial College Libraries: A Subject Analysis" (Ph.D. diss., University of Illinois, 1960), 75–146. The "Commonwealth" or "Real Whig" political treatises so conspicuous in these collections are summarized in terms of their "republican" orientation in Robbins, *The Eighteenth-Century Commonwealthman;*and Bailyn, *The Ideological Origins of the American Revolution*. Also conspicuous in the new library holdings were works from classical antiquity, especially the Roman republic. See Charles F. Mullett, "Classical Influences on the American Revolution," *Classical Journal*, 35 (1939), 92–104; Bolgar, *The Classical Heritage and its Beneficiaries* (Cambridge, England, 1954); and Richard M. Gummere, *The American Colonial Mind and the Classical Tradition* (Cambridge, Mass., 1963).

3. On collegiate speaking societies see Albert Goodhue, "The Reading of Har-

vard Students 1770–1781, As Shown by the Records of the Speaking Club," *Essex Institute Historical Collections*, 73 (1937), 107–29; and Morison, *Three Centuries of Harvard*, 140. The introduction of forensic oratory at Harvard and Yale is described, *ibid.*, 89–90; Tucker, *Puritan Protagonist: President Thomas Clap of Yale College*, 77; and David Potter, *Debating in the Colonial Chartered Colleges: An Historical Survey, 1642–1900* (New York, 1944), 33–63.

4. These totals are computed from Weis, *The Colonial Clergy and the Colonial Churches of New England*. In *The World of John Cleaveland*, 207–08, Christopher Jedrey traces the wide disparity in concentrations of college graduates from a ratio of 1 in 18 adult white males in Boston to 1 in 83 in Plymouth County.

5. See Ezra Stiles, *Discourse on Christian Union*, 50, 102. On the basis of admissions records from 54 Connecticut churches between 1700 and 1775, Gerald Moran discovered that "the greatest proportionate gains in new membership did not come during the Great Awakening, but in 1770–74, with the next largest increase in 1735–39; the third in 1740–44; the fourth in 1710–14; and the fifth in 1725–29." See "The Puritan Saint," 256. In Boston's Old South Church, high points of admissions were registered in 1742, 1756, and 1770. See Richard Shiels, "Revivals of Religion Among New England Congregationalists, 1730–1835," unpubl. paper, Graph 1. In Ipswich, Mass., revivals of church membership peaked in 1742–43 and 1763–64. See Jedrey, *The World of John Cleaveland*, 116.

6. In surveying the pamphlet literature of the Revolutionary era, Bernard Bailyn estimated that a total of 400 pamphlets were published in all 13 colonies. In this same period, the clergy of Massachusetts and Connecticut alone published over 1,800 sermons. See Bernard Bailyn, *Pamphlets of the American Revolution* (Cambridge, Mass., 1965), I, vii; and Hatch, *The Sacred Cause of Liberty*, 176. Between 1764 and 1783, 137 weekly newspapers were published in 44 urban locations throughout the colonies. Few of these survived more than a year, nor did they circulate widely. Isaiah Thomas's *Massachusetts Spy* set a colonial circulation record of 3,500. See G. Thomas Tansell, "Some Statistics of American Printing, 1764–1783," in Bernard Bailyn and John B. Hench, eds., *The Press and the American Revolution* (Worcester, Mass., 1980), 346–49; Arthur M. Schlesinger, *Prelude to Independence: The Newspaper War on Britain, 1764–1776* (orig. pub., 1958; reprinted New York, 1966), 303–04; and Philip Davidson, *Propaganda and the American Revolution* (Chapel Hill, N.C., 1941), 226.

7. On college reading see Goodhue, "The Reading of Harvard Students"; Robert F. Seybolt, "Student Libraries at Harvard, 1763–1764," Colonial Society of Massachusetts, *Publications*, 28 (1935), 449–61. Ministerial libraries corresponded closely to others listed in David Lundberg and Henry F. May, "The Enlightened Reader in America," *American Quarterly*, 28 (1976), 262–80. Virtually every minister's library included a copy of Josephus's *Antiquities*—a work that has not received sufficient attention in studies of 18th-century New England thought. The imported copies of Josephus were supplemented by eight reprintings on colonial presses. The works of Josephus are summarized in G. A. Williamson, *The World of Josephus* (Boston, 1964).

8. The long-term implications of war with France in terms of the American Revolution are traced in Lawrence Henry Gipson, "The American Revolution as an Aftermath of the Great War for Empire, 1754–1763," *Political Science Quarterly*, 65 (1950), 86–104. On American fears of Catholic and Anglican bishoprics in the New World see Carl Bridenbaugh, *Mitre and Sceptre: Transatlantic Faiths, Ideas, Personalities, and Politics, 1689–1775* (New York, 1962), chapters 7–9.

9. The events surrounding the Stamp Act and its repeal are traced in Edmund S. and Helen M. Morgan, *The Stamp Act Crisis: Prologue to Revolution*, rev. ed. (New York, 1962).

10. Otis's speech is summarized, *ibid.*, 53–54; and John J. Waters, Jr., *The Otis Family In Provincial and Revolutionary America* (orig. publ. 1968; reprinted New York, 1975), 121–25. Important pamphlets from 1764–65 include: Stephen Hopkins, *The Rights of Colonies Examined* (Providence, R.I., 1765); James Otis, *The Rights of the British Colonists Asserted and Proved* (Boston, 1764); Oxenbridge Thacher, *The Sentiments of a British American* (Boston, 1764); John Adams, *A Dissertation on the Canon and Feudal Law* (Boston, 1765); *Considerations Upon the Act of Parliament* (Boston, 1764); and [Thomas Fitch *et al.*], *Reasons Why the British Colonies in America Should Not Be Charged with Internal Taxes* (New Haven, 1764).

11. Andrew Eliot, *A Sermon Preached Before His Excellency* (Boston, 1765), 47–48. On Cooper's early activities with the press see Charles Akers, *The Divine Politician: Samuel Cooper and the American Revolution in Boston* (Boston, 1982), 54–55. Cooper's meetings with the Boston radicals are recorded in John Adams's diary. See Lyman H. Butterfield, ed., *The Adams Papers*, vol. 2, *Diary, 1771–1788* (orig. publ. 1961; reprinted New York, 1964), entries Feb. 14, 1771; Dec. 16, 1772; or July 16, 1773. On Stiles, see Morgan, *The Gentle Puritan*, 226–27.

12. On growing ministerial sentiment against the stamp tax, as reflected in the thought of Samuel Cooper and Charles Chauncy, see Akers, *The Divine Politician*, 61–71; and Griffin, *Old Brick: Charles Chauncy of Boston*, 138–43.

13. As quoted in George P. Anderson, "Ebenezer Mackintosh, Stamp Act Rioter and Politician," Colonial Society of Massachusetts, *Publications*, 26 (1924–26), 35. Gordon S. Wood describes the "ideological" character of mobs in America in contrast to Europe in "A Note on Mobs in the American Revolution," *William and Mary Quarterly*, 23 (1966), 635–42.

14. Douglas Adair and John A. Schutz, eds., *Peter Oliver's Origin and Progress of the American Revolution* (San Marino, Calif., 1961), 39, 58–60. For an account of the destruction of Hutchinson's home see Bernard Bailyn, *The Ordeal of Thomas Hutchinson* (Cambridge, Mass., 1974), 35–69.

15. As quoted in Oscar Zeichner, *Connecticut's Years of Controversy, 1750–1776* (Chapel Hill, N.C., 1949), 62. On the higher concentration of radical Sons of Liberty activities in "New Light" counties in Connecticut see Baldwin, *The New England Clergy*, 103.

16. On the calculating goals of mob behavior in the Stamp Act riots see Pauline Maier, *From Resistance to Revolution: Colonial Radicals and the Development of American Opposition to Britain, 1765–1776* (New York, 1972), 4–76. Robert Middlekauff parallels the rituals of riot and revival in "The Ritualization of the American Revolution," in Stanley Coben and Lorman Ratner, eds., *The Development of an American Culture* (Englewood Cliffs, N.J., 1970), 34.

17. Jonathan Mayhew, *Observations on the Charter and Conduct of the S. P. G.* (Boston, 1763), 39. Most colonial leaders criticized the destruction of Aug. 26, but not the protest activities of Aug. 14. See Nash, *The Urban Crucible*, 298.

18. The harsh debates surrounding elections in Boston are summarized in Warden, *Boston*, 169. On Windham see Mark A. Noll, "Ebenezer Devotion: Religion and Society in Revolutionary Connecticut," *Church History*, 45 (1976), 293–307.

19. *Resolves of the New London Sons of Liberty*, Dec. 30, 1765, reprinted in Edmund S. Morgan, ed., *Prologue to Revolution: Sources and Documents on the*

Stamp Act Crisis, 1764–1766 (Chapel Hill, N.C., 1959), 114. For a discussion of local resolutions as instruments of mass political indoctrination see Merill Jensen, *The Founding of a Nation: A History of the American Revolution, 1763–1776* (New York, 1968), 99.

20. On Johnson's influence on the drafting of the Lyme Resolves and his close associations with the Sons of Liberty see Baldwin, *The New England Clergy*, 103; and Zeichner, *Connecticut's Years of Controversy*, 52. Johnson's essays are reprinted in Bernard Bailyn, "Religion and Revolution: Three Biographical Studies," *Perspectives in American History*, 4 (1970), 125–39, and appendix.

21. Bailyn, "Religion and Revolution," 144–46, 148, 155, 163–64. Colonial fears of British conspiracy are traced in Bailyn, *The Ideological Origins of the American Revolution*, 144–59; Maier, *From Resistance to Revolution*, 183–91; and Wood, "Conspiracy and the Paranoid Style," 401–41.

22. Samuel Johnson, *Some Important Observations* (Newport, R.I., 1766), 5, 7, 20.

23. *Ibid.*, 20–21, 56.

24. Adair and Schutz, eds., *Peter Oliver's Origins and Progress of the American Revolution*, 73. The Declaratory Act is summarized in *The Ideological Origins of the American Revolution*, 202.

25. Edward Barnard, *A Sermon Preached* (Boston, 1766), 15, 38. Jonathan Lee's Connecticut election sermon echoed similar sentiments in its praise of "liberty, darling liberty . . . which these self-settled colonies . . . reserved, as a condition of submitting to the British crown." *A Sermon Delivered* (New London, 1766), 18.

26. Edward Barnard, "Sermon on Psalm 122:1–6," July 24, 1766, Sermons Collection, Folder 4, EI.

27. Joseph Emerson, *A Thanksgiving-Sermon Preached at Pepperell* (Boston, 1766), 9, 29–30. See also William Patten's *A Discourse Delivered at Halifax* (Boston, 1766), 21: "I rejoyce that America has resisted. Surely this is the Lord's doing, and it may be justly marvellous in our eyes."

28. Charles Chauncy, *Good News From a Far Country* (Boston, 1766), reprinted in Thornton, *Pulpit of the American Revolution*, 127–28, 139, 137.

29. Edward Barnard, "Sermon on Psalm 122:1–6"; and Jonathan Mayhew, *The Snare Broken* (Boston, 1766), 35. Mayhew's simultaneous apology for the destruction of property and defense of liberty is summarized in Akers, *Called Unto Liberty*, 202–07; and Bailyn, "Religion and Revolution," 111–24.

30. On the return to local concerns after the repeal see Gross, *The Minutemen and Their World*, 39–41.

31. Perez Fobes, "Sermon on Matthew 22:4," June 8, 1766, in Sermons Collection, 1 envelope, CL.

32. Jonathan Bowman, "Sermon on John 7:37," July 29, 1766, Sermons Collection, 1 volume, AAS; Samuel Williams, "Sermon on Matthew 11:28," Nov. 29, 1767, Sermons Collection, 1 envelope, EI; and Joseph Lathrop, "Sermon on 2 Corinthians 6:1," Jan. 18, 1767, Sermons Collection, 1 envelope, CL.

33. David White, "Sermon on John 3:36," Sept. 7, 1766 (repeated in 1768 and 1778), Sermons Collection, Box 3, Folder 3, AAS. For similar themes in evangelical preaching see: John Smalley, "Sermon on 1 Corinthians 13:12," Apr. 6, 1766, Sermons Collection, 1 envelope, CL; John Devotion, "Sermon on Luke 2:32," Apr. 30, 1769, Sermons Collection, Box 1, Folder 21, AAS; Stephen West, "Sermon on Titus 2:6," Mar. 22, 1767, Box 3, Folder 4, *Ibid.*; Jonathan Ashley, "Sermon on 1

Timothy 4:8," Dec. 6, 1767, "Sermons, 1738–1767," 1 folder, *ibid.*; Jonathan Edwards, Jr., "Sermon on Hebrews 9:27," Sept. 11, 1768, Sermons Collection, 1 envelope, CL; or Caleb Barnum, "Sermon on Luke 11:13," 1763 (repeated in 1768 and 1773), 1 envelope, *ibid.*

34. Samuel Wales, "Sermon on Matthew 22:37–38," 1772, "Sermons, 1769–1791," 1 folder, AAS. A major theme in American religious studies of the 1960s and 1970s was the emergence of a national-state "civil religion" in which allegiance to the "American Way of Life" became a religiouslike creed or faith. For a summary of the literature see Russell E. Richey and Donald G. Jones, eds., *American Civil Religion* (New York, 1974); and Martin E. Marty, *A Nation of Behavers* (Chicago, 1976), 180–203.

35. The radicalizing influence of these events in Boston and the conspiratorial framework in which they were interpreted are traced in Bailyn, *The Ideological Origins of the American Revolution*, 101–17; and Gary B. Nash, "Social Change and the Growth of pre-Revolutionary Urban Radicalism," in Alfred F. Young, ed., *The American Revolution*, 6–7.

36. Harry A. Cushing, ed., *The Writings of Samuel Adams*, 4 vols. (Boston, 1904–08), II, 256. For an assessment of Adams's importance to the Revolution see Pauline Maier, "Coming to Terms with Samuel Adams," *American Historical Review*, 81 (1976), 12–37.

37. "Samuel Cooper to Thomas Pownall," Mar. 26, 1770, reprinted in *American Historical Review*, 8 (1902–03), 316–17.

38. Charles Chauncy, *Trust in God* (Boston, 1770), 35; and Adair and Schutz, eds., *Peter Oliver's Origins and Progress of the American Revolution*, 91.

39. John Lathrop, *Innocent Blood Crying to God* (Boston, 1771), 5–7, 15–16.

40. [Auth. unk.], "A Sermon Prepared Soon After the Boston Massacre, March 5, 1770," Sermons Collection, 1 envelope, CL. I am indebted to Mary Morgan of the Congregational Library for calling this sermon to my attention. Internal evidence suggests that the author was either a Boston minister or serving a church in the immediate Boston "metropolis."

41. James Dana, *A Century Discourse* (New Haven, 1770); and Judah Champion, *A Brief View of the Distresses . . . Our Ancestors Encountered* (Hartford, 1770), 40.

42. Charles Chauncy, *Trust in God*, 6. The circumstances of this sermon are described in Griffin, *Old Brick*, 146–50; and Heimert, *Religion and the American Mind*, 431.

43. Charles Chauncy, *Trust in God*, 21, 32.

44. "Samuel Cooper to Thomas Pownall," Nov. 14, 1771, reprinted in *American Historical Review*, 8 (1902–03), 325.

45. The massacre orations were collected and printed by Peter Edes in *Orations Delivered at the Request of the Inhabitants of the Town of Boston* (Boston, 1785). For discussions of the orations see James Loring, *The Hundred Boston Orations Appointed by the Municipal Authorities* (Boston, 1852); and Barnet Baskerville, *The People's Voice: The Orator in American Society* (Lexington, Ky., 1979), 13–17. The extent to which 18th-century lay oratory—at least of formal occasions—was sermonic in form has yet to be explored. One lay oration, John Hancock's 1774 massacre oration, was so obviously sermonic in form ("let us play the man for our God, and for the cities of our God") that many loyalists supposed it was penned by Samuel Cooper. Charles Akers disputes this claim in *The Divine Politician*, 169–72, but the mere supposition suggests lay orators consciously framed their

discourse in sermonic molds fixed by occasional preaching. There were, after all, few other American oratorical models to follow.

46. Adam's oration notes are recorded in Butterfield, ed., *Diary, 1771–1788*, 57–61.

47. *Boston Gazette*, Nov. 11, 1771, reprinted in Cushing, ed., *The Writings of Samuel Adams*, II, 269.

48. The importance of pamphlet literature in articulating a constitutional defense of American resistance is described in Bailyn, *The Ideological Origins of the American Revolution.* The limited audience of pamphlet literature is discussed in Stout, "Religion, Communications, and the Ideological Origins of the American Revolution."

49. Cleaveland's essays are summarized in Jedrey, *The World of John Cleaveland*, 130–35.

50. See, e.g., Edward Barnard, "Sermon on 1 Kings 8:57–58," Apr. 2, 1772, Sermons Collection, Folder 4, EI; or Moses Parsons, *A Sermon Preached at Cambridge* (Boston, 1772), 29.

51. John Allen, *An Oration Upon the Beauties of Liberty* (Boston, 1773), 14, 16. Allen's sermon was exceeded in separate editions by only two pamphlets, including the "runaway best seller" *Common Sense.* See Thomas R. Adams, *American Independence, the Growth of an Idea: A Bibliographic Survey of the American Political Pamphlets Printed between 1764 and 1776* (Providence, R.I., 1965), xi–xii. For information on Allen's career and the significance of *An Oration*, see John M. Bumsted and Charles E. Clark, "New England's Tom Paine: John Allen and the Spirit of Liberty," *William and Mary Quarterly*, 21 (1964), 561–70.

52. John Allen, *An Oration*, 19–20.

53. The best discussion of the Committees of Correspondence is Richard D. Brown, *Revolutionary Politics in Massachusetts: The Boston Committee of Correspondence and the Towns, 1772–1774* (orig. publ. 1970; reprinted New York, 1976). See especially, 38–57, 92–121.

54. See Schlesinger, *Prelude to Independence*; and Davidson, *Propaganda and the American Revolution.*

55. Charles Turner, *A Sermon Preached Before His Excellency* (Boston, 1773), 16, 22, 29–30. Samuel Adams sent a copy of Turner's sermon to Arthur Lee, and Thomas Cushing forwarded a copy to Benjamin Franklin. See Baldwin, *The New England Clergy*, 119.

56. "Samuel Cooper to Benjamin Franklin," Dec. 17, 1773, reprinted in Massachusetts Historical Society, *Collections*, 4th Ser., 4 (1858), 374–75. The Boston Tea Party and its aftermath is described in Benjamin Labaree, *The Boston Tea Party* (New York, 1964); and Dirk Hoerder, *Crowd Action in Revolutionary Massachusetts, 1765–1780* (New York, 1977), 247–70. Local support for the Tea Party is described in Pauline Maier, *From Resistance to Revolution*, 275; and L.F.S. Upton, ed., "Proceedings of Ye Body Respecting the Tea," *William and Mary Quarterly*, 22 (1965), 287–300. Governor Hutchinson's role in provoking the Tea Party is discussed in Bernard Bailyn, *The Ordeal of Thomas Hutchinson*, 259–63.

57. Adair and Schutz, eds., *Peter Oliver's Origins and Progress of the American Revolution*, 102–03. The Coercive Acts are summarized and discussed in David Ammerman, *In the Common Cause: American Response to the Coercive Acts of 1774* (orig. publ. 1974; reprinted New York, 1975).

58. "Samuel Cooper to Benjamin Franklin," 374. Widespread support for Boston's defiance in the New England countryside is described in Hoerder, *Crowd*

Action in Revolutionary Massachusetts, 247–367; R. D. Brown, *Revolutionary Politics in Massachusetts,* 149–236; Nash, *The Urban Crucible,* 339–84; Jedrey, *The World of John Cleaveland,* 136–72; Gross, *The Minutemen and Their World,* 42–67; Jensen, *The Founding of a Nation,* 551–67; Ammerman, *In the Common Cause,* 103–24; and Richard L. Bushman, "Massachusetts Farmers and the Revolution," in Richard M. Jellison, ed., *Society, Freedom, and Conscience: The American Revolution in Virginia, Massachusetts, and New York* (New York, 1976), 77–124.

Chapter 14

1. Newspapers are discussed in Schlesinger, *Prelude to Independence;* Davidson, *Propaganda and the American Revolution,* 225–48; Stephen Botein, "'Meer Mechanics' and an Open Press: The Business and Political Strategies of Colonial American Printers," *Perspectives in American History,* 9 (1975), 127–228; and Thomas C. Leonard, "News for a Revolution: The Exposé in America, 1768–1773," *Journal of American History,* 67 (1980), 26–40.

2. For discussions of enduring "aurality" and its cultural significance see Rhys Isaac, "Dramatizing the Ideology of Revolution: Popular Mobilization in Virginia, 1774 to 1776," *William and Mary Quarterly,* 33 (1976), 357–85; and Stout, "Religion, Communications, and the Ideological Origins of the American Revolution." Both of these studies draw heavily on Walter J. Ong, *The Presence of the Word: Some Prolegomena for Cultural and Religious History* (New Haven, Conn., 1976).

3. Jonathan Boucher, *A View of the Causes and Consequences of the American Revolution in Thirteen Discourses . . .* (London, 1797; reprinted New York, 1967), 320, 321. On "government by committee," see Ammerman, *In the Common Cause,* 103–24.

4. The clergy's advocacy of nonconsumption is summarized in Baldwin, *The New England Clergy,* 155. The opposition of merchants and lawyers to nonconsumption is discussed in R. D. Brown, *Revolutionary Politics in Massachusetts,* 191–93, 200. Congregational clergymen who were active participants in their militias include Chandler Robbins, Caleb Barnum, Joseph Bowman, Jonathan Moore, Thomas Allen, Peter Thacher, Jonathan Todd, Eleazar May, Benjamin Boardman, Samuel Webster, John Treadwell, Joseph Willard, David Avery, David Grosvenor, Phillips Payson, Benjamin Balch, Jonathan French, and John Martin. See Baldwin, *The New England Clergy,* 163; and Shipton, ed., *Sibley's Harvard Graduates.* In his biographical listing of prominent loyalists, Lorenzo Sabine identified 45 loyalist clergymen in New England, of whom 29 were Anglican. [See *Biographical Sketches of Loyalists of the American Revolution,* 2 vols. (Boston, 1864).] This is not to say, of course, that there were no loyalists or "lukewarm" patriots among the Congregational clergy. Micah Lawrence (HC, 1759), for example, refused to sign the Association Test in 1776, and Lemuel Hedge (HC, 1759) was censured for having loyalties "inimical to the American States." See Shipton, ed., *Sibley's Harvard Graduates,* 440, 450. In general, however, among professional subgroups in New England the Congregational clergy was the least divided over the question of resistance and independence.

5. William Gordon, *A Discourse Preached Dec. 15, 1774* (Boston, 1775), 5. It is inaccurate to conclude, as Davidson does in *Propaganda and the American Revolution,* 91, that because the churches and ministers were never asked to take an "official vote" on independence they "lagged considerably behind public opin-

ion." For ministers to publish binding statements would be to deny the independent principle in church government that they upheld in civil government. More accurate is Alice Baldwin's recognition that the Congregational clergy "were organized and could easily communicate with each other. They were able and zealous propagandists with a remarkable opportunity for reaching the people. All through the struggle they used every means at their disposal to present the old arguments with new force. No clever lawyer, no radical mechanic gave more warmth and color to the cause than did some of these reverend divines. With a vocabulary enriched by the Bible they made resistance and at last independence and war a holy cause." *The New England Clergy,* 171.

6. Joseph Perry, *A Sermon Preached* (Hartford, 1775), 7. See also Gad Hitchcock's 1774 Massachusetts election sermon, *A Sermon Preached Before His Excellency* (Boston, 1774), 46: "Our danger is not visionary, but real—Our contention is not about trifles, but about *liberty* and *property,* and not only ours but those of posterity to the latest generation."

7. Richard L. Merritt, *Symbols of American Community 1735–1775* (New Haven, Conn., 1966), 111.

8. In the decade 1770–79, 281 sermons were printed of which 85% were of the occasional variety. See Hatch, *The Sacred Cause of Liberty,* 178; and Harry P. Kerr, "The Character of Political Sermons Preached at the Time of the American Revolution" (Ph.D. diss., Cornell University, 1962), 25. Public fast days increased 300% from an average of 6 per year between 1767 and 1774 to an average of 18 per year from 1775 to 1777. See Love, *The Fast and Thanksgiving Days of New England,* 501–03.

9. Timothy Hilliard, *The Substance of Two Sermons* (Boston, 1774), 5; Samuel Webster, *The Misery and Duty of an Oppress'd and Enslav'd People* (Boston, 1774), 21. For similar accusations and calls for repentance see: Thaddeus Maccarty, *Reformation of Manners, of Absolute Necessity* (Boston, 1774); Timothy Hilliard, *The Duty of a People* (Boston, 1774); Nathan Fiske, *The Importance of Righteousness* (Boston, 1774); Jeremiah Day, *The Ability of God to Restrain Sin* (New Haven, 1774); James Barry, *A Reviving Cordial for a Sin-Sick Despairing Soul* (Boston, 1774); John Lathrop, *A Discourse Preached Dec. 15, 1774* (Boston, 1774); or Peter Whitney, *The Transgressions of a Land* (Boston, 1774). For discussions of the theme of moral repentance and reformation in Revolutionary preaching see Perry Miller, "From the Covenant to the Revival," in James W. Smith and A. Leland Jamison, eds., *Religion in American Life* (Princeton, N.J., 1961), I, 322–334; and Edmund S. Morgan, "The Puritan Ethic and the American Revolution," *William and Mary Quarterly,* 24 (1967), 3–43.

10. Samuel Webster, *The Misery and Duty,* 21, 29, 31. See also, Samuel Sherwood, *A Sermon Containing Scriptural Instructions to Civil Rulers* (New Haven, 1774), 38.

11. William Gordon, *A Discourse Preached Dec. 15, 1774,* 13, 15; Elisha Fish, *A Discourse at Worcester* (Worcester, Mass., 1775), reprinted in Baldwin, *The New England Clergy,* appendix, 182. See also Samuel Sherwood, *A Sermon Containing,* 13; or Peter Whitney, *The Transgressions of a Land,* 10.

12. William Gordon, *A Discourse Preached,* 8, 11, 30–32. Alice Baldwin traces the circulation and influence of this sermon in *The New England Clergy,* 124. For similar exhortations see also Joseph Lyman, *A Sermon Preached at Hatfield* (Boston, 1775), 19; and Jonathan Bascom, *A Sermon Preached at Eastham* (Boston, 1775), 23.

13. Zabdiel Adams, *The Grounds of Confidence and Success in War* (Boston,

1775), 26; and John Lathrop, *A Sermon Preached* (Boston, 1774), 15, 32. In all, 35 militia sermons were printed in the Revolutionary era. See Kerr, "The Character of Political Sermons," 25.

14. Ebenezer Chaplin, "Sermon on 2 Samuel 1:18," July 25, 1774, Sermons Collection, 1 envelope, CL. The aggressive scriptural injunction to "Play the man" (2 Samuel 10:12) was a commonplace in militia sermons. See John Ferling, "The New England Soldier: A Study in Changing Perceptions," *American Quarterly*, 33 (1981), 26–45.

15. Flavius Josephus, *The Famous and Memorable Workes of Josephus* (London, 1602), pt. I, 206. For a summary of Israel's history during the divided kingdom see Simon Dubnov, *History of the Jews from the Beginning to Early Christianity*, trans. Moshe Spiegel, 5 vols. (New York, 1967), I, 159–70.

16. Emerson's local career and the events leading to battle are summarized in Gross, *The Minutemen and Their World*, 21–29, 110–14.

17. William Emerson, "Sermon on 2 Chronicles 13:12," Mar. 13, 1775, reprinted in Amelia Forbes Emerson, *Diaries and Letters of William Emerson, 1743–1776* (privately printed, Concord, Mass., 1972), 69. I am indebted to the Concord Historical Society for making this volume available to me.

18. *Ibid.*, 66, 61. Peter Whitney issued a similar warning to England in his published 1774 fast sermon: "These colonies, are to England, as the pillars were to the house which Sampson brake. . . . If we fall the whole British empire will fall with us; and possibly that may fall while we stand. Nothing will save the nation from ruin, if America does not." *The Transgressions of a Land*, 68.

19. William Emerson, "Sermon on 2 Chronicles 13:12," 66, 69.

20. *Ibid.*, 70.

21. The battle is described in Gross, *The Minutemen and Their World*, 114–32. Emerson's leading role in mobilization and the battle itself is summarized in Shipton, ed., *Sibley's Harvard Graduates*, 15: 42.

22. Most scholars agree that 1775 marked the critical time when, in Pauline Maier's words, thoughts of "resistance" turned to "revolution." See Maier, *From Resistance to Revolution*, 228–70; Bailyn, *The Ideological Origins of the American Revolution*, 118; Gordon S. Wood, *The Creation of the American Republic 1776–1787* (orig. publ. 1969; reprinted New York, 1972), 45; or Davidson, *Propaganda and the American Revolution*, 37.

23. Samuel Seabury, *Letters of a Westchester Farmer* (1774), reprinted in Leslie F. S. Upton, ed., *Revolutionary Versus Loyalist: The First American Civil War, 1774–1784* (Waltham, Mass., 1968), 27.

24. Samuel Seabury as quoted in G.N.D. Evans, ed., *Allegiance in America: The Case of the Loyalists* (Reading, Mass., 1969), 7.

25. The process by which Americans justified republican ideas by prior experience is described in Bernard Bailyn, "Political Experience and Enlightenment Ideas in Eighteenth-Century America," *American Historical Review*, 67 (1962), 339–51. In New England, Enlightenment ideas were supported both by prior experience and covenant theology. On the backward-looking aspects of Revolutionary thought see Richard Buel, "Democracy and the American Revolution: A Frame of Reference," *William and Mary Quarterly*, 21 (1964), 180–88; and Trevor H. Colbourn, *The Lamp of Experience: Whig History and the Beginnings of the American Revolution* (New York, 1965).

26. See Samuel West's 1776 election sermon, *A Sermon Preached* (Boston, 1776), reprinted in Thornton, *The Pulpit of the American Revolution*, 285. Bernard Bailyn

summarizes American's radical interpretation of popular sovereignty in *The Ideological Origins of the American Revolution*, 175–98, 201.

27. Reprinted in Baldwin, *The New England Clergy*, appendix, 178–79. On Cleaveland's activities in 1774–75 see Jedrey, *The World of John Cleaveland*, 136–39.

28. Nathan Perkins, *A Sermon Preached June 2, 1775* (Hartford, 1775), 6, 8–9.

29. For analyses of Independence that liken separation from the crown to the alienation of children from parents see Greven, *The Protestant Temperament*, 339–41; Edwin G. Burrows and Michael Wallace, "The American Revolution: The Ideology and Psychology of National Liberation," *Perspectives in American History*, 6 (1972), 167–306; and Jay Fliegelman, *Prodigals and Pilgrims: The American Revolution Against Patriarchal Authority, 1750–1800* (Cambridge, Mass., 1982).

30. Samuel Langdon, *A Sermon Preached* (Watertown, Mass., 1775), reprinted in Thornton, *The Pulpit of the American Revolution*, 242, 239.

31. *Ibid.*, 234–35, 238, 242, 256–57.

32. Robert Ross, *A Sermon in Which the Union of the Colonies is Considered and Recommended* (New York, 1776), 5, 16, 27–28. See also Moses Mather, *America's Appeal to the Impartial World* (Hartford, 1775); and Dan Foster, *A Short Essay on Civil Government* (Hartford, 1775).

33. Ebenezer Chaplin, "Sermon on 1 Samuel 30:6," May 11, 1775, Sermons Collection, 1 envelope, CL. Like other evangelical sermons in this period, Chaplin's notes were brief, but included with this particular sermon is a 13- page elaboration in Chaplin's handwriting, possibly transcribed after Independence.

34. Samuel Mather, "Sermon on Isaiah 48:10," July 9, 1775, in Mather Family Papers, Box 9, AAS. For similar sentiments see Caleb Barnum, "Sermon on Acts 22:28," July 20, 1775, in Emery, *The Ministry of Taunton*, II, 27–29.

35. Elias Smith, "Sermons on Romans 8:31," May 11, 1775, in "Sermons, 1755–1784," vol. 5 of 6 vols., EI. Smith repeated his sermon three times in the following weeks at Reading, Boxford, and Beverly. The same sentiments appeared in print in William Stearns, *A Sermon Preached* (Watertown, Mass., 1775), 11, 14.

36. Samuel Langdon, *The Co-Incidence of Natural and Revealed Religion* (Boston, 1776), 24–25.

37. Nathaniel Niles, *Two Discourses on Liberty* (Newburyport, Mass., 1774), 57. Among manuscript sermons dealing with redemption see, e.g., John Bacon, "Sermon on 1 John 4:10," Apr. 6, 1775, "Boston, Massachusetts Church Records," vol. 2 of 5 vols., "Sermons of John Bacon, 1772–1775," AAS. In 1775–76 the New England presses published many sermons whose central theme was spiritual regeneration. See, e.g.: Samuel Andrews, *A Discourse, Shewing the Necessity of Joining Internal Repentance with the External Profession of It* (New Haven, 1775); Ebenezer Cleaveland, *The Abounding Grace of God Towards Notorious Sinners* (Salem, 1775); Elijah Fitch, *A Discourse* (Boston, 1776); Eliphalet Wright, *A People Ripe for An Harvest* (Norwich, Conn., 1776); William Law, *The Grounds and Reasons of Christian Regeneration* (Boston, 1775); Benjamin Foster, *God Dwelling in the Tents of Shem* (Worcester, Mass., 1775); Ezra Sampson, *The Ceasing and Failing of the Godly* (Boston, 1776); David Rowland, *Ministerial Necessity In the Discharge of the Gospel Embassy* (Hartford, 1776); Samuel West, *A Sermon Preached* (Boston, 1775); or Joseph Huntington, *A Sermon Delivered* (Norwich, Conn., 1776).

38. Andrew Lee, *Sin Destructive of Temporal and Eternal Happiness* (Norwich, Conn., 1776), 18.

39. "A Letter from Jonathan Sewall to General Frederick Haldimand," May 30,

1775, in Jack P. Greene, ed., *Colonies to Nation, 1763–1789: A Documentary History of the American Revolution* (New York, 1975), 267. Philip J. Greven discusses "The Nature of Liberty" in *The Protestant Temperament*, 341–47. See also Heimert, *Religion and the American Mind*, 12.

40. Samuel West, *A Sermon Preached*, 307, 309. See also, Timothy Hilliard, *The Duty of a People* (Boston, 1774), 30; or John Lathrop, *A Discourse Preached Dec. 15, 1774* (Boston, 1774), 28.

41. Samuel West, *A Sermon Preached*, 317.

42. Judah Champion, *Christian and Civil Liberty and Freedom Considered and Recommended* (Hartford, 1776), 5–6. On Champion's active career as a patriot, and the importance of this sermon see J. T. Headley, *The Chaplains and Clergy of the Revolution* (Springfield, Mass., 1861), 318–26; and Baldwin, *The New England Clergy*, 124.

43. Judah Champion, *Christian and Civil Liberty*, 10, 17, 25–26.

44. The importance of these new occasions and commemorations in bringing New England history to bear on Revolutionary events is discussed in W. F. Craven, *The Legend of the Founding Fathers* (New York, 1956), 28–55.

45. Cooper's unpublished sermon is preserved in Sermons Collection, HL, and reprinted in Charles W. Akers, ed., "'A Place for My People Israel': Samuel Cooper's Sermon of 7 April 1776," *New England Historical and Genealogical Register*, 132 (1978), 128–29.

46. *Ibid.*, 130, 136–37, 139.

47. Enoch Huntington, *The Happy Effects of Union* (Hartford, 1776), 13, 15.

48. Samuel Baldwin, *A Sermon Preached at Plymouth, Dec. 22, 1775* (Boston, 1776), 21; Jonas Clark, *The Fate of Blood-Thirsty Oppressors* (Boston, 1776), 5–6, 10, 16, 27, 30.

49. Ebenezer Chaplin, "Sermon on Isaiah 33:13," Feb. 18, 1776, in "Sermons, 1759–1794," 2 oct. vols., I, AAS; and "Sermon on Psalm 81:7," July 28, 1776, *ibid.* See also Thomas Fessendon, "Sermon on Exodus 17:11," Mar. 24, 1776, "Sermons, 1773–1804," 1 Folder, *ibid.*

50. John Eells, "Sermon on Isaiah 31:1–3," May 17, 1776, Sermons Collection, CHS.

51. In *Inventing America: Jefferson's Declaration of Independence* (New York, 1978), 323–62, Gary Wills points out that in July 1776 the delegates to the Continental Congress had more important things on their minds than the declaration. A parchment copy of the declaration was not available until Aug. 2, 1776, and was still being signed six months later. The final text with completed signatures was not printed until Jan. 1777.

52. Peter Whitney, *American Independence Vindicated* (Boston, 1777), 43, 47.

53. *Ibid.*, 27, 29–30; and Butterfield, ed., *The Adams Papers: Diary and Autobiography*, II, 351.

54. Thomas Paine, *Common Sense* (1776), reprinted in Sidney Hook, ed., *The Essential Thomas Paine* (New York, 1969), 30–32. Italics are mine.

55. Peter Thacher, "Sermon on 2 Samuel 10:12, preached after Independence, 1777," in Sermons Collection, Box 2, Folder 37, AAS. For an account of Thacher's chronicle of the Battle of Bunker Hill see Kenneth Murdock, "Reverend Peter Thacher's Report on Bunker Hill," Massachusetts Historical Society, *Proceedings*, 59 (*Transactions*, 1925–56), 36–45. The theme of Israel's republic continued to sound in 1777. See, e.g., Samuel Webster's 1777 Massachusetts election sermon, *A Sermon Preached* (Boston, 1777), 28: "Had it not been for the Jews madness in

insisting to have their *wise* and *happy government* changed into a *monarchy*, I am persuaded, the world would have seen more of the excellency of that divine constitution."

56. This is not to say there was no millennial commentary in the decade 1765–75 or that ministers never identified political events with millennial prophecies. On Apr. 25, 1773, for example, John Adams noted in his *Diary* that "Dr. [Samuel] Cooper was up[on] Rev. 12:19. And the great Dragon was cast out, that old Serpent called the Devil and Satan . . . Q[uery]. Whether the Dr. had not some political Allusions in the Choice of this Text." Yet, it is significant that Cooper did not make explicit the political identification with England, forcing Adams to speculate on the "political Allusion." Similarly, in 1774, Samuel Langdon published a sermon on a *Rational Explanation of St. John's Vision of the Two Beasts* (Portsmouth, 1774), but noted in the foreword that public interest in the subject was not sufficient to underwrite a larger book-length commentary. Studies of millennial thought and republican ideology, including Hatch, *The Sacred Cause of Liberty*; Davidson, *The Logic of Millennial Thought*; Cushing Strout, *The New Heavens and the New Earth: Political Religion in America*, (New York, 1974); May, *The Enlightenment in America*, 153–76; or Bloch, *Visionary Republic*, do not make clear how preaching on the millennium built up only *after* 1775; it was not the framework within which resistance and violence were originally conceived or justified. By identifying religion's "role" in the Revolution in terms of millennial rhetoric, historians ironically minimize the importance of religion. If colonial pulpits were preoccupied with millennial themes regarding the end of time, they obviously had no singular influence on Revolutionary deliberations regarding life in this world. Millennial speculations, as James Davidson points out, could not "provide the rationale for mounting a revolution." (*The Logic of Millennial Thought*, 216.) But New England's covenant past and the "Jewish Republic" *could* provide the rationale for resistance, and *did* give religion a unique role in New England's revolution.

57. Thomas Paine, *Common Sense*, 66.

58. Sylvanus Conant, *An Anniversary Sermon Preached at Plymouth, Dec. 23, 1776* (Boston, 1777), 24–25.

59. Ebenezer Baldwin, *The Duty of Rejoycing Under Calamities and Afflictions* (New York, 1776), 38.

60. Samuel Sherwood, *The Churche's Flight into the Wilderness* (New York, 1776), 17, 49. Nathan O. Hatch discusses the "intellectual revolution" that shifted America's identification of Antichrist from France to Britain in *The Sacred Cause of Liberty*, 86–87. The notion that America was rewalking Israel's past and that the Revolution was a reenactment of the escape from Egypt was frequently stated in 1776–77. See, e.g., Eli Forbes, "Sermon on Revelation 6:2," Jan. 24, 1777, in "Sermons, 1752–1804," 1 envelope, AAS; or Nicholas Street, *The American States Acting Over the Part of the Children of Israel in the Wilderness* (New Haven, 1777), 7.

61. John Bacon, "Sermon on 1 John 4:10." Nathan O. Hatch describes the differences between Revolutionary and nineteenth-century millennialism in "The Christian Movement and the Demand for a Theology of the People," *Journal of American History*, 67 (1980), 545–66.

62. Peter Whitney, *American Independence Vindicated*, 51, 54. On the colonial insistence that "virtue" must accompany republican forms see Michael McGiffert, "The Question of '76," Davis Memorial Lecture IV, (Spokane, Wa., 1977); and Charles Royster, *A Revolutionary People at War: The Continental Army and Ameri-*

can Character, 1775–1783 (Chapel Hill, N.C., 1979), 16–24. In New England, as we have seen, "virtue" meant, above all else, "piety." In *The Creation of the American Republic*, 59, Gordon Wood observes how colonial patriots presented republican ideas as if "there was nothing new about [them]; John Winthrop would have found them congenial."

63. In *The Urban Crucible*, 361, Gary B. Nash observes that the main reason internal discord was muted in New England, in contrast to other regions, was that "the people were not nearly so heterogeneous in religion as in other parts."

64. The tendency of colonial patriots to identify with classical heroes from republican Greece and Rome is described in Wood, *The Creation of the American Republic*, 48–53. But in New England, where the sermon dominated public communications, references to and identifications with the founders or Old Testament patriarchs far outstripped classical allusions.

65. Ebenezer Parkman, "Sermon on Isaiah 64:9," 1760, Apr. 13, 1777, and July 4, 1780, in "Sermons, 1724–1781," Parkman Family Papers, 1707–1879, Box 1, AAS.

Epilogue

1. There is a wide body of literature on the internal social strains accompanying rebellion and independence. See, e.g.: John R. Howe, Jr., "Republican Thought and the Political Violence of the 1790s," *American Quarterly*, 19 (1967), 147–65; Kenneth A. Lockridge, "Social Change and the Meaning of the American Revolution," *Journal of Social History*, 6 (1973), 403–39; Jack P. Greene, "The Social Origins of the American Revolution: An Evaluation and Interpretation," *Political Science Quarterly*, 88 (1973), 1–22; or Robert E. Shalhope, "Toward a Republican Synthesis: The Emergence of an Understanding of Republicanism in American Historiography," *William and Mary Quarterly*, 29 (1972), 49–80.

2. See Bernard Bailyn's discussion of "The Contagion of Liberty," in *The Ideological Origins of the American Revolution*, 230–320. The transforming radicalism of the Revolution on all levels of American society is treated in Wood, *The Creation of the American Republic*.

3. Warren Association of Baptists, *Minutes . . . in Their Meeting at Middleborough Sept. 9 and 10, 1777* (Boston, 1777), 5. On the "double aspect" of Independence for New England dissenters, see McLoughlin, *Isaac Backus and the American Pietistic Tradition*, 135.

4. Samuel Hopkins, *A Dialogue Concerning the Slavery of the Africans* (Norwich, Conn., 1776) reprinted in Roger Burns, *et. al.*, *Am I Not a Man and a Brother: The Antislavery Crusade of Revolutionary America, 1688–1788* (New York, 1977), 399, 413. Hopkins's efforts on behalf of antislavery are summarized in Conforti, *Samuel Hopkins and the New Divinity Movement*, 125–41.

5. James Allen, *The Watchman's Alarm to Lord N---H* (Salem, 1774), reprinted in Burns *et al.*, *Am I Not a Man and a Brother*, 335; and Nathaniel Niles, *Two Discourses on Liberty*, 37–38. Other New England ministers who made pointed attacks against the institution of slavery included Joseph Bellamy, Levi Hart, Jonathan Edwards, Jr., Ebenezer Baldwin, Nathaniel Emmons, Ezra Stiles, James Allen, and Nathaniel Niles. Most, but not all, of these ministers were evangelicals. See Baldwin, *The New England Clergy*, 128; and Mark A. Noll, *Christians in the American Revolution* (Grand Rapids, Mich., 1977), 93–102.

6. Benjamin Rush as quoted in Bailyn, *The Ideological Origins of the American Revolution*, 230.

7. The post-Revolutionary divisions of rationalists and evangelicals are summarized in Perry Miller, *The Life of the Mind in America: From the Revolution to the Civil War* (New York, 1965), pt. I. The limits of Unitarianism's appeal are described in Howe, *The Unitarian Conscience*, 147–78.

8. On the growth of new denominations see Heimert, *Religion and the American Mind*, 397–98; and Hatch, "The Christian Movement and the Demand for a Theology of the People."

Index